Unique Tenets of the Middle Way Consequence School

Unique Tenets of the Middle Way Consequence School

by Daniel Cozort

Snow Lion Publications
Ithaca, New York

Snow Lion Publications
P.O. Box 6483
Ithaca, NY 14851 USA
607-273-8519

First Edition USA 1998

Printed in Canada on acid-free, recycled paper

ISBN 1-55939-077-8 (paper)
ISBN 1-55939-059-x (cloth)

Library of Congress Cataloging-in-Publication Data

Cozort, Daniel, 1953-
Unique tenets of the middle way consequence school / by Daniel Cozort. -- 1st ed. USA.
p. cm.
Includes bibliographical references (p.) and index.
ISBN 1-55939-077-8 (alk. paper). -- ISBN 1-55939-059-X
1. Prāsaṅgika. 2. Dge-lugs-pa (Sect)--Doctrines. I. Title.
BQ7477.C68 1998
294.3'420423--DC21 97-37351
CIP

Table of Contents

Part Two: Jamyang Shayba's "Unique Tenets of the Prāsaṅgika-Mādhyamika School" with the Annotations of Ngawang Belden

Part Three: Janggya's "Unique Tenets of the Prāsaṅgika-Mādhyamika School"

Note on Conventions

It is my hope that this book will be of some use to anyone interested in Buddhist philosophy. For specialists in Tibetan and Sanskrit, I have included key terms and book titles upon their first occurrence; noted emendations in the Tibetan texts; whenever possible, located and reproduced in the notes passages from Sanskrit texts that are cited in the translated texts; constructed three glossaries of technical terms; and have attempted to include in the bibliography all translations and critical editions of cited texts.

For others, I have followed several procedures in the main text as part of an effort to bring Tibetan Buddhism out of the arcane and make it accessible to other scholars of Buddhism, other scholars of religion and philosophy, and others who are simply interested in Buddhism, philosophy, or Tibetica:

1. Sanskrit and Tibetan words have been limited to parenthetical citation with two exceptions: a few Sanskrit terms are treated as English words and therefore are neither translated nor italicized, and proper names are not translated. The Sanskrit terms treated as English words are: abhidharma, Arhat, Bodhisattva, Buddha, dharma, karma, maṇḍala, nirvāṇa, saṃsāra, sūtra, tantra, vajra, yogi, Mahāyāna and Hīnayāna. Parenthetical citation and citation in the notes follow the Wylie transliteration system with the exception that I have not capitalized any letters.[1]

---

[1]Wylie 261-67. (See bibliography for complete references.)

2. Throughout the body of the book, I use a system of "essay phonetics" that renders Tibetan names in an easily pronounceable form. Devised by Professor Jeffrey Hopkins of the University of Virginia, it is fully explained on pp. 19-22 of his *Meditation on Emptiness* (1983). It approximates Hla-sa (= Lhasa) pronunciation. Hopkins' system enables readers who are not familiar with Tibetan and / or Sanskrit to gain access to the names of important Buddhist philosophers, a goal with which I am in complete agreement. Without a pronunciation system, the non-Tibetanist who might wish to refer to philosophers such as Janggya or Jamyang Shayba is faced with consonant-cluster nightmares like *lcang skya* or *'jams dbyangs bzhad pa*. Such strings of apparent typographical errors are destined to remain alien and instantly forgettable. The following table indicates the transliteration and basic pronunciation systems for each Tibetan consonant; marks over certain sounds indicate that such a letter would be pronounced with a sharper, higher tone:

ཀ	ka	ḡa	ཁ	kha	ka	ག	ga	ga	ང	nga	nga n̄ga
ཅ	ca	j̄a	ཆ	cha	cha	ཇ	ja	ja	ཉ	nya	nya n̄ya
ཏ	ta	d̄a	ཐ	tha	ta	ད	da	da	ན	na	na n̄a
པ	pa	b̄a	ཕ	pha	pa	བ	ba	ba	མ	ma	ma m̄a
ཙ	tsa	d̄za	ཚ	tsha	tsa	ཛ	dza	dza	ཝ	wa	wa
ཞ	zha	sha	ཟ	za	sa	འ	'a	a	ཡ	ya	ya
ར	ra	ra	ལ	la	la	ཤ	sha	s̄ha	ས	sa	sa
ཧ	ha	ha	ཨ	a	a						

In the Hopkins system, the nasals (far right columns) are low in tone except when there is a superscribed or prefixed letter; a subscribed *la* is high in tone, except for *zla* which is pronounced "da"; *dbang* is pronounced "wang," *dbyangs,* "yang"; and the letters *ga* and *ba* are phoneticized as *k* and *p* when they are found in the suffix position. Since my modest aim was to give readers an approximate pronunciation, I have not used high tone markers. I also differ from the Hopkins system by not inserting hyphens between the syllables of Tibetan names, for which I have several reasons. First, it seems to me that nonhyphenated names look less alien than those that are; second, Tibetans who come to the West or publish books in Western languages adopt nonhyphenated forms, and there are an increasing number of such persons; and third, persons who are not professional Buddhologists and who publish many translations, transcriptions, etc., seldom use hyphenated forms. Since the readership for even scholarly books now extends far beyond the circle of other scholars, some accommodation to widely used styles seems called for. The absence of hyphens occasionally leads to an awkward-looking result, such as in the name Janggya, but I have not found this to provide a difficulty with pronunciation, which is the point.

A list of Tibetan names in both easy pronunciation and transliterated form is found below. The proper names of those who have established a form for their names in the West are the only exceptions to the easy pronunciation system. For instance, I have not made an exception for the relatively famous name of Dzongkaba, although it is true enough that "Tsongkhapa" and "Tsong-kha-pa" have more renown than "Dzongkaba." (His is a rare name that can be pronounced more or less as it appears in transliterated form; such names have in some cases disguised the need for a pronunciation system. See the table below for more representative instances.) Tibetan studies are still in a developing state, and I feel that it is not yet too late for a different (and improved) convention to become accepted.

3. In the service of a more readable translation, I have usually shortened titles. Full titles can be found in the bibliography. Tibetans normally abbreviate, too, but often to an extreme degree. For instance, Jamyang Shayba sometimes refers to Dzongkaba's *Illumination of the Thought, Explanation of (Candrakīrti's) "Entrance to the Middle Way" (dbu ma la 'jug pa'i rgya cher bshad pa dgongs pa rab gsal)* simply as *Explanation (rnam bshad)*.

I have used few abbreviations. In the notes, "P" refers to the modern reprint of the Peking edition of the Tibetan canon, the *Tibetan Tripiṭaka* (Tokyo-Kyoto: Suzuki Research Foundation, 1956). Since I do not have, nor have easy access to, a copy of this, whereas I do have copies of many of the works referred to in this study, references in the notes, unless specified as "P," are to the first edition listed *after* the P number in the bibliography. In notes referring to the works of Jamyang Shayba and Ngawang Belden, "NG" denotes the Ngawang Gelek Demo edition, "DSK" the Drashikyil edition reprinted at Gomang College. See my introduction to the translations for more information on these editions.

Following is a list of all Tibetan names appearing in the book in "essay phonetics" and transliterated form:

Agya Yongdzin	a kya yongs 'dzin
Amdo	a mdo
Batsap Nyimadrak	pa tshab nyi ma grags
Belden Chöjay	dpal ldan chos rje
Belden Drakba	dpal ldan grags pa
Budön	bu ston
Daktsang Shayrab Rinchen	stag tshang shes rap rin chen
Drashi Chöpel	bkra shis chos 'phel
Drashikyil	bkra shis 'khyil
Drebung	'bras spungs
Dzongkaba Losang Drakba	tsong kha pa blo bzang grags pa

Gadamba	bka' gdams pa
Gagyuba	bka' rgyud pa
Ganden	dga' ldan
Ganden Jinchaling	dga' ldan byin chags gling
Ganggya Dingring	rgang gya'i lting ring
Gelukba	dge lugs pa
Gendün Gyatso	dge 'dun rgya mtsho
Gomang	sgo mang
Gönchok Jikmay Wangbo	dkon mchog 'jigs med dbang po
Gönchok Tsering	dkon mchog tshe ring
Gungtang Gönchok Denbay Drönmay	gung thang dkon mchog bstan pa'i sgron me
Gyeltsap Darma Rinchen	rgyal tshab dar ma rin chen
Gyumay	rgyud smad
Hlasa	lha sa
Jambel Sampel	'jam dpal bsam 'phel
Jambel Trinlay Yönden Gyatso	'jam dpal 'phrin las yon tan rgya mtsho
Jamyang Shaybay Dorjay Ngawang Dzöndrü	'jam dbyangs bzhad pa ngag dbang btson 'grus
Jangdzay	byang rtse
Janggya Rolbay Dorjay	lcang kya rol pa'i rdo rje
Jaydzün Chögyi Gyeltsen	rje btsun chos kyi rgyal mtshan
Jonangba	jo nang pa
Kaydrup Gelek Belsang	mkhas grub dge legs dpal bzang
Losang Chögyi Nyima	blo bzang chos kyi nyi ma
Losang Dayang	blo bzang rta dbyangs
Losang Denbay Nyima	blo bzang bstan pa'i nyi ma
Losang Gönchok	blo bzang kun mchog

Loseling	blo gsal gling
Ngawang Belden	ngag dbang dpal ldan
Ngawang Drashi	ngag dbang bkra shis
Paṇchen Sönam Drakba	Paṇ chen bsod nams grags pa
Purbujok	phur bu lcog
Rongta Losang Damchö Gyatso	rong tha blo bzang dam chos rgya mtsho
Sagyaba	sa skya pa
Sera	se ra
Sönam Rinchen	bsod nams rin chen
Tügen Losang Chögyi Nyima	thu'u bkwan blo bzang chos kyi nyi ma
Tupden Gyatso	thub bstan rgya mtsho
Üba Losel	dbus pa blo gsal
Yangjen Gaway Lodrö	dbyangs can dga' ba'i blo gros

Preface

This is a book about certain implications of the philosophy of emptiness (*stong pa nyid, śūnyatā*). It is, in several ways, a continuation of the work that Jeffrey Hopkins began in *Meditation on Emptiness* (1983) and *Emptiness Yoga* (1987). It too introduces and analyzes interpretations of the Prāsaṅgika-Mādhyamika "school" of Indian Buddhism by prominent scholars, past and present, of the Gelukba (*dge lugs pa*) monastic order of Tibetan Buddhism; it also uses as a textual base the encyclopedic works of Jamyang Shayba (*'jam dbyangs bzhad pa*, 1648-1721), Ngawang Belden (*ngag dbang dpal ldan*, b. 1797) and Janggya (*lcang skya*, 1717-86).

Hopkins' pioneering work brought to English-speaking readers the worldview of what might be call "Gelukba Buddhism," including much of the material that a monk would absorb in many years of study. In particular, he explored in great detail the system for meditation on emptiness that Gelukbas have constructed out of terse and ambiguous Indian sūtras and *śāstras*. Hopkins showed that for Gelukbas, the enigma of Nāgārjuna's first-century *Treatise on the Middle Way (dbu ma'i bstan bcos, madhyamakaśāstra)* has been solved. "Emptiness" means something quite precise; therefore, that of which things are empty can be described finely enough to enable the construction of specific practices to isolate and destroy harmful misconceptions. In short, Gelukbas have systematized a highly unsystematic philosophy, and Hopkins' important work has revealed this intricate and ingenious system.

Compared to *Meditation on Emptiness*, the present study is far more modest in scope and execution. It focuses upon certain implications of the Mādhyamika view which are well known among Gelukbas as the "unique tenets" of the Prāsaṅgika-Mādhyamika School. "Prāsaṅgika" is the Tibetan appellation for the tradition based primarily on Candrakīrti's seventh-century exegesis of the works of Nāgārjuna. The "unique tenets" are a list of positions that Gelukbas link to Nāgārjuna himself and which mainly comprise careful refutations of the tenets of non-Prāsaṅgikas, prominently those who are identified as Cittamātrins (=Yogācārins) or Svātantrika-Mādhyamikas.

The "unique tenets" are a kind of miscellany of topics, ranging from a qualified realism (in this case, a defense of the idea that there is an external world) to propositions about perception, nirvāṇa, the "extremes" of annihilation and permanence, etc. Some topics concern central issues in Buddhism; others merely clarify the way in which certain terms (e.g, *pratyakṣa*) are used by Prāsaṅgikas. All of them are difficult and controversial, even those that do not seem particularly crucial.

The "unique tenets" hinge upon a principle that Gelukbas regard as a kind of key that opens all philosophical doors. This key is called "ultimate analysis" and is discussed generally in the first chapter and specifically in every subsequent chapter. It is what Gelukbas say non-Prāsaṅgikas do, prompting those schools to invent things that don't exist and to deny the existence of things that do exist. The "ultimate analysis" key is a unique contribution of Gelukbas to Prāsaṅgika thought, although of course Gelukbas claim that it is a direct derivation of Nāgārjuna's own criticisms of the metaphysical entities propounded by others.

As a corollary to rejecting ultimate analysis, Gelukbas (in this case with much explicit support in Indian texts) maintain that the "unique tenets" are founded upon a respect for the way in which ordinary people see the world. Indeed, "ultimate analysis" and "worldly conceptions" are virtual antonyms. Thus, in the "unique tenets," Gelukbas claim that the Prāsaṅgikas perform a graceful philosophical pirouette that returns them to common sense, the place where all philosophy begins.

The attribution of particular tenets to "schools" is not well grounded in historical realities. There were no schools of Indian Buddhism as such; Indian Buddhism was never so organized! Monk-scholars did not identify themselves as belonging to this or that school (and certainly not to the many subschools identified in Gelukba literature), and it is hazardous and, I think, unhelpful to guess now at their affiliations. It is a mistake, we know, even to presume that the commentator of a text agrees with its positions. Then, as now, traditional Buddhist scholars have played roles in order to understand better the perspectives of their opponents. Moreover, the way in which these purported schools are fit into a hierarchy (see the table in chapter 1) is nothing that was self-evident in the Indian context, but is something done in a purely speculative way by Gelukbas who are looking at Indian Buddhist treatises through the lens of their own constructed version of Prāsaṅgika-Mādhyamika. It may not even be appropriate, for instance, to place the Sautrāntikas in the "Hīnayāna" camp; they may have been Mahāyānists who did not clearly identify themselves as such.

Nevertheless, the Gelukba view on the merits of "tenets" study, as pithily expressed by Losang Gönchok, is that "Understanding the views of the lower systems is also a platform or method of coming to understand the views of the higher systems."[1] The fiction of "four schools" is a heuristic device that allows a student to come gradually to the Prāsaṅgika view by way of absorbing, analyzing, and finally rejecting other points of view. (This rejection, it should be noted, is only of selected aspects; the "schools" do not disagree on most issues.) Implicitly, this teaches the student *how* to be a Prāsaṅgika, since the Prāsaṅgika method is precisely one of beginning with the assertions of others and revealing the absurd or at least awkward consequences (*prāsaṅga*) that they entail. The

[1]*Word Commentary* 12.4.

study of tenets is thought to sharpen the intellect and to give the student an exposure to coherent points of view that challenge his or her presuppositions.

The particular sections of the "tenets" books translated here are one means for Gelukba monks, particularly those of Drebung Monastery's Gomang College, to understand the implications of the works of Indian Mādhyamikas. It might be objected that they, and for that matter, we, ought not to try to understand the views of Nāgārjuna and Candrakīrti through the lens of seventeenth- and eighteenth-century works and twentieth-century interpreters. In the case of this book, such an objection would be misplaced, since I make no claim to have understood Nāgārjuna, et al. Rather, what is presented here is a particular interpretation of the thought of these figures. It might be seen as a piece of the puzzle of Tibetan Buddhism rather than a piece of the Indian puzzle. However, I would argue that this particular interpretation is interesting, plausible, and for the most part well argued and supported. It deserves the light of day more, I think, than, for instance, yet another speculative study of Nāgārjuna.

Also, inasmuch as any and all interpretations of the Indian tradition involve a hermeneutic, the relevant questions for any would-be interpreter are what that hermeneutic should be and how self-consciously one can use it. It has been my fortunate experience that deliberately reading the Buddhist philosophical past through the eyes of the contemporary and near-contemporary Gelukba tradition is rich and satisfying. It is a pleasure to work with Tibetan scholars, whose kindness and generosity are legendary, and it is instructive and stimulating to see them doing philosophy on their feet. They are, of course, biased; they revere Dzongkaba and cannot easily bring themselves to be critical of his views. But the best of them are also true philosophers who are willing to put everything on the table, who know the Indian sources and will put their formidable intellects to bear on extremely subtle points. Far from beings slaves to their own intellectual tradition, they are masters of it more than most Westerners could claim to be of theirs. Furthermore, the great scholars are, unfortunately, a dwindling resource. Even if one seems to be putting the cart before the horse to utilize a more contemporary tradition when work remains to be done on older texts, there seems to me to be great merit in working with members of a living tradition while they are still available, and to work with them on the sort of texts, such as monastic textbooks, with which they are intimately familiar.

Having said all of that, I cannot claim that this book does a particularly good job of contextualizing this piece of the Gelukba worldview in the overall picture of Indo-Tibetan Buddhism. That is, I have only looked in the original languages at those parts of the Indian sources (except for those already translated) that are cited by Tibetan authors. I am no expert in many areas of Indian Buddhism or in Tibetan Buddhism prior to Dzongkaba. I cannot be certain how significant are these limitations. On the very specific topics which comprise the "unique tenets," it is possible, if unlikely, that there are relevant passages in the Indian texts that were never cited by our Tibetan authors, for instance. And it may be, for instance, that Dzongkaba relied heavily upon, or for that matter, was rejecting, the interpretation by his own teacher Rendawa of specific points in Candrakīrti's work. So, I must again make clear my intention, which is to present, and, to the extent I am able, to analyze a particular Gelukba interpretation of points drawn from works the Gelukbas identify as "Prāsaṅgika" (mainly those of Nāgārjuna and Candrakīrti). As best I am able I have tried to determine whether or not the Gelukba positions are a justifiable reading of the Indian texts, but my principal goal has been to consider them on their own and to ask whether they are coherent and cogent. I hope that I have been able to present this philosophy in a way that is clear and accessible and that it will in some small measure be helpful to someone else.

Sources

This book is based on several levels of oral and textual commentary. Since my primary goal is to provide a picture of how one large and important segment of Tibetan Buddhism views these issues, I rely upon two normative texts and representative written and oral commentary. I call the texts—the tenets "encyclopedias" of Jamyang Shayba and Janggya—"normative" because they are among those upon which many contemporary Gelukba scholars rely for their understanding of these philosophical tenets. I have more to say about these works and their authors in the first chapter, so for now it will suffice to say that these works synthesize a vast amount of Indian sūtra and *śāstra* literature as well as the Tibetan works of Dzongkaba, founder of the Gelukba order, and his chief disciples. They are the culmination of several centuries that saw the composition of "tenets" books and monastic "textbooks" (*yig cha*). In fact, Jamyang Shayba is the last of the major writers of the latter, and Janggya the last of the former. They also reflect centuries of monastic courtyard debate (Jamyang Shayba's work, in particular, includes many hypothetical debates). My many sessions with eminent native scholars did not turn up a great many perspectives in addition to those already found in these pages; although monk-scholars continue to read and debate about the Indian and Tibetan sources utilized by the tenets-book authors, they seem to feel no pressing need for something even more thorough. I translated portions of these works and also translated two works commenting on Jamyang Shayba, the *Annotations* by Ngawang Belden (included here) and *Word Commentary* by Losang Gönchok (*blo bzang dkon mchog*). In addition, I read portions of many Indian and Tibetan works cited by the authors whose works I translated.

For oral commentary, I eventually gathered the opinions of a fairly wide range of Gelukba monastics. From Jeffrey Hopkins I got grounding in the teaching of the late Gomang College (Jamyang Shayba's college) scholar Kensur Ngawang Lekden; later, I clarified some questions with Gomang's Geshay Tupden Gyatso. I did a great deal of study with Kensur Yeshey Tupden and Geshe Belden Drakba, two scholars of Loseling College, Gomang's sister college in Drebung Monastery. Loseling's friendly rivalry with Gomang has made scholars of either place particularly sensitive to points of difference in their respective monastic textbooks. I also had several interviews with Geshay Gönchok Tsayring and Amchok Tulku of Ganden Monastery and with Geshay Sönam Rinchen of Sera Monastery. Finally, I was able to address many questions to the Dalai Lama, who is not a member of any of the three great Gelukba monasteries, and who is the rare scholar whose knowledge extends to non-Gelukba Tibetan writings. These scholars did not merely impart an oral tradition with which they were familiar, but, in our sessions, probed, questioned, reversed themselves, disagreed with the authors, and, most of all, threw consequences at *me*. It is difficult to imagine a more thorough thrashing of a text than that which they delivered. I am gratified to be able to place before others the result of this process, and I hope that it will prove to be stimulating and otherwise helpful.

Dedication

For Harry, with inexpressible gratitude

Acknowledgments

In the spring of 1980, with only a rudimentary command of Tibetan and only the vaguest notion of what I was getting myself into, I began slowly, a little bit week-by-week, to translate that portion of Janggya's *Presentation of Tenets* concerning the unique tenets. Jeffrey Hopkins suggested the topic and met with me privately to review my translations and annotations. At every turn, it seemed, more questions arose than were answered. Some of those were swept away in my first classes with a Tibetan lama, Gyumay Kensur Jambel Shenpen (who later became the Ganden Tri Rinbochay, head of the Gelukba order). However, we had only a half-dozen meetings. It was the late Kensur Yeshey Tupden, former abbot of Loseling College of Drebung Monastery (and great humanitarian), who really opened these texts for me. My classes with him over three years, in America and India, ranged over all of the texts translated herein and a good deal of the Losang Gönchok book upon which I often relied; readers will see that his many insights and suggestions leaven the footnotes with which I have annotated those translations.

In 1983, with the crucial assistance of an American Institute of Indian Studies fellowship, my wife and I left for nearly a year's stay in India. While there, I was able to complete my sessions with Kensur Yeshey Tupden at Drebung Monastery, where the problems of life in the Third World seemed tolerable in the spirited company of the marvelous monks of Drebung. Prior to that, I had been enamored only of the genius of the Buddha, but had no special feelings for the Tibetans or for India; our visit changed all of that.

During the remainder of our stay in India, I consulted with several other adroit Tibetan scholars. I benefitted greatly from studying for nearly three months with Geshay Belden Drakba, at that time the librarian of Tibet House in Delhi. The Ven. Losang Tarchin (Gordon Aston) participated in these sessions, asking excellent questions and helping me through numerous linguistic logjams. Later, in Dharamsala, I brought my most vexing questions to Geshay Gönchok Tsayring and Amchok Rinbochay of Ganden Monastery and to Geshay Sönam Rinchen of Sera Monastery (the latter two were then working at the Library of Tibetan Works and Archives). Most treasured of all such sessions, though, were two audiences with His Holiness the Dalai Lama, who showed himself to be not only a great spiritual leader but one of the greatest scholars of his tradition. His Holiness showed a remarkable capability to understand the thrust of my questions even when I was not able to express myself clearly, to come up with approaches to them that no one else had suggested, and to playfully speculate about the answers when the questions could not be settled. He exemplifies what is best about the Gelukba tradition—its commitment to the use of reason to jar the foundations of misconception, without losing sight of the higher purpose of religious practice. Ngari Rinbochay (Tendzin Choegyal), then His Holiness' secretary, not only arranged but participated in the interviews. Finally, back in the U.S., I addressed a number of questions to Geshay Tupden Gyatso, of Drebung's Gomang College, who resides at the Tibetan Buddhist Learning Center in New Jersey.

My greatest debt is to Jeffrey Hopkins, who spent hundreds of hours with me on these topics. It has been a privilege to be the apprentice to such a master craftsman. I am grateful to Paul Groner, Bryan Pfaffenberger, and Karen Lang for reading the entire manuscript and making many good suggestions. In particular, I am indebted to Karen Lang, who raised some very good questions about an earlier draft, discovered many errors that had crept into my Sanskrit citations, and gave me valuable bibliographic pointers. Craig Preston, Jules Levinson, and Guy Newland all discussed certain points with me and helped me to clarify those issues. I also am grateful to my former colleagues at Bates College and to my present colleagues at Dickinson College for their encouragement and friendship. I would also like to thank Alex Mast, a Dickinson student who helped me with many final details.

Finally, I would like to thank my wife, Christine Altieri, who has not even read this book, much less typed or proofread it. More importantly, she understood what I needed to do and let me do it despite the many sacrifices that entailed. That is why I think of this book as hers also.

Part One:

Introduction to the Unique Tenets and Analysis of Selected Topics

"My Doctrine has two modes,
Advice and tenets.
To children I speak advice
And to yogis, tenets."

— *Laṅkāvatāra Sūtra*

1 The Unique Tenets

Nearly two millennia ago, around the time Paul of Tarsus and his fellow apostles had begun to propagate the new and radical teaching of Jesus throughout the Roman Empire, the south Indian scholar and monk Nāgārjuna was attracting a following at the great Nālanda Monastic University in Magadha by teaching a new way of understanding the six-centuries-old message of Śākyamuni Buddha.[1] Like Paul, Nāgārjuna had an impact that was widespread, enduring, and continues to provoke creative thought.

Little is known of Nāgārjuna's life, except from a legendary account in a biography that survives only in Chinese translation.[2] He is said to have been so intelligent, and his memory so prodigious, that he was able to master the entirety

[1] Nāgārjuna's dates are controversial, since the Tibetan tradition considers Nāgārjuna to have been a master both of sūtra and tantra who lived for 600 years. Most Western scholars postulate the existence of at least two different people named Nāgārjuna, one who established the Mādhyamika School and another who taught about tantra. The former probably lived in the first or second century C.E. To some extent, Nāgārjuna's influence is also a matter of debate, since there is scant evidence that contemporary Indian thinkers reacted to his writings. On the other hand, the Mādhyamika philosophy that claims him as its founder became the most important current of thought in the Mahāyāna world.

[2] Richard Robinson (21-22) gives a summary that I have further condensed. The text on Nāgārjuna is #2047 of the Chinese *Tripiṭaka* in the *Taishō Shinshū Daizōkyō* published in Japan in the 1920s.

of the enormous Buddhist canon (but of which school is uncertain) in only ninety days. He sought even more scriptures, obtaining several of the long-hidden Mahāyāna ("Great Vehicle") discourses *(mdo, sūtra)* from a monk in the Himālayas. He absorbed these and traveled widely, debating with many Strivers (*śrāmana,* the spiritual seekers of the forest) and seeking more texts. A Nāga[3] then appeared to him and took him to a place in the ocean where he was presented with the Vaipulya ("extensive," i.e., Mahāyāna) sūtras; again he was able to memorize these in just ninety days, and was returned to south India where he taught the re-revealed Mahāyāna of the Buddha.

Through his teaching and writing, Nāgārjuna articulated a point of view that came to be regarded as distinctive and resulted in his being regarded as the founder of the first philosophical school of the Mahāyāna, the Mādhyamika ("Middle Way," *dbu ma*). His followers, ancient and contemporary, regard his teachings as expressing the very essence of the Buddha's discourses on the Perfection of Wisdom *(shes rab kyi pha rol tu phyin pa, prajñāpāramitā)*, the seminal texts of the Mahāyāna.

The "middle way" of the school's name and which is propounded by Nāgārjuna in his most famous work, the *Treatise on the Middle Way (dbu ma'i bstan bcos, madhyamakaśāstra)*, is a way he claims to have been articulated by the Buddha himself. It is a spiritual path that falls neither to the extreme of "existence" or "permanence" *(rtag mtha', śaśvatānta)* nor to the extreme of "non-existence" or "annihilation" *(chad mtha', ucchedānta)*. As set forth by the particular Tibetan tradition utilized in the present study, Nāgārjuna meant by these extremes the fallacies of either propounding the inherent existence *(rang*

---

[3] "Nāga" is a word with several meanings. Its basic meaning is "snake," but it is used especially with regard to great serpents or serpent-people of Indian mythology such as the snake Ananta upon which Viṣṇu reclines during the long sleep of the universe when it is in a cycle of dissolution. Nāgas are also a class of beings that are half-human, half-snake, and live under the ground or at the bottom of the ocean; it is probably such a being that is meant in this legend, which is controversial even in the Buddhist tradition.

bzhin gyis grub pa, svabhāvasiddhi) of phenomena or propounding the non-existence of phenomena even conventionally. The former extreme is a reification of things, conceiving them to exist exactly in the manner in which they appear—as if they existed in and of themselves, as if they could, for instance, be pointed to as the collection of their parts, or an individual part, or separate from them. The latter extreme of "non-existence" is the nihilistic rejection of the cause and effect of actions *(las, karma)* and consequently of transmigration in a cycle *('khor ba, saṃsāra)* of rebirth and the possibility of liberation from it. A few ancient Indian thinkers like the Cārvākas fell to the latter extreme, but most fell to the former, Nāgārjuna thought; non-Buddhists generally posited a permanent and unchanging soul or essence, of course, but even most Buddhists propounded some kind of "true" or independent existence.[4]

The Prāsaṅgika "School"

Tibetan traditions consider Nāgārjuna's school to have two branches, the split coming from Bhāvaviveka's (*legs ldan 'byed* c. 500-570, a.k.a. Bhāva or Bhāvya) criticism of Buddhapālita's (*sang rgyas bskyangs*, c. 470-540) commentary on Nāgārjuna's *Treatise on the Middle Way*. Candrakīrti (seventh century), in turn, defended Buddhapālita.[5] The schools of Bhāvaviveka on

---

[4]According to Gelukba exegetes, although it is true enough that Nāgārjuna's critique undermines all erroneous tenets, it is not concerned merely with philosophical positions, which constitute mere "artificial" errors. Much more serious, and a universal problem rather than just a malady of philosophers, is the "innate" misconception of inherent existence which occurs simply through one's assent to the false manner in which ordinary things appear.

[5]The three texts in question are Bhāvaviveka's *Lamp for (Nāgārjuna's) "Wisdom," Commentary on the "Treatise on the Middle Way" (prajñāpradīpamūlamadhyamakavṛtti, dbu ma rtsa ba'i 'grel pa shes rab sgron ma)*, Buddhapālita's *Commentary on (Nāgārjuna's) "Treatise on the Middle Way" (buddhapālitamūlamadhyamakavṛtti, dbu ma rtsa ba'i 'grel pa buddha pā li ta)* and Candrakīrti's *Clear Words, Commentary on (Nāgārjuna's) "Treatise on the Middle Way" (mūlmadhyamakavṛttiprasannapadā, dbu ma rtsa ba'i 'grel pa tshig gsal ba)*.

the one hand and Buddhapālita and Candrakīrti on the other are called the Svātantrika-Mādhyamika[6] (Middle Way "Autonomy," *dbu ma rang rgyud pa)* and Prāsaṅgika-Mādhyamika (Middle Way "Consequence," *dbu ma thal 'gyur pa)* Schools; these names reflect two different approaches to awakening in others a realization of the nature of reality, depending respectively on so-called "autonomous inferences" *(rang rgyud kyi rjes dpag, svatantrānumāna)* in which the members of a syllogism are held to be inherently existent and are asserted as being established in a common manner in the systems of both the stater and the hearer, and on consequences *(thal 'gyur, prasaṅga)* that contradict the listener's own positions.[7]

Candrakīrti may justifiably be considered the *de facto* founder of the Prāsaṅgika School because he clearly championed the method of flinging contradictory consequences and defended other aspects of Buddhapālita's thought over against the school of Bhāvaviveka.[8] For Tibetan Prāsaṅgikas, Candra-

---

For an extensive analysis of the Bhāvaviveka / Buddhapālita / Candrakīrti debate, see Hopkins (1983a: 441-530).

[6]These are not terms that appear in the Indian literature. They are probably a Tibetan distinction, made in the late eleventh or early twelfth century, after Batsap Nyimadrak (*pa tshab nyi ma grags*, 1055-1158 [?]) and Jayānanda translated the works of Candrakīrti into Tibetan (Lopez 1987: 26). Also, see Karen Lang's article on Batsap. Mimaki notes, for instance, that Yeshayday, the disciple of the eighth-century Indian masters Padmasambhava and Śāntarakṣita, never used the terms.

[7]Jamyang Shayba (*Great Exposition of the Middle Way* 424.2) glosses autonomous syllogism as that in which the "three modes exist from their own side" *(tshul gsum rang ngos nas grub pa)*. The three modes of a sign are the presence of the reason in the subject, the forward entailment and the reverse entailment. For example, in the syllogism "The subject, a pot, is impermanent because of being a product," the first mode—the presence of the reason in the subject—is the applicability of the reason (product) to the subject (pot), i.e., that pot is a product; the forward entailment, roughly speaking, is that whatever is a product is necessarily impermanent; and the reverse entailment, roughly speaking, is that whatever is not impermanent is necessarily not a product. Because the Svātantrikas are said to hold that conventionally, phenomena *do* inherently or autonomously exist, the phenomena used in their syllogisms, and the relationships between them, are said to inherently or autonomously exist.

[8]On Buddhapālita and Candrakīrti, see Ruegg (1981: 60-61, 71-81). Jamyang Shayba, whose works on the tenets of Indian Buddhism provide much

kīrti is, after Nāgārjuna, clearly the most important figure in the history of the school. According to Tāranātha,[9] Candrakīrti was a south Indian who learned all branches of knowledge at an early age and became a scholar's scholar at Nālanda University, learning about Nāgārjuna's treatises from both Bhāvaviveka's and Buddhapālita's disciples but favoring the latter. He was able to do many miraculous feats such as milking a picture of a cow and passing through walls. He defeated many non-Buddhist opponents in debate, converted many people to Buddhism, and wrote several profound treatises on the Middle Way philosophy.

According to the Gelukba scholar Losang Gönchok *(blo bzang dkon mchog)*, other Indian Prāsaṅgikas of great stature include Nāgārjuna's student Āryadeva (c. 170-270); Śāntideva (eighth century), who wrote the well-loved classic *Engaging in the Bodhisattva Deeds* (*byang chub sems dpa'i spyod pa la 'jug pa, bodhisattvacaryāvatāra*); Atīśa (982-1054), who was instrumental in the revitalization of Tibetan Buddhism in the eleventh century; and Jayānanda (latter half of eleventh century), who, as the translator of his works into Tibetan, promoted Candrakīrti's stature even though he was later criticized for his own commentary on Candrakīrti's *Entrance to (Nāgārjuna's) "Treatise on the Middle Way" (dbu ma la 'jug pa, madhyamakāvatāra)*.[10]

---

of the basis for this book, is perhaps unique in considering Buddhapālita the actual founder of the school. However, Janggya claims that Jamyang Shayba privately also considered Candrakīrti to be the founder. Janggya, *Presentation of Tenets* 288.20-89.5; see Lopez (1987: 256).

[9]Tāranātha (1970: 198-99).

[10]These authors and their works are listed by Losang Gönchok in his commentary (218.1-19.3) on the root verses of Jamyang Shayba's (*'jam dbyangs bzhad pa*, 1648-1721) massive *Great Exposition of Tenets*. It is called *Word Commentary on the Root Text of (Jamyang Shayba's) "Tenets," Clear Crystal Mirror (grub mtha' rtsa ba'i tshig ṭik shel dkar me long)*. In addition, he regards Aśvaghoṣa (also, according to Tāranātha [132], called Śūra and Mātṛceṭa) and Nāgabodhi as Mādhyamikas who also had the view of the Prāsaṅgika, though they did not identify themselves in a partisan way. Jayānanda wrote a large commentary to Candrakīrti's *Entrance* and was instrumental in establishing Prāsaṅgika in Tibet as the translator of the works of Candrakīrti. His commentary on Candrakīrti's *Entrance* is frequently criticized in Dzongkaba's commentary on the *Entrance* commonly called *Illumination of the Thought (dgongs pa rab gsal)*; see Hopkins (1980: *passim*). Nakamura (1987:

Together with Nāgārjuna and Candrakīrti they are the authors of the distinctive Prāsaṅgika literature, which includes the following nineteen works:

By Nāgārjuna:

1 ***Treatise on the Middle Way / Fundamental Treatise on the Middle Way, Called "Wisdom"*** *(dbu ma'i bstan bcos / dbu ma rtsa ba'i tshig le'ur byas pa shes rab ces bya ba, madhyamakaśāstra / prajñānāmamūlamadhyamaka-kārikā)*

2 ***Essay on the Mind of Enlightenment*** *(byang chub sems kyi 'grel pa, bodhicittavivaraṇa)*

3 ***Refutation of Objections*** *(rtsod pa bzlog pa'i tshig le'ur byas pa, vigrahavyāvartanīkārikā)*

4 ***Seventy Stanzas on Emptiness*** *(stong pa nyid bdun cu pa'i tshig le'ur byas pa, śūnyatāsaptatikārikā)*

5 ***Sixty Stanzas of Reasoning*** *(rigs pa drug cu pa'i tshig le'ur byas pa, yuktiṣaṣṭikākārikā)*

6 ***Treatise Called "The Finely Woven"*** *(zhib mo rnam par 'thag pa zhes bya ba'i mdo, vaidalyasūtranāma)*

7 ***Precious Garland of Advice for the King*** *(rgyal po la gtam bya ba rin po che'i phreng ba, rājaparikathāratnāvalī)*

By Āryadeva:

8 ***Four Hundred / Treatise of Four Hundred Stanzas*** *(bstan bcos bzhi brgya pa zhes bya ba'i tshig le'ur byas pa, catuḥśatakaśāstrakārikā)*

By Buddhapālita:

9 ***Buddhapālita's Commentary on (Nāgārjuna's) "Treatise on the Middle Way"*** *(dbu ma rtsa ba'i 'grel pa buddha pā li ta, buddhapālitamūlamadhyamakavṛtti)*

---

289) mentions some other later Mādhyamikas who wrote in criticism of Cittamātra and who were apparently Prāsaṅgikas: Prajñākaramati (c. 950-1000), who wrote an extensive commentary on Śāntideva's *Engaging in the Bodhisattva Deeds* (the only one extant by an Indian author) and Advayavajra (eleventh century), who wrote short outlines of the Buddhist philosophical schools. See also Ruegg (1981: 58, 107, 116). Dzongkaba refers to Prajñākaramati on several occasions (Hopkins, 1980: *passim*).

By Candrakīrti:

10 ***Entrance to (Nāgārjuna's) "Treatise on the Middle Way"*** *(dbu ma la 'jug pa, madhyamakāvatāra)*[11]

11 ***Autocommentary on the "Entrance to (Nāgārjuna's) 'Treatise on the Middle Way'"*** *(dbu ma la 'jug pa'i bshad*

[11]I have translated *'jug pa / avatāra* as "entrance" in accordance with most other translators. However, Hopkins (1983a: 868-71, n. 545) notes that according to former tantric abbot Kensur Lekden, the sense of "supplement" predominates in the Gelukba literature. The basis for that may be Dzongkaba's discussion of the term *avatāra* at the beginning of his *Illumination of the Thought* (adapted from Hopkins' translation [1980: 96-99]), which strongly suggests the translation "supplement." In what follows, each instance of *'jug pa* has been translated as "supplement."

> Our own system on this is that Candrakīrti supplements Nāgārjuna's *Treatise* in two ways, from the viewpoints of the profound and of the vast.
>
> With respect to the first, Candrakīrti says that he composed the *Supplement* in order to indicate that the meaning of the middle way that he ascertained is not shared with other Mādhyamikas....Also, refutation of the Cittamātra system, which was not done at length in Nāgārjuna's *Treatise* or in Candrakīrti's *Clear Words*, is extensive here in the *Supplement*. Therefore, one way in which this book supplements the *Treatise* is through its good determination of the meaning of the *Treatise* from the viewpoint of these two purposes [i.e., distinguishing its real meaning from its Cittamātra and Svātantrika interpretation].
>
> It also supplements the *Treatise* from the viewpoint of the vast....Although Nāgārjuna's *Treatise*, except for the topic of profundity, does not indicate the features of vastness in the Mahāyāna, his text was nevertheless composed in terms of the Mahāyāna rather than the Hīnayāna....Thus, [Candrakīrti thought that] it would be very good to fill in the gaps in the paths explained in the *Treatise on the Middle Way*—supplying the other Mahāyāna paths of vastness by way of the quintessential instructions of the Superior Nāgārjuna [as found in other of his works]....Thus, the second way that this text supplements Nāgārjuna's *Treatise on the Middle Way* is in supplementing the paths of the *Treatise* from the viewpoint of the vast.

In short, Dzongkaba argues that Candrakīrti aimed to clarify Nāgārjuna's thought by explaining how Nāgārjuna's middle way is not the one propounded by the Cittamātra or Svātantrika Schools and by adding explanations of the Mahāyāna paths—clearly attempts at augmentation rather than introduction.

pa / dbu ma la 'jug pa'i rang 'grel, madhyamakāvatāra-bhāṣya)

12 ***Commentary on (Nāgārjuna's) "Sixty Stanzas of Reasoning"*** *(rigs pa drug cu pa'i grel pa, yuktiṣaṣṭikāvṛtti)*

13 ***Clear Words, Commentary on (Nāgārjuna's) "Treatise on the Middle Way"*** *(dbu ma rtsa ba'i 'grel pa tshig gsal ba, mūlamadhyamakavṛttiprasannapadā)*

14 ***Commentary on (Āryadeva's) "Four Hundred Stanzas on the Yogic Deeds of Bodhisattvas"*** *(byang chub sems dpa'i rnal 'byor spyod pa bzhi brgya pa'i rgya cher 'grel pa, bodhisattvayogacaryācatuḥśatakaṭīkā)*

By Śāntideva:

15 ***Engaging in the Bodhisattva Deeds*** *(byang chub sems dpa'i spyod pa la 'jug pa, bodhisattvacaryāvatāra)*

16 ***Compendium of Learnings*** *(bslab pa kun las btus pa'i tshig le'ur byas pa, śikṣāsamuccayakārikā)*

By Atīśa:

17 ***Explanation of (Śāntideva's) "Engaging in the Bodhisattva Deeds"*** *(byang chub sems dpa'i spyod pa la 'jug pa'i bshad pa, bodhisattvacaryāvatārabhāṣya)*

18 ***Lamp for the Path to Enlightenment*** *(byang chub lam gyi sgron ma, bodhipathapradīpa)*

19 ***Quintessential Instructions on the Middle Way*** *(dbu ma'i man ngag, madhyamakopadeśa).*

These works have been a dominant force in Tibetan Buddhism. Monks of the Gelukba *(dge lugs pa)* order, the largest and, for more than four centuries, the most powerful of Tibet's Buddhist orders, explicitly identify themselves as Prāsaṅgikas and argue that all of the other principal Buddhist orders are basically Prāsaṅgika as well.[12] They are particularly committed to the writings of Candrakīrti. Though they study the

[12]The Gelukbas assert that all the major Tibetan sects are Prāsaṅgika, even if some of those sects do not explicitly identify themselves as such. For the Gelukba reasoning behind this assertion, see Hopkins 1983 (531-38—mostly a paraphrase of Janggya's *Presentation of Tenets* 291.9-99.8).

works of Nāgārjuna, Āryadeva, and others—of the nineteen works on this list, seven are by Nāgārjuna and five others are commentaries[13] on his works—they place particular emphasis on the *Entrance to the Middle Way* by Candrakīrti. They commit it to memory, work through monastic textbooks *(yig cha)* thick with detailed commentaries and hypothetical debates on it, and engage each other in hours of daily dialectical debate on its implications.

Despite the fact that they regard themselves as Prāsaṅgikas, the Gelukbas display a somewhat critical attitude toward the Prāsaṅgika texts; although they regard them with great reverence, they are at the same time willing, even eager, to creatively extend their conclusions. The Gelukba respect for Nāgārjuna and Candrakīrti—and their own founder, Dzongkaba Losang Drakba (*tsong kha pa blo bzang grags pa*, 1357-1419)—usually inhibits criticism. They cite the works of these scholars as authoritative in much the same way that earlier Buddhists cited the sūtras of Śākyamuni. On the other hand, since they are clearly committed to the pursuit of truth and prize logical consistency, they do not hesitate to "clarify" apparently incorrect statements with ingenious explanations that explicate what those Mādhyamika luminaries "must have meant." So, while it is true that the Gelukbas do not question the most fundamental aspects of Mādhyamika and Prāsaṅgika-Mādhyamika philosophy, regarding themselves as its conservators, they continue to struggle creatively toward a coherent *system* of Prāsaṅgika thought from the many sources they accept as authoritative. In this way they go far beyond Nāgārjuna and even Candrakīrti, neither of whom exhibits interest in the construction of a comprehensive system of tenets.

The translations (in parts two and three) of the works of Jamyang Shayba (*'jam dbyangs bzhad pa*, 1648-1721), Ngawang Belden (*ngag dbang dpal ldan*, b. 1797) and Janggya (*lcang skya*, 1717-86) demonstrate both conservative (uncritical) and liberal

---

[13]Kaydrup (Cabezón 1992: 82) identifies eight great Indian commentaries on Nāgārjuna's *Treatise on the Middle Way*, for instance, but only those of Buddhapālita and Candrakīrti made this list.

(extrapolating) tendencies. These seventeenth- and eighteenth-century Gelukbas, who wrote the most exhaustive works on comparative philosophical tenets in the history of Buddhism, attempt in their works to map a coherent system of Prāsaṅgika philosophy. In the process they make virtually no claims without the support of citations from the works, Indian and Tibetan, that they consider authoritative. This makes their texts a rich compendium of Prāsaṅgika writing (albeit one heavily weighted toward Candrakīrti and Dzongkaba).

Nevertheless, they will admit that there are apparent errors in those texts and will identify and correct them. To give just one example, in his annotations to the first chapter of Jamyang Shayba's text, Ngawang Belden notes that Candrakīrti says that one needs to interpret statements (by the Buddha) that a mind-basis-of-all *(kun gzhi rnam par shes pa, ālayavijñāna)*, person, and the five aggregates *(phung po, skandha)* substantially exist (*rdzas su yod pa, dravyasat*). The potential problem with Candrakīrti's statement is that it does not distinguish between the conventional, non-substantial existence of the person and aggregates on the one hand and the total non-existence of the mind-basis-of-all on the other hand. Thus, although he is "correct," Candrakīrti seems to have left himself open to potential criticism and this is being signaled.[14]

Moreover, Gelukba scholars explicate the rather terse and even obscure statements of Nāgārjuna, Candrakīrti, etc., making subtle distinctions that go well beyond those made in the Indian sources. This is evident in many of the unique tenets, such as those that concern the path attainments of non-Prāsaṅgikas (discussed in chapter 6). Crucial to the Gelukba exegesis of passages from Āryadeva, Candrakīrti, Śāntideva,

[14]However, Ngawang Belden defends Candrakīrti on the grounds that he says elsewhere that Buddha's statement about the mind-basis-of-all in particular was made sheerly for the benefit of those not ready to hear about emptiness and was not an indication that the mind-basis-of-all conventionally exists. Candrakīrti's basic statement is not in question: it is certainly true that since nothing substantially exists, statements about something that is held to be substantially existent must be interpreted in order to disclose the underlying thought of the speaker.

etc., is the distinction between different varieties of misconceptions of self: subtle versus coarse, innate versus artificial (i.e., acquired, not inborn), etc. Despite the fact that no such distinctions are made by any of those Indian philosophers, it would be difficult otherwise to explain many of the passages cited from their works.

Why the Unique Tenets are Unique: Conventional and Ultimate Analysis

The Gelukba presentation of Prāsaṅgika philosophy gives a somewhat different picture of Nāgārjuna's enterprise than has emerged from many studies that have not utilized Tibetan sources. Nāgārjuna subjected the assertions of Buddhist and non-Buddhist philosophers to withering analysis, reducing to absurdity all views that (according to Gelukba exegetes) depended on the postulation of inherently existent entities. Again and again he flung at opponents, real and hypothetical, consequences *(thal 'gyur, prasaṅga)* of their positions that demonstrated their untenability. For taking this approach of working from the assertions of others, Nāgārjuna has often been labeled a negativist without a system whose statement "I have no thesis of my own" indicates a refusal to make positive assertions.[15] An extreme version of this view is expressed by A. B. Keith, who characterizes Nāgārjuna as a nihilist:[16]

> Nāgārjuna denies consistently that he has any thesis of his own, for to uphold one would be wholly erroneous; the truth is silence, which is neither affirmation nor negation, for negation in itself is essentially positive in implying a reality.

---

[15]According to Gelukbas, Nāgārjuna meant by this statement only that he had no *inherently existent* theses, not that he had no theses at all. In fact, his works show that he has numerous theses. See Hopkins (1983a: 471-3, 847).

[16]Keith (1979: 239-41). That Nāgārjuna was a nihilist is the thesis of a more recent monograph by Wood (1994), based on translations from Sanskrit sources.

> He confines himself to reducing every positive assertion to absurdity, thus showing that the intellect condemns itself as inadequate just as it finds hopeless antimonies in the world of experience...If we accept the strict doctrine of Nāgārjuna, as interpreted by Buddhapālita and Candrakīrti, and accepted by Çāntideva, we must admit that the phenomenal world has not merely no existence in absolute truth, but has no phenomenal existence, difficult as this conception is, and numerous as are the failures of its holders to exactly express it.

Others, to be sure, have been more moderate in their assessment of Nāgārjuna and his method, but even if they have admitted that Nāgārjuna did not reject the existence of conventional phenomena, they maintain that he refused to make any positive assertions. B. K. Matilal concludes:[17]

> It needs to be emphasized, even at the risk of repetition, that the doctrine of emptiness does not actually consist in the rejection of the phenomenal world, but in the maintenance of a non-committal attitude toward the phenomena and in the non-acceptance of any theory of the phenomenal world as finally valid.

Of course, a number of writers have recognized that even Nāgārjuna's rejection of the views of others in some sense constitutes "views" of his own,[18] and that Nāgārjuna's assertion that things arise only dependently, not by their own character, is a positive assertion about dependent-arising *(pratītyasamutpāda, rten 'byung)*.[19] Still, the preponderance of scholarship, perhaps wary of distorting Nāgārjuna's intention by ascribing to him particular positions on such matters as the validation of perception, the Buddhist soteriological path

---

[17]Matilal (1971: 156).

[18]For instance, Richard Jones, "The Nature and Function of Nāgārjuna's Arguments," *Philosophy East and West* 28 (1978), p. 485.

[19]Alex Wayman, "Who Understands the Four Alternatives of the Buddhist Texts?" *Philosophy East and West* 27 (1977), p. 14. Also, Harris (1991) shows that Nāgārjuna does not always proceed by flinging consequences, but sometimes makes dogmatic statements.

structure, etc., has focused exclusively on Nāgārjuna's negative dialectic.

The topics with which this book is concerned reflect a radically different assessment, since they comprise a collection of Mādhyamika School tenets *(grub mtha', siddhānta)*[20] that are attributed directly or indirectly to Nāgārjuna himself. They show that those in Tibet who consider themselves Nāgārjuna's spiritual heirs have adopted particular positive metaphysical, epistemological, and soteriological positions that they believe are his. These topics are widely known among Gelukba scholars as the "unique tenets" *(thun mong ma yin pa'i grub mtha')* of the Prāsaṅgika-Mādhyamika School. Dzongkaba has explicitly identified them with Nāgārjuna, calling them the "great difficult points of (Nāgārjuna's) *Treatise on the Middle Way Called 'Wisdom.'*"[21]

They are, indeed, difficult points. Several of the prominent Gelukba scholars with whom I worked, when informed that my project concerned these topics, sucked in their breath and shook their heads: "Very difficult. Very difficult." Some are thorny problems of a highly technical nature; others are issues that go to the heart of the unique Prāsaṅgika view that no phenomenon exists inherently, but only as a mere nominal imputation, which even its adherents admit is a tenet notoriously difficult to understand properly and therefore not the appropriate view to be taught to a mass audience. Some of the topics of the "unique tenets" are all the more difficult because they pivot on these crucial bases.

The presentation of the Prāsaṅgika tenets occurs against the backdrop of a hierarchical arrangement of Buddhist philosophies. The historical verity of this arrangement is highly

[20]*Grub mtha' / siddhānta* is literally "established conclusion"; Gönchok Jikmay Wangbo defines it as "a thesis decided upon and established in reliance on scripture and / or reasoning and which, from the perspective of one's mind, will not be forsaken for something else" (3.14-4.1; translated in Sopa and Hopkins [150]).

[21]This is the title of a small book by Dzongkaba: *Explanation of the Eight Great Difficult Points of (Nāgārjuna's) "Fundamental Treatise on the Middle Way Called 'Wisdom'" (rtsa pa shes rab kyi dka' gnas chen po brgyad kyi bshad pa*; Sarnath: Pleasure of Elegant Sayings Press, 1970).

disputable; there is little evidence of real Indian "schools" in the sense of lineages dedicated to a certain systematic view. However, for Gelukbas the "schools" represent the distillation of certain definite and strong currents in Indian thinking, based on the intellectual heritage translated from Sanskrit to Tibetan during the formative period (sixth century C.E. onwards) of Tibetan Buddhism. Also, Tibetans have seen the schools as the natural outcome of the Buddha's three "Wheel Turnings" (as exemplified in the *Sūtra Unraveling the Thought* [*dgongs pa nges par 'grel pa'i mdo, saṃdhinirmocanasūtra*]); their hermeneutic stresses that the Buddha, the master pedagogue, fully intended to promote distinctive and contradictory views to serve different types of students. In ascending order of proximity to the correct position of the highest school, the Prāsaṅgika School, they are:

1 **Vaibhāṣikas** (Proponents of the "Great Exposition," *bye brag smra ba)*[22]
2 **Āgamānusāra-Sautrāntikas** (Proponents of Sūtra Following Scripture, *lung gi rje su 'brang pa'i mdo sde pa*)[23]
3 **Nyāyānusāra-Sautrāntikas** (Proponents of Sūtra Following Reasoning, *rigs gi rje su 'brang pa'i mdo sde pa*)[24]
4 **Āgamānusāra-Cittamātrins** (Proponents of Mind-Only Following Scripture, *lung gi rje su 'brang pa'i sems tsam pa*)[25]

---

[22]Vaibhāṣikas are so-called because they rely upon the *Mahāvibhāṣā* (*bye brag bshad mtsho chen mo*—although it was not translated into Tibetan). There are generally held to be eighteen subschools, although different ancient authors had different lists. See Hopkins (1983a: 713-19). Historically, the most important school seems to have been the Sarvāstivāda.

[23]These Sautrāntikas are followers of the views in Vasubandhu's *Treasury of Higher Knowledge* (*chos mngon pa'i mdzod kyi tshig le'ur byas pa, abhidharmakośakārikā*). On the translation of *chos mngon pa / abhidharma*, see my note in the next chapter at the point of discussion of the works of Vasubandhu.

[24]These Sautrāntikas follow the views in Dignāga's *Compendium on Prime Cognition* (*tshad ma kun las btus pa, pramāṇasamuccaya*) and the works of Dharmakīrti, the most famous of which is a commentary on Dignāga's work.

[25]These Cittamātrins embrace the views of Asaṅga.

5 **Nyāyānusāra-Cittamātrins** (Proponents of Mind-Only Following Reasoning, *rigs gi rje su 'brang pa'i sems tsam pa*)[26]

6 **Yogācāra-Svātantrika-Mādhyamikas** (Middle Way Autonomy Yogic Practitioners, *rnal 'byor spyod pa'i dbu ma rang rgyud pa*)[27]

7 **Sautrāntika-Svātantrika-Mādhyamikas** (Middle Way Autonomy Sūtra Practitioners, *mdo sde spyod pa'i dbu ma rang rgyud pa*)[28]

8 **Prāsaṅgika-Mādhyamikas** (Middle Way Consequentialists)

In the Gelukba monasteries, the positions of all schools are studied in order to fully understand the Buddhist context of the highest system, the Prāsaṅgika School. Jamyang Shayba, whose *Great Exposition of Tenets* is itself the greatest textbook for such a study, says that "the views of the lower systems are also a platform for [understanding] the views of the upper systems."[29] The twentieth-century Gelukba abbot, Kensur Yeshey Tupden, recommended that:[30]

> The student who has faith in emptiness but does not understand it begins by studying the Vaibhāṣika system, then Sautrāntika, Cittamātra, Svātantrika, and finally Prāsaṅgika.

---

[26]Like the Sautrāntikas following reasoning, these Cittamātrins rely upon the works of Dignāga and Dharmakīrti; however, they differ from Sautrāntikas in that they reject the existence of external objects and assert that all sentient beings eventually become Buddhas (a teaching known as "one final vehicle").

[27]These Svātantrikas are those who follow the views of the Indian abbot Śāntarakṣita, who was instrumental (along with Padmasambhava) in establishing the first monastery in Tibet. As their name implies, they combine views identified as Mādhyamika and as Cittamātra (which is also called Yogācāra).

[28]These Svātantrikas are identified with the views of Bhāvaviveka, who is also considered the founder of Svātantrika in general because of differences that Gelukbas have discerned between his and Buddhapālita's interpretations of Nāgārjuna.

[29]Jamyang Shayba's root verse, DSK II 56.3, cited in Losang Gönchok, *Word Commentary* 12.1-2.

[30]Klein 1994: 86.

> This method guards against undermining students' understanding of dependent arising, so that they will not [wrongly] conclude that validly established phenomena do not exist at all.

Partly as a result of giving these "lower" views a high degree of value in the overall soteriology, and partly because of their role-playing in the debate courtyard, Gelukba expositors of tenets attempt to present them in a fair and balanced way.[31]

Since Tibetans named those of the Nāgārjuna-Candrakīrti school "Prāsaṅgikas" ("flingers of consequences") because of their procedure of working with the assertions of others—adducing unwanted consequences to those positions rather than pushing their own conclusions—it will not be surprising that the "unique tenets" are largely a list of the faulty assertions of *others*, exposed as such by the unique standpoint of the Prāsaṅgika School. However, the Gelukbas who have collected these tenets are not content to merely propound the negative assertions of the Prāsaṅgikas; they also construct, out of the Indian source-material, Prāsaṅgika solutions to the difficulties they raise. For instance, the Prāsaṅgika School is hardly unique in denying the existence of a "mind-basis-of-all" *(kun gzhi rnam par shes pa, ālayavijñāna)*, a consciousness that contains all of the seeds for future experiences that have been deposited by past intentional actions *(las, karman)*. In fact, only one of the eight principal Buddhist schools or subschools identified by the Tibetan doxographers claim that such a consciousness exists. Nevertheless, the Prāsaṅgika refutation of the mind-basis-of-all reveals the unique viewpoint of the Prāsaṅgikas, who reject the existence of any entities that exist by their own nature, and it affords them an opportunity to articulate the unique assertion that the mere disintegratedness *(zhig pa, nāṣa)* of an action is sufficient to cause a later effect.

This example also is used to demonstrate that Prāsaṅgikas do not merely qualify the assertions of the lower schools by - labeling them "conventional," as some have thought. Because

[31]This seems to me to be true from my own limited experience; however, I am also replying on the judgements of Perdue (1992) and Hopkins (1983a, especially pp. 575-77).

the Prāsaṅgikas accept nothing as existing ultimately, but do accept things that exist conventionally, it has sometimes been thought that the only difference between Prāsaṅgikas and others is that what the lower schools assert as ultimate, Prāsaṅgikas assert to be conventional. In fact, Candrakīrti accuses the Svātantrika-Mādhyamikas of making this generalization about Nāgārjuna's positions:[32]

> May scholars ascertain that just as it is the case that except for this Mādhyamika textual system, in other treatises this doctrine of emptiness is not expressed without error,[33] so also this system appearing here, which I have expressed along with answers to objections, like the doctrine of emptiness, does not exist in other treatises. Because of that, the proposition by certain Mādhyamikas that just what Sautrāntikas and Vaibhāṣikas propound to be ultimate, Mādhyamikas assert to be conventional, is set forth by those who do not understand the suchness [explained] in (Nāgārjuna's) *Treatise on the Middle Way* because it is unreasonable for a supramundane doctrine to be similar to a mundane doctrine.[34]

According to Gelukba scholars, it is true enough that, because non-Prāsaṅgikas assert the existence of phenomena that are inherently or truly existent—what they consider "ultimate"—Prāsaṅgikas in general accept as "conventional" what others assert to be "ultimate." However, there are a number of other

---

[32]*Autocommentary on the "Entrance,"* 255.3-7 (P 5263, vol. 98, 166.2.1-5). This passage has been cited by Jamyang Shayba in the introduction to "unique tenets" as it has been altered slightly by Dzongkaba in his *Illumination of the Thought*; for a review of the alterations, see the list of emendations. It has been translated here in accordance with Dzongkaba's edition, on which Jamyang Shayba relies.

[33]In other words, the Mādhyamika School textual system of Nāgārjuna and Āryadeva is the only one that correctly sets forth the doctrine of emptiness (that phenomena are empty of inherent existence), and Candrakīrti is the only one who correctly understands Nāgārjuna's explanation of suchness (emptiness) in his *Treatise on the Middle Way*.

[34]That is, if Nāgārjuna's doctrine were as the Svātantrikas have explained it, the supramundane doctrine of Nāgārjuna, a doctrine that actually leads to passage beyond sorrow *(myang 'das, nirvāṇa)* would be no better than the mundane doctrine of other schools.

phenomena, such as a mind-basis-of-all, self-consciousness *(rang rig, svasaṃvedanā),* and autonomous syllogisms *(rang rgyud kyi sbyor ba, svatantra-prayoga),* that Prāsaṅgikas do not accept as existing even conventionally. Therefore, they *do* reject some positions entirely and, furthermore, provide alternative explanations for them.

On what basis are these phenomena rejected? I wish to argue that one major way in which Gelukba Prāsaṅgikas have creatively extended Candrakīrti's Prāsaṅgika philosophy is through distinguishing an implicit principle that Prāsaṅgikas can use to challenge and dispense with certain assertions of their opponents, and that in several of the "unique tenets" it is precisely this principle that is evoked. Simply put, the Gelukbas distinguish between two types of analysis, conventional and ultimate, the former being the proper establisher of all conventional phenomena (i.e., those phenomena other than emptinesses), the latter being employed by schools such as Cittamātra in the course of describing or attempting to prove the existence of entities such as the mind-basis-of-all or self-consciousness. The Gelukba authors whose works are translated in parts two and three explain that Prāsaṅgikas must reject some supposed existents outright because they cannot be established through conventional analysis, the only valid means of establishing phenomena other than emptiness. Thus, the distinction between ultimate and conventional analysis often becomes the analytical knife with which the Prāsaṅgikas distinguish themselves from other schools—not conventional and ultimate *existence,* which all schools propound, but conventional and ultimate *analysis,* which has to do with the way in which those phenomena are analytically established.

Following Dharmakīrti, Gelukbas say that conventional valid cognition, the means by which conventional analysis is carried out, is of two types: direct and inferential. Valid cognition is that which is correct and incontrovertible toward its main object. Sense direct valid cognition such as by the eye, ear, nose, tongue, and body is simply that sense cognition that is not affected by superficial causes of error such as a fault in the physical sense-power, distorting atmospheric conditions, movement, etc., and that apprehends its object without the medium of concepts. Direct valid cognition also includes mental direct valid cognition, which is induced by sense direct valid cognition, and yogic direct valid cognition. Nevertheless, all such cognition by ordinary beings is affected by an element of false appearance because objects that appear to ordinary beings seem to inherently exist. Still, Gelukbas say that Prāsaṅgikas regard such conventional cognition to be valid, since it is correct with regard to the basic entity of its object.

Inferential valid cognition of the conventional sort includes all types of reasoning processes with the exception of (1) those that are fallacious and (2) those that seek to establish an ultimately existent object. An instance of the former would be reasoning that because wherever there is smoke, there is fire, that it follows that wherever there is fire, there is smoke (which does not follow because there are many kinds of smokeless fire). An instance of the latter would be a conceptual consciousness that imputes a phenomenon *to* its parts—e.g., that thinks that the legs, back, and seat of a chair *are* a chair, rather than merely being the *basis* of the designation "chair," chair being a mere imputation or nominal designation *in dependence on* legs, seat, and back. Opponents are said to engage in ultimate analysis when they posit entities through this sort of process; in other words, they are being said to posit some objects that, if they could be established at all, could be established only by engaging in ultimate analysis. Candrakīrti and subsequent Prāsaṅgikas, on the other hand, are said to posit objects the way the world does, without (ultimate) analysis and investigation.

According to Dzongkaba,[35] something is established as existing conventionally if it is (1) well known to a conventional consciousness, (2) not damaged by conventional valid cognition, and (3) not damaged by ultimate valid cognition. In other words, a phenomenon must be perceivable by a con-

[35]*Great Exposition of Special Insight* (Dharamsala edition 405a.1-6b.4); the complete discussion can be found in Wayman's confusing translation (1978: 236-38).

sciousness that is not involved in realizing its emptiness of inherent existence, such as an eye, ear, nose, tongue, body, or mental consciousness not investigating the ultimate;[36] it must not be vulnerable to refutation by conventional valid cognition, such as occurs when "blue" snowy mountains seen from a distance are discovered to be white or when a reflection is discovered not to function in the manner of the object reflected; and it must not be vulnerable to refutation by ultimate valid cognition, such as occurs when something is claimed to be inherently existent but in fact cannot be found when sought by ultimate analysis (for instance, the mind-basis-of-all or self-consciousness asserted by the Cittamātra School).[37]

The first criterion—that something be well known to a conventional consciousness—is not logically necessary,[38] since the remaining two will exclude all non-existent and ultimate phenomena, but it is useful because it indicates that Prāsaṅgikas begin with the conceptions of ordinary worldlings, limiting that class only by excluding what valid cognition refutes. That something is *well known* to a conventional consciousness does not have to mean that ordinary beings have to know about it. If that were the case, then emptiness and many other phenomena could not be said to exist. The point is that if ordinary beings *did* know about it, their ordinary non-analytical awarenesses would not be seeking the mode of being of those phenomena. Concerning this criterion, Dzongkaba says:[39]

> [The relationship between] actions and effects, the grounds and paths, and so forth are not well known to the common

---

[36]According to Kensur Yeshey Tupden (Klein 1994: 46), these phenomena may include well-known things that don't exist, such as water (in the case of a mirage) or the "horns of a rabbit" (a well-known non-entity).

[37]Kensur Yeshey Tupden (Klein 1994: 138) contends that "ultimate valid cognition" is a misnomer, since all valid cognitions are conventional, meaning that their objects are conventionally existent phenomena. Rather, this refers to ultimate analysis.

[38]As pointed out by Guy Newland (1992: 85).

[39]Newland translation (1992: 84) of Dzongkaba's *Great Exposition of the Stages of the Path* 842.2-4.

> person. However, when [such things] are taken as objects through hearing and experience, etc., they appear to ordinary minds that do not analyze how [their final] mode of being exists. Thus, [while it would be] a fault [if such things] were not well known in the world, this is not the case.

All things that exist, exist conventionally, for nothing exists ultimately. Even emptiness, despite being an ultimate *truth*, exists only conventionally, not ultimately. Furthermore, emptiness exists only conventionally despite the fact that it is realized as the result of an ultimate analysis, the point being that it was not what was sought in the analysis but is itself precisely the non-finding of an ultimately existing phenomenon by ultimate analysis.[40] Emptiness, too, is empty; it does not withstand ultimate analysis.

The distinction between ultimate and conventional analysis is not used to make blanket rejections of other schools. Prāsaṅgikas are in fact rejecting only what they see as those schools' *hypotheses*—phenomena that can be certified by neither valid sense cognition nor valid inference, phenomena invented to paper over certain perceived philosophical conundrums. For instance, the Cittamātra School's assertion of a mind-basis-of-all is really a hypothesis formulated to meet the perceived need for a stable, neutral medium for the transmittal of karmic latencies; but of course it is not put forward as a mere hypothesis, since it is said to exist. Gelukbas object not to the imputation of a basis for karmic latencies—according to them, the Prāsaṅgikas have their own, the "mere I"[41]—but to treating a mere imputation as if it existed in and of itself. Otherwise, as stated earlier, Prāsaṅgikas are content to accept the conventional existence of phenomena that other schools assert.

---

[40]Kensur Yeshey Tupden (Klein 1994: 48) adds that, therefore, a consciousness directly realizing emptiness, which is not involved in analysis, is a conventional consciousness whose object is a conventionally existent phenomenon.

[41]The "mere I" is a mere imputation of "I" in dependence on the aggregates of mind and body, not a substantial entity like a mind-basis-of-all.

The prohibition against ultimate analysis does not prohibit analysis in general, and Prāsaṅgikas demonstrate this by some of their discriminations with respect to conventional phenomena. Candrakīrti distinguishes between objects that are real and unreal from the viewpoint of the world:[42]

> Objects realized by the world [and] apprehended
> By the six unimpaired sense powers
> Are true from just [the viewpoint of] the world. The rest
> Are posited as unreal from just [the viewpoint of] the world.

Dzongkaba, commenting on this, identifies phenomena such as reflections as unreal in relation to the world:[43]

> The rest—that is, reflections, and so forth—that appear as objects when the sense powers are impaired, are posited as being unreal in relation to just the world. The word "just" indicates that without relying on a reasoning consciousness, just conventional valid cognition is sufficient to posit those consciousnesses as mistaken.

According to Dzongkaba, the ordinary worldly discrimination involved in recognizing that a mirror-image of a face is not a face, etc., is not a search for an object that can be found upon analysis, but merely the use of conventional valid cognition to overcome error or potential error based on one's initial perception of the mirror-image. The distinctions of Candrakīrti and Dzongkaba are further refined by Ngawang Belden, who distinguishes between what is real in relation to the perspective of the world *('jig rten shes ngo la ltos te yang dak)* and what is unreal in that perspective.[44] The first category includes those phenomena that cannot be realized as unreal without depending upon ultimate analysis—conventional phenomena such as trees, rocks, etc. The second category comprises phenomena that can be realized as unreal by conven-

---

[42]*Entrance* (VI.25) 5b.5-6. This quotation and the next follow the translations of Newland (1988: 252, 253-54). Also translated in Huntington 160.

[43]*Illumination of the Thought* 200.2-4.

[44]*Annotations* 180, 201, 203 (Sarnath edition). See Newland (1988: 268-69).

tional valid cognition, such as reflections or mirages. Presumably, the latter, when just considered *as* reflections, mirages, etc., are also real in relation to the perspective of the world—a reflection is really a reflection, though it is not really that which it reflects. Many other kinds of distinctions might be made with regard to how conventional phenomena may be analyzed without falling into the extreme of ultimate analysis.

To recapitulate, the Gelukba extension of Candrakīrti's Prāsaṅgika philosophy provides the implicit rationale for Candrakīrti's rejection of certain positions by demonstrating a principle at the heart of his work that is used to cut down mistaken tenets. Those assertions that are not supported by worldly renown and must involve the use of ultimate analysis, since they cannot be established by conventional analysis, must be rejected. Thus, the Cittamātra School's fabrication of self-consciousness is rejected in part because it involves ultimate analysis of the cause and effect of memory; its rejection of external objects is repudiated in part because it involves ultimate analysis into the cause and effect of consciousness; its theory of a mind-basis-of-all is opposed because it involves ultimate analysis of the relationship between a thing and its bases of designation; and those who deny that disintegratedness is a functioning thing are disputed because their reasoning is based on ultimate analysis into the relationship between disintegratedness and its basis of designation, that which has disintegrated.

But as was said earlier, the Gelukbas go even further, not only elaborating Candrakīrti's criticisms of the positions of others but also proposing *solutions* to those problems. That is, their analysis is not purely negative, but extends to an explanation of positive principles. The crucial question to be considered now is whether or not they violate their own principles by inventing entities that, no less than those proposed by the Cittamātra or other schools, require ultimate analysis for their establishment. I would argue that they do *not*.

For instance, an enduring problem in Indian religion is the provision of a way to account for the transmittal of karmic potencies from one incarnation to the next. Non-Buddhist theories have been built upon the postulation of an enduring metaphysical self or soul, the *ātman*, in which karmic potencies can be infused or (as in Jainism) upon which karmic potencies can become encrusted. Buddhist schools, which for the most part have never admitted the possibility of an *ātman* (the Pudgalavādins—"Proponents of the Person" [*gang zag smra ba*]—being a possible exception) have invented a number of substantial entities that could serve to link two incarnations: "obtainers" *(thob pa, prāpti)*, the basic continuum of the mind *(sems rgyud, cittasaṅtāna)*, "non-wastage" *(chud mi za ba, avipranāśa)*, and mind-basis-of-all.[45]

On this topic, the Gelukbas assert, in effect, that the Prāsaṅgikas find it unnecessary to posit any such entity at all. Rather, the mere fact that actions have ceased, or disintegrated—their disintegratedness *(zhig pa, naṣṭa)*—is sufficient to cause a future effect to issue forth from those actions. An action's disintegratedness is neither a substantial entity separate from it nor a permanent, unchanging phenomenon; hence, disintegratedness does not accrue the same unwanted consequences flung by Prāsaṅgikas at the other possibilities. In order to construct the "solution" of disintegratedness, Gelukbas put together Candrakīrti's statements in two sources—statements in his *Clear Words* (his commentary on Nāgārjuna's *Treatise on the Middle Way*) in which he establishes that a state of disintegratedness is caused and acts as a cause and statements in his *Commentary on (Āryadeva's) "Four Hundred,"* where he says that even though many eons have passed since an action has ceased, its effects can be experienced.

---

[45]According to Gönchok Jikmay Wangbo (*Precious Garland of Tenets* 21.14-22.2, translated in Sopa and Hopkins [193]), the Kashmiri Vaibhāṣikas and the Sautrāntikas both identify the continuum of mind as the basis of infusion of predispositions (as do Svātantrika-Mādhyamikas). Other Vaibhāṣikas posit a vague factor, neither matter nor consciousness, called an "obtainer" as that which prevents the loss of the karmic potency until it ripens into an effect. According to Dzongkaba (*Extensive Commentary on the Difficult Points of the "Afflicted Mind and Basis-of-All"* 14b.6), Cittamātrins also refer to these latencies as obtainers. The five Saṃmitīya sub-schools of the Vaibhāṣikas say that actions produce an impermanent phenomenon called "non-wastage" that prevents the loss of the action's potency (Lamotte, "Le traité de l'acte de Vasubandhu" 162-63).

These statements are used explicitly to construct an alternative to substantialist positions that cannot be established through conventional valid cognition. The Gelukba solution to the problem is unique in that it does not involve the postulation of a metaphysical entity.

Another strategy employed by Gelukbas in formulating Prāsaṅgika solutions to the problems for which others resort to the postulation of substantial entities is to argue that since things do not inherently exist, it is *unnecessary* to posit a way to bridge apparent differences; rather, the conventions of the world can be taken at face value. For instance, refuting the notion of self-consciousness, they argue that since a remembering consciousness and the previous consciousness, such as an eye consciousness that apprehended a patch of blue, are not inherently other, there is no need to make a distinction between the two. We merely say, "*I* saw blue," not distinguishing between the self of the time of seeing and the time of remembering, between an eye consciousness and a later memory consciousness. Candrakīrti says in his *Entrance to (Nāgārjuna's) "Treatise on the Middle Way"* (VI.75):[46]

> Because for me this memory is not [inherently] other
> Than that [mind] by which the object was experienced,
> One remembers, "I saw [this earlier]."
> This is also the way of worldly convention.

Ngawang Belden, commenting on this, says:[47]

> One does not think, "The self of the time of remembering is the self of the time of [previous] experience," and one does not use the verbal convention, "Previously I saw the blue which was qualified by being the object which subsists [both] at the time of this utterance and the time of the [previous object]."

---

[46]*Entrance to the Middle Way* 7b.9. Dzongkaba's commentary is in *Illumination of the Thought* 159a.4-60a.4. Translated by Lamotte in *Muséon* 11: 353 and by Huntington (166).

[47]*Annotations* 116b.

The postulation of inherently existent entities only serves to unnecessarily complicate matters. In this way, the Prāsaṅgikas can simultaneously affirm the conventions of the world and avoid the creation of a substantialist solution.

The theme of the acceptance of worldly conventions is frequently sounded in both Indian and Tibetan Prāsaṅgika philosophy. Among Candrakīrti's numerous affirmations of the value of the world's conventions is this passage in his *Entrance to the Middle Way* (VI.22):[48] "We assert that worldly [people], abiding in their own views, are valid." In his *Commentary on (Nāgārjuna's) "Sixty Stanzas of Reasoning,"* he says:[49]

> Worldly things are not to be asserted through scrutiny and analysis. How then? In accordance with what is well known in the world.

In his *Clear Words,*[50] he says that this acceptance of what the world asserts is for the sake of ordinary persons, who may not be able to understand the Buddha's teaching about emptiness (also called "suchness"): "...the Buddhas help beings who are trainees, and who do not know suchness, with reasoning as it is well known to them." For this reason, Prāsaṅgikas are sometimes called "Mādhyamikas who take what is well known in the world" *('jig rten grags sde spyod pa'i dbu ma pa, lokaprasiddhavargacārimādhyamika).*[51]

In general, Prāsaṅgikas agree with the world about the existence of worldly things, though they do not always agree with the world's assessment of those things, such as the efficacy of ritual sacrifice or bathing.[52] And of course Prāsaṅ-

---

[48]*Entrance to the Middle Way* 5b.2-3. Also translated in Huntington (160).

[49]P 5265, vol. 98, 177.4.2. Toh. 3864, vol. 7, 8.3.6.

[50]Translated by Hopkins (1983a: 526). Also translated by Sprung (1979: 42): "The Buddhas themselves, out of concern for those they were guiding, who were ignorant of logic, made their points in terms of the conventional ideas of these people themselves." Sanskrit edited by Poussin 36.1-2.

[51]Budön (Obermiller 1931: vol. 2, 135).

[52]For instance, Candrakīrti, in his *Commentary on (Nāgārjuna's) "Sixty Stanzas of Reasoning,"* says that the four conceptions of the body as clean, blissful, as a self, or as permanent, are wrong even for a worldly perspective (cited in Jamyang Shayba's *Great Exposition of the Middle Way* 558). This is

gikas cannot approve of phenomena as the world perceives them, for the world conceives of phenomena as if they existed inherently, from their own side, and Prāsaṅgikas regard that conception to be the very root of cyclic existence. To be true to both the conventions of the world and to the tenet of the lack of inherent existence requires the Gelukbas to use numerous subtle distinctions, distinctions not always made in Candrakīrti's works. Candrakīrti's insistence upon respect for the conventions of the world stopped short of schemes to classify and order conventionalities. Gelukbas place great emphasis on respecting the conventions of the world, perhaps stemming from Dzongkaba's experience of a vision of Mañjushrī, who advised him to value appearances.[53]

Of things about which ordinary people do *not* speak, I would argue that Gelukbas consider Prāsaṅgikas to accept only those that are supramundane aspects of the Buddhist path such as the special consciousnesses that occur as a result of building the accumulations of merit and wisdom necessary to progress toward Buddhahood and the extraordinary powers such as levitation, clairvoyance, etc., that are by-products of that development. On what grounds can Prāsaṅgikas accept these phenomena without giving up the principle of rejecting what is not accepted by the world? Perhaps it is because these phenomena can at least be certified by yogis whereas those the Prāsaṅgikas reject cannot. Since these can be empirically verified in one's own experience without resorting to ultimate analysis, they are distinct from the postulated entities of the Cittamātra School, such as self-consciousness and the mind-

admittedly difficult to square with his general approval of the conventions of the world, since it seems that at least the first of these, that the body, if washed, is clean, is well accepted in the world. However, if what is meant by worldly perspective is conventional valid cognition, it can be argued that conventional valid cognition, establishing that the body always contains foul substances such as bile, phlegm, urine, and excrement, establishes that it cannot be made clean by superficial washing and hence, its cleanliness is not actually upheld in the world.

[53]Thurman (1984: 79) translates a portion of Kaydrup's biography of Dzongkaba, found in volume *ka*, 3a.4, of the Ngawang Gelek Demo edition of the collected works of Dzongkaba.

basis-of-all, which cannot, according to Prāsaṅgika, be objects of knowledge.

Enumeration of the Unique Tenets

A number of Gelukba authors have written about the "unique tenets"; most of them comment only on the eight points identified by Dzongkaba,[54] who may have been the first to produce such a list.[55] Translations of the relevant portions of two Gelukba works on philosophical tenets comprise the last two parts of this book. Those are Jamyang Shayba's *Great Exposition of Tenets*, published in 1699, and Janggya's *Presentation of Tenets (grub mtha'i rnam bzhag)*, composed between 1736 and 1746. Jamyang Shayba's list, comprising eight *pairs* of tenets, is by far the largest. The following is a collation of lists of the "unique tenets," beginning with the sixteen identified by Jamyang Shayba:

---

[54]The list of eight appearing in Dzongkaba's *Illumination of the Thought* is also found in two short works in the "Collected Works" *(gsung 'bum)* of Dzongkaba's close disciple Gyeltsap (*rgyal tshab*, 1364-1432): *Eight Great Difficult Points of (Nāgārjuna's) "Treatise on the Middle Way" (dbu ma'i rtsa ba'i dka' gnas chen po brgyad)* and *Notes on the Eight Great Difficult Points, Preventing Forgetfulness of the Foremost One's Speech (dka' gnas brgyad gyi zin bris rje'i gsung bzhin brjed byang du bkod pa bcugs)*. They are also found in a short work by Rongta Losang Damchö Gyatso (*rong tha blo bzang dam chos rgya mtsho*, 1863-1917): *Mode of Asserting the Unique Tenets of the Glorious Prāsaṅgikas, A Few Letters of Beginning, Moonlight by Which the Intelligent Distinguish Errors (dpal ldan phal 'gyur ba'i thun mong ma yin pa'i bzhed tshul las brtsams pa'i yi ge nyung du blo gros kun da 'byed pa'i zla 'od)*. As far as I can tell from my own search and from asking Gelukba scholars, these and the works that have been translated here are the only Gelukba works specifically commenting on the "unique tenets," but there may be others of which I am not aware scattered throughout Gelukba literature.

[55]Dzongkaba probably was the first to distinguish a group of unique tenets for the Prāsaṅgika School. For instance, in pre-Gelukba presentations of tenets such as the *Treasury of Explanations of Tenets (grub pa'i mtha' rnam par bshad pa'i mdzod)* of Üba Losel (dbus pa blo gsal, fourteenth century), a Gadamba (*bka' gdams pa*, the sect of Atīśa and predecessor of Gelukba), these topics go virtually unmentioned.

1 External objects *(phyi don, bāhyārtha)* exist because they are not refuted by a conventional analytical awareness *(tha snyad dpyod byed kyi blo)*.
2 A mind-basis-of-all *(kun gzhi rnam par shes pa, ālaya-vijñāna)* does not exist because it cannot be posited except through a search for an imputed object.
3 The selflessness of the person *(gang zag gi bdag med, pudgalanairātmya)* is as subtle as the selflessness of other phenomena *(chos kyi bdag med, dharmanairātmya)*.
4 There are instances of conceptual, mental, directly perceiving consciousnesses *(yid kyi mngon sum, mānasa-pratyakṣa)* such as feelings *(tshor ba, vedanā)*.
5 Even common beings can have yogic directly perceiving consciousnesses *(rnal 'byor mngon sum, yoga-pratyakṣa)*.
6 One can directly realize the sixteen aspects of the four noble truths even before the path of preparation *(sbyor lam, prayogamārga)*.
7 The three times—past, present, and future—are all functioning things *(dngos po, bhāva)*.
8 Disintegratedness *(zhig pa, naṣṭa)*—a functioning thing's state of having ceased—is itself a functioning thing.
9 There are no autonomous syllogisms *(rang rgyud kyi sbyor ba, svatantra-prayoga)*.
10 There is no self-consciousness *(rang rig, svasaṃvedanā)*.
11 *Pratyakṣa* refers principally to objects, not subjects.
12 True cessations *('gog bden, nirodha-satya)* are both emptinesses *(stong pa nyid, śūnyatā)* and ultimate truths *(don dam bden pa, paramārtha-satya)*.
13 The terms "nirvāṇa with remainder" *(lhag bcas myang bdas, sopadhiśeṣa-nirvāṇa)* and "nirvāṇa without remainder" *(lhag med myang bdas, nirupadhiśeṣa-nirvāṇa)* refer to the presence or absence, respectively, of the appearance of true existence *(bden yod, satya-sat)* to a person (who has overcome all afflictive obstructions), depending on whether or not that person is out of or in meditative equipoise directly realizing emptiness.

14 One cannot begin to destroy the obstructions to omniscience *(shes bya'i sgrib pa, jñeyāvaraṇa)* until one has destroyed all of the obstructions to liberation *(nyon mong pa'i sgrib pa, kleśāvaraṇa).*

15 In addition to afflictive ignorance, there is also non-afflictive ignorance *(nyon mong can ma yin pa'i ma rig pa, akleśāvidyā[?]).*

16 The extreme of permanence or eternalism is avoided through the appearance of conventional truths *(kun rdzob bden pa, saṃvṛtisatya)*, and the extreme of annihilation is avoided through positing them as empty of inherent existence.

To these points we can add two from Dzongkaba's list in his *Illumination of the Thought, Explanation of (Candrakīrti's) "Entrance"*:[56]

17 Hearers *(nyan thos, śrāvaka)* and Solitary Realizers *(rang sang rgyas, pratyekabuddha)* realize the selflessness of phenomena just as Bodhisattvas do.

18 The conception of a self of phenomena is an affliction *(nyon mong, kleśa).*

Also, we can add three points from Dzongkaba's *Eight Great Difficult Points of (Nāgārjuna's) "Fundamental Treatise on the Middle Way"*:

19 Even conventionally, nothing exists inherently.[57]

20 There is a unique way of positing the obstructions to omniscience and liberation.[58]

21 There is a unique way to explain how a Buddha's omniscient awareness knows impure phenomena without itself being mistaken.[59]

---

[56]*Illumination of the Thought* 124b.2-5.

[57]*Explanation of the Eight Great Difficult Points* 6.1-15.12.

[58]*Explanation of the Eight Great Difficult Points* 31.16-40.12.

[59]*Explanation of the Eight Great Difficult Points* 40.12-42.11.

The eight tenets identified by Dzongkaba in the small latter work are numbers 1, 2, 9, 10, 17, 19, 20, and 21. He also identified eight topics in his *Illumination of the Thought, Explanation of (Candrakīrti's) "Entrance,"*[60] numbers 1, 2, 7, 8, 9, 10, 17, and 18; this is the list used by Janggya.

Dzongkaba saw eight difficult topics (or twelve, if one wants to collate his two lists), but their enumeration seems to have been quite arbitrary. He himself found "limitless subtle distinctions."[61] Indeed, since the basic viewpoint of the Prāsaṅgika School—that there is no inherent existence, even conventionally—is unique, it could be said that every assertion that is qualified in that way by a Prāsaṅgika is a unique tenet. Indeed, in many of the unique tenets it is this basic point that provides the means to distinguish the Prāsaṅgikas from others.

As noted earlier, most commentators have chosen to include only the eight points identified by Dzongkaba in his *Illumination of the Thought*. This is not the case with Jamyang Shayba, who has clearly been prodded into expansion of the list in reaction to the withering attack leveled against Dzongkaba by the fifteenth-century Sagya *(sa skya)* order scholar Daktsang Shayrap Rinchen (*stag tshang shes rap rin chen*, b. 1405), known as Daktsang the Translator *(lo tsā ba)*.[62] Daktsang (at least according to Jamyang Shayba) explicitly asserts the contraries of many of the points found on Jamyang Shayba's list, and can be construed, with a little work, to assert even more; thus Jamyang Shayba found many more topics, indeed, twice as many as Dzongkaba, to assemble under the rubric of "unique tenets." At least five of Jamyang Shayba's topics (1, 2, 5, 8, and 13) are connected with accusations he makes against Daktsang. In the introduction to the Mādhyamika School section of the *Great Exposition of Tenets*, Jamyang

[60]*Illumination of the Thought* 124b.2-5.

[61]*Explanation of the Eight Great Difficult Points* 1.4.

[62]In his *Ocean of Good Explanations, Explanation of "Freedom from Extremes through Understanding All Tenets" (grub mtha' kun shes nas mtha' bral grub pa zhes bya ba'i bstan bcos rnam par bshad pa legs bshad kyi rgya mtsho)*, itself an encyclopedic treatment of Buddhist philosophy.

Shayba ridicules Daktsang for asserting that actions produce effects without disintegrating, that nirvāṇa without remainder is utterly without form (i.e., that one who possesses it has no body), that a mind-basis-of-all exists and external objects do not, and that those who are not Superiors *('phags pa, ārya)* cannot have yogic direct perception.[63]

Jamyang Shayba seems to have wished in his own list to reflect Dzongkaba's pioneering list of eight, so he referred to his own list as eight *pairs* of topics. It is clear, however, that the pairing of these topics was somewhat arbitrary, for Jamyang Shayba found it most sensible to discuss them in eleven sections. In the translation section, I have retained Jamyang Shayba's plan of organization rather than creating chapter headings for each of his topics because it is sometimes important to note what he has paired together.

In the first section of this book, several of these topics are examined in greater detail: the Prāsaṅgika School refutation of "mind-only" in the sense of no external objects (chapters 2 and 3); its refutation of self-consciousness (chapter 4); and its position on disintegratedness and the three times (chapter 5). It would have been a massive task, beyond the scope of this book, to have discussed every topic in such detail, and thus I have commented on the other topics in a briefer way in chapter 6 and through explanatory footnotes in the translations.

The topics treated in greater detail have been chosen because (1) they are important topics to which Janggya and Jamyang Shayba give much space, (2) they are topics that have not already been extensively discussed in Western sources, and (3) they are topics that illustrate the Gelukba principles of rejecting what requires ultimate analysis on the one hand and of preserving the conventions of the world on the other. As will be seen, the existence of external objects (the rejection of "mind-only") is upheld on the grounds that external objects are found in the conventions of the world and are not refuted by conventional analysis; self-consciousness is rejected because it falls outside of the conventions of the world and cannot be certified by conventional valid cognition;

[63]See Losang Gönchok, *Word Commentary* 176.5 ff.

and disintegratedness is shown to be a convention of the world, upheld by conventional analysis, whereas all other solutions to the basic problem of the connection between karmic cause and effect would require the postulation of a metaphysical entity.

Topics that do not meet these criteria are discussed more briefly. For instance, I do not choose to discuss autonomous syllogisms, a very important topic in the debate between the Svātantrika and Prāsaṅgika schools, both because Jamyang Shayba barely mentions the topic in this selection and because his treatment of the subject has been analyzed in detail elsewhere.[64]

Sources for the Unique Tenets

This book concerns itself principally with several, but by no means all, of the perspectives within the Gelukba order on Candrakīrti's Prāsaṅgika-Mādhyamika School. For the most part, it is not an exploration of the Indian antecedents to Tibetan Gelukba Prāsaṅgika philosophy except where the Gelukbas cite Indian sources. Nevertheless, many if not all of the pertinent comments of past masters such as Nāgārjuna and Candrakīrti are cited by Jamyang Shayba or Janggya (particularly the former), and in any case, the Indian sources tend to be few in number and terse in manner on the "unique tenets" with which we are concerned.

Nor is this book a presentation of the Prāsaṅgika School's philosophy of emptiness or its methods for gaining a realization of emptiness. That is unnecessary, for several recent works on the Prāsaṅgika School as defined in the Tibetan Gelukba tradition have already greatly enhanced our understanding of the Prāsaṅgika-Mādhyamika School's definition of the object to be negated in the view of emptiness and the reasonings used to negate it. They include Jeffrey Hopkins's *Meditation on Emptiness* and *Emptiness Yoga*, Robert A. F. Thurman's translation of Dzongkaba's *The Essence of the Good*

[64]Hopkins (1983a: 441-530).

Explanations (entitled *Tsongkhapa's Speech of Gold in the Essence of Eloquence*), Geshe Rabten and Stephen Batchelor's *Echoes of Voidness*, Elizabeth Napper's *Dependent-Arising and Emptiness*, and Guy Newland's *The Two Truths* (see the bibliography for references). The present book complements these outstanding works by exploring the application of the Prāsaṅgika School's principles to a number of persistently puzzling points in Buddhist philosophy.

Specifically, this book explores the views of several closely associated seventeenth- and eighteenth-century eastern Tibetan and Mongolian Gelukba scholars. Jamyang Shayba, Ngawang Belden (*ngag dbang dpal ldan*, b. 1797, also known as Belden Chöjay [*dpal ldan chos rje*]), and several other authors whose works were consulted are associated with Gomang *(sgo mang)* College of Drebung *('bras spungs)* Monastery outside of Hlasa (= Lhasa), and their presentation of the unique Prāsaṅgika tenets contains some positions unique to Gomang, as can be seen in the notes to the translation. Although Janggya is not formally associated with any one of the colleges of the great Gelukba monasteries, he studied at several, including Gomang.

This exposition of the unique tenets of the Prāsaṅgika School cannot be equated with Nāgārjuna's views, nor with those of Candrakīrti, Dzongkaba, or even Drebung Monastery. However, the explanations of Jamyang Shayba, Janggya, and others, are careful, reasoned analyses that seem to me to have as much claim on the truth as do any other interpretations of Candrakīrti; they cite his works copiously; and they rely heavily on the works of Dzongkaba. They are, in short, close to the heart of the Gelukba understanding of Mādhyamika and are worthy of study. They are, no doubt, not completely reliable, but the extent to which these Gelukbas have used, ignored, distorted, clarified, or extended their Indian and Tibetan antecedents is a large question that I am able to address only in a preliminary way as the material unfolds in subsequent chapters.

Jamyang Shayba's full name is Jamyang Shaybay Dorjay Ngawang Dzöndrü; he was born in 1648 in lower Amdo *(a mdo),* the easternmost region of Tibet (now in Qinghai Province of the People's Republic of China), in the area of Ganggya Dingring *(rgang gya'i lting ring).*[65] A serious student, he became a novice monk in his teens, traveling to Hlasa at the age of 21 to enter the Gomang College of Drebung Monastery. At age 27 he became a fully ordained monk, and at 29 he entered the Tantric College of Lower Hlasa, Gyumay *(rgyud smad).* Among his teachers were the great Fifth Dalai Lama Losang Gyatso *(blo bzang rgya mtsho)* and the first of the line of reincarnating Janggya lamas, Ngawang Chöden *(ngag dbang chos ldan).*

At the age of 33 he entered a two-year meditation retreat in a cave near Drebung, thereby attaining yogic powers *(dbang, siddhi).* He wrote prolifically for the rest of his life. Among the dozens of texts collected in the fifteen volumes of his "Collected Works" *(gsung 'bum)* are his famous monastic textbooks *(yig cha)* on the five "root" topics: Valid Cognition *(tshad ma, pramāṇa)*;[66] the Perfection of Wisdom; Mādhyamika; Abhidharma *(chos mngon pa)*; and Monastic Discipline *('dul ba, vinaya).* His textbook on Mādhyamika (a commentary on Candrakīrti's *Entrance to the Middle Way*), commonly called the *Great Exposition of the Middle Way* (*dbu ma chen mo,* 442 folios in the Ngawang Gelek edition), has been frequently used in this study to elucidate points made in what is perhaps his greatest work, the *Great Exposition of Tenets* (*grub mtha' chen mo,* 530 folios in the Drashikyil edition), a portion of which has been translated in the second part of this book.

The *Great Exposition of Tenets* is a commentary on Jamyang Shayba's own terse 16-folio verse treatise on tenets, which was written ten years earlier.[67] The *Great Exposition of Tenets* was

---

[65]The following account of Jamyang Shayba's life and literary activities has been gleaned from Lokesh Chandra (1963: 45-49), who in turn relies on a sketch by a "Dr. Rinchen of Ulanbator."

[66]Study of this topic is based on Dharmakīrti's *Commentary on (Dignāga's) "Compendium on Prime Cognition" (tshad ma rnam 'grel, pramāṇavārttika).*

[67]Information on the *Great Exposition of Tenets* is from Geshay Tupden Gyatso, a contemporary Gomang scholar. According to him, the root text of the *Great Exposition of Tenets* was written at the behest of the Fifth Dalai

written at the request of Sanggyay Gyatso *(sangs rgyas rgya mtsho)*, whom Jamyang Shayba tutored, and was published in 1699, a year before he became abbot of Gomang College, a position he held for seven years. The verse treatise, or "root text," is normally memorized by Gomang monks early in their studies, prior to the classes on the Perfection of Wisdom. The *Great Exposition of Tenets* itself is not the focus of any class, but rather is used as an encyclopedia of philosophy to which teachers and their students refer again and again as relevant topics arise in their major texts.

In 1709 Jamyang Shayba returned to Amdo, and in the following year he founded the Drashikyil *(bkra shis 'khyil)* Monastery, which grew into a major Gelukba center (and a tantric college was also established there in 1717). Its first abbot was Ngawang Drashi *(ngag dbang bkra shis)*, who, using Jamyang Shayba's writings, authored the "Collected Topics" *(bsdus grwa)* textbook still studied by those beginning the Gomang curriculum. Jamyang Shayba died at age seventy-three or -four in 1721 or 1722.

Ngawang Belden,[68] author of the *Annotations for the "Great Exposition of Tenets," Freeing the Knots of the Difficult Points, Precious Jewel of Clear Thought*, was a Mongolian, born in 1797, and is often referred to as "Belden Chöjay of Urga" because his career centered around Urga (later called Ulanbator, the capital of Outer Mongolia). Most of his study took place in Mongolia, in the Drashi Chöpel *(bkra shis chos 'phel)* College of Ganden *(dga' ldan)* Monastery in Urga. In his fortieth year, he became the Chöjay (*chos rje*, a rank just beneath that of abbot [*mkhan po*]) of Urga. He visited Tibet at least once, but spent most of his latter years in China and Mongolia. In addition to his *Annotations* on the *Great Exposition of Tenets*, he is well known for his books setting forth the paths of the four tantra

---

Lama, and the commentary was written ten years later at the urging of Sanggyay Gyatso, who was a student of Jamyang Shayba. However, the Fifth Dalai Lama died in 1682; his death was concealed by the regent, Sanggyay Gyatso, for fourteen years. Thus it must have been the latter, not the Dalai Lama, who asked Jamyang Shayba to compose the root text.

[68]Biographical information on Ngawang Belden has been drawn from Lokesh Chandra (1963: part 2, 10-13, 282-84 and 1961: 22-24, 50-52).

sets,[69] setting forth the differences between the Gomang and Loseling Colleges of Drebung Monastery on the Prāsaṅgika School and the Perfection of Wisdom, and setting forth the teachings on the two truths in the four systems of tenets.[70] Ngawang Belden's *Annotations*, which is even longer than Jamyang Shayba's massive text, sheds a great deal of light—and a little heat, since he sometimes is critical of Jamyang Shayba's conclusions—on topics that Jamyang Shayba does not always make clear.

Janggya Rolbay Dorjay, the author of the *Clear Exposition of the Presentation of Tenets, Beautiful Ornament for the Meru of the Subduer's Teaching*, is the second of the line of Janggya reincarnate lamas *(sprul sku)*.[71] He was born in 1717 in the Amdo region of Tibet, but spent little of his life in Tibet. Recognized as the reincarnation of the former Janggya at the age of three (with the assistance of the aged Jamyang Shaybay Dorjay), he was taken to the Janggya monastery, Gönlung Jambaling, but stayed there only a few years before being taken to Beijing.

There he became friends with a fellow schoolmate who would later become the Ch'ienlung Emperor, who in 1736, having ascended the throne, appointed Janggya the lama of the seal, the highest position for a Tibetan lama in the Chinese court. Janggya at the time was only nineteen years old and had just the previous year received the full ordination of a monk.

The Emperor asked Janggya to organize and carry out the translation of the Indian commentaries *(bstan 'gyur)* in the

---

[69]My summary of the Highest Yoga Tantra *(rnal 'byor bla med kyi rgyud, anuttarayogatantra)* section of this work, supplemented by Gelukba commentaries, was published by Snow Lion in 1986 as *Highest Yoga Tantra*.

[70]A portion of the latter was translated by John Buescher in "The Buddhist Doctrine of Two Truths in the Vaibhāṣika and Theravāda Schools." Doctoral dissertation at the University of Virginia, 1982.

[71]Biographical information on Janggya can be found in Hopkins (1987: 15-35; helpful bibliography in note 1, p. 448), who draws on several sources, including Gene Smith's introduction to the *Collected Works of Thu'u-bkwan Blo-bzang-chos-kyi-nyi-ma*, vol. 1, pp. 2-12, and a short biography in Lokesh Chandra's *Materials for a History of Tibetan Literature* (38-45). The present account gives a few details from the biography by Hopkins.

Tibetan canon into Mongolian; he began by compiling an extensive Tibetan-Mongolian glossary in the remarkably brief time of one year (helped presumably by many scholars) and accomplished the translation by the end of seven years. With the Emperor, Janggya established the monastery of Ganden Jinchaling *(dga' ldan byin chags gling)* in Beijing, a teaching monastery like those of Tibet, which later became known as the "Lama Temple."

Janggya had many eminent teachers, including Losang Denbay Nyima (head of the Gelukba order) and the Seventh Dalai Lama; he in turn had many eminent students, including Gönchok Jikmay Wangbo, the second Jamyang Shayba, and Tügen Losang Chögyi Nyima, who became his biographer. Janggya gave many teachings and initiations to thousands of people, including the Emperor, who when receiving initiation performed the required prostrations, etc., to Janggya. His final great work was to oversee the translation of the Buddha-word *(bka' 'gyur)* portion of the Tibetan canon into Manchu. He died in 1786.

As has been indicated, the relations between these authors are close and complex. Jamyang Shayba Ngawang Dzöndrü, the first of a lineage of Jamyang Shayba lamas, was tutored in tantric studies by Janggya Ngawang Chöden *(lcang skya ngag dbang chos ldan)*, the first Janggya; the second Jamyang Shayba, Gönchok Jikmay Wangbo (1728-91), and third Tügen, Losang Chögyi Nyima (1737-1802), were students of the second Janggya, Rolbay Dorjay. Gungtang Denbay Drönmay, whose work clarifies a number of points involved in the Mādhyamika School critique of the philosophy of the Cittamātra School, was a disciple of Gönchok Jikmay Wangbo. There is an "eastern" flavor to this circle, as it centers around Drashikyil Monastery (founded by Jamyang Shayba) and Gönlung Jambaling Monastery (Janggya's home monastery) in Amdo and because the group contains several Mongolians—the Janggyas and Ngawang Belden.

Thus, there is a certain unity in the translated works upon which this presentation of the "unique tenets" relies. However, there are significant differences in style, and some in content.

Janggya does not go into nearly the same degree of detail as does Jamyang Shayba, nor does he pepper his text with hypothetical debates; on the other hand, he is relatively clear and straightforward and often goes more deeply into issues than does Jamyang Shayba, who is sometimes content merely to cite Indian sources without elaboration. He sometimes disagrees with Jamyang Shayba, though not by name. Jamyang Shayba, on the other hand, does not always express his point clearly and occasionally omits details that would be helpful; in those instances, the annotations of Ngawang Belden are indispensable. The annotations are frequently many times as long as an entire section of a chapter in Jamyang Shayba's work, and sometimes put the annotator at odds with his subject. However, when Ngawang Belden disagrees with Jamyang Shayba, which is not infrequent, he does not distort Jamyang Shayba's points in order to make his own.

In addition to the selections translated in parts two and three, I have also made frequent recourse, in the introductory chapters and in the notes to the translations, to Jamyang Shayba's *Great Exposition of the Middle Way* (his massive commentary on Candrakīrti's *Entrance to the Middle Way*), to Losang Gönchok's *Word Commentary on the Root Text of "Tenets"* (a compact summary of the *Great Exposition of Tenets*), and the slim but pithy *Precious Garland of Tenets* by Gönchok Jikmay Wangbo, the second Jamyang Shayba. These works are, as might be expected, useful supplements that do not depart in any significant way from the material in the translations. I received some further clarification of Gomang College traditions by addressing questions to Gomang's Geshay Tupden Gyatso. By way of contrast, I have attempted to point out those arguments and textual interpretations with which Gelukba scholars from other monasteries or monastic colleges would disagree and to present their positions in the notes. For this purpose, it has been very helpful to study the translated texts with several non-Gomang College scholars, principally those of Gomang's surviving rival college within Drebung monastery, Loseling *(blo gsal gling)* College. Due to their physical and intellectual proximity to Gomang the Loseling scholars tend to be familiar with the issues that divide the two schools.[72] The illuminating commentary of Loseling's Kensur Yeshey Tupden and Geshay Belden Drakba, and the answers of Sera *(se ra)* Monastery's Geshay Sönam Rinchen and Ganden *(dga' ldan)* Monastery's Geshay Gönchok Tsayring to my specific questions, have provided other angles to issues raised by Jamyang Shayba, et al.

Also, a thought-provoking contrast to this Gelukba explanation of Candrakīrti's system is included by way of the many references to the counter-arguments of Daktsang the Translator, who wrote his own book on the tenets of Indian Buddhism[73] and whose criticisms of Dzongkaba served as a major source of Jamyang Shayba's inspiration for his *Great Exposition of Tenets*. Reading Daktsang is a reminder that Candrakīrti's works are sufficiently ambiguous on numerous points to permit a variety of interpretations and forces us to consider the way in which Dzongkaba, Jamyang Shayba, Ngawang Belden, Janggya, and others marshal the evidence for their interpretations.

In conclusion, let us raise a question related to the use of these specific sources for an exploration of the unique tenets of the Prāsaṅgika School: if the "unique tenets" at least nominally stem from the work of Nāgārjuna, the founder of the Mādhyamika School, what purpose is there in studying the opinions of Tibetans sixteen centuries or more removed from him? We might answer that in the first place, certainly it is not necessary to justify the study of Gelukba monastic literature on the basis of its value for understanding Indian Buddhism, for it is surely also important to understand Tibetan Buddhism on its own terms. Even if it could be shown that the

---

[72]Jamyang Shayba's annotator, Ngawang Belden, wrote an entire book cataloguing those differences on the topics of the Prāsaṅgika School and the Perfection of Wisdom, called *Stating the Mode of Explanation in the Textbooks on the Middle Way and the Perfection of Wisdom in the Loseling and Gomang Colleges: Festival for Those of Clear Intelligence (blo gsal gling dang bkra shis sgo mang grva tshang gi dbu phar gyi yig cha'i bshad tshul bkod pa blo gsal dga' ston).*

[73]*Freedom from Extremes through Understanding All Tenets (grub mtha' kun shes nas mtha' bral grub pa)* along with his own commentary, *Ocean of Good Explanations (legs bshad kyi rgya mtsho).*

Gelukbas have totally misunderstood the philosophy of the Indian Mādhyamika School, the Tibetan Mādhyamika School is itself a worthy subject for investigation. These works of Tibetan scholars of the Mādhyamika School draw us into a world of thought that has considerable coherence and subtlety and may be appreciated on that level alone.

However, I believe that it *can* be shown that works such as Janggya's *Presentation of Tenets*, Jamyang Shayba's *Great Exposition of Tenets*, and Ngawang Belden's *Annotations* to the latter are valuable for the study of the Indian Mādhyamika School in that they suggest definite, concrete avenues of interpretation for the typically terse, difficult Sanskrit texts of Nāgārjuna, Candrakīrti, etc., and because they extend the arguments made by those Indian masters. A study of the unique tenets based on Nāgārjuna alone would be slim, for as we shall see, the statements of Nāgārjuna cited by the Gelukbas are few in number and tend to be pointers rather than maps. The Tibetan authors are careful scholars who liberally cite both the seminal Indian sources and the exegeses of Dzongkaba and his closest disciples, providing an anthology of Prāsaṅgika literature interspersed with their own commentaries and hypothetical objections and replies. They provide a rich medium for the exploration of some of Buddhism's most controversial doctrinal questions.

2 The Prāsaṅgika Critique of "Mind-Only" Idealism

Candrakīrti's *Entrance to (Nāgārjuna's) "Treatise on the Middle Way,"* the well from which Gelukbas draw their understanding of Nāgārjuna's Mādhyamika School, is the principal Indian source for Jamyang Shayba's criticism of the philosophy of Cittamātra in the *Great Exposition of Tenets*.[1] Candrakīrti is generally regarded by Tibetan scholars as the founder of the Prāsaṅgika-Mādhyamika School; ironically, Jamyang Shayba diverges, as he identifies its founder as Buddhapālita (fifth century), whom Candrakīrti defended against the criticisms of Bhāvaviveka (sixth century, considered the founder of the Svātantrika-Mādhyamika School). Jamyang Shayba clearly intends no slight to Candrakīrti, but rather sees himself as merely following the lead of Dzongkaba, who calls Buddhapālita the "revealer" of the Prāsaṅgika path.[2]

---

[1]Other than a single citation of Nāgārjuna, the only Mādhyamika prior to Candrakīrti (seventh century) cited by the Gelukba authors in refutation of Cittamātra is Bhāvaviveka (c. 490-570), who criticizes the Cittamātra interpretation of certain sūtras.

[2]Interpreting Dzongkaba's statement, at the end of *The Essence of the Good Explanations*, that the path is "revealed by Buddhapālita," Jamyang Shayba calls Buddhapālita the "establisher" of the Prāsaṅgika School, although "for its chariot a great way was made by the honorable Candrakīrti" (*Great Exposition of Tenets* 282.6 [DSK edition]; see translation of beginning of Prāsaṅgika chapter in Hopkins [1983a: 584]). Janggya feels that

The seventeenth-century Buddhist historian Tāranātha tells us that Candrakīrti had extensive experience debating against Cittamātra.[3] As a *paṇḍita* of the monastic university of Nālanda, he is said to have engaged in a seven-year-long debate with Candragomin (*zla ba dge bsnyen*), who followed the views of Asaṅga and would therefore be regarded as a Cittamātrin Following Scripture. (Regrettably, none of Candragomin's Cittamātra writings are extant, though he wrote copiously on many topics.) Apparently the debate went miserably for Candrakīrti despite his renown for brilliant disputation, for Tāranātha tells us that spectators were heard to declare, "Nāgārjuna's doctrine is medicine for some, poison for others, but Asaṅga's is nectar for all." Candrakīrti was quite bewildered by Candragomin's unexpected prowess until one night he followed Candragomin, and discovered that each night his adversary was receiving coaching from a statue of Avalokiteśvara, the Bodhisattva who personifies compassion; when he saw this, he conceded the debate, judging that it was folly to continue against such competition.

This story of Candrakīrti's defeat at the hands of Candragomin is perhaps entirely apocryphal (Tāranātha was an important figure of the Jo-nang-ba [*jo nang pa*] sect, which was often accused by members of other Tibetan sects of being a Tibetan version of Cittamātra).[4] However, Nālanda was apparently the sort of place where Buddhist scholars of all stripes

---

Jamyang Shayba has misconstrued Dzongkaba:

> Some scholars of our own [Gelukba] sect say that this means that Buddhapālita is the founder of Prāsaṅgika. However, this is not the opinion of the foremost great being Dzongkaba. Although Buddhapālita did not use autonomous reasons and commented on the meaning of the text only through consequences, this alone is not sufficient to make him the founder of Prāsaṅgika. For in order to be designated as the founder of this or that system, one must clearly delineate proofs for the correctness of that system and [prove] why interpretation in any other way is unsuitable.

This is adapted from the translation by Lopez (1987: 254) of Janggya's *Presentation of Tenets* 286.16-287.2.

[3] Tāranātha 203-6.

[4] Snellgrove (1987: 489-90). They were also accused of being crypto-Vedāntins (Hopkins 1983a: 535).

lived side by side and where there developed the distinctive style of monastic debate still practiced daily in the monasteries of Tibetan Buddhism. Whatever its historicity, the story points to an active competition in an arena of ideas between proponents of the Cittamātra and Mādhyamika viewpoints (whatever was the degree of actual self-identification with a "school"), a competition reflected in the writings of Candrakīrti, to a lesser degree in subsequent Indian Mādhyamika works such as Śāntideva's *Engaging in the Bodhisattva Deeds*,[5] and in Tibetan Gelukba works on Mādhyamika.

Prāsaṅgika authors have criticized several positions identified with the Cittamātra School, such as its assertion of a mind-basis-of-all, self-consciousness, and three distinct vehicles for liberation. However, Candrakīrti was most concerned with what he saw as the core assertion of Cittamātra Buddhism, that there are no external objects. Basically, Gelukbas interpret "no external objects" to mean that there are no objects of mind that are *different substantial entities* from the minds that apprehend them. Roughly, but perhaps more evocatively, then, "mind-only" means that an object arises only along with a particular consciousness, not prior to it, and that objects therefore are inseparably related with the minds that observe them. The present chapter concerns the Cittamātra presentation of this tenet and Prāsaṅgika responses to it as it is addressed in the seminal works of Indian Buddhists such as Asaṅga, Vasubandhu, and Candrakīrti; the following chapter will explore the works of Gelukba scholars such as Jamyang Shayba and Janggya.

---

[5]The most famous of the subsequent Prāsaṅgikas, Śāntideva, refuted Cittamātra just with respect to the existence of self-consciousness. See *Engaging in the Bodhisattva Deeds* IX.15b-29. There is not yet, to my knowledge, any indication that a post-Candrakīrti Indian Cittamātra movement persisted. It would be interesting to see whether later Indian Cittamātrins responded to Candrakīrti's criticisms; Cittamātrins such as the Yogācāra-Svātantrika-Mādhyamika, Śāntarakṣita, and his disciple Kamalaśīla seem not to have done so, at least in the *Compendium of Suchness* (*de kho na nyid bsdus pa, tattvasaṃgraha*) and commentary.

The Cittamātra "School"

According to the Gelukba reckoning, the seminal writings of the Cittamātra School were composed last of the four major Indian Buddhist schools of tenets. This is not a fact that is particularly important to them because they assume that the sūtras upon which the Cittamātrins relied are authentic, genuine utterances of the Buddha. It is relevant only because of the possibility mentioned by Dzongkaba that a major purpose for Candrakīrti's *Entrance to the Middle Way* was to refute Cittamātra misunderstandings of Nāgārjuna's teachings.[6]

Mahāyāna tradition explains that the philosophical systems required "openers of a chariot-way" (*shing rta srol 'byed*)[7] because those sūtras upon which they rely remained hidden from view and from widespread practice for an extensive period. Janggya explains that in the first centuries following the passing (*parinirvāṇa*, complete passage beyond sorrow) of the Buddha, only a few humans openly held the positions of the Mahāyāna; fortunately, many of the Mahāyāna scriptures were solicited by gods and divine serpents (*nāga*) and eventually came to be found in those places.[8] Then, as the Buddha had prophesied, the south Indian Buddhist monk Nāgārjuna brought the scriptures up from the depths of the ocean where the serpents lived and disseminated them.[9] Most Western scholars consider the Perfection of Wisdom sūtras and Cittamātra sūtras to have been fabricated by Mahāyāna monks in the early centuries of the Common Era.

The Cittamātrins are also called Yogācārins (*rnal 'byor spyod pa*; "Practitioners of Yoga"), Vijñānavādins (*rnam shes smra ba*; "Proponents of Knowledge"), or Vijñāptivādins (*rnam*

---

[6]See chapter 1, note on the title of *Entrance*.

[7]As Donald Lopez puts it, Buddha blazed the trail, but the chariot-way openers widened and smoothed it so that the way would be clearer and easier to follow (1987: 14).

[8]*Presentation of Tenets* 71.19 ff. It is interesting that Tāranātha has no explanation for the appearance of Mahāyāna teachings other than that suddenly a sufficient number of teachers appeared (chapter 13).

[9]*Presentation of Tenets* 72.14-15.

rig smra ba; "Proponents of Knowledge-Only"). Asaṅga (c. 310-90) is almost universally held to be the founder of the school,[10] and he and his half-brother Vasubandhu (320-400)[11] wrote most of the foundational literature of Cittamātra, setting forth its unique doctrines.[12] Ironically, Gelukbas say that although Asaṅga did indeed found the Cittamātra system, since it was he who set forth Cittamātra as a separate system, his own final view was that of the Prāsaṅgika School, as can be seen from the way in which he commented on several sūtras in his *Explanation of (Maitreya's) "Sublime Continuum of the Mahāyāna."*[13]

Little can be said with certainty about the careers of Asaṅga and Vasubandhu. Asaṅga lived in the late third and early

---

[10]On Asaṅga's dates, see Nakamura (1987: 264). Some regard Maitreya (or Maitreyanātha) to be the founder of the Cittamātra School. Traditionally, the "Maitreya" who is the author of such works as the *Discrimination of the Middle Way and the Extremes* (*dbus dang mtha' rnam par 'byed pa, madhyāntavibhāga*) is considered to be the coming Buddha Maitreya, who dictated his books to Asaṅga. Modern scholars tend to consider Maitreya to have been a monk who lived in the third and fourth centuries (Nakamura [1987: 256] estimates his dates as C.E. 270-350). As Griffiths notes, it will take an extensive study of the style and content of the works ascribed to Maitreya in order to determine whether, say, "Maitreya" is just an Asaṅga pen-name (1986: 174, n. 9).

[11]Nakamura 1987: 268.

[12]Janggya lists some of the many other works by authors such as Jñānaśrī, Sthiramati, Asvabhāva, Guṇaprabha, Jinaputra, Vinītadeva, Guṇamati, Ratnākaraśānti, Dignāga, Dharmakīrti, Dharmapāla, Suvarṇadvipa, and Ratnākaraśāntipāda, whom he considers to be Cittamātrin, in his *Presentation of Tenets* 155.17-56.17. (I have been helped by a rough unpublished translation of those pages by Joe Wilson.)

[13]Jamyang Shayba, *Great Exposition of Tenets* II: 10b.2 (DSK *ca* 6b.7 ff.) Gungtang asserts that before Asaṅga, there were no Cittamātrins (*Explanation of the Difficult Topics of Afflicted Mentality and Mind-Basis-of-All* 4a.1, translated by Joe Wilson [1984: 228]). He is probably following Dzongkaba's lead, for Dzongkaba says that before Asaṅga and Nāgārjuna there may have been proponents of the "Middle Way" and "Mind-only" but no one who laid out a system (*Difficult Topics* 3a.1-8, translated by Wilson [1984: 71-73]). B. K. Matilal (1974: 141) considers Cittamātra to be contemporaneous with the Mahāyāna though not systematized until Asaṅga and Vasubandhu and not a full-fledged philosophy until Dharmakīrti.

fourth century.[14] According to Tāranātha,[15] Asaṅga had a prodigious command of the Three Baskets of the Hīnayāna canon and many Mahāyāna sūtras as well, being able to memorize 100,000 verses per year. But because he had difficulty understanding the Perfection of Wisdom scriptures, he took up a practice in which he meditated on Maitreya, hoping for enhancement of his capacity for comprehension. He meditated for twelve years in the hopes of seeing a sign from Maitreya. Every three years, on the verge of abandoning his quest, he saw something that inspired him to renew his effort: the slow but steady wearing away of a mountain due to its being brushed by the wings of birds; stones that were being worn away by drips of water; and an old man making needles by rubbing ingots of iron with a soft cotton cloth. However, in the twelfth year, discouraged again, he left his cave. He encountered a dog on the road, infested with worms and crying out in pain. Moved by the dog's suffering, he resolved to remove its worms; but not wanting to hurt the worms, he cut off a strip of his own flesh to which to transfer them. At that moment, the dog was transformed into Maitreya, who took Asaṅga to his abode, Tuṣiṭa heaven, where he taught Asaṅga his five great treatises.[16]

Among Asaṅga's Cittamātra works translated into Tibetan are:

Compendium of the Mahāyāna (*theg pa chen po bsdus pa, mahāyānasaṃgraha*)

Compendium of Ascertainments (*rnam par gtan la dbab pa bsdu ba, viniścayasaṃgrahaṇī*, sometimes called *nirṇayasaṃgraha*)

---

[14]Warder 1980: 236.

[15]This is condensed from Tāranātha 1980: 156 ff.

[16]*Discrimination of Phenomena and the Nature of Phenomena* (*dharmadharmatāvibhaṅga, chos dang chos nyid rnam par 'byed pa*); *Discrimination of the Middle Way and the Extremes* (*madhyāntavibhaṅga, dbus dang mtha' rnam par 'byed pa*); *Ornament for the Mahāyāna Sūtras* (*mahāyānasūtrālaṃkārakārikā, theg pa chen po'i mdo sde'i rgyan gyi tshig le'ur byas pa*); *Ornament for Clear Realization* (*abhisamayālaṅkāra, mngon par rtogs pa'i rgyan*); and *Sublime Continuum of the Mahāyāna* (*mahāyānottaratantraśāstra, theg pa chen po rgyud bla ma'i bstan bcos*).

Explanation of (Maitreya's)[17] ***"Sublime Continuum of the Mahāyāna"*** *(theg pa chen po'i rgyud bla ma'i bstan bcos kyi rnam par bshad pa, mahāyānottaratantraśāstravyākhyā* or *ratnagotravibhāgavyākhyāna)*

Explanation of the "Sūtra Unraveling the Thought" *(dgongs pa nges par 'grel pa'i rnam par bshad pa, saṃdhinirmocanabhāṣya)*[18]

Of these, the *Compendium of the Mahāyāna* is a particularly important source for those positions identified by Gelukbas as Cittamātra.

Vasubandhu[19] was Asaṅga's younger half-brother, born the year after Asaṅga's ordination as a monk. He too became a monk and studied at Nālanda. But while Asaṅga meditated in his cave, Vasubandhu trekked to Kashmir to master the texts of abhidharma (*chos mngon pa*).[20] Later, Asaṅga converted him to the Mahāyāna by having two monks recite first the *Teachings of Akṣhayamati (blo gros mi zad pas bstan pa'i mdo,*

---

[17]According to Warder (1980: 403), the Chinese tradition regards the *Ratnagotravibhāga* to have been written by Sthiramati (though not the person of that name who is a famous later Cittamātrin).

[18]This is commonly attributed to Asaṅga (e.g., Obermiller 1931: 140), although Dzongkaba does not accept Asaṅga's authorship.

[19]This account is condensed from Tāranātha (1980: 167 ff.).

[20]Vasubandhu's most famous work is the *Abhidharmakośa* (*chos mngon pa'i mdzod*), which I translate as *Treasury of Higher Knowledge.* "Higher knowledge" is being used as a translation term because the *Treasury of Higher Knowledge* speaks mainly of two kinds of abhidharma, both being kinds of knowledge: the wisdom that realizes nirvāṇa and ordinary correct knowledge. See A. Hirakawa (1980: 159-75, especially 167). Many other translations are possible. Ngawang Belden, in his commentary (*Collected Works,* vol. *ga* 5.3) on Vasubandhu's *Treasury of Higher Knowledge* gives four etymologies for *chos mngon pa / abhidharma*, their diversity reflecting the extensive range of meanings for *mngon pa* and *chos*: (1) "approaching nirvāṇa," nirvāṇa being the highest (*mngon pa, abhi*) of phenomena (*chos, dharma*); (2) "repeated examination of aggregates, constituents, sources, etc.," an intensive or repeated (*mngon pa*) examination of phenomena; (3) "overwhelming the assertions of opponents"; and (4) "manifesting the meaning of the collection of discourses," that is, manifesting (*mngon pa*) the teaching (*chos*). According to Hirakawa, the *Mahāvibhāṣa* gives twenty-five meanings for *abhidharma.*

akṣayamatinirdeśa-sūtra) and then the *Sūtra on the Ten Grounds* (*sa bcu pa'i mdo, daśabhūmika-sūtra*). Among Vasubandhu's Cittamātra works are:

> ***Twenty Stanzas*** (*nyi shu pa'i le'ur byas pa, viṃśikākārikā*, with his own commentary, *nyi shu pa'i 'grel pa, viṃśikāvṛtti*)
>
> ***Thirty Stanzas*** (*sum cu pa'i tshig le'ur byas pa, triṃśikākārikā*)
>
> ***Commentary on (Maitreya's) "Discrimination of the Middle and the Extremes"*** (*dbus dang mtha' rnam par 'byed pa' 'grel pa, madhyāntavibhāgaṭīkā*)
>
> ***Commentary on (Asaṅga's) "Compendium of the Mahāyāna"*** (*theg pa chen po bsdus pa'i 'grel pa, mahāyānasaṃgrahābhāṣya*).

Of these, the *Twenty Stanzas* is particularly important.

These works by Asaṅga and Vasubandhu are, in turn, largely dependent upon a small number of second- or third-century sūtras expounding Cittamātra doctrine:[21]

> ***Sūtra Unraveling the Thought*** (*dgongs pa nges par 'grel pa'i mdo, saṃdhinirmocanasūtra*)[22]
>
> ***Sūtra on the Ten Grounds*** (*daśabhūmikasūtra, sa bcu pa'i mdo*, part of the *Buddha Garland Sūtra* [*sangs rgyas phal po che'i mdo, buddhāvatamsakasūtra*])
>
> ***Descent to Laṅka Sūtra*** (*lang kar gshegs pa'i mdo, laṅkāvatārasūtra*)

---

[21]For discussion of these sūtras, see Nakamura (1987: 254-55). These are sūtras listed by Gungtang. Wilson notes (1984: 42-43) that Daktsang and Janggya have similar lists, Janggya adding the *Ratnakūṭa* (Jewel Heap) sūtras, among which is the *Lion's Roar of Queen Śrīmāla*, which Jacques May (1971: 274-79) adds to the list. The Cittamātra philosophers consider these sūtras to be definitive, which for them means that they can be literally accepted; however, there are some *passages* in the *Descent to Laṅka Sūtra* and the *Sūtra on the Heavily Adorned* that require interpretation for at least some Cittamātrins (Gungtang 10b.3-4, translated by Wilson [1984: 304-5]).

[22]Nakamura (255, n. 15) regards this to be the oldest Cittamātra sūtra, as he considers it to be post-Nāgārjuna (who lived c. 150-250) and pre-Maitreya (who lived c. 270-350), i.e., late third century.

Mahāyāna Abhidharma Sūtra (*theg chen chos ngon pa'i mdo, mahāyānābhidharmasūtra*)

The *Sūtra Unraveling the Thought* is Asaṅga's principal source.[23] The *Mahāyāna Abhidharma Sūtra* seems also to have been important. It is no longer extant, but on the basis of its remaining fragments (such as those cited by Asaṅga) it seems to have contained the basic ideas of the Cittamātra system. The Gelukba roster of later Cittamātra thinkers includes Dharmakīrti, Sthiramati, Dharmapāla, and Asvabhāva; however, since, on the particular issue of mind-only, the earlier works of Vasubandhu and Asaṅga are those to which Candrakīrti seems to respond and are those on which Tibetan Prāsaṅgikas focus, we need not be concerned with them here.

Before outlining the specific aspects of Cittamātra philosophy to which the Prāsaṅgikas reacted so robustly, let us put it in perspective by reflecting that it was perhaps inevitable that "mind-only" idealism would arise in Buddhism, which must itself broadly be considered an idealism due to its emphasis on the primacy of mind. Idealism is a perennial philosophy that regards with skepticism the data of the senses, perhaps arising in reflection on ordinary human experience such as mirages, optical illusions, solar phenomena, hallucinations, visionary experiences, and vivid dreams; the latter, particularly, throw doubt on the reality of all of waking life. An apt illustration, though not Buddhist, is found in the well-known story about the Daoist master Zhuang-zi:[24]

> Once Chuang Chou dreamt he was a butterfly, a butterfly flitting and fluttering around, happy with himself and doing as he pleased. He didn't know he was Chuang Chou. Suddenly he

---

[23]This is according to Janggya (158), who quotes Asaṅga's *Compendium of Ascertainments* (*gtan la dbab pa bsdu ba, nirṅayasaṃgraha*) to demonstrate Asaṅga's reliance on it. See Janggya translation in Wilson (1984: 53-54). John Powers has recently published a fine new translation of the sūtra under the title *Wisdom of Buddha*.

[24]Watson 1964: 45. Chuang Chou is the personal name of the "Master Chuang," i.e., Chuang-tzu, which is transliterated Zhuang-zi in modern Pinyin.

> woke up and there he was, solid and unmistakable Chuang Chou. But he didn't know if he was Chuang Chou who had dreamt he was a butterfly, or a butterfly dreaming he was Chuang Chou.

In very broad strokes, all Buddhists are idealists because they believe, in H. B. Acton's words, that "mind and spiritual values are fundamental in the world as a whole,"[25] and secondly, they oppose the view that mind is derived from or reducible to material processes. The first aspect of the idealistic outlook, the primacy of mind over matter, is affirmed in the basic Buddhist notion that the mind is the source of cyclic existence (*'khor ba, saṃsāra*), the round of rebirth in various forms of existence brought about by actions (*las, karma*) contaminated by ignorance (*ma rig pa, avidyā*). In the *Saṃyutta-nikāya*[26] the Buddha says:

> The world is led by mind and drawn along by mind. All phenomena are controlled by one phenomenon, mind.

Similarly, Candrakīrti, commenting on the *Sūtra on the Ten Grounds* in his *Entrance to the Middle Way* (VI.84), says:[27]

> The Bodhisattva of the Manifest [sixth ground]...realizes that the creator is only mind.

---

[25]H. B. Acton 1967: 110. Thomas Kochumuttom (1982: 1) characterizes even Vasubandhu's Cittamātra thought as "realistic pluralism," because it recognizes a plurality of beings and phenomena. He seems to restrict the use of the term "idealism" to monistic idealism, perhaps because so many in the past (e.g., Stcherbatsky) have seen Cittamātra that way, but I see no need to do so.

[26]*Saṃyuttanikāya* I.39.10-11 (Pāli Text Society translation, 1917). The Pāli is: *cittena nīyati loko, cittena parikassati / cittasa ekadhammassa sabbheva vasam anvagū.*

[27]The Manifest (*mngon gyur, abhimūkhī*) is the sixth of the ten Bodhisattva "grounds" (*sa, bhūmi*) or levels that Mahāyānists pass over to attain Buddhahood. The *Sūtra on the Ten Grounds* is P 761.31, vol. 25; the passage in question is: "He thinks as follows, 'What belongs to the triple world, that is (of) mere mind.'" It is translated in Honda (189). Candrakīrti's passage is found in P 5262, vol. 98, 103.1.8.

Stripped of its reference to the Bodhisattva grounds (a concept present only in Mahāyāna Buddhism), this naming of mind as the creator of the world could be accepted by Buddhists of all persuasions. Specifically, Buddhists consider the ignorant mind (*ma rig pa, avidyā*), the misconception of self, to be the root from which cyclic existence issues.[28]

The second aspect of the idealistic outlook, the insistence that the mind cannot be reduced to physical processes, is also a fundamental principle of Buddhist doctrine. For instance, if the mind were not distinct from the body, reincarnation would not be possible, for the continuum of mind and the vitality of the body would cease in concert. Also, there could be no Formless Realm (*gzugs med khams, ārūpyadhātu*)—in which there are no physical processes, since all the beings there have a disembodied existence—as specified in Buddhist cosmology.

In addition to being idealists in the broadest sense, all Mahāyāna doctrinalists are anti-realists insofar as they deny that forms exist independently of being perceived.[29] In general, Buddhists speak of the very existence of phenomena in terms of mind: one definition of "existent" is, in fact, "that which is observed by valid cognition" (*tshad mas dmigs pa, pramāṇālambana*).[30]

---

[28]In the sūtras, the Buddha often said that attachment (*sred pa, tṛṣṇā*) is the cause of suffering, but when he explained the twelve links in the chain of dependent-arising (*rten 'byung, pratītyasamutpāda*) it was ignorance that he identified as the root of suffering, with attachment, grasping (*len pa, upādāna*), and existence (*srid pa, bhava*) acting to nourish and actualize potentials for suffering. Based on the mental condition of ignorance, sentient beings perpetrate intentional actions (*las, karma*) that create potentials for the manifestation of future environments and bodies. Thus, the mind is really the creator of the world as we know it.

[29]For widely used definitions of idealism, realism, and anti-realism, see Acton (1967: 110).

[30]Sanskrit is uncertain. In Gönchok Jikmay Wangbo's presentation of the Sautrāntika School, much of whose epistemology (from Dignāga and Dharmakīrti) is adopted by the higher schools, an object of knowledge (*shes bya, jñeya*) is defined as "that which is suitable to be an object of mind" (*blo'i yul du bya rung ba*), and is a synonym for "existent." In the *Collected Topics* (*bsdus grwa*) entitled *Festival for the Wise* written by Jambel Trinlay (*'jam dpal 'phrin las*) and used by young students of Drebung Monastic University's

The philosophy of Cittamātra is sometimes called Buddhist Idealism, which in the light of the preceding discussion should be understood to indicate that it is the *most* idealistic form of Buddhist thought. Although all Buddhists emphasize the primacy of mind and resist its reduction to physical processes, most stop short of rejecting the validity of perceptions that affirm an external world. Interpreters agree that the Cittamātra School, on the other hand, at the very least denies that one can directly apprehend an external object (an object that is a separate entity from the mind that apprehends it); moreover, the Tibetan tradition, and the greater part of the Indian tradition, has understood the Cittamātra School to deny the very *existence* of any external object.

Gönchok Jikmay Wangbo, the second Jamyang Shayba, defines a Cittamātrin as:[31]

> a person propounding Buddhist tenets who asserts the true existence (*bden grub, satyasat*) of dependent natures (*gzhan dbang, paratantra*) but does not assert external objects (*phyi don, bāhyārtha*).[32]

This definition brings out two crucial aspects of Cittamātra thought as it is understood by Gelukba interpreters: (1) the assumption that if impermanent things exist at all, they must exist by way of their own character, i.e., truly or ultimately,

---

Loseling College, the definition of "existent" (*yod pa*) is "that which is observed by valid cognition" (*tshad mas dmigs pa*); an "established base" (*gzhi grub*) is "established by valid cognition" (*tshad mas grub pa*); an "object of comprehension" (*gzhal bya*) is "an object of realization by valid cognition" (*tshad mas rtogs par bya ba*), and so forth. (See p.3; there are eight synonyms altogether).

[31] *Precious Garland of Tenets* (40). Translated by Hopkins and Sopa (249). Janggya's definition (*Presentation of Tenets* 157.7-8) is similar.

[32] These two qualifications are not necessarily held together. The Yogācāra-Svātantrikas (*rnal 'byor spyod pa'i dbu ma rang rgyud pa*) do not consider phenomena to be truly existent even though they also refute the existence of external objects (Gönchok Jikmay Wangbo, *Precious Garland of Tenets* [55-56], translated in Sopa and Hopkins [283-85]). The Sagya scholar Daktsang is accused of arguing that some Cittamātrins—the so-called False Aspectarians (*rnam rdzun pa, alīkākāravādin*)—actually assert external objects, but that view is refuted by Jamyang Shayba (Losang Gönchok, *Word Commentary* 152.3 ff.). About the False Aspectarians, see Sopa and Hopkins (284-85).

and (2) that they do not exist as objects that are a separate entity from the awarenesses that apprehend them, though that is how they appear.

With regard to the first of these aspects, the conception of "true existence" refers to the conception that a phenomenon does not merely exist in dependence on being imputed by terms and thought, but rather exists by way of its own nature (*rang gi mtshan nyid kyis grub pa, svarūpa-siddhi*) and is analytically findable among its bases of designation, such as its parts. For instance, to conceive of a chair as truly existent is to conceive that the chair exists in its own right either as its back, seat, and legs, or as the collection of these parts, or apart from them.[33] That is, one would expect to be able to point to the chair either as *being* one or more of those parts, the collection of them, or as a thing apart from them, not having to settle for a chair that is a mere nominal designation. Cittamātrins are said to feel that what they call dependent natures (*gzhan dbang, paratantra*; literally, "other-powered")—the appearances of objects that arise from causes and conditions—and thoroughly established natures (*yongs grub, pariniṣpanna*)—the absence, in those dependent natures, of a difference in entity from the awarenesses apprehending them—must truly exist, or they would not exist at all.

However, according to Gelukba scholars, the term "true existence" has a slightly different meaning for Prāsaṅgikas than for Cittamātrins. For the Cittamātra School, existent imputational natures (*rnam grags pa'i kun btags, parikalpita*) are *not* truly existent. These phenomena include space[34] and cessations (*'gog pa, nirodha*)—mere negatives or absences such as

[33]In the *Entrance to the Middle Way*, Candrakīrti uses the example of a chariot to explore seven possibilities for the inherent existence of the chariot: the chariot does not inherently exist because of not being its parts, not being other than its parts, not being in its parts, not being that in which its parts exist, not possessing its parts, not being the composite of its parts, and not being the shape of its parts. See Wilson (1980).

[34]"Space" refers to the uncaused space which is nothing more than a lack of obstructive contact as opposed to space in the sense of what appears to the eye in a room or outdoors; the latter is visible form, hence, a dependent nature rather than an imputational nature

emptiness or the cessation of an affliction (*nyon mongs, kleśa*) upon its destruction. Space and cessations exist, but they must be imputed in dependence on terms and thought. They do not exist from their own side, but rather must be posited by the negation of another phenomenon. Still other imputational natures, such as a phenomenon's difference in entity from the awareness that apprehends it (i.e., a phenomenon's being an external object), lack true existence for Cittamātrins because they do not exist at all. Because of these problems, Gönchok Jikmay Wangbo has deliberately excluded imputational natures by specifying, in his definition of Cittamātrins, that they assert the true existence of *dependent* natures.

Gelukbas attempt to become even more precise: they say that according to Cittamātrins, existent imputational natures have inherent existence (*rang bzhin gyis grub pa, svabhāva-siddhi*) and existence in their own right (*rang ngos nas grub pa, svarūpa-siddhi*) but do not have true existence, existence by way of their own nature (*rang gi mtshan nyid kyis grub pa, svalakṣaṇa-siddhi*), or ultimate existence (*don dam par grub pa, paramārtha-siddhi*). All phenomena are *inherently* existent, etc.; but because phenomena such as space are only *imputedly* existent, they are not also *truly* existent, etc. Therefore, "true existence" may be summed up as meaning that which exists from its own side *and* is not merely imputed. For Prāsaṅgikas, on the other hand, all of these terms are equivalent, equally implying an object that can be found upon analysis.

All phenomena have dependent, thoroughly established, and imputational natures: impermanent phenomena are themselves dependent natures because they depend on causes and conditions; they are falsely imagined to be different entities from the awarenesses that apprehend them; and their emptiness of such an imputational nature is thoroughly established. Hence, that dependent natures are truly existent does not mean that they necessarily exist the way they appear to ordinary beings, for they appear to be external objects; thus, although these phenomena truly exist, they do not truly exist *as external objects*. They are falsities that truly exist.

With regard to the second aspect of Gönchok Jikmay Wangbo's definition, there are numerous statements in the sūtras on which the Cittamātra School relies to suggest that external objects—objects separate from, i.e., a different entity from, the consciousnesses apprehending them—do not exist. The *Sūtra on the Ten Grounds* is the source of perhaps the most famous statement:[35]

> [The Bodhisattva] thinks as follows, "What belongs to the triple world, that is (of) mere mind. The *Subhāṣitasaṃgraha* quotes as follows: "This triple world is mind-only."

The *Descent to Laṅka Sūtra* says:[36]

> Through relying on mind-only
> One does not conceive of external objects.
> Abiding in correct observation
> One passes beyond mind-only as well.

and:[37]

> [Objects] do not appear as external objects as perceived.
> The mind appears as various [objects through the power of predispositions].
> [Because the mind is generated] in the likeness of bodies [senses], enjoyments [objects of senses], and abodes [physical sense organs and environments],
> I have explained [that all phenomena are] mind-only.

In interpreting these passages, Gelukbas take "mind-only" to mean that although minds and their objects, such as a visual consciousness and a visible object, seem to us to be unconnected entities, they are actually one inseparable entity. Minds and appearances arise simultaneously from a single cause, the

---

[35]Translation from Honda (189).

[36]This is the Lopez (1987: 346) translation of the sūtra as cited in Śāntarakṣita at P 5285, vol. 101, 13.2.8-3.1. Lopez also translates Jñānavajra's Prāsaṅgika interpretation of this passage (1987: 472, n. 7).

[37]P 775, vol. 29, 53.4.2. This is translated by Hopkins (1983a: 613).

ripening of a predisposition (*bag chags, vāsanā*)[38] established by a previous action (*las, karma*). Actions are themselves primarily the mental factor of intention (*sems pa, cetanā*). All appearances of objects are caused by these karmic predispositions that are contained within a neutral, continuously operating consciousness called the mind-basis-of-all (*kun gzhi rnam par shes pa, ālayavijñāna*). A single potency in this consciousness simultaneously causes both the appearance of an object and a consciousness apprehending it; hence, an apprehended object such as an orange and its apprehending subject such as an eye consciousness are simultaneous and are said to be a single substantial entity within being conceptually diverse. In other words, they occur inseparably. As Janggya says:[39]

> Although there are no external objects, on account of latencies for the perception of external objects having been infused [and subsequently ripening in the mind-basis-of-all], there occur knowledges [i.e., phenomena] that are perceived as [external] objects.

According to Gelukba scholars, the Cittamātra School regards external objects to be not only not ultimately existent, but not even conventionally existent, for although the world believes in them, they cannot be established by a valid conventional awareness.[40] On the other hand, Cittamātra accepts objects that are one entity with the minds that apprehend them and can be certified by conventional valid cognition. Thus, even

---

[38]Predispositions or latencies, seeds (*sa bon, bīja*), and potencies (*nus pa, śakti / bāla*) are equivalent. They are neither form nor consciousness, but non-associated compositional factors (*ldan min 'du byed, viprayuktasaṃskāra*), i.e., not associated with minds or mental factors in the way that a mind is always associated with mental factors or a mental factor is always associated with other mental factors or with a main mind.

[39]Janggya 157. Translated by Wilson (1984: 51).

[40]According to Gönchok Jikmay Wangbo, in the Cittamātra system a conventional truth is an "object found by a prime cognition that is a correct consciousness distinguishing a conventionality" (Sopa and Hopkins [1976: 264]), i.e., all existent phenomena except for thoroughly established natures. All conventional truths exist conventionally, and all except for imputational natures exist ultimately as well.

though Cittamātra rejects utterly the existence of external objects, it accepts the existence of objects other than mind. In other words, "mind-only" is not an absolute idealism in which only mind exists.

According to the Gelukba exegesis of Dharmakīrti on mind-only, that objects are "one entity with mind" means that the two must arise concomitantly and must be observed together. Thus, objects cannot be considered "external objects," even though it is not the case that, for instance, the objects of the senses such as sights, sounds, and odors are contained within the mind-body aggregates (*phung po, skandha*) of the person apprehending them. Objects and subjects are different, but not different *entities*. Because there are no external objects acting as conditions for consciousnesses, Cittamātrins do not explain, as other Buddhists do, sense experience on the basis of the coming together of three conditions—an empowering condition (*bdag rkyen, adhipatipratyaya*) such as an eye sense-power, an immediately preceding condition (*de ma thag rkyen, samanantarapratyaya*) such as a previous moment of consciousness, and an observed-object condition (*dmigs rkyen, ālambana-pratyaya*) such as an external object. In other versions of the working of karma, it can be said that other beings and the environment itself can set up the conditions under which one's karmic potentials can ripen; in the Cittamātra scheme, since there are no external objects appearing to consciousness, it can only be the fruition of one's own karma and one's reactions to those events that determine the chain of latency-generated appearances that is one's stream of experience.

Although the Cittamātra school maintains that there are no external objects, that is usually the way that objects appear to ordinary beings and are conceived by them to exist. The assent to the appearance of subject-object duality is extremely important, for the Cittamātra system considers it to be a type of ignorance that prevents the attainment of omniscience and Buddhahood.[41] The realization of the emptiness (*stong pa nyid,*

---

[41]According to Gelukba scholars, the Cittamātra School regards the conception of a self of persons—the conception of the person being a self-sufficient entity—to be the ignorance that prevents liberation from cyclic

śūnyatā) of subject and object being different entities is the wisdom (*ye shes, jñāna*) that overcomes the obstructions to omniscience, i.e., achieves Buddhahood.

Some modern interpreters have suggested that although Asaṅga and Vasubandhu deny the theories of realists such as the Vaibhāṣikas, they do *not* actually deny the existence of external objects.[42] They raise the possibility that Vasubandhu and other Cittamātrins assert only that external objects cannot appear directly to the mind; the mind instead processes mere representations of those phenomena, with those representations being the same entity as the mind. In other words, the philosophy of mind-only can be considered as merely an epistemological rather than ontological judgement. This is a case difficult to prove and which depends on the unlikely possibility that (1) Asaṅga and Vasubandhu have been consistently misinterpreted throughout subsequent Buddhist doctrinal history[43] and (2) that they themselves did not see that in order to avoid misunderstanding it was necessary to clarify the sūtras they cite that seem so clearly to indicate a denial of external objects. Actually, not only Buddhists, but the Nyāya,

---

existence. Thus, according to them it is not necessary to realize the most subtle emptiness—the lack of a difference in entity between subject and object and of objects naturally being a basis of names—in order to achieve liberation, though it must be overcome in order to attain Buddhahood.

[42]For example, Lambert Schmithausen (1976: 241); Thomas Kochumuttom (1982: 48); Janice Willis (1979: 20-36). Some scholars make a distinction between the two seminal figures of early Cittamātra: Diana Paul (1984: 215) feels that although Asaṅga perhaps denies external objects, Vasubandhu probably does not. Stephen Anacker (1984: 159) agrees with her about Vasubandhu. Schmithausen distinguishes between phases of Asaṅga's writings: earlier parts of the *Yogācārabhūmi* are consistent with Hīnayāna ontology, whereas the later addition, the *Bodhisattvabhūmi*, is a "Mahāyāna illusionism" that propounds epistemological (but not necessarily ontological) dualism.

[43]Harris (83) concludes that, in fact, Bhāvaviveka and Candrakīrti did deliberately misinterpret them, "taking issue with a point of view that was never held by classical interpreters." This is certainly possible; there are many cases in which Indian commentators engage in exaggeration and hyperbole, possibly out of habits formed in the debating courtyard. However, there is also quite enough textual evidence to justify the interpretation of these Mādhyamikas.

Vaiśeṣika, Mīmāṃsaka, Jain, and other schools[44] understood the Cittamātra position to be a rejection of external objects.

Often the evidence of the revisionists seems rather thin. Anacker[45] cites one passage in Vasubandhu's *Commentary on (Asaṅga's) "Compendium of the Mahāyāna,"* in which he refers to the causes of a visual consciousness, to show that Vasubandhu asserts that there are forms separate from consciousness: "An eye consciousness occurs in dependence on an eye and a form together with the mind-basis-of-all." However, this statement does *not* to seem to preclude the possibility that the eye and form are one entity with the eye consciousness. To give another example, Kochumuttom[46] argues that Vasubandhu's position is that there are external objects, even though only "forms of consciousness" (*rnam rig pa, vijñāna*) appear to minds. He gives the example of mistaking a coiled rope for a snake. The problem with this example, if this is indeed his model, is that mistaking a rope for a snake can be explained simply as a matter of mixing something from the side of consciousness with what exists outside, so that a speckled, coiled form is imbued with the additional attributes of animation and danger. This is far short of a "form of consciousness." If "mind-only" means nothing more than acknowledging that in an act of cognition there is a subjective element as well aṣ an objective one, then it is hardly worthy of being called a distinct tenet system.

Rather, the best evidence, it seems to me, is that some Cittamātra arguments against external objects are so poor that it is difficult to believe that the Cittamātra philosophers themselves found them convincing. For instance, it does seem odd that if Cittamātra thinkers actually disbelieved the existence of external objects that they refuted only the possibility of *partless* particles, not those *with* parts, leaving open the possibility that they were refuting only external objects *as defined* by the Sautrāntikas and Vaibhāṣikas, not external objects in general. (On the other hand, since Gelukbas consider Asaṅga to

[44]Matilal (1974: 147-68).

[45]159.

[46]48.

have been a Prāsaṅgika, it is not the case that he had to be convinced by his own Cittamātra arguments!)

Whether or not it is reasonable to read some Cittamātra texts as not denying external objects, the subsequent Indian and Tibetan traditions alike have accepted no-external-objects as the Cittamātra School's final position. Since we are mainly concerned with the Prāsaṅgika refutation of what is taken to be the Cittamātra position, the outcome of the modern investigation of Cittamātra, though interesting, is not relevant here. Also, it may not ever be possible to determine precisely what Asaṅga and Vasubandhu meant or even that they composed the works attributed to them.

In any case, the idealism of Cittamātra must be distinguished from an absolute idealism in which only one mind exists, for Vasubandhu, in particular, makes it clear that there are a plurality of subjects.[47] Nor is it an immaterialism, holding that only minds exist, for the objects of consciousness are not themselves called mind, but form, etc., albeit form that is one entity with mind. Jamyang Shayba is very critical of Daktsang the Translator for what he sees as the latter's misinterpretation of Cittamātra by equating mind and its objects:[48]

> Daktsang's saying that all phenomena are mind is also incorrect. It is the sign of a very coarse awareness that is the system of analysis of a fool. It is as follows: Then it [absurdly] follows that all faults and good qualities are one because when all faults and good qualities appear to one consciousness that one consciousness must *be* all faults and good qualities. If that is accepted, the two, cyclic existence and nirvāṇa, would [absurdly] be one. Furthermore, there are many faults such as that one would eat consciousness and drink consciousness.[49]

---

[47]Although he often speaks in such a way that it seems as though he is referring to only one mind, in his *Twenty Verses* (18-20), he is concerned to show that different beings can have an influence on each other. This is discussed toward the end of the present chapter.

[48]This is Jamyang Shayba's thought as condensed by Losang Gönchok, *Word Commentary* 153.5-54.2.

[49]Moreover, we would be very hungry, for "mental food and drink" would not be filling. Moore's famous objection to Berkeley's idealism was

A Cittamātrin might say, for instance, that a table and the mind apprehending it may not be different entities, but they are not identical; neither *is* the other. Similarly, a table and the space it occupies are one entity, but no one would claim that the space *is* the table or that the table *is* the space.

According to Gelukba scholars, Prāsaṅgikas do not refute all of the Cittamātra positions, although those they accept are sometimes creatively adapted. For instance, it is said that Prāsaṅgikas *do* refute the true existence of any phenomenon and the non-existence of external objects, but they do *not* deny that subject-object dualism is transcended in the experience of the direct realization of emptiness by an exalted wisdom consciousness, for they do not wish to deny that one's experience of directly realizing emptiness is as if the mind and emptiness are fused, like fresh water poured into fresh water. They merely resist the conclusion that the experience of fusion means that the mind and emptiness are the same. The Prāsaṅgikas also do not deny that phenomena have the three natures. As Janggya says:[50]

> The presentation of the three characters [i.e., natures] in our own Prāsaṅgika system is: those conventionalities that are the substrata [of emptiness] just like those appearing [to our minds now] are posited as other-powered [or dependent] natures; factors of superimposition that are their own objective mode of subsistence or mode of disposition are posited as imputational natures; and the factors of the emptiness of such superimpositions are posited as thoroughly established natures.

Thus, for Prāsaṅgikas, a dependent nature is a conventional truth (conventional truths comprising all existents other than emptinesses); the inherent existence conceived with respect to a dependent nature is a non-existent imputational nature; and a thoroughly established nature is the emptiness of inherent existence of any phenomenon. In other words, like the Citta-

---

that the fire I remember does not warm me, nor the food I remember sate me.

[50]*Presentation of Tenets* 494.15-18.

mātrins, they explain that in terms of a dependent nature, its thoroughly established nature is its emptiness of an imputational nature. For example, for a table, its dependent nature is the table itself; its thoroughly established nature is the table's emptiness of inherent existence; and the opposite of that, the inherent existence of table, is its imputational nature, i.e., the nature that does not exist despite the fact that ignorance imputes it to the table.

Indian Sources for the Mind-Only Controversy

Let us turn now to the specific issue of the Cittamātra refutation of external objects and the Prāsaṅgika rebuttal of their positions. In their citation of Indian sources for the debate, Jamyang Shayba and Janggya draw almost exclusively upon the works of Asaṅga and Vasubandhu for the Cittamātra view and upon the sixth chapter of Candrakīrti's *Entrance to the Middle Way* for the Prāsaṅgika critique. Although we are principally concerned with the Tibetan exposition of the arguments, before exploring the full range of the arguments set forth by the two Tibetan philosophers let us briefly review what is propounded in the seminal works of the great Indian Buddhists.

The principal arguments made by Cittamātra thinkers in their denial of the existence of external objects are set forth in Asaṅga's *Compendium of the Mahāyāna* (which in turn cites the *Mahāyāna Abhidharma Sūtra*) and in Vasubandhu's *Twenty Stanzas*.

Asaṅga's principal treatment of external objects is in the second chapter of the *Compendium of the Mahāyāna*.[51] The following is a list of his arguments, which will be examined in more detail in the next chapter:

[51]Section numbers correspond to those assigned by Lamotte (1973; Tome I [Tibetan]: 26-31, Tome II [French translation]: 92-107). A number of these arguments from the *Compendium of the Mahāyāna* are from a sūtra not identified by Asaṅga but identified by Lamotte as the *Mahāyāna Abhidharma Sūtra* (1973: 19*-20*).

1. External objects are not needed for the production of consciousness, since in a dream (or magical emanation, or mirage, or optical illusion) we perceive objects without there having been any actual objects. Waking and dreaming are different mainly because upon waking we realize that our dream-objects do not exist, whereas an ordinary person has no break from the delusion that the objects of waking life exist as they appear (II.6).

2. Buddha said in the *Sūtra on the Ten Grounds* that all phenomena are mind-only and explained this further to Maitreya in the *Sūtra Unraveling the Thought* (II.7).

3. Objects, such as a blue totality (*kaṣina*)[52] or the appearance of a skeleton-covered area, perceived by yogis who have achieved special meditative states, are not external objects that have been recalled through memory, but rather are just internal images. Hence, consciousness can occur without external objects (II.8, II.14.2).

4. Hungry ghosts, animals, humans, and gods see one thing—a running stream—as blood and pus, as an abode, as water, and as nectar, respectively. Since it would be impossible for a single external object to have many natures, there must be no external object (II.14.1).

5. One can observe past objects, future objects, dream-objects, or reflections even though those are not external objects[53] (II.14.2).

---

[52]As explained by Buddhaghosa in the *Path of Purification* (*visuddhimagga*) for meditators in the Theravāda tradition, *kaṣina* are circular patterns used as foci of concentration. Some are simply spots of intense color; others are circular sections, marked off in various ways, of earth, water, sky, fire, etc. One meditates on the external *kaṣina* itself until one achieves a "learning sign," a clear mental image of it, at which point the external prop may be abandoned. The "learning sign" eventually develops into a "counterpart sign," an abstract, luminous image with which one can then practice "extension of the sign," enlargement of the image until it eventually fills all of space. The term "totality" conveys the meditator's experience that the *kaṣina* is the totality of sensible reality.

[53]Past objects no longer exist, future objects do not yet exist, dream-objects have never existed, and a reflection is not what it seems to be.

6. If external objects existed as they appear, one could correctly know suchness without effort. Therefore they must not exist as they appear (II.14.3).

7. Bodhisattvas who have gained meditative power in a concentration cause things to appear through the power of their belief. Yogis who have obtained calm abiding (*zhi gnas, śamatha*) and special insight (*lhag mthong, vipaśyanā*) can, with effort, see things such as subtle impermanence when they take them to mind (II.14.4).

8. No external objects appear to one who has attained a non-conceptual exalted wisdom consciousness (II.14.4).

In his approach to the existence of external objects in the *Twenty Stanzas*, Vasubandhu is primarily concerned with two points: showing that external objects are not necessary to explain the production of consciousness; and refuting the existence of the types of objects posited by the Hīnayāna schools. The following is a summary of his arguments:

1. External objects are not needed for the production of consciousness, since they are generated even in the absence of external objects, such as when someone with amblyopia[54] (an eye condition diminishing sight) sees non-existent "hairs" or when someone (with crossed eyes) sees a "double-moon" (verse 1).

2. External objects are not needed for the production of consciousness in the instance of a dream, where non-existent objects appear to the mind. Dream-objects can even be consistent with respect to time and place, just like "external" objects (verses 3, 16).

3. It makes as much sense to consider the guards, etc., of the hells as projections of consciousness rather than external reality as it does to claim that they are not sentient beings but rather are appearances of external elements generated by the karma of beings born in the hells (verses 4-7).

[54]"Dimness of sight"; it has also been suggested that this eye disease is ophthalmia, an inflammation of the eye (Fenner).

4. There could be no external objects composed of directionally partless particles (*rdul phra rab cha med, paramāṇu*) because either a particle touches other particles, in which case it has different parts where the other particles touch it, or else all the particles surrounding the particle touch the same place on it, in which case there could be only one particle (verse 12).

5. If there were partless particles, there could be no gross objects composed of them because the aggregation of those particles would necessitate their having parts. On the other hand, if the partless particles did aggregate, there could be just one "part." Hence, the earth could be covered in a single stride, etc. (verses 13-15).

The arguments made by Vasubandhu and Asaṅga are in many respects the same. They fall into three basic categories: (1) the refutation of external objects made from directionally partless particles; (2) examples that show that external objects are unnecessary; and (3) consequences contradictory to the assertion of external objects. Candrakīrti does not appear to have been concerned with refuting all of them; instead, demonstrating why he is aptly called the "opener of the chariot-way" for the Prāsaṅgika School, he concentrates on exposing the internal contradictions in the Cittamātra positions.

Candrakīrti's critique of Cittamātra comes in the context of the second part of his explanation of the famous tetralemma of the Mādhyamika School with respect to production, the inquiry into whether things are produced from things that are different from them. This is found in the sixth chapter of the *Entrance to the Middle Way*, verses 45-71 and 84-97 (the intervening verses are concerned with refuting the notion of self-consciousness).[55] The following is a summary of his arguments:

---

[55]For translations, see the French translation of La Vallée Poussin and the English translations of C. W. Huntington, Stephen Batchelor, and Peter G. Fenner. (These are cited in the bibliography under Candrakīrti.)

1. The Cittamātra School points out that in a dream, there is apprehension of a dream-object, and one can later remember that dream-object, even though there is no external object. For them, the absence of the object after the dream shows that it had no external existence whereas its recollection when one is awake shows that consciousness truly exists. However, this is fallacious; if a subsequent recollection could establish the existence of an (inherently existent) mind, an external object would also be established, since it was recalled as an external object (VI.48-49).

2. Similarly, the Cittamātra School likes to point out that the objects of a dream function just like external objects, since a dream-object can be the cause of attachment. Thus, they say that there really is no difference between a dreaming and waking mind, nor between internal dream-objects and so-called external objects. However, this does not establish the true existence of the dreaming mind, but rather only proves that *both* a waking mind and a dreaming mind are false. Both a dream consciousness and a waking consciousness are mistaken with respect to their objects, for their objects do not inherently exist even though that is the way they appear. Hence, the visual object, the eye, and the eye consciousness are all false. When one awakens from the sleep of ignorance, one understands that one's ordinary cognition was mistaken, just as upon awakening from a dream one realizes that the dream-objects did not exist (VI.50-53).

3. As another illustration of perception without an external object, the Cittamātra School likes to point to the instance of persons with the eye disease amblyopia who see "falling hairs" in front of them. However, this example establishes merely that the awareness is defective, without valid perception, and thus not truly existent, since people with good vision see nothing in the place where "falling hairs" are seen. If a mind were truly existent, it could not be contradicted by the perceptions of others; hence, others would also see the falling hairs. (VI.54-55). (This, then is like the example of dreaming: perception "without an object" occurs only when one's consciousness is under the control of a distorting force such as

sleep or amblyopia; and if the consciousness in question truly existed, its objects would absurdly exist for others.)

4. The Cittamātra contention that the appearance of objects and the perception of them arise from seeds that are in the mind-basis-of-all is not feasible. A potential must be the cause of either a present consciousness or a future consciousness. If it is the cause of a present consciousness, then as a cause it would exist at the same time as its effect, which is absurd, since a cause must exist prior to its effect. On the other hand, if it were the cause of a future consciousness, it would not exist when its effect did, in which case it would have no connection to it (VI.56-61).

5. If the appearance of objects is dependent only on karmic seeds, and not on one's sense organs, then the blind absurdly should be able to see things while awake just as they do when they are asleep and dreaming (VI.62-67).[56]

6. A yogin can perceive the ground to be covered with skeletons as the result of meditative stabilization. If the mind truly existed, its object would always be visible to others, but that is obviously not the case here, since others do not see the skeletons. The same holds true with respect to a hungry ghost's perception of blood and pus in a river. If the blood and pus truly existed, everyone would see those substances there. The Cittamātra reply that the hungry ghost's perception would be like that of a person with amblyopia is inadmissible, for there is nothing invalid about the hungry ghost's perception (VI.69-71).

7. The notion of self-consciousness (a consciousness that non-dualistically realizes a consciousness that in turn apprehends an object) is refuted. If the dependent natures that consciousness experiences are one entity with it, they are not apprehended-objects of that consciousness; how then can consciousness be posited, since there is nothing separate from it that it can be said to know? That is, how could consciousness be known if there is no object for it to know? The Cittamātra

[56]This is another variation on the argument about the dream state. The Cittamātra School has argued that waking and dreaming objects are equivalent in terms of being able to produce consciousness.

School replies that a consciousness knows itself. In fact, they maintain that only if a consciousness knew itself could recollection of that consciousness come about at a later time. However, this is both unnecessary and absurd.[57] It is unnecessary because recalling the object experienced previously serves as a sufficient cause for the recollection of the awareness; we remember, "I saw blue," for instance, and that serves as recollection not only of blue but of the *seeing* of blue. It is absurd because something posited as truly existent could not be the cause for something else that is also truly existent, as both the consciousness and its self-consciousness are. Also, self-consciousness is absurd because something cannot be both agent and recipient of action, just as a sword cannot cut itself nor an eye see itself (VI.72-77).[58]

8. The Cittamātrins have rejected the conventions of the world without warrant; they have fallen from both conventional truths and from ultimate truths (since they assume the true existence of consciousness) (VI.78-83).

9. The scriptures upon which the Cittamātra School relies either have been misinterpreted in the sense that they have been treated too literally or have not been understood to be merely provisional teachings for those incapable of hearing the more profound doctrine of the emptiness of inherent existence. First, in some sūtras such as the *Sūtra on the Ten Grounds,* Buddha said "The three realms are mind-only" just to indicate that, rather than a god who created the world and beings, the creative agency is only the intentional actions of beings. Second, in sūtras such as the *Descent to Laṅka Sūtra,* Buddha taught that what appear to be external objects are actually mental forms, but he did this only to help certain persons give up their attachment to forms and to make it easier for some to later understand the non-inherent existence of consciousness. Buddha said that both forms and conscious-

[57]Candrakīrti apparently does not deal with the additional wrinkle introduced by Dharmapāla (530-61 C.E.), who spoke also of self-self-consciousness. See Nakamura (1987: 278).

[58]The analogies are in Candrakīrti's Autocommentary 104.7-5.1. This is cited in the Jamyang Shayba / Ngawang Belden translation, chapter 7.

nesses equally exist conventionally and equally do not exist ultimately (VI.84-97).

In the next chapter, we will examine Gelukba approaches to these arguments by exploring several works, primarily those of Jamyang Shayba, Ngawang Belden, and Janggya. Before passing on to those matters, let us consider the more fundamental question that divides the Cittamātra and Prāsaṅgika viewpoints—whether or not the Cittamātrins are accurate in their assertion that the Buddha actually taught that external objects do not exist.

Cittamātra and Prāsaṅgika Perspectives on Mind-Only Scriptures

As noted earlier, the Cittamātra works of Asaṅga and Vasubandhu are dependent upon a small number of sūtras from which they derive Cittamātra doctrine: the *Sūtra Unraveling the Thought*, the *Sūtra on the Ten Grounds*, the *Descent to Laṅka Sūtra*, and the *Mahāyāna Abhidharma Sūtra*. The first of these is Asaṅga's principal source.

What should be noted first about the Prāsaṅgika stance toward the scriptural sources of the Cittamātra School is that the most obvious ground for the dismissal of the Cittamātra philosophy is not employed. Prāsaṅgikas might be expected to deny the authenticity of Cittamātra scriptural sources by showing through various modes of literary or deductive criticism that those words were never uttered by the Buddha and hence must be regarded as a sheer fabrication by certain Mahāyāna monks. However, such a tactic is not used against Cittamātra. One reason, perhaps, is that it was realized that such a move might have the undesirable side-effect of casting doubt on the authenticity of the Mahāyāna scriptures in general. That is, it would be difficult for Mādhyamikas, as Mahāyānists, to reject any scripture on the grounds of authenticity; to convince the Hīnayānists who doubt the Mahāyāna because of its apparent contradictions with previously canonized scriptures, Mahāyānists have generally argued that the Blessed One, from the depths of his compassion, taught a broad range of doctrines to captivate diverse types of people. Hence, the Cittamātra and Mādhyamika Schools alike characterize the sūtras accorded primacy by the other as authentic, but "requiring interpretation" (*drang don, neyārtha*), whereas their own authoritative sūtras are labeled "definitive" (*nges don, nītārtha*).[59]

According to Gelukba scholars, the Prāsaṅgikas, therefore, do not use historical inquiry or literary criticism to distinguish definitive and non-definitive sūtras; rather, these categories are established on the basis of what stands up to reasoning, for of course the Buddha's own final view, the definitive view, could not be logically subordinate to any other.[60] This is not a new idea, for even if there were not competing interpretations of the Buddha's own final view, it is a common notion that the Buddha's doctrine is not to be blindly accepted without analysis. The Buddha's own dictum was that his doctrine be subjected to reasoning in the way in which a goldsmith analyzes a gold nugget.

Accordingly, Bhāvaviveka, said to be the founder of the Svātantrika-Mādhyamika School, does not deny the authenticity of so-called Cittamātra scriptures. His criticism of Cittamātra is to deny that the Buddha literally taught in *any* of those scriptures that there are no external objects, implying that the basic thrust of the philosophy of Cittamātra is based on a misunderstanding. In saying this, he goes far beyond Candrakīrti, who is willing to say that in most cases, Buddha actually *did* mean to say that there are no external objects (although that was not the Buddha's own final view). According to Bhāvaviveka, when, in scriptures such as the *Sūtra on the Ten*

---

[59]To be precise, the question of definitive and interpretable sūtras is quite a bit more complex than this, since *sūtra* can mean a *portion* of a larger text; hence, there are parts of sūtras that the other school finds generally authoritative that might be definitive rather than requiring interpretation, and vice versa. The Janggya translation, section C, discusses issues related to these.

[60]For a discussion of the criterion of truth as established by reasoning in the classification of Buddhist scriptures, see Cabezón (1981: 7-23).

Grounds, Buddha said that the "three realms"—the Form Realm (*gzugs khams, rūpadhātu*), Formless Realm (*gzugs med khams, ārūpyadhātu*), and Desire Realm (*'dod khams, kāmadhātu*)—which comprise the whole of cyclic existence (*'khor ba, saṃsāra*), are "mind-only," he did not mean that there are no external objects. He meant only that mind, in the sense of intentions (*sems pa, cetanā*) to act or in the sense of karmic latencies with the mind, is the creator of cyclic existence.[61] Thus, in Bhāvaviveka's view, these sūtras not only are in need of clarification regarding their presentation of ultimate truths, but are not even literal. Bhāvaviveka says:[62]

> In the sixth Bodhisattva stage, the Bodhisattva...thinks: the three realms are mind-only, they are established by mind-only, and are brought about by mind-only. God (Īśvara) is not an agent. When this is clear to him he says, "O Jinaputra, it is so, the three realms are mind-only." The word "only" should be understood as negating an agent [other than mind]; but it should not be understood as negating [external] objects.

Janggya explains:[63]

> The term "only" in the *Sūtra on the Ten Grounds* statement "The three realms are only mind" does not eliminate external objects; rather, [it means that] since all three realms[64] are constructed by actions and since actions are limited to the two, intention and thought [i.e., intentional and operational

---

[61]The context in which this famous statement appears in the *Sūtra on the Ten Grounds* suggests to me that Bhāvaviveka and Candrakīrti are correct, for it is followed by a statement that the twelve links of dependent-arising depend on the mind; that mind is ignorance, and it conditions the rest of the process (Honda 1968: 189).

[62]The following translation of Bhāvaviveka's *Lamp for (Nāgārjuna's) "Wisdom," Commentary on the "Treatise on the Middle Way"* (*dbu ma rtsa ba'i grel pa shes rab sgron ma, prajñāpradīpamūlamadhyamakavṛtti*) is from Eckel (1980: 337). Also, see Lopez (1987: 312-13).

[63]*Presentation of Tenets* 482.9-13.

[64]The Desire Realm (*'dod khmas, kāmadhātu*), Form Realm (*gzugs khams, rūpadhātu*), and Formless Realm (*gzugs med khams, ārūpyadhātu*), the realms of rebirth for sentient beings.

> actions], the three realms are constructed by mind. Therefore, the term "only" is stated for the purpose of negating the existence of a creator of the world other than the mind, such as Īśvara, who is different than the mind, and so forth.

The Prāsaṅgikas did not go to the same lengths as Bhāvaviveka. True, they, like other Buddhists, understood the mind to be the creator of cyclic existence in the sense described by Bhāvaviveka. And it is also true that they consider that in general the "Cittamātra scriptures" require interpretation because they do not explicitly identify the mode of being of their subjects as the lack of inherent existence. However, Prāsaṅgikas do not say that those sūtras are necessarily non-literal; it is accepted that often "mind-only" is what the Buddha intended his listeners to understand when he spoke. As Candrakīrti says, Buddha taught mind-only just provisionally and for certain persons—those not yet capable of understanding the absence of inherent existence. As he says in his *Entrance to the Middle Way* (VI.43):[65]

> The teachings that a basis-of-all exists, that the person [inherently] exists,
> And that only the aggregates [inherently] exist
> Should be taken as teachings for those who would not understand
> The very profound meaning [of emptiness].

And (VI.94):[66]

> These sūtras teaching no external objects of perception, i.e.,
> Teaching that the mind appears as the variety of objects,
> Turn away from forms those extremely attached to forms.
> These also require interpretation.

---

[65]*Entrance to the Middle Way* 6b.2. Also cited in Jamyang Shayba, chapter 1; there is more bibliographic information there. For another translation, see Huntington 162.

[66]*Entrance to the Middle Way* 8b.6-8. The translation is from Hopkins (1983a: 614).

In this way, the Buddha acts like a doctor who acts for the good of his patients; the *Descent into Laṅka Sūtra* states:[67]

> Just as a doctor distributes
> Medicines to the ill,
> So Buddha teaches
> Mind-only to sentient beings.

Therefore, Prāsaṅgikas maintain that the teaching of the Cittamātra School is an authentic teaching of the Buddha and, within the sphere of those suffering from over attachment to forms, is an appropriate "medicine" to relieve symptoms such as the reification of subject-object dualism, even if it does not teach the final mode of being of phenomena as does the tradition of the Mādhyamika School.

However, although the Prāsaṅgika hermeneutic relies principally on logic, establishing the true mode of existence of phenomena so as to be able to explain that the Buddha's teaching of other systems was a matter of skillful pedagogy, it does not rely only on logic when assessing the scriptures upon which Cittamātra depends. Prāsaṅgikas also take note of sūtras that appear to directly contravene the teaching of mind-only. According to Candrakīrti:[68]

> [Truly existent mind and form] were equally abandoned by Buddha in the sūtras on the mode of wisdom and [conventionally existent mind and form] were equally set forth
> In the Abhidharma [scriptures].

According to Candrakīrti, the Perfection of Wisdom sūtras teach that all five aggregates of body and mind lack true existence, and the abhidharma scriptures accord all five equivalence in terms of conventional existence. Therefore, there is

---

[67]P 775, vol. 29, 34.3.5. This is found in chapter 2. Cf. Suzuki 44 (123). It is cited in Janggya, *Presentation of Tenets* 482.20-83.1.

[68]*Entrance to the Middle Way* (VI.92) 8b.5. Dzongkaba's commentary is *Illumination of the Thought* 175a.5 ff.; the material in brackets is from him.

no difference between mind and its objects in terms of true or conventional existence.

Hence, with regard to Cittamātra texts, Prāsaṅgikas argue both that those texts are valid, serving a useful function for appropriate persons, and that those texts are contradictory with the Buddha's higher teachings in the Perfection of Wisdom sūtras and abhidharma texts. It is then presumably for the sake of those who do not require the diluted teachings of Cittamātra that they develop their arguments against its central tenet; these arguments will be explored in the next chapter.

3 Gelukba Renditions of the Mind-Only Controversy

Now that we have made a brief survey of the Indian sources for the analyses of Jamyang Shayba and Janggya, let us consider the issues in more detail. According to those Gelukba authorities, the Prāsaṅgika rebuttal of the Cittamātra refutation of external objects includes the arguments listed below. That the Gelukbas feel free to extend the analysis of mind-only beyond Candrakīrti is clear: only the second through fifth arguments are drawn directly from Candrakīrti.[1] The first four are direct replies to points made by the early Cittamātra School.

1 The Cittamātra refutation of partless particles does not preclude the existence of external objects.
2 Several of the examples used by the Cittamātra School to establish the feasibility of consciousness in the absence of external objects in fact only indicate that consciousness lacks true existence.

[1]Candrakīrti's *Entrance to the Middle Way* is a direct source for the second (VI.48-53), third (VI.78-83), fourth (VI.72-77) and fifth (VI.32) arguments. Cf. Huntington 161, 163, 166-67. Janggya discusses the first, second, fourth, and fifth; Jamyang Shayba (or his commentators, Losang Gönchok or Ngawang Belden) the third through tenth. Gungtang, disciple of the second Jamyang Shayba, Gönchok Jikmay Wangbo, is the source of the eleventh.

3 The Cittamātra use of ultimate analysis to refute external objects does not refute their conventional existence.
4 The Cittamātra assertion of simultaneous observation of both subject and object is not possible.

In addition to those four direct replies, another seven arguments and contradictory consequences are asserted:

5 Scriptures—the Perfection of Wisdom Sūtras and the abhidharma scriptures—say that both form and consciousness conventionally exist but do not ultimately exist.
6 There is no conventional validly cognizing consciousness that refutes external objects.
7 Objects that were mere mental representations could not appear to conventional valid cognition.
8 Whatever is one entity with mind would absurdly *be* mind.
9 Although the existence of a mind-basis-of-all would entail the non-existence of external objects, a mind-basis-of-all does not exist.
10 Without external objects, nothing would exist.
11 Without external objects, shared objects of perception would be impossible.

Of the three authors whose works are translated in parts two and three, Jamyang Shayba is the most laconic on this subject, contributing only a short statement that contains the fifth and sixth arguments listed above. Janggya devotes much of his treatment to the issue of the interpretation of sūtras (see chapter 2), an issue not addressed by Jamyang Shayba and Ngawang Belden in the context of the unique tenets of the Prāsaṅgika School. Like Ngawang Belden, he denies that the Cittamātra refutation of partless particles (the first argument listed above) serves as a refutation of external objects; unlike either of the others, he examines the Cittamātra examples such as dreams and argues, in reliance on Candrakīrti, that such examples can be turned against Cittamātra (the second argument listed above). Ngawang Belden, relying in part on Candrakīrti and Dzongkaba (to make the point that the Cittamātra refutation of external objects, relying on ultimate analysis, undermines the teaching on conventional and ultimate truths), supplies most of the remaining criticisms; of the three authors, his is the most extensive analysis.

These arguments will be organized around four headings: (1) the Cittamātra School's allegation of contradictions in the assertion of external objects; (2) the Cittamātra School's refutation of directionally partless particles; (3) the Cittamātra School's refutation of the necessity of external objects for the production of consciousness; and (4) miscellaneous criticisms of Mind-Only by the Prāsaṅgikas.

Cittamātra Arguments That the Assertion of External Objects Contradicts Meditative Experiences

Cittamātra philosophers, as understood by Gelukbas, argue that the assertion of external objects contradicts other common Buddhist tenets. The illustrations for these arguments fall into two categories: (1) there are meditative experiences in which external objects are not found, either because there is simply an absence of any positive appearance or because an internal mental image has blocked out the appearance of external objects; and (2) there are cases in which different types of individuals validly perceive different objects in the same place, which would be contradictory if external objects existed.

First, let us consider instances of meditative experience in which no external objects are found. One, suggested by Asaṅga, is that no external objects appear to the mind at the time the mind is absorbed in meditative equipoise on emptiness.[2]

[2]Some Western scholars, such as Schmithausen (1976: 247), have suggested that the philosophy of Mind-Only (which they feel may not mean that no external objects exist, but only that they cannot appear to the mind) stems from the meditative experience of having the object itself disappear

He assumes that the most valid consciousness is the wisdom that realizes an ultimate truth (*don dam bden pa, paramārtha-satya*), i.e., an emptiness (which in the Cittamātra system is principally the lack of a difference of entity of subject and object—the absence of an external world). He argues that if external objects actually existed, they would have to appear to this consciousness, since it is the knower of reality (*chos nyid, dharmatā*), and the externality of the objects would be their very nature. The Cittamātra School and the Mādhyamika School agree that at the time of direct realization of emptiness, when one is in meditative equipoise (*mnyam bzhag, samāhita*) on emptiness, only emptiness itself appears to the mind;[3] even Prāsaṅgikas agree that external objects do not appear to a consciousness absorbed in the direct realization of an ultimate truth. Asaṅga takes this as an indication that those objects do not exist.

The principal Prāsaṅgika reply, according to the Gelukba authorities, is that this sort of analysis is obviously ultimate analysis and hence proves nothing in terms of the conventional existence of external objects. As Ngawang Belden says:[4]

> That forms, sounds, and so forth, are external objects is not refuted by valid cognition distinguishing conventionalities which does not depend on valid cognition distinguishing the ultimate because: (1) there is no instance of valid cognition distinguishing conventionalities that refutes external objects and (2) consciousnesses also are not established when they are analyzed by valid cognition distinguishing the ultimate.

Conventional valid cognition—direct perception or inference—certifies external objects. Only a consciousness analytically searching for an object, i.e., a validly cognizing consciousness distinguishing the ultimate, fails to find an external object.

---

at the moment of realizing its emptiness. I think it quite likely that the tenet followed the experience in this way; thus, although neither Asaṅga nor Vasubandhu leads off with this argument, it seems appropriate to use it to initiate our review since it may have been the one most important to them.

[3]Losang Gönchok, *Word Commentary* 146.3-4.

[4]*Annotations* 109a.2-3.

However, this failure to find an external object that can bear analysis refutes only the existence of truly existent external objects, not the existence of external objects conventionally. In other words, it is not surprising that an analytical awareness seeking an external object fails to establish one, since there is nothing, even consciousness, that can withstand such analysis. That is, when one attempts to designate an object that can be apprehended apart from the consciousness that realizes it, no such object appears, and one might erroneously conclude that no such object exists even conventionally. In this case, ultimate analysis involves the investigation into the relationship between a cause and effect, namely, the object and the consciousness for which it is an object of knowledge.

Even if Asaṅga's point did not entail ultimate analysis, Gelukbas might answer that it is not necessarily the case that external objects do not appear to an exalted wisdom consciousness, since they can appear to a Buddha. This is not an answer given in the context of their discussion of the tenet of mind-only, but is clearly indicated by Jamyang Shayba, for instance, in the root verses of his section on Buddhahood in the *Great Exposition of Tenets*, where he says of a Buddha:[5]

> With respect to the effect [of Buddhahood], meditative equipoise and subsequent attainment do not alternate; they have become one entity....
> All elaborations have vanished for the perspective of [the Buddha's] perception of the element of [Superior] qualities (*chos dbyings*, *dharmadhātu*, i.e., emptiness), but
> [For the perspective] of [the Buddha's] non-analytical [perception], the varieties are known, like an olive.

His commentator, Losang Gönchok, explains:

> For the perspective of [the Buddha's] perception of emptiness—the element of qualities—all elaborations of conventionalities have vanished and do not exist. Still, for the perspective of [the Buddha's] non-analytical perception of conventionalities, all the phenomena of the varieties are known

[5]In Losang Gönchok, *Word Commentary* 284.2-85.3.

> individually without confusion, like a wet olive fruit set in the palm of the hand.

Therefore, meditative absorption on emptiness does not necessarily preclude the appearance of objects; that is the case only for those who have not yet overcome the obstructions to omniscience. Since Buddhas are omniscient, they are able to cognize simultaneously both the bases of emptinesses, such as tables and chairs, and emptinesses themselves; hence, the realization of emptiness does not itself preclude the appearance of external objects. According to Jamyang Shayba, then, Prāsaṅgikas may assert that it is only the obstructions to omniscience that prevent the appearance of external objects while one is absorbed in the realization of emptiness, not the non-existence of such objects.

Other examples adduced by the Cittamātra thinkers to contradict the validity of the perception of external objects have to do with particular perceptions of external objects that, if true, would entail that more than one object could exist in one place or that one object had several contradictory natures. We have already referred to one instance, cited by Asaṅga, of yogis who practice a type of meditation in which all that appears to their minds is water or earth, the water "totality" or earth "totality." The yogi's cognition of only water or only earth, produced by profound concentration, is considered valid.[6] Asaṅga raises the difficulty that if these are external objects, the cognitions of other persons who are unable to see what appears to the yogi would be invalidated. If, on the other hand, there are no external objects and all appearances are produced from seeds that ripen simultaneously to produce appearances and consciousnesses, different cognitions are not necessarily contradictory.

---

[6]Jamyang Shayba (*Great Exposition of the Middle Way* 638.7), considering a hypothetical debate about a yogi's cognition of the ground being covered with skeletons, denies that all such appearances are just imaginary form, because to him it would absurdly entail that, "the actual appearance of such emanated by the two [types of Hīnayāna] Arhats and Bodhisattva Superiors on the pure grounds is [an imaginary form-source]."

Another of Asaṅga's examples[7] is particularly evocative. It concerns a certain trio consisting of a human, a god (*lha, deva*), and a hungry ghost (*yi dvags, preta*). In the *Compendium of the Mahāyāna*, Asaṅga says:[8]

> One thing [appears] to hungry ghosts, animals, humans
> And gods in accordance with whatsoever type [is appropriate to those beings]
> Because their minds are different;
> Therefore it is asserted that [external] objects are not established.

Asvabhāva (c. 450-530),[9] commenting on this example in his *Connected Explanation of (Asaṅga's) "Compendium of the Mahāyāna"* (*theg pa chen po'i bsdud pa'i bshad sbyar, mahāyānasaṃgrahopanibandhana*), suggests a curious situation: suppose that a god, a hungry ghost, and a human were to stand together, viewing a flowing river. As described in Buddhist cosmologies such as that found in Vasubandhu's *Treasury of Higher Knowledge* (*chos mngon pa'i mdzod, abhidharmakośa*), these three types of beings are extremely diverse in terms of their physical and mental characteristics and occupy vastly different environments. Gods and goddesses live long, blissful lives in sublime surroundings; hungry ghosts live in continual desperation in hot, dry, filthy places.[10] Their physical proxi-

---

[7]See Lamotte (1973 II: 104). Dharmakīrti, in his *Commentary on (Dignāga's) "Compendium on Prime Cognition,"* (III: 341) makes a similar argument. See explanation in Masaaki Hattori (1968: 105).

[8]Vasubandhu also refers to the seeing of pus, etc., by hungry ghosts (*Twenty Stanzas*, verse 3), but he does not mention any other beings and what they see. His point, however, is much the same as Asaṅga's: the hungry ghost's perception of pus is just of its own projection, not of an external object. Tibetan edited by Étienne Lamotte, *La Somme du Grande Véhicule D'Asaṅga* I: 31; translation into French, II: 105.

[9]Nakamura (1987: 276).

[10]In Vedic cosmology, *pretas* are spirits of the dead that have not yet become "fathers" (*pitṛ*), ghostly beings that make a long journey to the moon and are then reborn on earth. It was believed that during the year of "development" into a "father" it was very important to make daily food offerings to the *preta* to nourish it. Hence, the *preta* is by definition a being that has hunger, and if not fed by its former family would suffer from

mity is therefore unlikely. But if we suppose that gods, ghosts, and humans were spatially and temporally proximate, we can speculate about what each would see.

According to Asvabhāva:[11]

> By the power of their own karma, hungry ghosts see a river as full of pus, etc.; animals take that very river as a dwelling with the thought that it is a dwelling; humans think that it is water that is sweet, pure, and cool—they bathe in it, drink it, and enter it; and gods that dwell in the meditative equipoise of the sphere of limitless space (*nam kha' mtha' yes, ākāśānantya*) see it as space—that is, their discrimination of form has been destroyed.

Jamyang Shayba's explanation of this adds that gods (other than those in the levels of meditative equipoise) see the river as nectar.[12] Hence, the following scenario can be constructed: among the beings at the river-bank, some gods would perceive nothing but space; other gods, who evidently in their previous lives possessed the karmic predispositions to "ripen" upon death into a new lifetime full of sensual delights, would

---

continual hunger and thirst. Translators rendered *preta* into Tibetan as *yi dvags*, "those who think of food." In Buddhist literature, these hungry ghosts are of various sorts, though all are "hungry" because they cannot obtain sufficient food and drink. Some have huge bellies and needle-thin throats, so that they cannot swallow what they find; others cannot find anything other than blood, pus, excrement, and urine; others are constantly fooled by visions that turn out to be mirages; and so forth. One of the peculiarities of hungry ghosts is that they apparently are affected differently than are humans, and so forth, by natural events. Dzongkaba notes that hungry ghosts are not warmed, but cooled, by winter sunlight and are burned by summer moonlight (*Illumination of the Thought* 153b.6). See also Lati Rinbochay (1983: 33-35). Nāgārjuna refers to a number of their difficulties in his *Friendly Letter* (*bshes pa'i spring yig, suhṛllekha*).

[11]P 5552, vol. 113. This passage is cited in Jamyang Shayba's *Great Exposition of the Middle Way* 639.3 and in Dzongkaba's *Illumination of the Thought* 153b.2-4.

[12]*Great Exposition of the Middle Way* 641.5. Jamyang Shayba's long treatment of this topic may be based on Kaydrup's long treatment (see Cabezón 1992: 334-45). Kaydrup adds that those appearances are individual. Not all of the desire-realm gods would see nectar, and not all of the hungry ghosts would see blood and pus (Cabezón 1986: 684).

see a stream of nectar, perhaps with a delicious fragrance wafting upwards. The poor hungry ghost, always surrounded by a disgusting and frustrating environment, would observe yet another slow-moving stream of blood and pus. The human, of course, would see a river. It is notable that there is no suggestion that any Buddhist school would reject this scenario.

Each of the three beings would perceive only that which would be appropriate to their characteristic natures. That such would be the case must have seemed to Buddhist doctrinalists to be the only possibility that would preserve traditional cosmology; for it would be unseemly that gods experience anything unpleasant or that hungry ghosts experience anything pleasurable. However, at the same time it presented the puzzling result that apparently one stream of fluid can appear in many guises to different beings.

Is this simply analogous to the differences in perception that would occur amongst a fish, bird, or human momentarily located at a certain point on a river? The water of a stream undoubtedly looks vastly different to such different beings due to (1) great differences in their optical structures and capacity, which would affect factors such as hue, resolution of detail, depth perception, etc.; (2) the respective size and position of the observers, which would result in great variations in perspective; and (3) other factors such as familiarity with water, desire for and use of water, and so forth. However, even though a stream undoubtedly looks, feels, smells, sounds, etc., vastly different to a fish, a bird, and a human, it could not be experienced in a way that is *completely* different. All would be moistened by it; all would feel its weight, its pressure, its movement. It is quite another thing to say that what a hungry ghost experiences as a hot, barren desert a god can experience as empty space or as a garden of delights. The differences in the perspectives of the god and hungry ghost are much more extreme than can be explained through mere differences in optical structure or environment; not only are their experiences even of the color and texture of the fluid entirely different, but it is perfectly possible that what one god experiences as empty space, another can experience as nectar, and a hungry ghost will experience as a barren desert. There need not be the slightest correspondence between their experiences.

How, then, can these parties all be correct? It seems that the possibilities are limited to three: (1) that only one of the beings has correct perception, the other two being deluded—in a sense, suffering from elaborate hallucinations; (2) that all of the beings have deluded perception such that none of them sees what is really there; and (3) that all of the beings have correct perception, entailing that water, nectar, and blood and pus are all actually present in the same place.

The first of these possibilities is the one that surely most people would regard as the commonsense notion (especially from a human perspective). A naive realism would insist that there is an external basis for what is perceived and that it would be impossible for that basis to have a multiple nature—to be at once water, nectar, and blood and pus. In that case, only one of the three beings could be correct. Presumably, this would be the human, with the god and hungry ghost presumed to be seeing water mistakenly as nectar or as blood and pus.

The second interpretation, that all three beings are deluded, is essentially that of the Cittamātrins. In one sense, this is not their unique claim, for all Buddhist schools assert that ordinary (unenlightened) beings of every type are under the sway of the delusion that the objects of their experience exist exactly the way that they appear. However, the Vaibhāṣika and Sautrāntika schools would consider an epistemic delusion with respect to objects other than a person to be the exception rather than the rule.

For the Cittamātra School , there is for the cognition of ordinary persons a continual layer of delusion in the very appearance of subject-object duality. It explains that the *prima facie* appearance of objects as independent of the sense or mental consciousness apprehending them is delusory. Along with the Mādhyamika School, the Cittamātra School says that objects exist in dependence upon minds, but the Prāsaṅgikas do not find it necessary thereby to conclude that objects have no entity other than the mind that apprehends them. According to Gelukbas, the Cittamātra School does.

The third interpretation of the example—that all three beings are correct—is the explanation of the Prāsaṅgikas. The basic assumption is that existence is established by valid cognition and that the six consciousnesses of all beings are capable of such. Since all three beings have awarenesses that are neither affected by a deep cause of error—such as a defect in the eye—nor a superficial cause of error—such as fog, dim light, etc.—they respectively establish the existence of water, nectar, and blood and pus. All three substances must exist. Yet it is not possible for water also to *be* blood and pus or to *be* nectar, so it cannot be the case that all three substances exist in one entity. Rather, three entities are present in one place, each seen only by beings with the karmic propensities to be able to see them.

To illustrate this, Jamyang Shayba uses two analogies. First, each being has six types of consciousness that certify different types of objects. The fact that an eye consciousness cannot certify a sound does not preclude the existence of the sound, just as the fact that an ear consciousness cannot certify a visible form does not preclude the existence of that form. Jamyang Shayba says:[13]

> That [the eye consciousnesses of such hungry ghosts and gods are not validly cognizing consciousnesses] cannot be accepted because (1) at that time the production of pus as part of the river is established by the valid cognition of the hungry ghost's eye consciousness and (2) although the production of part [of the fluid] as water is established by the valid cognition of the eye consciousness of a human, pus is *merely* not established [by the human]. Therefore, although both are validly cognizing consciousnesses, the objects are discrete and the object established by one is not harmed by the other. For example, it is like the fact that the objects of the two sense consciousnesses, eye and ear, are contradictory and although the object of one is not mutually

[13]*Great Exposition of the Middle Way* 649.2-50.1.

> held by the other, they are not mutually invalidating. This is because Dzongkaba's *Illumination of the Thought, Explanation of (Candrakīrti's) "Entrance"* says:
>
> > Although there are two objects which are established by valid cognition, since they are discrete [functioning] things, how could it be that with respect to just that object established by one of those two, the other establishes its opposite?

Due to their difference in capacity, each consciousness exercises a discrete function that does not contradict another. That is, the eye consciousness merely certifies a visible form, not also the *absence* of sound. In the same way, the eye consciousness of a hungry ghost has a different purview than that of a human and does not contradict the human's perception. It certifies only blood and pus, not non-water. It is simply the case that what is sensate for one type of being is supersensory for another. This is not mere relativism: one eye consciousness can contradict another, such that if one person with amblyopia sees falling hairs, another without that defect can establish non-hairs. However, the first party's *ear* consciousness, for instance, could not establish non-hairs because such are not within its purview.

This is much like the Gelukba characterization of the difference between an ordinary being's perception of phenomena and that of a Buddha. Non-Buddhas, even Superiors (*'phags pa, āryan*) who have realized emptiness, are restricted to a view of either ultimate or conventional truths, not both simultaneously; and ultimate truths are cognized only by a few, who at the time of meditative equipoise on emptiness (that which is an ultimate truth) are unable to cognize conventional truths (the bases of the ultimate truths). Nevertheless, the cognition of only an ultimate truth does not negate the existence of conventional truths, nor does the later cognition of conventional truths negate the existence of ultimate truths. Still, the simultaneous cognition of the two truths requires omniscience, just as the simultaneous cognition of the water, blood and pus, and nectar would require at least the removal of obstructing predispositions, if not omniscience.

The other metaphor Jamyang Shayba uses concerns the partial viewing of an object; when we see an object we typically see only that part of it that faces us; we do not see its far side or interior. Just so, we do not see the nectar or blood and pus that are hidden from us, only the water that appears. Only the water casts its aspect toward our eye consciousness and forms it in its image. The other substances are, for us, supersensory.

Unfortunately, the *exact* relationship of the three worlds is not spelled out even by Jamyang Shayba, but there seem to be three possible delineations. One is that there is an external substratum of some fluid that remains the same, but which each being experiences in a different way, just as two people might experience a third person as being attractive or repulsive. A second possibility is that there is a substratum that is continually changeable, being at one time nectar, at another water, and at another blood and pus.[14] A third possibility is that the three universes interpenetrate, so that all three fluids exist in the same place at the same time.

The first of these options, that there is a common substratum—generic fluid, generic container, etc.—is contradicted by the very terms of the example, which states that gods of the Formless Realm validly perceive only space where others experience some form of fluid. To this we can add Jamyang Shayba's approving citation of Kaydrup's statement that not all hungry ghosts or gods have the same experience. That there is a common substratum is a tempting, but not viable, solution.

The second option, that the environment is continually changing depending on the beings for which it serves as a basis of experience, depends on extrapolating from Kaydrup's remark that the hungry ghost comes upon water, which then

[14]Cabezón (1992: 336) suggests a variant: in the dominant human realm, the substance is water, changing to nectar or pus as a god or hungry ghost approaches. In a heaven, the substances would be nectar, changing at the approach of a human, etc.

changes into blood and pus as he raises the vessel to his mouth to drink. In other words, the environment is depicted as changing as different kinds of beings come to inhabit it; it may change before they are aware of it (as would be the case with us) or it may change perceptively (as would be the case with a hungry ghost, as part of the frustration to which hungry ghosts are prone). In this view, the essential fluidity of existence "coagulates" in different ways, as blood and pus for the disgusting hungry ghost world, as water for the bland human world, and as nectar for the rich god world. However, this model of a world of substances that continually change in type falters where we postulate the existence of different types of beings in one place; in that case, the substratum would have to change in three ways, in which case it would not be any different than the third option.

The third option, that the three universes interpenetrate, seems to be the clear implication of our example. It is not extraordinary for Buddhists to postulate levels of existence that are beyond an ordinary person's ken, for the Form Realm and Formless Realm are such. The surprise here is that these other worlds are no place other than the same temporal and spatial dimension in which we ourselves reside. For instance, Jamyang Shayba says that the hungry ghost, god, and human that simultaneously view the stream may all stand on the same spot (though there is a problem in saying "same" since even the surface of the land would be different for these three beings). And that is not because the god and hungry ghost have immaterial or non-obstructive bodies, for we are told that their bodies are coarse and obstructive. It is simply the case that their coarse obstructive bodies are not coarse and obstructive for humans or for each other, but only for others of their own type and the phenomena created by their karma. He constructs a hypothetical debate:[15]

---

[15]*Great Exposition of the Middle Way* 647.4-48.1. To clarify this debate, I have prefaced the conflicting positions with "incorrect position" and "correct position," though no such terms are used by Jamyang Shayba.

Incorrect Position: It [absurdly] follows that at that time a human does not see the water under the pus because the pus is obstructive and coarse, as is the case, for example, with the water that underlies pus at the present time.

Correct Position: There is no entailment [that because the pus is coarse and obstructive, a human cannot see the water beneath it]. It [absurdly] follows that at that time the ground that is covered by a hungry ghost is not seen by that human because the form of that hungry ghost is obstructive and coarse, as is the case, for example, with the ground that is the underlying basis on which a human stands. You asserted the entailment. The three circles!

Incorrect Position: Even though a hungry ghost's form is obstructive and coarse, a human does not perceive it due to the power of karma. Therefore the ground that is covered by that does not appear to be obscured.

Correct Position: It follows that nectar and pus are very similar in that way because the other two do not appear in that way to that human, whereby only water appears. The three circles!

A debater seeks to capture his opponent in the three "circles" of self-contradiction: (1) the opponent has accepted the reason; (2) the opponent has accepted the entailment; and (3) the opponent has accepted the opposite of the consequence.[16] Here, the opponent has accepted that the body of a hungry ghost is coarse and obstructive; that if something is covered by a coarse, obstructive form, it cannot be seen; and that, nevertheless, the ground covered by a hungry ghost is seen by a human. Realizing the absurdity of the entailment (no one holds that a hungry ghost's body would obstruct a human's view), the opponent would realize that the ground underneath a hungry ghost's body would be visible and therefore would realize the absurdity of the original contention that a human would not see water where a hungry ghost sees blood and pus.

---

[16]I have relied on an oral explanation of Amchok Rinbochay of the Library of Tibetan Works and Archives for my understanding of the three circles of self-contradiction.

But there is a hedge, it seems, and it comes in the form of explaining that each of the three substances or beings that occupy the same *area* are in fact located in their own *space*, even though those spaces interpenetrate in the same area. What this means is mysterious, but seems to be a distinction constructed to prevent the *mixture* of the substances; they preserve their integrity. Perhaps if they did not have their own spaces, it would absurdly (and revoltingly) follow that when we drink water, we also drink blood and pus.

Whichever of the final two options represents Jamyang Shayba's thinking, we are left with a remarkable conclusion about the radical relativity of the external world. Jamyang Shayba apparently says that these universes interpenetrate, that the totality of *samsāra* is immeasurably richer than we are capable of apprehending. This is itself taken as a very powerful indication that phenomena lack any kind of enduring substantial existence. For the Gelukba interpreters, and doubtless also for Candrakīrti, the interpenetration of phenomena (in this sense) precludes their true existence. An important aspect of our basic ignorance is to conceive of phenomena as though they existed independently of our karma, which actually is the *basic* cause for their very existence.

A different instance of apparently contradictory perception of external objects is raised by Dharmakīrti, who points to the fact that when one person is simultaneously seen by a friend and an enemy, the former sees the person as attractive whereas the latter sees the person as repulsive.[17] Or, as Nāgārjuna says in his *Essay on the Mind of Enlightenment* (verse 20), an ascetic, a lover, and a wild dog respectively see a woman as a corpse, a mistress, and a tasty morsel. How can one person be both attractive and repulsive? Rather, beauty and ugliness must be in the "eye of the beholder"; i.e., they must be mental representations rather than external objects.

---

[17]Dharmakīrti's *Commentary on (Dignāga's) "Compendium of Prime Cognition"* is cited in Jamyang Shayba's *Great Exposition of the Middle Way* 652-57; this quotation seems to be 110.10-13 (Dharamsala edition). See also Losang Gönchok, *Word Commentary* 146.5-47.2.

This is another example without a direct reply from the Prāsaṅgikas. It lacks the force of the previous one, for it has to do only with an intangible quality of the observed object rather than its basic entity. That is, it would be easy enough to concede that beauty or ugliness is a mere superimposition without conceding that the beautiful or ugly *person* is a mere projection or superimposition.

Cittamātra and Prāsaṅgika Perspectives on "Partless Particles"

Having considered the Cittamātra allegation of contradictions in the assertion of external objects, let us turn to its refutation of external objects by way of refuting partless particles, the basic elements that, according to the Vaibhāṣikas and perhaps some Sautrāntikas, comprise gross objects.[18] These tiny or "subtle" (*phra ba*) particles are for them the principal units of impermanent physical entities, the "building blocks" for gross objects. Hypothetically, these particles are partless because they are too minute to be physically subdivided.[19]

Technically, that particles could not be physically divided does not preclude the possibility that they could be *mentally* subdivided; but in order for these particles to retain their ultimacy, it would be necessary that the consciousness that apprehends them not be canceled out by that cleavage. In this way, according to Gönchok Jikmay Wangbo,[20] the Vaibhāṣika

---

[18]Losang Gönchok, *Word Commentary* 99.3-4. With respect to the Sautrāntikas, Gönchok Jikmay Wangbo does not mention *any* Sautrāntikas that do not assert partless particles (*Precious Garland of Tenets* 36.4-6, translated in Sopa and Hopkins [186]). However, Losang Gönchok, commenting on Jamyang Shayba's *Great Exposition of Tenets*, says that some assert partless particles, some do not. Of those that do assert partless particles, some say that they touch, some do not (*Word Commentary* 112.3-5).

[19]According to Geshay Gendün Lodrö, they could not be further reduced without disappearing (Hopkins 1983: 894, n. 758).

[20]Gönchok Jikmay Wangbo, *Precious Garland of Tenets* 36.4-6, translated in Sopa and Hopkins 186.

School and the Sautrāntikas Following Scripture consider partless atoms to be "ultimate truths," an ultimate truth for them being something for which the consciousness apprehending it is not canceled if it is broken physically or distinguished mentally into parts.[21] A partless particle is in fact only *directionally*, i.e., spatially partless, without north, south, east, west, top, or bottom; it is, however, temporally divisible, the particle of one moment not being the same as the particle of a past or future moment, and can be distinguished as a cause and as an effect.[22]

There is, however, controversy over whether or not partless particles touch one another or have interstices.[23] The difficulty of maintaining that particles can touch each other is that it would seem to imply that they have parts, since certainly if a particle touched a particle below it, the part that touched the bottommost particle would not also be touching a particle above it. On the other hand, it is difficult (without being able to postulate a theory of nuclear forces) to explain the cohesiveness of conglomerations of particles.

Vasubandhu's refutation of directionally partless particles is two-pronged.[24] First, he says that if we imagine several particles in an array, surely a different part of the central particle would touch (or come close to touching) a particle to its west than would touch (or come close to touching) a particle to its east. That being the case, it is argued, subtle particles are not "directionless" after all. Second, he argues that if one side of a particle were also its opposite side—that is, if there were no "sides" at all, the particle being without directions—it would

---

[21]From Vasubandhu, *Treasury of Higher Knowledge* (*chos mngon pa'i mdzod, abhidharmakośakārikā*) VI: 4 (P 5590, vol. 115, 124.2.1-2; translated in Poussin 139-40).

[22]Sopa and Hopkins 186.

[23]Losang Gönchok (99.4) makes the general statement that Vaibhāṣikas assert that particles do not touch, but according to other Gelukba authorities this is apparently a position only of the Kashmiri Vaibhāṣikas (Hopkins 1983: 337-38).

[24]These are the essential arguments from Vasubandhu's *Twenty Stanzas* (12-15) and its autocommentary. Losang Gönchok, *Word Commentary* 144.5-45.

be impossible to construct gross forms out of them. All other particles would touch the same place; effectively, there would be just one particle, for no matter how many of the particles were put together, the aggregate could not get any larger. Hence, the notion of directionally partless particles is not viable.

According to Janggya, the Cittamātra School considers this refutation of directionally partless particles to effectively undermine the assertion of external objects:[25]

> The Cittamātra School thinks that when partless external objects are refuted, sense consciousnesses that are non-mistaken with respect to their appearing [objects] are refuted; in that case, since [for them,] mistaken sense consciousnesses are unable to posit objects, external objects would be negated.

This conclusion is based on what is taken to be the view of the Vaibhāṣika School that only a non-mistaken sense consciousness can validly posit objects and that only sense consciousnesses that apprehend partless particles or objects constructed of them can be non-mistaken. Hence, if there are no partless particles, the sense consciousnesses to which such appear must be mistaken; if there are no non-mistaken sense consciousnesses, there is no way to validly posit external objects. Since what cannot be posited by valid cognition cannot be said to exist, external objects are not feasible.

Prāsaṅgikas agree with Cittamātrins that directionally partless atoms or particles cannot be asserted.[26] In fact, the

---

[25]*Presentation of Tenets* 482.3-5.

[26]According to Losang Gönchok (145.4-46.1), Daktsang is said to hold the position that both the Mādhyamika and Cittamātra schools actually accept partless particles. I have not found such a passage in Daktsang, and it seems to be a rather extreme position for him to have taken. He would have been aware of Vasubandhu's *Twenty Stanzas*, which explicitly refutes partless particles, and of Nāgārjuna's *Essay on the Mind of Enlightenment*, where Nāgārjuna himself clearly denies partless particles in verse 18:

> When divided into directions
> Even a subtle particle is seen to have divisions.

Cittamātra School's rejection of partless particles is said to make them superior to the lower schools, even though they assert external objects. Ngawang Belden gives a hypothetical objection and reply:[27]

> *Objection*: It follows that in that case the Cittamātrins are inferior to the Sautrāntikas because (1) they are similar in asserting that consciousnesses are truly established and (2) propounding that external objects exist is better than propounding that they do not exist.
>
> *Response*: This is a wrong conception, manifesting complete ignorance of the respective status of tenet systems, because the Sautrāntikas assert, upon analysis by reasoning, partless particles and gross objects that are composed of them whereas the Cittamātrins are able to refute thoroughly such external objects by means of reasoning.

The partless particles described by the philosophers of the Vaibhāṣika and Sautrāntika schools are also truly existent particles, things able to withstand analysis, things that exist from their own side and are not just imputations; it is better to assert, as the Cittamātra School does, that there are no external objects than to speak of truly existent partless particles. In this case, the Cittamātrins have performed ultimate analysis and have properly concluded that the object under analysis cannot withstand it. Hence, Prāsaṅgikas quarrel only with the Cittamātra failure to extend the analysis to other phenomena, such as consciousnesses.

However, according to Gelukbas, Prāsaṅgikas do not agree that the rejection of directionally partless particles amounts to a rejection of external objects. As Janggya says,[28]

> How could what is analyzed into parts
> Be feasible as a subtle particle?

The Tibetan translation of this passage (only Sanskrit fragments are extant) is in Lindtner (1986b: 38-39) along with his translation into English.

[27] Ngawang Belden, *Annotations* 109a.7-b.1.

[28] *Presentation of Tenets* 482.1-8.

> The Cittamātra School thinks that when partless external objects are refuted, sense consciousnesses that are non-mistaken with respect to their appearing [objects] are refuted; in that case, since [for them,] mistaken sense consciousnesses are unable to posit objects, external objects would be negated. In this excellent system the thought is that although it is true that a mistaken sense consciousness is unable to posit a *true* object of comprehension, such [mistaken sense consciousnesses] serve as assisters in positing *false* objects of comprehension; therefore, there is no proof of the non-existence of [external] objects.

In other words, even if there are no truly existent partless particles, it is possible for objects composed of *mere* particles to be posited by sense consciousnesses. The Cittamātrins maintain that those sense consciousnesses would be mistaken with respect to their objects (by which they mean that the sense consciousnesses mistakenly apprehend the objects composed of particles to be a different entity from the awarenesses apprehending them). Prāsaṅgikas agree that the sense consciousnesses of ordinary beings are mistaken; Jamyang Shayba, commenting on Candrakīrti's statement that the awarenesses of ordinary beings are polluted by error, says:[29]

> Until Buddhahood is attained, one has no non-mistaken consciousnesses except for a Superior's exalted wisdom of meditative equipoise. Also, due to that, for childish persons,

---

[29]*Great Exposition of Tenets* 37a.2-3 (Jamyang Shayba translation, chapter 3). Also discussed in Losang Gönchok, *Word Commentary* 276.4-77.1. The passage Jamyang Shayba is commenting on is in Candrakīrti's *Clear Words*, 9b.3-4 (Sanskrit in Poussin, 30.3-4):

> The erroneous and the non-erroneous (*phyin ci log dang phyin ci ma log pa dag, viparyāsāviparyāsa*) are different [i.e., a dichotomy]. Therefore, like the falling hairs [seen by] one with cataracts / dimness of sight, and so forth, when what does not [inherently] exist is apprehended by [that is, appears to] an erroneous [consciousness] as just [inherently] existing, how could even a portion of an [inherently] existent object be observed?

This seems to be the only place in the works of Candrakīrti where he can be construed to be saying that valid cognition can be mistaken.

> i.e., common beings, even [the exalted wisdom] of meditative equipoise of the supreme mundane qualities path of preparation (*sbyor lam chos mchok, laukikāgradharma-prayoga-mārga*) is polluted by error with respect to what appears. Therefore, that all consciousnesses of common beings are mistaken is also a unique [tenet of the Prāsaṅgika School].

The eye, ear, nose, etc., consciousnesses of ordinary persons are mistaken because objects appear to those awarenesses to be inherently existent whereas they are not. However, a consciousness does not have to be non-mistaken in order to posit the existence of its object. For example, when we view distant mountains, they appear to be blue because of the haze between our eyes and the mountains; we suffer from a superficial cause of error and thus are mistaken with regard to the actual color of the mountains. Nevertheless, we can correctly identify the mountains as mountains. Similarly, even though we might mistake a mirage for a lake, we can nevertheless certify the existence of the mirage, which is itself an external object. In the same way, the existence of mere particles can be established by sense consciousnesses, even though those consciousnesses are mistaken with respect to the appearance of the particles as truly existent.

Arguments Concerning the Necessity of External Objects for the Production of Consciousness

Both Asaṅga and Vasubandhu adduce several examples to demonstrate the plausibility of the production of consciousness in the absence of external objects, concluding that such objects are not necessary. They refer to dreams, illusions, faults in the sense powers, the experiences of yogis and the experiences of beings in the hells; all involve the generation of consciousnesses, apparently without external objects.

Both Asaṅga and Vasubandhu refer first to dreams, noting that objects that appear to dreamers have no external counterparts; nevertheless, dream-objects are capable of producing effects in dreamers, such as a pleasant or unpleasant feeling,[30] and even physical effects such as perspiration or talking out loud. Similarly, because mirror-images falsely appear to be the objects of which they are reflections they can provoke a reaction. Just so, the non-external objects posited by the Cittamātra School function to produce effects in those to whom they appear, even though they have no external reality.

Along the same lines as the dream example is that of a person with amblyopia (*rab rib, timara*), an eye condition that, like cataracts, causes the appearance of squiggly lines in the air that can be mistaken for hairs, insects in one's food, and so forth. Vasubandhu refers to this example in the first stanza of his *Twenty Verses*. Similarly, Asaṅga refers to a person who sees a "double moon," i.e., a double-image of the moon, voluntarily or not. As in the case of dreaming, there is a consciousness generated without an external object (that is, at least the "second" moon is not an external object).

Another instance, cited by Asaṅga, of an awareness in which apparently no external objects appear is that of yogis who practice a type of meditation in which all that appears to their minds is water or earth, the water "totality" (*kaṣina*) or earth "totality."[31] The water or earth is called an object for one with "meditative power" (*dbang 'byor ba, vaibhūtvika*),[32] these being phenomena that appear only to the mental consciousness, and then only to the mental consciousness of the person who has performed the meditation. Asaṅga considers these phenomena to be obviously only internal objects (since there

---

[30]Asaṅga, *Mahāyānasaṃgrāha* (II: 27.3); in Lamotte (1973 I: 38; French translation II: 123).

[31]Losang Gönchok, *Word Commentary* 147.2. The status of these minds is controversial. Lati Rinbochay discusses the various possibilities in *Mind in Tibetan Buddhism* 112-14.

[32]This is one of the five types of forms that are phenomena-sources (*chos kyi skye mched, dharmātyatana*), i.e., forms that appear only to the mental consciousness (*yid shes, manovijñāna*), according to Asaṅga's *Compendium of Higher Knowledge* (*mngon pa kun btus, abhidharmasamuccaya,* cited in Jamyang Shayba's *Great Exposition of the Middle Way* 634.2-3).

is obviously more in the world than just earth or just water), produced without the need for an external object.[33]

Finally, Vasubandhu writes about the guards, tormenters, creatures, etc., of the Buddhist hells.[34] As he points out, it is not fitting that these beings be themselves sentient beings who have been born in the hells, since the hells exist as places of suffering and these beings do not suffer from the hells' intense heat or cold or other discomfitures. Hence, he argues, their appearance is not based on an external reality; rather, they are mere projections of consciousness. Others who explain this phenomenon are forced to say that the guards are appearances of external elements generated by the karma of beings born in the hells but are not real sentient beings.

In response to these examples, Prāsaṅgikas argue that the fact that a dream-horse, a mirage, or a mirror-image can be an object of a consciousness does not necessarily demonstrate that external objects are not needed for the production of awareness, only that the observed objects of consciousnesses are not necessarily objects that exist the way they appear. Candrakīrti implies that even forms such as dream-images, reflections, and echoes are external objects even though they are deceptive and immaterial, serving as the observed-objects of the awarenesses that perceive them:[35]

> It is not the case that it is not renowned that empty [i.e., delusive] things such as reflections

---

[33]One could argue with Asaṅga over the original meditation object, a patch of water or earth (or a skeleton, in the meditation on foulness), since even in the conventions of the world these are external objects. However, his point is that one begins with an object and mentally multiplies or expands it far beyond its original scope; this "extra" then is like the "second" moon in the double-moon example, or the mirror-image (for instance, one could set up several mirrors and multiply one's own image).

[34]There are eight hot and eight cold hells, and in several of these there are guards who inflict torture on those born there as hell-beings.

[35]*Entrance to the Middle Way* VI.37cd. Cf. Huntington 161-62. Also, see Jamyang Shayba's *Great Exposition of the Middle Way* 636. Candrakīrti's *Entrance* VI.67 also speaks of dream-objects as acting as external objects. Dzongkaba comments on this verse in *Illumination of the Thought* 149a.5-b.2. The cause of perception in dreams is called form (*gzugs, rūpa*).

> [Arise] in dependence on the collection [of causes and conditions].
> Just as reflections, and so forth, [arise] from empty [things],
> So consciousnesses are produced from empty [things] in those aspects.

Dzongkaba explains:[36]

> Here, it is said that an eye consciousness apprehending a reflection is produced from it....Since [a reflection] is the basis of observation of an eye consciousness, it is asserted to be a form-source (*gzugs kyi skye mched, rūpāyatana*); the appearance of a double-moon or falling hairs, mirages, and so forth, and echoes, and so forth, also should be understood [as form-sources].

Candrakīrti and Dzongkaba say that even though phenomena such as reflections are deceptive, they arise in dependence on causes and conditions and are capable of serving as a cause for consciousnesses that are produced in the aspect of those objects. The appearance of imaginary "falling hairs" to a person with amblyopia[37] is similar. Although the hairs, like the reflection, do not exist in the way they appear, the false appearance of hairs nevertheless functions as an external object by serving as a cause for the eye consciousness that apprehends them.

But beyond this, Prāsaṅgikas argue that these examples demonstrate only that external objects have no true or ultimate existence (*don dam du yod pa, paramārtha-sat*), something with which they have no quarrel, for the false appearance of these objects precludes their being truly existent. Instead, they criticize Cittamātrins for not being sufficiently radical—for failing to extend their reasoning similarly to consciousness, which also lacks true existence. The Cittamātra School is taken to propound the true existence of consciousness[38] (as well as

---

[36]The passage is cited in Jamyang Shayba's *Great Exposition of the Middle Way* 637.5-6.

[37]*Entrance to the Middle Way* (VI.41) 6a.9-b.1. Cf. Huntington 162.

[38]Nakamura (1987: 279) says that Asaṅga, in his *Compendium of the Mahāyāna*, concludes that consciousness also is empty, that being the

its objects, except of course for the imputational nature superimposed upon them) because for them, anything impermanent that exists must truly exist. (As noted earlier, there are permanent phenomena that are existent imaginaries, such as space and cessations such as the absence of afflictions due to insight, that are said by the Cittamātra School to be merely imputedly existent, not truly existent.) The realization of ultimate truths in their system is only the realization of a lack of a difference in entity between subject and object; nowhere is it said that mind and its objects are mere nominalities, that they are only imputed in dependence on their bases of designation, etc., as would be the case if they were not regarded as truly existent. According to Gelukba scholars, the fact that they call "imputational" only the subject-object appearance, not the appearance of true existence, indicates that they accept true existence. As Dzongkaba says:[39]

> This [Prāsaṅgika] system also indeed asserts that external objects are not established by way of their own character but with respect to that disagrees [with the Cittamātra School] in terms of whether or not this necessitates that external objects do not exist. Therefore, in general, if one knows how to posit any phenomenon as existing even though it does not exist by way of its own character, one can understand well the reasoning concerning the impossibility of distinguishing [external] objects and consciousnesses as existing or not

---

implication of the doctrine that all phenomena have three natures; so, for Asaṅga, both subject and object are empty. According to him, it is Dharmapāla who shifts the emphasis to only consciousness being truly existent. Nakamura does not identify the passage in question; in any case, it seems to me that since Asaṅga would mean by "empty" only the mind's emptiness of being a different entity from the mind apprehending it, it would not be imputedly rather than truly existent. Perhaps this is similar to misunderstanding Asaṅga's commentary on the passage in Maitreya's *Discrimination of the Middle Way and Extremes* I.3-4 which says that because there are no external objects, there are no awarenesses (that perceive external objects; this passage is translated in the Jamyang Shayba section, chapter 1). This *could* be read as saying that both objects and consciousnesses are equally false, but it seems to mean only that there are no consciousnesses actually engaged in the perception of external objects.

[39]*The Essence of the Good Explanations* 171.6-11.

> existing, whereas if one does not [understand the first], one cannot [understand the second].

From a Prāsaṅgika perspective, the failure to extend the analysis to consciousnesses has led the Cittamātra philosophers inaccurately to conclude that consciousness truly exists and that external objects do not exist even conventionally (*tha snyad du yod pa, saṃvṛti-sat*). It has been suggested by some Western scholars that the Cittamātra philosophers made this error because their tenets were propounded on the basis of meditative experience[40] (they were, after all, called the Practitioners of Yoga, *yogācāra*) in which no external objects appear, and felt, as do all Buddhist tenet-holders with the exception of Mādhyamikas, that denying the true existence of consciousness would be nihilistic.

In fact, the examples used by Asaṅga and Vasubandhu are said by Candrakīrti and Janggya to demonstrate only the absence of true existence of consciousness, for they show that consciousness is produced in dependence on an object, that it has no independent existence. Candrakīrti[41] points out that the Cittamātra School itself admits, in the dream example, that dream-images can deceive dreamers, making them think, for instance, that an elephant is charging toward them when it is not. For Janggya, the very fact that the dream consciousness can be deceived is an "extremely powerful reasoning" demonstrating that consciousness does not truly exist, since it indicates that the mind is dependent on an object:[42]

> The Mind-Only School offers a dream consciousness and a sense consciousness to which falling hairs appear as examples of inherently established consciousnesses without there being external objects. When, in the root text and commen-

[40]Schmithausen (1976: 247), among others, has suggested that the impetus for the philosophy of Cittamātra is the meditative experience of having the object itself disappear at the moment of realizing its emptiness. This seems quite plausible; indeed, the non-appearance of an object in meditative equipoise is one of the arguments given for the non-existence of external objects.

[41]*Entrance to the Middle Way* (VI.51-52) 6b.8-9. Cf. Huntington 163.

[42]*Presentation of Tenets* 483.2-9, translated in Janggya section chapter 4.

> tary to his *Entrance to the Middle Way* (VI.50-55), [Candrakīrti] refutes this, he says that the examples are not correct. For at the time of those [consciousnesses], although within [the range of] external objects there are no [dream-] elephants, falling hairs, and so forth, they appear as though they do exist. Therefore, the consciousnesses that have [such] as their objects are also false and do not inherently exist. Therefore, objects and consciousnesses are equally established by their own nature or not. This is an extremely powerful reasoning that refutes the unfeasibility of external objects.

In that case, there is no basis for giving subjects ontological priority over objects. If the mind were truly existent, it would be non-deceptive; then, in the case of a person with amblyopia, others would absurdly be able to see the "hairs" that appear to that person.[43] In other words, there would be no way to distinguish between a valid and a non-valid conventional awareness.

Cittamātra philosophy is also criticized for denying the conventional existence of external objects. Here, "conventional existence" does not mean to exist according to the opinions of ordinary people, for there is no denying that the ordinary convention of the world is that external objects exist. The Cittamātra School does not at all deny that things *appear* to be external objects. However, since those convictions are based on a false conception of the mode of existence of impermanent phenomena, they are invalid. What conventionally exists must, first of all, exist, and external objects are no more conventionally existent than is the horse that appears in a dream, the oasis that appears in a mirage, or the "body" that appears in a mirror.

According to Gelukba interpretations of the Prāsaṅgika School, on the other hand, all phenomena equally exist conventionally and do not exist ultimately. Again, Candrakīrti says (*Entrance to the Middle Way* VI.92):[44]

---

[43]Candrakīrti, *Entrance to the Middle Way* VI.53-55. Cf. Huntington 163.

[44]*Entrance to the Middle Way* 8b.5. Cf. Huntington 168. Dzongkaba's commentary is in *Illumination of the Thought* 175a.5 ff.; the material in brackets is taken from him.

> [Truly existent mind and form] were equally abandoned
> by Buddha in the sūtras on the mode of wisdom
> and [conventionally existent mind and form] were
> [equally] set forth
> In the abhidharma [scriptures].

Buddha rejected truly existent form *and* mind in the Perfection of Wisdom Sūtras and set out conventionally existent mind and form in the abhidharma scriptures. Phenomena are said to exist conventionally because there is no conventional valid cognizing awareness that refutes them. That is, among the six types of valid consciousness, other than a mental consciousness investigating ultimate existence, there is no valid awareness that can contradict the existence of external objects. In brief, this says that (1) we must assume that our ordinary awarenesses are valid unless shown otherwise and (2) that the reasonings put forward by the Cittamātra School are not valid since a reasoning consciousness could not be produced that would refute external objects.

Conventional valid cognition is not a mere affirmation of what appears to the senses, for there are many causes for the deception or faulty functioning of the senses. The sense organ may be damaged or otherwise affected, as in the case of cataracts or jaundice, or may be influenced by atmospheric or other disturbances that create phenomena such as mirages. Hence, something is established for conventional valid cognition if and only if it is not contradicted by another's valid cognition. For instance, one's perception of distant mountains as blue, caused by the intervening haze, could be easily contradicted by the testimony of someone closer to the mountains who saw them as green and brown.

But no matter what vantage point is assumed by another person with valid cognition, there is no way in which that person could contradict one's perception of an external object. One might be corrected with respect to the color of the mountains, or their distance, or even one's identification of them as mountains (if, for instance, the "mountains" turn out to have been a low bank of clouds)—but it cannot be denied that an eye consciousness was caused, and for Prāsaṅgikas that means that an external object existed, since that which causes a sense consciousness is external to it. Another valid cognition could show that there was no conventionally existent mountain, but not that there was no external object.

In the arguments discussed thus far, the Gelukbas, relying on Candrakīrti, have established only that it cannot be shown through conventional valid cognition that external objects do not exist. However, in his root verse, Jamyang Shayba seems to make the much broader claim that it can be assumed that external objects *exist* because they are not *refuted* by conventional valid cognition:[45]

> Because of not being refuted by and not being established by an awareness distinguishing conventionalities [respectively],
> It is asserted that external objects exist but that a mind-basis-of-all does not exist.

Ngawang Belden seems to support this claim:[46]

> The final reason why Prāsaṅgikas assert that external objects exist conventionally is as follows: That forms, sounds, and so forth, are external objects is not refuted by valid cognition distinguishing conventionalities which does not depend on valid cognition distinguishing the ultimate because: (1) there is no instance of valid cognition distinguishing conventionalities that refutes external objects and (2) consciousnesses also are not established when they are analyzed by valid cognition distinguishing the ultimate.

It should be noted first of all that Candrakīrti did not himself make the claim that the failure to refute external objects establishes their existence. He refuted only the non-assertion of external objects without going on to claim that this meant that external objects were established. Jamyang Shayba seems to be saying that the non-refutation of external objects implies their existence. If he means what he says, there would seem to be several problems. For instance, for ordinary human beings,

---

[45]*Great Exposition of Tenets* 36b.1 (DSK II: 202b.2).

[46]*Annotations* 109a.2-3.

conventional valid cognition is unable to refute countless claims about past events for which there is now no evidence one way or the other. For instance, we might consider the claims of supermarket tabloids: Did Jesus spend his twenties in India, as some have claimed? Has Elvis risen from the dead? Both claims seem preposterous, but they cannot be *dismissed* by conventional valid cognition.

On the other hand, Jamyang Shayba's seemingly objectionable statement is found only in his terse root verse; in his commentary we can see that it is probable that he means that external objects are at least established by *scripture* and that they are not refuted by conventional valid cognition:[47]

> External objects exist because: (1) Nāgārjuna's *Essay on the Mind of Enlightenment]* (*byang chub sems kyi 'grel pa, bodhicittavivaraṅa*) and the Perfection of Wisdom Sūtras say that the two, object and subject, equally exist conventionally and equally do not exist in the context of ultimate analysis, (2) [external objects] are set forth at length in the abhidharma texts and (3) [external objects] are not refuted by any awareness distinguishing conventionalities.

In other words, Jamyang Shayba is not trying to say that external objects are established just because they are not refuted by conventional valid cognition, but is saying merely that not only have they been established by scripture, they are not refuted by the reasonings articulated by the Cittamātra School. Moreover, the section on valid cognition in his *Great Exposition of the Middle Way*[48] demonstrates that he, like all other Prāsaṅgikas, regards external objects as being certified by conventional valid cognition. Ngawang Belden, like Jamyang Shayba, precedes his problematic assertion that external objects are established because they are not refuted by conventional valid cognition with a reference to the same sources as Jamyang Shayba, showing that external objects are established by scripture.

---

[47]*Great Exposition of Tenets* 36b.2.

[48]*Great Exposition of the Middle Way* 701 ff.

External objects are also asserted to exist in the conventions of the world, and the acceptance of ordinary worldly awareness is a frequent theme in Mādhyamika School writings. Candrakīrti, for instance, says in his *Entrance to the Middle Way* (VI.22),[49] "We assert that worldly [people], abiding in their own views, are valid." In his *Clear Words* he says,[50] "...the Buddhas help beings who are trainees, and who do not know suchness, with reasoning as it is renowned to them."

In keeping with the spirit of Candrakīrti's statements, Prāsaṅgikas generally accept whatever a reasonable person would accept; this, of course, excludes some of what people tend to think and say. Ordinary people are mistaken with respect to the ultimate nature of things, since they assent to the way things appear to them, which is as though they were inherently existent. Furthermore, they may believe in the efficacy of sacrifices and prayers to their gods; they may believe that they are spiritually purified by washing; they may not believe in the cause-and-effect of actions. However, none of these convictions are upheld by conventional valid cognition.

It should be noted that Cittamātrins do not rest their rejection of external objects on the claim that such objects are refuted by conventional valid cognition; thus, Prāsaṅgikas do not have that burden of proof toward Cittamātrins. Ngawang Belden states:[51]

> The Cittamātrins themselves do not propound that [external objects] are refuted by valid cognition that distinguishes conventionalities because: (1) they assert that the refutation of external objects needs to depend on valid cognition that distinguishes the ultimate [as described in] the Cittamātra system itself, such as a [reasoning consciousness realizing that subject and object are the same entity in dependence on]

[49]*Entrance to the Middle Way* 5b.2-3. Cf. Huntington 160.

[50]Translated by Hopkins (1983a: 526). Also translated by Sprung (1979: 42): "The Buddhas themselves, out of concern for those they were guiding, who were ignorant of logic, made their points in terms of the conventional ideas of these people themselves." Sanskrit edited by Poussin 36.1-2.

[51]Ngawang Belden, *Annotations pha* 109a.3-5.

> the logical mark of the definite simultaneous observation [of objects and the consciousnesses realizing them] and (2) the emptiness of establishment in accordance with the appearance of [objects as] external is an ultimate truth and a suchness in the Cittamātra system itself.

Dharmakīrti refutes external objects by reasoning that if an object and the consciousness which realizes it are observed to necessarily occur simultaneously they could not be separate entities.[52] In the statement, "The subject, the two, an apprehending subject and an apprehended object, are not different entities because they are observed to necessarily occur simultaneously (*lhan cig dmigs pa nges pa, sahopalambhaniyama*)," the sign (the reason, "because they are observed...simultaneously") of definite simultaneous observation serves to cause one to realize that an apprehending subject and an apprehended object are not different entities. Simultaneous observation is assumed to be possible because of the existence of self-consciousness (*rang rig, svasaṃvedanā*, the subject of the next chapter) a consciousness that apprehends another consciousness simultaneous with its knowledge of its object. That reasoning consciousness would be an instance of valid cognition distinguishing the ultimate because its object, the lack (or emptiness) of a difference in entity of subject and object, is an

[52]Dignāga, *Compendium on Prime Cognition* I: 9-10 and *vṛtti*, translated by Hattori (1968: 28-29). Hattori's notes cite Dharmakīrti's commentary. Dharmakīrti also explains that subject and object are *not* simultaneous (see Wilson [1984: 885, n. 33, and translation of Gung-tang 10a.2]), but it must be understood that when Dignāga and Dharmakīrti explain perception, they do it as though there were external objects. (This is Stcherbatsky's observation [1962: II: 7], as noted by Klein [1986: 43-44].)

One considerable difficulty with Dharmakīrti's assertion, as Jamyang Shayba and Losang Gönchok understand it (*Word Commentary* 142-44), is that it implies the following: if one can establish, through the logical sign of definite simultaneous observation, that subject and object are not separate substantial entities, it is then established that they are the *same* substantial entity. This, of course, would mean that the thoroughly established nature or emptiness posited in the Cittamātra system, the absence of a difference in entity of subject and object, would not be a non-affirming negative (*med dgag, prasajyapratiṣedha*), i.e., a mere absence that implies nothing positive in its place. This would contradict the *Sūtra Unraveling the Thought*.

ultimate truth, or suchness, in the Cittamātra system itself. In the Cittamātra system, ultimate truths are (1) the person's emptiness of being substantially existent or self-sufficient, (2) an object's emptiness of naturally being the basis of names, and (3) the emptiness of object and subject being different entities.

According to Ngawang Belden, then, Cittamātrins refute external objects by ultimate analysis (as they themselves have defined ultimate analysis, the search for an object that is a different entity from consciousness). No conventional valid awareness is able to refute external objects, because such consciousnesses are not investigators of the mode of being of the objects that appear to them, and such objects appear to be external objects. However, when external objects are subjected to reasoning, such as the reasoning that since subject and object definitely are produced simultaneously, they must not be different substantial entities, they are found not to exist.

Prāsaṅgikas agree with Cittamātra that forms, etc., do not exist ultimately, but not for the same reasons. Cittamātrins base their analyses on the unfindability of partless particles and the absence of external objects at the time of realizing ultimate truths. In the Prāsaṅgika system, phenomena are said not to exist ultimately because the Perfection of Wisdom sūtras refute inherent existence—true existence—for all five aggregates, including the aggregates of consciousness and its accompanying mental factors, not just the aggregate of form (*gzugs kyi phung po, rūpa-skandha*).[53] In fact, nothing can withstand the brunt of ultimate analysis (such as the analysis Nāgārjuna performs on causation, time, motion, etc., in his *Treatise on the Middle Way*), not even consciousness. If consciousness were ultimately (inherently, truly) existent, it would be findable among its bases of designation, either be the same as or different from its bases of designation, etc. However, lack of ultimate existence is no proof of a lack of conventional existence.

---

[53]Candrakīrti, *Entrance to the Middle Way* (VI.92) 8b.5. Cf. Huntington 168.

Moreover, according to Ngawang Belden, the Cittamātra identification of objects as being "internal" rather than external because they are not separate entities from their apprehending consciousnesses would entail that such objects ultimately existed:[54]

> Moreover, in the Prāsaṅgika system, if external objects did not exist conventionally, one would have to assert that forms, and so forth, conventionally are mental things (*shes pa'i dngos po*). In that case, there would be no way that they could be established by an ordinary conventional consciousness that operates without investigating through reasoning and without analysis. Therefore, analyzing by way of a reasoning which examined whether forms, and so forth, are established as the nature of consciousness, one would have to find that they are the nature of consciousness. In that case, form, and so forth, would have to be established by way of its own character, whereby that [this] is the Prāsaṅgika system would be a thorough deprecation.

Ngawang Belden is pointing out that the consequence of asserting objects that are not external is that they would be of the nature of consciousness, which the Cittamātra School considers to be truly or ultimately established. Hence, the Prāsaṅgika School cannot accept the existence of non-external objects, since that would mean accepting objects that exist by way of their own character. He concludes,[55] "Therefore, the Prāsaṅgikas' assertion of external objects meets back to their assertion of imputedly existent nominalities."

Let us conclude this section by taking one last look at the Cittamātra equation of dreams with waking reality in terms of their ability to produce effects. I wish to suggest that Prāsaṅgikas *might* have argued, though they did not, that the Cittamātra explanation that all appearances are equally the manifestation of seeds with the mind-basis-of-all would mean that a dream and a waking experience would have an equal status. This would present several difficulties. For instance,

[54]*Annotations* 109a.5-7.

[55]*Annotations* 109b.2.

suppose that last night I dreamt that my house burned down, but today I see it standing as though nothing happened. Someone other than a Cittamātrin would naturally say that the dream experience is unreal, having been invalidated by the waking experience; a Cittamātrin, on the other hand, would be forced to admit that both appearances are brought about in the same fashion, leaving no basis for preferring one over the other. Cittamātrins would presumably say that predispositions (*bag chags, vāsanā*) for the appearance of a burning house ripened at one time whereas predispositions for the appearance of an unburnt house ripened at another. Hence, our guidelines for action in this universe must be purely pragmatic; since I note that when I appear to be awake (for ripening predispositions are causing the appearance of wakefulness as well as the objects of that experience) my house appears to be whole, I would be prudent to act as though the burnt house of my dream were an illusion. Otherwise, the beings who appear as my relatives and companions in waking life might reasonably conclude that I am no longer mentally competent.

Vasubandhu seems to be aware of such a potential objection, for he apparently denies that the dream experience has the validity of a waking experience, saying:[56]

> Because the mind is overcome by sleepiness,
> A dream and its effects are different [from a wakeful
> mind and its object].

In other words, sleep is like a mental impairment that causes a hallucination; thus, one cannot trust the results of such a state of consciousness. Moreover, in such an impaired state, one cannot be held responsible for one's actions, e.g., dreaming of killing an irritating person.

However, Vasubandhu's reply seems somewhat less than convincing since it seems to be inconsistent with his other pronouncements. He has already argued for the reliability and efficacy of dreams—that they can be consistent with respect to

[56] *Twenty Verses* 18.

place and time, that they can cause physical effects, etc. Moreover, in Cittamātra terms, the "mental impairment" of sleep to which he refers is itself an appearance generated by the ripening of latencies with the mind-basis-of-all. It is a different experience but no more or less real than the experience of being "awake." Thus, in conclusion, Prāsaṅgikas might have argued that the example of the dream merely raises new difficulties with the Cittamātra position.

Other Prāsaṅgika Criticisms of Mind-Only

Let us conclude this survey of Prāsaṅgika arguments against Mind-Only philosophy by considering three points that were not linked to specific Cittamātra School claims concerning the non-existence of external objects. The first is also purportedly[57] the first Mādhyamika School refutation of Mind-Only—a passage from Nāgārjuna's *Essay on the Mind of Enlightenment (byang chub sems kyi 'grel pa, bodhicittavivaraṇa)*[58]

---

[57]The universally acknowledged "opener of the chariot-way" for the Mādhyamika School, Nāgārjuna, is traditionally said to have lived over six hundred years. If he actually lived for that period, then he would have seen his system challenged by the Mind-Only philosophy of Maitreya, Asaṅga, and Vasubandhu. But here Jamyang Shayba reverts to one (but only one) statement of Nāgārjuna's as evidence that the founder of the Mādhyamika School responded to the Cittamātra challenge by implicitly asserting the existence of external objects and rejecting any other position.

[58]P 2665, vol. 61, 286.1.6. Oddly, Jamyang Shayba does not cite stanza 27, which seems to be a direct response to Cittamātra:

> The Subduer's teaching that,
> "All of this is mind-only"
> Is for the sake of removing the fear of the childish;
> It is not a statement of reality.

The Sanskrit is: *cittamātram idaṃ sarvam iti yā deśanā muneḥ / uttrāsaparihārārthaṃ bālānaṃ sa nā tattvataḥ*. The translation is by Lopez (1987: 444). This stanza is also cited in Jamyang Shayba's *Great Exposition of Tenets* (see Hopkins' translation [1983a: 614]). Nāgārjuna's authorship of this work has been disputed by Ruegg (1981: 104) but upheld by Lindtner (1986: 248). Lindtner considers Nāgārjuna to be responding to the idealism of the in which Nāgārjuna says that objects and minds are equivalent in terms of existence or non-existence:

> A consciousness realizes an object of knowledge.
> Without objects known there are no consciousnesses.
> In that case, why not assert
> That [both] object of knowledge and knower [absurdly] do
> not exist?

This is taken to mean that without conventionally existent external objects, there would be no objects of knowledge, i.e., nothing would exist (since what cannot be known cannot be said to exist).

The passage in question is ambiguous at best. There is nothing in Nāgārjuna's passage to preclude a hypothetical Cittamātra objection that he is referring not to *external* objects, but only to "knowledges" (*rnam rig, vijñāna*), the dependent natures that Cittamātrins say arise from seeds with the mind-basis-of-all and are one entity with the mind. Asaṅga, in his *Compendium of the Mahāyāna* (2.5), lists fifteen knowledges, all of which are dependent natures.[59] Moreover, if Nāgārjuna had truly been aware of Cittamātra criticisms of his philosophy, he surely would have replied to them in no uncertain terms. Nevertheless, this statement has been taken to say that the alternative to the existence of external objects is nihilism, since there would be no objects to be known. The conclusion is that since all Buddhists reject nihilism,[60] external objects must exist. Candrakīrti's *Entrance* (VI.92) seems to echo this sentiment:[61]

Descent to Laṅka Sūtra, to which he finds references in several of Nāgārjuna's other works (349, n. 38). The sūtra seems to be a loosely organized collection of smaller texts written at different times, so that some parts might antedate Nāgārjuna whereas others do not. One portion even seems to have a reference to Nāgārjuna! (Sangharakshita 1985: 208). See Lopez (1987: 444, n. 4) for a discussion of this and other passages from Nāgārjuna.

[59]Wilson 1984: 359.

[60]Of course, there are some (e.g., Thomas Wood, A. B. Keith) who claim that Nāgārjuna himself was a nihilist, and would read the cited passage as clear proof.

[61]*Entrance to the Middle Way* 8b.5. Dzongkaba's commentary is in *Illum-*

If [external] form does not exist, do not hold that mind exists.
Also, if [internal] mind just exists, do not hold that [external] form does not exist.

Jamyang Shayba takes these statements to mean that external objects and minds both either exist or do not exist (the latter being precluded as nihilism).

The second argument we will consider is not one made by Candrakīrti or found in the "unique tenets" sections of the tenets books of Janggya or Jamyang Shayba, but comes from observations made by Gungtang, a disciple of Gönchok Jik-may Wangbo (the second Jamyang Shayba), in his book on Cittamātra.[62] This is the argument that without external objects, there could be no objects of perception shared by two or more persons. Gungtang gives one such argument:[63]

> *Statement of Opinion*: Concerning [the way in which the external environment is produced by internal latencies], it then follows that there does not exist a single functioning thing that is an object of perception shared [with another person] because whatever appears to Devadatta's basis-of-all necessarily does not appear to Yajñadatta's basis-of-all. This reason follows because whatever [appears to Devadatta's basis-of-all] is necessarily not an empowered effect of an action by Yajñadatta.

Since all appearances would be generated solely by individual awarenesses (due to individual karmic latencies, established by individual past actions, with the mind-basis-of-all), there could be no object that appeared to more than one person. Hence, Mind-Only thought ultimately entails solipsism.

Even though this argument is not made by Candrakīrti or the Gelukba authors whose works are herein translated, it is an obvious criticism that warrants attention since it is one that

ination of the Thought 175a.5 ff.; the material in brackets is taken from him.

[62] *Explanation of the Difficult Topics of Afflicted Mentality and Mind-Basis-of-All* 25b.3-26b.5, translated by Wilson (1984: 530-48).

[63] *Explanation of the Difficult Topics of Afflicted Mentality and Mind-Basis-of-All* 26a.6-26b.1. This is Wilson's translation (1984: 540).

Vasubandhu anticipated. Vasubandhu considered how one person can affect another in his *Twenty Verses* (18a):[64]

> Knowledges (*rnam rig, vijñapti*) are mutually determined by
> The force of one on another.

Vasubandhu, unfortunately, does not explain *how* persons can mutually influence one another, but simply makes the assertion. In the following two verses (19-20), he gives examples of ways in which the mental power of one person, such as a demon, causes in others a loss of memory, mental anguish, nightmares, or even death. In any case, he seems clearly to deny that persons are so separate that they cannot have mutual objects.

We might also note that even if he were *not* to deny the mutual influence of persons, he would not have an insurmountable logical problem for Mind-Only theory. It is quite possible that even if all appearances are generated only by an individual's karmic latencies, there might still be real communication between two individuals or they might simultaneously perceive some third thing or person, but it would be necessary that there be a precise coordination of ripening seeds with those bases-of-all to produce a common appearance. According to Gungtang, the Cittamātra response to the question of solipsism is just that:[65]

> It is not the case [that whatever is an empowered effect of an action by Devadatta is necessarily not an empowered effect of an action by Yajñadatta] because there exists a common locus of both. This reason follows because even though there do not exist fruitional effects shared [with another person] there do exist shared empowered effects.[66]

---

[64]*Twenty Verses* 18a. Sanskrit is: *anyonyādhipatitvena vijñaptiniyamo mithaḥ*.

[65]*Explanation of the Difficult Topics of Afflicted Mentality and Mind-Basis-of-All* 26b.1. This is Wilson's translation (1984: 540-41).

[66]"Fruitional effect" refers to something in an individual's five aggregates, i.e., something that is unique to an individual, and hence could not be shared with anyone else. "Empowered effect" is a broader term referring to the effects of actions and thus is not limited to an individual's aggregates.

In other words, there is no reason why an appearance should not be caused by the ripening of a latency with not only one individual, but two. Still, according to Janggya,[67] although the Cittamātra position is that there are indeed such shared empowered effects, individuals experience different aspects of them—e.g., when two people stand on opposite sides of an object, one sees the front while the other sees the back. This is due to the force of different latencies ripening to produce different appearances in the minds of two different individuals; nevertheless, despite the differences in perspective, etc., the appearance bears many similarities and is in that sense "shared."

Finally, to conclude this survey of Prāsaṅgika objections to Mind-Only it is interesting to note that the Cittamātra School does *not* use the argument that the existence of a mind-basis-of-all, asserted so frequently in the Cittamātra sūtras and Cittamātra School treatises, entails the non-existence of external objects. Nevertheless, it is an implicit argument that is set up and demolished by the Gelukbas and thus warrants mention.

It is a little puzzling that the Cittamātrins do not refer to their proofs for the existence of a mind-basis-of-all in the context of their assertions on external objects. It would seem to be a persuasive move, establishing at least the implausibility of external objects, since an important function of a mind-basis-of-all is to account for the possibility of appearances without the stimulus of external objects. There are many proofs given for the existence of a mind-basis-of-all. Among those presented in Asaṅga's *Compendium of Ascertainments*[68] are that if there were no mind-basis-of-all, there would be no continuously operating consciousness to appropriate a new body at the time of rebirth or to be present during "mindless" states such as the meditative equipoise of cessation (*'gog pa'i snyoms*

[67]*Presentation of Tenets* 264.2-9. Cited by Wilson (1984: 547).

[68]Gungtang 17b.2-20a.6, translated by Wilson (1984). Eight proofs are given by Asaṅga, but most actually are a defense of the possibility that more than one consciousness can operate at one time, a necessity if one is to assert the existence of a mind-basis-of-all.

'jug, nirodhasamāpatti), and there would be no basis for the infusion of karmic latencies.

Despite the absence of a Cittamātra source that even implicitly links the existence of a mind-basis-of-all and the nonexistence of external objects, it is clear that Gelukbas see the issues as related and have raised for themselves the question of whether the establishment of the one would establish the other. Ngawang Belden cites Dzongkaba's argument that one reason for not asserting the existence of a mind-basis-of-all is that external objects are asserted:[69]

> Moreover, because Prāsaṅgikas assert external objects it is also established that they do not assert a mind-basis-of-all. Dzongkaba's *The Essence of the Good Explanations* says:[70]
>
> > Also, a mind-basis-of-all is not posited due to the essential point of asserting external objects. If [a mind-basis-of-all] were asserted, it would have to be asserted in accordance with the statement in Maitreya's *Discrimination of the Middle and the Extremes* (I.4):[71]
> >
> > > Consciousnesses that perceive
> > > Objects, the sentient, selves, and knowledges are thoroughly produced.
> > > They have no [external] objects.
> > > Because there are no [external objects], there are no [minds apprehending external objects].

Maitreya's statement is taken to mean that minds that apprehend the objects of the senses, the sense-powers, and the mind-basis-of-all—all of which are appearances generated

[69] *Annotations* 110a.3-5.

[70] *The Essence of the Good Explanations*, 174.16-20.

[71] P 5522, vol. 108, 19.4.6-7. Sanskrit in Pandeya (1971: 13, 194): *arthasattvātmavijñāptipratibhāsaṃ prajāyate / vijñānaṃ nāsti cāsyārthastadabhāvāttadapyasat*. For another translation, see Stcherbatsky (1971: 64-65) or Kochumuttom (1982: 46-47 and 236-37). There is a similar statement in Asaṅga's *Compendium of the Mahāyāna* (Tibetan in Lamotte [1973 I: 31]; French translation in II: 105).

from karmic latencies with the mind-basis-of-all—are all truly existent and have no external objects.

If the existence of a mind-basis-of-all could be established, it would entail the non-existence of external objects, for a mind-basis-of-all just serves the function of accounting for experience in the absence of external objects. Dzongkaba's position, though it is not universally held in Tibet, is just that: the existence of external objects would entail the non-existence of a mind-basis-of-all and conversely the existence of a mind-basis-of-all would entail that there be no external objects. Therefore, because a mind-basis-of-all is refuted, the existence of a mind-basis-of-all cannot serve as a reason for the rejection of external objects (though it does not prove that external objects exist).

In this chapter, we have looked at a number of Cittamātra School arguments against the existence of external objects and at Prāsaṅgika rebuttals and counter arguments. We cannot be certain with the Gelukbas that Nāgārjuna initiated this debate, but evidently later Prāsaṅgikas saw Cittamātrins as a threat of some magnitude because a good deal of space and hostile rhetoric is reserved for them in places such as Candrakīrti's *Entrance to the Middle Way*.

Despite this, Candrakīrti and his followers seem to have equivocal attitudes toward Mind-Only. On the one hand, they admit that it can be useful for some people to hear the doctrine of Mind-Only initially, since that will help them to overcome their attachment to forms, i.e., to external objects.[72] That explains the acceptance of the "mind-only" scriptures as authentic, for Buddha would not have taught them if they could not have been of use to certain people. There is irony, then, in the fact that the very debate in which the Prāsaṅgikas

[72] *Entrance to the Middle Way* VI.96. Cf. Huntington 168. In the same spirit, Tenzin Gyatso, the Fourteenth Dalai Lama, said that he feels that the Mind-Only view can be helpful, removing the "grosser dirt." (Interview in Dharamsala, 6/15/84.)

engage the Cittamātrins would seem to undermine the soteriological purpose served by the preservation of distinct, viable systems of thought. However, perhaps the Prāsaṅgikas can be defended by the tradition of Buddhist logic, which rests on the assumption that a process of reasoning brings one closer to the realization of ultimate reality, that wisdom comes in part from the successful identification and reversal of one's most deeply held beliefs. In any case, those persons not yet capable of understanding the Prāsaṅgika view will probably not be swayed by Candrakīrti's arguments; but he presumably hopes that those who are ready to hear about the Middle Way of Nāgārjuna will have the good fortune to shed their erroneous Mind-Only conceptions.

The other concern that Candrakīrti displays in regard to Mind-Only is that adepts under the sway of Cittamātra philosophy might lose their opportunity for liberation, since they would not gain the liberating realization of ultimate truths, the absence of inherent existence of phenomena. In his *Entrance to the Middle Way* (VI.79-80), he says:[73]

> Those outside of the path of the glorious Nāgārjuna
> Do not obtain peace.
> They fall from conventional truths and the truth of suchness.
> There is no liberation for those who fall from those [truths].
>
> For those who achieve [i.e., understand] conventional truths
> The achievement of ultimate truths arises.
> Those who do not understand how to distinguish those
> Enter into bad paths because of their erroneous conceptions.

Because the Cittamātra School does not properly understand conventional truths, considering dependent phenomena to be truly existent and not external to the minds apprehending them, they cannot properly understand ultimate truths, the knowledge of which can deliver one from suffering. Thus, it can be speculated that Candrakīrti opposes Mind-Only because he wants to prevent those capable of penetrating the profound Mādhyamika view from fruitlessly pursuing a real-

---

[73]*Entrance to the Middle Way* (VI.79-80) 8a.3-4. Cf. Huntington 166-67.

ization of the non-existence of external objects, even though he admits that the Cittamātra approach is suitable for certain persons. With regard to those capable of understanding the Mādhyamika but trapped in the Cittamātra view, he might agree with what Bhāvaviveka says: adopting the Cittamātra view and then using the Mādhyamika philosophy to reject the true existence of the mind is like wallowing in mud so that one can wash and get clean; it would be better not to get dirty in the first place.[74]

Finally, although, as we have seen, there are significant differences between Mādhyamika and Cittamātra thought, we should note that historically this did not preclude their conflation.[75] Śāntarakṣita, who founded the Yogācāra-Svātantrika-Mādhyamika (Yogic Practice-Middle Way-Autonomy School, *rnal 'byor spyod pa'i dbu ma rang rgyud pa*) is one who found the two views basically compatible, for his school rejects inherent existence (ultimately) but also rejects the existence of external objects. According to Gelukba scholars, Prāsaṅgikas find Śāntarakṣita's views untenable because he admits that conventionally, things inherently exist, even if they do not exist that way ultimately. For Prāsaṅgikas, however, conventional valid cognition does not establish the mode of being of the object, and certainly does not certify it as being inherently existent. Therefore, things do not inherently exist even conventionally.

Indeed, without careful analysis, Prāsaṅgikas might well seem to reject external objects themselves, for they certainly refute *truly existent* external objects and describe phenomena as existing only as nominal designations in dependence on

---

[74]In Jamyang Shayba, *Great Exposition of Tenets* 16a.4-5 (DSK *ca* 10a.7-b.3). Cited by Lopez (1984: 20). I suggest that there may also be a concern with the devaluation of ordinary perception. The devaluation of worldly conventions might have been seen as leading to a devaluation of other persons also (since others could mistakenly be understood to be *mere* projections of one's own karma, the error of solipsism), resulting in the loss of compassion for others; or, simply, the devaluation of the world that might result from the Cittamātra view might cause people to take lightly their own worldly situations instead of working within them, resulting in their failure to make spiritual progress.

[75]The theme of Ian Harris' recent monograph, for instance, is that there is substantial continuity between the two schools.

thought; and they are like the Cittamātra School in the broad sense that they propound that phenomena do not stand by themselves, independently of apprehending awarenesses. Indeed, the twentieth-century Gelukba abbot Kensur Yeshey Tupden felt that the Cittamātrins come closer to the Prāsaṅgika view than do the other Mādhyamikas, the Svātantrikas, primarily because they give more primacy to the mind and less to the mind's object.[76] The Svātantrikas, after all, do not deny that objects exist from their own side, only that they have a mode of subsistence other than that which can be posited due to the force of the object appearing to consciousness.

However, Prāsaṅgikas are unwilling to reject phenomena merely because they cannot withstand analysis, and they are unwilling to suspend the conventions of the world in order to agree that objects do not exist as separate entities from mind. In the end, the Prāsaṅgikas attempt to take a middle way between a naïve acceptance of the world's conventions—accepting objects to exist in the way they appear to exist, whether this means as inherently existent as in the Prāsaṅgika view or as external objects as in the Cittamātra view—and rejection of the world's conventions.

[76]Klein 1994: 127, 128-29.

4 Refutation of Self-Consciousness

When we gaze at an impressive vista or behold the face of a loved one, it is the operation of the eye consciousness, says the Buddhist epistemological tradition of Dignāga and Dharmakīrti, that enables us to recall at a later time what we have seen. But sometimes, if not always, we can recall not merely that which was seen, but the very *seeing* itself. That is, we remember not only the mountain range and the feelings and conceptions that arose as we beheld it, but also the *mere awareness* that was the seeing itself. This subtle reflexive action occurs, say the epistemologists, through the agency of "self-consciousness" (*rang rig, svasaṃvedanā*), a type of consciousness whose object is only another consciousness.[1]

That even ordinary persons can remember not only an object previously experienced but also the awareness that experienced the object is generally accepted, and not only by those who assert self-consciousness, such as the Cittamātrins, but also by the Prāsaṅgikas. Proponents of self-consciousness contend that knowledge is like a lamp, not like a measuring

[1]An entirely different interpretation of self-consciousness is given by Jadunath Sinha (1972: 33), who contends that "self-consciousness" just refers to the fact that according to Cittamātra all appearances are mental; hence, any act of cognition is an act of self-consciousness, since what a consciousness apprehends is nothing other than itself. Sinha's conjecture both misunderstands the nature of objects according to Cittamātra and fails to fit Dignāga's use of the concept of self-consciousness to explain memory.

weight.[2] A lamp illuminates itself at the same time that it illuminates other things; so, they say, just as we see the lamp itself by the same light with which we see other things, in our acts of knowing we are aware of our knowing—for instance, our visual consciousness itself—at the same time we are aware of the object that is known (in this case, being seen). Opponents of the concept of self-consciousness assert that knowledge is like a measuring weight; it cannot be itself measured at the same time that it measures other things. A weight in one pan of a balance is that by which the heaviness of the object in the other pan is known, but we do not thereby also know the heaviness of the weight; another weight must be set against it to measure *it*. Similarly, in this model, knowledge knows only its object and must itself subsequently be known by another knowledge.

Within the four principal Buddhist systems of tenets identified by Gelukba scholars, self-consciousness is accepted only by certain Sautrāntikas, certain Cittamātrins, and the Yogācāra-Svātantrika-Mādhyamikas. Both the Sautrāntikas and Cittamātrins are subdivided into those who are "Followers of Reasoning"—followers of the logicians Dignāga and Dharmakīrti—and others who are "Followers of Scripture." The Followers of Reasoning of these two schools assert the existence of self-consciousness; they are joined by some Followers of Scripture[3] (though not, apparently, Asaṅga himself)[4] and the

---

[2]This metaphor is employed by Hattori (1988: 49).

[3]There is no consensus among Gelukbas as to whether Sautrāntikas Following Scripture assert self-consciousness. Lati Rinbochay points out that according to Jamyang Shayba, they do not (and that is clear from *Great Exposition of the Middle Way*—see the next note), but that according to Jamyang Shayba's subsequent reincarnation, Gönchok Jikmay Wangbo, they do (Lati Rinbochay and Napper, [1980: 64-65]). However, Sopa and Hopkins, in the annotations to their translation of Gönchok Jikmay Wangbo's *Precious Garland of Tenets* in *Cutting through Appearances*, follow Jamyang Shayba when they repeatedly state that Sautrāntikas Following Scripture do *not* assert self-consciousness. Also, Jamyang Shayba (*Great Exposition of the Middle Way* 714.1) says that some Cittamātrins Following Scripture assert the existence of self-consciousness. They are not following Asaṅga on this particular point.

[4]According to Jamyang Shayba's *Great Exposition of the Middle Way*

Yogācāra-Svātantrika-Mādhyamikas. Vaibhāṣikas,[5] Sautrāntika-Svātantrika-Mādhyamikas, and Prāsaṅgikas do not accept self-consciousness.[6]

According to Jamyang Shayba, the definition of self-consciousness is: "that having the aspect (*rnam pa, ākāra*) of the apprehender (*'dzin pa, grāhaka*)."[7] That is, a self-consciousness takes on the "aspect"—the semblance—of a consciousness that itself "has the aspect of the apprehended (*bzung ba, grāhya*)," the aspect of the object it apprehends.[8]

The relation of a self-consciousness to the consciousness it apprehends is a subtle one. A self-consciousness is said to be in a non-dualistic simultaneous relationship with the apprehending consciousness, one in which there is no appearance of subject and object, for the two just seem to be fused. Because of the invariability of their appearance together, they are "one entity" (*ngo bo gcig, ekavastu*), incontrovertibly concomitant. Nevertheless, a self-consciousness and the consciousness

---

694.5-6, Asaṅga himself does not assert self-consciousness, for it is not mentioned in his *Actuality of the Grounds* (*sa'i dngos gzhi, bhūmivastu*) and when he enumerates types of consciousness, he either asserts only three types of direct valid cognition (sense, mental, and yogic), or does not include self-consciousness in his list of four, consisting of sense, mental, worldly (a category that includes the first two, i.e., sense and mental), and pure consciousnesses.

[5]Losang Gönchok, *Word Commentary* 105-6; Gönchok Jikmay Wangbo *Precious Garland of Tenets* 23.1, translated in Sopa and Hopkins (198).

[6]According to Hattori (1968: 101) self-consciousness is also asserted by the Jainas, the Prabhākara-Mīmāṃsaktas, and the Advaita-Vedāntins, and rejected by the Sāṃkhyas and Naiyāyikas. It is also refuted in Pātañjali's *Yoga-sūtras*.

[7]In the *Great Exposition of the Middle Way* 714.6, Jamyang Shayba gives two definitions: (1) "an isolated phenomenon that has the aspect of the apprehender" (*'dzin pa'i rnam pa yan gar ba*); and (2) "a consciousness that realizes only the solitary aspect of the apprehender" (*'dzin pa'i rnam pa ya rkyang tsam rtogs pa'i shes pa*).

One problem that arises as a result of denying self-consciousness is that it would seem to deny the functioning of a Buddha's omniscient consciousness that, after all, knows all subjects and objects in all three times simultaneously. For a thorough discussion, see Newland (1992: 196-208).

[8]For a discussion of types of aspects, assertions on aspected perception, etc., see Klein (1986: 102 ff.).

it knows are not identical, and so it is not the case that a consciousness such as an eye consciousness is "self-conscious." That this would seem to be the implication of the term "self-consciousness" is unfortunate, since a "self"-consciousness is, in fact, a consciousness of *another* consciousness.

For instance, a self-consciousness of a visual consciousness is not that visual consciousness itself, since as a type of consciousness a self-consciousness is a mental consciousness (*yid shes, manovijñāna*) and a visual consciousness is a sense consciousness (*dbang shes, indriyavijñāna*). For that reason, Lati Rinbochay[9] says that although a wrong consciousness—e.g., a visual consciousness that sees snow-covered mountains in the distance as blue, although they are really brown, green, etc.—and its self-consciousness are one entity, the self-consciousness is not itself a wrong consciousness (since it is merely the observer of the visual consciousness).

Also, a consciousness and its self-consciousness have different empowering conditions (*bdag rkyen, adhipatipratyaya*), that is, different media through which they work. For instance, a visual consciousness is empowered by the eye *indriya* (sense-power), an invisible but physical aspect of the eye organ, whereas a mental consciousness is empowered by a previous moment of consciousness itself.[10] To give another instance, when Lati Rinbochay discusses whether a yogic directly perceiving consciousness (*rnal 'byor mngon sum, yogipratyakṣa*) and its self-consciousness can have the same causal conditions,[11] he says that they *cannot* have the same empowering condition because self-consciousness, of course, does not arise through the power of meditation. It may seem confusing to impute such differences to things that are said to

---

[9]1980: 60.

[10]A sense consciousness' empowering condition is its respective sense-power. Each of the five senses has a clear internal form that is its sense power. The empowering condition of a mental consciousness is a consciousness that precedes it. The other two conditions for perception are the immediately preceding condition (that there be a previous moment of consciousness) and the observed-object condition (the object observed). See Lati Rinbochay and Napper (1980: 68).

[11]Lati Rinbochay and Napper (1980: 62-63).

be *one entity*, but it needs to be borne in mind that it is not contradictory that two different phenomena that are the same entity have differences, even to the extent of having different empowering conditions. For instance, a table and its emptiness of inherent existence are one entity, but emptiness, a permanent phenomenon, does not have causes, whereas the table itself has many. That a table and its emptiness, or an eye consciousness and its self-consciousness, are one entity means that they are not found apart from one another, not that they are conceptually indistinguishable.

Self-consciousness should not be confused with the mental factor (*sems byung, caitta*) called "introspection" (*shes bzhin, saṃprajanya*), which also involves the apprehension of consciousness. Introspection has been described as the use of a "corner" of the mind to observe subtly the rest of the mind, "like a spy in wartime."[12] In meditation practice, introspection is essential for the application of mindfulness to mental states. However, introspection is not held to be in a non-dualistic, simultaneous relationship with the consciousness under observation, as is self-consciousness; rather, it is described as either a "corner" of consciousness observing the main consciousness or the observation of a previous moment of consciousness.

Sources for the Debate on Self-Consciousness

Let us first look at the basic assertions of Dignāga, found in the first chapter of his *Compendium on Prime Cognition* (*pramāṇasamuccaya, tshad ma kun las btus pa*).[13] First, Dignāga argues that if self-consciousness were absent, people would be uncertain about the sources of knowledge and would absurdly be unable to exercise the reflective aspect of awareness.

[12]Lati Rinbochay and Napper (1980: 62). And like the spy, introspection must be as unobtrusive as possible, or risk the termination of the operation it is observing. Meditators know how difficult it can be to observe one's own mind without allowing the "observer" to become the "actor."

[13]See Hattori (1968).

He argues that if there were no self-consciousness, an awareness would not be later remembered; therefore, when we reflected on how an object came to be known, we could not be certain whether it appeared all by itself or appeared due to the activity of consciousness being trained upon it. In other words, we would not be able to say that we know things because we deliberately attempted to know them; they would just have appeared. Moreover, this would further imply that because we could have no memory of our instances of knowledge, we also could not achieve the sort of self-consciousness that everyone accepts, the ability to reflect on how we know things and the ability to plan to know in the future what we do not now presently know.

Second, he shows that self-consciousness must exist because a consciousness is necessarily simultaneously known as it knows its own object. He relies on a Cittamātra assumption that a knower and object known are simultaneous to argue: since it is (1) the case that a present awareness knows a present object and (2) we *do* remember the knowing of something as well as the thing that is known, proving that a knowing of that knowing occurred, that knowing of knowing must have occurred simultaneous with the knowing of an object. As long as we accept that a present mind knows a present object, not one separated from it in time, we are logically led to accept self-consciousness.

Now that we have considered the basic position of proponents of self-consciousness, let us turn to the Mādhyamika refutation of that tenet, both in India and Tibet. According to Gelukba scholars, Prāsaṅgikas refute the notion of self-consciousness by arguing that (1) it is not necessary for the functions it is held to perform, (2) its assertion would entail the use of ultimate analysis, which in turn would mean that it is unfindable, and (3) its existence would entail several absurd consequences. The refutation of self-consciousness is traced back to the early Mahāyāna sūtra *Questions of Ratnacūḍa Sūtra* (*ratnacūḍaparipṛcchasūtra, gtsug na rin po ches zhus pa'i mdo*), which says:[14]

---

[14]This sūtra is P 47, vol. 24, 229-51. Stephen Batchelor (1979: 185) notes

> If just that which is observed is the mind, how could the mind see the mind? For, for example, a sword-edge is unable to cut just that sword-edge, and a fingertip is unable to touch just that fingertip.

Also, Gelukbas cite several passages in the works of Nāgārjuna. In his *Refutation of Objections,* he says that "Valid cognition is not established by itself,"[15] which is taken to mean that there is no self-consciousness. In his *Treatise Called "The Finely Woven"* (*zhib mo rnam par 'thag pa zhes bya ba'i mdo, vaidalya-sūtranāma*) he says,[16] "A lamp does not illuminate itself because it is without darkness," a statement taken to imply that self-consciousness is superfluous because consciousness requires no illumination to be known (an argument to which we will return later). Similar statements are made in his most famous work, the *Treatise on the Middle Way.*

However, the main arguments are from Candrakīrti, who is the source of four arguments against self-consciousness.[17] Of the three Gelukba authors whose works are translated here, Jamyang Shayba mainly cites Nāgārjuna's arguments that no valid cognition can establish itself and that consciousness, while having a nature of illumination, does not need to illuminate itself, adding little more. Ngawang Belden mentions Nāgārjuna's arguments, but is more concerned with extensively working through Candrakīrti's four arguments

---

that this quotation is similar to a passage in the *Descent to Laṅka Sūtra;* he points to Tokmay Sangbo's commentary on Śāntideva (*Ocean of Good Explanations, Commentary to Engaging in the Bodhisattva Deeds* 205), which quotes the *Descent to Laṅka Sūtra* for this point. Candrakīrti quotes this in his *Clear Words* (Sanskrit in Poussin 62.4, translated by Sprung [55]).

[15]P 5228, vol. 98, 15.3.1-2. Translation by K. Bhattacharya is on p. 34 of *Dialectical Method of Nāgārjuna,* translation section; the Sanskrit is on p. 40 of the text section. This passage comes in the context of refuting all possibilities for establishment that would involve the positing of an inherently existent entity. For a validly cognizing consciousness to certify itself, it would have to be able to observe itself, whereby it would be self-conscious.

[16]P 5226, vol. 95, 12.3.4.

[17]Note that he is replying to Dignāga; it is not clear that Candrakīrti was aware of, or at least responding to, the work of his near-contemporary Dharmakīrti.

against self-consciousness, mixing in citations from the works of Śāntideva, Dzongkaba and Kaydrup and providing his own insight into how the postulation of self-consciousness amounts to ultimate analysis. Janggya mainly summarizes the material from Candrakīrti and Śāntideva, without quite as much analysis as Ngawang Belden.

Refutation of the Necessity of Self-Consciousness for Later Memory of Consciousness

The basic approach taken by Prāsaṅgika critics of self-consciousness is to argue that it is unnecessary, since memory of the subjective aspect of experience can be generated without it. Of the points made by Jamyang Shayba and Janggya, most are drawn from Candrakīrti, but Śāntideva and Kaydrup also are cited.

Those who assert the existence of self-consciousness regard it as essential for the production of memory. Candrakīrti refutes the notion that the existence of memory is a proof of its existence. Ngawang Belden summarizes Candrakīrti's presentation in his *Entrance to the Middle Way* and Candrakīrti's own commentary:[18]

> The Prāsaṅgika School method of refuting those is that it is not feasible to prove [self-consciousness] by the sign of memory because (1) if it were said, "Self-consciousness exists because inherently established memory exists," the sign would not be established, just as the probandum would not be established[19] and (2) if it were said that self-consciousness exists because memory exists, since the two, self-consciousness and memory consciousnesses, do not have the relation of [memory] not occurring if [self-consciousness] does not occur, the entailment is indefinite; it would be similar to the proof that since water and fire exist, a water-crystal and fire-

[18] *Annotations* 116a.3-6.

[19] The sign "inherently established memory" is not established because there is no such thing.

crystal exist.[20] For Dzongkaba's *The Essence of the Good Explanations* says:[21]

> [Candrakīrti's *Commentary on the "Entrance"*] says:[22]
>
> > Here, if this is treated as proving a substantially established [memory consciousness], since such a memory consciousness does not exist, it is the same as what is being proved [i.e., self-consciousness, in terms of not existing and thus being incapable of serving as a proof]. If it is taken in terms of conventionalities, since self-consciousness is not established for a second party [e.g., a Prāsaṅgika], then it and memory are not established as cause and effect. Also, it is explained that the two, (1) the proof that since water and fire exist, [respectively] water-crystals and fire-crystals exist, and (2) the proof that since a memory exists, self-consciousness exists, are similar[ly fallacious].
>
> This is done in terms of treating [memory] as an effect sign and holding self-consciousness to be the predicate of what is proved.

Candrakīrti, Dzongkaba, and Ngawang Belden here contend that the existence of memory as the Cittamātrins have described it would not entail self-consciousness. When they propound that self-consciousness exists because memory exists, they posit consciousnesses that are inherently established. Prāsaṅgikas assert that if inherently existent or sub-

---

[20]Fire and water crystals are believed to produce fire and water. However, the existence of water or fire does not entail the existence of these crystals, since there are many other sources for those elements. Similarly, the mere existence of memory does not entail self-consciousness, since Prāsaṅgikas show that there are other explanations for the production of memory.

[21]*Essence of the Good Explanations* 175.14-76.1.

[22]It would seem likely that this is from Candrakīrti's *Commentary on the "Entrance,"* but this passage does not appear there in exactly this way. Thurman (1984: 318) assumes this is Dzongkaba's statement based on Candrakīrti's *Entrance to the Middle Way* VI.72. Poussin's translation in *Muséon* 11 (1910) of VI.72-76 is found on pp. 349-54.

stantially established memory is the reason or sign in such a proof, then both the sign (memory) and the predicate of what which is to be proved, i.e., the probandum[23] (self-consciousness), are equally non-existent.

Those who propound self-consciousness claim that memory, the sign of their proof for self-consciousness, is an "effect sign" (*'bras rtags, phalaliṅga*), one in which the sign is an effect of the predicate of the probandum. For example, in the proof "the subject, fire, exists because smoke exists," smoke, an effect of fire, indicates its existence. Similarly, it is being said that in the proof "the subject, self-consciousness, exists because memory exists," memory is the effect of self-consciousness and indicates its existence.

Prāsaṅgikas deny that relationship. Dzongkaba notes that using memory as a sign of self-consciousness would be like using "object of eye consciousness" as a sign to prove sound is impermanent (which is absurd because sound is an object of an ear consciousness) or inferring the existence of a water-crystal from mere water (which is absurd because there are many other sources of water). One would either be using an inappropriate sign or would have switched the predicate and sign of the syllogism.

Candrakīrti argues that self-consciousness is not necessary for the function it is imputed to serve—facilitating later memory of the subjective aspect of experience—because the memory of a previous consciousness and that previous consciousness are not inherently different. He says, in his *Entrance to (Nāgārjuna's) "Treatise on the Middle Way"* (VI.74-75):[24]

> If self-consciousness were to be established,

---

[23]The predicate of the probandum (*bsgrub bya'i chos*) is the term that is being predicated of the subject in a syllogism, the probandum being the thesis that is to be proved. For instance, the proposed syllogism here is: "The subject, self-consciousness, exists because memory exists." The probandum is: "self-consciousness exists." The predicate of the probandum is "exists."

[24]*Entrance to the Middle Way* 7b.9; other translations in Geshé Rabten (1983: 66), Huntington (166), and Poussin, *Muséon* 11 (1910: 353).

It would not be reasonable that the remembering consciousness have a memory of [a former consciousness]
Because [the previous consciousness and present memory] would be [inherently] other. No such consciousness [could] be generated in one's continuum.
This reasoning precludes any relation [between them].

Because for me this memory is not [inherently] other
Than that [consciousness] by which the object was experienced,
One remembers, "I saw [this earlier]."
This is also the way of worldly conventions.

Candrakīrti sees the assertion of self-consciousness as entailing the assertion of an inherent difference between the consciousness that experiences an object and the consciousness that later remembers that earlier consciousness. Perhaps his thought is that the Cittamātra School asserts the existence of self-consciousness precisely because it sees the earlier and later awarenesses as being unrelated and uses self-consciousness to bridge them. In any case, he implicitly argues that since what is *inherently* other is *unrelatedly* other, there could be no causal connection between a previous awareness and the later memory of it. Since it is clearly not feasible that there be no connection between a previous experience and the later memory of it, the Cittamātra School is tempted to postulate the existence of self-consciousness, which can somehow mediate between the two.

Candrakīrti simply asserts that since these two awarenesses are *not* inherently other (since, in the Mādhyamika view, there is nothing that is inherently other than something else), they are not inherently unrelated (and therefore do not need to be bridged). This is borne out by the fact that no hard distinction between them is made in the conventions of the world; for instance, when referring to a former perception, we merely say, "*I* saw blue," not, "The self now, of the time of remembering, which is also the self of the time of the original experience, saw blue," or "Previously I saw blue, which exists now just as it existed then." In other words, the world does not analyze; there is no thought that the self of the past and the present are the same or that the object of the past and the present are the same.[25] Since it is not necessary, in ordinary worldly conventions, to distinguish between a previous experience and present memory, it is unnecessary to posit an intermediary agent that originally was conscious of the experience.

Put another way, self-consciousness is considered to be unnecessary because the original experiencer of the object—e.g., a visual consciousness that sees a blue patch—and the later recollection of that blue patch *have the same object*. As Dzongkaba boldly says,[26]

> ...it is established that a memory consciousness thinking, "I saw it previously," is generated through the force of the two, the earlier experience of the object, blue, and a later remembering consciousness, engaging in one object.

Dzongkaba is saying that in the conventions of the world, one's recollection of having seen blue is nothing other than a *re-engagement* with the original blue, not a special engagement with a subsequently generated mental construct. This is an idea at odds with a philosophical model of memory, in which we consider the mechanism of recollection to involve mental images, e.g., as being like the retrieval of stored records which are then displayed on the screen of consciousness. The convention of the world on recollection is simply that the remembering awareness engages the original object: one says, "I saw that," as though the object remembered is the original object, but without any thought that the object seen is the same as or different from the original object. Dzongkaba's solution does not itself explain the memory of a previous awareness; but

---

[25]As Ngawang Belden points out (based on Candrakīrti), it is like the fact that in the world people have no conception of a seed and sprout as being inherently different; so, they say, "I planted that tree," when they mean that they planted the seed that grew into the tree; or they say, "*I* hurt," when it is their hand that hurts, without thinking "I am my hand." This is cited later in this chapter, in the context of the Prāsaṅgika rejection of ultimate analysis.

[26]*Essence of the Good Explanations* 176.18-20. This is cited by both Jamyang Shayba and Janggya.

since memory has the power to reach back to the original object without mediation, it can, presumably, also reach back to the previous awareness, as the world itself implies. It would also seem to be concordant with Śāntideva's explanation, to be examined later, that required *no* previous experience of an awareness in order for that awareness to be recalled later.

Moving on from the issue of how memory can occur without self-consciousness, let us briefly consider the issue of how consciousness can be certified as existing without it. It is a commonplace that objects are validated as existing by consciousnesses; then, is it not reasonable to assume that awarenesses themselves have to be validated by an awareness? Candrakīrti's reply is that self-consciousness is not needed as the "certifier" of the previous consciousness—the "registrar" of its existence—in the manner that an eye consciousness is the certifier of a visual object. Candrakīrti says,[27] "Mere realization of the aspects of the objects of comprehension establishes the entity of the valid cognition." In other words, consciousnesses are certified simply by operation; the mere apprehension of an object by a sense consciousness or mental consciousness certifies the existence of that consciousness. It might be objected that in a sense, then, it *does* certify itself; however, this occurs not by a double movement in which one movement is reflexive and the other directed outward. It is unnecessary that there be a self-consciousness present to certify the awareness.

This also disposes of a pair of objections made by proponents of self-consciousness, who argue that it is necessary that the consciousness that experiences another consciousness be an instance of self-consciousness because if it were a different

---

[27]According to Janggya (478.13-19), who cites this, this is from Candrakīrti's *Clear Words.* I have not yet located the passage in *Clear Words*, but the Tibetan (*gzhal bya'i rnam pa'i rjes su byed pa tsam gyis tshad ma dag gi rang gi ngo bo rnam par 'jog pa'i phyir*) roughly corresponds to Poussin's edition (p. 73, line 7): *samāsaditātmabhāvasattākayoḥ pramānayoḥ svarūpasya vyavasthāpanāḥ*, which, according to Yamaguchi's index, should be P 5260, vol. 98, 13.3.4, and Derge, folio 25a.3 (thanks to Karen Lang).

substantial entity, absurd consequences would follow. Ngawang Belden provides a hypothetical opponent's argument:[28]

> It follows that the subject, the experience of the earlier subject [the consciousness], is a self-experience because it is either a self-experience or other-experience and there is the damage that if it is an other-experience, (1) it would follow that the experiencers would be endless and (2) it would follow that the later consciousness would not distinguish another object. The mode of establishment of the latter two reasons should be known from extensive statements in Dzongkaba's *Illumination of the Thought, Explanation of (Candrakīrti's) "Entrance."*[29]

The proponent of self-consciousness alleges that two absurd consequences would stem from identifying the experiencer of an earlier consciousness as an other-experiencing consciousness: (1) an infinite regress of consciousnesses and (2) that consciousness would be unable to distinguish another object. This person thinks that if one remembered an earlier consciousness apprehending blue, one would need yet another consciousness to apprehend that remembering consciousness while it apprehended the consciousness apprehending blue, and another to apprehend that consciousness, *ad infinitum*. Moreover, this remembering consciousness would not be able to distinguish *blue* because it would be full of its apprehension of the *eye consciousness* apprehending blue.

However, Candrakīrti, by saying that an eye consciousness needs no certifier of its existence other than its own operation, diffuses the criticism that there would be an infinite regress of certifiers. If it is not necessary that a consciousness be remembered in order to be certified, then the first step in the regress is not taken. Also, Dzongkaba, by saying that a previous eye consciousness and a later memory engage in the same object, undermines the argument that a later remembering consciousness is full of its apprehension of the previous eye consciousness and therefore could not remember that eye

---

[28] *Annotations* 116a.1-3.

[29] See *Illumination of the Thought* 158 ff.

consciousness's object. Presumably, Dzongkaba would argue that the memory of the previous eye consciousness is simply a different memory than that of the memory of the object seen; or he might argue, as Śāntideva does below, that the memory of the previously seen object induces the memory of the previous consciousness.

Kaydrup, one of Dzongkaba's two chief disciples, is apparently unsatisfied with Candrakīrti's explanation of the certification of consciousness and arrives at his own alternative. He contends that memories of awarenesses are *directly induced* by the awarenesses themselves—for instance, that the memory of seeing a patch of blue is directly induced by the eye consciousness; this later remembering consciousness certifies the earlier eye consciousness. This explanation is one that Janggya finds "easier" to understand. Janggya says:[30]

> A subsequent remembering consciousness also certifies [a consciousness] because (1) through the power of comprehending blue, without needing the mediation of any other valid cognition, an eye consciousness apprehending blue directly induces a consciousness remembering the apprehension of such and that remembering consciousness itself eliminates the superimpositions of both the non-existence of blue and the non-existence of the eye consciousness apprehending blue, and (2) the remembering consciousness itself validly cognizes the existence of the eye consciousness. This appears to be the thought also of Kaydrup's *Opening the Eyes of the Fortunate* and it is a little easier to realize than the former [i.e., Candrakīrti's presentation in his *Clear Words*].

This would appear in some ways to be just as difficult as Candrakīrti's explanation. The simpler aspect is the explanation of the certification of consciousness; an eye consciousness, for instance, is not certified by self-consciousness, nor simply by its own operation (as in Candrakīrti's system), but it *is* certified by another consciousness, namely, the later remem-

---

[30]*Presentation of Tenets* 479.1 ff. That Janggya cites Kaydrup's explanation immediately after Candrakīrti's and notes that it is "easier to understand" seems to be an indication that he finds Candrakīrti's explanation unfathomable.

bering consciousness. (It is not clear whether Kaydrup and / or Janggya feels that *all* awarenesses can later be remembered and can therefore be certified in this manner.)

On the other hand, with regard to the generation of memory, Kaydrup seems to be making the rather problematic argument that one's present memory can be induced by one's previous experience without any mediation. For example, Kaydrup seems to be arguing that the eye consciousness with which I saw my friend ten years ago can be said to be the cause both of my memory of that friend today and of my memory of seeing, itself. The apparent difficulty with this explanation is that it allows cause and effect to be separated by a great deal of time. Still, it might be noted that this is parallel to the notion that since an action is not inherently other than the karmic latency that it establishes, it is possible for that action, many eons hence, to produce an effect. (This is the concept of "disintegratedness" [*zhig pa, naṣṭa*], the subject of the next chapter.) To make the parallel explicit, just as the factor of disintegratedness of the action produces an effect, so here the disintegratedness of the eye consciousness produces a later memory. Once again, like Candrakīrti's hypothesis, the argument depends on the assertion that an eye consciousness and the later memory of it are not inherently different.

A third type of explanation for the production of memory without self-consciousness is that proposed by Śāntideva. In his *Engaging in the Bodhisattva Deeds* (IX.23), he says that the memory of a previous consciousness can be generated even without any previous *experience* of the subject:[31]

> If self-consciousness did not exist,
> How would a consciousness be remembered?
> Memory [of consciousness] occurs due to the relation [of an object] with other-experiencers[32]

---

[31]The quotation has been expanded to include the first two lines of the stanza. The Sanskrit (V. Bhattacarya 191) is: *yadi nāsti svaṃsavintirvikṣānaṃ smaryate kathaṃ / ānyānubhūte saṃbandhat smrtirākhuvishaṃ yathā*. Cf. Batchelor's translation 136-7. Also, according to Geshay Belden Drakba, there is a very good commentary by Akya Yongdzin (Yangjen Gaway Lodrö).

[32]An "other-experiencer" is just any consciousness, i.e., any conscious-

Like [being mindful of] the poison of a rodent.

According to Śāntideva, self-consciousness is unnecessary because the earlier object and the consciousness that experienced it are relatedly remembered. For instance, when one remembers having seen a patch of blue, one does so by first of all remembering the patch of blue and then remembering the eye consciousness that saw the patch of blue. It seems that this is not a case of merely *inferring* that an eye consciousness must have been present,[33] since that would not actually be a memory of a previous awareness, but of experiencing newly what was previously experienced, if it was at all, only in a *subliminal* way.

Śāntideva's example ("...like [experiencing] the poison of a rodent") concerns a hibernating bear that is bitten by a rodent but does not fully awaken from its slumber.[34] When it awakens in the springtime, it feels the pain of the infection from the bite, and through that remembers the experience of having been bitten. The bite was not experienced at the time it occurred, but only later. Similarly, one does not experience one's eye consciousness seeing a blue patch at the time it occurs (but only the blue patch itself), only later experiencing the eye consciousness at the time of remembering the blue. In short, Śāntideva does not claim that there need be *any* previous experience of a consciousness in order for there to be a subsequent recollection of that awareness.[35]

---

ness other than self-consciousness. In this case, the "other-experiencer" is a body consciousness aware of the pain of the bite of a rodent.

[33]Kensur Yeshey Tupden said that it is not just inference of a previous eye consciousness, but *experience* of it.

[34]"Bear" is not present in the Sanskrit, but all of my informants assumed that it was the animal spoken of in the example.

[35]Kaydrup also found this explanation "extremely difficult to understand" (Cabezón 1992: 350).

The Argument That Mind Is Self-Conscious But Is Not a Self-Consciousness

In addition to their refutation of the need for self-consciousness in the production of the memory of the subjective aspect of experience, Prāsaṅgikas argue that since consciousness is *itself* knowledge, it is self-certifying and therefore needs knowing no more than a lamp needs illumination. That is, the very entity of consciousness is knowing (it is defined as "clear and knowing"[36]), just as the very entity of a lamp is light. (Note that a "lamp" is a vessel of oil with a wick that has been lit; an unlit vessel is not a lamp.[37]) A mind is self-knowing but does not *itself* know itself, acting as agent on itself, just as a lamp does not itself illuminate itself.

Many Prāsaṅgika authorities have made this point. Nāgārjuna's *Treatise Called "The Finely Woven"* (*zhib mo rnam par 'thag pa zhes bya ba'i mdo, vaidalyasūtranāma*) says,[38] "A butter-lamp does not illuminate itself because it is without darkness." Śāntideva's *Engaging in the Bodhisattva Deeds* (IX.19ab) says,[39] "The butter-lamp is not an object of illumination. / Why? It is not obscured by darkness." And Dzongkaba's *Illumination of the Thought, Explanation of (Candrakīrti's) "Entrance"* comments,[40]

> . . . because just as a butter-lamp itself does not illuminate itself but nevertheless its having luminosity is not precluded, so even though consciousness itself does not experience itself in the manner asserted by those who hold the contrary position, that it has mere experience is not precluded.
>
> *Objection*: The butter-lamp itself does illuminate itself.

---

[36]*gsal zhing rig pa*. See Jambel Sampel 1b.3, translated in Lati Rinbochay and Napper (1980: 45).

[37]Kensur Yeshey Tupden.

[38]P 5226, vol. 95, 12.3.4.

[39]*Engaging in the Bodhisattva Deeds* 189. The Sanskrit is: *naiva prakāśyate dīpo yasmānna tamasāvṛtaḥ*. Cf. translation by Batchelor (136).

[40]*Illumination of the Thought* 158b.2-4.

> *Response*: If that were the case, darkness itself would obscure itself, and if that were asserted, just as a pot is not seen in a mass of darkness, darkness also would not be seen.[41]

Since the lamp is not obscured by darkness, it requires no illumination; the darkness that exists prior to the light is not something in the nature of the lamp. In fact, Prāsaṅgikas deny that a lamp and darkness even *meet*. Ngawang Belden states:[42]

> Darkness and a butter-lamp do not meet. This is because the two, light and darkness, are contradictory in the sense of not abiding together.[43] Nāgārjuna's *Treatise on the Middle Way* (VII.10,11) says:[44]
>
> > If at the time of a butter-lamp's state of being produced,[45]

---

[41]According to Kensur Yeshey Tupden, a butter-lamp is self-luminous (*rang gsal ba*) in the sense that it has a nature of illumination and needs no other source, but it does not illuminate itself by itself (*rang nyid gyis rang gsal ba*), a formulation which implies that it *requires* illumination and that it illuminates itself in the same way it illuminates other things.

[42]*Annotations* 115b.4-7.

[43]According to Jambel Trinlay's textbook for Drebung's Loseling College (14.10-11), the definition of phenomena that are contradictory in the sense of not abiding together (*lhan cig mi gnas 'gal*) is: phenomena that do not have a common locus, that is, do not abide together harmlessly (*gnod med du lhan cig mi gnas pa'i gzhi mthun mi sri pa'i chos*). An example is hot and cold, which cannot exist together without harming each other. Phenomena that are contradictory in the sense of mutual abandonment (*phan tshun spangs 'gal*) are defined as: abiding in mutual abandonment in terms of objects of awareness (*blo'i yul du phan tshun spangs te gnas pa).* An example is existence and non-existence, which are contradictory and cannot mutually appear as objects of awareness to a single mind. Technically, the former type of contradiction does *not* preclude the meeting of two things. For instance, a crow and an owl are said to be contradictory in the sense of not abiding together because of their natural mutual enmity, but of course these creatures could meet and fight. In general, however, except for meetings between living beings, things that are contradictory in the sense of not abiding together harmlessly cannot meet.

[44]P 5224, vol. 95, 4.4.2-4. Sanskrit is in Poussin, 152.10-11, 153.1-2.

[45]The "state of being produced" (*skye bzhin pa*) is the moment just *before* its production, when it still does not exist.

It does not meet with darkness,
How, by a butter-lamp's being produced,
Would darkness be illuminated?

If, even without a butter-lamp's meeting darkness,
Darkness is cleared away,
Then the darkness dwelling all over the world
Would definitely be removed.[46]

With respect to that reasoning, Dzongkaba's *Ocean of Reasoning, Explanation of (Nāgārjuna's) "Treatise on the Middle Way"* says:[47]

> Also, with respect to asserting that conventionally a butter-lamp clears away darkness, although the two, a butter-lamp's state of being produced and darkness, must indeed meet, at the time of a butter-lamp's state of being produced a butter-lamp does not exist; therefore, [a butter-lamp] need not meet with darkness.
>
> In accordance with the assertion that a butter-lamp's clearing away of darkness is established by its own character, if a butter-lamp's state of being produced met with darkness, a butter-lamp would have to exist at that time whereas it does not. Therefore, [Nāgārjuna's] is a reasoning which indicates that since [darkness] does not meet [inherently] with a butter-lamp's state of being produced, it is not feasible for a butter-lamp to clear away darkness.[48]

---

[46]Nāgārjuna is exploring the possibilities for a meeting between a lamp and darkness: If they do not exist at the same time, how can light get rid of darkness? That is, if they do not meet, the production of a lamp would not cause the cessation of darkness. Or, if the lamp cleared away darkness without meeting it, then how could there be any darkness? On the other hand, if a lamp *does* exist at the same time as the darkness, how can it do away with the darkness? Dzongkaba explains the second stanza in *Illumination of the Thought* 164.5 ff.

[47]*Ocean of Reasoning* 163.19-64.5 (Varanasi ed.).

[48]Kensur Yeshey Tupden noted (12/14/83) that although conventionally a butter-lamp's state of being produced and darkness meet, they do not meet *ultimately*, for that would require that a butter-lamp would already exist (for something ultimately existent is never non-existent) entailing the absurdity that it would already exist at the time it is being produced. At that time, darkness is approaching destruction and the butter-lamp is approach-

If a light and darkness met, then light would have to clear away the darkness before it could be seen. Similarly, if consciousness and obscuration met, then consciousness would have to clear away the obscuration before it could be seen. Implicitly, those who propound the existence of self-consciousness are being accused of saying that consciousness is obscured and must be illuminated. Rather, it is being implied, because consciousness has a nature of illumination (or knowing), it is self-certifying (which again, is not a certification of itself *by itself*, which implies an extra reflexive movement; it is self-certifying simply through its operation) and *simply* knowable. Also, it would follow that if light illuminated itself, darkness would obscure itself; and if darkness obscured itself, then absurdly darkness could not be seen. Darkness would obscure itself just as it obscures objects like pots in unlit places.

Consciousness shines forth as it knows its objects, and that shining forth is why it needs no further knower in order to be seen clearly at a later time. This, it seems, is finally how these explanations of memory without self-consciousness are justified; we can easily remember even that of which we were not specifically aware earlier simply because awareness shines forth just as does a previously experienced object. To engage in recollection, whether of the previously experienced object or of the consciousness that knew the object, is simple because one was illuminated and the other was simply luminous.

The Objection That Positing Self-Consciousness Would Require Ultimate Analysis

Janggya argues that self-consciousness is not only unnecessary, but it cannot be established by conventional valid cognition:[49] "No matter how much one aims the mind, there is no appearance of [the mind] itself as the known and itself as

---

ing production. In the following moment, the butter-lamp is produced and darkness has ceased. There is no moment in which both exist; hence, they do not meet.

[49]*Presentation of Tenets* 476.3-4.

the knower." Those who assert the existence of self-consciousness are not being said to claim that self-consciousness is in turn observed by another consciousness such as another self-consciousness, *ad infinitum*; even if they did, Janggya says, there could be no such direct observation. If self-consciousness can be established at all, it must be established through reasoning. But it cannot be established merely through *conventional* reasoning—reasoning that investigates conventionalities—since self-consciousness, the object about which the reasoning revolves, is held to be *inherently* or *ultimately* established. Therefore, the reasoning upon which proponents of self-consciousness depend is that investigating the ultimate—ultimate analysis. Ngawang Belden asserts that the establishment of self-consciousness would "obviously" require ultimate analysis:[50]

> If self-consciousness were asserted it would be necessary to assert that it is able to bear the analysis of a reasoning [consciousness] searching for the imputed object, because searching for a means of positing [or certifying] a consciousness, that is, whether it is self-experiencing or the object of experience of another [consciousness], is a mode of searching for an imputed object which is even more obviously [a case of ultimate analysis] than searching [to see whether] a sprout is produced from self or produced from [that which is inherently] other.[51]

---

[50]*Annotations* 114b.5-15a.1.

[51]The term "inherently" has been inserted in brackets before "produced" in order to reflect the Gelukba explanation, stemming from Dzongkaba, that Nāgārjuna and his followers do not mean to exclude even *conventional* production from other as a possibility, since that is the way things are actually produced. For instance, a sprout is produced from a seed, the seed being conventionally other than it. In other words, the reasoning is aimed at eliminating all possibilities for inherently existent production, including production from self and production from what is inherently other. As it happens, it is unnecessary to qualify production from self as just meaning inherently existent production from self because there is not even any *conventionally* existent production from self. Hence, there is also no possibility of both production from self and other. The final option, production from neither, is rejected because there *is* conventional production from other.

What does Ngawang Belden mean in this context by ultimate analysis? Let us first consider the reasoning concerning a sprout and seed that he uses as an analogy. Beginning with Nāgārjuna, Prāsaṅgika explorations of the possibilities for the production of a sprout consider four options; in Gelukba exegeses these are presented as the possibilities that: (1) a sprout is produced from itself; (2) it is produced from that which is inherently other than it; (3) it is produced both from itself and from that which is other than it; and (4) it is produced causelessly. Such analysis is ultimate analysis because it constitutes a search for that which exists ultimately, in this case a mode of production in which the sprout does not arise in dependence on a seed.

The Prāsaṅgika method to ascertain whether or not a sprout inherently exists (which for them also means that it ultimately exists) is to search analytically for a sprout as being produced in any of these four ways. Such ultimate analysis into the cause and effect of seed and sprout is bound to fail at its proposed goal of finding the cause of the sprout. A sprout cannot produce itself, since that would entail that it already existed at the time of its production, in which case its reproduction would be unnecessary; or, since it must produced even though it already exists, its production and re-production would be endless. Nor can a sprout be produced from that which is inherently other than it. Things that are inherently other must be completely unrelated, since if they were related, they would be posited in dependence on each other and would not be inherently different. If something can be a cause of something that is unrelated to it, then it would absurdly follow that darkness could be caused by a lamp, or that rice could absurdly grow from a barley seed, and so forth.[52] Since neither self-production nor production from (what is inherently) other is feasible, the third possibility, the conjunction of both, is rejected; the fourth possibility is rejected

[52]A problem with dispensing with this particular corner of the reason is that if one realized that there were no inherently existent others, one would already have realized emptiness. If that were the case, why continue with the reasoning?

because, for instance, if a sprout were causeless, it would be absurd to plant a field since it would arise without seeding.

With regard to the production of a sprout, it is *not* ultimate analysis to merely observe that a sprout is produced from a seed and that the two are different. Rather, this is a determination based not on the sort of analysis just indicated, but on the most mundane sort of inquiry. It is simply well known in the world that a sprout arises from a seed, but when people in the world assert that relationship, they do not do so within assuming that a seed and sprout are inherently other. Hence, a seed and a sprout are conventionally, or nominally, cause and effect.

This brings us to the question of how the relationship between a previous experience and later memory is like that of a seed and sprout. The question concerns the production of a later memory of a previous experience: is the consciousness at a previous time self-experienced, or is it experienced by another consciousness? For instance, was the eye consciousness that apprehended a patch of blue (and which is currently being remembered) apprehended by self-consciousness at the time it occurred, or is the memory of this eye consciousness the result of a later consciousness? (Note that in order for this example to be parallel, the latter option would have to be understood to be a case of inherent otherness, i.e., that the eye consciousness and its experiencer are inherently other.) The latter option is easy to dispose of through the same sort of analysis done with respect to a seed and sprout that are conceived to be inherently other: if the eye consciousness and its experiencer (such as a later remembering consciousness) are inherently other, they would be unrelatedly other, entailing the absurd consequence that an eye consciousness apprehending blue could cause a later memory of an eye consciousness apprehending red or an ear consciousness hearing an echo, since there would be no definite relation between the cause and the effect. But the first option is absurd as well, for as the *Questions of Ratnacūḍa Sūtra* says, and all the Prāsaṅgikas repeat, if a consciousness could know itself then absurdly a sword can cut itself, a finger touch itself, an eye see itself, gymnasts stand on their own shoulders, and so on.

Again, since none of those possibilities can withstand analysis, the only acceptable possibility for the production of later memory is to posit merely nominal experience by other: a later memory occurs because a previous experience, such as an eye consciousness, is apprehended by a later consciousness. In the conventions of the world, it is well known that one only later recalls a previous experience: "I saw that." By "I saw" is indicated the recollection of previous experience, and by "that" is indicated the object of that experience (which is, at the same time, the object of one's present experience, the subject of the statement). However, as we have seen earlier in this chapter, often not even this much is said in the conventions of the world. For instance, one might plant a seed, and later point to the sprout and say, "I planted that," not explicitly or implicitly distinguishing between the seed that was planted and the sprout that was the effect of the seed. Just so, when one sees a blue patch and later points to the patch, saying, "I saw that," one does not distinguish the previous blue from the blue that is its effect (a later moment of similar type of blue, but not, due to the moment-by-moment disintegration of impermanent things, the *same* patch of blue).

The Prāsaṅgika authors, avoiding ultimate analysis when positing conventional phenomena, simply say that one remembers at a later time what was experienced earlier, without qualifying the relationship of the two. Ngawang Belden uses ordinary examples to make this point:[53]

> The two, previous experience and later memory, are not others established by way of their own character. It has already been explained [earlier in the sixth chapter, verse 32 of the *Entrance*] that the conception of substantial cause and effect—for instance, seed and sprout—as others established by their own character does not exist in an ordinary worldly awareness. Just so, the two, previous experience and later memory, not only are not conceived by an innate worldly awareness to be others established by their own character,

[53]*Annotations* 116b.4-17a.2.

> but also when one later remembers the object seen in the previous apprehension of blue, one uses the verbal convention, "*I* saw this previously also."
>
> Although such is indeed the case, one does not think, "The self of the time of remembering is the self of the time of [previous] experience," and one does not use the verbal convention, "Previously I saw the blue which was qualified by being the object which subsists [both] at the time of this utterance and the time of the [previous object]." Therefore, the verbal convention is not factually discordant. For example, it is like the fact that in the world, even though one uses the verbal convention, "*I* hurt," when one's hand hurts, it is not a case of thinking, "This hand is me," and so forth, and hence the verbal convention is not factually discordant.[54] An ordinary worldly [awareness] does not have the conception that such experience and memory or the two objects at those times are others established by their own character. Therefore, it is not the case that the [object] experienced and distinguished by the consciousness that earlier experienced it is not later experienced or distinguished by the consciousness which remembers that, whereby the remembering consciousness thinking, "I saw this earlier too," comes to be generated. This is the way of worldly convention; it is not to be taken as a case of positing something upon analysis by way of searching for an imputed object because it is a worldly convention that has a sense of falseness in that when the imputed object is sought it is not found.

Gelukbas *do* explain that conventionally, a seed and sprout, or a previous and later moment of a patch of blue, *are* different substantial entities, even though they are not substantially existent (since, for them, that would mean that they are inherently existent). That is, conventional valid cognition such as a sense consciousness can determine the difference between a seed and a sprout and a former and a later moment of blue. However, Ngawang Belden points out that in the world they are not ordinarily conceived to be so. They are

[54]Daktsang is said to contend that it is contradictory that seed and sprout be different substantial entities but that there be no production from other. Gelukbas reply that production from other means inherently other, whereas a seed and sprout are only conventionally other.

ordinarily not even conceived to be *other*, as when we say, of a tree, "I planted this," when in fact we planted a seed. Similarly, we do not ordinarily conceive that the blue we experienced in the past and the blue of our current recollection are different.

To reconcile the apparent contradiction between what ordinary people say and what conventionally exists, Ngawang Belden appears to be making a difference between what is **well known to the world** (*'jig rten la grags pa*) and what is **well known to an ordinary worldly awareness** (*'jig rten rang 'ga' ba'i blo la grags pa*). The first category appears to be broader; everything established for conventional valid cognition except emptiness, i.e., all conventional truths, is well known to the world. Perhaps this means that these phenomena are all within the purview of an awareness that is not turned toward emptiness, even if that awareness belongs to someone who is not ordinary, i.e., is a Superior, one who has realized emptiness directly, but who is not engaged in meditation on emptiness at that time. Moreover, the distinctions that philosophers make *about* ordinary and non-ordinary worldly conventions—such as that eyes have as their own unique objects of apprehension only color and shapes, not bodies, etc., or that the deceptiveness of reflections is an appropriate metaphor for the deceptiveness of conventional phenomena, which appear to inherently exist but do not—may be well known to the world, but certainly are not well known to an ordinary worldly awareness.

The second category—renown to an ordinary worldly awareness—precludes anything not obvious to an ordinary person; for example, that there is a difference between the seed that is the substantial cause of a tree and the tree itself is well known to the world but is not well known to an ordinary worldly awareness because an ordinary person, considering the production of a tree, does not even conceive of the seed and tree as different: "I planted that." Excluded from either category, of course, are beliefs that are not established by valid cognition.

Distinctions such as these seem to be a natural outcome of reflections on Candrakīrti's call to respect the conventions of the world; but do they in fact exceed his intentions by over-analyzing what the world says? I would argue that they do not, since the Gelukbas do not actually affirm anything that Candrakīrti himself does not affirm and do not reject anything that Candrakīrti himself does not reject. Still, we can see that the very existence of the distinctions made by Jamyang Shay-ba and Ngawang Belden indicates that it is not easy to determine what it means to uphold the world's conventions.

In conclusion, Prāsaṅgikas see self-consciousness as a concept in opposition to worldly conventions and one that is not necessary to explain the formation of memory. They propose several models of memory that reflect the conventions of the world and avoid the assumption of a metaphysical entity the establishment of which would require ultimate analysis. As in their defense of external objects, their reasoning stems from the fundamental rejection of inherent existence even conventionally.

5 Disintegration and the Three Times

Traditional accounts of the Buddha's enlightenment such as the introduction to the *Life Stories* (*skyes pa rabs kyi gleng gzhi, jātakanidāna*)[1] state that in the last watch of that night he discovered the causal chain that binds sentient beings in cyclic existence (*'khor ba, saṃsāra*), the round of transmigration. With the insight produced by profound mindfulness, he saw the causation of suffering: that death is caused by birth; birth by the "ripening" of a seed for rebirth; that ripening by grasping; grasping by attachment; attachment by contact; contact by the six senses; the six senses by mind and body; mind and body by consciousness; consciousness by action; and action by ignorance. These he called the twelve links of dependent-arising (*rten 'byung, pratītyasamutpāda*), the chain of cause and effect originating with ignorance and terminating in death that underlies cyclic existence.

This chapter is concerned with the final link, in particular with the implications arising from the seemingly innocuous assertions that death is something that is *produced* and something that can act as a *cause*. In a wider sense, we will be concerned with issues surrounding the disintegration of impermanent things. Gelukba treatments of the topic of disintegration begin with Buddha's statement, in the *Sūtra on the Ten Grounds* (*mdo sde sa bcu pa, daśabhūmika-sūtra*,[2] "Aging and

---

[1]P 748, vol. 21. Cf. selection in Warren (82).

[2]P 761.31, vol. 25. For translation and context, see Honda (190).

death [are produced] by the condition of birth," which is taken to indicate the Buddha's realization that death is not a mere absence of life, but life's destruction, a state *produced* indirectly but inexorably from the creation of life itself. That is, since death does not come into existence without birth, it belongs to the sphere of conditioned or compounded phenomena (*'dus byas kyi chos, saṃskṛtadharma*). Moreover, in that sūtra he identified two functions that death performs:[3]

> Death subsists in two activities: (1) it causes a compounded phenomenon to disintegrate and (2) it issues forth the cause of the non-severance of the continuum of thorough non-knowingness [i.e., ignorance].

Armed with these passages, which undeniably indicate a scriptural basis for the position that death is both caused and acts as a cause, Gelukba Prāsaṅgikas have attempted to demonstrate that, analogously, the "death" or, more strictly, "deadness" of past actions (*las, karma*)—their state of having disintegrated after being produced, or, in an abbreviated way, their "disintegratedness" (*zhig pa, naṣṭa*)[4]—is also produced and may have effects. Actions, like all impermanent phenomena, disintegrate moment-by-moment. For example, swatting a fly in anger, immediately disintegrating, gives rise to the "disintegratedness" of the action of swatting. In brief, Prāsaṅgikas from Candrakīrti onward assert that this action's state of having ceased has been caused (by the disintegratedness of the action's causes) and that it is capable of producing the effect of the action (such as an episode or entire lifetime of experience) in the future.

By identifying "disintegratedness" as a functioning thing, i.e., an impermanent, caused, potent phenomenon that disintegrates moment-by-moment and is able to perform a function,[5] Prāsaṅgikas contradict most other Buddhist tenet sys

---

[3]P 761.31, vol. 25.

[4]*zhig pa* is the past tense of *'jig pa* ("disintegration").

[5]Throughout the book, "functioning" often precedes "thing" because the Perfection of Wisdom sūtras often use the word *bhāva* (*dngos po*) to refer to all phenomena—conditioned or unconditioned, impermanent or permanent.

tems, which identify disintegratedness as a permanent, uncaused, non-disintegrating phenomenon. The sole exception among other Buddhist schools is the Vaibhāṣika School, which also labels disintegratedness as a functioning thing, but the Prāsaṅgika School diverges from it as well: Gelukba Prāsaṅgikas explain that even though the disintegratedness of an action may exist at the present time, the action that has disintegrated no longer exists, whereas the Vaibhāṣika School holds that the past action exists as an action even at the time of its having disintegrated.[6] Similarly, the Vaibhāṣika School asserts that the futureness of an action—the fact that its basic causes exist although its supporting conditions are not yet complete—exists even at the present time. For instance, for them, a sprout actually exists even at the time of the seed from which it will sprout (a position also said to be held by the non-Buddhist Sāṃkhyas). Other Buddhist schools, including the Prāsaṅgika School, deny that a sprout exists at the time of the seed; Gelukba exegetes say that it is permissible to say only that even though at that time the sprout does not exist, the sprout exists *as the entity of the seed*, which amounts to saying that a *seed* exists that will, upon the aggregation of the proper conditions, become a sprout.

The disagreement between the various Buddhist schools over the status of disintegratedness does not extend to the *mere* disintegration of things, for disintegration is one of the three characteristics of compounded phenomena set forth by the Buddha (the other two being production and endurance). No one denies that disintegration exists as an impermanent phenomenon, but according to Gelukba scholars, all schools other than the Prāsaṅgika and Vaibhāṣika Schools make a

---

The term "functioning," therefore, excludes permanent phenomena. Vaibhāṣikas are said to assert that even permanent phenomena perform functions—space, for instance, performing the function of allowing the movement of an object. However, Gelukbas limit "functioning" to the production of *effects*. Therefore, it must be understood that "functioning" is meant to imply that a thing has been produced and is able to act as a cause, whereas permanent phenomena are uncaused and have no effects.

[6]Gönchok Jikmay Wangbo, *Precious Garland of Tenets* 21.9.12, translated in Sopa and Hopkins (192).

radical distinction between disintegration (*'jig pa*) and disintegratedness (*zhig pa*), saying that disintegratedness is the mere absence of the phenomenon that has been extinguished, and therefore is a mere negative or non-affirming negative (*med dgag, prasajyapratiṣedha*), a permanent phenomenon that is both uncaused and incapable of acting as a cause.

According to Gelukba explanations of the Prāsaṅgika School, on the other hand, disintegration and disintegratedness are generally related in the same way that dying and death are related. For instance, when a person is dying, that person exists; however, when that person has died, it is no longer possible to posit a person, for a corpse cannot serve as the basis of imputation for a person (in other words, a dead "person" is not a person). Only that person's "deadness"—the actuality of his/her having died—exists. In the same way, *while* a thing disintegrates, that thing exists, for its production, endurance, and disintegration occur simultaneously and comprise the thing's "own time," its presentness. However, when that thing has disintegrated, it no longer exists; only its disintegratedness, its factor of having disintegrated, exists. Disintegration and disintegratedness, like dying and death, are, in general, sequential.[7]

From a different angle, it could also be said that when a thing disintegrates, its disintegration *continues*, for disintegratedness is said to be part of the "activity" of disintegration. Ngawang Belden says,[8]

> In the Prāsaṅgika system, it is asserted that since disintegratedness and disintegration are not mutually exclusive, a pot's disintegratedness is also a pot's disintegration. Moreover, the assertion that "a pot's disintegration" is the *activity* of a pot's disintegration is an assertion agreeing with the

---

[7]Technically, as will be seen, disintegratedness is *part* of the activity of disintegration, and hence, disintegration includes disintegratedness. Here, however, when disintegration is grouped with production and endurance, it refers only to something's "own time," its moment of being present, and does not include disintegratedness, which occurs in the subsequent moment.

[8]*Annotations* 113a.1-3.

> Sautrāntikas and above. However, Prāsaṅgikas assert that both a pot's not enduring and not having endured in the second [moment after] its own time are activities of a pot's disintegration; therefore both a pot's *approaching to* disintegratedness and a pot's disintegratedness are activities of a pot's disintegration.
>
> For example, it is asserted that [disintegratedness being an activity of disintegration] is similar to the fact that both a sprout's *approaching to* production and a sprout's production are activities of a sprout's production.

Prāsaṅgikas find that a pot's disintegratedness, its "not having endured," is part of the activity of a pot's disintegration, its "not enduring." Since disintegratedness is included within disintegration, a thing's disintegratedness is also its disintegration.[9] Like disintegration, then, disintegratedness is an impermanent phenomenon. The other Buddhist schools hold that a pot's disintegration is just its *approaching* to disintegratedness, which is simultaneous with pot's own time and does not include its disintegratedness, which occurs in the moment after its own time. (A thing's "own time" is just the moment in which it is present, so the following moment is not its own time, but rather is the moment of its disintegratedness.) Ngawang Belden asserts that the same relationship holds for *approaching to* production and to production itself, which are both *activities* of production.

However, disintegration is not necessarily disintegratedness; for instance, at the moment a pot is present, it is disintegrat*ing* (as are all impermanent phenomena) but has not disintegrat*ed*, and hence, its disintegrated*ness* does not yet exist. This relationship is a further indication that disintegratedness is impermanent, because disintegration, of which it is a part, is impermanent.

---

[9]Geshe Gendün Lodrö said that most Buddhists accept that at the time of the seed, a sprout exists as the *entity* of the seed; but a sprout *itself* does not exist then. This implies that, similarly, a sprout's disintegratedness exists at the time of its disintegration *as the entity of disintegration*.) The Vaibhāṣikas are said to differ from other Buddhist schools in saying that a sprout *actually* exists at that time, a position similar to that of the non-Buddhist Sāṃkhyas. For a discussion of Sarvāstivāda arguments, see Bastow.

Moreover, there is a sense in which the process of disintegration never ends, since disintegratedness itself disintegrates, producing its own disintegratedness, and so forth, in an endless series that begins with the production of the thing itself. There must, in fact, be an infinite regress, for once something has disintegrated, it *always* has disintegrated; even when an action, via its disintegratedness, has brought forth an effect, its status as something that *has* disintegrated could not change. (This may be why disintegratedness is said to be the *main* activity of disintegration.) The Sagya (*sa skya*) scholar Daktsang,[10] who is Jamyang Shayba's favorite target due to his criticisms of Dzongkaba, is held by Jamyang Shayba to have objected to this endless series on the grounds that it constituted an absurd endless regress:[11]

> *Daktsang*: It [absurdly] follows that the disintegratedness of a pot is endless because there is disintegratedness also of pot's disintegratedness!
>
> *Reply*: There is no entailment [that because there is disintegratedness also of pot's disintegratedness that the disintegratedness of pot is endless]. Then, it would [absurdly] follow [for you] that although pot is impermanent it is endless because there is impermanence also of pot's impermanence. You asserted the entailment.
>
> *Another Incorrect Position*: It [absurdly] follows that pot's disintegratedness and another disintegratedness of that and yet another are endless because of your assertion.
>
> *Response*: That is acceptable.
>
> *Incorrect position*: It [absurdly] follows that the disintegratedness of a pot is not established because the disintegratedness of that and another and another are endless.
>
> *Response*: There is no entailment [that because disintegratedness involves an endless progression, that the disintegratedness of a pot is not established]. It [absurdly] follows that pot's production is not established because [according to you,] with respect to the time of pot's production, the time

[10] Daktsang Lotsawa was born in 1405, during the period in which Dzongkaba (1357-1419) was establishing the Gelukba order. He is infamous among Gelukba scholars for his scathing denunciations of Dzongkaba's views.

[11] Jamyang Shayba, *Great Exposition of the Middle Way* 628.5-29.2.

of pot's cause, the time of the cause of that, [etc.], would be endless.

This seems to be a disjointed dialogue because Jamyang Shayba at first claims that there is endless regress and then, admitting that the series is endless, denies any fallacy involved with it. In any case, he finds it just as reasonable to say that upon the disintegration of a disintegratedness, a disintegratedness of a disintegratedness is produced, and so on, as it is to say that a pot's impermanence is impermanent, as is the impermanence of a pot's impermanence, and so on, or to say that a pot's cause has a cause, its cause's cause has a cause, and so on.

Other schools consider disintegration and disintegratedness to be mutually exclusive. They admit that disintegration is an activity, but hold that disintegratedness is not, being a mere absence of something upon its disintegration. Hence, they claim that disintegratedness is a "non-affirming" negative (*med dgag, prasajyapratiṣedha*), a phenomenon neither caused nor capable of producing an effect. (Non-affirming negatives are phenomena such as emptiness, the negation of a phenomenon's inherent existence; they are *mere* negatives, negatives that imply nothing positive in their place. On the other hand, a phrase like "treeless plain" involves an affirming negative, since "plain" is affirmed.)[12]

The seemingly minor topic of disintegratedness becomes important because Gelukba Prāsaṅgikas are interested in avoiding the pitfalls of the various explanations put forward by other schools to account for the transmission of karmic potentials from one life to the next. Other tenet systems posit various substantially existent entities to serve as karmic seed-holders or as bases of the "infusion" of karmic seeds that are themselves conceived to be substantially existent. The problem faced by all Buddhist tenet systems, which share with most other Indian philosophical systems a cosmology based on the notions of karma and reincarnation, is that there must

[12]For an extensive discussion of the divisions of negatives according to Gelukba sources, see Hopkins (1983a: 721-27).

be a continual basis for such latencies or, otherwise, actions and their effects would not necessarily be related.

Gelukbas contend that most of the subschools comprising the Vaibhāṣika School[13] (from what they have gathered from close reading of Vasubandhu's *Treasury of Higher Knowledge*) assert that karmic latencies have "acquisition" (*thob pa, prāpti*), a factor of adherence that causes the latencies to remain attached to the continuum of the sentient being who has acquired them.[14] Several other subsects—the Sarvāstivāda, Vibhajyavāda, and Saṃmitīya—assert "non-wastage" of actions (*las chud mi za ba, karmāvipraṇāśa*), that the potencies of karma persist until their fruition without being "wasted."[15] Kashmiri Vaibhāṣikas, Sautrāntikas, and the Sautrāntika-Svātantrika-Mādhyamika School consider the continuum of mind to be the basis of infusion,[16] while Cittamātrins and the Yogācāra-Svātantrika-Mādhyamika School propound a mind-basis-of-all.

According to Gelukba scholars, Prāsaṅgikas hold that it is not necessary to posit any of these possibilities. Rather, a factor of actions themselves (their disintegratedness), which requires neither intervening causes nor making actions into permanent entities, is responsible for the production of effects. The Prāsaṅgikas have, in fact, made it possible to change the terminology of karmic cause and effect. It is no longer necessary to say that actions establish "seeds" for future effects. It is also no longer necessary to say that they are held in a neutral

---

[13]The Tibetan traditions follow ancient authorities such as Bhāvaviveka in identifying eighteen Vaibhāṣika schools. For a survey of the various ways in which Bhāvaviveka and others distinguished the relationships of the schools, see Hopkins (1983a: 339-41 and 713-19).

[14]Gönchok Jikmay Wangbo, *Precious Garland of Tenets* 21.14-22.2, translated in Sopa and Hopkins (1989: 194). According to Dzongkaba (*Extensive Commentary on the Difficult Points of the "Afflicted Mind and Basis-of-All"* 14b.6), Cittamātrins also assert *prāpti*, although they also assert the mind-basis-of-all.

[15]Lamotte, 1936: 162-63. William Ames gave an interesting paper on "Death and the Non-Disappearance of Karma" on *karmāvipraṇāśa* according to the Sāṃmitīyas at the 1986 AAR meetings.

[16]Gönchok Jikmay Wangbo, *Precious Garland of Tenets* 21.14, translated in Sopa and Hopkins (193).

medium until ripened by appropriate conditions into an individual fruition, for each virtuous or non-virtuous action has a later continuum—its continuum of disintegratedness—that serves to link the action and its effect. It might be said that for Prāsaṅgikas, the disintegratedness of actions simply performs the same functions that, in other explanations, are performed by a karmic seed.

In addition, saying that the disintegratedness of actions produces future effects allows Prāsaṅgikas to avoid explaining that actions persist without disintegrating. This is a consequence that could be flung at proponents of "acquisition" and "non-wastage" and is flung at Daktsang:[17]

> If [as Daktsang says] that which has been done—the utterance of harsh speech, and so forth—produced effects by means of not having disintegrated, then even though many aeons had passed, those [actions which had] not issued forth their effects would have to exist even now. Hence, why is it that even though [the actions of] the three—body, speech, and mind—which were performed in earlier [lifetimes] also would not have been destroyed, they not only are not seen but not remembered? Whoever makes such an explanation has already been refuted earlier.

Daktsang has been interpreted by Jamyang Shayba to hold the idea that actions themselves persist without disintegrating in some manner over time until their effects issue forth. It would then absurdly follow that those actions would exist now, and we would see (experience) them, remember them, and endlessly re-live them.

The remainder of this chapter will, after a section on the position of non-Prāsaṅgikas, examine specific arguments, based on either scripture or reasoning, for considering disintegratedness to be a functioning thing. Whereas the Indian sources for previous "unique tenets" have been somewhat

---

[17] *Great Exposition of Tenets* 39a.2-3. I have not found any place where Daktsang says something like this; it seems likely that Jamyang Shayba is attributing this position to him on the basis of his rejection of disintegratedness as a functioning thing.

slim, in this area there is much to cite from the sūtras and from the seminal Mādhyamikas, Nāgārjuna, Āryadeva, and Candrakīrti. All of the Gelukba authors in this study quote liberally from the Indian sources; Jamyang Shayba, as usual, makes that his main concern, whereas Ngawang Belden often adds the commentaries of Dzongkaba and occasionally cites Kaydrup. As has been the case previously, Candrakīrti is the principal Gelukba source, particularly with regard to four sets of reasonings. However, each Gelukba author treats this material differently. Janggya ignores the reasonings altogether; Jamyang Shayba just announces them and cites a passage from a luminary such as Candrakīrti. Ngawang Belden, however, supplies an analysis of each argument. On the other hand, with regard to the ancillary topic of the three times, Ngawang Belden uncharacteristically adds no annotations to Jamyang Shayba's explanation (which relies on Candrakīrti); also, both Jamyang Shayba and Janggya, but not Ngawang Belden, carefully explain why positing disintegratedness as a functioning thing does not involve ultimate analysis.

Why Non-Prāsaṅgikas Do Not Consider Disintegratedness to Be a Functioning Thing

Proponents of True Existence (*dngos smra ba, bhāvavādin*) is the name Gelukbas give to those who belong to Buddhist tenet systems that propound, explicitly or implicitly, that phenomena necessarily inherently exist. (As before, Gelukbas make such designations based on their interpretation of the manner in which those schools posit phenomena, not necessarily on explicit statements made by them.) As noted earlier, except for the Vaibhāṣika School these schools consider disintegratedness to be a permanent phenomenon. Why? The first reason identified by Janggya and Ngawang Belden[18] (who expand on Dzongkaba's *Illumination of the Thought*), is that the

[18]Janggya, *Presentation of Tenets* 487 (translation chapter 7), and Ngawang Belden, *Annotations* 113b (translation chapter 6).

Proponents of True Existence assume that when an object such as a sprout is destroyed, everything that is part of that sprout is destroyed. Dzongkaba says:[19]

> In the former systems, they think: When a [functioning] thing such as a sprout has disintegrated, everything that is part of the sprout is obliterated. Since one does not get any other thing that is different from a sprout, such as a pot, they assert that disintegratedness is utterly not a [functioning] thing. [Also,] neither the [functioning] things among the separate sense-spheres, such as blue, nor that which is a collection of the [functioning] things which are its parts, such as a pot, are suitable to be illustrations of that [sprout's] disintegratedness. Therefore, [they think that disintegratedness] is not a [functioning] thing.
>
> In the latter [i.e., Prāsaṅgika] system, for example, one cannot posit (1) Upagupta's individual five aggregates, (2) their collection, or (3) that which is a different entity from those two as an illustration of Upagupta, and Upagupta is also unsuitable to be an illustration of those three. However, it is not contradictory that despite that, what is designated as Upagupta in dependence on his aggregates is a [functioning] thing. Similarly, even though disintegratedness also cannot [be posited] as an illustration of either the thing which has been destroyed or anything which is the same type as that [former object], it is a [functioning] thing because it is produced in dependence on a thing that is destroyed.

In other tenet systems it is felt that for something to be a functioning thing there must be an illustration that one can point to, as is the case with a patch of blue or a pot. But concerning the disintegratedness of a pot, what can one point to? Neither a part or quality of the pot, such as its color, nor the pot itself (the whole comprising many parts) is suitable to be an illustration of disintegratedness. Non-Prāsaṅgikas conclude from this that there is no functioning thing that can be a disintegratedness, and hence, disintegratedness must be permanent.

[19]*Illumination of the Thought* 127b.2-6.

For them, a mere nominal designation could not be a functioning thing. An illustration of something must *be* that thing. However, Dzongkaba says that Prāsaṅgikas, who assert that all phenomena are mere nominal designations, have no such problem. Just as it is possible to designate a person named Upagupta in dependence on a certain collection of the aggregates of mind and body even though Upagupta is *not* any of the aggregates, their collection, or a different entity from them (being a mere nominal designation *in dependence on* those aggregates), so it is possible to designate the phenomenon disintegratedness even though it is *not* the thing which has been destroyed or a later moment of similar type of that thing. The crucial point is that Upagupta is merely designated *in dependence upon* his aggregates, not *to* those aggregates.

The Proponents of True Existence do admit the mere nonexistence of the sprout, but they consider this non-existence to be a permanent phenomenon, just as space, the absence of obstructions, is permanent, i.e., non-disintegrating. According to Gelukbas, Prāsaṅgikas reply that although when a sprout is destroyed, it no longer exists, there is in addition to the absence of that sprout a functioning thing, namely, the disintegratedness that is its factor of having disintegrated.[20]

[20]I think that we might add the following points, though they are not explicitly indicated in this context by the Gelukba authors. (1) In principle, that an *aspect* of a thing could exist even when the thing itself does not exist is something accepted even by non-Prāsaṅgikas, for a sprout's futureness (its factor of not yet having arrived despite the existence of its causes because its cooperative conditions have not yet been completed) exists at a time when the sprout does not yet exist. (2) It seems to me that Prāsaṅgikas might further object that if all of something's parts were destroyed along with it, it would not be able to produce an effect in the future. For instance, if all of a virtuous action's parts were destroyed along with it, there would be no way to connect that action to a future effect such as birth as a human being.

Scriptural Proofs That Disintegratedness Is a Functioning Thing

The scriptural proofs used by Janggya, Jamyang Shayba, and Ngawang Belden are based on the passage from the *Sūtra on the Ten Grounds* cited at the beginning of this chapter (though it is asserted that many Perfection of Wisdom sūtras agree): "Aging and death [are produced] by the condition of birth"; and, "Death subsists in two activities: (1) it causes a compounded phenomenon to disintegrate and (2) it issues forth the cause of the non-severance of the continuum of thorough non-knowingness [i.e., ignorance]." They also depend, though to a lesser degree, on the writings of Nāgārjuna, which are considered virtually as authoritative as Buddha's own words. In his *Sixty Stanzas of Reasoning* (*rigs pa drug cu pa, yuktiṣaṣṭika*, 20ab), he says,[21] "Peace [i.e., death] due to exhaustion of causes / Is realized as 'exhaustion.'" That passage is adduced to show that disintegratedness is both caused and acts as a cause.

The first proof from the *Sūtra on the Ten Grounds* is simply the assertion that disintegratedness is a caused phenomenon, based on the statement in that sūtra that, "Aging and death [are produced] from the condition of birth." Because disintegratedness is a caused phenomenon, it is necessarily impermanent and a functioning thing, since caused phenomenon, impermanent phenomenon, and functioning thing are equivalent. None of the Gelukba authors goes on to explain precisely *how* birth causes death; however, on the basis of the example of a butter-lamp dying out, where the lighting of a lamp is the cause of the disintegratedness of the wick and fuel, which in turn causes the disintegratedness ("death") of the lamp, it can be supposed that it is birth that causes the exhaustion of life that in turn causes the death of a person.

The second proof from scripture concerns the statement in that sūtra that "Death subsists in two activities: (1) it causes a

[21]P 5225, vol. 95, 11.4.1. Translations have been produced by Lindtner (1986b: 79) and Tola and Dragonetti (1983: 112).

compounded phenomenon to disintegrate and (2) it issues forth the cause of the non-severance of the continuum of thorough non-knowingness [i.e., ignorance]." Death's two activities are its causing (1) the disintegration of a sentient being and (2) the continuation of ignorance, i.e., the continuity of the karmic residues established directly or indirectly by ignorance, the misconception of an inherently existent self. None of the Gelukba authors explain further the first of these two functions, that death causes the disintegration of a sentient being. Dzongkaba clearly states with reference to the *Sūtra on the Ten Grounds* that[22] "Death is the disintegratedness of a sentient being who has died," but if by "death" in this passage is meant a sentient being's disintegratedness, it in fact could *not* be the cause of a sentient being's disintegration. Disintegration occurs prior to disintegratedness and is *its* cause; similarly, death (or deadness) is caused by dying and is the second phase of the activity of dying. Rather, the passage must either indicate that death is not the disintegratedness of a sentient being or must refer to a second meaning for "death," viz., that death is the disintegratedness not of a sentient being but of the *causes* for the sentient being's life. That "death" has the latter meaning is consistent with the illustration that Dzongkaba himself uses (and which is examined in the following section) of the consumption of the wick and fuel of a butter-lamp. With regard to the consumption of the wick and fuel being the cause of a butter-lamp's dying out he says that the consumption, or disintegratedness, of the wick and fuel is not the disintegratedness of the lamp itself, but only of the *causes* of the lamp. Similarly, with death being understood as the disintegratedness of the *causes* for life and not the disintegratedness of the sentient being who has died, death is indeed the cause of a sentient being's having disintegrated.

Except for the Vaibhāṣika School, Buddhist schools, operating from the Buddha's teaching that all things are impermanent (*mi rtag pa, anitya*), hold that something that disintegrates requires no causes other than its own production in order to

---

[22]Dzongkaba, *Illumination of the Thought* 128a.1.

disintegrate, for disintegration is in its nature. Also, all but the Vaibhāṣika School[23] hold that a thing's production, endurance, and disintegration occur simultaneously. That is because products last for only a single moment, and therefore all the activities associated with its present moment—its "own time"—must occur in that single moment.[24] Since something disintegrates in the same moment it is produced, without the need for any further causes, the causes for the production of something are also the causes for its disintegration. Similarly, the disintegratedness of those causes is the cause for the disintegratedness of the thing itself. If something's causes did not disintegrate, the thing would continue, whereas if they disintegrate, the thing also disintegrates. The causes of a thing's production, endurance, and disintegration occur in the moment prior to its "own time" (the moment it is present). The disintegrated*ness* of those causes occurs in the next moment, the "own time" of the thing itself, the moment of its production, endurance, and disintegration. Therefore, the disintegratedness of a thing's causes brings about the disintegratedness of the thing itself in a subsequent moment.

Death is also said to cause the non-severance of the continuum of ignorance. That is, death causes the continuation of the karmic latencies generated directly or indirectly by ignorance (for even latencies produced by desire, hatred, etc., are produced on a basis of ignorance). As long as death and disintegratedness are equated (i.e., that death is taken to mean "deadness"), this is basically another way of saying that the disintegratedness of an action preserves its potency to produce an effect until the time of its fruition. The latencies, of course, must be carried over to succeeding transmigrations or the whole doctrine of action and effect would collapse. Actually, death must preserve more than just the continuum of ignorance, for Arhats, who also die and are reborn (though

---

[23]Gönchok Jikmay Wangbo, *Precious Garland of Tenets* 22.4-7. Translated in Sopa and Hopkins (1989: 195).

[24]Hopkins (1983a: 350), paraphrasing Ngawang Belden, *Annotations*. See the chart, later in this chapter, for all the possibilities of a single moment.

not due to the force of afflictive karma) have predispositions for mistaken dualistic appearance—the obstructions to omniscience—that are established by ignorance and must be carried over.

In addition to these proofs based on the *Sūtra on the Ten Grounds*, Jamyang Shayba also attempts to show that Nāgārjuna himself held that disintegratedness is a functioning thing, because in the *Treatise on the Middle Way* in the chapter on nirvāṇa (XXV.13) Nāgārjuna says:[25]

> How can nirvāṇa
> Be both a thing and the non-existence of a thing?
> Nirvāṇa is an uncompounded phenomenon
> And things and the non-existence of things [i.e., their disintegratedness] are compounded phenomena.

This stanza forms a portion of Nāgārjuna's refutation of the four extremes concerning nirvāṇa, which are, according to Gelukba exegetes: that it is a [functioning] thing; that it is a non-thing [i.e., a thing's having become non-existent, its disintegratedness, which is also a thing]; that it is both a thing and a non-thing; or that it is neither. Here he says that nirvāṇa is not both a thing and non-thing because those are both caused whereas nirvāṇa is uncaused. This unusual interpretation of the term "non-thing" (*dngos med, abhāva*) as a disintegratedness, and hence a functioning thing, rests on Candrakīrti's comments[26] that a thing is caused and thus is a compounded phenomenon, but so also is a non-thing, since it arises in dependence on a thing and the *Sūtra on the Ten Grounds* says that aging and death are caused by birth. In brief, according to Gelukba exegetes, even though the main point of the pas-

---

[25]P 5224, vol. 95, 10.1.5-6. The Sanskrit (Poussin 531) is: *bhaved abhāvo bhāvaś ca nirvāṇam ubhyaṃ kathaṃ/ asaṃskrtaṃ ca nirvāṇaṃ bhāvābhāvau ca saṃskṛtau.* The quotation has been lengthened by including the first two lines of the stanza. A similar passage from Gyeltsap can be found in the Jamyang Shayba translation, chapter 8, in the section on true cessations.

[26]*Clear Words* 356.2-3. Following upon this, Jamyang Shayba glosses "sprout's disintegratedness" by "*dngos med* of a sprout" which could only refer to a sprout's non-existence upon its disintegration, not non-existence, which, unlike disintegratedness, is not an impermanent phenomenon.

sage is to show that nirvāṇa is uncompounded, it also shows that Nāgārjuna classifies disintegratedness as a thing, i.e., as a compounded phenomenon. Ngawang Belden relates Nāgārjuna's statement on non-things to not asserting inherent existence:[27]

> [Nāgārjuna] says that both a [functioning] thing and its absence upon its destruction are compounded phenomena because that also has its source in not asserting that [a phenomenon is established] by its own character (*rang mtshan, svalakṣaṇa*).

Ngawang Belden sees Nāgārjuna as rejecting the attempt to label disintegratedness as a permanent phenomenon, i.e., a non-affirming negative, because that would involve the assertion of an inherently existent entity, one findable upon analysis. Ngawang Belden does not explain this further, but clearly sees this as a support for the sort of argument that Jamyang Shayba makes, discussed later in this chapter, that the assertion of disintegratedness as a non-affirming negative involves ultimate analysis.

Logical Proofs That Disintegratedness Is a Functioning Thing

In addition to their scriptural proofs, Prāsaṅgikas set forth a number of reasonings concerning disintegratedness. The principal arguments are made by Candrakīrti in his *Clear Words,* where he sets forth four reasons to prove that disintegratedness is a functioning thing. However, let us first turn to the earlier statements of Nāgārjuna and his chief disciple, Āryadeva.

Nāgārjuna, in his *Sixty Stanzas of Reasoning* (*rigs pa drug cu pa, yuktiṣaṣṭika*) states that death (the disintegratedness of a

[27]*Annotations,* note *ra,* 113b.1.

sentient being) is caused by the exhaustion of causes for the continuation of life:[28]

> Peace [i.e., death] due to exhaustion of causes
> Is realized as "exhaustion."

Candrakīrti comments that:[29]

> . . . since if the conditions for remaining are not complete, it disintegrates. In accordance with that, in the world that which is extinct or used up is observed as "exhausted" due to only the exhaustion of its causes....According to those whose thought is that the cessation of things is only causeless, ceasedness also would [absurdly] not depend on [functioning] things because of being causeless like a flower in the sky.

Dzongkaba comments:[30]

> The subsistence of [functioning] things depends upon conditions that cause subsistence because if the conditions for subsistence are not present, [the continua of things] would disintegrate. Therefore, the extinguishment and cessation of a butter-lamp's light, which arises from the extinguishment and cessation of the causes that make [the butter-lamp] subsist—the wick, oil, and so forth—is observed to be "extinguishment and cessation."

---

[28]P 5225, vol. 95, 11.4.1. The stanza (20) continues: "How is what is not [inherently] exhausted/ Called 'exhausted'?" See translations by Lindtner (1986b: 79) and Tola and Dragonetti (1983: 112).

[29]In Jamyang Shayba's text, this work is referred to simply as "the commentary on that" (*de'i 'grel pa*); since Nāgārjuna's own commentary has not been preserved in any language (see Tola and Dragonetti [1983: 95, 177, n. 1]), it is assumed that this refers to Candrakīrti's commentary, *Commentary on (Nāgārjuna's) "Sixty Stanzas of Reasoning"* (*rigs pa drug cu pa'i 'grel pa, yuktiṣaṣṭikavṛtti*), and a passage similar to this occurs there (P 5265, vol. 98, 177.2.4-5). However, this appears to be a paraphrase rather than a quotation. There is a debate on the consumption of the wick and butter in Candrakīrti's commentary (Toh. 3864, vol. 7) 15b.5 ff.

[30]*Ocean of Reasoning, Explanation of (Nāgārjuna's) "Treatise on the Middle Way,"* cited in Ngawang Belden's *Annotations* 113b.6.

They say that disintegratedness obviously has a cause because a lamp dies out as a result of the consumption of its wick and fuel. Since the lamp would endure unless its causes came to be absent, it must be forced to go out. The destruction of the wick and fuel serves as the cause for the lamp's disintegratedness. Also, the example of the lamp shows that disintegratedness is a functioning thing because it *acts* as a cause; the disintegratedness of the wick and fuel causes the dying out of the lamp.[31]

Āryadeva adds that the disintegratedness of a cause is generated by the production of an effect. Dzongkaba cites him immediately after the passage quoted above:

> Āryadeva's *Four Hundred* (IX.18ab) says:[32]
>
> > Effects destroy causes.
> > Therefore, a non-existent is not what is produced.
>
> This explains that the cause's ceasedness is caused by the effect's being produced, whereby [such] is the assertion of the Superior (Nāgārjuna) and his spiritual son (Āryadeva).
>
> Through the essential point of asserting that the pastness that is the disintegratedness of a sprout is a [functioning] thing, even the futureness of a sprout is likewise [a functioning thing]. Therefore, [that] is the meaning of [Āryadeva's saying], "a non-existent is not what is produced."

For instance, the "being produced" (*skye bzhin pa*) or "approaching production" (*skye ba la mngon du phyogs pa*) of an effect is simultaneous with the disintegration or approaching to disintegratedness of the cause. Since, if the causes for something's subsistence are not destroyed, it remains, it is neces-

---

[31]In the same way, it seems, the disintegratedness of the impelling karma of a sentient being causes the death of that person. None of the authors under consideration explicitly makes this connection, but it seems to follow.

[32]P 5246, vol. 95, 136.5.7. P reads: *'bras bu yi ni rgyu bshig pa/ des na rgyu ni rtag ma yin* ("Effects destroy causes./ Therefore, causes are not permanent.") Ngawang Belden's version is quite different: *'bras bu yis ni rgyu bshig pa/ des na med pa skye mi 'gyur*. Cf. Sonam 210.

sary that an effect be produced to interrupt the continuance of the thing. Hence, the production of a thing serves as a cause of the disintegratedness of the causes; Āryadeva says, "Effects destroy causes." Applied to the example of seed and sprout, the production of a sprout brings about the destruction of the seed that is *its* cause.[33]

Candrakīrti's First Argument

Let us now turn to arguments employed by Candrakīrti. Candrakīrti uses four sets of reasonings in his *Clear Words* to show that disintegration (and, according to Gelukbas, disintegratedness) is a functioning thing. Although Candrakīrti himself does not seem to explicitly distinguish between "disintegration" and "disintegratedness," it seems clear, from his fourth reasoning if nowhere else (it uses the example of a crop perishing due to water *having* evaporated), that he wishes to show that something's absence upon its disintegration—its disintegratedness—is a functioning thing.

The first of the those four is: if disintegratedness were not a functioning thing, it would absurdly follow that disintegration could not be a characteristic of compounded phenomena. Candrakīrti says, in his *Clear Words*:[34]

> According to those who, having asserted that disintegration [i.e., disintegration and disintegratedness] is causeless, propound that all compounded phenomena are momentary, disintegration would be non-existent because of being causeless like a flower in the sky. Therefore, it would be contradictory to establish that things are momentary and that those [things you propound that are] devoid of disinte-

[33]It seems to me that this also shows that causes are dependent on effects in the sense that it is through the production of an effect that something comes to be designated as a cause.

[34]*Clear Words*, 117.4-5 (59a.4-5). Sanskrit is in Poussin (1970: 174). The quotation has been restored to full length by filling in the middle, from "disintegration would be non-existent" to "Because of that."

> gration are compounded phenomena. Because of that, all of these [assertions] would not fit together.

A "sky-flower" is a famous instance of a non-existent (like "son of a barren woman," "cloak of turtle hairs," or "horns of a rabbit"). Candrakīrti flings the absurd consequence that if disintegration were causeless, it would be a "sky-flower." If compounded phenomena did not disintegrate, there would be no disintegration. However, those phenomena would absurdly not be momentary or compounded.

Disintegration, along with production, endurance, and aging, is a characteristic of compounded phenomena—functioning things—that also characterizes something *as* a compounded phenomenon. Some terms that are characteristics *of* compounded phenomena do not characterize them *as* compounded phenomena. For instance, emptiness is a characteristic *of* all phenomena, but does not characterize something *as* a compounded phenomenon because it is not unique to compounded phenomena and therefore would not help one to understand something as a compounded phenomenon. Jamyang Shayba cites Dzongkaba's *Ocean of Reasoning, Explanation of (Nāgārjuna's) "Treatise on the Middle Way"*:[35]

> The activity of blue's disintegration includes the disintegratedness in its second period. And, whatever are non-associated compositional factors must be compounded by their causes and conditions, whereby they are established as having causes.

Jamyang Shayba concludes:

> It follows that blue is the agent and that the four, blue's activities of production, disintegration, abiding, and aging, characterize blue as a compounded phenomenon because (1) it is contradictory for blue itself to be its own activity and (2) blue's own activity of characterizing blue as a compounded phenomenon exists.

---

[35]*Great Exposition of the Middle Way* 610.6-11.3.

Thus, disintegratedness is a characteristic that causes one to understand what a compounded phenomenon is. It is argued that if disintegration were not a functioning thing, it would be causeless and therefore not a characteristic of compounded phenomena. Then, how could things be momentary? They would not disintegrate.

In Jamyang Shayba's *Great Exposition of the Middle Way*[36] the argument takes a slightly different tack: he asks how disintegration could be a characteristic that causes one to understand compounded phenomena if the activity of disintegration had no causes:

> It [absurdly] follows that the disintegration of a sprout is not suitable as a characteristic that causes one to understand compounded phenomena because [according to you] the disintegrating of a sprout and the activity of disintegration [of a sprout] have no causes.

In that case, disintegration would be like emptiness in the sense that although it would be a *characteristic* of compounded phenomena, it would not *characterize* compounded phenomena because it could not help one understand compounded phenomena *as* compounded phenomena.

Other schools might reply that although *disintegration* is caused, disintegrat*edness* is uncaused. According to Kaydrup, the Prāsaṅgika response to this is that if there were no causes for something's disintegratedness, there would be no causes for its disintegration, and then the thing itself could not be momentary. Kaydrup makes the parallel that "approaching to production" (*skye ba la mngon du phyogs pa*) has causes and so does production, a premise that no one would deny; his *Opening the Eyes of the Fortunate* says:[37]

> In brief, does the disintegratedness of a sprout exist or not exist without relying on causes? If it does, it is contradictory that a sprout does not disintegrate without depending on

---

[36]*Great Exposition of the Middle Way* 609.6 ff.

[37]*Opening the Eyes of the Fortunate* (Mādhyamika Text Series, vol. 1, New Delhi, 1972), 371.6-72.2. Cf. Cabezón (1992: 313).

> causes, and if it does not, it is contradictory that the disintegratedness of a sprout does not depend on causes. Since "approaching to disintegratedness" is called "disintegration" (*'jig pa*) it is very contradictory that approaching to disintegratedness depends on causes whereas disintegratedness does not depend on causes. Otherwise, it would [absurdly] equally follow that even though approaching to production is caused by causes, producedness is not caused by causes.

Just as both approaching to production and production have causes, so approaching to disintegratedness (i.e., disintegration) has causes and so also must its effect, disintegratedness.

Of course, in one sense, disintegration *is* causeless, for it requires no causes *in addition to* the object's own causes; the same causes that produce a sprout cause its disintegration. But it is not actually causeless, for it does have *those* causes. Just so, disintegratedness has the causes of the thing as its indirect causes and has disintegration as its direct cause. Disintegration's principal activity is disintegratedness.[38] In fact, Dzongkaba goes so far as to say (in his *Ocean of Reasoning*) that something's disintegratedness is its *impermanence* because it is its having disintegrated after a time when it had not disintegrated:[39]

> The reason why a disintegratedness that is blue's activity of disintegrating must be posited is that the two, blue's not having disintegrated at its own time and having disintegrated at a second time, are indicated as equally [functioning] things or not [functioning] things; in that case, its disintegratedness also is its impermanence.

However, just because a thing's disintegration and disintegratedness—respectively, its not enduring and not having endured—equally do or do not have causes does not mean that

[38] *Great Exposition of the Middle Way* 610.1.

[39] Cited in Jamyang Shayba's *Great Exposition of the Middle Way* 611.6-12.1. This indicates that the thing is impermanent—but does it show that disintegratedness is equivalent to impermanence? Perhaps disintegratedness, being something's not having endured, i.e., not having been permanent, is also something's impermanence.

they are produced simultaneously from one cause. This would be absurd because, for example, a pot and a rabbit equally have causes but do not have the *same* causes. A pot's disintegration and a pot have the same causes, and a pot's disintegratedness is caused by the disintegration of the pot or the disintegratedness of the pot's causes. For example, the disintegratedness of a lamp is due to the exhaustion or disintegratedness of the lamp's causes (i.e., the disintegration of the lamp), the causes for the lamp's remaining having become incomplete.[40]

Candrakīrti's Second Argument

Candrakīrti's first argument was that if disintegratedness were not a functioning thing, it could not be posited as characterizing compounded phenomena. His second argument is that if disintegratedness were not a functioning thing, nothing would be produced by causes. He says, in his *Clear Words*:[41]

> *Objection:* Since this called disintegration [i.e., disintegratedness[42]] is a non-[functioning] thing, of what use are causes to a non-thing?
>
> *Response*: Is it not the case that [functioning] things also would be causeless? For [functioning] things already exist, and of what use are causes for that which exists? What already exists is not produced again. Hence, it would [absurdly] follow that [functioning] things would be causeless in all respects. Therefore, that is not feasible.

The argument is a response to a hypothetical opponent who thinks that because, for instance, the disintegratedness of a seed already exists as a non-thing (in his view), it needs no

---

[40]*Great Exposition of the Middle Way* 613.5.

[41]*Clear Words*, 117.7-18.1; Sanskrit is in Poussin, 174.2-4. The quotation has been lengthened by adding to first sentence, the objection, and filling in between, "For..." and "...in all respects."

[42]According to Ngawang Belden, Candrakīrti considers disintegration and disintegratedness equally to be functioning things.

causes. Candrakīrti points out that, of course, something that already exists needs no causes and that if this person's position were taken to its logical extreme, it would absurdly follow that causes would be unnecessary for anything because nothing that exists needs causes. What the person really means to say is that something that already exists needs no *further* causes, that is, no causes in addition to those that produced it, to which Candrakīrti replies that disintegratedness also needs no further causes than those that produced it.

In fairness to the opponent, it seems that Candrakīrti may have ignored a vital part of his argument, namely that since disintegratedness is a non-thing, it is an uncaused phenomenon. In other words, the opponent's argument is not really that since disintegratedness exists, it needs no causes, for no school denies that although some phenomena that exist (i.e., permanent phenomena) require no causes, all others do; but rather, it is that the uncaused phenomenon disintegratedness needs no causes. In that case, Candrakīrti's response ought to have been to prove that disintegratedness is caused. Jamyang Shayba apparently notices this,[43] remarking:

> Candrakīrti says that it is feasible to assert that the disintegratedness of a sprout is a [functioning] thing because the disintegratedness of a sprout is a [functioning] thing in relation to its own entity and is the non-existence of a thing in relation to a sprout. That follows because it is both (1) a thing due to not having disintegrated in relation to its own entity and (2) the non-existence upon cessation of a thing that is a sprout in relation to a sprout.

In other words, Candrakīrti says that although disintegratedness is the non-existence of a thing, it is a "non-thing" in relation to a sprout but a thing in relation to its own entity.

---

[43]*Great Exposition of the Middle Way* 614.1 ff.

Candrakīrti's Third Argument

The third argument Candrakīrti makes in his *Clear Words* is that disintegratedness is a functioning thing because it is newly produced. He says:[44]

> Furthermore, just as production has causes because [something] did not previously exist and because it did exist later, just so, disintegration [i.e., disintegration and disintegratedness] also should be asserted [to have causes].

The argument is simply that since it is admitted that, for instance, a seed's disintegratedness exists at the time of a sprout, but did not exist earlier, it must have been caused. Its earlier non-existence and later existence are adduced as proof of its having been newly produced.

This would be a powerful reasoning were it not flawed by the fact that there are "occasionally permanent" phenomena that earlier do not exist, but later do, and nevertheless are not functioning things.[45] For instance, until the production of a table, there is no space of a table nor is there an emptiness of inherent existence of the table, but after its production those come into being. They are not considered "newly produced," for "production" is a term appropriately applied only to functioning things. Being mere absences, the space and emptiness of the table are simply "occasional permanent phenomena," permanent not in the sense of being everlasting but in the basic sense of not disintegrating moment-by-moment. Therefore, the fact that a seed's disintegratedness once did not exist but now exists does not itself prove that the seed's disintegratedness is a functioning thing. The argument is saved if by "exist later" is meant "arises later," that is, produced later.

---

[44]*Clear Words* 118.1. Sanskrit is in Poussin 174.5-6.

[45]On occasional permanent phenomena, see Hopkins (1983a: 216).

Candrakīrti's Fourth Argument

The fourth reason given in Candrakīrti's *Clear Words* is that it is well known in the world that disintegratedness is a functioning thing. Candrakīrti frequently sounds the theme of accepting what the world accepts, so it is not surprising that in the end he appeals to the common sense of the world. In the *Heap of Jewels Sūtra* (*dkon mchog btsegs pa'i mdo, ratnakūṭa-sūtra*), Buddha says, "What is asserted to exist in the world, that I also assert to exist." Āryadeva adds in his *Four Hundred* [VIII.21cd]):[46] "Except with the worldly, one is unable to approach the world." Candrakīrti himself says in his *Commentary on (Nāgārjuna's) "Sixty Stanzas of Reasoning"*:[47]

> Worldly things are not to be asserted through scrutiny and analysis. How then? In accordance with what is well known in the world.

In general, whatever is well known in the world is accepted as existing conventionally, except for what cannot be established by valid cognition. In the last chapter, we saw that Ngawang Belden makes a distinction between what is well known in the world (which seems to be synonymous with what conventionally exists) and what is well known to an ordinary worldly awareness (which does not have to meet the criterion of being established by valid cognition). Since Candrakīrti criticizes some of what ordinary people say, his use of the phrase "well known in the world" must refer to what conventionally exists.

In any case, that disintegratedness is well known in the world is a necessary if not sufficient condition for the conventional existence of disintegratedness that is a thing. Worldly conventions are the phenomena established by conventional valid cognition. They are not to be refuted by reasoned investigation (*'thad pa*), that is, ultimate analysis.

---

[46]P 5246, vol. 95, 136.3.5-6. The two lines prior to this are: *ji ltar kla klo skad gzhan gyis / gzung bar mi nus de bzhin du.* Cf. Sonam 197.

[47]P 5265, vol. 98, 177.4.2. Toh. 3864, vol. 7, 8.3.6.

With regard to disintegratedness, the world often says that disintegratedness acts as a cause. For instance, if a farmer's field of wheat withers due to drought, it is said that the lack of water—its having been consumed through evaporation—is the cause of the crop's failure. Similarly, a child that perishes from starvation is said to die from lack of food—food's having been consumed.[48] Candrakīrti says:[49]

> In the world, even non-existence exists as just a cause. For as in "If there is no water, my grain will be ruined," and "My child will die from lack of food," the loss of grain and child is propounded to occur due to the non-existence of water and food [respectively].

Hence, according to Candrakīrti, the world clearly holds that disintegratedness, though negative, is an affirming negative rather than a non-affirming negative, implying a positive phenomenon, i.e., a causal phenomenon. Similarly, Jamyang Shayba asserts that "disintegratedness of a sprout" implies the sprout in dependence on which disintegratedness arises,[50] and Dzongkaba asserts that it implies a functioning thing:[51]

> That which has disintegrated [i.e., a disintegratedness] is not a mere elimination, but implies a [functioning] thing that involves an elimination of that.

Janggya adds:[52]

---

[48]An obvious objection would seem to be that it *is* a mere absence—of water and of food—that causes the death of the wheat and the child. It could be the case that in those spots there was no water or food to begin with—that the wheat and/or child are abandoned in a rocky place, for instance. Thus, no "having been consumed" is involved. On the other hand, perhaps one could say that the dryness of the place has been caused through previous evaporation, making it a functioning thing that in turn can bring about the death of that which attempts to depend on it for life.

[49]*Commentary on (Nāgārjuna's) "Sixty Stanzas of Reasoning"* (P 5265, vol. 98, 177.4.2-4; also in chapter 6 of the Jamyang Shayba translation.

[50]*Great Exposition of the Middle Way* 625.5.

[51]In *Illumination of the Thought*, cited in the *Great Exposition of the Middle Way* 626.1.

[52]Janggya, *Presentation of Tenets* 489.20.

> The term "sprout's disintegratedness" serves both to eliminate a sprout's not having disintegrated and to imply that the disintegration of a sprout occurs in dependence on the sprout.

Thus, disintegratedness is an affirming negative because it implies an activity of a sprout, not merely an elimination. That is, a sprout's merely not existing is a non-affirming negative, but the non-existence of a sprout upon its destruction is its disintegratedness, a functioning thing.

In a similar way, a futureness is an affirming rather than a non-affirming negative. Both Janggya and Jamyang Shayba contend that "sprout's futureness" implies (1) that the sprout will be produced when its conditions are complete or (2) a thing that is the non-completion of conditions. A sprout is implied, a sprout being a positive phenomenon. The sprout does not yet exist, but it is not necessary that the existent implied by an affirming negative exist at the present time.

Dzongkaba's Argument

Let us now turn to an argument made by Dzongkaba and commented upon by Janggya. Dzongkaba in his *Illumination of the Thought, Explanation of (Candrakīrti's) "Entrance"* contends that there is a parallel between birth and death on the one hand and disintegration (a thing's not remaining for another moment beyond its own time) and disintegratedness (its not *having* remained for another moment beyond its own time) on the other:[53]

> This [example of a sentient being's death has concerned] the disintegratedness of a continuum, but it is the same for the disintegratedness of the first moment [of a phenomenon] at its next period, and it also indicates that the first moment [of a phenomenon] is a cause of its disintegratedness in the next period. Therefore, with respect to the two, the birth and death of a sentient being, [and the two,] not enduring in the

[53]*Illumination of the Thought* 127b.6-28a.4.

> next period and not having endured in the next period, whether they are posited or not posited as [functioning] things and whether they are produced or not produced by causes is the same in every way.

Janggya paraphrases this:[54]

> The reasoning is: (1) the birth and death of a sentient being and (2) something not remaining for a second moment and not having remained for a second moment are proved to be thoroughly similar in terms of whether or not they are posited as [functioning] things and whether or not they depend on causes.

The present moment of a thing, its existing but not enduring for another moment, is the cause of its own disintegratedness, its not having endured. In other words, moment A is the cause of the disintegratedness of moment A, which occurs in moment B. Similarly, birth, a sentient being's having been born, is that sentient being's life or endurance and his/her not remaining for another moment after his/her (karmically allotted) time, just as disintegration corresponds to the time in which something is present and is that thing's not remaining for another moment beyond that time. Death, the sentient being's having died, is his/her not *having* remained for another moment beyond that time, just as disintegratedness is something's not having remained for another moment beyond its own time.

There are also parallels to disintegration and disintegratedness just with birth itself and just with death itself.[55] Regarding birth, a sentient being's "being born" (*skye bzhin pa*) or "approaching birth" (*skye ba la mngon du phyogs pa*), the moment before birth (birth in this case being the moment of conception, which then is the first moment of life), is a sentient being's not remaining for another moment in the state of

---

[54]Janggya, *Presentation of Tenets* 488.

[55]This paragraph is based on the discussion of the three times in the *Great Exposition of Tenets* and *Great Exposition of the Middle Way* by Jamyang Shayba and the *Presentation of Tenets* by Janggya, which are summarized near the end of this chapter.

futureness, or, put another way, is a sentient being's futureness not remaining for another moment. Birth, the sentient being's having been born, is that sentient being's futureness not having remained for another moment. Similarly, with regard to death, dying (approaching death) is a sentient being's not remaining for another moment; death, a sentient being's having died, is that being's not having remained for another moment. (A table setting out some of these relationships and those that are similar is at the end of this chapter in the discussion of the three times.)

These examples have involved the severance of some continuum—the continuum of a sentient being's futureness, for birth, and the continuum of the sentient being himself or herself, for death—but the parallels can be upheld for any moment in that continuum. For instance, the present moment of a pot has been produced by its previous moment and will produce a subsequent moment of that pot unless a necessary condition for its production has ceased. If, for instance, someone were to break the pot, the pot would no longer produce another moment of itself.

Jamyang Shayba on Ultimate Analysis

Having surveyed the various arguments made by Indian and Tibetan Prāsaṅgikas in support of the thesis that disintegratedness is a functioning thing, let us turn to Jamyang Shayba's discussion of ultimate analysis, which occurs in the context of his criticism of Daktsang. Among the many contradictions Daktsang thought he had discovered in Dzongkaba's works, one concerned Dzongkaba's alleged positing of disintegratedness as something found upon analysis. Jamyang Shayba, in turn, used Daktsang's objection to accuse him of holding that disintegratedness is not a functioning thing.

What Daktsang actually said was:[56]

---

[56] *Ocean of Good Explanations* 235.3-5.

> No pot other than the phenomena that are its discrete parts is found when the parts of a pot—its form, odor, and so forth—are analyzed by reasoning. It is contradictory to assert this and yet find, in the face of analysis, a thing that is a disintegratedness that is different from an action's continuum of similar type (*las rang gi rigs 'dra'i rgyun*) due to analyzing the moments of an action, because both the object analyzed and the mode of analysis are completely the same.

In other words, Daktsang seems to be saying that if one holds that when a pot's parts are analyzed, no pot is found apart from or among them (a statement with which all Prāsaṅgikas would presumably agree, for a pot is not its parts or separate from them, but merely imputed in dependence on them), then similarly, when the moments of an action are analyzed, one should hold that no disintegratedness is found among or apart from the action's continuum of similar type. However, this is precisely what he sees in Dzongkaba's analysis. Let us again look at what Dzongkaba said in his *Illumination of the Thought, Explanation of (Candrakīrti's) "Entrance"*:[57]

> In the former systems, they think: When a [functioning] thing such as a sprout has disintegrated, everything that is part of the sprout is obliterated. Since one does not get any other thing that is different from a sprout, such as a pot, they assert that disintegratedness is utterly not a [functioning] thing [i.e., they assert that it is a permanent or non-disintegrating phenomenon. Also,] neither the [functioning] things among the separate sense-spheres, such as blue, nor that which is a collection of the [functioning] things which are its parts, such as a pot, are suitable to be illustrations of that disintegratedness [of a sprout]. Therefore, [disintegratedness] is not a [functioning] thing.
>
> In the latter [i.e., Prāsaṅgika] system, for example, one cannot posit (1) Upagupta's individual five aggregates, (2) their collection, or (3) that which is a different entity from those two as an illustration of Upagupta, and Upagupta is also unsuitable to be an illustration of those three. However, it is not contradictory that despite that, what is designated as Upagupta in dependence on his aggregates is a [function-

[57] *Illumination of the Thought* 127b.2-6.

> ing] thing. Similarly, even though disintegratedness also cannot [be posited] as an illustration of either the thing which has been destroyed or anything which is the same type [i.e., same causal continuum] as that, it is a [functioning] thing because it is produced in dependence on a thing that is destroyed.

Dzongkaba says that concerning the disintegratedness of a pot, neither a part or quality of the pot, such as its color, nor the pot itself (the whole comprising many parts) is suitable to be an illustration of disintegratedness. The other tenet systems conclude from this that there is no functioning thing that can be a disintegratedness, and hence, disintegratedness must be permanent. In other tenet systems, it is felt that for something to be a functioning thing there must be an illustration that one can point to, as is the case with a patch of blue or a pot. For them, a mere nominal designation could not be a functioning thing.

Dzongkaba replies that even though someone called Upagupta is not his five aggregates, nor vice versa, nevertheless, Upagupta can be posited *in dependence on* those aggregates. He then goes on to say that disintegratedness can be posited neither as an illustration of the thing nor of the continuum of similar type of that thing (for an illustration of something must *be* that thing). This may be how Daktsang got the notion that Dzongkaba considers the disintegratedness of an action to be different from its continuum of similar type. A subtle distinction must be made: disintegratedness is *not* the continuum of similar type of, for instance, an act of giving, for that would mean that the disintegratedness of that action would itself *be* an act of giving. Nevertheless, it is possible to designate the phenomenon, disintegratedness, in dependence on the act of giving, even though it is *not* the giving which has been destroyed or some other thing like it. It is merely designated *in dependence on* the thing that has been destroyed, just as Upagupta is merely designated *in dependence upon* his aggregates, not *to* those aggregates. On the other hand, it is not found separate from the continuum of similar type of the action, for that is the basis in dependence on which it is imputed. Thus, the disintegratedness of an action can be found neither as nor separate from its continuum of similar type; to posit it as either of these possibilities would be to claim that something can be found upon ultimate analysis.

With regard to ultimate analysis, Jamyang Shayba specifically denies that disintegratedness is posited by way of performing an analytical search. He cites Candrakīrti's *Commentary on (Āryadeva's) "Four Hundred"*:

> Even though a very long time has passed and gone after the cessation of an action which was done and accumulated, [the action itself] indeed does not persist, but nevertheless, effects actually arise even from actions with many aeons intervening after their cessation.

Jamyang Shayba then comments:[58]

> His mere propounding that disintegratedness is a [functioning] thing is not a matter of searching for the imputed object, a disintegratedness, because merely analyzing whether disintegratedness is a thing or a non-thing does not constitute ultimate analysis. And, for example, it is like propounding that a pot is a [functioning] thing. Otherwise, there would be much that is damaging and contradictory, such as that even your propounding that disintegratedness is not a [functioning] thing would be a matter of searching for an imputed object; however, as was said earlier, merely analyzing whether or not disintegratedness has causes does *not* constitute a search for an imputed object because it merely explains the way in which [things] act as cause and condition conventionally, like, for example, the explanation in the texts of manifest knowledge of the causes and conditions of compounded phenomena.

In other words, it is not being claimed that disintegratedness is findable as, or apart from, an action's later continuum of similar type, simply that disintegratedness conventionally has causes and effects, as the world says. It is no different than positing a pot as a functioning thing because one can observe

---

[58]*Great Exposition of Tenets* 38b.7-39a.1.

its causes, such as the clay, potter, and fire. One would cross over into ultimate analysis if in searching for the cause of an object one were to claim that it was either the object itself or inherently other than the object, as would be the case if in the analysis of the going out of a butter-lamp one claimed that the going out was self-generated—that the lamp itself caused its own going-out—or that it was inherently different from the exhaustion of the wick and fuel, which conventionally is its cause. Investigating the *mere* causes of something is not ultimate analysis; it is only when one holds that those causes are inherently one or different from their effect that the line between conventional and ultimate analysis has been crossed. Once again, whether or not one's analysis constitutes ultimate analysis stems from whether or not one holds the Prāsaṅgika view that denies inherent existence but that allows nominal conventional existence.

Ngawang Belden's Objections to Jamyang Shayba

Before passing on to the topic of the three times, let us look briefly at two criticisms of Jamyang Shayba by Ngawang Belden on the subject of disintegratedness. Ngawang Belden is not afraid to disagree with Jamyang Shayba or to point out ambiguities in his writings (though often he does so discreetly, citing Jamyang Shayba and adding, this "should be analyzed"). With regard to disintegratedness, Ngawang Belden calls into question two statements of Jamyang Shayba in the *Great Exposition of the Middle Way*: (1) there is no disintegratedness of the obstructions to omniscience in the continuum of a Buddha Superior; and (2) if something is to be posited as a pastness or a futureness, it must not be totally consumed. Jamyang Shayba's statement is:[59]

> *Incorrect Position*: It follows that there is disintegratedness of subtle obstructions to omniscience in the continuum of a

[59]*Great Exposition of the Middle Way* 628.3-5.

Buddha Superior because those have disintegrated in the continuum of a Buddha Superior.

Correct Position: Although some assert that, there is no entailment [that because subtle obstructions to omniscience have disintegrated in the continuum of a Buddha Superior that there necessarily is disintegratedness of those in the continuum of a Buddha Superior]. Then, [for you] it would [absurdly] follow that the horns of a rabbit are a future phenomenon because the horns of a rabbit have not come. The three circles!!!

If the [consequence] above were accepted, it would [absurdly] follow that past obstructions to omniscience would exist in the continuum of a Buddha Superior because of that assertion. That cannot be accepted because those have been totally exhausted without remainder in the element of qualities in the continuum of a Buddha Superior. The reason is easy [to prove]. There is entailment [that because obstructions to omniscience have been totally exhausted without remainder in the element of qualities it cannot be accepted that the disintegratedness of subtle obstructions to omniscience exists in the continuum of a Buddha Superior] because to posit [something as a] pastness or futureness it is necessary that it not be totally consumed or totally destroyed.

In other words, the fact that the obstructions to omniscience have disintegrated does not mean that their disintegratedness exists. Disintegratedness implies an effect to come out, but there is none here. Still, why not say that Buddha's omniscience is the effect? Ngawang Belden cites Dzongkaba to make his point:[60]

Dzongkaba's *Ocean of Reasoning, Explanation of (Nāgārjuna's) "Treatise on the Middle Way"* says:[61]

Therefore, these causes and effects such as seeds and sprouts must be posited in the manner seen by people in the world. In the world, saying, "My rice spoiled due to lack of water," and, "My son died due to lack of food,"

---

[60]*Annotations* 114b.3-6.

[61]*Ocean of Reasoning*, 191.6-12.

> are cases of propounding that through the non-existence of the former the latter is lost. Moreover, just as the non-extinction of food and water are taken to be the causes of a child's being alive and rice being good, the extinction of those is posited as the cause of the extinction of [child and rice]. Therefore, those [things] which have not become extinct are different from those which do not exist [i.e., have become extinct]; through that the class of effects from those [things which have become non-existent] should also be understood.

That explains that the disintegratedness of a continuum is a [functioning] thing; even though those [actions] are totally consumed or totally destroyed, [their effects] appear to exist.[62] Therefore, there appear to be great bases for analysis with respect to the statements in Jamyang Shayba's *Great Exposition of the Middle Way (dbu ma chen mo)*[63] that (1) the disintegratedness of obstructions to omniscience does not exist in the continuum of a Buddha Superior and (2) that in order to posit [something] as a pastness or as a futureness it is necessary that it not be totally consumed or totally destroyed. However, I will not write [more about these] because I fear it would be too much.

With regard to the first of these, it is easy to appreciate the paradox Ngawang Belden sees. Buddhahood is attained upon the destruction of the last of the obstructions to omniscience, the appearance of true existence that prevents simultaneous cognition of objects and their emptinesses, that is, of conventional and ultimate truths. For a Buddha Superior, then, the obstructions to omniscience have been destroyed; why then is it not possible to say that the disintegratedness of those obstructions exists as a factor in the mental continuum of that Buddha?

---

[62]As will be seen shortly, Jamyang Shayba apparently does not agree with Ngawang Belden that disintegratedness is a cause of total consumption or destruction, for disintegratedness preserves something's continuum of similar type and there is an effect to come out from it. That is apparently also why Jamyang Shayba says that there is no disintegratedness of the obstructions to omniscience for a Buddha.

[63]*Great Exposition of the Middle Way* 628.3-5.

Jamyang Shayba's discussion of this question implies that for him, the mere fact that something has disintegrated does not entail that its disintegratedness necessarily exists, any more than the fact that something has not come yet implies that it *will* come. For instance, the imaginary "horns of a rabbit" have of course not come to be, but that does not make them a future object. For something to be future, its causes must exist, whereas there are no existing causes for rabbit-horns; likewise, for something to be a disintegratedness, which is a functioning thing, it must be able to cause an effect. In order to produce an effect it must not be totally consumed or destroyed. Contrary to this, the disintegratedness of the obstructions to omniscience is totally destroyed. The obstructions to omniscience have been totally exhausted without remainder in the "element of qualities" (*chos 'bying, dharmadhātu*), i.e., emptiness. The "remainder" that is lacking for those obstructions to omniscience is their disintegratedness, which is posited in dependence on the continuum of similar type of those obstructions to omniscience (though the obstructions to omniscience themselves no longer exist).

Jamyang Shayba wants to avoid saying that somehow there is a continuation of the obstructions to omniscience for a Buddha. Geshay Gönchok Tsering, a contemporary Gelukba scholar, suggested[64] that Jamyang Shayba's thought is that although there is an abandonment and elimination of the obstructions to omniscience, "abandonment" or "elimination" are not effects of the obstructions to omniscience and so would not contaminate a Buddha's continuum, whereas disintegratedness would (as an effect of the obstructions to omniscience and their continuum of similar type); moreover, the continuum of the obstructions to omniscience would not have been cut.

If this is what he means, Jamyang Shayba would seem to have a defensible position. Still, he seems inconsistent: he claims that the disintegratedness of obstructions to omniscience is not possible because it would have no effect, but in a similar case, the disintegratedness of a sentient being, he

[64]Conversation, 6/6/84.

says that such a disintegratedness causes the non-severance of the continuum of ignorance; why not, then, say that the disintegratedness of the obstructions to omniscience causes the continuation of the absence of obstructions to omniscience? Note that such an absence would not be a non-affirming negative because the positive phenomenon of omniscience is implied by the absence of obstructions to it.

On the other hand, it is possible to make a good argument that an *effect* of the obstructions to omniscience—their disintegratedness—*without* the obstructions to omniscience themselves, must be considered contaminating, and hence that it is not possible for it to occur in the continuum of a Buddha. Such a view seems reasonable when it is considered that a Buddha's Truth Body (*chos sku, dharmakāya*) and Form Body (*gzugs sku, rūpakāya*), which comprise a Buddha's continuum, are the "imprints" of merit and wisdom; how could the disintegratedness of the obstructions to omniscience, for instance, be the result of merit or wisdom? Although a Buddha's continuum contains virtues such as non-hatred and non-desire, these are not mere factors of the destruction of hatred and desire, but are positive qualities that are their opposites.

We have already alluded to Ngawang Belden's second objection, concerning Jamyang Shayba's statement that in order to posit a pastness or futureness, it must not be totally consumed or destroyed. Perhaps what Jamyang Shayba means is nothing more than that disintegratedness, which is a pastness, is not a disintegratedness of itself. Elsewhere (in the section on the Svātantrika-Mādhyamikas), he points out that although, when something is destroyed, it itself no longer exists, its "continuum of similar type" is not destroyed, for its disintegratedness *is* that continuum. Therefore, what *is* destroyed is the action, not its disintegratedness. It is all the more puzzling that Ngawang Belden makes this objection, since he himself refutes the contention of most other schools that when a sprout is destroyed, everything that is part of it is destroyed. It appears that Ngawang Belden failed to grasp the referent of what is posited as a pastness or futureness, which is not the present object itself but a factor of its having disintegrated or not having come.

The Three Times

The topic of the three times—past, present, and future—is a debater's delight; there are so many terms and relations to keep straight that it is relatively easy for a challenger to make a defender's head spin. It might be helpful to place a number of these terms in tabular form and review them before proceeding further.

The following chart illustrating the three times by the last two moments of a seed and first moment of a sprout shows a few of the many possible ways of expressing their relationship. It should be remembered that since many terms within each column are synonymous, the horizontal matchups are somewhat arbitrary. Also, it is very important to note that, in general, the terms of columns A and C are set out in relation to the term of column B, which represents the present seed. Thus, "seed's futureness" in the first column indicates the futureness of a seed that is present in moment B. Moment A would also be a time of "seed's presentness," namely the presentness of the seed of the next-to-last moment of a seed, but it would take a far larger chart to begin to express all the possible relationships of these three moments.

The Three Times Illustrated by The Last Two Moments of a Seed and First Moment of a Sprout

Moment A	Moment B	Moment C
next-to-last moment of seed	last moment of seed	first moment of sprout
seed's futureness	seed's presentness	seed's pastness
seed's futureness	seed (seed's own time)	seed's disintegratedness
seed's approaching to production	seed's production	seed's effect

seed's non-existence despite having causes	seed's existence	seed's non-existence upon having disintegrated
seed's cause	effect of seed's cause	seed's effect
seed's, sprout's non-existence	sprout's non-existence	sprout's existence
futureness of sprout's futureness	sprout's futureness	sprout (sprout's own time, presentness)
sprout's indirect cause	sprout's direct cause	effect of sprout's cause
past at time of seed	past at time of sprout	future at time of seed
seed's approaching to production	sprout's approaching to production	sprout's production
seed's being produced	sprout's being produced	sprout's production
seed's approaching to disintegration	seed's disintegration	seed's disintegratedness
	seed's not enduring another moment	seed's not having endured another moment
seed's approaching to cessation	seed's cessation	seed's ceasedness

Jamyang Shayba gives identical definitions for the three times in his *Great Exposition of Tenets* and *Great Exposition of the Middle Way*, and Janggya, possibly following him, cites the same definitions.[65] They are based on Candrakīrti's statements in his *Commentary on (Āryadeva's) "Four Hundred"*:[66] "The past is what has passed beyond just this [present time]," "The present has been produced but has not ceased," and "The future is what has not come at the present time."

---

[65]Janggya differs from Jamyang Shayba only in not beginning his definition of futureness with "a factor of."

[66]P 5266, vol. 98, 247.3.2.

A presentness—a phenomenon's factor of being present—is defined as:[67]

> that which (1) is neither a factor of disintegratedness nor a factor of futureness of another [functioning] thing and (2) has been produced but has not ceased.

Candrakīrti said merely that the present has been produced but has not ceased, but, as Jamyang Shayba shows, that is not itself sufficient for a definition of presentness.[68] A pastness—a factor of disintegratedness of another functioning thing that has already been produced—would absurdly be a presentness, for at its own time (its moment of existing) it has, of course, been produced but has not ceased. It would absurdly be the case that the disintegratedness of a seed would be both the seed's presentness and its pastness. Similarly, a futureness—a factor of non-production of another functioning thing due to the non-completion of its conditions, though its substantial causes exist—would absurdly be a presentness, since at its own time it has been produced but has not ceased. All things are present at their own times, but that does not necessarily indicate that they are presentnesses.

Nor are past and future present merely because they are known at the present time. One can remember a past object or clairvoyantly know a future object at the present time, but one does not know that thing at its own time. Even when a past or a future object is known at its own time, as by a Buddha's omniscient consciousness, the past or future object is not established at the present time.[69] Analogously, Jamyang Shayba points out that although a person on the plain sees a distant mountain, that mountain is not established in the plain with that person.

---

[67]Jamyang Shayba, *Great Exposition of Tenets* 38b.4-5.

[68]*Great Exposition of the Middle Way* 600.2-6 and 606.2 ff. In some debates Jamyang Shayba uses the short definition "produced but not ceased," (e.g., *Great Exposition of the Middle Way* 606.2 ff.) qualified by "itself"—i.e., it need not be specified that it is not those two factors if a presentness is "itself produced but not ceased."

[69]*Great Exposition of the Middle Way* 591.2.

Since the three times are mutually exclusive, pastnesses and futurenesses cannot be presentnesses, even though at their own time they are present. This does not mean that it is not possible to posit a presentness *for* a sprout's futureness or its disintegratedness; a disintegratedness's presentness is its factor of having been produced but not having ceased, that factor being a different functioning thing from that disintegratedness, and a futureness's presentness is its factor of having been produced but not having ceased, that factor being a different functioning thing from that futureness.

Also, it must be understood that even though something has itself been produced and has itself not ceased, it has not necessarily itself been produced without having ceased.[70] That is, pastnesses and futurenesses have themselves been produced and have themselves not ceased, but they are not said to have themselves been produced without ceasing, that term being reserved for presentnesses. For these reasons, it is necessary to specify that a presentness is neither a factor of disintegratedness nor a factor of futureness of some other thing.

Moreover, futureness, although it has been produced without having ceased, is *not* a presentness because it is not the producedness-but-not-ceasedness of some other thing and because it *is* a factor of non-production of another thing. As Dzongkaba says in his *Ocean of Reasoning*:[71]

> Similarly, moments of similar type of futureness arise, but since its entity must be posited from the point of view of only the nonproduction of some other thing, it is very different from the two, past and present.

---

[70]For a hypothetical debate in which this point is made, see *Great Exposition of the Middle Way* 606.2 ff. In Tibetan, the distinction is that even though something might be *rang nyid skyes* and *rang nyid ma 'gag*, it is not necessarily *rang nyid skyes la ma 'gag pa*.

[71]Cited in *Great Exposition of the Middle Way* 607.4; the passage has not yet been located in the original but is probably a commentary on a passage in the nineteenth chapter of Nāgārjuna's *Treatise on the Middle Way*, the chapter on time.

The definition of a futureness is:

> a factor of non-production of another [functioning] thing due to the non-completion of its conditions, even though the causes for its production exist.

For instance, a seed does not sprout in the wintertime because even though the sprout's substantial cause—the seed—exists, the cooperative conditions such as moisture and warmth are not present. The sprout's factor of not having come due to incomplete conditions, even though it has causes, is its futureness.

Again, Candrakīrti's statement is not itself sufficient as a definition of a futureness. Candrakīrti said only, "The future has not come at the present time." This would leave open the possibility that even permanent phenomena and non-existents could be posited as futurenesses.[72] For example, space, a non-disintegrating phenomenon, can be said not to have come at the present time, as can the traditional illustration of a non-existent, the horns of a rabbit. It is necessary to add that (1) a futureness is not a futureness of *itself*, but of another thing; (2) for a futureness to exist, the causes of the thing of which it is a factor must exist; and (3) it is a factor of non-production.

That *as which* the future has not come is the present; i.e., when the future comes, it will come as the present.[73] For example, a "future sprout" is a sprout's factor of not having come, though its causes exist, due to the temporary incompleteness of its cooperative conditions. This future sprout is not itself a sprout, for no sprout exists prior to a sprout's production. However, when a future sprout comes, it will come as a present sprout. A sprout *is* what will come and thus can be posited as that which has not (but will) come.

It might be thought that since this sprout will come in the future, it should be posited as future.[74] But, when the sprout

---

[72]For a hypothetical debate in which this point is made, see *Great Exposition of the Middle Way* 602.5.

[73]For a hypothetical debate in which this point is made, see *Great Exposition of the Middle Way* 603.4.

[74]For a hypothetical debate in which this point is made, see *Great*

comes, it will be present. What is posited as future is just the futureness of a sprout. That is, the sprout that *will come* is not future since when it exists, it exists at the present time. What is posited as the future is that sprout's futureness.

Futurenesses have causes, because the non-completion of conditions for the arising of something causes a futureness. Candrakīrti says in his *Commentary on (Nāgārjuna's) "Sixty Stanzas of Reasoning"*:[75]

> . . . the non-completion of [a future phenomenon's] conditions subsists as the cause for the non-production of a future phenomenon. If its conditions were not incomplete, it would definitely be produced.

The futureness of something is different than that which is future in relation to it.[76] The futureness of a pot occurs prior to it and, hence, is past at the time of a pot. That is, when a pot is produced, its futureness is finished. Thus, a pot's futureness is actually *past* in relation to a pot. It is also true that being something's futureness or its "being produced" (*skye bzhin pa*) does not mean that it itself is future or not yet produced.[77] It has been produced, but that of which it is a futureness has not been produced. Also, although a futureness is "produced but not ceased," it is not posited as a presentness.[78] It is a factor of the non-production of another thing, whereas a presentness is not.

A futureness is not only caused, but acts as a cause—it causes the temporary non-production of something.[79] Still, a disintegratedness is not the same as a futureness even though

---

Exposition of the Middle Way 603.5.

[75]Cited in Jamyang Shayba's *Great Exposition of Tenets* 38b.3-4.

[76]For a hypothetical debate in which this point is made, see *Great Exposition of the Middle Way* 605.3 ff.

[77]For a hypothetical debate in which this point is made, see *Great Exposition of the Middle Way* 607.5 ff.

[78]For a hypothetical debate in which this point is made, see *Great Exposition of the Middle Way* 606.6 ff.

[79]For a hypothetical debate in which this point is made, see *Great Exposition of the Middle Way* 616.6 ff.

the disintegratedness of a butter-lamp's wick and fuel is the cause of the non-production of a future butter-lamp. That is because the futureness of something does not exist unless that thing's causes exist, and in the case of a spent lamp, there are no causes present for a future lamp.

A pastness is defined as:

> a factor of disintegratedness of another [functioning] thing that has already been produced (*skyes zin*).

Candrakīrti describes the past simply as that which has passed beyond the present, referring to something that was present but has passed, not to something that has passed beyond the current present time (for something that will pass beyond the current present time is future at the present time, not past).

Janggya points out that it is not sufficient to define the past as "not present," for a pastness is a factor of disintegratedness of something that has already arisen.[80] Also, it could be said that such a definition would allow futurenesses and non-existent phenomena to be posited as pastnesses, for the futureness of a sprout is, in relation to the sprout, not present, and non-existent phenomena such as the horns of a rabbit are none of the three times.

It is not necessary to add to the definition of a pastness that this factor of disintegratedness be something that has *itself* ceased.[81] It might be thought that a disintegratedness is not actually a pastness but a presentness, since at its own time it has been produced but has not ceased. Then, it might be thought that if a disintegratedness is a pastness, it absurdly must have ceased. However, this is irrelevant. A disintegratedness is not posited as a pastness because it has itself ceased, but because it is the disintegratedness of something else. In relation to that thing of which it is a factor of disintegratedness, it is a pastness. In fact, whenever we say that something is past, it is past only in relation to some other

[80]Janggya, *Presentation of Tenets* 489.

[81]Janggya, *Presentation of Tenets* 490.

thing; for instance, the 1995 bombing in Oklahoma City is past in relation to the present, future in relation to the 1994 elections, and present in its own time.

Vasubandhu defines the past by saying, "Having arisen, disintegrated (*byung nas zhig pa*)." It might be thought that what "arisen" refers to is also past.[82] Rather, what has arisen is a sprout, which has disintegrated. Even though the sprout has *passed*, it is not a *pastness*. It is non-existent, but its pastness, the disintegratedness of a sprout, exists. This disintegratedness is a disintegratedness of a present object, even though a present object no longer exists, because it is only a disintegratedness in relation to something, and that something was the present sprout.

Also, what has passed has partaken of both the causes for being present and of being present, the effect of those causes.[83] The present has partaken of causes for being present, but has not partaken of *being* present—rather, it *is* partaking of being present.

A pastness also cannot be defined as that which is past in relation to something such as a pot, for the pastness of a pot is not past in relation to a pot.[84] What is past in relation to a pot occurs prior to a pot, whereas the pastness of a pot can occur only *after* that pot. For example, a pot's futureness is past in relation to that pot (that is, it occurs prior to that pot) and its disintegratedness is future in relation to that pot (because of occurring subsequent to it, for disintegratedness is the effect of the thing of which it is a disintegratedness). The same sort of distinction applies to futurenesses and the future. The futureness of a pot occurs prior to that pot and is its cause, and so forth.

Finally, a pastness, being a functioning thing, lasts only for a single moment; hence, the pastness or disintegratedness of

---

[82]For a hypothetical debate in which this point is made, see *Great Exposition of the Middle Way* 604.1 ff.

[83]For a hypothetical debate in which this point is made, see *Great Exposition of the Middle Way* 604.3 ff.

[84]For a hypothetical debate in which this point is made, see *Great Exposition of the Middle Way* 604.5.

a thing occurs only in the moment following the existence of the thing, when the disintegratedness of the thing also disintegrates. This means that the later moments of similar type of a pot's disintegratedness are not pot's disintegratedness. All such moments are posited as pastnesses, but only a pot's disintegratedness is a pot's pastness.[85] The disintegratedness of a pot's disintegratedness is not that pot's pastness, but rather is the pastness of that pot's pastness, and so on. At the time of the disintegratedness of a pot's disintegratedness, a pot's disintegratedness has already ceased.

From among the three times, the present is main and the past and future are secondary, because the present is posited by way of having been produced and not having disintegrated.[86] Past and future, on the other hand, are posited not in their own terms but in terms of the present. They must be posited in dependence on the disintegration or non-production of another thing, whereas the present does not.[87] Also, the present is main because it is observed now (whereas past and future are not directly perceived by ordinary persons). Candrakīrti's *Commentary on (Āryadeva's) "Four Hundred"* says,[88] "The present is main because it is observed now."

Still, even though the past and future are secondary, there is mutual interdependence of all three times such that in order for one to appear to a person's mind, aspects of the others also must appear. The present cannot be posited without relying on the other two times. Why? It is necessary to say, "has been produced," in order to eliminate the possibility that something has not come (due to temporarily incomplete conditions, though the causes exist) and "not ceased," to eliminate the

---

[85]This does not mean that those moments are past in relation to a pot, for in fact they are future in relation to that pot. Rather, when they are posited as pastnesses, it is in relation to that pot that they are so posited.

[86]For a hypothetical debate in which this point is made, see *Great Exposition of the Middle Way* 600.6.

[87]See Janggya, *Presentation of Tenets* 490.3-7. As we have seen, the present must also be posited by way of reference to the two other times.

[88]Cited in *Great Exposition of the Middle Way* 600.4. This seems to be inconsistent with the general Prāsaṅgika School position that inference is as valid as direct perception.

possibility of it being past. In other words, to realize "present," which requires realization of the present's defining characteristics, necessitates a negative route, an elimination of what it is not. Candrakīrti says in his *Commentary on (Āryadeva's) "Four Hundred,"*[89] "Those three times also are interdependent because each does not exist without depending on the [other] two," and Dzongkaba's *Ocean of Reasoning* says:[90]

> Since one must posit the present with regard to what has not crossed or not passed beyond that, it is contradictory for the present not to depend on the past. Therefore, the future also must indirectly depend on the past because something is posited as future due to not having come in the present.

Hence, not only does presentness depend upon pastness and futureness, but the futureness of a pot depends on both present and past. It is obvious that the future depends on the present, for the future is posited in relation to the present, and it is equally obvious that the present depends on the past, for the present is not established without eliminating the past. In addition, by this route it can be said that futureness depends on pastness. Even though futureness occurs before the object, it is dependent not on that object but also on that thing's having disintegrated.

---

[89]This passage is cited in *Great Exposition of the Middle Way* 601.4.

[90]This passage is cited in *Great Exposition of the Middle Way* 601.5-6.

6 Other Unique Tenets

As we have seen in the preceding chapters, the Prāsaṅgikas (according to their Gelukba followers) not only criticize the views of other schools, usually by asserting that their opponents have improperly engaged in ultimate analysis, but also tender their own solutions to the sticky problems that comprise the "unique tenets." This chapter will turn toward the unique Prāsaṅgika tenets that we have not yet explored to consider what sort of critical stance the Prāsaṅgikas are said to take and whether they have devised a positive thesis to replace the one refuted.

Let us begin by briefly reviewing what, in the preceding chapters, has been identified as ultimate analysis. We have already seen that Prāsaṅgikas are said to reject, on a number of grounds, the Cittamātra thesis that there are no external objects. Gelukbas explain that one of these grounds is that the Cittamātra refutation of external objects depends on ultimate analysis because the Cittamātrins look for, but do not find, objects that are different entities from consciousness and which occur prior to, and act as causes for, the production of consciousness. Dharmakīrti, for instance, is said to argue that since a consciousness and the self-consciousness that observes it act upon their objects simultaneously, a consciousness and its object arise simultaneously. This precludes the existence of objects that are a separate entity from their apprehenders, i.e., are external objects. Prāsaṅgikas, on the other hand, maintain that external objects exist simply because they are asserted to exist in the conventions of the world and are not refuted by a conventional analytical awareness.

We have also seen that Prāsaṅgikas reject the postulation of self-consciousness on the grounds that it requires that one regard an experience and its recollection at a later time to be inherently other. This constitutes ultimate analysis because it is an investigation into whether a memory is inherently other than its cause (what is being remembered). Prāsaṅgikas, on the other hand, give several explanations for the production of memory of previous experience without self-consciousness, none of which involve the assumption of a mediating entity. These explanations also just accept the conventions of the world.

We have also seen that Prāsaṅgikas reject the notion that disintegratedness lacks the capacity to act as a cause. Here too, their opponents such as the Sautrāntikas and Cittamātrins are accused of engaging in ultimate analysis by searching for a disintegratedness that can be imputed either as the thing destroyed or apart from it. Because they have not found such a self-sufficient disintegratedness, those others have concluded that disintegratedness is a mere negative. Prāsaṅgikas, on the other hand, assert positively that disintegratedness is a functioning thing that can cause a future effect to arise from an action that has ceased and, moreover, show that this assertion is nothing other than what the world accepts.

Let us now examine the other "unique tenets" to see what kind of analysis and positive alternatives the Gelukba authors of this study see as being offered by Prāsaṅgikas. Looking over the many tenets analyzed by Jamyang Shayba (which include all of those subsequently enumerated by Janggya and many more) we can see roughly three categories. First, there are those **tenets that involve the rejection of specific assertions of one or more Buddhist schools on the basis that those assertions result from ultimate analysis**. Prāsaṅgikas:

- Reject the Cittamātra School's assertion of a mind-basis-of-all (*kun gzhi rnam par shes pa, ālayavijñāna*).

- Deny that there are non-defective sense consciousnesses among non-Buddhas that are non-mistaken with regard to the appearance of inherent existence.

- Deny that autonomous syllogisms must be stated to an opponent to cause that person to understand emptiness.

- Deny that there can be destruction of the obstructions to omniscience even while one is working on the destruction of the obstructions to liberation.[1]

- Reject the claims of the lower schools that *pramāṇa* necessarily means new realization of an object and that mental direct perception is necessarily non-conceptual.

- Reject the claim of the lower schools that nirvāṇa "with remainder" and "without remainder" refer to nirvāṇas with and without aggregates impelled by contaminated actions and afflictions.

In this category of tenets, the Gelukbas often say that the basis of the Prāsaṅgika rejection of the other schools' views is the Prāsaṅgika rejection of positing objects upon ultimate analysis—which in turn is based on its assertion of non-inherent existence—and acceptance of what the world accepts.

A second category of tenets is concerned with implications of the Mahāyāna and Hīnayāna path structures. For the most part, they are **tenets propounded to demonstrate that some persons who are regarded by other schools as Arhats—liberated beings—are only ersatz Arhats,** having realized only a coarse selflessness and having thereby suppressed, but not removed from the root, the obstructions to liberation. These tenets, then, revolve around the unique Prāsaṅgika assertion that the root of cyclic existence is the conception of

---

[1]The preceding three assertions are mainly identified with the Svātantrika School (but are held by others as well).

inherent existence, which is more subtle than the conception of a self described by other systems of tenets. Five assertions are elucidated in this regard:

- One must realize emptiness in order to become liberated and therefore some "Arhats" who have only realized a coarse selflessness are not actually liberated.

- There is desire that either is, or is thoroughly mixed with, the conception of true existence, and so-called Arhats still have this sort of desire.

- Although some of these "Arhats" do indeed have yogic direct perception of the four noble truths, one does not have to be an Arhat or even a Superior (one who has directly realized emptiness) in order to have such yogic direct perception.

- Although some of these "Arhats" have indeed realized the coarse aspects of the four noble truths, such a realization is not sufficient to overcome the obstructions to liberation.

- Since true cessations, the irrevocable cessation of some portion of the afflictions of desire, hatred, etc., are also emptinesses, such "Arhats" who have not realized emptiness could not have experienced true cessations, i.e., could not have overcome the afflictive obstructions.

The final category of unique Prāsaṅgika tenets seems to involve neither the rejection of a specific position posited by others upon using ultimate analysis nor to bear on the authenticity of persons regarded by non-Prāsaṅgikas as Arhats. Included in this category is the Prāsaṅgika use of the term *pratyakṣa* to accord with its use in the world and the unique way in which the Prāsaṅgikas, by not asserting inherent existence, can explain the avoidance of the two extremes of permanence and annihilation. Thus, all of these tenets in one way or another are connected to the fundamental viewpoint of the Prāsaṅgika School that nothing inherently exists and that in general one should accord with the conventions of the world.

Only four of the tenets to be discussed in the present chapter are propounded by Janggya (the other Janggya tenets having been discussed in previous chapters): (1) the non-existence of a mind-basis-of-all, (2) the non-existence of autonomous reasons, (3) that one must realize emptiness in order to be liberated from cyclic existence, and (4) that the conception of a self of phenomena is an obstruction to liberation. These are all included in the many tenets set forth by Jamyang Shayba and further explained by Ngawang Belden.

Refutation of a Mind-Basis-of-All

First, let us consider those tenets that involve the rejection of entities posited by other schools upon engaging in ultimate analysis. Let us begin with Asaṅga's Cittamātra assertion of a mind-basis-of-all—a neutral, continuously operating consciousness the function of which is to hold the seeds of actions (*las, karman*). The mind-basis-of-all is not accepted by Prāsaṅgikas because they claim that it cannot be posited except through a search for an imputed object. According to Gelukbas, the Cittamātra School asserts that the mind-basis-of-all is the person (*gang zag, puruṣa*)—that which bears the karmic latencies or seeds—and is findable upon analysis. That is, the Cittamātra School is considered to hold that if one sought the basis of imputation of *the person* one would discover the mind-basis-of-all. Ngawang Belden states:[2]

> Moreover, if a mind-basis-of-all which is a different entity from the six collections [of consciousness] were asserted, it would have to be asserted in accordance with the explanation that just that [mind-basis-of-all] is the object of observation of the innate view of the transitory [collection of aggre-

[2]*Annotations* 110a.2-3.

> gates] that conceives of an [inherently existent] "I" and which is associated with the afflicted mentality. Therefore, it would have to be asserted that the mind-basis-of-all is the illustration of the person and that when the person—the imputed object—is sought, it is findable.

In place of a mind-basis-of-all, Prāsaṅgikas are held to assert that the mere disintegratedness of actions can bring about the future occurrence of effects. Also, they claim that the "mere I" (*nga tsam*)—the "I" that is designated in dependence on the aggregates of mind and body—is a sufficient basis with which to associate the factors of disintegratedness, it being unnecessary to posit an additional consciousness such as a mind-basis-of-all. Janggya states:[3]

> In a system that does not assert inherent existence, there is no assertion of a mind-basis-of-all, non-wastage, acquisition, and so forth, but there is no need to assert those because [Prāsaṅgikas] are able to posit a presentation of actions and effects [without them].
>
> *Question*: How are you able to posit [actions and effects]?
>
> *Answer*: Even without asserting a mind-basis-of-all, it is feasible to posit the arising of effects from an action that has been accumulated[4] and has ceased, because the cessation of actions is not inherently established. There is a way in which that ["not inherently ceased"] serves as a reason for [the arising of effects from actions that have been accumulated and that have ceased] because the reason, "because it has not inherently ceased," establishes that later effects arise from an action's having disintegrated.

Janggya is saying that if an action had *inherently* ceased, that action's ceasedness or disintegratedness could indeed not possibly produce a later effect; however, since phenomena are neither inherently produced nor are inherently destroyed, the possibility of mere production of a later effect is not pre-

[3]*Presentation of Tenets* 473.16-20.

[4]That an action has been accumulated means that a seed for a future experience of pleasure or suffering has been established.

cluded. We can note that this does not establish that a later effect *will* emerge, but we are probably meant to put this statement together with all of the arguments adduced for disintegratedness that were explored in the previous chapter.

Valid Cognition Is Mistaken but Reliable

The unique tenets of the Prāsaṅgika School also include three positions that are mainly refutations of tenets identified with the Svātantrika School (but which also apply to the other non-Prāsaṅgika schools). The first of these Prāsaṅgika tenets is that until Buddhahood, all instances of conventional valid cognition, whether those of childish persons or of Superiors, are mistaken in the sense that their objects falsely appear to be inherently existent. Only the direct realization of emptiness in meditative equipoise is unmistaken cognition. Jamyang Shayba states:[5]

> In that way, until Buddhahood is attained, one has no non-mistaken consciousnesses except for a Superior's exalted wisdom of meditative equipoise. Also, due to that, for childish persons, i.e., common beings, even [the exalted wisdom] of meditative equipoise of the supreme mundane qualities path of preparation (*sbyor lam chos mchog, laukikāgradharma-prayogamārga*) is polluted by error with respect to what appears. Therefore, that all consciousnesses of common beings are mistaken is also a unique [tenet of the Prāsaṅgika School].[6]

Among non-Buddhas, only a Superior's exalted wisdom of meditative equipoise, the direct realization of emptiness, is a non-mistaken consciousness. All awarenesses that are not

---

[5]*Great Exposition of Tenets* 37a.2.

[6]The supreme mundane qualities path of preparation is the highest level of the path of preparation, where a yogi is still realizing emptiness conceptually but has not yet developed the ability to cognize it directly. Since even this consciousness is a conceptual consciousness, it is necessarily a mistaken consciousness because to it emptiness appears to truly exist.

direct realizations of emptiness, even the conceptual realization of emptiness on the highest level of the path of preparation, are mistaken because their object—emptiness—appears to be inherently existent.

Jamyang Shayba cites Candrakīrti's *Clear Words*, which seems to indicate that any consciousness to which something appears to be inherently existent must be labelled "erroneous" (*phyin ci log*):[7]

> The erroneous and the non-erroneous are different [i.e., a dichotomy]. Therefore, like the falling hairs [seen by] one with cataracts /dimness of sight, and so forth, when what does not [inherently] exist is apprehended by [that is, appears to] an erroneous [consciousness] as just [inherently] existing, how could even a portion of an [inherently] existent object be observed?

Despite the fact that most validly cognizing consciousnesses are mistaken in this way, Gelukbas assert that these consciousnesses are able to certify the basic entity of their objects of knowledge. Their basis seems to be to accept the worldly convention that these awarenesses are valid but to reject claims that they are correct with regard to the inherent existence of their objects; that would entail an affirmation of inherent existence, since objects undeniably appear to exist this way. This then becomes an issue involving the use of ultimate analysis, since those who would claim that conventional valid cognition was correct with respect to the inherent existence of its object would have to maintain that such objects were findable upon analysis. The Svātantrikas are, then, wrong to claim that the non-defective sense consciousnesses that certify their objects also certify the manner in which those objects appear, i.e., their appearing to be inherently existent.

---

[7]*Clear Words*, 9b.3-4. Sanskrit in Poussin, 30.3-4. This has also been translated by Hopkins (1983a: 613, 615) and by Sprung (1979: 41). The bracketed material is from Ngawang Belden's commentary.

Refutation of Autonomous Syllogisms

Another Prāsaṅgika criticism of the Svātantrika School is embodied in its rejection of autonomous syllogisms (*rang rgyud kyi sbyor ba, svatantra-prayoga*). This topic is barely touched upon in Jamyang Shayba's exposition of Prāsaṅgika tenets, because he has discussed it extensively elsewhere, but it is an important topic for Janggya. He describes autonomous syllogisms as follows:[8]

> Svātantrikas assert that the mere establishment of the three modes of a sign[9] in the proof of non-true [existence] for either of the parties of a dispute is not sufficient; rather, [the three modes] must be established from within an objective mode of subsistence (*don gyi sdod lugs*).

In this interpretation of the Svātantrika School, all three aspects of a correct reason or logical sign—the subject, predicate, and reason (e.g., pot, impermanence, and being a product, in the syllogism "The subject, a pot, is impermanent because of being a product")—must be inherently existent and inherently related. In the Gelukba presentation of the Svātantrika School, Svātantrikas are held to propound that conventionally, objects inherently exist; i.e., objects *do* exist the way they appear, as if inherently existent, to non-defective sense consciousnesses. For them, a phenomenon cannot be a mere imputedly existent nominality, as for the Prāsaṅgikas; it *must* have its own inherent nature (*rang bzhin, svabhāva*) in the sense of being findable among its bases of designation. Prāsaṅgikas

---

[8] *Presentation of Tenets* 479.8.

[9] A correct sign (reason) must possess three modes or qualities: the presence of the sign in the subject, the forward entailment, and the reverse entailment. For instance, in the syllogism "The subject, a pot, is impermanent because of being a product," all three modes are established. There is presence of the sign in the subject because the sign, product, is a quality of the subject, a pot. Roughly speaking, there is forward entailment because whatever is a product is necessarily impermanent; there is reverse entailment because whatever is not impermanent is necessarily not a product.

reject this, saying that even conventionally, nothing inherently exists.

As will be seen later, Svātantrikas do not want to have to say that all sense consciousnesses, to which things appear to be inherently existent, are mistaken, for then how could objects be validly posited? Prāsaṅgikas take the plunge of asserting that even though sense consciousnesses are mistaken, they can validly posit objects (though not as existing the way they appear). Janggya continues:

> The meaning of autonomy (*rang rgyud, svatantra*) is asserted as: the generation of inferential cognition realizing the probandum (*bsgrub bya*)[10] within the [context of the three modes] being established in that manner. The reason for that is that in their system any non-conceptual or conceptual valid cognition must definitely be non-mistaken with respect to the inherent nature (*rang bzhin, svabhāva*) of the appearing object or referent object [respectively] with respect to which it is a valid cognition, because, if [a consciousness] is mistaken with respect to that, it cannot be posited that an object of comprehension is found by valid cognition. Furthermore, this meets back to the fact that they cannot posit a phenomenon as existent if conventionally it does not have its own nature that is not an imputedly existent nominality.
>
> Therefore, they think that if the bases [that is, the subjects] on which depend the predicates about which the two parties debate—permanence, impermanence, true existence, non-true existence, etc.—do not exist within being established as commonly appearing and as demonstrably established objectively, they are not able to prove the modes of the sign in terms of such [a subject] because it is not feasible that there be a predicate of a non-existent substratum. That is the meaning of a commonly appearing subject.

For the Svātantrikas, the systems of the stater and the hearer of a syllogism must agree that the consciousness that certifies the existence of the subject, etc., of the syllogism also certifies its inherent existence. Therefore, the subject must be inher-

[10]The probandum is that which is to be proved, i.e., the thesis. To again use the "pot" syllogism, the probandum is "pot is impermanent."

ently existent, because (1) objects appear to Svātantrikas and to their hearers alike as if they were inherently existent and (2) both systems agree on the validity of this appearance. Prāsaṅgikas do not need to posit this, since their principal method is to reveal contradictions that arise from their opponent's convictions, without insisting, as the non-Prāsaṅgikas do, that the two systems agree that the inherent existence of objects is certified by the validly cognizing consciousnesses that certify the subject, etc. Therefore, for Prāsaṅgikas there need not be, nor could there be, a commonly appearing subject. Janggya continues:

> According to this excellent [Prāsaṅgika] system, once such [a subject and sign] are demonstrable, both of those have become objects that exist by way of their own entity, and just that is the meaning of being ultimately established. Therefore, the assertion that there exists the establishment of a commonly appearing subject for both parties in a debate—that is, a mode of proving a predicate within taking just that [subject] as the substratum—is very wrong. According to the Mādhyamika who is the first party, this is because existence by way of [an object's] own entity is not feasible even conventionally, whereby such [a commonly appearing subject] necessarily does not exist. As long as the other parties have not generated the [correct] view in their continua, they cannot distinguish the difference between existing by its own entity and mere [conventional] existence; therefore, until they realize the view, they cannot be shown the mode of mere conventional existence.
>
> Therefore, a mode of objective establishment which exists in the manner of common appearance [in the systems of] both parties is asserted by those who do not just lead from an opponent's assertions [i.e., non-Prāsaṅgikas]; this mode is not found, whereby it is asserted that a commonly appearing subject does not exist.
>
> Also, this meets back to asserting or not asserting conventionally phenomena that exist by way of their own character. Even the essential points such as that Svātantrikas distinguish real and unreal conventionalities and that Prāsaṅgikas do not assert real conventionalities in their own system must be known in dependence on this [position].

According to Janggya, because Prāsaṅgikas do not accept that things inherently exist even conventionally whereas non-Prāsaṅgikas do, they do not think that a Mādhyamika and an opponent could possibly have a commonly appearing subject. Moreover, they are not drawn into the additional difficulty of distinguishing between real and unreal conventionalities except on the level of ordinary worldlings themselves, who correctly assert, for instance, that the appearance of a mirage can be mistaken for water. Prāsaṅgikas assert that since *all* appearances are unreal in the sense that they appear to inherently exist whereas they do not, there are no real conventionalities. However, from the point of view of the world they also say that most objects, with the exception of those of consciousnesses affected by superficial causes of error such as those that apprehend mirages as water, are real in relation to a worldly consciousness.[11]

The Prāsaṅgikas themselves mainly work with their opponent's own assertions, which they will demonstrate to entail unwanted consequences. However, although when addressing sharp opponents they do not depend on, nor consider necessary, the use of syllogisms, they use them for opponents who are not as sharp. The syllogisms used are not *autonomous* syllogisms because they are not regarded as being about inherently existent objects or to entail inherent relationships. Again, Janggya states:[12]

> Although autonomous reasons are not asserted in the Prāsaṅgika School, signs with the three modes definitely must be asserted, and the three modes also must definitely be established by valid cognition. Also, that [establishment of the three modes] is accomplished by other-renowned reasons.
>
> In accordance with the earlier explanation, there is no objective mode of establishing, for the two parties of a debate, an object of comprehension that appears commonly [without contradicting their respective systems]. Therefore, leading from the assertions of an opponent, one states rea-

[11]See Lopez (1987: 207-12).

[12]*Presentation of Tenets* 480.13-20.

> sons that are well known to the opponents themselves. [One may also state reasons that are] well known to [the opponent who is] other in relation to the first party, i.e., a Mādhyamika. Therefore, the two, self-renowned reasons and other-renowned reasons, are equivalent.[13]

The Prāsaṅgikas use reasonings that play upon an opponent's own knowledge and beliefs. From their own point of view, then, *all* of their reasonings are "other-renowned," i.e., those well known to the person with whom they are debating.

Prāsaṅgika Perspective on the Destruction of the Obstructions to Omniscience

The third Prāsaṅgika tenet in this list, directed against assertions said to be made by schools such as the Svātantrika and Cittamātra upon engaging in ultimate analysis, is the assertion that one cannot begin to destroy the obstructions to omniscience (*shes bya'i sgrib pa, jñeyāvaraṇa*) until one has destroyed all of the obstructions to liberation (*nyon mong pa'i sgrib pa, kleśāvaraṇa*). This contradicts the Svātantrikas, who assert that beginning on the first Bodhisattva ground (the path of seeing) one simultaneously destroys the obstructions to liberation and the obstructions to omniscience.[14] The obstructions to omniscience "pollute" the mind, causing the appearance of inherent existence even for Arhats, persons who have overcome the afflictions of ignorance, desire, and aversion

---

[13]The other party is "self" to himself or herself, "other" to us, and vice versa. Whichever of the two expressions is used, it can refer to a reason that the opponent holds. Since Prāsaṅgikas lead from an opponent's assertions, not from their own, they would in general not use reasons well known only to themselves but not their opponents. See Jamyang Shayba, *Great Exposition of the Middle Way* 418.2-5.

[14]Gönchok Jikmay Wangbo, *Precious Garland of Tenets* 63.13-17, translated in Sopa and Hopkins (291). The two branches of the Svātantrika School share this assertion except that Sautrāntika-Svātantrikas do not contend that one *finishes* abandoning the two obstructions at the same time, for over the last three Bodhisattva grounds one removes only obstructions to omniscience.

through realizing the emptiness of inherent existence. According to Janggya:[15]

> Since the two [Hearer and Solitary Realizer] Arhats and Bodhisattvas who abide on the pure [eighth through tenth] grounds have removed all the seeds of the afflictions, the consciousness that conceives of true existence is not produced [in their continua]. However, since their [minds] are polluted by the predispositions [established by] those [afflictions], awarenesses are produced that are mistaken with respect to their appearing objects.
>
> In that case, the predispositions [established by] the afflictions are the chief of the obstructions to omniscience, and the effects of those—the factors of mistaken dualistic appearance—are also included in those [obstructions to omniscience].

Further meditation on emptiness conjoined with the practice of the perfections is required to remove the obstructions to omniscience, which are like the stubborn stains that persist in a piece of cloth that has been thoroughly washed. Jamyang Shayba, depending on Dzongkaba, asserts that one does not begin to abandon them until after the obstructions to liberation have been removed:[16]

> The bottom limit of an exalted wisdom that releases one from any of the impedimentary obstructions [i.e., the obstructions to omniscience] is posited from the ground of irreversibility, the eighth [Bodhisattva] ground.[17] In consideration of many such meanings, Dzongkaba's *Illumination of the Thought, Explanation of (Candrakīrti's) "Entrance"* says:[18]
>
> > ...because obstructions that are predispositions and that are different from those seeds [producing the

---

[15]*Presentation of Tenets* 486.1.

[16]*Great Exposition of Tenets* 41a.3-4.

[17]In the Mahāyāna path structure, there are five levels called paths; the fourth of these, the last before Buddhahood, is the path of meditation, which is divided into ten Bodhisattva grounds.

[18]*Illumination of the Thought* 25b.1-2. Bracketed material comes from Dzongkaba's previous sentence. Also translated by Hopkins (1980: 147).

> afflictions] are posited as obstructions to omniscience, they are not [begun to be] abandoned until one attains the eighth [Bodhisattva] ground.

Jamyang Shayba's principal Indian Prāsaṅgika source is Candrakīrti; Jamyang Shayba cites Candrakīrti's graphic examples:[19]

> When one has abandoned all afflictions on the eighth [Bodhisattva] ground, one must [then begin to] abandon the obstructions to omniscience but not earlier than that because until the afflictions have been abandoned, there is no way to abandon their predispositions. For example, until one removes the oil in something fouled with oil, one is unable to remove its befoulment. That is because Candrakīrti's *Autocommentary on the "Entrance"* says:[20]
>
> > Those that are involved in stopping up and infusing the mental continuum are predispositions. "The aftermath of the afflictions," "conditioning of the afflictions," "the root of the afflictions," and "predispositions of the afflictions" are synonymous.
> >
> > Even though they have abandoned the afflictions by an uncontaminated path, all Hearer and Solitary Realizer [Arhats] are unable to abandon [the obstructions to omniscience]. This is like the fact that because a pot and [a piece of] woolen cloth have contacted [sesame oil and flowers, respectively], even though the sesame oil and flowers, and so forth, have been removed, a subtle quality [of those can be] observed.

Jamyang Shayba also wants to show that the obstructions to omniscience can be described as "non-afflictive ignorance" (*nyon mong can ma yin pa'i ma rig pa*) and that there are instances of obstructions to omniscience that are consciousnesses. His reasoning appears to be that since ignorance is a consciousness, that which is ignorance is a consciousness,

---

[19]*Great Exposition of Tenets* 40b.6.

[20]P 5263, vol. 98, 164.1.5-7. The quotation has been lengthened by filling in material indicated by "etc." (*sogs*), beginning with, "This is like the fact..."

whereby the obstructions to omniscience, being non-afflictive ignorance, must be consciousnesses. Otherwise, it would be necessary to admit that non-afflictive ignorance is not actually ignorance. He first cites a passage from Candrakīrti that specifically mentions non-afflictive *ignorance*:[21]

> There is non-afflictive ignorance and ignorance that is an obstruction to omniscience because Candrakīrti says in his *Autocommentary on the "Entrance,"*[22] "...because of being thoroughly involved in ignorance that is not afflictive..." and his *Seventy Stanzas on the Three Refuges* (*skyabs gsum 'gro bdun cu pa, triśaraṇasaptati*) says:[23]
>
> > For the sake of abandoning non-afflictive ignorance,
> > [Arhats] are later urged on by the Buddhas.
>
> And:[24]
>
> > Since non-afflictive ignorance exists,
> > [It must be] abandoned [in order to attain] omniscience.

However, his contention that these passages show that there are obstructions to omniscience that are consciousnesses is opposed by Janggya and Ngawang Belden; Janggya refers to many authorities who also oppose that view:[25]

> In dependence on Candrakīrti's *Seventy Stanzas on the Three Refuges* which says, "For the sake of abandoning non-afflictive ignorance..." and "...non-afflictive ignorance exists...." and his statement in his *Autocommentary on the "Entrance,"* "...ignorance that is not afflictive..." Paṇchen Sönam Gyeltsen (*paṇ chen bsod nams rgyal mtshan*)[26] and the great scholar and

[21]*Great Exposition of Tenets* 40b.4-6.

[22]Candrakīrti also mentions non-afflictive ignorance in his *Brilliant Lamp, Commentary on the Guhyasamāja Tantra* (*rgyud 'grel sgron gsal, pradīpoddyotana*), cited in Losang Dayang *Grounds and Paths* 119.2.

[23]P 5366, vol. 103, 175.4.5. No Sanskrit text is extant.

[24]P 5366, vol. 103, 175.1.4.

[25]Janggya, *Presentation of Tenets* 486.17-87.14.

[26]None of the half-dozen scholars I asked knew who this was.

adept Jamyang Shaybay Dorjay [Jamyang Shayba] say that the existence of obstructions to omniscience that are consciousnesses is correct.

Nevertheless, with respect to the Foremost Omniscient [Dzongkaba's] interpretations of the ignorance that is an obstruction to omniscience, except for his interpretation [of it] as predispositions of mistaken dualistic appearance, he does not appear to have interpreted it as ignorance that is a consciousness.

Most scholars and adepts such as the omniscient Kaydrup, the lord of reasoning Jaydzün Chögyi Gyeltsen (*rje btsun chos kyi rgyal mtshan*) of Sera (*se-ra*) and his [spiritual] sons, as well as the great treasure of wisdom Jamyang Gaway Lodrö (*'jam dbyangs dga' ba'i blo gros*), the foremost omniscient Gendün Gyatso (*dge 'dun rgya mtsho*), and Paṇchen Sönam Drakba,[27] assert that there are no obstructions to omniscience that are consciousnesses. Also, the omniscient Paṇchen Losang Chögyi Gyeltsen (*paṇ chen blo bzang chos kyi rgyal mtshan*),[28] a keeper of the teaching of both the transmission of explanation and the transmission of achievement of the Foremost Lama [Dzongkaba], says:

> The subtle obstructions [preventing] the perception
> Of the two truths directly and simultaneously by one consciousness
> Are designated "ignorance" [but] are not actual consciousnesses;
> Hence there is not even partial contradiction.

His statements along with his reasons are very concordant with the great mass of the speech of the Foremost [Dzong-

[27]Kaydrup (1385-1438) is one of Dzongkaba's two chief disciples; Jaydzün Chögyi Gyeltsen (1469-1546) is the author of monastic textbooks for Jay college of Sera Monastery; I have not yet found biographical information on Jamyang Gaway Lodrö, except for his dates (1429/30-1503); Gendün Gyatso (1476-1542) is the second Dalai Lama; and Paṇchen Sönam Drakba (1478-1554) is the author of monastic textbooks for Loseling College of Drebung Monastery.

[28]He is the first Paṇ-chen Lama (1569-1662). Losang Dayang (*Grounds and Paths*, 119.4-5) calls him the All-Seeing Paṇchen Losang Chögyi Gyeltsen (*paṇ chen kun gzigs blo bzang chos kyi rgyal mtshan*), and the name of his book is *Answer to the Objections of the Translator [Daktsang] Shayrap Rinchen* (*sgra pa shes rab rin chen gyi rtsod lan*).

> kaba]. Therefore, [this topic] still should be finely analyzed by the intelligent.

Though no reasons are given for Janggya's denial of obstructions to omniscience that are consciousnesses, it could be speculated that Janggya and the others want to avoid saying that even sense consciousnesses such as an eye consciousness are instances of obstructions to omniscience just because they have predispositions for mistaken dualistic appearance.

Pramāṇa Is Not Necessarily New Cognition

In addition to their criticisms of the Cittamātra and Svātantrika Schools, Prāsaṅgikas also refute the notion, held by all the lower schools, that prime cognition (*tshad ma, pramāṇa*) is necessarily *new* realization of an object. The Prāsaṅgika School interprets the "*pra*" of "*pramāṇa*" as meaning "prime," but not in the sense of first; rather, it is in the sense of main. Hence, all valid awarenesses are *pramāṇa*, including *subsequent* cognition (*bcad shes, paricchinajñāna*[?]), a category that includes all valid consciousnesses other than those which occur in the first moment of cognizing an object. Jamyang Shayba says:[29]

> The statement in Nāgārjuna's *Refutation of Objections* (*rtsod zlog, vigrahavyāvartanī*, vs. 32):[30]
>
>> If it is thought that [valid cognition] is established
>> By other validly cognizing consciousnesses, it would be endless.
>> Furthermore, the first is not established,
>> Nor the middling, nor the last . . . [31]

[29]*Great Exposition of Tenets* 37a.3.

[30]P 5228, vol. 95, 15.1.3-4. The quotation has been expanded by adding the first two lines. Nāgārjuna's commentary is P 5232, vol. 98, 61.1.6-2.2. Also found in K. Bhattacharya (1978: 25).

[31]If a valid cognition must be certified by another valid cognition, there would be an endless regress, in which case no valid cognition would be established—first, middle, or end.

> refutes that [*pramāṇa* necessarily means] *new* realization and refutes that [consciousnesses are certified by] self-consciousness or other-knowing consciousnesses.[32]

Ngawang Belden, relying on Dzongkaba's student Kaydrup, explains that the reason why it is inappropriate to indicate that *pramāṇa* must mean new realization is that it would constitute ultimate analysis. He does not specify exactly the manner in which the ultimate analysis would take place, but it seems reasonable to speculate that he would regard that assertion about *pramāṇa* to be an investigation to determine whether or not a certain consciousness was the first, or a subsequent, moment of a continuum of perception, in other words, investigation of whether or not the object imputed—the consciousness—*is* its basis of imputation—the moments of a continuum of consciousness. He says:[33]

> Both of the assertions that all awarenesses of common beings are mistaken consciousnesses and that subsequent [valid] cognition is prime cognition have their source in the non-assertion of [establishment by a phenomenon's] own character, because (1) whatever is an awareness of a common being necessarily perceives [phenomena] to be established by their own character and (2) whatever might be a new incontrovertible consciousness would have to be an object that is findable through analysis by a reasoning consciousness. The first [reason] is easy. The second is established because Kaydrup's *Opening the Eyes of the Fortunate* (*bskal bzang mig 'byed/stong thun chen mo*) says:
>
>> The assertion that [prime cognition] is necessarily newly incontrovertible—[that an awareness] cannot be posited as prime cognition merely by being incontrovertible with respect to the object of comprehension that is its object of the mode of apprehension—is incorrect because (1) mere conventional prime cognition does not establish that

[32]Valid cognition is certified neither by self-consciousness nor by other-knowing consciousness; it is certified simply by its own operation toward its objects (see introduction chapter 3 and chapter 7 of Jamyang Shayba).

[33]*Annotations*, note *wa*, 111b.1.

> prime cognition must be newly incontrovertible and (2) prime cognition analyzing the ultimate does not in any way find prime cognition. That the former [reason—that mere conventional prime cognition does not establish that prime cognition must be newly incontrovertible—] is so follows (1) because an ordinary innate awareness of a worldly being that is not affected by adventitious causes of error and operates without investigation or analysis designates as prime cognition what is merely incontrovertible with respect to the object it comprehends and does not in any way designate [a consciousness as prime cognition] by way of it being *newly* incontrovertible and (2) because in all logicians' statements of proofs for the necessity of mentioning the term "newly" as part of the definition of prime cognition, the way something becomes prime cognition is put in terms of positing as prime cognition an object found by analysis through reasoning.

Kaydrup says that conventional valid cognition does not establish that prime cognition must be a new awareness; thus, Ngawang Belden thinks, if an instance of prime cognition which must be newly incontrovertible does exist, it must be established by ultimate valid cognition, in which case it would be findable through analysis by a reasoning consciousness. Similarly, Kaydrup also notes that prime cognition is not found by ultimate valid cognition either; indeed, in the Prāsaṅgika system, nothing is findable upon analysis by ultimate valid cognition. It seems that in this case, Prāsaṅgikas accept the conventions of an ordinary worldly awareness, for whom *pramāṇa* is simply correct awareness; they reject the conclusions of those who designate it as just the first moment of awareness by noting that this would be an attempt to find consciousness *as being* its basis of designation—a moment of consciousness—and thus would be ultimate analysis.

Mental Direct Perception Can Be Conceptual

In another tenet that stands in opposition to at least those followers of Dharmakīrti in the Sautrāntika and Cittamātra Schools, Prāsaṅgikas accept the existence of instances of mental direct perception (*yid kyi mngon sum, mānasapratyakṣa*) that are conceptual (*rtog pa, kalpanā*). Jamyang Shayba cites Candrakīrti's *Clear Words:*[34]

> Since in scripture it is also not the case that only non-conceptual consciousnesses are directly perceiving consciousnesses (*mngon sum, pratyakṣa*), this [contrary assertion that there is only non-conceptual direct perception] is untenable.

One reason is that, according to Dzongkaba, there are instances of mental direct perception that are remembering consciousnesses, which are always conceptual consciousnesses. He says:[35]

> Candrakīrti's *Commentary on (Āryadeva's) "Four Hundred,"* at the point of explaining the meaning of the passages in the abhidharma texts that the five, forms, and so forth, are individually known by the [corresponding] sense consciousnesses and the mental consciousness, says:[36]
>
>> The two [types of] perception [sense and mental] do not perceive the same object. One, [a sense consciousness] which is generated first, directly distinguishes the aspect of the object. The second [the mental consciousness] does not know [the object] in the sense of just acting [on it] directly; [however,] since, by the power of a sense consciousness, it is produced thinking of such, it is designated that it also knows that object.

---

[34]*Clear Words* 50.1-2. Sanskrit in Poussin 75.1-2: *nāgamādapi kalpanāpohasyaiva vijñānasya pratyakṣatvamiti na puktametat.* Translations by Sprung (1979: 63) and Stcherbatsky (1927: 251).

[35]*Illumination of the Thought* 162b.5-63a.2.

[36]P 5266, vol. 98, 251.3.6-8 (202b.7-8, 203a.6). Variant readings: for "generated," P reads *skyes* for *skye;* for "aspect," P reads *rnam par* for *rnam pa;* for "second," P reads *gnyis pas na* for *gnyis pa ni.*

> Initially, a sense consciousness directly knows an object such as a form, and through the power of that sense consciousness, the mental consciousness knows it, but it is said [that the mental consciousness] does not know it directly like a sense consciousness. It is also said that the mental consciousness that knows its object through the force of a sense consciousness is a memory consciousness.

Jamyang Shayba also seems to assert that there are instances of these conceptual, mental directly perceiving consciousnesses that are *feelings* (*tshor ba, vedanā*), although he does not elaborate. The main meaning of feeling is a mental factor that accompanies a main consciousness and that experiences an object. Dzongkaba (who is cited by Ngawang Belden) indicates how feeling is also an experiencer of an object:[37]

> "Feeling" is a word related with an agent, an activity, or an object; thus there come to be three: (1) feeling in the sense of the person [who feels]; (2) feeling in the sense of the activity [of feeling]; and (3) what is felt. The second of these is the valid [i.e., actual] one, the mental factor feeling. The third is the object of comprehension [of a feeling], that is, pleasure, pain, or neutral feeling. This is in terms of a mental consciousness.

Feeling can include not only the mental factor that accompanies a mental consciousness following sense experience, but also "internal feelings." Dzongkaba identifies two types of direct comprehension, one having to do with internal feelings, in his *Illumination of the Thought, Explanation of (Candrakīrti's) "Entrance"*:[38]

> Therefore, with respect to direct comprehension, there are two, (1) the distinguishing by a sense consciousness of forms, and so forth, for instance, and (2) the thorough distinguishing by internal experience of pleasant and painful feel-

[37] *Illumination of the Thought* 163a.2-63b.1. 327.2 in Peking *ca.*

[38] *Illumination of the Thought* 163a.2-63b.1, 327.2 in Peking *ca.* This quotation immediately follows the preceding quotation.

ings, and so forth, for instance. The latter of those two has to be asserted [to occur] even during the ordinary state.

Thus, Jamyang Shayba interprets the second, "internal experience," as feeling that, since it is a "direct comprehension" and is in a category separate from sense consciousnesses, must be a mental direct perception. For instance, the mental factor feeling that accompanies a pleasant memory is a direct comprehension of pleasantness but is not sense direct perception; hence, it would seem that for Jamyang Shayba it would necessarily be mental direct perception.

Also, the Prāsaṅgikas are held to assert that direct perception can be conceptual, in contradistinction to those Sautrāntikas and Cittamātra who follow the great epistemologists, Dignāga and Dharmakīrti. Their expansion of the range of mental direct perception to include conceptual instances is, based, it seems, on the assertion of feelings that are instances of mental direct perception and does not seem to be related to a deeper issue, such as the use of ultimate analysis.

Prāsaṅgika Perspectives on Nirvāṇa

The final tenet of this category—rejection of the assertions of other schools on issues other than path structure—is that according to Gelukba scholars, over against the lower schools, Prāsaṅgikas define the terms "nirvāṇa with remainder" (*lhag bcas myang 'das, sopadhiśeṣa-nirvāṇa*) and "nirvāṇa without remainder" (*lhag med myang 'das, nirupadhiśeṣa-nirvāṇa*) not by whether or not a liberated person is or is not still alive, but to whether or not such a person is experiencing the appearance of true existence (*bden yod, satya-sat*). The term "nirvāṇa with remainder" (*lhag bcas myang 'das, sopadhiśeṣa-nirvāṇa*) refers to the persistence of the appearance of true existence to a person who has overcome all afflictive obstructions when that person is not in meditative equipoise directly realizing emptiness. "Nirvāṇa without remainder" (*lhag med myang 'das, nirupadhiśeṣa-nirvāṇa*) refers to the absence of the appearance of true existence to such a person when that person is meditating on emptiness.

In general, the nirvāṇas posited by the lower schools are contradictory with those posited by the Prāsaṅgika School, since they mean very different things by "with remainder" and "without remainder." Both sides agree that nirvāṇa occurs when the afflictions of desire, hatred, etc., have been utterly destroyed; that much is shared. But according to the Prāsaṅgika School one first manifests a nirvāṇa without remainder because in the meditative equipoise in which the afflictions are finally abandoned, there is no remainder of an appearance of true existence. The lower schools would identify that nirvāṇa as a nirvāṇa *with* remainder because unless one dies at that time there is no discontinuation of the continuum of aggregates impelled by contaminated actions and afflictions.

Subsequent to meditative equipoise, both would identify one's nirvāṇa as a nirvāṇa with remainder, but within meaning different things by "remainder." For the lower schools, it means that there is a remainder of aggregates impelled by contaminated actions and afflictions; for the Prāsaṅgika School, that there remains an appearance of true existence due to obstructions to omniscience, here specifically predispositions established by the ignorant consciousness that conceives true existence. Similarly, all schools would identify the nirvāṇa of an Arhat at the time of death as being a nirvāṇa without remainder, but within meaning different things by "without remainder." For the lower schools, it means that the continuum of the aggregates of the Arhat have been completely cut off; for the Prāsaṅgika Schools, it means that at that time an Arhat in meditative equipoise on emptiness experiences no conventional appearances whatsoever, and therefore experiences no mistaken dualistic appearances.

Jamyang Shayba argues that there are three reasons why the assertions of the lower schools are incorrect: (1) if a nirvāṇa without remainder meant the nirvāṇa experienced upon death, it would not be actualized; (2) the way in which Arhats attain a nirvāṇa in which the contaminated aggregates are completely abandoned is just that the aggregates are primordially extinguished into emptiness, not that they are irrevocably cut off, and (3) there is a Hīnayāna sūtra in which Śariputra, having actualized a nirvāṇa without remainder, spoke, demonstrating that one need not die to have such a nirvāṇa. With regard to the first of these reasons, Jamyang Shayba relies on Candrakīrti's *Commentary on (Nāgārjuna's) "Sixty Stanzas of Reasoning"*:[39]

> Since there is nothing whatsoever in an entity which is a severance of the continuum of the aggregates, in whom is that cessation actualized? ...For the time being, as long as there is an impelling force for the continuation of those aggregates by the power of causes and conditions, so long can [the continuum of the aggregates] not be fully understood as extinct because it has production.

No person would be able to actualize a nirvāṇa without a remainder of aggregates because the mental and physical aggregates are the basis of imputation for persons. A person whose aggregates had been destroyed would be dead. In most Mahāyāna systems (the Mādhyamika School and the followers of Dharmakīrti in the Cittamātra School) there is no instance in which the aggregates of a person are completely extinguished in the sense of irrevocably cutting their continuum (although the form aggregate is temporarily absent in the case of persons born in the Formless Realm). From the point of view of the Mahāyāna schools (other than the followers of Asaṅga in the Cittamātra School), all sentient beings eventually attain Buddhahood. Those who have attained nirvāṇa have purified their aggregates of afflictions and are no longer powerlessly reborn in cyclic existence, but the process of transformation from ordinary being to Arhat and from Arhat to Buddha does not disturb the basic continuum of the aggregates.

The lower schools would probably answer that there is after all an attainer of their version of nirvāṇa without remainder—one in which the continuum of the aggregates is cut

---

[39]P 5265, vol. 98, 174.4.5. The second part of this quotation, the portion following the ellipses, seems to be a very loose paraphrase of the text following the first part.

off—because the person who is about to attain that nirvāṇa in the next moment may be designated as the attainer of a nirvāṇa without remainder. Such a designation would be a coarse worldly convention, analogous to the way in which the world refers to persons and death. For example, although it is not possible to posit a person who is dead (because persons are imputed in dependence on their aggregates, and a corpse has neither a living body nor a consciousness associated with it) people in the world often speak as though such a person could be posited.

To Jamyang Shayba this is not a satisfactory answer. It is no more admissible to talk about persons who have attained a nirvāṇa in which the aggregates have been utterly destroyed than to talk about persons who are dead.

With regard to the second reason, that Arhats just attain a nirvāṇa in which the aggregates are "extinguished into emptiness" but not irrevocably destroyed, Jamyang Shayba following the lead of Candrakīrti and Dzongkaba, cites a Hearer sūtra:[40]

> This which is suffering is completely abandoned, definitely abandoned, purified, extinguished, freed from desire, stopped, thoroughly pacified, vanished, not connected to other sufferings, not arisen, not produced. This is peace, this is auspiciousness. It is like this: since all the aggregates are abandoned, attachment is extinguished, one is freed from desire, has cessation, nirvāṇa.

Dzongkaba explains that this sūtra indicates that there is no destruction of the aggregates upon the attainment of this nirvāṇa:[41]

---

[40]This sūtra is cited in Candrakīrti's *Commentary on (Nāgārjuna's) "Sixty Stanzas of Reasoning,"* but is not identified by him or by Nāgārjuna, Dzongkaba or Jamyang Shayba. According to Jamyang Shayba's *Great Exposition of the Middle Way* 188a.3 (Buxaduor edition), it is a sūtra set forth by Śaripūtra after his enlightenment. Perhaps it is the *Repetition Sūtra*. Translated by Hopkins (1980: 170).

[41]*Illumination of the Thought* 35a.2-5. Translation, Hopkins (1980: 170-71). The differences between this translation and that in *Compassion in Tibetan Buddhism* reflect Hopkins' subsequent re-interpretation of the passage.

Otherwise, according to the Proponents of True Existence, it is not fit to explain [the Hearer sūtra] as primordial extinguishment in the sense that the aggregates have been primordially without inherently existent production, as [the line] in Maitreya's *Sublime Continuum of the Mahāyāna*, "The afflictions are primordially extinguished," is explained; rather, it must [incorrectly] be explained as an utter abandonment [of the aggregates] by means of the path.

If it is [explained this way, then there are the following faults:] when the nirvāṇa that is to be actualized existed, the actualizer would not [and thus could not report on the extinguishment that was realized, as was done in the *Repetition Sūtra*]. Also, when the actualizer existed, the nirvāṇa to be actualized would not because the aggregates would not have been extinguished. Hence, they are unable to explain this sūtra.

According to us, it is permissible to explain extinguishment here in accordance with the statement:[42]

> Extinguishment [in this case] does not [occur] by
> means of an antidote;
> It is so called because of primordial extinguishment.

We are able to explain well the meaning of the sūtra [as referring to a natural or primordial absence of inherent existence in phenomena].

Since the Proponents of True Existence—the proponents of the lower tenet systems—interpret this sūtra as being concerned with a nirvāṇa without remainder in the sense of an irrevocable extinguishment of the aggregates, they would not interpret it as Dzongkaba has done or as Maitreya would, as being concerned with the primordial extinguishment of the aggregates into emptiness. In the section in which the quoted passage occurs, Maitreya speaks about the natural purity of the mind and the adventitious nature of the afflictions defiling it; he does not mean that the afflictions are removed by the path from beginningless time. They would then have the

[42]This passage appears neither in Maitreya's nor Asaṅga's texts. It may be in Gyeltsap's commentary on Maitreya.

problem of explaining how there could be an actualizer of that nirvāṇa (since the aggregates would have been abandoned at the point of attaining the nirvāṇa), or, vice versa, how there could be an actualized nirvāṇa without remainder if there were a person who had actualized it.

The Two Selflessnesses of Persons and Phenomena Are Equally Subtle

The second category of unique tenets revolves around the issue of defining Arhats; the Prāsaṅgikas deny that status to certain so-called Arhats who have only realized what, for them, is a coarse selflessness and, although they have thereby suppressed the coarse afflictions, have not removed any of the obstructions to liberation from the root.

First, Prāsaṅgikas take issue with the Svātantrika School's assertion that it is necessary only to realize the selflessness of the person (*gang zag gi bdag med, pudgalanairātmya*) in order to attain liberation from cyclic existence. In all schools other than the Prāsaṅgika School, the selflessness of the person is the non-existence of a self-sufficient person (*rang rkya ba'i gang zag*), which (in the non-Prāsaṅgika Mahāyāna schools) is coarser than the selflessness of phenomena; essentially, then, other schools allow for the possibility of gaining liberation even if one realizes only a less subtle level of selflessness. According to Gelukba explanations of Prāsaṅgika, the selflessness of the person is as subtle as the selflessness of phenomena; all phenomena are devoid of inherent existence, the subtle selflessness.

In this case, the explicit basis for the rejection of the view of other schools is just scripture. The Indian Prāsaṅgika source is Śāntideva's *Engaging in the Bodhisattva Deeds* (IX.41cd), which says:[43]

> Therefore, scripture says that without this path

---

[43]V. Bhattacharya (195). The Sanskrit is: *na vinānena mārgeṇa bodhirityāgamo yataḥ*. Stephen Batchelor identifies this *śloka* as 40cd.

There can be no enlightenment.

Gyeltsap expands on this in his *Explanation of (Śāntideva's) "Engaging in the Bodhisattva Deeds"* (*spyod 'jug dar ṭīk*):[44]

> It follows that one definitely needs to realize emptiness in order to obtain the fruit of a Hearer or Solitary Realizer Arhat.[45] Why? Because it is said in passages of the Perfection of Wisdom Sūtras that without familiarity with this path of realizing emptiness one attains none of the three enlightenments [of a Hearer Arhat, a Solitary Realizer Arhat, or a Buddha].

Thus, it is insufficient merely to realize a coarse selflessness of the person; one must realize emptiness, the absence of inherent existence and the subtle selflessness, in order to be liberated.

Desire and Aversion Conceive True Existence

The second tenet related to Arhats is Jamyang Shayba's claim that it is a unique Prāsaṅgika tenet that there are instances of desire and aversion, in addition to ignorance, that are consciousnesses that conceive true existence. That is, since all afflictions such as desire and aversion have ignorance as their basis, and there are instances of them arising only after an ignorant consciousness (one conceiving true existence) has determined an object to be inherently attractive or unattrac-

---

44*Collected Works (gsuṅ 'bum) of Rgyal-tshab rje Dar-ma-rin-chen* (New Delhi: Lama Guru Deva, 1982), vol. 4, 258.6-59.2. See also *Collected Works (gsuṅ 'bum) of Rgyal-tshab rje Dar-ma-rin-chen* (New Delhi: Ngawang Gelek Demo, 1981), vol. 3, 253.5-54.1.

45Hearers (*nyan thos, śrāvaka*) and Solitary Realizers (*rang sang rgyas, pratyekabuddha*) are Hīnayāna practitioners who respectively depend and do not depend on the instructions of a teacher in their last lifetime prior to attaining liberation. *Arhan* was translated into Tibetan as *dgra bcom pa,* meaning, "one who has destroyed the foes of the afflictions," i.e., become liberated. For a discussion of his translation of this as "Foe Destroyer," see Hopkins (1983a: 871-73, n. 553).

tive, those afflictions are mixed with a conception of true existence. The Indian source is Āryadeva's *Four Hundred* (VI.11):[46]

> Like the body sense-power in the body,
> Delusion[47] serves as the basis for all [afflictions].
> Therefore, all afflictions are overcome
> Through overcoming obscuration.

The body sense power is the physical basis for touch. It is said that where it is absent, such as in most of the hair, the ends of the nails, etc., no other senses may operate. In the same way, desire and hatred are absent or inoperable in the absence of the consciousness conceiving true existence. Gyeltsap, in his *Commentary on (Āryadeva's) "Four Hundred"* (*bzhi rgya pa'i dar ṭīk*) makes this connection explicitly:[48]

> In the body, the body sense power pervades the other sense powers such as the eye and dwells as the basis of those. If it did not exist, the other sense powers would also not dwell [in the body]. In just that way, the afflictive ignorance—the obscuration which [mistakenly] determines that dependent-arisings, which are empty of inherent existence, are truly existent—pervades and dwells in all the afflictions such as desire and hatred. That is because one adheres to desire, hatred, and so forth, upon determining a thing [falsely] imputed by obscuration to be inherently attractive or unattractive. Therefore, the manner in which the mode of apprehension of both desire and hatred and the mode of apprehension of the consciousness conceiving true existence are mixed should be known.

---

[46]P 5246, vol. 95, 135.2.8-3.1. The quotation has been expanded to include the last two lines. Cf. Sonam 156.

[47]"Delusion" (*gti mug, moḥa*) is usually synonymous with ignorance. However, according to Geshay Tupden Gyatso, since Prāsaṅgikas assert non-afflicted ignorance, and delusion is an affliction, in their system the two are not synonymous.

[48]*Collected Works (gsuṅ 'bum) of Rgyal-tshab-rje Dar-ma-rin-chen* (New Delhi: Lama Guru Deva, 1981), vol. 1, 597.6. Cf. Sonam 156.

According to Jamyang Shayba,[49]

> This is because of the unique assertion that just as those two [levels, coarse and subtle][50] exist with respect to ignorance, they also [exist] with respect to attachment, and so forth.

Arhats are those persons who have abandoned ignorance and thus have also abandoned all of the afflictions such as desire that are based on it. A controversy arose over the status of certain persons who some regarded as Arhats, but who still manifested a kind of craving. Prāsaṅgikas such as Śāntideva are reacting against the designation of "Arhat" for some persons who have only realized a coarse selflessness and have thereby gotten rid of only coarse levels of desire, aversion, and so forth. Jamyang Shayba cites Śāntideva's *Engaging in the Bodhisattva Deeds* (IX.47cd):[51]

> This attachment is not afflictive but
> Why is it not like obscuration?

Ngawang Belden explains this passage:[52]

> This craving in the continuum of the person whom you [wrongly] assert to be an Arhat is [afflictive, but not] in the manner explained in the abhidharma texts. Also, it is said in those abhidharma texts that thorough obscuration—ignorance—is of two [types], afflictive and non-afflictive. Just so, in accordance with the explanation in the abhidharma texts that there is one type [of ignorance] that is afflictive and one which is not afflictive, why do you not also [absurdly] assert craving [as afflictive and non-afflictive]? You should assert this.

According to Ngawang Belden, Śāntideva admits that the so-called "Arhats" do not have afflicted craving *based on a coarse*

---

[49]*Great Exposition of Tenets* 36b.7-8.

[50]Identified by Geshay Tupden Gyatso.

[51]V. Bhattacharya (197). The Sanskrit is: *kimaktiṣāpitaṣṇaiṣām nāsti saṃamohavat satī*. Also cited in Hopkins (1980: 157).

[52]*Annotations*, note *tsa*, 111a.2.

conception of self (the misconception of a self described in the abhidharma texts). However, he wants to make the point that they do have afflicted craving *based on a subtle conception of self.* He does this by arguing that the lower schools should admit that the so-called "Arhats" still have craving, and invites them to call it "non-afflicted craving," since that is the only conceivable kind of craving that could exist in the continuum of an Arhat. However, Śāntideva considers this to be absurd: craving is craving; "non-afflictive craving" is an oxymoron. For him, the fact that these "Arhats" have craving indicates that they are not Arhats at all, for they retain at least a subtle level of ignorance. Therefore, what the proponents of the abhidharma texts call "non-afflictive" ignorance is in fact just a subtle level of afflictive ignorance.

Hence, this tenet is linked to the fact that one must overcome subtle ignorance and not merely the conception of a self of persons as defined in the lower schools; otherwise, one might be an ersatz "Arhat" who manifests some kinds of desire or aversion based on having a remainder of ignorance. The Prāsaṅgika basis of refutation in this case is simply a refusal to dilute the achievement of becoming an Arhat by permitting it to include a residue of what to them is obviously ignorance-based action. Their "innovation" is the assertion of desire or aversion that is thoroughly mixed with the conception of true existence, making it clear that "Arhats" with even subtle craving are mislabeled.

Common Beings Can Have Yogic Direct Perception

The third tenet concerning Arhats is Jamyang Shayba's argument, based on a sūtra cited by Candrakīrti, that even common beings can have yogic directly perceiving consciousnesses (*rnal 'byor mngon sum, yoga-pratyakṣa*). Yogic direct perception is a special type of mental direct perception that arises from meditative stabilization, but most definitions of it specify that it occurs only in the continuum of a Superior.[53] However, Jamyang Shayba refers to the so-called "Arhats" who have obviously had yogic direct perception, since they *have* been able to realize the sixteen coarse attributes of the four noble truths.[54] However, they are not Superiors, but only common beings, because they have not realized the subtle aspects of the four noble truths. Dzongkaba's *Illumination of the Thought, Explanation of (Candrakīrti's) "Entrance"* says:[55]

> Also, in the *Sutra on the Miserliness of One in Trance* (*bsam gtan dpe 'khyud kyi mdo, dhyānitamuṣi*), which is quoted in [the twenty-fourth chapter of] Candrakīrti's *Clear Words*,[56] Buddha says, "Mañjuśrī, sentient beings, whose minds are mistaken due to four errors through not seeing the noble truths correctly as they are in reality, do not pass beyond this unreal cyclic existence." Mañjuśrī responds, "Oh, Supramundane Victor,[57] please indicate what is apprehended by sentient beings that causes them not to pass beyond cyclic existence." The Teacher said that sentient beings are not liberated because they do not know the four

[53]The definition of yogic direct perception (based on Dignāga and Dharmakīrti) in Geshay Jambel Sambel's typical Gelukba text (4a.1-2; translated in Lati Rinbochay and Napper [61-62]) is: "a non-conceptual non-mistaken exalted knower in the continuum of a Superior that is produced from a meditative stabilization that is a union of calm abiding and special insight and that has become its own unique empowering condition." Obviously, Jamyang Shayba would delete "of a Superior," since he holds that even common beings can have yogic direct perception.

[54]The sixteen attributes of the four noble truths consist of the four attributes of true sufferings—impermanence, misery, emptiness, and selflessness; the four attributes of true origins—cause, origin, strong production, and condition; the four attributes of true cessations—cessation, pacification, auspicious highness, and definite emergence; and the four attributes of true paths—path, suitability, achievement, and deliverance (Losang Gönchok, *Word Commentary* 258.4-59.1). For an explanation of each of these attributes and the manner in which they are contemplated in meditation, see Hopkins (1983a: 292-96).

[55]*Illumination of the Thought* 31b.5-32a.5. This is basically unaltered from Hopkins' translation (1980: 162-63).

[56]*Clear Words* 342.4 ff. (Poussin's Sanskrit text is 516.5-18.6).

[57]On the justification for translating *bcom ldan 'das* (*bhagavan*) as Supramundane (or Transcendent) Victor, see Lopez (1987: 196, n. 46).

> truths as they are in reality, and Mañjuśrī requested Buddha to explain what is misconceived by sentient beings that causes them not to be liberated from cyclic existence. In answer to this, Buddha says that they think, "I will pass beyond cyclic existence, and I will attain nirvāṇa," with a sense of adhering to the true existence of these. Therefore, when they have meditated on impermanence and so forth, they think, "I know suffering, I have abandoned its sources, I have actualized its cessation, I have cultivated the path." They then think, "I have become an Arhat." When they have temporarily abandoned the manifest [coarse] afflictions explained above, they think, "I have extinguished all contaminations." It is said that at the time of death they perceive that they will be reborn; thereby, they doubt Buddha, and this fault causes them to fall into a great hell. This applies to some who abide on such a path but not to all.

These persons conceive of things as truly existent even in their meditation on subtle impermanence, and so forth. Therefore, they manage to abandon, or suppress, coarse afflictions only temporarily.

Jamyang Shayba's stand that yogic direct perception is not necessarily included only in the continuum of a Superior is a conclusion drawn from Dzongkaba's analysis of the *Sūtra on the Miserliness of One in Trance*, a sūtra cited in Candrakīrti's *Clear Words*. What is gained or lost by this position? Jamyang Shayba allows the possibility that the so-called Arhats have yogic direct perception while carefully stipulating that they have not achieved liberation. This, of course, is an attack on the way in which the lower schools define the four noble truths, particularly the way in which they define ignorance. Because their identification of the self to be negated in the view of selflessness has been too coarse, no one could become an Arhat by merely adhering to their tenets.

One Can Directly Realize the Sixteen Aspects of the Four Noble Truths Even before the Path of Preparation

Jamyang Shayba makes essentially the same point concerning the fourth tenet of this type when he contends that one can directly realize the sixteen aspects of the four noble truths even before the path of preparation (*sbyor lam, prayogamārga*). These sixteen attributes have both coarse and subtle aspects; e.g., coarse sufferings arise from the coarse actions and afflictions established by the coarse conception of self, subtle sufferings from the subtle conception of self.[58] Hence, it is possible for one to directly realize the *coarse* sixteen attributes of the four noble truths without having reached the path of preparation, i.e., without having had special insight with respect to the subtle emptiness. Hypothetically, this could be done without reaching even the first path, the path of accumulation (*tshogs lam, saṃbhāramārga*), though it seems unlikely that one might realize impermanence or selflessness without having generated the spirit of renunciation.

The point being made here is that although there are some persons who claim to be Arhats on the basis of having realized the sixteen aspects of the four noble truths, it is easy to see that they have not attained special insight that realizes the subtle emptiness and hence have not attained the heat path of preparation because, as Jamyang Shayba points out, they are boastful whereas real Arhats are not:[59]

> Because the attainment of special insight realizing emptiness and the heat (*drod, uṣmagata*) path of preparation are simultaneous,[60] when those are attained such pride of wrong

[58]Losang Gönchok, *Word Commentary* 259.2.

[59]*Great Exposition of Tenets* 37b.2.

[60]From among the five paths comprising the spiritual course, the path of preparation (*sbyor lam, prayogamārga*) is the second, attained upon achieving special insight with emptiness as its object. Special insight is defined as "a wisdom of thorough discrimination of phenomena conjoined with special

> conceit [i.e., boasting] is not produced. Therefore, one does not arrive even at the path of preparation by just directly realizing the sixteen coarse attributes of the four truths.

This is essentially the same point as was made with regard to yogic direct perception, where persons who considered themselves to be Arhats were obviously mistaken since they, upon having realized the sixteen aspects of the four noble truths, generated doubt with respect to the Buddha's enlightenment, demonstrating that they had only temporarily suppressed the manifest afflictions.

True Cessations Are the *Dharmadhātu*

Finally, Jamyang Shayba, citing Nāgārjuna and Dzongkaba argues that true cessations (*'gog bden, nirodha-satya*), absences of afflictions in the minds of persons who have irrevocably eliminated a portion of the afflictions, are the element of a [Superior's] qualities (*chos dbyings, dharmadhātu*),[61]

---

pliancy induced by the power of analysis" (Jamyang Shayba, *Great Exposition of the Concentrations and Formlessnesses*, 81b.3, cited in Hopkins (1983a: 92). Special insight may be directed at the sixteen aspects of the four noble truths such as the coarse selflessness of the person (thus, even ordinary beings can have yogic direct perception, as Jamyang Shayba argues in chapter 4). However, unless special insight has the subtle emptiness as its object one cannot use it to reach the path of preparation. Although Jamyang Shayba's college, Gomang, asserts that a coarse selflessness of the person *is* an emptiness, this is a coarse emptiness and the realization of it is not liberating. The "heat" path of preparation is the first of four parts of that path, the path over which one's conceptual realization of emptiness is deepened. Upon completing the remaining three parts of the path of preparation, one is brought to the point of non-conceptual direct realization of emptiness.

[61]Maitreya, in his *Discrimination of the Middle and the Extremes* (I.15-16) explains that the term *chos dbyings* (*dharmadhātu*) is synonymous with emptiness and etymologizes it as "the cause of the qualities (*chos, dharma*) of Superiors" (*'phags pa'i chos kyi rgyu, hetutvāccāryadharmā*). Tibetan is P 5522, vol. 108, 30.4.4-5. For Sanskrit, see Pandeya (1971: 38-39). Dzongkaba explains that emptiness is the cause of the qualities of Superiors because meditation on it acts as a cause for becoming a Superior; his interpretation

i.e., emptiness. The import of this is that it then follows that all Superiors are persons who have realized emptiness, not anything more coarse such as the absence of a self-sufficient person, since Superiors are necessarily those who have realized true cessations. Jamyang Shayba makes this point through his exegesis of Nāgārjuna's *Sixty Stanzas of Reasoning*:[62]

> True cessations are understood to be the element of a [Superior's] qualities, i.e., [emptiness]) by way of how they are included in the four truths and two truths. Nāgārjuna's *Sixty Stanzas of Reasoning* (4cd) says:[63]
>
> > Through [believing in inherent] existence one is not released.
> > Through [believing in total] non-existence one does not transcend cyclic existence.
> > By thoroughly understanding [the nature of] things and non-things (*dngos med, abhāva*),[64]
> > The great beings are released.
>
> Thereby, it is also explained that Superiors realize emptiness.

What is not so clear is why Jamyang Shayba considers true cessations to be emptinesses, and hence to be ultimate truths within the division of all phenomena into two truths, ultimate truths (*don dam bden pa, paramārthasatya*) and conventional

---

relies on Vimuktisena's *Illumination of the 25,000 Stanza Perfection of Wisdom Sutra* (see Hopkins [1980: 178-79]; also see Ngawang Belden, *Annotations dbu* 8b.6 (Hopkins [1983: 383]).

[62]*Great Exposition of Tenets* 39b.5.

[63]P 5225, vol. 95, 11.2.6-7. The citation has been expanded by adding the first two lines. The Tibetan, and the Sanskrit reconstruction by Uriūtso Ryūshin, reproduced in Tola and Dragonetti (98), are: *yod pas rnam par mi grol te/ med pas srid pa 'di las min. // idaṃ bhavas ca nirvāṇam ubhayaṃ naiva vidyate/ bhava eva parijñāto nirvāṇam iti kathyate.*

[64]According to Candrakīrti (*Entrance to the Middle Way* VI.220 [14b.1]), *abhāva* means uncompounded phenomenon (*'dus ma byas kyi chos, asaṃskṛta-dharma*). In other words, the "great beings" understand all phenomena, impermanent and permanent.

truths (*kun rdzob bden pa, saṃvṛtisatya*). True cessations are absences of afflictions in the minds of persons who have irrevocably eliminated a portion of the afflictions; but are they emptinesses of inherent existence, as Jamyang Shayba says? According to Jamyang Shayba:[65]

> Candrakīrti's *Clear Words* (XVIII.1):[66]
>
> > Internal and external things are not observable [as truly existent]. Therefore, the consciousnesses conceiving the internal and external as [inherently existent] self and as [inherently existent] mine are extinguished totally. Here, this is suchness.
>
> The meaning of this is set forth in Dzongkaba's *Great Exposition of the Stages of the Path* (*lam rim chen mo*):[67]
>
> > The total extinguishment of all conceptions of [inherently existent] I and mine through the thorough pacification of all these appearances of the varieties of internal and external phenomena as [their own] suchness, whereas they are not [their own] suchness, along with their predispositions, is the suchness that is to be attained here, the Truth Body.
>
> This explains that true cessations are ultimate truths.[68]

"Suchness," i.e., emptiness, here is explained to be the elimination of the object of the conception of an inherently existent I and mine. Thus, in Jamyang Shayba's view, a true cessation is being explicitly indicated by Candrakīrti and Dzongkaba to be an emptiness.

---

[65]*Great Exposition of Tenets* 40b.1.

[66]*Clear Words* 220.3. The Sanskrit is in Poussin 340.6-7: *ādhyātmikabāhyāśeṣavastvanupalambhenādhyātmaṃ bahiśca yaḥ sarvathāhaṃkāramamatāraparijñaya idamatra tattvaṃ.* Also translated by Sprung (165).

[67]Dzongkaba, *Great Exposition of the Stages of the Path*, 371b.2-3.

[68]The "suchness to be attained" is the adventitiously pure Nature Truth Body (*ngo bo nyid sku, svabhāvika-kāya*), the emptiness of the Buddha's omniscient consciousness and the ultimate true cessation.

Not all Gelukbas agree with Jamyang Shayba; Paṇchen Sönam Drakba (*paṇ-chen bsod-nams-grag-pa*, 1478-1554), author of textbooks for Loseling College of Drebung Monastery, regards true cessations to be ultimate truths but not necessarily to be the element of qualities, emptiness.[69] His position is that a true cessation, being the abandonment of a specific affliction (such as desire, hatred, or ignorance) in a yogi's mental continuum, is merely the negation of that affliction and not a negation of true existence. They argue that the object of negation of a true cessation is an existent (an affliction), whereas the object of negation of a wisdom consciousness realizing emptiness is a non-existent (inherent existence). However, Jamyang Shayba can avoid the possible problem of explaining how, without switching objects of observation, persons realizing an absence of inherent existence on the uninterrupted path of a path of meditation in one moment are in the next moment able to realize the factor of an absence of an affliction in their own continua.

Pratyakṣa Refers to Objects

Finally, several Prāsaṅgika tenets do not fall into either of the previous two categories. For instance, Prāsaṅgikas make what seems to be a rather minor point that the term *pratyakṣa* refers principally to objects, not the consciousnesses that realize them. It is not necessary to reserve the term for valid directly perceiving consciousnesses. Jamyang Shayba explains:[70]

> The [Sanskrit] translation equivalent of *mngon sum*, *pratyakṣa*, was used for both *mngon sum* [which often refers to a directly perceiving consciousness] and *mngon gyur* ["manifest phenomenon," synonymous with manifest object]. Hence, when the two, a pot and the directly perceiving sense

[69]According to Geshay Belden Drakba, this is the position taken in Paṇchen Sönam Drakba's *General Meaning of (Maitreya's) "Ornament for Clear Realization."*

[70]*Great Exposition of Tenets* 39b.2.

consciousness apprehending it, are considered together, it is asserted that the pot is the actual *pratyakṣa* and that the term *pratyakṣa* is used imputedly with respect to the directly perceiving sense consciousness. Candrakīrti's *Commentary on (Āryadeva's) "Four Hundred"* says:[71]

> In that way [when considering a subject and object together], a consciousness is not fit to be considered a *pratyakṣa*. It is fit for the object [to be considered a *pratyakṣa*].

And, his *Clear Words* says:[72]

> Furthermore, because the term *pratyakṣa* expresses the meaning, "not hidden," *pratyakṣa* means to manifest to a sense-power. With respect to [*pratyakṣa*], since it is taken to mean "manifesting to a sense power," non-hidden phenomena such as a pot or blue are established as manifest objects (*mngon sum, pratyakṣa*), and the consciousnesses which thoroughly distinguish those are called manifest (*mngon sum, pratyakṣa*) due to having as their cause a manifest object like hay-fire or grass-fire.[73]

In general, then, the Prāsaṅgika School does not consider consciousnesses to be *pratyakṣa*. However, a consciousness that has its objects "before the eyes," that is, a directly perceiving consciousness, is also often called *pratyakṣa*. Candrakīrti explains that they come to have that name only by way of their association with their objects. Just as fire in the instances of a hay-fire or grass-fire has been given the name of its object,

---

[71]P 5266, vol. 98, 259.3.4.

[72]*Clear Words* 48.1-3. The Sanskrit is in Poussin 71.10-11. The quotation has been restored to full length. Translations by Sprung (61) and Stcherbatsky (1927: 244).

[73]There are several etymologies for the term *pratyakṣa*. Poussin gives sources (1970: 71-72, n. 4); Stcherbatsky (1927: 250, n. 2) says that Vasubandhu's definition in *Nyāyavārti* (42—edition unspecified) is quite different from Dignāga's in his *Compendium of Prime Cognition* (*pramāṇa-samuccaya*) I.15 (P 5700, vol. 130, Toh. 4203). The etymology followed by the Prāsaṅgika School appears to be "before the eyes" (*prati*, before, + *akṣa*, eyes), in the sense of objects obvious to the senses.

the substance being burned, so consciousnesses are given the name *pratyakṣa* ("manifest") because their objects are *pratyakṣa* ("manifest"). Still, this is not the only sense in which consciousnesses are *pratyakṣa*; minds themselves can be manifest objects for other minds, such as the eye consciousness apprehending a form that is later recalled by a memory consciousness. This does not contradict Candrakīrti's point, since in this sense minds are being considered as objects rather than as apprehending subjects, and it is the latter sense that is being rejected as the main meaning of *pratyakṣa*. As Ngawang Belden states:[74]

> Whatever is an established base (*gzhi grub*) is necessarily an actual manifest object (*mngon sum, pratyakṣa*) in relation to an awareness that clearly realizes it, and with regard to whatever consciousness is a valid directly perceiving consciousness with respect to an object, that consciousness is necessarily an imputed directly perceiving consciousness (*mngon sum, pratyakṣa*) in relation to that object.

Ngawang Belden himself thinks that not only is *pratyakṣa* not restricted to only sense-objects (which would have excluded consciousnesses), but that *all* phenomena are *pratyakṣa* to awarenesses that clearly, i.e., directly realize them. This would imply that for him, even a permanent phenomenon such as an emptiness can be considered a *pratyakṣa* in relation to the wisdom consciousness of meditative equipoise directly realizing it.

How Prāsaṅgikas Avoid the Two Extremes

Finally, according to Dzongkaba, it is a unique Prāsaṅgika tenet that the extreme of permanence or eternalism is avoided through the appearance of conventional truths, and the extreme of annihilation is avoided through positing them as empty of inherent existence. This is based on Dzongkaba's

[74] *Annotations*, note *cha*, 117b.2-3.

statements regarding the compatibility of emptiness and dependent-arising in his *Three Principal Aspects of the Path* (*lam gyi gtso bo rnam gsum*, stanza 13):[75]

> When [the two realizations of dependent-arising and emptiness exist] simultaneously without alternation
> And when from only seeing dependent-arising as infallible,
> Definite knowledge entirely destroys the mode of apprehension [of the conception of inherent existence],
> Then the analysis of the view [of reality] is complete.
> ...
> Further, the extreme of [inherent] existence is excluded [by knowledge of the nature] of appearances [existing only as nominal designations],
> And the extreme of [total] non-existence is excluded [by knowledge of the nature] of emptiness [as the absence of inherent existence and not the absence of nominal existence].

Ngawang Belden explains:[76]

> For persons who have completed analysis of the view as in this passage, the force of the awareness conceiving inherent existence decreases to the extent they apply their minds to the meaning of dependent-arisings which are [understood to be] posited by names and terms. This is the way the extreme of [inherent] existence is eliminated through appearance.
>
> Also, for such persons, the force of the awareness that lacks conviction in the cause and effect of actions and conceives those to be non-existent decreases to the extent they apply their minds to the emptiness of inherent existence. This is the way the extreme of non-existence [i.e., no conventional existence] is eliminated through emptiness.

---

[75]P 6087, vol. 153. Thurman (1982) identifies the first part as Dzongkaba *Collected Works*, vol. *kha*, 230b.4-31b.5. This translation follows that of Hopkins in Tenzin Gyatso, Dalai Lama XIV (1984: 148, 153). First part also translated by Hopkins and Sopa (101-2) and by Hopkins (1987: 22). Janggya cites this passage (see Hopkins, 1987: 348-49) and explains that it means that the more one comes to understand emptiness, the better is one's understanding of phenomena as being merely dependent imputations, and vice versa.

[76]*Annotations* 119a.2.-3.

All Buddhist philosophers might say that the extreme of existence is avoided through realizing selflessness and that the existence of non-existence is avoided through the appearance of conventional phenomena, but, according to Gelukba scholars, the Prāsaṅgikas are asserting that the opposite also is true. It seems that by switching these terms, the Prāsaṅgikas are emphasizing the compatibility of emptiness and dependent-arising. The observation of dependent-arisings is a sign of their lack of inherent existence, and the realization of emptiness makes possible one's understanding of conventionalities *as* conventionalities. Similarly, Dzongkaba says in the beginning of the sixth chapter of his *Illumination of the Thought* that understanding that phenomena are merely imputed by thought assists one in understanding emptiness, whereas usually it is said that until one has realized emptiness one is unable to understand conventionalities as mere conventionalities, imputed by thought.

This tenet does not seem to be directed against any particular school, although it implicitly rejects any explanation of the avoidance of the two extremes that does not reject inherent existence, since otherwise one would fall to an extreme of permanence. All other Buddhist schools would fall to that extreme.

This concludes our survey of the unique tenets of the Prāsaṅgika School as described by some of the luminaries of the Gelukba tradition.

7 Conclusion

Now that we have concluded our survey of the unique tenets of the Prāsaṅgika School as identified and developed in Tibetan Gelukba sources, we can address several questions of a general nature. The most general question is whether or not these tenets are actually those of the Indian founders of the Mādhyamika and Prāsaṅgika-Mādhyamika Schools, recalling that according to Dzongkaba, all of these tenets stem from the writings of the father of the Mādhyamika School, Nāgārjuna. Of course, since Nāgārjuna himself claims only to be propounding the thought of the Buddha in the Perfection of Wisdom Sūtras, his special inspiration and original source for these tenets would have to be the Buddha himself. But did the Sage of the Śākyas ever counsel his monks not to use "autonomous syllogisms"? Did he speak of "obstructions to omniscience"? Did he assert "conceptual mental direct perception"? Certainly he did not do so explicitly. But if, as is claimed in these Gelukba sources, he denied inherent existence, he logically would also deny autonomous syllogisms. If he taught the Mahāyāna sūtras, he denied that Hearer Arhats have destroyed the predispositions established by ignorance, even though they have destroyed ignorance itself, and therefore he would affirm the existence of obstructions to omniscience. If he did not deny that memory is mental direct perception, he might well affirm it if asked. And so forth.

The sūtras are cited on a number of occasions: to show that there are so-called Arhats who actually have subtle afflictions and, in their disappointment over not being liberated, cause their own births in a hell; that Hearer Arhats have not overcome the obstructions to omniscience; that death (disintegratedness) acts as a cause; that even the Buddha accepted what the world accepted; and that self-consciousness is absurd. On other points, the product of philosophical development in the centuries after Śākyamuni's *parinirvāṇa,* it is only the much later writings of Nāgārjuna and his followers that provide direct authority for the collectors of unique tenets.

Nāgārjuna, as the articulator of the unique view that nothing can withstand ultimate analysis, is cited a little more frequently than are the sūtras. He is cited to show that external objects exist, since minds and objects equally conventionally exist; that *pramāṇa* need not mean new realization; that self-consciousness is absurd; that disintegratedness is a functioning thing; and that one cannot become a Superior without realizing the subtle aspects of the four noble truths. His disciple, Āryadeva, is cited to demonstrate that ignorance is the basis of all the afflictions; that disintegratedness is itself caused; and that the conventions of the world must be respected.

These citations are insufficient in themselves to justify Dzongkaba's characterization of the "unique tenets" as difficult points in Nāgārjuna's *Treatise on the Middle Way*, except in the sense that many of them are rooted in the basic viewpoint of the Mādhyamika School. Nevertheless, they do support the Gelukba contention that Nāgārjuna, far from being "without any thesis," definitely held positions on a variety of epistemological, metaphysical, and soteriological issues, and that he respected the conventions of the world.

Despite Dzongkaba's nod to Nāgārjuna, the Gelukba authors whose works we have been considering have clearly founded their analysis of the unique tenets of the Prāsaṅgika School on the rock of Candrakīrti, who in turn is seen as supplementing and clarifying the work of Nāgārjuna. Occasionally, other Indians such as Śāntideva are cited, but on relatively few occasions. Jamyang Shayba, who has put together the most extensive list of the unique tenets, refers to Candrakīrti at every opportunity; Ngawang Belden, his annotator, glosses the quotations with which Jamyang Shayba peppers his text and offers many passages from Dzongkaba's commentary on Candrakīrti's *Entrance* and his *The Essence of the Good Explanations*. Janggya cites authorities far less frequently, and when he does tends to cite Dzongkaba, but obviously has drawn arguments from Candrakīrti even when he does not cite him.

From Candrakīrti has come an insistence on the uniqueness of Nāgārjuna's system. Indeed, one could find little better justification than these topics for translating the *avatāra* in the title of Candrakīrti's *Madhyamakāvatāra* as "supplement," since that work explicitly distinguishes the system founded by Nāgārjuna from the systems of Cittamātra and Svātantrika-Mādhyamika. There were obviously many topics, such as that of a mind-basis-of-all, that Nāgārjuna either did not anticipate or on which he did not comment (presuming, as the tradition does, that he was still alive at the time of the founding of the Cittamātra School); on such matters, Candrakīrti supplied what Gelukbas accept would be Nāgārjuna's view. Candrakīrti also is the source for the bulk of the unique tenets; only a few of the topics we have considered are built on anything other than a passage from his works.

However, it is also obvious that Candrakīrti did not attempt to lay out his own system of tenets; his greatest works are his *Clear Words*, a commentary on the *Treatise on the Middle Way*, and his *Entrance* to Nāgārjuna's text, and even in the latter he identifies Mādhyamika tenets only to the extent that he is defending Nāgārjuna's thought against the emerging Cittamātra and Svātantrika-Mādhyamika systems. Thus, it is really the Gelukbas who systematize. We have seen that they do not openly innovate, but rather modestly advertise their project as the distillation, the creation of an anthology, of many sources on a topic. But they do much more than this. For instance, we have seen that of twelve arguments made against the Cittamātra School refutation of external objects, Candrakīrti is the explicit source of only four.

The question of whether or not these Tibetans have accurately represented their Indian antecedents is one that cannot be answered here. In the first place, the terseness and ambiguity of many passages in the Indian texts make it difficult to definitively assess their intent. This is particularly true of Nāgārjuna. Second, the establishment of the full context in which the citations are found remains a desideratum. Many of the texts on which the Gelukbas have relied remain unstudied or have not themselves been adequately contextualized. I have attempted here, with all citations I was able to locate in their original sources, to read enough of the surrounding material to determine their context, but I did not study these texts in depth.

The crux of the Gelukba presentation of the unique Prāsaṅgika tenets has been the two-fold assertion, based on Candrakīrti, that no phenomenon inherently exists and that, in general, what is well known to the world should also be accepted by philosophers. By making the first assertion, the Gelukba Prāsaṅgikas have been able to make a distinction between ultimate and conventional analysis, since positing of objects upon engaging in ultimate analysis involves the imputation of inherently existent entities or relationships. Thus, the Cittamātra refutation of external objects can be rejected in part because it involves ultimate analysis into the causes of consciousnesses; the existence of a mind-basis-of-all can be rejected because, in part, its assertion involves the notion that it is findable under analysis; self-consciousness is rejected because its postulation involves the assertion of an analytically findable, inherent difference between the object of one's recollection and the object originally experienced; objections to positing disintegratedness as a functioning thing are dismissed because they would involve ultimate analysis into the findability of a state of having been destroyed apart from that which has been destroyed; that conventional valid cognition is necessarily non-mistaken with regard to the mode of being of its object is rejected as involving the assertion of analytically findable objects; autonomous syllogisms are rejected because they would involve the assertion that the three modes of the sign in such syllogisms are analytically findable; and that *pramāṇa* must mean "new realization" is rejected because it would involve ultimate analysis to find a basis of designation—moments of consciousness—identical to the objected designated—*pramāṇa*. Thus, non-Prāsaṅgikas are criticized for either postulating an inherently existent entity that could supposedly withstand analysis, or for using such analysis to overturn legitimate conventions of the world.

The second basic Gelukba assertion on the unique Prāsaṅgika tenets, directly drawn from Candrakīrti, is that the world's conventions should generally be accepted. Even if this were not clearly stated by Candrakīrti, Dzongkaba's legendary encounter with Mañjushrī (the Bodhisattva personifying wisdom), who reportedly advised him to value appearances even as he sought to understand their emptiness, would have influenced the Gelukba stance.[1] For the most part, this is clearly stated: the world obviously accepts external objects; the world's language shows that it thinks of death or disintegratedness as being caused and acting as a cause; the world does not conceive that memory requires an intermediary consciousness; the world uses the term *pramāṇa* in the sense of "correct," not necessarily "first."

Even though these and other points are asserted by awarenesses to which things appear falsely, and which are therefore mistaken, Gelukbas affirm them; in the midst of mistakenness about the mode of being of phenomena is a *non*-mistaken aspect that deserves respect. Still, what of questions about which ordinary persons have no opinion? How is it "upholding the conventions of the world" when it comes to questions such as how nirvāṇa with and without remainder should be defined, or whether yogic direct perception can be attained by common beings, or what kinds of selflessness are realized by Arhats. In these cases, Gelukbas sometimes try to distinguish between ordinary and non-ordinary conventions, or between

[1]Dzongkaba's biography is summarized and elucidated by Thurman (1984: 65-89); this episode is recounted on p. 79.

what is well known to the *world* and well known to *ordinary people in the world,* etc., though in the sources we have examined there is not sufficient explanation of these distinctions to make them fully useful. Principally, Gelukbas assert that these tenets can be adopted because they can be established by conventional valid cognition, without relying on ultimate analysis.

But *why* should the conventions of the world be so honored? Are not the descriptions of philosophers, qualified in such a way as to clarify the nature and relationships of phenomena, better to rely upon? There is no direct answer to this question in the sources we have at our disposal, but it seems to me that the Prāsaṅgikas /Gelukbas feel that it is essential to the project of liberating sentient beings that people not have their faith in worldly conventions weakened. That might seem to be an odd assertion, since they have identified the root of saṃsāra to be the assent to the false appearance of the world; but we must remember that only one part of that appearance is declared to be false, and it is from the remainder that the Prāsaṅgikas can work with people, or they can work with themselves. The salvific process called "meditation on emptiness" begins with identifying the precise way in which phenomena, personal or otherwise, appear to the mind. It introduces an unhelpful level of complexity to declare that sense perception is fundamentally unveridical or that there are types of consciousness, such as the mind-basis-of-all, that exist but cannot be experienced. The Prāsaṅgika, says the Gelukba, wants to simplify matters so as to be able to focus on the analysis of ordinary experience. Thus, upholding the conventions of the world as a way to abet the all-important work of coming to realize emptiness is one aspect of the religious significance of the unique tenets. Another, it seems to me, is that in order to keep good ethics, one needs to have conviction in a convincing presentation of conventional phenomena. Dzongkaba implies this when he says:[2]

---

[2]Dharamsala edition of the *Great Exposition of the Stages of the Path* 408b.1.

> Therefore, in the system of the masters Buddhapālita and Candrakīrti, inherent existence, that is, establishment by way of the object's own entity, is refuted even conventionally. Hence, it appears to be very difficult to posit conventional objects. If one does not know how to posit these well, without damage [by reasoning], one does not gain ascertainment with respect to the class of deeds whereby it appears that most fall to a view of deprecation.

Dzongkaba's thought seems to be that if one feels that the appearances of the world have no validity, one treats them with contempt; how, then, could one act properly? How could it be possible for one to generate compassion for others?

Also, the acceptance of the world's conventions is a principal way for the Prāsaṅgikas to demonstrate that they have many theses, positive as well as negative, and not merely on the topics mentioned in the "unique tenets," but in all other areas as well. For to fully live up to Candrakīrti's acceptance of the world's conventions, Prāsaṅgikas must accept as part of their world-view all that can be verified by valid cognition. This is virtually a reversal of the critical stance, cited in chapter 1, that characterizes Nāgārjuna's system as nihilistic and single-minded and would lead one to expect that the Prāsaṅgika system, to the extent that any system existed, would be mere negation. However, the Prāsaṅgika philosophy of Candrakīrti, particularly as it is developed in the Tibetan Gelukba sources to which we have referred, is actually a school rich with ideas, freed by the dynamic principle that nothing has inherent existence, and holds its own as a conceptual system within the traditions of Buddhist philosophy. The "unique tenets" are themselves only a few of the many issues to which the unique Prāsaṅgika viewpoint could be applied.

Indeed, while noting that this book is but a beginning to the project of understanding the unique tenets of the Prāsaṅgika School, we should also recognize that their philosophical development is clearly not finished, at least within Gelukba scholasticism. The Gelukba tradition is a living force, and at least as long as it can survive, monks will study Dzongkaba's discussion of the unique tenets; as long as Jamyang Shayba is revered, young monks will memorize his verses on the schools of tenets, including the unique tenets of the Prāsaṅgika School. And they will debate about them. Dzongkaba's or Jamyang Shayba's or Janggya's interpretation of the points comprising the unique tenets is not sacrosanct; their positions can be effectively undermined in the crucible of debate. Indeed, an extension of this book would include a record of the sorts of debates a monastic class would create in their study of each of these tenets. With regard to the endurance of this tradition, the mirror is now clouded: perhaps the whole tradition will fade away under the pressure of the tragic events of this century, or perhaps it will be firmly rooted in India or the West and be continued. I conclude the present work in 1995, with guarded optimism that for a long time to come it will still be possible to find Tibetan philosophers for whom the unique tenets of the Prāsaṅgika School are living questions.

Part Two

Jamyang Shayba's "Unique Tenets of the Prāsaṅgika-Mādhyamika School"

from Jamyang Shayba Ngawang Dzöndrü's *Great Exposition of Tenets / Explanation of "Tenets," Sun of the Land of Samantabhadra Brilliantly Illuminating All of Our Own and Others' Tenets and the Meaning of the Profound, Ocean of Scripture and Reasoning Fulfilling All Hopes of All Beings*

With the Annotations of Ngawang Belden

from Ngawang Belden's *Annotations for the "Great Exposition of Tenets," Freeing the Knots of the Difficult Points, Precious Jewel of Clear Thought*

Translator's Introduction

The portion of Jamyang Shayba's *Great Exposition of Tenets* translated in the following pages is only a small part of the twelfth chapter of that massive work. The first third of the chapter, concerning the interpretation of scripture, the object of negation in meditation on emptiness, and the reasonings used to generate realization of emptiness, has been translated by Jeffrey Hopkins.[1]

The twelfth is the penultimate chapter, followed only by a short "elimination of doubts" with respect to tantra, the Vajrayāna (Diamond Vehicle). In previous chapters Jamyang Shayba discusses the nature of philosophical tenets *(grub mtha', siddhānta)*; refutes the positions of the six orthodox systems of Indian philosophy (Vedānta, Mīmāṃsa, Nyāya, Vaiśeṣika and Sāṃkhya / Yoga), their minor variants, and the theologies of Vaiṣṇavism and Śaivism; refutes the positions of the materialist Cārvāka and heterodox Jaina systems; discusses Buddhist tenets in general; presents the Vaibhāṣika and Sautrāntika systems; presents a traditional history of the Mahāyāna; presents the Cittamātra system; introduces the Mādhyamika system; and presents the Svātantrika-Mādhyamika system.

There are three published editions of the *Great Exposition of Tenets*: the "Drashikyil edition," recently reprinted by Go-

[1]Hopkins 1983.

mang and also included in *The Collected Works of 'Jam-dbaṅs-bzad-pa'i-rdo-rje* published in New Delhi in 1973 by Ngawang Gelek Demo; the "Musoorie edition" published by Dalama in 1962; and the "Gomang edition" published by Gomang College in India (n.d.).[2] The Musoorie and Gomang editions are essentially identical[3] and contain numerous errors not present in the Drashikyil edition. I began with the Musoorie edition but later compared the entire text to the Drashikyil edition (in the Ngawang Gelek printing); emendations based on that comparison will be found after the translations, "NG" denoting the Ngawang Gelek text. There are also references to "DSK" (the Gomang publication of the Drashikyil text), which I have been using for the past few years.

The translation of Jamyang Shayba's *Great Exposition of Tenets* has been interspersed with a translation of Ngawang Belden's *(ngag dbang dpal ldan,* b. 1779, known as Belden Chöjay [*dpal-ldan-chos-rje*]) *Annotations for the "Great Exposition of Tenets," Freeing the Knots of the Difficult Points, Precious Jewel of Clear Thought*. Page numbers from the *cha* section of the 1962 Musoorie edition used for the Jamyang Shayba translation and from the *dbu ma pa* section of the 1964 Sarnath edition used for the Ngawang Belden translation have been placed in the text, in brackets and boldfaced for greater contrast.

The chapter headings follow the organization of Jamyang Shayba's text, but the sub-headings often are my own, introduced for the sake of clarity. Ngawang Belden's annotations

[2]For a concordance of these three editions, see Mimaki (1982: 257-67). The Gomang and Ngawang Gelek printings of the Drashikyil edition are essentially identical although it is likely that the former was copied from the latter. The orthography is obviously different and the Gomang scribe sometimes finishes his copying before the end of the corresponding page in the Ngawang Gelek version and has to use ellipses or has to squeeze a bit more on the next page because he was not able to get a few words into the space available. The pagination of the two versions is different because in the Ngawang Gelek version each folio *side* in the entire volume has been counted separately, though it also has the usual folio numbers. The "unique tenets" are found in the Gomang edition, *cha* 48a.2-55a.1, in the Musoorie edition *cha* 36a.3-41a.6, and in the Drashikyil edition part II 201b.6-11a.1, enumerated as 1014.6-33.1 in the Ngawang Gelek printing.

[3]Hopkins (1983a: 568).

have been inserted at what seemed to be the proper place based on Ngawang Belden's comments on a particular text or point. However, Ngawang Belden does not quote or otherwise indicate, at the start of his notes, the precise passage in Jamyang Shayba on which he is commenting; thus, there are a few occasions where the Ngawang Belden annotation may have been inserted a little ahead or behind of the place in Jamyang Shayba's text where Ngawang Belden would have placed it himself.

Jamyang Shayba's Introduction: Why Prāsaṅgika Tenets are Unique

Jamyang Shayba:[1] The presentation of unique Prāsaṅgika-Mādhyamika School *(dbu ma thal 'gyur ba, prāsaṅgika-mādhyamika)* tenets has two parts: a brief indication and an extensive explanation.

A. Brief Indication of the Unique Tenets

Candrakīrti's *Autocommentary on the "Entrance to the Middle Way" (dbu ma la 'jug pa'i bshad pa, madhyamakāvatārabhaṣya)* says,[2] "The learned should determine that this system[3] is

[1]*Great Exposition of Tenets cha* 36a.3.

[2]*Autocommentary on the "Entrance"* 255.5; also, P 5263, vol. 98, 166.2.5-6. This is a citation of the *Entrance to the Middle Way* 17b.9 (epilogue). Cf. Huntington 196.

[3]"This system" can be taken as either the Mādhyamika of Nāgārjuna or the Prāsaṅgika School, for Candrakīrti certainly saw no difference between Nāgārjuna's thought and his own. Candrakīrti justified his own rejection of autonomous syllogisms *(svatantra-prayoga)* and use of contradictory consequences by Nāgārjuna's example. See *Clear Words* 24.7-5.2; translation by Sprung (1979: 38-39). As Dzongkaba notes in the beginning of his *Illumination of the Thought, Explanation of (Candrakīrti's) "Entrance"* (6.3.-8.2), Candrakīrti wrote his *Entrance to the Middle Way* in order to demonstrate the unsuitability of interpreting Nāgārjuna, the founder of the Mādhyamika system, according to other tenet systems (such as Cittamātra and Svātantri-

unique." Although there are many subtle [tenets] unshared with the Svātantrika-Mādhyamikas *(dbu ma rang rgyud pa)* and below, when they are condensed into the greater distinguishing features, there are eight pairs[4] of great distinguishing features. These may be known from Dzongkaba's *Illumination of the Thought, Explanation of (Candrakīrti's) "Entrance" (dbu ma dgongs pa rab gsal)*, Candrakīrti's *Autocommentary on the "Entrance"* and so forth. Because I have mentioned [some] of these earlier [in this book] and have also explained it extensively in other places, what follows is treated as a mere textual commentary.[5]

Ngawang Belden:[6] This is as Dzongkaba's *Illumination of the Thought, Explanation of (Candrakīrti's) "Entrance"* says:[7]

Candrakīrti's *Autocommentary on the "Entrance"* says:[8]

---

ka) and to fill in gaps on the Bodhisattva practices.

[4]Although Jamyang Shayba refers to Dzongkaba and Candrakīrti in connection with eight pairs of tenets, only he himself has composed such a list. Candrakīrti had no list of "unique Prāsaṅgika School tenets" (of course, he would not have applied the term "Prāsaṅgika" to himself or Buddhapālita). Dzongkaba's list of unique tenets had only eight items, not eight pairs. See the Introduction for a comparison of the lists of Dzongkaba, Jamyang Shayba, and others.

[5]When Jamyang Shayba says that the Prāsaṅgika School tenets should be known from Dzongkaba's *Illumination of the Thought*, and so forth, he means that those texts are important sources for these unique tenets, not that there is a list of points as such or that all of those topics are necessarily extensively discussed in those works. As will be seen, Jamyang Shayba often cites Candrakīrti and Dzongkaba and then expands upon their themes. Jamyang Shayba has mentioned some of these points earlier in the book, particularly in the "Introduction to the Mādhyamika School" chapter (chapter 10) where he refutes some of the assertions he has found in Daktsang (or at least has imputed to Daktsang). That what follows is considered a "mere textual commentary" *(gzhung 'grel tsam)* seems to indicate that he will not digress into hypothetical debates, as he often does elsewhere in the *Great Exposition of Tenets*.

[6]Note *pa*, 108a.5.

[7]*Illumination of the Thought* 264a.4-b.3.

[8]*Commentary on the Entrance* 255.3-7 (P 5263, vol. 98, 166.2.1-5). This passage appears similarly in these two editions and the Sarnath edition of Dzongkaba's *The Essence of the Good Explanations* (140), where this passage

May scholars ascertain that except for this Mādhyamika School textual system, in other treatises this doctrine of emptiness is not expressed without error;[9] just so, this system appearing here, which I have expressed along with answers to objections, does not, like the doctrine of emptiness, exist in other treatises. Because of that, the proposition by certain Mādhyamikas *(dbu ma pa)* that just what Sautrāntikas *(mdo sde pa)* and Vaibhāṣikas *(bye brag smra ba)* propound to be ultimate, Mādhyamikas assert to be conventional, is set forth by those who do not understand the suchness [explained] in (Nāgārjuna's) *Treatise on the Middle Way (dbu ma'i bstan bcos, madhyamakaśāstra)* because it is unreasonable for a

---

has also been cited, but here in *Illumination of the Thought* Dzongkaba has considerably edited it: for "Mādhyamika School textual system" *(dbu ma'i gzhung lugs)*, P (etc.) reads *"Treatise on the Middle Way" (dbu ma'i bstan bcos)*; for "other" *(gzhan na)*, P reads *gzhan las* (same meaning); for "not expressed" *(brjob pa med pa)*, P reads *mi brjod pa* (same meaning); for "this system appearing here" *('dir 'byung pa'i lugs kyang)*, P reads *lugs 'di nas 'byung pa de yang* (same meaning); for "certain Mādhyamikas" *(dbu ma pa kha cig)*, P reads just "someone" *(kha cig)*; the sentence concerning Sautrāntikas and Vaibhāṣikas is a combination of two nearly identical sentences in P; and for "do not understand the suchness" *(de kho na nyid ma shes pas)*, P reads *don gyi de kho na nyid mngon par mi shes pa kho nas* (same meaning). Dzongkaba's substantive alterations appear to be for the sake of clarifying Candrakīrti. He has altered *dbu ma'i bstan bcos* to *dbu ma'i gzhung lugs*, perhaps to indicate that in addition to Nāgārjuna's *Treatise on the Middle Way* there are other Mādhyamika School treatises that express the doctrine of emptiness correctly, for Candrakīrti certainly would not denigrate Nāgārjuna's other works on emptiness by suggesting that only the *Treatise on the Middle Way* is correct. He has also specified the persons who are mistaken about the Mādhyamika School's presentation of the ultimate and conventional as "certain Mādhyamikas"—in other words, the Svātantrika-Mādhyamikas. This is an important source for Dzongkaba's argument that the recognition of distinct branches of the Mādhyamika School is based on Candrakīrti's own assessments. See his *The Essence of the Good Explanations* 139.18 ff. (translated by Thurman [1984: 288]).

[9]In other words, the Mādhyamika School textual system of Nāgārjuna and Āryadeva is the only one that correctly sets forth the doctrine of emptiness, that phenomena are empty of inherent existence, and Candrakīrti is the only one who correctly understands Nāgārjuna's explanation of suchness (emptiness) in his *Treatise on the Middle Way*.

supramundane doctrine to be similar to a mundane doctrine.[10]

This is a system that posits all conventional presentations it asserts as being without establishment by their own character. Therefore, it asserts that tenets such as those of the two proponents of [truly existing external] objects which are presented only within establishment by the object's own character **[108b]** lack establishment not only ultimately but even conventionally.[11] Thus, [Candrakīrti] advises that this system of his is not only unshared even with the Cittamātrins *(sems tsham pa)* but should be known as unique in relation to the systems of other Mādhyamikas[12] who comment on the thought of the Protectors,[13] Nāgārjuna and Āryadeva.

---

[10]That is, if Nāgārjuna's doctrine were as the Svātantrika-Mādhyamikas have explained it, the supramundane doctrine of Nāgārjuna, a doctrine that actually leads to passage beyond sorrow *(myang 'das, nirvāṇa)* would be no better than the mundane doctrine of other schools.

[11]The "two proponents of truly existing external objects" are the Vaibhāṣikas and Sautrāntikas, who, according to Gelukbas, consider it impossible for an object to exist if it does not exist ultimately, i.e., is not established by its own character. The Cittamātrins also are proponents of true existence, and the Svātantrika-Mādhyamikas are proponents of inherent existence, but they assert inherent existence only conventionally, not ultimately. It is a unique Prāsaṅgika School tenet that objects lack inherent existence not only ultimately, but even conventionally.

[12]The Prāsaṅgika School also diverges from other Mādhyamikas, viz., the Svātantrika-Mādhyamikas, on this point, because the Svātantrika-Mādhyamikas assert that phenomena are established by their own character conventionally, though not ultimately. The sources for this in Indian Buddhist literature are few in number and without any clear, strong expression; it is a distinct contribution of later scholars in Tibet to have explored the differences between Candrakīrti and Bhāvaviveka, the founder of the Svātantrika-Mādhyamikas. For a discussion of the issues see Lopez (1987) and Hopkins (1983a).

[13]Nāgārjuna and Āryadeva are called "Protectors" because of protecting the kingdom of doctrine and conquering the foe of cyclic existence. Nāgārjuna is called Nāga-Arjuna, because like Arjuna he protects and destroys enemies (Hopkins 1983a: 356-57, paraphrasing Jamyang Shayba's *Great Exposition of Tenets* 4a.2 ff. [Musoorie ed.]).

Dzongkaba's *Great Exposition of Special Insight (hlag mthong chen mo)* says:[14]

> That which is asserted to be ultimate by those two schools [the Vaibhāṣika School and the Sautrāntika School] and not asserted [even] conventionally by Mādhyamikas refers to things such as partless [particles or moments of consciousness].[15] However, [Candrakīrti] is not indicating that what those two schools assert to be truly established is not asserted by Mādhyamikas conventionally, for even though they assert forms, sounds, and so forth, to be truly established, Mādhyamikas assert them conventionally.[16]

---

[14]*Great Exposition of Special Insight* 402a.1-2.

[15]Directionally partless particles and partless moments of consciousness are asserted by Vaibhāṣikas and Sautrāntikas Following Scripture (those who follow Vasubandhu's *Treasury of Higher Knowledge [abhidharmakośa]* instead of Dharmakīrti's *Seven Treatises on Valid Cognition*). For them, an ultimate, or ultimate truth, is something that cannot be reduced or analyzed in such a way that one's apprehension of it is cancelled. It is a "building block" out of which are made conventions or conventional truths, objects that cannot bear such analysis. They contend that the ultimate unit of matter is a particle too minuscule to be further divided, and the ultimate unit of consciousness is a moment too brief to be divided. Mādhyamikas (and Cittamātrins) accept neither directionally partless particles nor partless moments of consciousness, maintaining that no directionally partless particle nor partless moment can bear analysis; thus these are not asserted even conventionally. This will be discussed at greater length in chapter 1.

[16]Both Mādhyamikas and Sautrāntikas, for instance, assert the existence of tables and chairs. Thus, Mādhyamikas do assert the conventional existence of phenomena such as forms and sounds that Sautrāntikas and Vaibhāṣikas assert to be truly established. They simply do not assert that those phenomena truly exist.

However,[17] Dzongkaba's *The Essence of the Good Explanations (legs bshad snying po)* says:[18]

> Because our own system is unique in relation to other Mādhyamikas [i.e., the Svātantrika-Mādhyamikas, some persons] assert that what is propounded as ultimate by the two [schools that] propound [truly existent external] objects is asserted conventionally by Mādhyamikas. They are to be posited as not knowing the middle way suchness, the reason being that in our system phenomena that are established by their own character are not asserted even conventionally whereas they posit [phenomena] within [establishment by their own character].[19] If one falls from either of the two truths, one would fall from the other also, whereby it is unsuitable for the supramundane doctrine that does not fall from the mode of the two truths to be similar to a mundane doctrine which has fallen from the two truths in terms of either of the two truths.[20] Therefore, this system of the Supe-

---

[17]Ngawang Belden seems to imply that there is a conflict between Dzongkaba's texts by introducing them with "however" *(kyang)*. But there seems to be no contradiction, and Ngawang Belden surely realized this; although objects which are truly established do not exist even conventionally, objects which are merely asserted to be truly existent but which are in fact not truly existent do exist conventionally. The only objects not included are those which have no basis whatsoever, such as a mind-basis-of-all, self-knowing consciousnesses, partless particles, and so forth. It must be understood that in the first quotation Dzongkaba's referent is simply phenomena such as forms, considered without any qualification such as "truly existent"; however, in the second quotation his referent is truly existent forms, and so forth. As Kensur Yeshey Tupden said, his instances *(mtshan gzhi)* are different.

[18]*The Essence of the Good Explanations* 140.17-41.9. Also translated by Thurman (1984: 289).

[19]Sautrāntikas and Vaibhāṣikas assert objects that are established by their own character, but the Prāsaṅgika School rejects propounding such objects even conventionally. However, although the Prāsaṅgika School cannot assert objects such as tables and chairs in the same manner as the Sautrāntikas and Vaibhāṣikas, they can assert them in the manner of existing as mere imputations by thought.

[20]As Kensur Yeshey Tupden said, if one does not understand ultimate truths, one does not understand conventional truths, and vice versa. Others cannot posit ultimate truths because they assert inherently existent objects; they say that conventional truths are found upon analysis, whereas the Prā-

rior (Nāgārjuna)[21] is unique in relation to the tenets of the proponents of true existence not only ultimately but even conventionally.[22]

Jamyang Shayba:[23] The root text says:

Because they do not assert establishment by way of [the object's] own character even conventionally,
There are many distinguishing features—the eight unique [pairs of tenets] and so forth.

In general, [asserting] the existence of external objects and the non-existence of a mind-basis-of-all, and so forth, is not unique.[24] However, it is unique to assert certain [tenets] within imputedly existent mere nominalism *(ming rkyang)* due to not asserting [phenomena] as existing by way of their own character.[25] This is the unexcelled thought of the Perfection of Wisdom Sūtras *(phar rol du phyin pa'i mdo, prajñapāramitāsūtra)* and the Superior [Nāgārjuna]—the Father—and his spiritual sons.[26] As Candrakīrti's *Entrance to the Middle Way* says:[27]

---

saṅgika School says that they are found without analysis and investigation.

[21]"Superior" is one of the epithets of Nāgārjuna and translates *'phags pa (ārya)*. For a discussion of this translation, see Hopkins (1983a: 840, n. 495). Superiors are those who have attained the path of seeing *(mthong lam, darśana-mārga)* and first bodhisattva ground *(sa, bhūmi)*, i.e., who have experienced a direct realization of emptiness.

[22]Nāgārjuna's system is (1) unique in relation to the ultimate because the object of negation is unique and (2) unique in relation to the conventional because inherently existent objects do not exist even conventionally.

[23]*Great Exposition of Tenets* 36a.5.

[24]Only the Cittamātra and Yogācāra-Svātantrika-Mādhyamika (Middle Way Autonomist Yogic Practice) Schools (the latter "founded" by Śāntarakṣita) deny the existence of external objects, and only Cittamātrins Following Scripture (the followers of Asaṅga) assert the existence of a mind-basis-of-all. Thus, there are many schools in addition to the Prāsaṅgika School that reject these Mind-Only positions.

[25]Only the Prāsaṅgika School bases its criticism of the tenets of others on a standpoint of rejecting inherent existence, asserting that phenomena exist as mere imputations by thought, designated in dependence on their bases of designation.

[26]The Prāsaṅgika School standpoint is set forth by Candrakīrti, who

With respect to this system, the monk Candrakīrti,
Having collected it from the *Treatise on the Middle Way*,
Has expressed it in accordance with scripture
And quintessential instructions.[28]
Just as, in places other than this *Treatise*
This doctrine [of emptiness][29] does not exist
So also the mode of what has arisen here does not exist in
 other places.
The learned should determine that this system is unique.

---

draws it from Nāgārjuna, who in turn is said to be expressing Buddha's thought in the Perfection of Wisdom Sūtras.

[27]*Entrance to the Middle Way* 17b.9. Dzongkaba's commentary is in *Illumination of the Thought* 264a.3 ff. Cf. Huntington 196.

[28]Huntington translates this just as "Mādhyamika texts," but I assume that Jamyang Shayba would follow the explanation of Dzongkaba (*Illumination of the Thought* 264a.3), who identifies the quintessential instructions as those of Nāgārjuna. This would seem to indicate that Dzongkaba regarded Candrakīrti as Nāgārjuna's actual student (which implies that he regarded Nāgārjuna as having a six-hundred-year lifespan). Candrakīrti, in his *Clear Words* (P 5260, vol. 98, 92.2.3), says:

> And having seen the *Four Hundred* and so forth [by Āryadeva, etc.] and likewise many profound sūtras as well as the commentary done by Buddhapālita, I have gathered together the good explanations of Bhāvaviveka [and those of these masters] which were transmitted from one to another [and the texts of Śūra, Jñānagarbha, etc.] as well as what I received from [Nāgārjuna's own] analysis [of the meaning of his words] and have expounded this in order to please those of great intelligence.

The material in brackets is from *Great Exposition of Tenets* DSK II.70b.6-71a.1; it is translated in Hopkins (1983a: 591-92, 862-63). Some scholars think that the analysis Candrakīrti refers to is his own; others, like Jamyang Shayba, that it was Nāgārjuna's. Kaydrup, Dzongkaba's student, says that the view that Candrakīrti was Nāgārjuna's actual student is supported by *Guhyasamāja Tantra* masters, scriptural citation, and reasoning (Lessing and Wayman 91).

[29]"This doctrine" is the doctrine of emptiness, according to Kensur Yeshey Tupden (3/10/83).

B. Extensive Explanation of the Unique Tenets

This section has eleven parts:

1 The distinctive tenets that external objects *(phyi don, bāyārtha)* and a mind-basis-of-all *(kun gzhi rnam par shes pa, ālayavijñāna)* [respectively] exist and do not exist.

2 The distinctive tenets concerning the two selflessnesses *(bdag med, nairātmya)*.

3 The distinctive tenets that subsequent cognition *(bcad shes, paricchinna-jñāna*[30]*)*is prime cognition *(tshad ma, pramāṇa)* and that [all] conventional *(tha snyad)* [validly cognizing consciousnesses are mistaken].

4 The distinctive tenets concerning mental direct perception *(yid kyi mngon sum, mānasa-pratyakṣa)* and yogic direct perception *(rnal 'byor mngon sum, yoga-pratyakṣa)*.

5 The distinctive tenets on the mode of asserting the sixteen aspects of the four noble *('phags pa, āryan)* truths and the three times.

6 The distinctive tenets that disintegratedness *(zhig pa)* is a [functioning] thing *(dngos po, bhāva)* and that effects [from actions that have ceased] are feasible, along with a dispelling of objections.

7 The distinctive tenets that autonomous syllogisms *(rang rgyud kyi sbyor ba, svatantra-prayoga)* and self-consciousness *(rang rig, svasaṃvedanā)* are not asserted **[36b]**.

8 The distinctive tenets concerning direct perception *(mngon sum, pratyakṣa)* and true cessations *('gog bden, nirodha-satya)*.

9 The distinctive tenet concerning [nirvāṇas] with remainder *(lhag bcas, sopadhiśeṣa)* and without remainder *(lhag med, nirupadhiśeṣa)*.

---

[30]This is a possible reconstruction of the Sanskrit.

10 The distinctive tenet concerning the two [types of] obstructions *(sgrib pa, avaraṇa)* and their mode of abandonment.
11 The distinctive tenet concerning the mode of eliminating the two extremes, along with subsidiary topics.

1 External Objects Exist But a Mind-Basis-of-All[1] Does Not

Jamyang Shayba:[2] The root text says:

Because of not being refuted by and not being established by an awareness distinguishing conventionalities[3] [respectively],

---

[1]"Mind-basis-of-all" translates *kun gzhi rnam par shes pa/ālayavijñāna*. I usually render *rnam par shes pa/vijñāna* as "consciousness," but in this phrase it will be translated as "mind" for the sake of brevity.

[2]*Great Exposition of Tenets cha* 36b.1 (DSK II: 202b.2).

[3]A conventional validly cognizing consciousness *(tha snyad pa'i tshad ma)* is a directly perceiving or inferential awareness. (This twofold division of valid cognition comes from the Pratyakṣa chapter [1 ff.] of Dharmakīrti's *Commentary on (Dignāga's) "Compendium of Prime Cognition."*) It is (1) valid because it is not invalidated by any cause of error and (2) conventional because it is not involved in ultimate analysis, such as searching for an object among its bases of designation, e.g., trying to find a chair that is either the same as or different from its parts. Its objects include all phenomena except for ultimate truths *(don dam bden pa, paramārtha-satya)*, which in the Prāsaṅgika system are the emptinesses *(stong pa nyid, śūnyatā)* of conventional truths *(kun rdzob bden pa, saṃvṛti-satya*, literally "truths for concealers"), which comprise all other phenomena. (Kensur Yeshey Tupden considers even emptinesses to be objects of such a consciousness, since emptinesses conventionally exist. See Klein [1994: 48, 138].) Jamyang Shayba intends to show that there is no validly cognizing consciousness that

It is asserted that external objects exist but a mind-basis-of-all does not exist.

A. External Objects Exist

External objects exist because: (1) Nāgārjuna's *Essay on the Mind of Enlightenment (byang chub sems kyi 'grel pa, bodhicitta-vivaraṇa)* and the Perfection of Wisdom Sūtras say that the two, object and subject, equally exist conventionally and equally do not exist in the context of ultimate analysis, (2) [external objects] are set forth at length in the abhidharma *(chos mngon pa)* texts, and (3) [external objects] are not refuted by any awareness distinguishing conventionalities.

Ngawang Belden:[4] Nāgārjuna's *Essay on the Mind of Enlightenment* (39) says:[5]

> A consciousness realizes an object of knowledge.
> Without objects known there are no consciousnesses.
> In that case, why not assert
> That [both] object of knowledge and knower do not exist?

---

establishes the non-existence of external objects and no validly cognizing consciousness that establishes a mind-basis-of-all.

[4]*Annotations,* note *pha,* 108b.6.

[5]P 2665, vol. 61, 286.1.6; see *Great Exposition of Tenets cha* 48b.5. Also translated by Lindtner (1986b: 47). According to the Gelukba tradition, Nāgārjuna lived for six hundred years and therefore was still alive at the time of Asaṅga's "founding" of the Cittamātra system; for evidence, they point to the *Essay on the Mind of Enlightenment,* which seems to be a reply to Asaṅga. (See Hopkins [1983a: 359]. Of course, it is possible that Nāgārjuna is responding to an earlier variety of Mind-Only thought. Some scholars (e.g., B. K. Matilal [1974: 141]) assume that Mind-Only arose simultaneously with the Mahāyāna, though there is no clear evidence for its existence prior to the "Mind-Only" sūtras and their elucidation by Asaṅga and Vasubandhu.

In such passages he says that [external] objects and consciousnesses similarly exist [conventionally] and do not exist [ultimately]. Candrakīrti's *Entrance to the Middle Way* (VI.92) says:[6]

> If form does not exist, do not hold that mind exists.
> Also, if mind just exists, do not hold that form does not exist.
> [Truly existent mind and form] were equally abandoned by Buddha in the sūtras on the mode of wisdom, and [conventionally existent mind and form] were [equally] set forth
> In the abhidharma [scriptures].

Through this, he explains that when it is asserted that external forms do not exist, one should not hold that mind exists **[109a]**. Also, when it is asserted that internal mind exists, one should not hold that external forms do not exist.[7]

Also, he explains that with respect to the five aggregates,[8] in the Perfection of Wisdom Sūtras Buddha refutes inherent existence similarly for all five and that the abhidharma [scriptures] say that all five are similar in terms of having specific characteristics and [sharing] general characteristics, and so forth.[9]

---

[6]*Entrance to the Middle Way* 8b.5. Cf. Huntington 168. Dzongkaba's commentary is in *Illumination of the Thought* 175a.5 ff; the material in brackets is taken from him.

[7]The Cittamātrins are said to apply analysis to external objects made of partless particles (it being assumed that all physical objects are made of such) and thereby demonstrate, through denying that anything is indivisible, that such external objects cannot be found. Gelukba Prāsaṅgikas agree that external objects cannot bear such analysis, but add that if such reasoning were applied to a consciousness, it also would be unable to bear analysis.

[8]The five aggregates *(phung po, skandha)* are a fivefold division of impermanent phenomena into forms *(gzugs, rūpa)*, feelings *(tshor ba, vedanā)*, discriminations *('du shes, saṃjñā)*, compositional factors *('du byed, saṃskāra)*, and consciousnesses *(rnam shes, vijñāna)*. Forms are physical phenomena; the other four aggregates comprise mental phenomena and phenomena that are neither physical nor mental, such as impermanence.

[9]There is a passage similar to this one in Dzongkaba's *The Essence of the Good Explanations* 172.6-12, and in his *Illumination of the Thought* 176a.3 ff. The passage indicates that Buddha refutes inherent existence for all five

The final reason why Prāsaṅgikas assert that external objects exist conventionally is as follows: that forms, sounds, and so forth, are external objects is not refuted by valid cognition distinguishing conventionalities which does not depend on valid cognition distinguishing the ultimate because: (1) there is no instance of valid cognition distinguishing conventionalities that refutes external objects[10] and (2) consciousnesses also are not established when they are analyzed by valid cognition distinguishing the ultimate.[11]

The Cittamātrins themselves do not propound that [external objects] are refuted by valid cognition that distinguishes conventionalities because: (1) they assert that the refutation of external objects needs to depend on valid cognition that distinguishes the ultimate [as described in] the Cittamātra system itself, such as a [reasoning consciousness realizing that subject and object are not different entities[12] in dependence

---

aggregates, signifying that the mental aggregates are no different from the physical aggregate in not being truly existent. The scriptures of abhidharma agree in the sense that they hold that the five aggregates share the general characteristics *(spyi mtshan, sāmānyalakṣaṇa)* of being impermanent, unsatisfactory, and selfless, but all have their own specific defining characteristics *(rang mtshan, svalakṣaṇa).*

[10]Conventional valid cognition—direct perception or inference—certifies external objects. Only a consciousness analytically searching for an object, i.e., a validly cognizing consciousness distinguishing the ultimate, fails to find an external object. However, this failure to find an external object that can bear analysis refutes only the existence of truly existent external objects, not the existence of external objects conventionally. There is no non-analytical, conventional awareness that establishes the non-existence of external objects.

[11]Whenever one searches analytically for an imputed object, it is unfindable. For instance, if one looked among the parts of a table for the table, one would not be able to find any part that *is* the table. In the same way, consciousness is unfindable when sought.

[12]In this chapter, the position of the Cittamātra School that the objects that are apprehended by consciousnesses are one entity *(ngo bo gcig, ekabhāva)* with those consciousnesses is sometimes abbreviated, "one entity with consciousness." This should not be construed to indicate that apprehended objects are one entity with consciousness in some larger sense, like the monistic idealism of an Absolute Mind into which everything coalesces; rather what is meant is that objects are only one entity with exactly that consciousness that apprehends them and is produced with them from a single

on] the logical mark of the definite simultaneous observation [of objects and the consciousnesses realizing them] and (2) the emptiness of establishment in accordance with the appearance of [objects as] external is an ultimate truth and a suchness in the Cittamātra system itself.[13]

Moreover, in the Prāsaṅgika system, if external objects did not exist conventionally, one would have to assert that forms, and so forth, conventionally are mental things. In that case, there would be no way that they could be established by an ordinary conventional consciousness that operates without investigating through reasoning and without analysis.[14]

---

potency of the mind-basis-of-all. That they are one entity indicates that they are necessarily produced simultaneously or necessarily observed simultaneously; nevertheless, they can be distinguished conceptually.

[13]Dharmakīrti refutes external objects by reasoning that if an object and the consciousness which realizes it are observed to necessarily occur simultaneously they could not be separate entities. In the statement "The subject, the two, an apprehending subject and an apprehended object, are not different entities because they are observed to necessarily occur simultaneously," the sign (the reason, "because they are observed...simultaneously") of definite simultaneous observation *(lhan cig dmigs nges)* serves to cause one to realize that an apprehending subject and an apprehended object are not different entities. Simultaneous observation is possible because of the existence of self-consciousness *(rang rig, svāsaṃvedanā)*, that consciousness that knows a consciousness that in turn apprehends an object (see chapter 7). That reasoning consciousness would be an instance of valid cognition distinguishing the ultimate because its object, the lack (or emptiness) of a difference in entity of subject and object, is an ultimate truth, or suchness, in the Cittamātra system itself. According to Jamyang Shayba, in the Cittamātra system, ultimate truths are (1) the person's emptiness of being substantially existent or self-sufficient, (2) an object's emptiness of naturally being the basis of names, and (3) the emptiness of object and subject being different entities.

[14]According to the Prāsaṅgika School, since objects do conventionally exist, if they are not external objects they must exist as "mental things" *(shes pa'i dngos po)* in the sense of being objects that are the same entity as the minds apprehending them. According to the Cittamātra School, such objects are truly established and are conventional truths. But the Prāsaṅgika School maintains that "mental things" could not appear to a conventional validly cognizing consciousness; hence, only a validly cognizing consciousness distinguishing the ultimate could establish a chair as a mental thing. The reason is that an ordinary conventional awareness does not distinguish a chair as a mental thing, but just as a chair. Going beyond that point requires

Therefore, analyzing by way of a reasoning which examined whether forms, and so forth, are established as the nature of consciousness, one would have to find that they are the nature of consciousness.[15] In that case, form, and so forth, would have to be established by way of its own character, whereby that [this] is the Prāsaṅgika system would be a thorough deprecation.[16]

Objection: It follows that in that case the Cittamātrins are inferior to the Sautrāntikas because (1) they are similar in asserting that consciousnesses are truly established and (2) propounding that external objects exist is better than propounding that they do not exist.

Response: This is a wrong conception, manifesting complete ignorance of the respective status of tenet systems, because the Sautrāntikas assert, upon analysis by reasoning, partless particles and gross objects that are composed of them whereas **[109b]** the Cittamātrins are able to refute thoroughly such external objects by means of reasoning.[17]

However, because (1) the Cittamātrins are unable to posit objects that are established merely conventionally without

---

ultimate analysis.

[15]One would be forced to this conclusion simply because if objects conventionally exist and are not external to consciousness they are perforce one entity with consciousness.

[16]If forms, etc., were findable under analysis, they would be established by way of their own character. According to the Prāsaṅgika system, objects are not established by way of their own character even conventionally.

[17]From the point of view of the Prāsaṅgika School, it is true (1) that both the Sautrāntika School and the Cittamātra School assert that impermanent phenomena are truly established and (2) that it is better to assert external objects than to deny their existence. Nevertheless, it is better to refute external objects than to assert "partless particles" which are found upon analysis, as the Sautrāntikas do. Partless particles are conceived to be basic units of matter so tiny that they cannot be physically subdivided, and they assert that these units can be found upon analysis. For Prāsaṅgikas, the Cittamātra analysis of such "partless particles" demonstrates that external objects cannot withstand analysis in the sense that, at the very least, they must be designated in dependence on their parts. Someone who understands the Cittamātra analysis can then agree with the Prāsaṅgika School that external objects are not findable upon analysis and be in a position to understand that they are merely imputed by thought.

investigation or analysis by reasoning and (2) the Prāsaṅgikas have the distinguishing feature of being able to posit such, there comes to be a difference in their asserting or not asserting external objects.[18] Therefore, the Prāsaṅgikas' assertion of external objects meets back to their assertion of imputedly existent nominalities. Hence, Dzongkaba's *The Essence of the Good Explanations* says:[19]

> The presentation of the Prāsaṅgika School's unique mode of commenting on the thought of the Superior [Nāgārjuna] in dependence on [its refutation of inherent existence] has three parts: (1) the unique distinction of realizing selflessness, the coarse and subtle conceptions of self, and so forth; (2) the unique distinction of positing external objects while not asserting a mind-basis-of-all or self-knowing consciousness; and (3) the unique distinction of not asserting autonomous [syllogisms].

And:[20]

> This system also indeed asserts that external objects are not established by way of their own character but with respect to that disagrees [with the Svātantrikas][21] in terms of whether or not this necessitates that external objects do not exist. Therefore, in general, if one knows how to posit any phenomenon as existing even though it does not exist by way of its own character, one can understand well the reasoning concerning the impossibility of distinguishing [external]

[18]From the Prāsaṅgika School's point of view, the Cittamātrins make two critical errors: they do not limit the scope of their analysis to ultimate existence, thereby refuting even the conventional existence of external objects; and they do not extend their analysis from external objects to internal consciousnesses.

[19]*The Essence of the Good Explanations* 161.14-18. The quotation has been expanded to include the entire sentence.

[20]*The Essence of the Good Explanations* 171.6-11.

[21]Dzongkaba is speaking here of "other Mādhyamikas," i.e., Svātantrika-Mādhyamikas. According to Gelukbas, this school asserts that whatever exists must conventionally be established by way of its own character, i.e., be inherently established. Therefore, all Svātantrikas would be forced to say that if external objects lack inherent existence even conventionally, as the Prāsaṅgikas contend, they could not exist.

> objects and consciousnesses as existing or not existing, whereas if one does not [know how to so posit objects without their being established by way of their own character] one cannot [understand the reasoning].[22]

Therefore, that the Cittamātrins assert the non-existence of external objects and the true establishment of the mind destroys the presentation of the two truths and causes [the Cittamātrins] to fall from both truths. This is because those assertions are harmed by valid cognition distinguishing the conventional and valid cognition distinguishing the ultimate, respectively, because:

(1) Candrakīrti's *Entrance to the Middle Way* (VI.93) says:[23]

> Also, having destroyed those stages of the two truths,[24]
> Your [Cittamātra assertion of] substantial entities is refuted,
> whereby [the true existence of mind and the non-existence of external objects] is not established.

and (2) Dzongkaba's *The Essence of the Good Explanations* says:[25]

> Therefore, to distinguish a difference of existence and non-existence with respect to such as those [consciousnesses and external objects] is to contravene worldly conventions and

---

[22]If one knows that both minds and external objects can be posited without being inherently existent, it is easy to understand that objects and subjects are similar in not being inherently existent and in being conventionally existent. Svātantrikas do not share this view, contending that if something does not exist by way of its own character it cannot exist at all. Hence, although Prāsaṅgikas and some Svātantrikas (the Sautrāntika-Svātantrikas) agree that external objects exist, they differ because these Svātantrikas are unwilling to affirm external objects that do not exist by way of their own character.

[23]Candrakīrti's *Entrance to the Middle Way* 8b.6. Dzongkaba's commentary is in *Illumination of the Thought* 176b.1-2.

[24]The Cittamātra School contravenes conventional truths because in refuting external objects it negates the valid convention of the world that external objects exist. It contravenes ultimate truths because in asserting the true establishment of mind it negates the ultimate truth of minds, their lack of true existence.

[25]*The Essence of the Good Explanations* 172.12-18.

to contravene the presentation of the ultimate as well, whereby one falls from both truths. Āryadeva's *Four Hundred (bzhi bgya pa, catuḥśataka)* (XVI.24) says:[26]

> "One exists, one does not"
> Is not so in reality and also not in the world.
> Therefore, "this exists, that does not"
> Cannot be said.

B. A Mind-Basis-Of-All Does Not Exist

Jamyang Shayba:[27] Even though many sūtras describe a mind-basis-of-all,[28] many [other] profound sūtras explain that [the former sūtras] require interpretation. With respect to positing [a mind-basis-of-all], since it cannot be posited without searching for the imputed object of the seeds for the fruition of actions, it is not established by a conventional

---

[26]*Four Hundred* (P 5246, vol. 95, 140.2.3-4). Sanskrit (Bhattacharya 295) is: *ekaṃ sadasadekuṃ ca naidaṃ tattvaṃ na laukikam / tenedam sadidamasad vaktum eva na śakyate.* This *śloka* is found near the end of the *Four Hundred* and is interpreted by Dzongkaba to show that it contravenes Nāgārjuna's presentation of the ultimate to assert, as the Cittamātra School does, that there is any difference between minds and external objects in terms of true existence. Cf. Sonam 299 (stanza 399).

[27]*Great Exposition of Tenets cha* 36b.2 (DSK II: 202b.3).

[28]A mind-basis-of-all is asserted only by Cittamātrins Following Scripture *(lung gi rje su 'brangs pa, āgamānusārin)*, the followers of Asaṅga. It is distinct from the five sense consciousnesses and the mental consciousness, and its function is nothing more than to bear the seeds or latencies of actions. It does not distinguish objects, is neither virtuous nor non-virtuous, and is undefiled by the accompaniment of any afflicted mental factors. See Wilson (1984) for an extensive explanation of these characteristics according to Gelukba sources, especially Gungtang.

reasoning consciousness.[29] Therefore, a mind-basis-of-all necessarily does not exist.

Ngawang Belden:[30] Another reason why Prāsaṅgikas do not assert a mind-basis-of-all that is a different entity from the six collections [of consciousness][31] is founded on not accepting inherent establishment in terms of both truths, because if a mind-basis-of-all which is a different entity from the six collections were asserted, it would have to be asserted in accordance with the explanation of the *Sūtra Unraveling the Thought (dgongs pa nges par 'grel pa'i mdo, saṃdhi-nirmocanasūtra)*, Asaṅga's *Compendium of the Mahāyāna (theg pa chen po bsdus pa, mahāyānasaṃgraha)*, his *Compendium of Ascertainments (rnam par gtan la dbab pa bsdu ba, viniścayasaṃ-*

---

[29]According to Gelukbas, the mind-basis-of-all *as described in* the Cittamātra School's texts is an object that can be found by an analyzing consciousness. As a consciousness, it must be truly existent; as a truly existent phenomenon, it can be found by analysis. It is said to be a "different entity from the six collections of consciousness," for instance, suggesting its findability apart from them. Indeed, if a mind-basis-of-all were not asserted to be findable under analysis, other than the fact that it is a consciousness there would be no essential difference between it and the "mere I" *(nga tsam,* a non-associated compositional factor *[ldan min 'du byed, viprayuktasaṃskāra])* that Prāsaṅgikas posit as the bearer of karmic latencies from one lifespan to another and which is asserted to be merely imputed in dependence on the aggregates. According to Prāsaṅgikas, whatever can be found by an analysis that searches for it is not established by a conventional reasoning consciousness and therefore does not conventionally exist. (Emptiness is "found" upon analysis, but is not found as the result of a search for *it;* rather, emptiness is what one realizes upon searching analytically for something *else.*) The "mere I," on the other hand, is posited without investigation and analysis. Here, a "conventional reasoning consciousness" means only conventional valid cognition of some sort; the point is that no conventional valid cognizing consciousness certifies a mind-basis-of-all. Some scholars reserve the term "reasoning consciousness" for ultimate valid cognition.

[30]*Annotations* 109b.7.

[31]According to Kensur Ngawang Lekden, (? -1971), former abbot of the Tantric College of Lower Lhasa *(rgyud smad grwa tshang)* and a geshay of Gomang College, consciousnesses are called "collections" because there are many examples of each type according to their objects of experience or apprehension. (Oral communication from Jeffrey Hopkins.)

grahaṇī), the root text and commentaries on Maitreya's *Discrimination of the Middle and the Extremes (dbus dang mtha' rnam par 'byed pa, madhyāntavibhaṅga),* and so forth **[110a]**. If such [a mind-basis-of-all] were asserted, there would be no way that it could be established by a non-defective conventional consciousness that neither investigates nor analyzes.[32] Therefore, when one sought the object that is imputed by the name "basis-of-all," it would have to be findable by reasoning; were that the case, inherently established objects would also have to be asserted even while one was not asserting such.

Moreover, if a mind-basis-of-all which is a different entity from the six collections [of consciousness] were asserted, it would have to be asserted in accordance with the explanation that just that [mind-basis-of-all] is the object of observation of the innate view of the transitory [collection of aggregates] that conceives of an [inherently existent] "I" and which is associated with the afflicted mentality. Therefore, it would have to be asserted that the mind-basis-of-all is the illustration of the person and that when the person—the imputed object—is sought, it is findable.[33]

Moreover, because Prāsaṅgikas assert external objects, it is also established that they do not assert a mind-basis-of-all.[34] Dzongkaba's *The Essence of the Good Explanations* says:[35]

> Also, a mind-basis-of-all is not posited due to the essential point of asserting external objects. If [a mind-basis-of-all]

---

[32]The mind-basis-of-all as described in those texts would have to be truly established, and thus findable under analysis.

[33]The Cittamātrins assert that the mind-basis-of-all is the illustration of the person, as it is the basis for bondage and liberation, and that it is that which is found by an analysis that seeks the person. (This is an argument made by the Gelukba scholar Gungtang; see chapter 3.) The Prāsaṅgikas contend that nothing is findable under analysis; rather, the "mere I" is the illustration of the person, being merely imputed in dependence upon one or more of the five aggregates. That it is a *mere* imputation by thought means that it cannot be found upon analysis.

[34]There would be no need to assert a mind-basis-of-all if external objects existed, since they, not latencies deposited on the mind-basis-of-all, would be the causes of consciousnesses which perceive external objects.

[35]*The Essence of the Good Explanations* 174.16-20.

were asserted, it would have to be asserted in accordance with the statement in Maitreya's *Discrimination of the Middle and the Extremes* (I.4):[36]

> Consciousnesses that perceive
> Objects, the sentient, selves, and knowledges are thoroughly produced.[37]
> They have no [external] objects.
> Because there are no [external objects], there are no [minds apprehending external objects].

Jamyang Shayba:[38] Because these two [tenets—the existence of external objects and the non-existence of a mind-basis-of-all—] also have their source in an imputed object's non-existence upon analysis, they are unique [Prāsaṅgika tenets].

[Also,] as Candrakīrti's *Entrance to the Middle Way* (VI.92cd) says:[39]

> [Truly existent mind and form] were equally abandoned by Buddha in the sūtras on the mode of wisdom and [conventionally existent mind and form] were [equally] set forth
> In the abhidharma [scriptures].

---

[36]P 5522, vol. 108, 19.4.6-7. The material in brackets has been inserted to reflect Dzongkaba's understanding of the passage. The Sanskrit in Pandeya (1971: 13 and 194) is: *arthasattvātmavijñāptipratibhāsaṃ prajāyate/ vijñānaṃ nāsti cāsyārthastadabhāvāttadapyasat.* For other translations, see Stcherbatsky (1971: 64-5) and Kochumuttom (1982: 46-7 and 236-7). There is a similar statement in Asaṅga's *Compendium of the Great Vehicle* (Tibetan in Lamotte 1973, I: 31]; French translation in II: 105).

[37]That is, minds that apprehend the objects of the senses, the sense-powers, and the mind-basis-of-all—all of which are appearances generated from karmic latencies with the mind-basis-of-all—are all truly existent and have no external objects.

[38]*Great Exposition of Tenets cha* 36b.3.

[39]Candrakīrti's *Entrance to the Middle Way* 8b.5. Cf. Huntington 168. The quotation has been restored to full length. Dzongkaba's commentary is in *Illumination of the Thought* 176a.4 ff. and is the basis for the bracketed material.

And (VI.43):[40]

> The teachings that a basis-of-all exists,[41] that the self [inherently] exists,
> And that only the aggregates [inherently] exist
> Should be taken as teachings for those who would not understand
> The very profound meaning [of emptiness].

Ngawang Belden:[42] The teaching from some sūtras that a mind-basis-of-all exists, that persons substantially exist, and that the mere aggregates substantially exist were spoken in consideration of trainees who [for the time being] are unable to realize the profound meaning previously explained.

Without making any difference, [Candrakīrti] says that the statements that all three—mind-basis-of-all, person, and aggregates—are substantially existent requires interpretation.[43] However, the basis of [Buddha's] thought[44] when he said that

---

[40]Candrakīrti's *Entrance to the Middle Way* 6b.2. (P 5262, vol. 98, 102.2.6). Candrakīrti's commentary is P 5263, vol. 98, 127.2.4 ff. Dzongkaba's commentary is in *Illumination of the Thought* 132a.4-134b.1 (P 6143, vol. 154, 55.5.8). Cf. Poussin (*Muséon* 11: 322). The material in brackets follows Ngawang Belden's explanation, with "inherently" substituted for its synonym, "substantially," for the sake of consistency. Ngawang Belden's citation of the same quotation has been deleted to avoid redundancy.

[41]Prāsaṅgikas regard the sūtras in which a mind-basis-of-all is mentioned either to have been taught for the sake of persons who are for the time being incapable of penetrating the subtle Mādhyamika view or to be referring to something other than a latency-bearing consciousness.

[42]*Annotations* 110a.6.

[43]Candrakīrti, in making this statement, did not distinguish between the conventional existence of the person and the aggregates and the total non-existence of a mind-basis-of-all. He simply said that none of those three can literally be said to substantially exist, since for him (according to Gelukbas), substantial existence is equated with inherent existence and cannot be predicated of any object. Therefore, statements that something substantially exists require interpretation to reveal the thought underlying them. Because Candrakīrti did not distinguish between the person and the aggregates, which conventionally exist, and the mind-basis-of-all, which does not exist even conventionally, Dzongkaba and later Gelukbas had to clarify this point.

[44]The three criteria of Prāsaṅgika hermeneutics are: (1) the basis of

the person and the aggregates are substantially existent is that he spoke within thinking that the person and aggregates conventionally exist; therefore, the basis of his thought does not [need to be] set forth as something separate from [persons and aggregates]. However, the basis of his thought [when he said that the mind-basis-of-all is substantially existent] *is* set forth separately in accordance with [Candrakīrti's] saying in his *Autocommentary on the "Entrance"* that Buddha's statement that the mind-basis-of-all is substantially existent was made in consideration of emptiness [its purpose being directed for those not ready to hear about emptiness].[45] By that also, one

---

thought *(dgongs gzhi)*, (2) the purpose *(dgos pa)*, and (3) the damage to the literal teaching *(dngos la gnod byed)*. The basis of thought is what the speaker, usually Śākyamuni, had in mind—was aware of—when he spoke. For a scripture requiring interpretation, the basis of thought is not something that is communicated either directly or indirectly, for the speaker does not intend to talk about it. For instance, Candrakīrti says that when Buddha spoke about the mind-basis-of-all, he was thinking about emptiness (in the sense that emptiness is the basis of all phenomena and is to be minded well). In other words, emptiness was the basis of his thought. See Jamyang Shayba's *Great Exposition of the Middle Way* 814.

[45]However, Buddha's intention was just to communicate provisionally the idea of a mind-basis-of-all, in the sense of a basis for holding karmic latencies, for those trainees not yet ready to hear about emptiness. It is said to be clear that Buddha's intention must have been to teach the mind-basis-of-all only provisionally and that the basis of his thought was emptiness, for the literal teaching of a mind-basis-of-all is contradicted by the faults outlined earlier: a mind-basis-of-all cannot be established by conventional valid cognition, and once it is established that external objects exist, a mind-basis-of-all would have no function. When Buddha said that the person and the aggregates substantially exist, the basis in his own thought from which he was speaking was the conventionally existent person and aggregates, but since he was speaking to people who would not understand non-substantial existence, he spoke of a substantially existent person and aggregates. It is not necessary to analyze the meaning of "person" and "aggregate" in Buddha's own thought. However, when Buddha spoke of a mind-basis-of-all, he could not have had a conventionally existent mind-basis-of-all as the basis from which he was speaking since the mind-basis-of-all does not exist even conventionally; therefore, it was necessary for Candrakīrti to explain that Buddha taught a mind-basis-of-all to persons not ready to hear about emptiness even though he knew that a mind-basis-of-all did not exist. Jamyang Shayba discusses the differences between Candrakīrti and Bhāvaviveka on this point in the *Great Exposition of the Middle Way* 814.2 ff.:

can understand that Prāsaṅgikas do not assert that a mind-basis-of-all conventionally exists.

Candrakīrti says that for Buddha, "mind-basis-of-all" means emptiness, whereas Bhāvaviveka says he meant that the mind is the world-creator.

2 The Two Selflessnesses

Jamyang Shayba:[1] The root text says:

There is no liberation for those who conceive of true existence, an afflictive [obstruction].
The selflessnesses are similarly [subtle].[2]

---

[1]*Great Exposition of Tenets cha* 36b.4.

[2]Afflictive obstructions are, in brief, the afflictions of desire, hatred, and ignorance and the predispositions established by them. Ignorance is the principal affliction and desire and hatred are merely secondary because desire and hatred occur in dependence upon ignorance. The most important sense of ignorance is not mere not-knowing, but rather is the consciousness that conceives persons and other phenomena to inherently or truly exist.

There are two levels of ignorance, coarse and subtle. Coarse ignorance occurs only with respect to the person and is the conception of a self-sufficient person; the subtle ignorance with respect to both persons and other phenomena is the conception of inherent existence. Coarse ignorance, the conception of a self-sufficient person, is the conception that "I" am autonomous and like a master over my mind and body. This misconception is not merely coarse, but is also *artificial*, i.e., merely the result of false teachings, if it takes the form of conceiving of the I and aggregates to be separate entities, like a lord and his subjects; it is *innate* if there is no such further misconception, the aggregates being conceived to be like salesmen and the I being conceived to be like the head salesman, in charge of but not a different type than the other salesmen. (However, this latter conception would also be artificial if it were the result of false teachings rather than merely arising naturally.) Subtle ignorance, the conception of inherent existence, is that "I" exist from my own side; the "I" just seems to be fused with the aggregates. According to Gelukba scholars, Svātantrikas wrongly

A. Liberation Depends on Realizing Emptiness

Śāntideva's *Engaging in the Bodhisattva Deeds* (IX.41cd) says:[3]

> Therefore, scripture says that without this path
> There can be no enlightenment.

Ngawang Belden:[4] **[110b]** This is as Gyeltsap's *Explanation of (Śāntideva's) "Engaging in the Bodhisattva Deeds" (spyod 'jug dar ṭīk)* says:[5]

> It follows that one definitely needs to realize emptiness[6] in order to obtain the fruit of a Hearer or Solitary Realizer Arhat.[7] Why? Because it is said in passages of the Perfection of Wisdom Sūtras that without familiarity with this path of

---

identify the conception of true existence as the obstructions to liberation, the seeds established by former actions. In fact, in their presentation of the Prāsaṅgika School, both levels of ignorance are obstructions to liberation, for one cannot be liberated without realizing the most subtle selflessness. The second point that Jamyang Shayba is making is that the two selflessnesses—the absence of inherent existence with respect to the person and the absence of inherent existence with respect to all other phenomena—are different only with respect to the basis of selflessness, not with respect to the subtlety of the object of negation.

[3]V. Bhattacharya (195). The Sanskrit is: *na vinānena mārgeṇa bodhirityāgamo yataḥ*. Stephen Batchelor identifies this *śloka* as 40cd.

[4]*Annotations*, note *ba*, 110b.1

[5]*Collected Works (gsuṅ 'bum) of Rgyal-tshab rje Dar-ma-rin-chen* (New Delhi: Lama Guru Deva, 1982), vol. 4, 258.6-259.2. See also *Collected Works (gsuṅ 'bum) of Rgyal-tshab rje Dar-ma-rin-chen* (New Delhi: Ngawang Gelek Demo, 1981), vol. 3, 253.5-254.1.

[6]That is, one must definitely overcome subtle ignorance, the conception of inherent existence, realizing the emptiness of inherent existence with respect to persons and all other phenomena.

[7]Hearers (*nyan thos, śrāvaka*) and Solitary Realizers (*rang sang rgyas, pratyekabuddha*) are low vehicle practitioners who respectively do and do not depend on the instructions of a teacher in their last lifetime prior to attaining liberation. "Foe Destroyer" is the Tibetan translation of *arhan* (for which the nominative singular form is Arhat), etymologized as "one who has destroyed the foes (*ari* + *han*) of the afflictions," i.e., become liberated. For a discussion of this translation, see Hopkins (1983a: 871-73, n. 553).

realizing emptiness one attains none of the three enlightenments [of a Hearer Arhat, a Solitary Realizer Arhat, or a Buddha]. Prajñāmokṣa, in his *Explanation of (Śāntideva's) "Engaging in the Bodhisattva Deeds" (spyod 'jug 'grel chen, bodhisattvacaryāvatārabhāṣya),* cites the statement in the Mother [Perfection of Wisdom] Sūtras that one who has the discrimination of things *(dngos po, bhāva)* does not have liberation, and that the completely perfect Buddhas of the three times and [others] ranging from Stream-Enterers to Solitary Realizers attain [liberation] in dependence upon just this perfection of wisdom. In accordance with that, the meaning of [Śāntideva's] passage is not that it refers to only the unexcelled enlightenment [of a Buddha].[8]

"Having the discrimination of things *(dngos po)*" is the same as "having the discrimination of true establishment *(bden grub)*" because it is said that the two, "true establishment" and "thing," have a common [Sanskrit] original [i.e., *bhāva*].

Jamyang Shayba:[9] Like that passage [in Śāntideva], the Perfection of Wisdom Sūtras explain that there is no liberation for one who has the discrimination of true existence. Therefore, it is necessary to assert that the consciousness conceiving true existence[10] is the mental affliction that prevents the attainment of liberation—in which the mind is released from afflictions—whereby it is asserted that the consciousness conceiving true existence is an afflictive obstruction.[11] For this reason,

[8]In other words, "enlightenment" *(byang chub, bodhi)* does not refer only to the *final* enlightenment of a Buddha, which is unexcelled because it is a complete, final abandonment of both the obstructions to liberation and the obstruction to omniscience. It also refers to the enlightenment of a Hearer Arhat or Solitary Realizer Arhat, who have abandoned only the obstructions to liberation.

[9]*Great Exposition of Tenets cha* 36b.5.

[10]*bden 'dzin (satyagrāha)* is being translated not as "the conception of true existence" but as "consciousness conceiving true existence" in order to emphasize that "conception" refers to a consciousness actively misconceiving reality.

[11]For the other schools, a person is considered to have overcome the afflictions of desire, hatred, and ignorance obstructing liberation from cyclic existence through realizing a selflessness that is the absence of a self-

although there is no difference between the modes of emptiness of the two selflessnesses, they must be posited [merely] by way of the bases of emptiness [i.e., persons and other phenomena]. Therefore, the two selflessnesses are equally subtle. Candrakīrti's *Entrance to the Middle Way* (VI.179) says:[12]

> So that transmigrators might be liberated [from the two obstructions]
> This selflessness was set forth [by the Buddha] in two aspects by way of the divisions of phenomena and persons.

Ngawang Belden:[13] Dzongkaba's *Illumination of the Thought, Explanation of (Candrakīrti's) "Entrance"* says:[14]

> This selflessness which is the absence of inherent establishment of phenomena was set forth by the Supramundane Victor (Buddha) in two aspects, the divisions of the selflessness of persons and of the selflessness of [other] phenomena. The mode of dividing [selflessness] into two is not a differentiation by way of two different selves which are nonexistent in terms of their bases, persons and [other] phenomena. For that [one type of self] which does not exist is inherent establishment. Because of this, the two selflessnesses [the subtle selflessness of the person and the subtle selflessness of phenomena] are distinguished by way of the divisions of the bases—the subjects—(1) phenomena such as the aggregates and (2) persons.
>
> *Question*: For what purpose did he teach those two?
>
> *Answer*: The selflessness of *persons* was taught so that transmigrators who are Hearers and Solitary Realizers might be liberated from cyclic existence. *Both* selflessnesses

sufficient person. The Prāsaṅgika School would label this only a "coarse" selflessness, enabling one only to suppress manifest forms of the afflictions; it might seem even to oneself that one has overcome hatred and desire, but since these would not have been removed from the root (ignorance), it is possible for them to return. According to the Prāsaṅgika reading of the Perfection of Wisdom Sūtras, one cannot attain *any* enlightenment without realizing the subtle selflessness that is the emptiness of true existence.

[12]*Entrance to the Middle Way* 13a.2. Cf. Huntington 179. Dzongkaba's commentary is in *Illumination of the Thought* 230b.1-31b.3.

[13]*Annotations*, note *ma*, 110b.4.

[14]*Illumination of the Thought* 230b.1-4.

are taught so that transmigrators who are Bodhisattvas could be liberated through attaining omniscience.[15]

B. Ignorance Is the Basis of All Afflictions

Jamyang Shayba:[16] Āryadeva's *Four Hundred* (VI.11) says:[17]

Like the body sense power in the body,[18]
Delusion[19] serves as the basis for all [afflictions].
Therefore, all afflictions are overcome
Through overcoming obscuration.

---

[15]Dzongkaba seems to be saying that Hearers and Solitary Realizers need only to realize the selflessness of the person to be liberated from cyclic existence, but from several other statements in the same book it is clear that this is not what he intends. He shows that Hearers and Solitary Realizers must realize subtle selflessness—the absence of inherent existence—to be liberated, and there is no difference in subtlety between the selflessnesses of persons and phenomena. What is probably meant is that Buddha's teaching of the selflessness of persons was particularly helpful to Hearers and Solitary Realizers, who are not as sharp as Bodhisattvas, because the selflessness of persons is easier to realize than the selflessness of phenomena. Still, both selflessnesses need to be taught for anyone to achieve liberation. Also, it seems that Dzongkaba implies that Bodhisattvas attain liberation only upon attaining omniscience, i.e., Buddhahood; however, it is clear from many other contexts that this is not what he intends. Possibly, he is referring to the Bodhisattva's vow to become omniscient for the sake of all sentient beings, or "liberation" here means both liberation from cyclic existence and liberation from the obstructions to omniscience.

[16]*Great Exposition of Tenets* 36b.7.

[17]P 5246, vol. 95, 135.2.8-3.1. The quotation has been expanded to include the last two lines. Cf. Sonam 156 (stanza 135).

[18]The body sense power is the physical basis for touch. It is said that where it is absent, such as in most of the hair, the ends of the nails, etc., no other senses may operate. In the same way, desire and hatred are absent or inoperable in the absence of the consciousness conceiving true existence.

[19]"Delusion" *(gti mug, moḥa)* is usually equated to ignorance. However, according to Geshay Tupden Gyatso, since Prāsaṅgikas assert non-afflicted ignorance, and delusion is an affliction, in their system the two are not equivalent.

Ngawang Belden:[20] Also, with respect to the meaning of "the body sense power in the body," and so forth [from Āryadeva's *Four Hundred*], Gyeltsap's *Commentary on (Āryadeva's) "Four Hundred" (bzhi rgya pa'i dar ṭīk)* says:[21]

> In the body, the body sense power pervades the other sense powers such as the eye and dwells as the basis of those. If it did not exist, the other sense powers would also not dwell [in the body]. In just that way, the afflictive ignorance—the obscuration which [mistakenly] determines that dependent-arisings, which are empty of inherent existence, are truly existent—pervades and dwells in all the afflictions such as desire and hatred **[111a]**. That is because one adheres to desire, hatred, and so forth, upon determining a thing [falsely] imputed by obscuration to be inherently attractive or unattractive. Therefore, the manner in which the mode of apprehension of both desire and hatred and the mode of apprehension of the consciousness conceiving true existence are mixed should be known.

This can be known extensively from the two, Dzongkaba's *Illumination of the Thought, Explanation of (Candrakīrti's) "Entrance"* and Dzongkaba's *The Essence of the Good Explanations*.[22]

Jamyang Shayba:[23] Hence, the Svātantrikas and below do not assert desires, and so forth, that are consciousnesses that conceive true existence, but here it is asserted not only that [desire and hatred] have the aspect of a coarse consciousness conceiving of self but also that there are [instances] of the three poisons[24] that have the aspect of conceiving true exis-

---

[20] *Annotations*, note *ma* (continued), 110b.7.

[21] *Collected Works (gsuṅ 'bum) of Rgyal-tshab-rje Dar-ma-rin-chen* (New Delhi: Lama Guru Deva, 1981), vol. 1, 597.6. Cf. Sonam 156-57.

[22] In fact, it seems to me that neither of these works explains this even as extensively as Gyeltsap just has. See *Illumination of the Thought* (26a.6-31a.2, translated in Hopkins, 1980: 150-60, especially 158), and *The Essence of the Good Explanations* (165.1-66.1, translated in Thurman, 1984: 308-9).

[23] *Great Exposition of Tenets cha* 36b.7.

[24] The three poisons are desire, hatred, and ignorance.

tence.[25] This is because of the unique assertion that just as those two [levels, coarse and subtle][26] exist with respect to ignorance,[27] they also [exist] with respect to attachment, and so forth. Śāntideva's *Engaging in the Bodhisattva Deeds* (IX.47cd) says:[28]

> This attachment is not afflictive but
> Why is it not like obscuration?

Ngawang Belden:[29] This craving in the continuum of the person whom you [wrongly] assert to be an Arhat is [afflictive, but not] in the manner explained in the abhidharma texts.[30] Also, it is said in those abhidharma texts that thorough

---

[25]According to Jamyang Shayba, Prāsaṅgikas assert not only that there is desire based on consciousnesses conceiving true existence, but desire that *is* a consciousness conceiving true existence in the sense that desire and ignorance are conjoined. That is because just as there are coarse and subtle levels of ignorance, so there are coarse and subtle levels of desire and hatred based upon those.

[26]Identified by Geshay Tupden Gyatso.

[27]Geshay Tupden Gyatso said that there are consciousnesses conceiving true existence that are desires *('dod chags yin mkhan gyi bden 'dzin)*, but desires *('dod chags)* are not necessarily ignorance *(ma rig pa)*. According to him, the process of the occurrence of an action involving desire is that first, one conceives that an object truly exists; second, one has desire for that object; and third, one acts *(las, karman)*. The point here is that Prāsaṅgikas claim that there are coarse and subtle afflictions such as desire based on coarse and subtle ignorance, respectively.

[28]V. Bhattacharya (197). The Sanskrit is: *kimakliṣāpitaṣṇaiṣām nāsti saṃamohavat satī*. Also cited in Hopkins (1980: 157).

[29]*Annotations*, note *tsa*, 111a.2.

[30]Arhats are those persons who have abandoned ignorance and thus all of the afflictions such as desire that are based on it. A controversy arose over the status of certain persons who some regarded as Arhats, but who still manifested a kind of craving. Śāntideva admits that the so-called "Arhats" do not have afflicted craving *based on a coarse conception of self* (the misconception of a self described in the abhidharma texts). However, he wants to make the point that they do have afflicted craving *based on a subtle conception of self.* He does this by arguing that the lower schools should admit that the so-called "Arhats" still have craving, and invites them to call it "non-afflicted craving," since that is the only conceivable kind of craving that could exist in the continuum of an Arhat. However, Śāntideva considers this to be absurd: craving is craving; "non-afflictive craving" is an oxy-

obscuration—ignorance—is of two [types], afflictive and non-afflictive. Just so, in accordance with the explanation in the abhidharma texts that there is one type [of ignorance] that is afflictive and one which is not afflictive, why do you not also [absurdly] assert craving [as afflictive and non-afflictive]? You should assert this.

---

moron. For him, the fact that these "Arhats" have craving indicates that they are not Arhats at all, for they retain at least a subtle level of ignorance. Therefore, what the proponents of the abhidharma texts call "non-afflictive" ignorance is in fact just a subtle level of afflictive ignorance.

3 Prime Cognition and Conventional Valid Cognition

Jamyang Shayba:[1] The root text says:

Because of not being unpolluted and because new realization is unsuitable [respectively] [37a],
All consciousnesses of childish persons are mistaken and subsequent cognition is established as prime cognition.[2]

---

[1]*Great Exposition of Tenets cha* 36b.8.

[2]Jamyang Shayba has two points to make in this section. The first is that all consciousnesses of childish persons—ordinary beings who have not realized emptiness and thereby become Superiors—are mistaken in the sense that they are not unpolluted by the appearance of true existence. This is an understatement because, in fact, all instances of conventional valid cognition, whether those of childish persons or of Superiors, are mistaken in the sense that their objects appear to be truly existent. Only ultimate valid cognition, the direct realization of emptiness in meditative equipoise, is unmistaken cognition. Second, subsequent cognition, a category that includes all valid consciousnesses other than those which occur in the first moment of cognizing an object, is prime cognition *(tshad ma, pramāṇa)* because "new realization" is unsuitable to be the definition of prime cognition; in other words, since prime cognition need not be new realization, even subsequent cognition may be prime cognition. The Prāsaṅgika School interprets the *"pra"* of *"pramāṇa"* as meaning "prime," but not in the sense of first; rather, it is in the sense of main. Hence, all valid awarenesses are *pramāṇa*.

A. Conventional Valid Cognition Is Necessarily Mistaken

Candrakīrti's *Clear Words (tshig gsal, prasannapadā)* says:[3]

> The erroneous and the non-erroneous[4] *(phyin ci log dang phyin ci ma log pa dag, viparyāsāvaiparyāsa)* are different [i.e., a dichotomy]. Therefore, like the falling hairs [seen by] one with cataracts / dimness of sight, and so forth, when what does not [inherently] exist is apprehended by [that is, appears to] an erroneous [consciousness] as just [inherently] existing, how could even a portion of an [inherently] existent object be observed?

Ngawang Belden:[5] An erroneous object of knowledge—a falsity—and a non-erroneous object of knowledge—a truth—are different in the sense of being a dichotomy. Mistaken object of knowledge, falsity, object found by a mistaken consciousness, and truth for a concealer are equivalent.[6] Hence, it is said that

---

[3]*Clear Words* 9b.3-4. Sanskrit in Poussin 30.3-4. This has also been translated by Hopkins (1983a: 613, 615) and by Sprung (1979: 41). The bracketed material is from Ngawang Belden's commentary.

[4]Sometimes "erroneous and non-erroneous" are taken as referring to objects of knowledge, as in Dzongkaba's *The Essence of the Good Explanations* (192); sometimes as consciousnesses, as in his *Great Exposition of the Stages of the Path* (448b.3 of Shes rig par khang edition). Ngawang Belden takes it according to the former, Dzongkaba's later work.

[5]*Annotations*, note *tsha*, 111a.4.

[6]These are equivalent to conventional truths, which comprise all objects of knowledge except for emptinesses and are truths only in a special sense, since they do not exist as they appear. One problem with this is that even an emptiness does not exist as it appears to a conceptual reasoning consciousness (although it does exist as it appears to a directly perceiving consciousness). So, according to Kensur Yeshey Tupden, whose position is that of Loseling College, in one sense it too is a falsity. (See Ngawang Belden, *Stating the Mode of Explanation in the Textbooks on the Middle Way and the Perfection of Wisdom in the Loseling and Go-mang Colleges* 469.2; see also Newland 1992.) Conceptual consciousnesses are always mistaken because what appears to them is a generic image or concept *(don spyi, arthasāmānya)* of an object, which appears to be the object itself. However, although a conceptual consciousness realizing emptiness does not conceive that the generic image of emptiness is emptiness, the generic image appears to be emptiness. Thus,

just as "falling hairs," and so forth, do not exist even though they appear to exist to a person with cataracts, truths for a concealer are objects found by a mistaken consciousness which, although they do not ultimately exist, appear to [ultimately] exist.

Jamyang Shayba:[7] Candrakīrti's *Entrance to the Middle Way* (VI.29) says:[8]

> One with pure eyes would see the nature—suchness —
> Of the falling hairs, and so forth, in the place
> Where these unreal entities are imputed
> Through the force of cataracts.[9]

Ngawang Belden:[10] The meaning of "through the force of cataracts" is: when someone without cataracts concentrates his vision on that place where falling hairs, and so forth, are seen by one with cataracts, he does not observe the falling hairs, and so forth, and sees that they do not exist. Just as the mode of being [of the falling hairs] is seen by one without cataracts

---

it is mistaken with regard to its appearing object even if it is not wrong with regard to its apprehended object. However, emptiness is not generally said to be a falsity; it is a truth in the important sense that it exists in the way it appears to its uncommon certifying awareness, a consciousness directly realizing emptiness. Emptiness is not a falsity merely because it can be cognized falsely by a mistaken consciousness.

[7]*Great Exposition of Tenets cha* 37a.2.

[8]*Entrance to the Middle Way* 5b.8-9. Cf. Huntington 160-61 (he translates the first line as "spontaneously perceives what is real"). Jamyang Shayba's citation has been expanded to include the first line of this stanza. Dzongkaba's commentary in *Illumination of the Thought* is 109a.4-10a.5, with "dispelling objections" continuing to 113a.3.

[9]Dzongkaba comments on this in his *Middling Exposition of Special Insight* (translations in Hopkins, unpublished ms., p. 98, and Thurman [1982: 159]). Just as a person with good eyes will not see falling hairs in the place where they are seen by a person with cataracts (or amblyopia), so one who has destroyed all the taints that cause the false appearance of true existence will not "see" inherent existence in the places where such is seen by ordinary persons and Superiors who have not overcome the obstructions to omniscience.

[10]*Annotations* 111a.5.

but is not seen by one with cataracts, so even though a Buddha, who has abandoned the predispositions of ignorance, turns his mind toward the bases—aggregates, constituents, sources, and so forth—which are perceived by a person who is polluted by ignorance to be truly existent, he does not observe even a mere speck of true establishment in those places and sees such to be non-existent. Know that this object [i.e., non-true establishment] is an ultimate truth.[11]

Jamyang Shayba:[12] In that way, until Buddhahood is attained, one has no non-mistaken consciousnesses except for a Superior's exalted wisdom of meditative equipoise. Also, due to that, in childish persons, i.e., common beings, even [the exalted wisdom] of meditative equipoise of the supreme mundane qualities path of preparation *(sbyor lam chos mchog, laukikāgradharma-prayogamārga)* is polluted by error with respect to what appears. Therefore, that all consciousnesses of common beings are mistaken is also a unique [Prāsaṅgika tenet].[13]

---

[11]The predispositions of ignorance are latencies for the appearance of inherent existence that have been established by ignorance—the conception of inherent existence. By causing phenomena to appear in a way different than they actually exist, those predispositions are like cataracts that cause the appearance of falling hairs wherever one looks. Just as a person without cataracts not only is not obscured by the appearance of falling hairs but can also validly establish the non-existence of falling hairs, so a Buddha not only is not obscured by the appearance of inherent existence but can also establish the non-existence of inherent existence. There is no appearance of inherent existence to a Buddha except by way of the appearance of inherent existence to beings whose minds the Buddha knows. Although a Superior other than a Buddha can also establish non-true existence, it is necessary to specify a Buddha in this example because only a Buddha is capable simultaneously of cognizing both conventional phenomena, such as the aggregates, and ultimate phenomena, emptinesses. Other Superiors are incapable of cognizing anything other than emptiness when in meditative equipoise on emptiness. Moreover, because non-Buddhas have yet to abandon the obstructions to omniscience (the predispositions of ignorance), phenomena continue to appear to them to be inherently existent, even if they no longer assent to that appearance.

[12]*Great Exposition of Tenets cha* 37a.2.

[13]Among the consciousnesses of sentient beings (= non-Buddhas) only

B. Prime Cognition Is Not Necessarily New Realization

The statement in Nāgārjuna's *Refutation of Objections (rtsod zlog, vigrahavyāvartanī,* vs. 32):[14]

> If it is thought that [valid cognition] is established
> By other validly cognizing consciousnesses, it would be endless.
> Furthermore, the first is not established,
> Nor the middling, nor the last...[15]

refutes that [*pramāṇa* necessarily means] new realization and refutes that [consciousnesses are certified by] self-consciousness or other-knowing consciousnesses.[16]

---

a Superior's exalted wisdom of meditative equipoise, the direct realization of emptiness, is a non-mistaken consciousness. The beginning of this statement seems to imply that after one becomes a Buddha, one will have non-mistaken consciousnesses which are not also exalted wisdoms of meditative equipoise. However, because Buddhas are omniscient they have no consciousnesses that are not also continually in meditative equipoise on emptiness. The supreme mundane qualities path of preparation is the highest level of the path of preparation, where a yogi is still realizing emptiness conceptually but has not yet developed the ability to cognize it directly because emptiness still appears to truly exist. Because even this consciousness is conceptual, it is necessarily a mistaken consciousness.

[14]P 5228, vol. 95, 15.1.3-4. The quotation has been expanded by adding the first two lines. Nāgārjuna's commentary is P 5232, vol. 98, 61.1.6-2.2. Also found in K. Bhattacharya (1978: 25).

[15]If a valid cognition must be certified by another valid cognition, there would be an endless regress, in which case no valid cognizer would be established—first, middle, or end.

[16]Valid cognition is certified neither by self-consciousness nor by other-knowing consciousness; they are certified simply by their own operation toward their objects (see chapter 4 of the introduction and chapter 7 of the Jamyang Shayba translation).

Ngawang Belden:[17] Furthermore, the meaning of "the first is not established" was explained in the context of the Svātantrika School.[18]

Jamyang Shayba:[19] Also, it is explained in Candrakīrti's *Clear Words*[20] that it is unsuitable to analyze in this way [i.e., whether or not prime cognition involves new realization of an

---

[17]*Annotations*, note *dza*, 111a.8.

[18]In note *ma* (Ngawang Gelek edition, vol. *ca* 17a.5 ff.), an annotation to Jamyang Shayba's polemical attack on Daktsang at the beginning of the Mādhyamika chapter, Ngawang Belden says:

> Nāgārjuna's *Refutation of Objections* says: "If your objects / Are well proven by valid cognition, / How also are your valid cognitions / Well established in just that way?" With respect to certifying valid cognition, in answer to the question, [Nāgārjuna says]: "If it is thought that [valid cognition] is established / By other valid cognitions, it would be endless. / Moreover, the first is not established, / Nor the middle, nor the last." If it is thought that valid cognition is established by a different factuality, valid cognition would be endless [i.e., an infinite regress], and if it is endless, the first would not be established; and if the first does not exist, the middle is not established and the last also is not established. The meaning has been set forth in Nāgārjuna's *Commentary on the "Refutation of Objections"* to be thus. Here, [Jamyang Shayba's] saying that it is refuted that the meaning of prime cognition is new realization should be analyzed.

In other words, Ngawang Belden doubts that this passage can be used to prove that prime cognition need not mean new realization.

[19]*Great Exposition of Tenets cha* 37a.4.

[20]I have found no passage yet in *Clear Words* that states this. However, Candrakīrti says in 49.6-7 (Sanskrit is in Poussin 74, translated in Sprung [1979: 63]) that there is no conception in the world that direct perception *(mngon sum, pratyakṣa)* is a consciousness free from conceptuality *(rtog pa dang brel pa'i shes pa)*. *If* this is the passage that Jamyang Shayba is thinking of, the bracketed material is inappropriate, since this passage supports the idea that it is unsuitable to analyze whether direct perception is conceptual or nonconceptual, not whether prime cognition is new realization or not. (The assertion that there is conceptual direct perception is explained in the next chapter.) Still, Candrakīrti's point is that it is contrary to the conventions of the world to analyze prime cognition, and that would include an investigation into its newness.

object],[21] and it is explained that the definition of prime cognition is "an incontrovertible consciousness" *(mi bslu ba'i shes pa).*

Therefore, the establishment of subsequent cognition as prime cognition is unique, and these two [assertions—that prime cognition need not be new realization and that all consciousnesses of common beings are mistaken—] have their source in the non-assertion of [establishment by a phenomenon's] own character.[22]

Ngawang Belden:[23] **[111b]** Both of the assertions that all awarenesses of common beings are mistaken consciousnesses and that subsequent [valid] cognition is prime cognition have their source in the non-assertion of [establishment by a phenomenon's] own character, because (1) whatever is an awareness of a common being necessarily perceives [phenomena] to be established by their own character and (2) whatever might be a new incontrovertible consciousness would have to be an object that is findable through analysis by a reasoning consciousness. The first [reason] is easy. The second is established because Kaydrup's *Opening the Eyes of the Fortunate (bskal bzang mig 'byed / stong thun chen mo)* says:

> The assertion that [prime cognition] is necessarily newly incontrovertible—[that an awareness] cannot be posited as prime cognition merely by being incontrovertible with respect to the object of comprehension that is its object of the mode of apprehension—is incorrect because (1) mere conventional prime cognition does not establish that prime cognition must be newly incontrovertible and (2) prime cognition analyzing the ultimate does not in any way find prime cognition.[24] That the former [reason—that mere con

[21]Material in brackets from Kensur Yeshey Tupden.

[22]Losang Gönchok, *Word Commentary* 257.2-4, says that the proofs for *pramāṇa* being new realization in the texts of the proponents of true existence are a case of analyzing for an imputed object and are therefore unsuitable.

[23]*Annotations*, note *wa*, 111b.1.

[24]Kaydrup says that conventional valid cognition does not establish that prime cognition must be a new awareness; thus, Ngawang Belden thinks, if an instance of prime cognition which must be newly incontrovertible does

ventional prime cognition does not establish that prime cognition must be newly incontrovertible —] is so follows (1) because an ordinary innate awareness of a worldly being that is not affected by adventitious causes of error and operates without investigation or analysis designates as prime cognition what is merely incontrovertible with respect to the object it comprehends and does not in any way designate [a consciousness as prime cognition] by way of it being *newly* incontrovertible and (2) because in all logicians' statements of proofs for the necessity of mentioning the term "newly" as part of the definition of prime cognition, the way something becomes prime cognition is put in terms of positing as prime cognition an object found by analysis through reasoning.[25]

---

exist, it must be established by ultimate valid cognition, in which case it would be findable through analysis by a reasoning consciousness. Likewise, Kaydrup also notes that prime cognition is not found by ultimate valid cognition either; indeed, in the Prāsaṅgika system, nothing is findable upon analysis by ultimate valid cognition.

[25]An ordinary awareness would designate a consciousness as prime cognition simply because it is incontrovertible with respect to its object. It would not engage in investigation to determine if that consciousness was the first or a subsequent moment of a continuum of perception. To investigate the relationship between the object imputed—the consciousness—and the basis of imputation—the moments of a continuum of consciousness—would be ultimate analysis. According to Kensur Yeshey Tupden, the "logicians" *(rtog ge pa)* are tenet-holders of Svātantrika and below. In all of their statements about prime cognition, they presume that prime cognition is findable under analysis because their general position is that objects are findable under analysis.

4 Mental and Yogic Direct Perception

Jamyang Shayba:[1] The root text says:

Because feeling is mental direct perception *(yid kyi mngon sum, manasa-pratyakṣa)*, conceptual mental direct perception exists.
Because even when one actualizes the sixteen [aspects of the four noble truths] one is not [necessarily] a Superior,
It is asserted that there are common beings who actualize the sixteen aspects of the [four noble] truths.

A. Mental Direct Perception May Be Conceptual

Furthermore, the statement in Candrakīrti's *Commentary on (Āryadeva's) "Four Hundred" (bzhi rgya pa'i grel pa, catuḥśatakaṭīkā)*:[2]

---

[1]*Great Exposition of Tenets cha* 37a.4.

[2]I have expanded the passage cited by Jamyang Shayba by depending on Dzongkaba's larger citation in *Illumination of the Thought* 163a.2-3 (296 in Varanasi edition). The context of Dzongkaba's citation is distinguishing sense and mental consciousnesses: sense consciousnesses directly know their objects whereas mental consciousnesses know their objects indirectly through the power of sense consciousnesses. Explaining Candrakīrti, Dzongkaba says he shows that feelings are distinguished by *internal* exper-

> [???] are not aspects of experience like feelings *(tsor ba, vedanā)*, and so forth, nor objects distinguished by way of sense [consciousnesses] like forms, sounds, and so forth.

explains that ordinary feelings that have a conventional aspect are mental direct perception. Also, Candrakīrti's *Clear Words* says:[3]

> Since in scripture it is also not the case that only non-conceptual consciousnesses are directly perceiving consciousnesses *(mngon sum, pratyakṣa)*, this [contrary assertion that there is only non-conceptual direct perception] is untenable.

Therefore, because [Candrakīrti] refutes [the idea] that direct perception is necessarily non-conceptual, conceptual mental direct perception is asserted.

Ngawang Belden:[4] Whatever is direct prime cognition is not necessarily a non-conceptual consciousness (1) because the mental direct perception indicated here, i.e., that [like the] one which is renowned to Epistemologists *(tshad ma pa, prāmāṇika)*,[5] is asserted in this context [of the Prāsaṅgika School] to be a memory consciousness and (2) because [the experience of] feeling that is a mental consciousness is asserted to be mental direct perception.[6]

---

ience.

As will become a little clearer in Ngawang Belden's subsequent citation of Dzongkaba, the main meaning of feeling is the mental factor that is an *object* of experience. It is unusual to consider feeling to *be* mental direct perception. In fact, Jamyang Shayba may not be arguing that feeling *is* mental direct perception, but that the mental direct perception *of* feeling must be *conceptual*, since feeling is not an object experienced by a sense consciousness first—it is an object of "internal" experience.

[3]*Clear Words* 50.1-2. Sanskrit in Poussin 75.1-2: *nāgamādapi kalpanāpohasyaiva vijñānasya pratyakṣatvamiti na yuktametat*. Translated by Sprung (1979: 63) and Stcherbatsky (1927: 251).

[4]*Annotations*, note *zha*, 111b.5.

[5]*Prāmāṇika* is a possible construction for *tshad ma pa*. This refers to the followers of Dignāga and Dharmakīrti.

[6]The Epistemologists, followers of Dignāga and Dharmakīrti, assert that in mental direct perception of an object, the object is directly known without

The first reason [—that the mental direct perception indicated here is a memory consciousness—] is established because (1) Dzongkaba's *Illumination of the Thought, Explanation of (Candrakīrti's) "Entrance"* says:[7]

> Mental direct perception is not asserted in accordance with explanations in [texts] of the Epistemologists. Candrakīrti's *Commentary on (Āryadeva's) "Four Hundred,"* at the point of explaining the meaning of the passages in the abhidharma texts that the five, forms and so forth, are individually known by the [corresponding] sense consciousnesses and the mental consciousness, says:[8]

---

conceptuality. That is the "mental direct perception indicated here." "Indicated here" *(skobs 'dir bstan)* refers to a sūtra passage, "Consciousnesses of forms are of two types, those depending on the eye and those depending on the mind" (Lati Rinbochay and Napper [1980: 54]). This is taken to indicate the cognition of forms, and so forth, by a mental consciousness in dependence on prior cognition of those objects by sense consciousnesses. Jambel Sampel (3a.2-3b.4, translated in Lati Rinbochay and Napper 56-57) distinguishes three systems for explaining the relationship of the mental and sense direct perception; (1) alternating, where moments of mental and sense direct perception alternate; (2) simultaneous production of three types, that there is simultaneous production of the second moment of sense direct perception, the first moment of mental direct perception, and the second moment of self-consciousness; and (3) production of a moment of mental direct perception at the end of a continuum of sense direct perception. For a summary according to Dharmakīrti see Jackson (1994: 123). Jamyang Shayba considers the third type to be the one explicitly indicated by Dharmakīrti, but does not consider a single moment of mental direct perception to be viable (Lati Rinbochay and Napper [1980: 165, n. 35]). According to Prāsaṅgikas, mental direct perception subsequent to sense direct perception is a *conceptual* mental consciousness engaging in recollection of the object. For the followers of Dignāga, mental direct perception is necessarily non-conceptual and thus it is not possible that it be a memory consciousness.

With regard to the second reason, the principal meaning of "feeling" is the mental factor that accompanies either a sense or mental consciousness. However, here "feeling" refers to a mental factor that accompanies a conceptual consciousness that experiences pleasure, pain, and neutral feeling. Since such a mental factor accompanies a main conceptual consciousness, it also is a conceptual consciousness.

[7]*Illumination of the Thought* 162b.5-63a.2 (Dzongkaba's sentence begins before what is cited here). 326.4 in NG edition.

[8]P 5266, vol. 98, 251.3.6-8 (202b.7-8, 203a.6). Variant readings: for "gen-

> The two [types of] perception [sense and mental] do not perceive the same object. One, [a sense consciousness] which is generated first, directly distinguishes the aspect of the object. The second [the mental consciousness] does not know [the object] in the sense of just acting [on it] directly; [however,] since, by the power of a sense consciousness, it is produced thinking of such, it is designated that it also knows that object **[112a]**.

> Initially, a sense consciousness directly knows an object such as a form, and through the power of that sense consciousness, the mental consciousness knows it, but it is said [that the mental consciousness] does not know it directly like a sense consciousness. It is also said that the mental consciousness that knows its object through the force of a sense consciousness is a memory consciousness.

and (2) Kaydrup's *Opening the Eyes of the Fortunate* says:[9]

> It is said that a sense consciousness clearly and directly knows the object such as a form whereas the mental consciousness knows [the object] through the power of a sense consciousness but does not know it clearly and directly like a sense consciousness, and it is said that the mental consciousness, which knows objects through the power of a sense consciousness, is a memory consciousness. Therefore...

The second [reason—that the experience of feeling, which is a mental consciousness, is mental direct perception—] is also established because Dzongkaba's *Illumination of the Thought, Explanation of (Candrakīrti's) "Entrance"* says:[10]

> Also, Candrakīrti's *Commentary on (Āryadeva's) "Four Hundred"* says:

---

erated," P reads *skyes* for *skye;* for "aspect," P reads *rnam par* for *rnam pa;* for "second," P reads *gnyis pas na* for *gnyis pa ni.*

[9] *Opening the Eyes of the Fortunate* 453. Cf. Cabezón 1992: 372-73.

[10] *Illumination of the Thought* 163a.2—63b.1. 327.2 in Peking *ca.* This quotation follows the immediately preceding quotation.

> ...are not aspects of experience, like feelings, and so forth, nor objects thoroughly distinguished by way of sense [consciousnesses] like forms, sounds, and so forth.

Therefore, with respect to direct comprehension, there are two, (1) the distinguishing by a sense consciousness of forms, and so forth, for instance, and (2) the thorough distinguishing by internal experience of pleasant and painful feelings, and so forth, for instance. The latter of those two has to be asserted [to occur] even during the ordinary state.[11]

Because it is not explained here that there are more than four [types of] direct valid cognition and since [the experience of feeling] is not suitable to be posited as yogic, sense, or self-conscious direct valid cognition, it is posited as mental direct perception. Such mental direct valid cognition is indeed discordant with the [assertions of] the Epistemologists. Nevertheless, it is not the case that mental direct valid cognition is not asserted.[12]

In that case, "feeling" is a word related with an agent, an activity, or an object; thus there come to be three: (1) feeling in the sense of the person [who feels]; (2) feeling in the sense of the activity [of feeling]; and (3) what is felt. The second of these is the valid [i.e., actual] one, the mental factor feeling. The third is the object of comprehension [of a feeling], that is, pleasure, pain, or neutrality. This is in terms of a mental consciousness; the three [types] of feelings of sense consciousnesses thoroughly distinguish forms, sounds, and so forth [as pleasurable, painful, or neutral]. The way those are established is as before.

Question: If [the experience of] feeling, a mental consciousness, manifestly distinguishes pleasure, pain, and so forth,

---

[11]I am not certain as to the meaning of "ordinary state." In tantra, there is discussion of the basic or ordinary state, the path state, and the effect (Buddha) state; or it could refer to one's lifetime with the exclusion of the birth state and intermediate state between death and rebirth, or to waking life as opposed to dreaming and deep sleep. Either way, the point is that we experience, through the mental consciousness, not just sensory information but also internal feelings.

[12]The quotation has been expanded to include, "Because it is not explained...is not asserted," and the last sentence.

would [that mental consciousness] not then be self-conscious?[13]

Answer: There is no fault because (1) the self-consciousness which is refuted [by Prāsaṅgikas] is an isolated factor *(yan 'ga' ba)* of all consciousnesses that has the aspect of the apprehender, is directed inside, and for which the appearance of the known and knower as different has vanished; (2) here it is said in the sets of sūtras that "special experience" *(nyams su myong ba khyad par can)* is the definition of feeling; and (3) even in the conventions of the world it is said, "[I] experience pleasure and pain." Because the object of experience and the experiencer appear to be just different **[112b]**, it is not the same as the self-consciousness of the other party. Therefore, feeling is established through the fact that happiness and so forth are established by experience.

B. Common Beings Have Yogic Direct Perception

Jamyang Shayba:[14] Śāntideva's *Engaging in the Bodhisattva Deeds* (IX.46cd) says:[15]

Though [manifest] afflictions are [temporarily] absent,
They are seen to have [rebirth by] the power of actions.[16]

---

[13]Self-consciousness *(rang rig, svasaṃvedanā)* is a mind that observes another consciousness simultaneously with that consciousness's observation of an object. It is mainly the followers of Dignāga and Dharmakīrti among the Sautrāntikas and Cittamātrins and the Yogācāra-Svātantrikas who assert the existence of self-consciousness. The Prāsaṅgika School regards self-consciousness to be logically impossible (see chapter 7). The questioner thinks that since the mental consciousness experiencing pleasure, etc., apparently knows its own entity (since it has been said that feeling *is* a mental consciousness, an instance of mental direct perception) it would be an instance of self-consciousness. In other words, if feeling *is* pleasure, pain, etc., then it must know itself. Dzongkaba will reply that since we say "*I* experience pleasure and pain," it obviously is the case that this awareness is not non-dualistic self-consciousness.

[14]*Great Exposition of Tenets cha* 37a.6.

[15]V. Bhattacharya (196). Sanskrit: *drṣaṃ ca hetu sāmarthyaṃ / niḥkleśasyāpi karmaṇaḥ*. Batchelor (1979: 142) counts this as stanza 48cd.

[16]In Śāntideva's text, a hypothetical Vaibhāṣika, a Hīnayānist, maintains

Ngawang Belden:[17] Even though manifest afflictions which are described in the abhidharma texts do not operate temporarily in the continua of persons you assert to be Arhats, it is seen that through the force of actions there is still the capacity to impel later rebirths.

Jamyang Shayba:[18] It is seen that those asserted to be Arhats—for instance, those described in the abhidharma texts who are without the afflictions of conceiving of a permanent self, and so forth—doubt the Buddha and through that bad karma are born in a hell. The *Sutra on the Miserliness of One in Trance (bsam gtan dpe 'khyud kyi mdo, dhyānitamuṣi)* says:

> Having gone alone to a solitary place...This [so-called Arhat] is thinking, "I know I have been liberated from all suffering; I have nothing at all further to be done later, and I have become an Arhat." At the time of his death **[37b]**, he sees that he will be born [again], and becomes doubtful and uncertain about the enlightenment of the Buddha. He falls into doubt and after the time of his death falls into a great hell.[19]

---

that there are persons who, following the Hīnayāna abhidharma texts, have destroyed all craving and become Arhats (see chapter 2). Śāntideva replies that these persons have only temporarily suppressed the manifest form of their afflictions and therefore have not attained freedom from rebirth. As Jamyang Shayba will add below, these persons have abandoned only the conception of a permanent self, etc., which, according to the Prāsaṅgika School, is merely an artificial, learned conception and not the innate ignorance that conceives phenomena to inherently exist. Therefore, they could not have abandoned any afflictions from the root, though their success in suppressing them has led them to believe they have won final deliverance. The Sagya scholar Daktsang considers it contradictory to have yogic direct perception realizing impermanence without having reached the path of preparation and contradictory that clairvoyance is only mental direct perception whereas realizing the four noble truths is yogic direct perception. See his *Ocean of Good Explanations* 238.1-3.

[17] *Annotations*, note *za*, 112b.1.

[18] *Great Exposition of Tenets cha* 37a.7.

[19] It is a measure of the destructive capacity of doubt that it apparently is capable of destroying great virtue. Perhaps what is assumed is that these persons come to hate the Buddha for having "deceived" them.

Ngawang Belden:[20] Dzongkaba's *Illumination of the Thought, Explanation of (Candrakīrti's) "Entrance"* says:[21]

> Also, in the *Sutra on the Miserliness of One in Trance*, which is quoted in [the twenty-fourth chapter of] Candrakīrti's *Clear Words*,[22] Buddha says, "Mañjuśrī, sentient beings, whose minds are mistaken due to four errors through not seeing the noble truths correctly as they are in reality, do not pass beyond this unreal cyclic existence." Mañjuśrī responds, "Oh, Supramundane Victor,[23] please indicate what is apprehended by sentient beings that causes them not to pass beyond cyclic existence." The Teacher said that sentient beings are not liberated because they do not know the four truths as they are in reality, and Mañjuśrī requested Buddha to explain what is misconceived by sentient beings that causes them not to be liberated from cyclic existence. In answer to this, Buddha says that they think, "I will pass beyond cyclic existence, and I will attain nirvāṇa," with a sense of adhering to the true existence of these. Therefore, when they have meditated on impermanence and so forth, they think, "I know suffering, I have abandoned its sources, I have actualized its cessation, I have cultivated the path." They then think, "I have become an Arhat." When they have temporarily abandoned the manifest [coarse] afflictions explained above, they think, "I have extinguished all contaminations." It is said that at the time of death they perceive that they will be reborn; thereby, they doubt Buddha, and this fault causes them to fall into a great hell. This applies to some who abide on such a path but not to all.[24]

---

[20]*Annotations*, note *'a*, 112b.2.

[21]*Illumination of the Thought* 31b.5-32a.5. I use Hopkins' translation (1980: 162-63).

[22]*Clear Words* 342.4 ff. (Poussin's Sanskrit text 516.5-18.6).

[23]On the justification for translating *bcom ldan 'das* (bhagavan) as Supramundane (or Transcendent) Victor, see Lopez (1988: 196, n. 46).

[24]These persons not only do not realize emptiness, they are conceiving true existence in their meditation on impermanence, and so forth. This brings out an important point: it is not possible to cause the consciousness conceiving true existence to become non-manifest through any type of meditation other than meditation on emptiness. It is possible only temporarily to abandon coarse afflictions.

[With regard to a textual corruption in Jamyang Shayba's citation of that sutra—the presence of a superfluous *bshad*[25]—] it should read, "I know I have become an Arhat."

Jamyang Shayba:[26] This passage explains that even though [such a person] had actualized the coarse four noble truths as [explained] before, he is born in a great hell through the force of doubting the Buddha's enlightenment, whereby it is unsuitable for [such a person] to be a Superior. Therefore, it is a unique assertion [of the Prāsaṅgika system] that there are common beings who have in their continua yogic direct perception[27] manifestly realizing the sixteen coarse attributes of the four noble truths.[28]

[25]In other words, one should read *bdag gis shes* for *bdag gis bshad shes* (37a.8). See the note for the earlier passage where this was quoted.

[26]*Great Exposition of Tenets cha* 37b.1.

[27]The definition of yogic direct perception (based on Dignāga and Dharmakīrti) in Geshay Jambel Sampel's typical Gelukba text (4a.1-2; translated in Lati Rinbochay and Napper [61-62]) is: "a non-conceptual non-mistaken exalted knower in the continuum of a Superior that is produced from a meditative stabilization that is a union of calm abiding and special insight and that has become its own unique empowering condition."

[28]Note that none of the sources cited above—the sūtra, Śāntideva, or Dzongkaba—explicitly said that these persons had yogic direct perception. Jamyang Shayba seems to assume that these persons have been able to realize subtle impermanence *(phra ba'i mi rtag pa)* directly, which would indeed require yogic direct perception. Dzongkaba's discussion above merely says "impermanence," but it would not require anything more than ordinary reasoning to realize coarse impermanence. According to Jamyang Shayba, then, it is not necessary that yogic direct perception be in the continuum of a Superior.

5 The Sixteen Attributes of the Four Noble Truths and the Three Times

Jamyang Shayba:[1] The root text says:

Because special insight *(lhag mthong, vipaśyanā)* with respect to emptiness and the path of preparation *(sbyor lam, prayogamārga)* are simultaneous,
Even though one has directly[2] realized the sixteen [attributes of the four noble truths]
One has not reached the path of preparation,
And because disintegratedness *(zhig pa)* is a [functioning] thing *(dngos po, bhāva)*, the three times are asserted to be [functioning] things.

---

[1]*Great Exposition of Tenets cha* 37b.2.

[2]In the root verse, *mngon sum gyis* could be taken either as "by direct perception" or "directly." Jamyang Shayba's commentary makes it clear that he takes *mngon sum gyis* in the root verse to mean just "directly"; Ngawang Belden, in his word commentary on Jamyang Shayba's root verses found in the *Three Commentaries* (509.4), glosses it as "by mere direct realization" (*mngon sum du rtogs pa tsam gyis*).

A. Direct Realization of the Four Noble Truths Is Not the Path of Preparation

Because the attainment of special insight realizing emptiness[3] and the heat *(drod, uṣmagata)* path of preparation are simultaneous,[4] when those are attained such pride of wrong conceit [i.e., boasting] is not produced. Therefore, one does

---

[3]Gelukbas say that since the Sautrāntikas do not accept the possibility of direct realization of a mere negation such as emptiness, for them, yogic direct perception that realizes the selflessness of the person is realization by direct perception *(mngon sum gyis rtogs pa)* but is not direct realization *(mngon sum du rtogs pa)* because it only realizes the selflessness of the person implicitly. Therefore, in that system it may make a difference whether *mngon sum gyis* means realization by direct perception or merely means direct realization. Mādhyamikas are said to have no such problem, since they contend that there is yogic direct perception that *directly* realizes a non-affirming negative such as emptiness. Still, even for Mādhyamikas, not all cases of realization by direct perception are instances of direct realization. That is because they consider conceptual realization subsequent to inferential realization—such as realizing that sound is impermanent upon realizing that sound is a product and that all products are impermanent—to be direct perception *(mngon sum, pratyakṣa)* after its first moment, but since such an inferential realization depends initially upon a reason, it is not considered direct realization *(mngon sum du rtogs pa)*.

[4]From among the five paths comprising the spiritual course, the path of preparation *(sbyor lam, prayogamārga)* is the second, attained upon achieving special insight with emptiness as its object. Special insight is defined as "a wisdom of thorough discrimination of phenomena conjoined with special pliancy induced by the power of analysis" (Jamyang Shayba, *Great Exposition of the Concentrations and Formlessnesses*, 81b.3, cited in Hopkins [1983a: 92]). Special insight may be directed at the sixteen aspects of the four noble truths such as the coarse selflessness of the person (thus, even ordinary beings can have yogic direct perception, as Jamyang Shayba argues in chapter 4). However, unless special insight has the subtle emptiness as its object one cannot use it to reach the path of preparation. Although Jamyang Shayba's college, Gomang, asserts that a coarse selflessness of the person *is* an emptiness, it is a coarse emptiness and the realization of it is not liberating. The "heat" path of preparation is the first of four parts of that path, the path over which one's conceptual realization of emptiness is deepened. Upon completing the remaining three parts of the path of preparation, one is brought to the point of non-conceptual direct realization of emptiness.

not arrive even at the path of preparation by just directly realizing the sixteen coarse attributes of the four truths.[5]

B. Disintegratedness Is a Functioning Thing

Because the *Sūtra on the Ten Grounds (mdo sde sa bcu pa, daśabhūmikasūtra)*[6] and many Perfection of Wisdom *(shes rab kyi pha rol tu phyin pa, prajñāpāramitā)* Sūtras say that aging and death [are caused] by the condition of birth, it is established that the death of a sentient being, disintegratedness *(zhig pa)*, and pastness *('das pa)* are [functioning] things.[7]

---

[5]The sixteen attributes of the four noble truths consist of the four attributes of true sufferings—impermanence, misery, emptiness, and selflessness; the four attributes of true origins—cause, origin, strong production, and condition; the four attributes of true cessations—cessation, pacification, auspicious highness, and definite emergence; and the four attributes of true paths—path, suitability, achievement, and deliverance (Losang Gönchok, *Word Commentary* 258.4-59.1). For an explanation of each of these attributes and the manner in which they are contemplated in meditation, see Hopkins (1983a: 292-96). These sixteen attributes have both coarse and subtle aspects; e.g., coarse sufferings arise from the coarse actions and afflictions established by the coarse conception of self, subtle sufferings from the subtle conception of self (Losang Gönchok 259.2). Hence, it is possible for one to directly realize the *coarse* sixteen attributes of the four noble truths without having reached the path of preparation, i.e., without having had special insight with respect to the subtle emptiness. Hypothetically, this could be done without reaching even the first path, the path of accumulation *(tshogs lam, saṃbhāramārga)*, though it seems unlikely that one might realize impermanence or selflessness without having generated the spirit of renunciation. The point being made here is that although there are some persons who claim to be Arhats *(dgra bcom pa, arhan)* on the basis of having realized the sixteen aspects of the four noble truths, it is easy to see that they have not attained special insight that realizes the subtle emptiness and hence the heat path of preparation because they are boastful whereas real Arhats are not. This is the same point as was made in the last chapter, where persons who considered themselves to be Arhats were obviously mistaken since they, upon having realized the sixteen aspects of the four noble truths, generated doubt with respect to the Buddha's enlightenment, demonstrating that they had only temporarily suppressed the manifest afflictions.

[6]P 761.31, vol. 25. This is also cited in Janggya and in the next chapter. For translation, see Honda (1968: 190).

[7]A sentient being's death, "deadness," or "having died" is also that sentient being's disintegratedness, having disintegrated, or pastness. Whatever

Therefore, all three times—past, future, and present—are implicitly established as [functioning] things; this will be explained later.[8]

Ngawang Belden:[9] In the systems of other proponents of tenets it is asserted that because disintegratedness *(zhig)* and disintegration *('jig)* are mutually exclusive, the two, a pot's disintegratedness and a pot's disintegration, are mutually exclusive. A pot's not enduring in the next [moment after] its own time is the meaning of a pot's disintegration, and a pot's **[113a]** not having endured in the next [moment after] its own time is the meaning of a pot's disintegratedness.[10] The first is asserted to be [included in] the aggregates of compositional factors, and the second is uncompounded.[11]

---

is caused is necessarily impermanent and a functioning thing. The Prāsaṅgika School holds that death, disintegratedness, or pastness are caused and therefore are functioning things.

[8]As will be seen in chapter 6, section 3, pastness is a functioning thing because of being caused, and a futureness—a thing's factor of not having yet come, despite the existence of its causes, due to the incompleteness of its cooperative conditions—is also caused because it exists due to the non-aggregation of those conditions.

[9]*Annotations*, note *ya*, 112b.8.

[10]An existing pot's aspect of *disintegration* is its inability to endure past its own time, i.e., the present moment (for all impermanent phenomena are destroyed every moment) or, put another way, its inevitability of not enduring. A pot's disintegration, then, is concurrent with it. On the other hand, a pot's *disintegratedness* is its aspect of not having endured, the fact of its having disintegrated. A pot's disintegratedness, then, occurs *after* it has disintegrated, when the pot itself no longer exists. The non-Prāsaṅgika systems, except for the Vaibhāṣika School, maintain that this disintegratedness is a mere absence and conclude from this that disintegration and disintegratedness are mutually exclusive, but the Prāsaṅgikas hold that disintegratedness is itself an impermanent phenomenon which, therefore, itself disintegrates. Thus, they maintain that the two are not mutually exclusive.

[11]Buddha said that compounded phenomena are characterized by production, abiding, and disintegration (Jamyang Shayba, *Great Exposition of the Middle Way* 610.4-5). An impermanent phenomenon such as a chair is momentary in the sense that it disintegrates moment-by-moment. However, even though in each moment there is a new chair, it is not impossible to posit a continuum of chair; that is, even though in each moment the chair simultaneously is produced, endures, and disintegrates, the phenomenon

In the Prāsaṅgika system, it is asserted that since disintegratedness and disintegration are not mutually exclusive, a pot's disintegratedness is also a pot's disintegration. Moreover, the assertion that "a pot's disintegration" is the *activity* of a pot's disintegration is an assertion agreeing with the Sautrāntikas and above. However, Prāsaṅgikas assert that both a pot's not enduring and not having endured in the second [moment after] its own time[12] are activities of a pot's disintegration; therefore both a pot's approaching to disintegratedness and a pot's disintegratedness are activities of a pot's disintegration.[13]

---

chair is nevertheless validly imputed in dependence on the continuum of moments that comprise its existence. The manner in which the chair is in one moment created, endures, ages, and disintegrates is: its production is its being the new creation of what did not exist; its enduring is its similarity to what preceded it; its aging is its being a different entity from the previous moment; and its disintegration is its not lasting another moment.

A pot's disintegration is its quality of not enduring after the moment of its "own time," the moment it endures, the moment in which it is present. Disintegration is something that the pot has at the present time, part of its nature; hence, it is an impermanent phenomenon, and from among the five aggregates of impermanent phenomena would be included in that of compositional factors (*'du byed, saṃskāra).*

Gelukbas say that except for the Vaibhāṣika and the Prāsaṅgika-Mādhyamika schools, Buddhist schools assert that a pot's disintegratedness is its absence after having disintegrated. Being a mere negative, it is a permanent phenomenon, one that is not compounded—put together—like impermanent phenomena.

[12]A thing's "own time" is just the moment in which it is present, so the following moment is not its own time, but rather is the moment of its disintegratedness.

[13]Prāsaṅgikas find that a pot's disintegratedness, its "not having endured," is part of the activity of a pot's disintegration, its "not enduring." Like disintegration, then, disintegratedness is an impermanent phenomenon. The other Buddhist schools hold that a pot's disintegration is just its *approaching* to disintegratedness, which is simultaneous with a pot's own time and does not include its disintegratedness, which occurs in the moment after its own time. (Geshe Gendün Lodrö said that most Buddhists accept that at the time of the seed, a sprout exists as the entity of the seed; but a sprout itself does not exist then. This implies that similarly, a sprout's disintegratedness exists at the time of its disintegration as the entity of disintegration.) The Vaibhāṣikas differ from other Buddhist schools in saying that a sprout *actually* exists at that time, a position similar to that of the non-

For example, it is asserted that [disintegratedness being an activity of disintegration] is similar to the fact that both a sprout's approaching to production and a sprout's production are activities of a sprout's production.[14] However, the three—Sautrāntikas, Cittamātrins, and Svātantrikas—assert that even though both a sprout's approaching to production and a sprout's production are activities of a sprout's production, it is not the case that both a sprout's approaching to disintegratedness and a sprout's disintegratedness are activities of a sprout's disintegration. That is because [for them,] a sprout's disintegratedness is not an activity of a sprout's disintegration because it is not a [functioning] thing.

Dzongkaba's *Illumination of the Thought, Explanation of (Candrakīrti's) "Entrance"* says:[15]

> Candrakīrti's *Clear Words* sets forth[16] the two, scripture and reasoning, in order to prove that in the Prāsaṅgika system, disintegratedness is a [functioning] thing. With respect to the first [i.e., scriptural proofs], the *Sūtra on the Ten Grounds* says, "Aging and death [are produced] by the condition of birth." Death is the disintegratedness of a sentient being who has died, and [the sūtra] says that it is produced by the condition of birth. Also, [the sūtra] says:
>
> > Death subsists in two activities: (1) it causes a composed phenomenon to disintegrate and (2) it issues forth the cause of the non-severance of the continuum of thorough non-knowingness [i.e., ignorance].

Buddhist Sāṃkhyas. It should be noted that disintegratedness *(zhig pa)* and disintegration *('jig pa)* are not synonymous, for although disintegratedness is disintegration because of being part of the activity of disintegration and of course because of being impermanent, disintegration is not necessarily disintegratedness. For example, the disintegration of a pot at its own time—its nature of disintegration even when it is present —is not its disintegratedness, its not having endured.

[14]That is, approaching to disintegratedness and disintegratedness are parallel to approaching to production and production.

[15]*Illumination of the Thought* 127b.6-128a.4.

[16]*Clear Words* 59a.5 ff. Sanskrit is in Poussin 174.10 ff.

This says that two activities are performed by death; it also says that death is generated by causes and that death produces ignorance. Therefore, disintegratedness is produced by causes, and disintegratedness is able to produce effects.[17]

This [example has concerned] the disintegratedness of a continuum, but it is the same for the disintegratedness of the first moment [of a phenomenon] at its next period, and it also indicates that the first moment [of a phenomenon] is a cause of its disintegratedness in the next period.[18] Therefore, with respect to the two, the birth and death of a sentient being, [and the two,] not enduring in the next period and not having endured in the next period, whether they are posited or not posited as [functioning] things and whether they are produced or not produced by causes **[113b]** is the same in every way.[19]

---

[17]Even though it is said that a compositional phenomenon needs no cause other than its production for its disintegration, Geshay Gönchok Tsering (6/ 16/84) said that disintegratedness is the *cooperative condition (lhan cig byed rkhyen, sahakāripratyaya)* of disintegration; the substantial cause *(nyer len, upādāna)* of a thing's disintegration is its production. In general, a cooperative condition is a necessary but not sufficient cause. For instance, water, sun, and nutrients are cooperative conditions of a plant, but its seed is its substantial cause. In the case of the exhaustion of a butter-lamp, the substantial cause of its exhaustion is its own production, and the cooperative condition of that exhaustion is its disintegratedness. With regard to death, Kensur Yeshey Tupden pointed out that first, one dies *('chi ba)*, then one is dead *(shi ba)*. (There is no person who is dead, for that which is dead is not a person, but a corpse.) The first (dying) causes the second (death), which is a disintegratedness of a person and the cause of the non-severance of the continuum of ignorance, etc. The substantial cause of dying (= approaching death) is birth, the cooperative condition, disintegratedness (deadness).

[18]The present moment of a thing, its existing but not enduring for another moment, is the cause of its own disintegratedness, its not having endured. In other words, moment A is the cause of the disintegratedness of moment A, which occurs in moment B.

[19]Just as both birth and death are caused and hence are functioning things, so also both disintegration and disintegratedness are caused and hence are functioning things. Moreover, there are the parallels that with respect to birth, being born is like not enduring for another moment and having been born is like not having endured for another moment, and that with respect to death, dying is not enduring for another moment and having died is not having endured for another moment.

6 Disintegratedness Is a Thing and Effects Are Feasible

Jamyang Shayba:[1] The root text says:

Because of being produced, disintegratedness is a [functioning] thing. Although many [aeons pass after an action has ceased,
Effects issue forth, even though obtainers *(thob pa, prāpti)*, [mental] continua [in which predispositions are infused], and non-wastage *(chud mi za ba, avipranāśa)* do not exist.[2]
The mere propounding that disintegratedness is a [functioning] thing is without analysis, like [saying] pots are things.

---

[1]*Great Exposition of Tenets cha* 37b.5.

[2]These are different entities posited by various schools to explain the transmission of karmic latencies such that future effects can arise from past actions. According to Gönchok Jikmay Wangbo (*Precious Garland of Tenets* 21.14-22.2, translated in Sopa and Hopkins 193-94), the Kashmiri Vaibhāṣikas and the Sautrantikas both identify the continuum of mind (Geshay Tupden Gyatso identified "continuum" as the continuum of consciousness) as the basis of infusion of predispositions (as do Svātantrika-Mādhyamikas). Other Vaibhāṣikas posit a factor, neither matter nor consciousness, called an "obtainer" as that which prevents the loss of the karmic potency until it ripens into an effect. The five Saṃmitīya subschools of the Vaibhāṣikas say that actions produce an impermanent phenomenon called "non-wastage" that prevents the loss of the action's potency (Lamotte 1936: 162-63).

If harsh speech of long ago had not disintegrated but appeared to an innate [awareness],
Why is all that one did previously not remembered?[3]

This can be known extensively in my *Final Analysis* [the *Great Exposition of the Middle Way*].

A. Disintegratedness Is a Functioning Thing

Here, since there are causes for the three times, the three times are established as [functioning] things. If mere characterizations *(so so'i mtshan nyid tsam)* of them are stated, from among the three—past, future, and present—it is explained in scripture that a pastness or disintegratedness is a [functioning] thing and thus its causes exist, due to which it has both cause and effect. For at the time of teaching dependent-arising, in the third scriptural collection [the abhidharma scriptures] it is said,[4] "Aging and death [are caused] by the condition of birth." [Disintegratedness] is also said to issue forth effects; the *Sūtra on the Ten Grounds* says:[5]

[3]The last sentence of the root text does not make Jamyang Shayba's point as forcefully as his commentary does. If, as Daktsang is held to say, actions do not disintegrate over time, then there are the absurdities that not only would one's mind be flooded with the awareness of everything one had ever done, but those actions would still be occurring since they had never disintegrated. This is discussed in the final section.

[4]In his *Great Exposition of the Middle Way* (609.1), Jamyang Shayba says that this is taught in *all three (gsum ga)* scriptural collections, whereas in both editions of the *Great Exposition of Tenets* he says that it is taught in the *third (gsum pa)*. Certainly the *abhidharma-piṭaka* would be a likely place to find a discussion on death and birth, but the sūtra-*piṭaka* certainly would have many passages as well. The argument against "all three" might be that a discussion on death and birth is not likely to be found in the *vinaya-piṭaka*.

[5]The *Sūtra on the Ten Grounds* is P 761.3.1, vol. 25. This passage is translated in Honda (1968: 190), and cited by Candrakīrti in his *Clear Words* (118.4), by Dzongkaba in his *Ocean of Reasoning* (190.6-8) and his *Illumination of the Thought* (127b.7; see chapter 5), and by Jang-gya (see chapter 8). Part of the quotation is missing in the Sanskrit (174.12; see Poussin's note).

> Deadness subsists in two activities: (1) it causes a composed phenomenon to disintegrate and (2) it issues forth the cause of the non-severance of the continuum of thorough non-knowingness [i.e., ignorance].[6]

Also, Nāgārjuna's *Treatise on the Middle Way* (XXV.13) says:[7]

> How can nirvāṇa
> Be both a thing and the non-existence of a thing?
> Nirvāṇa is a non-compounded phenomenon *('dus ma byas kyi chos, asaṃskṛtadharma)*
> And things and the non-existence of things [their disintegratedness] are compounded phenomena *('dus byas kyi chos, saṃskṛtadharma)*.

Ngawang Belden:[8] [Nāgārjuna] says that both a [functioning] thing and its absence upon its destruction are compounded phenomena because that also has its source in not asserting that [a phenomenon is established] by its own character *(rang mtshan, svalakṣaṇa)*. That is because Dzongkaba's

---

[6]Death, the last of the twelve links of dependent-arising *(rten 'byung, pratītyasamutpāda)*, is caused by birth, the eleventh link, and is the cause of ignorance, the first link (of another round of dependent-arising). See my earlier note on this passage in chapter 5.

[7]P 5224, vol. 95, 10.1.5-6. The Sanskrit (Poussin, 531) is: *bhaved abhāvo bhāvaś ca nirvāṇam ubhyaṃ kathaṃ / asaṃskrtaṃ ca nirvāṇaṃ bhāvābhāvau ca saṃskṛtau.* The quotation has been lengthened by including the first two lines of the stanza. This stanza forms a portion of Nāgārjuna's refutation of the four extremes concerning nirvāṇa: that it is a [functioning] thing; that it is a non-thing [i.e., a thing's having become non-existent, its disintegratedness, which is also a thing]; that it is both a thing and non-thing; or that it is neither. Here he says that nirvāṇa is not both a thing and non-thing because those are both caused whereas nirvāṇa is uncaused. This unusual interpretation of the term "non-thing" as a disintegratedness, and hence a functioning thing, rests on Candrakīrti's comments (*Clear Words* 356.2-3) that a thing is caused and thus is a compounded phenomenon, but so also is a non-thing *(dngos po med pa)*, since it arises in dependence on a thing and a sūtra passage says that aging and death are caused by birth. A similar passage from Gyeltsap can be found in chapter 8 in the section on true cessations.

[8]*Annotations*, note *ra*, 113b.1.

Illumination of the Thought, Explanation of (Candrakīrti's) "Entrance" says:[9]

> Moreover, in all positions that assert that things are inherently established it is not feasible that disintegratedness be a [functioning] thing, but in the system of the [Prāsaṅgika-][10] Mādhyamikas who assert that [phenomena] are not inherently established, it is an essential point that disintegratedness is established as a [functioning] thing.
>
> In the former systems, they think: When a [functioning] thing such as a sprout has disintegrated, everything that is part of the sprout is obliterated. Since one does not get any other thing that is different from a sprout, such as a pot, they assert that disintegratedness is utterly not a [functioning] thing [i.e., they assert that it is a permanent or non-disintegrating phenomenon. Also,] neither the [functioning] things among the separate sense-fields, such as blue, nor that which is a collection of the [functioning] things which are its parts, such as a pot, are suitable to be illustrations of that disintegratedness [of a sprout].[11] Therefore, [disintegratedness] is not a [functioning] thing.
>
> In the latter [i.e., Prāsaṅgika] system, for example, one cannot posit (1) Upagupta's individual five aggregates, (2) their collection, or (3) that which is a different entity from those two as an illustration of Upagupta, and Upagupta is also unsuitable to be an illustration of those three. However, it is not contradictory that despite that, what is designated as Upagupta in dependence on his aggregates is a [functioning] thing. Similarly, even though disintegratedness also cannot [be posited] as an illustration of either the thing which has been destroyed or anything which is the same type [i.e., same causal continuum] as that, it is a [function-

---

[9] *Illumination of the Thought* 127b.2-6.

[10] It is necessary to add this because Svātantrikas do not agree that disintegratedness is a functioning thing.

[11] Concerning the disintegratedness of a blue pot, neither a part or quality of the pot, such as blue, nor the pot itself (the whole comprising many parts) is suitable to be an illustration of disintegratedness. They conclude from this that there is no functioning thing that can be a disintegratedness, and hence, disintegratedness must be permanent.

ing] thing because it is produced in dependence on a thing that is destroyed.[12]

Jamyang Shayba:[13] It is said that the consumption or disintegratedness of the wick is the cause of a butter-lamp's dying out.[14] Nāgārjuna's *Sixty Stanzas of Reasoning (rigs pa drug cu pa, yuktiṣaṣṭika)* (20ab) says:[15]

Peace [i.e., death] due to exhaustion of causes
Is realized as "exhaustion."

And, Candrakīrti's *Commentary on (Nāgārjuna's) "Sixty Stanzas of Reasoning" (rigs pa drug cu pa'i 'grel pa, yuktiṣaṣṭikavṛtti)* says:[16]

---

[12]In other tenet systems it is felt that for something to be a functioning thing there must be an illustration that one can point to, as is the case with a patch of blue or a pot. For them, a mere nominal designation could not be a functioning thing. For Prāsaṅgikas, who assert that all phenomena are mere nominal designations, there is no such problem. Just as it is possible to designate a person named Upagupta in dependence on a certain collection of the aggregates of mind and body, even though Upagupta is *not* any of the aggregates, their collection, or a different entity from them (being a mere nominal designation *in dependence on* those aggregates), so it is possible to designate the phenomenon disintegratedness even though it is *not* the thing which has been destroyed or some other thing like it. An illustration of something must *be* that thing. The difference is that Upagupta is merely designated *in dependence upon* his aggregates, not *to* those aggregates.

[13]*Great Exposition of Tenets cha* 37b.7.

[14]More will be said on this topic later. Here, it is implied that while the disintegratedness of the person is the cause of the non-severance of the continuum of ignorance upon a person's death, the cause of the person's death is also disintegratedness, that is, the disintegratedness of a person's life-impelling karma, just as the consumption of a wick is the cause of a butter-lamp's extinguishment.

[15]P 5225, vol. 95, 11.4.1. The stanza continues: "How is what is not [inherently] exhausted / Called 'exhausted'?" See translations by Lindtner (1986b: 79) and Tola and Dragonetti (1983: 112).

[16]In Jamyang Shayba's text, this work is referred to simply as "the commentary on that" *(de'i 'grel pa)*; since Nāgārjuna's own commentary has not been preserved in any language (see Tola and Dragonetti [1983: 95, 177 n.1]), it is assumed that this refers to Candrakīrti's commentary, and a passage similar to this occurs there (P 5265, vol. 98, 177.2.4-5). However, this

> ...since if the conditions for remaining are not complete **[38a]**, it disintegrates. In accordance with that, in the world that which is extinct or used up is observed as "exhausted" due to only the exhaustion of its causes.

Also, the same text says:[17]

> According to those whose thought is that the cessation of things is only causeless, ceasedness also would [absurdly] not depend on [functioning] things because of being causeless like a flower in the sky.

Ngawang Belden:[18] Dzongkaba's *Ocean of Reasoning, Explanation of (Nāgārjuna's) "Treatise on the Middle Way" (rigs pa'i rgya mtsho / rtsa she ṭīk chen)* says:[19]

> The subsistence of [functioning] things depends upon conditions that cause subsistence because if the conditions for subsistence are not present, [the continua of things] would disintegrate. Therefore, the extinguishment and cessation of a butter-lamp's light, which arises from the extinguishment and cessation of the causes that make [the butter-lamp] subsist—the wick, oil, and so forth—is observed to be "extinguishment and cessation." Also, Āryadeva's *Four Hundred* (IX.18ab) says:[20]

---

appears to be a paraphrase rather than a quotation. There is a debate on the consumption of the wick and butter in Candrakīrti's commentary (Toh. 3864, vol. 7) 15b.5 ff.

[17]P 5265, vol. 98, 177.3.3-4.

[18]*Annotations*, note *la*, 113b.6.

[19]I speculate that this passage is somewhere in chapter 7.

[20]P 5246, vol. 95, 136.5.7. P reads: *'bras bu yi ni rgyu bshig pa / des na rgyu ni rtag ma yin* ("Effects destroy causes. / Therefore, causes are not permanent") which is how Ruth Sonam (210; stanza 218ab) translates the line. Ngawang Belden's version, translated here, is quite different: *'bras bu yis ni rgyu bshig pa/ des na med pa skye mi 'gyur*. The context of the quotation is that Āryadeva is refuting Vaiśeṣika assertions of permanent, minute particles (that serve as "building blocks" for coarse objects). Here he says that when a particle becomes an object, it no longer exists (just as a seed ceases upon production of a sprout). We can make sense of Ngawang Belden's version if we understand it to mean that when an effect is produced, it causes (or "produces") a functioning thing—namely the ceasedness/disintegratedness

Effects destroy causes.
Therefore, a non-existent is not what is produced.

This explains that the cause's ceasedness is caused by the effect's being produced, whereby [such] is the assertion of the Superior (Nāgārjuna) and his spiritual son (Āryadeva).

Through the essential point of asserting that the pastness that is the disintegratedness of a sprout is a [functioning] thing, even the futureness of a sprout is likewise [a functioning thing].[21] Therefore, [that] is the meaning of [Āryadeva's saying], "a non-existent is not what is produced **[114a]**."

Jamyang Shayba:[22] There are proofs that disintegratedness is a [functioning thing because of (1) the [absurd] consequence that [otherwise] the explanation of [disintegration] as a characteristic of compounded phenomena would be incorrect, (2) the [absurd] consequence that [otherwise] nothing would be produced by causes, (3) the reasoning concerning the new production [of disintegration] that did not previously exist, and (4) being established by worldly renown.

With respect to the first consequence [that the explanation of disintegration as a characteristic of compounded phenomena would be incorrect], Candrakīrti's *Clear Words* says:[23]

According to those who, having asserted that disintegration [i.e., disintegration and disintegratedness] is causeless, propound that all compounded phenomena are momentary, disintegration would be non-existent because of being causeless like a flower in the sky.[24] Therefore, it would be

---

of the cause—not a non-existent.

[21]That is, using the same reasoning, it is possible to show that futureness is caused and acts as a cause.

[22]*Great Exposition of Tenets cha* 38a.2.

[23]*Clear Words* 117.4-5 (59a.4-5). Sanskrit is in Poussin (1970: 174). The quotation has been restored to full length by filling in the middle, from "disintegration would be non-existent" to "Because of that."

[24]It would be causeless not in the sense of being a permanent phenomenon, but in the sense of being non-existent, because none of these momentary things would require disintegration. However, if they did not require disintegration, they would not be momentary or compounded. A "sky-flower" is a famous instance of a non-existent (like "son of a barren woman,"

> contradictory to establish that things are momentary and that those [things you propound that are] devoid of disintegration are compounded phenomena. Because of that, all of these [assertions] would not fit together.[25]

Ngawang Belden:[26] The meaning of the first consequence is as follows: Our own schools who assert that disintegratedness and disintegration are contradictory assert that since the disintegration which consists of [functioning] things' not enduring in the next period after the time of their establishment is produced from just the causes of this and that thing, it does not depend on causes that occur later and are other than [the thing's] own causes, and they assert that since the disintegratedness [of a thing] at that second period is a non-thing, it is utterly uncaused.[27] Here it is demonstrated that there is damage [to their assertions] by drawing a parallel between production by causes and non-production by causes of the two, that which has not disintegrated [i.e., disintegration] and disintegratedness, as follows. If there were no causes for something's not having endured [i.e., its disintegratedness]

"cloak of turtle hairs," or "horns of a rabbit").

[25]Even for Prāsaṅgikas, disintegra*tion* is causeless in the sense that something disintegrates with no further cause than its production, whereas disintegrat*edness* is caused. So, disintegration occurs in the same moment as production, disintegratedness subsequently. (Vaibhāṣikas, on the other hand, say that disintegration occurs in the next moment.) The characteristics of compounded phenomena are their production, endurance, and disintegration. In addition, all phenomena are empty of inherent existence. But unlike the characteristics of production, etc., emptiness does not characterize something *as* a compounded phenomenon in addition to being a characteristic *of* a compounded phenomenon, for even uncompounded phenomena are empty.

[26]*Annotations*, note *sha*, 114a.1.

[27]According to the Prāsaṅgikas, if *zhig pa* is uncaused, then *'jig pa* would absurdly be uncaused; if that is true, how could things be momentary? Prāsaṅgikas assert that disintegratedness does not depend merely on a thing's own causes, but has later causes (i.e., *'jig pa*), just as the production of a thing does not depend merely on the causes of approaching to production, but has its own causes. It is held to be absurd in either case that the "approaching" is caused but the result is uncaused. This raises the problem: what is the direct cause of the pot's disintegratedness? The pot's disintegration (i.e., the previous moment)?

in its next period, there would also have to be no causes for its not enduring [i.e., its disintegration] in its next period, whereby [that thing] would not be momentary. In that case, [that thing] would not be established as a compounded phenomenon, and it would also be incorrect to propound that compounded phenomena are momentary.[28] It is as Kaydrup's *Opening the Eyes of the Fortunate* says:[29]

> In brief, does the disintegratedness of a sprout exist or not exist without relying on causes? If it does, it is contradictory that a sprout does not disintegrate without depending on causes, and if it does not, it is contradictory that the disintegratedness of a sprout does not depend on causes. Since "approaching to disintegratedness" is called "disintegration" (*'jig pa)*, it is very contradictory that approaching to disintegratedness depends on causes whereas disintegratedness does not depend on causes.[30] Otherwise, it would [absurdly] equally follow that even though approaching to production is caused by causes, producedness is not caused by causes.

---

[28]As Kaydrup is about to point out, it is absurd to say that disintegration, the state of approaching to disintegratedness, has causes but that disintegratedness does not. He contends that if disintegratedness does not have causes, then disintegration would not have causes, and it would then absurdly follow that things would not disintegrate and that they would not be momentary.

[29]*Opening the Eyes of the Fortunate* (Madhyamika Text Series, vol. 1, New Delhi, 1972), 371.6-72.2. Cf. Cabezón 1992: 311-12.

[30]Although disintegration does not depend on causes in the sense of causes other than those for the thing's production, disintegration, a characteristic of compounded phenomena, has those causes.

This text [i.e., Jamyang Shayba] says,[31] "The [absurd] consequence that [if disintegratedness were not a functioning thing] the explanation of [disintegration] as a characteristic of compounded phenomena would be incorrect." Whether or not the printing is corrupt [at that point] should be analyzed, because (1) the explanation in Kaydrup's *Opening the Eyes of the Fortunate* of the meaning of the passage in Candrakīrti's *Clear Words* which [Jamyang Shayba] cites as his source is what I have just cited,[32] and (2) a statement such as that in Dzongkaba's *Ocean of Reasoning, Explanation of (Nāgārjuna's) "Treatise on the Middle Way,"* which, after the earlier passage, says, "That is a refutation *by reasoning*, and with respect to a refutation *by scripture*..." and so forth, says that the earlier proof is a refutation by reasoning and that the statement that the characteristics of compounded phenomena are included in the aggregate of compositional factors is a refutation [of uncaused disintegratedness] by scripture.[33] Hence, if [Jamyang Shayba's] text read, "It would follow that propounding that compounded phenomena are momentary is incorrect," it would be fitting.

---

[31]*Great Exposition of Tenets cha* 38a.2. Jamyang Shayba interprets Candrakīrti's statement to mean that it would not be suitable to assert both that disintegration is a characteristic of compounded phenomena and that disintegratedness is causeless because the latter implies that disintegration is causeless whereas whatever is a characteristic of a caused phenomenon must itself be caused. Selflessness also is a characteristic of compounded phenomena, but does not characterize them *as* compounded phenomena, since it is also a characteristic *of* uncompounded phenomena. Production, endurance, and disintegration, on the other hand, characterize something *as* a compounded phenomenon; if something has those characteristics, it is necessarily a compounded phenomenon.

[32]According to Kaydrup, the meaning of the passage in Candrakīrti's *Clear Words* is that if disintegratedness were caused, things would not disintegrate, whereby they would not be momentary, not that disintegratedness could not be a characteristic of compounded phenomena (although that certainly would also be true).

[33]In other words, Jamyang Shayba has mixed together this reasoning and a scriptural passage that comes later.

Jamyang Shayba:[34] With respect to the second consequence [that if disintegratedness were not a functioning thing, nothing could be produced by causes], Candrakīrti's *Clear Words* says:[35]

> *Objection:* Since this called disintegration [i.e., disintegratedness[36]] is a non-[functioning] thing, of what use are causes to a non-thing?
>
> *Response:* Is it not the case that [functioning] things also would be causeless? For [functioning] things already exist, and of what use are causes for that which exists? What already exists is not produced again. Hence, it would [absurdly] follow that [functioning] things would be causeless in all respects. Therefore, that is not feasible.

Ngawang Belden:[37] The meaning of the second consequence is as follows:

Objection: The disintegratedness of a sprout is a non[-functioning] thing. What could causes do for that? Therefore, [disintegratedness] has no causes **[114b]**.

Response: Then, a sprout also exists, and what use are causes to it? What is already produced is not produced again. This draws the parallel that if causes cannot do anything for a sprout's disintegratedness, there is no need for causes to act on what has not disintegrated.[38]

Objection: Since what has not disintegrated has already been established, at this time it need not be caused; however, since just that establishment is caused, it has causes.

---

[34]*Great Exposition of Tenets cha* 38a.3.

[35]*Clear Words* 117.7-18.1; Sanskrit is in Poussin 174.2-4. The quotation has been lengthened by adding to first sentence, the objection, and filling in between, "For..." and "...in all respects."

[36]As can be seen in the discussion below, Ngawang Belden considers Candrakīrti to be referring to disintegratedness.

[37]*Annotations*, note *sa*, 114a.6.

[38]That is, if disintegratedness is said not to require causes because it exists (as a non-thing), then things that have not disintegrated also absurdly would not need causes.

Response: I also do not assert that a sprout's disintegratedness which is already [established] is further caused, but I do say that just that sprout's disintegratedness is caused.

Jamyang Shayba:[39] The third reasoning [that disintegratedness is a functioning thing because it is newly produced] exists because Candrakīrti's *Clear Words* says:[40]

> Furthermore, just as production has causes because [something] did not previously exist and because it did exist later, just so, disintegration [i.e., disintegration and disintegratedness] also should be asserted [to have causes].

Ngawang Belden:[41] The meaning of the third consequence is as follows: because [a sprout] did not exist earlier at the time of the seed but later does exist, the production of a sprout has causes. Similarly, a sprout's disintegratedness also has causes because it did not exist earlier at the time of the sprout but later it does exist.

Jamyang Shayba:[42] The fourth reason is establishment [that disintegratedness is a functioning thing] even by worldly renown, (1) because it is seen that through the lack of water due to its consumption, grain is lost, and through the lack of food due to its consumption, a child is lost, (2) because what is seen by the world is not suitable to be taken as non-existent upon analysis by reasoning, and (3) because even Buddhas accept [phenomena] in terms of such [worldly conventions]. For:

(1) the *Chapter Showing the Three Vows Sūtra (sdom pa gsum bstan pa'i le'u'i mdo, trisambaranirdeśapartivartasūtra)* says, "What is asserted to exist in the world, that I also assert to exist."[43]

---

[39]*Great Exposition of Tenets cha* 38a.4.

[40]*Clear Words* 118.1. Sanskrit is in Poussin 174.5-6.

[41]*Annotations,* note *ha,* 114b.2.

[42]*Great Exposition of Tenets cha* 38a.5.

[43]This is a chapter of the *Heap of Jewels Sūtra (dkon mchog btsegs pa'i mdo,*

(2) Both Buddhapālita and Candrakīrti explain it similarly, and there are many instances, such as Āryadeva's saying (in his *Four Hundred* [VIII.21cd]):[44]

> Just as a barbarian cannot be
> Guided in a foreign language,
> Except with the worldly
> One is unable to approach the world.

(3) Candrakīrti's *Commentary on (Nāgārjuna's) "Sixty Stanzas of Reasoning"* says:[45]

> Worldly things are not to be asserted through scrutiny and analysis. How then? In accordance with what is renowned in the world.

(4) The same text says:[46]

> In the world, even non-existence exists as just a cause. For as in "If there is no water, my grain will be ruined" and "My child will die from lack of food," the loss of grain and child is propounded to occur due to the non-existence of water and food [respectively].

Moreover, since all the conventions of the world are without reasoned investigation, the meaning of being renowned in the world **[38b]** is that [something] is to be posited through only its renown in the world but not by reasoned investigation because the conventions of the world are contradictory with reasoned investigation.[47]

---

ratnakūṭa-sūtra).

[44]P 5246, vol. 95, 136.3.5-6. I have expanded the quotation by including two lines prior to Ngawang Belden's translation. They are: *ji ltar kla klo skad gzhan gyis / gzung bar mi nus de bzhin du*. Cf. Sonam 196 (stanza 194).

[45]P 5265, vol. 98, 177.4.2. Toh. 3864, vol. 7, 8.3.6. The following citations have numerous small differences with the texts as they appear in the canon.

[46]P 5265, vol. 98, 177.4.2-4.

[47]This sentence ("Moreover, since all the conventions...investigation") presumably is Jamyang Shayba's own conclusion, although he has indicated it as included within the quotation from Candrakīrti. It is not found in the Peking recension of the canon. According to Kensur Yeshey Tupden, "rea-

Therefore, food having been consumed and so forth are affirming negatives,[48] not non-affirming negatives, like, for instance, non-desire, non-hatred, non-obscuration, endless life *(amitāyus)*, and endless light *(amitābha])*.[49]

Therefore, even though Daktsang pretends to be a follower of Candrakīrti, he refutes that disintegratedness is a [functioning] thing by means of the reasonings of the Sautrāntikas and the Cittamātrins, and even though he acts astonished [at Dzongkaba], he errs because he is not aware of the necessity of the two distinctions of worldly conventions, coarse and subtle.[50] Since he does not appear to reply to any of

---

soned investigation" is ultimate analysis. Nothing can withstand ultimate analysis. On the other hand, one can use conventional analysis on something "renowned in the world," that which is established by conventional valid cognition. One avoids ultimate analysis by not investigating matters, such as a thing's relation to its causes or bases of designation, that bear on whether or not that thing exists from its own side or exists as a mere nominal imputation. This still leaves open the possibility of eliminating many perceptual and logical errors through conventional valid cognition.

[48]Affirming negatives *(ma yin dgag, paryudāsa-pratiṣedha)* are existent phenomena that are expressed in a manner involving a negation, but which suggest a positive phenomenon in place of what is negated, such as "treeless plain" or "non-partisan committee." Non-affirming negatives *(prasajya-pratiṣedha, med dgag)* such as emptiness, the negation of a phenomenon's inherent existence, are *mere* negatives, negatives that imply nothing positive in their place. They are also permanent phenomena, neither caused nor capable of producing an effect. Because "food having been consumed" and so forth are affirming negatives rather than non-affirming negatives, they can be posited as impermanent phenomena, having causes and causing results.

[49]Non-desire, non-hatred, and non-obscuration are affirming negatives, as these terms imply positive moral attributes. "Endless life" and "endless light," of course, imply the positive phenomena of life and light. Jamyang Shayba is probably making a pun on two names of the Buddha Amitābha. According to Chandra Das, the Buddha Amitābha has three names, Amitābha being his name in his aspect as an Emanation Body *(sprul sku, nirmāṇakāya)* and Amitāyus as a Complete Enjoyment Body *(longs sku, saṃbhogakāya)*.

[50]Daktsang "acts astonished" at Dzongkaba because Dzongkaba has said that disintegratedness is a functioning thing, but had to use reasoned investigation to reach his conclusion, asking, for instance, "What is the cause of the child's death?" Jamyang Shayba's reply is that this sort of analysis is not ultimate analysis, merely analysis involving subtle (as opposed to coarse) worldly conventions. It is not ultimate analysis because it is not a search for

these scriptural passages or reasonings, the analytical should throw away [his works] like poison.

Ngawang Belden:[51] The meaning of the fourth reasoning [that it is established by worldly renown that disintegratedness is a functioning thing] is as follows: it is as Dzongkaba's *Ocean of Reasoning, Explanation of (Nāgārjuna's) "Treatise on the Middle Way"* says:[52]

> Therefore, these causes and effects such as seeds and sprouts must be posited in the manner seen by people in the world. In the world, saying, "My rice spoiled due to lack of water," and, "My son died due to lack of food," are cases of propounding that through the non-existence of the former the latter is lost. Moreover, just as the non-extinction of food and of water are taken [respectively] to be the causes of a child's being alive and rice being good, the extinction of those is posited as the cause of the extinction of [child and rice]. Therefore, those [things] which have not become extinct are different from those which do not exist [i.e., have become extinct]; through this the class of effects from those [things which have become non-existent] should also be understood.

This explains that the disintegratedness of a continuum is a [functioning] thing; even though those [actions] are totally consumed or totally destroyed, [their effects] appear to exist.[53]

---

an inherently existent entity among its bases of designation, such as would be done (or assented to) by proponents of the lower schools. The difference between subtle and coarse worldly conventions is not one made in the Prāsaṅgika literature, except perhaps for this very instance. The half-dozen or so scholars I asked knew of no source for making such a distinction, although several made educated guesses themselves. For instance, Geshay Gönchok Tsayring told me that subtle worldly conventions are those that are conventionally existent but which ordinary people know nothing about. For instance, impermanence is a mere coarse worldly convention, but *subtle* impermanence, the moment-by-moment disintegration of things, is a subtle convention.

[51]*Annotations*, note *a*, 114b.3.

[52]*Ocean of Reasoning*, 191.6-12.

[53]As will be seen, Jamyang Shayba apparently does not agree with Nga-

Therefore, there appear to be great bases for analysis with respect to the statements in Jamyang Shayba's *Great Exposition of the Middle Way (dbu ma chen mo)*[54] that (1) the disintegratedness of obstructions to omniscience do not exist in the continuum of a Buddha Superior and (2) that in order to posit [something] as a pastness or as a futureness it is necessary that it not be totally consumed or totally destroyed.[55] However, I will not write [more about these] because I fear it would be too much.

B. The Three Times

Jamyang Shayba:[56] There are causes even for futurenesses because they exist due to the force of the non-completion and non-aggregation of the causes and conditions of something's coming about at this time even though the causes for that exist. This is because Candrakīrti's *Commentary on (Nāgārjuna's) "Sixty Stanzas of Reasoning"* says:[57]

> With respect to that, then, the non-completion of [a future phenomenon's] conditions subsists as the cause for the non-production of a future phenomenon. If its conditions were not incomplete, it would definitely be produced.

---

wang Belden that disintegratedness is a cause of total consumption or destruction, for disintegratedness preserves something's continuum of similar type and there is an effect to come out from it. That is apparently also why Jamyang Shayba says that there is no disintegratedness of the obstructions to omniscience for a Buddha.

[54]*Great Exposition of the Middle Way* 628.3-5.

[55]Jamyang Shayba appears to mean that disintegratedness, which is a pastness, is not a disintegratedness of itself. It itself is a functioning thing that can produce an effect. Elsewhere (in the section on the Svātantrikas) he points out that although, when something is destroyed, it itself no longer exists, its continuum of similar type is not destroyed. Disintegratedness *is* that continuum. Thus, while the thing itself is destroyed, perhaps it could be said that it is *merely* destroyed, not *totally* destroyed.

[56]*Great Exposition of Tenets cha* 38b.3.

[57]This appears to be a paraphrase of P 5265, vol. 98, 177.3.1-2.

The definition of a pastness is:

> a factor of disintegratedness of another[58] [functioning] thing that was already produced.

An illustration is, for instance, the disintegratedness of a sprout. Candrakīrti's *Commentary on (Āryadeva's) "Four Hundred"* says,[59] "A pastness is what has passed beyond just this [present time]."

The definition of a presentness is:

> that which (1) is neither a factor of disintegratedness nor a factor of futureness of another [functioning] thing and (2) has been produced but has not ceased.

For instance, a sprout. Candrakīrti's *Commentary on (Āryadeva's) "Four Hundred"* says,[60] "The present has been produced but has not ceased."

The definition of a futureness is:

> a factor of non-production of another [functioning] thing due to the non-completion of its conditions, even though the causes for its production exist.

For instance, a sprout's not having arrived at the present time even though the causes for a future sprout exist. For Candrakīrti's *Commentary on (Āryadeva's) "Four Hundred"* says,[61] "With respect to that, the future has not come at the present time."[62]

---

[58]Because the factor is itself a thing, that of which it is a factor is a different thing than it.

[59]P 5266, vol. 98, 247.3.2.

[60]P 5266, vol. 98, 247.3.2.

[61]P 5266, vol. 98, 247.3.2.

[62]Kensur Yeshey Tupden felt that a sprout that is future *(ma 'ongs pa'i myu gu)* and the futureness of a sprout *(myu gu ma 'ongs pa)* are probably different. A sprout that is future is not a sprout, for it is not present, and whatever is a sprout is necessarily present. A futureness of a sprout comes before that sprout, a pastness of a sprout after. The futureness of a sprout exists as the entity of the seed.

Since disintegratedness is a [functioning] thing, an action that has been done and accumulated,[63] even though many aeons have gone after its having disintegrated, actually issues forth its fruit. Therefore, "obtainer," mind-basis-of-all, non-wastage [of actions, mental[64]] continua and so forth do not have to be asserted.[65] Candrakīrti's *Commentary on (Āryadeva's) "Four Hundred"* says:

> Even though a very long time has passed and gone after the cessation of an action which was done and accumulated, [the action itself] indeed does not persist, but nevertheless, effects actually arise even from actions with many aeons intervening after their cessation.

His mere propounding that disintegratedness is a [functioning] thing is not a matter of searching for the imputed object, a disintegratedness, because merely analyzing whether disintegratedness is a thing or a non-thing does not constitute ultimate analysis. And, for example, it is like propounding that a pot is a [functioning] thing. Otherwise, there would be

---

[63]Virtuous and non-virtuous actions that have been completed are said to be "accumulated" because they leave seeds and predispositions that will come to fruition at a later time. However, only if one clearly *intends* to perform an act of virtue or non-virtue is a "path of action" or karmic path established—one that can result in future good or bad rebirths. For instance, angrily swatting a fly is definitely an action that causes the accrual of seeds and predispositions for bad states, one aspect of karma, but unintentionally squashing an ant while walking is an act of killing that bears only minor consequences. There is also a category of acts *not* done but for which karma is accumulated, such as when one intends to swat a fly but misses. One does not accumulate the type and degree of karma that one might have if one had oneself successfully completed the act of killing, but bad karma is accumulated because of the anger/harmful intent that was produced in one's mind. These examples were suggested by Geshay Sönam Rinchen and Geshay Gönchok Tsayring.

[64]"Continuum" *(rgyun)* was identified by Kensur Yeshey Tupden as the continuum of virtuous and non-virtuous karma. However, since this passage concerns various means for holding and transmitting karmic potencies, it seems that the author probably meant the mental continuum, which even the Prāsaṅgika School identifies as at least the temporary basis for seeds.

[65]See note on root verse at the beginning of this chapter.

much that is damaging and contradictory, such as that even your propounding that disintegratedness is not a [functioning] thing would be a matter of searching for an imputed object **[39a]**; however, as was said earlier, merely analyzing whether or not disintegratedness has causes does not constitute a search for an imputed object because it merely explains the way in which [things] act as cause and condition conventionally, like, for example, the explanation in the abhidharma texts of the causes and conditions of compounded phenomena.[66]

If [as Daktsang says] that which has been done—the utterance of harsh speech and so forth—produced effects by means of not having disintegrated, then even though many aeons had passed, those [actions which had] not issued forth their effects would have to exist even now. Hence, why is it that even though [the actions of] the three—body, speech, and mind—which were performed in earlier [lifetimes] also would not have been destroyed, they not only are not seen but not remembered? Whoever makes such an explanation has already been refuted earlier.[67]

---

[66]This is all a reply to Daktsang's objection that finding "disintegratedness that is different from the continuum of similar type of the action" *(las rang gi rigs 'dra'i rgyun las gzhan pa'i zhig pa)* is like finding a pot among its parts, i.e., ultimate analysis. (See *Ocean of Good Explanations* 235.3-4.) Jamyang Shayba says that disintegratedness is posited *without* analysis, being simply designated to a basis of designation, the later continuum of similar type of the action (not something found apart from it). If making such a mere designation were ultimate analysis, then Daktsang's supposed assertion that disintegratedness is not a functioning thing (which in fact he never makes) would also involve ultimate analysis.

[67]Daktsang has been interpreted by Jamyang Shayba to hold the idea that actions themselves persist without disintegrating in some manner over time until their effects issue forth. It would then absurdly follow that those actions would exist now, and we would see (experience) them, remember them, and endlessly relive them. It seems that there is little difference between what is called the "seed" established by an action, an impermanent phenomenon that can later "ripen" into an effect, and the disintegratedness of an action, which is also an impermanent phenomenon and said to be the cause of an action's later coming to fruition. Perhaps it could be said that a "seed" established by an action *is* that action's disintegratedness.

7 The Non-Assertion of Autonomous Syllogisms and Self-Consciousness

Jamyang Shayba:[1] The root text says:

Because they cannot [be posited] without analysis,[2] autonomous [reasons] and self-consciousness do not exist.

A. Autonomous Reasons Are Not Asserted

Autonomous [reasons] cannot be posited without finding something positable upon analyzing for the imputed object.[3]

---

[1]*Great Exposition of Tenets cha* 39a.3.

[2]Both autonomous syllogisms and self-consciousness are asserted by those schools that regard those entities to be able to withstand analysis, i.e., to inherently exist. Prāsaṅgikas show that no phenomenon can withstand analysis, but they do assert that there are entities that exist in a merely nominal way. However, autonomous reasons and self-consciousness do not exist even nominally.

[3]This is a very important topic in Prāsaṅgika literature, since it is the issue that provides the basis for the division of the Mādhyamika School into Svātantrika and Prāsaṅgika branches. Jamyang Shayba barely mentions the topic here, certainly because he has already discussed it in great detail earlier in the Prāsaṅgika chapter. For a critical analysis of Jamyang Shayba's presentation and a translation of relevant texts, see Hopkins (1983a: 441-530).

Self-consciousness also does not exist because if one also analyzed for the imputed object—consciousness—there is no mode of analysis [more] obvious than this [to be ultimate analysis]. These are unique assertions [of the Prāsaṅgika School]. Candrakīrti's *Clear Words* says:[4]

> [It is not admissible] for one who is a Mādhyamika to use an autonomous inference because another position [among the four extremes] is not asserted.

B. Self-Consciousness Is Not Asserted

Nāgārjuna's *Refutation of Objections* (LI) says:[5]

> Valid cognition is not established by itself,
> Neither mutually
> Nor by other valid cognition,
> Not by its object of comprehension nor causelessly.

[4]The quotation has been restored to full length. Hopkins translates this passage (1983a: 475; 818, n. 374, for information on texts he used). Sprung's translation (1979: 7) is: "It is meaningless for a Mādhyamika, because he cannot accept his opponent's premises, to propound a self-contained argument from his own point of view *(svatantra-prayoga)*." This translation reflects a commonly held view that Prāsaṅgikas reject syllogisms of all types since they have no tenets of their own. However, Dzongkaba and his followers do not at all object to syllogisms *per se*, but only to those which are held to exist under their own power *(rang dbang du grub pa, svairīsiddhi)*, i.e., to be inherently established. Also, see Jamyang Shayba's *Great Exposition of the Middle Way* 423.4. For a discussion of the importance of these issues in Gelukba monasticism, see Hopkins (1983a: 846-47).

[5]P 5228, vol. 98, 15.3.1-2. Translation by K. Bhattacharya is on p. 34 of *Dialectical Method of Nāgārjuna*, translation section; the Sanskrit is on p. 40 of the text section: *naiva svataḥ prasiddhir na parasparataḥ parapramāṇair vā. / na bhavati na ca prameyairna cāpyakasmāt pramāṅānām*. Cf. Della Santina (1986: 109-15), Lindtner (1986b: 214).

Ngawang Belden:[6] Dzongkaba's *Illumination of the Thought, Explanation of (Candrakīrti's) "Entrance"*[7] says that this system's refutation of self-consciousness also meets back to not asserting establishment by way of [a phenomenon's] own character. Why? It is by reason of the fact that if self-consciousness were asserted it would be necessary to assert that it is able to bear the analysis of a reasoning [consciousness] searching for the imputed object, because searching for a means of positing [or certifying] a consciousness, that is, whether it is self-experiencing or the object of experience of another [consciousness] **[115a]**, is a mode of searching for an imputed object which is even more obviously [a case of ultimate analysis] than searching [to see whether] a sprout is produced from self or produced from other.[8]

With[9] respect to the four [types of valid cognition]—a directly perceiving consciousness, inferential cognition, [inference] comprehending through an example, and scriptural valid cognition—a directly perceiving consciousness is not established by that directly perceiving consciousness itself, inferential cognition is not established by inferential cognition itself, [inferential cognition] comprehending through an example is not established by [inferential cognition] compre-

---

[6]Annotations, note *ka*, 114b.7.

[7]*Illumination of the Thought* 124b.5.

[8]One mode of ultimate analysis is an inquiry into the relation between an object and its basis of designation. With regard to the production of a sprout, it is *not* ultimate analysis merely to observe that a sprout is produced from a seed, and that the two are different. However, if we search for those two entities among their parts or for their relationship, we will not find them. Is the seed the hull, or the germ, or the bran? (etc.; Candrakīrti goes through seven possibilities). Is a sprout inherently produced from a seed? If so, if a seed exists, a sprout must exist, and if it already exists, there is no need for it to be produced—and so forth. Similarly, a consciousness is conventionally different from the later recollection of it, but is it inherently different? If so, the two are utterly unrelated and hence it is impossible for the previous consciousness to be remembered.

[9]*Annotations*, note *kha*, 115a.1. What follows is a slightly expanded paraphrase of Nāgārjuna's *Commentary on "Refutation of Objections,"* P 5232, vol. 95, 62.3.4-8. Here, Nāgārjuna demonstrates the non-inherent existence of valid cognition by refuting all possibilities for the establishment of inherently existent valid cognition.

hending through an example itself, and scriptural valid cognition is not established by scriptural valid cognition itself. To explain this, [Nāgārjuna] says, "Valid cognition is not established by itself."

A directly perceiving consciousness is not established by the [other] three [types of] valid cognition, that is, [the four types] with the exception of itself; inferential cognition is not established by the [other] three [types of] valid cognitions; [inferential cognition] comprehending through an example is not established by the [other] three [types of] valid cognitions; scriptural valid cognition is not established by the [other] three [types of] valid cognitions. To explain this, [Nāgārjuna] says, "[Valid cognition] is not [established] mutually."

A directly perceiving consciousness is not established by other directly perceiving consciousnesses; inferential cognition is not established by other inferential cognition; [inferential cognition] comprehending through an example is not established by other [inferential cognition] comprehending through an example; and scriptural valid cognition is not established by other scriptural valid cognition. To explain this, [Nāgārjuna] says, "[Valid cognition] is not [established] by other valid cognition." [Valid cognition] is also neither established by way of its object of comprehension that is its object or the object of other [valid cognition] together or individually, nor is it established causelessly. To explain this, [Nāgārjuna] says, "[Valid cognition] is neither [established] by its object of comprehension nor causelessly."

Jamyang Shayba:[10] The *Questions of Ratnacūḍa Sūtra (gtsug na rin po ches zhus pa'i mdo, ratnacūḍaparipṛicchāsūtra)* says:[11]

---

[10]*Great Exposition of Tenets cha* 39a.4.

[11]This sūtra is P 47, vol. 24, 229-251. Stephen Batchelor (1979: 185) notes that this quotation is similar to a passage in the *Descent to Laṅkā Sūtra;* he points to Tokmay Sangbo's commentary on Śāntideva, *Ocean of Good Explanations, Commentary to Engaging in the Bodhisattva Deeds* (205), which quotes the *Descent to Laṅkā Sūtra* for this point. Candrakīrti quotes this in his *Clear Words* (Sanskrit in Poussin 62.4, translated by Sprung 55).

> If that mind is sought everywhere...However, if just that which is observed is the mind, how could the mind see the mind? For, for example, a sword-edge is unable to cut just that sword-edge, and a finger-tip is unable to touch just that fingertip.

Śāntideva's *Engaging in the Bodhisattva Deeds* (IX.17cd-18ab) says:[12]

> Also, the Protector of the World [Buddha] said
> "The mind does not see the mind."
> Just as the edge of the sword does not cut itself
> The mind also [does not know itself].

Passages such as these refute [self-consciousness].

Ngawang Belden:[13] Dzongkaba's *Illumination of the Thought, Explanation of (Candrakīrti's) "Entrance"* says:[14]

> With respect to that, it is not feasible that a consciousness apprehends that same consciousness because it is contradictory that its activity operate on itself. For a sword-edge does not cut just that same [sword-edge], a finger-tip does not touch itself, even well-trained gymnasts are unable to mount their own shoulders, fire does not burn itself, and an eye does not see itself.

Jamyang Shayba:[15] [The Prāsaṅgikas] also refute [the reasoning that] just as a butter-lamp illumines both itself and other [things], the mind knows both itself and other [things]. Nāgārjuna's *Refutation of Objections* (XXXV, XXXVI) says:[16]

---

[12]The Sanskrit is found in V. Bhattacharya (1960: 189): *uktaṃ ca lokānathena cittaṃ na paśyati / na cchinatti yathātmānamasidhārā tathā manaḥ*. Cf. Batchelor (1979: 135).

[13]*Annotations*, note *ga*, 115a.5.

[14]*Illumination of the Thought* 155a.2-4. This is virtually identical to Candrakīrti's *Autocommentary on the "Entrance"* 51b.7-52a.1.

[15]*Great Exposition of Tenets cha* 39a.6.

[16]P 5228, vol. 95, 15.1.6-7. His own commentary is P 5232, vol. 95, 61.3.3-8. The quote has been restored to full length. Missing in this edition, but present in the NG edition, were the first two lines of stanza XXXVI. The

If, as you say,
Fire illuminated itself [just as it illumines other things],
Then fire would burn itself
Just as it [burns] other things.

If, as you say,
Fire illumines itself and other things,
Then just as a butter-lamp [illumines itself and other things], darkness also
Would obscure both itself and other things.

Ngawang Belden:[17] The statements "If fire illumined itself" and so forth were explained in the context of the Svātantrika School.[18] Also, that letters are left off and that there are errors in this citation in this [Prāsaṅgika School] context can be understood from [my annotation there in the Svātantrika School section].[19]

Jamyang Shayba:[20] Nāgārjuna's *Treatise on the Middle Way* (VII.12) says:[21]

If a butter-lamp illumines
Itself and other things,
There is no doubt that darkness also would obscure
Itself and other things.

Sanskrit (from Johnston a Kunst 131) is: *yadi ca svātmānamayaṃ tvadvacanena prakāśayatyagniḥ paramiva nanvātmānaṃ paridhakṣyatyapi hutāśaḥ. (35) / yadi ca svaparātmānau tvadvacanena prakāśayatyagniḥ pracchādayiṣyati tamaḥ svaparātmānau hutāśa ivā.* (36) According to Kensur Yeshey Tupden, an unlit butter-lamp is not a butter-lamp, just a cup of butter. But Geshay Tupden Gyatso felt that the unlit lamp could still be called a lamp, for that is the name given even to a cup of butter.

[17] *Annotations,* note *nga,* 115a.7.

[18] Ngawang Belden is referring to note *ma* on p. 26 of *dbu ma* in this edition (NG vol. *ca*: 35).

[19] Ngawang Belden, in the annotation just referred to, notes that Jamyang Shayba skipped several lines in his citation of Nāgārjuna.

[20] *Great Exposition of Tenets cha* 39a.8.

[21] P 5224, vol. 95, 4.4.4. Sanskrit is in Poussin 154.8-9: *pradīpaḥ svaparātmānau saṃprakāśayate yadi / tamo 'pi svaparātmānau chādayiṣyatyasaṃśayaṃ.* Candrakīrti's commentary is in *Clear Words* 103.

It would [absurdly] follow that even darkness, upon being obscured by itself, does not appear. Also, there is no need for an illuminator [of the butter-lamp] other than the butter-lamp [itself] **[39b]** because darkness does not exist in it. Nāgārjuna's *Treatise Called "The Finely Woven" (zhib mo rnam par 'thag pa zhes bya ba'i mdo, vaidalyasūtranāma)* says:[22]

> A butter-lamp neither clears away darkness that it meets nor clears away darkness that it does not meet.
>
> *Question:* Here it would be like the harms of [the eighth] planet?[23]
>
> *Answer:* No, because [that is] contradictory with the example [of light and darkness].

Also,[24] "A butter-lamp does not illuminate itself because it is without darkness." Also, Śāntideva's *Engaging in the Bodhisattva Deeds* (IX.19ab) says:[25]

> The butter-lamp is not an object of illumination.
> Why? It is not obscured by darkness.

Ngawang Belden:[26] It is as Dzongkaba's *Illumination of the Thought, Explanation of (Candrakīrti's) "Entrance"* says:[27]

> ...because just as a butter-lamp itself does not illuminate itself but nevertheless its having luminosity is not precluded, so even though consciousness itself does not experience itself in the manner asserted by those who hold the contrary position, that it has mere experience is not precluded.
>
> *Objection:* The butter-lamp itself does illuminate itself **[115b]**.

---

[22]P 5226, vol. 95, 12.3.2-4. No Sanskrit text is extant. The quotation has been expanded. This passage will be quoted again by Ngawang Belden 31.7-8.

[23]According to Geshay Belden Drakba, this refers to a paralysis-like affliction caused by contact with (the rays of) the eighth planet.

[24]P 5226, vol. 95, 12.3.4.

[25]*Engaging in the Bodhisattva Deeds* 189. The Sanskrit is: *naiva prakāśyate dīpo yasmānna tamasāvṛtaḥ*. Cf. Batchelor 1979: 136.

[26]*Annotations*, note *ca*, 115a.7.

[27]*Illumination of the Thought* 158b.2-4.

> *Response:* If that were the case, darkness itself would obscure itself, and if that were asserted, just as a pot is not seen in a mass of darkness, darkness also would not be seen.[28]

Nāgārjuna's *Treatise Called "The Finely Woven"* says:[29]

> A butter-lamp neither clears away darkness that it meets nor clears away darkness that it does not meet.
>
> *Question:* Here it would be like the harms of [the eighth] planet?
>
> *Answer:* No, because [that is] contradictory with the example [of light and darkness].

The meaning of that statement is that the butter-lamp does not *inherently* clear away darkness which it either meets or does not meet.[30]

Opponent: Just as someone such as Devadatta[31] is harmed by meeting with the faults brought about by [the eighth] planet, a butter-lamp harms darkness through meeting it.

---

[28]According to Kensur Yeshey Tupden, a butter-lamp is self-luminous *(rang gsal ba)* in the sense that it has a nature of illumination and needs no other source, but it does not illuminate itself by itself *(rang nyid gyis rang gsal ba)*, a formulation which implies that it *requires* illumination and that it illumines itself in the same way it illumines other things. Also, if darkness obscured itself, then absurdly darkness could not be seen. Darkness would obscure itself just as it obscures objects like pots in unlit places.

[29]See the previous citation in the Jamyang Shayba section.

[30]Neither a meeting nor a non-meeting of a lamp and darkness can be found analytically. Nāgārjuna shows (see below) that if they meet, then absurdly light and dark exist in one place simultaneously. If they do not meet, how can one harm the other? Or, if darkness is cleared away even though they do not meet, how could there ever be any darkness? Rather, their "meeting" is just an imputation in dependence upon the absence of light in the presence of darkness, and vice versa. Moreover, a lamp and darkness do not meet even conventionally, since they do not exist at the same time. As the Prāsaṅgika will say, they are never found together, being contradictory in the sense of not abiding together harmlessly.

[31]I have searched biographical material on the Devadatta who was the Buddha's cousin, but have found no episode that would indicate that this is a reference to a legend about him.

Prāsaṅgika: That is incorrect because the example and meaning are discordant, since even though there is a meeting of Devadatta and the faults brought about by [the eighth] planet, darkness and a butter-lamp do not meet. This is because the two, light and darkness, are contradictory in the sense of not abiding together.[32] Nāgārjuna's *Treatise on the Middle Way* (VII.10, 11) says:[33]

> If at the time of a butter-lamp's state of being produced[34]
> It does not meet with darkness,
> How, by a butter-lamp's being produced,
> Would darkness be illuminated?
> If, even without a butter-lamp's meeting darkness,
> Darkness is cleared away,
> Then the darkness dwelling all over the world
> Would definitely be removed.[35]

With respect to that reasoning, Dzongkaba's *Ocean of Reasoning, Explanation of (Nāgārjuna's) "Treatise on the Middle Way"* says:[36]

---

[32]According to Jambel Trinlay's textbook for Drebung's Loseling College (14.10-11), the definition of phenomena that are contradictory in the sense of not abiding together *(lhan cig mi gnas 'gal)* is: phenomena that do not have a common locus, that is, do not abide together harmlessly *(gnod med du lhan cig mi gnas pa'i gzhi mthun mi sri pa'i chos)*. An example is hot and cold, which cannot exist together without harming each other. The import of this category is that wisdom and the consciousness conceiving true existence, being contradictory in this way, do not meet.

[33]P 5224, vol. 95, 4.4.2-4. Sanskrit is in Poussin 152.10-11, 153.1-2.

[34]The "state of being produced" *(skye bzhin pa)* is the moment just *before* its production, when it still does not exist.

[35]Nāgārjuna is exploring the possibilities for a meeting between a lamp and darkness: if they do not exist at the same time, how can light get rid of darkness? That is, if they do not meet, the production of a lamp would not cause the cessation of darkness. Or, if the lamp cleared away darkness without meeting it, then how could there be any darkness? On the other hand, if a lamp *does* exist at the same time as the darkness, how can it do away with the darkness? Dzongkaba explains the second stanza in *Illumination of the Thought* 164.5 ff.

[36]*Ocean of Reasoning* 163.19-64.5 (Varanasi ed.).

> Also, with respect to asserting that conventionally a butter-lamp clears away darkness, although the two, a butter-lamp's state of being produced and darkness, must indeed meet, at the time of a butter-lamp's state of being produced a butter-lamp does not exist; therefore, [a butter-lamp] need not meet with darkness.

In accordance with the assertion that a butter-lamp's clearing away of darkness is established by its own character, if a butter-lamp's state of being produced met with darkness, a butter-lamp would have to exist at that time, whereas it does not. Therefore, [Nāgārjuna's] is a reasoning which indicates that since [darkness] does not meet [inherently] with a butter-lamp's state of being produced,[37] it is not feasible for a butter-lamp to clear away darkness. It can be understood [more] extensively in just that [source].

Here, let us abbreviate the mode of asserting self-consciousness and refuting it in accordance with how it is set forth in the root text and (auto-)commentary of Candrakīrti's *Entrance to (Nāgārjuna's) "Treatise on the Middle Way."*[38]

Opponent: In the continuum of a common being who is seeing blue with his eyes, there is both an experience of the object, blue, and an experiencer of the subject, [the consciousness] apprehending blue **[116a]**, because when this is remembered at a later time, there is both a memory of the object—"This blue was previously seen"—and a memory of the subject—"I saw."

If that is accepted, it follows that the subject, the experience of the earlier subject [the consciousness], is a self-experience because it is either a self-experience or other-experience

[37]Kensur Yeshey Tupden noted (12/14/83) that conventionally, a butter-lamp's state of being produced and darkness meet. They do not meet *ultimately*, for that would require that a butter-lamp would already exist (for it is the basis of the activity of being produced) entailing the absurdity that it would already exist at the time it is being produced. At that time, darkness is approaching destruction and the butter-lamp is approaching production. In the following moment, the butter-lamp is produced and darkness has ceased. There is no moment in which both exist, hence they do not meet.

[38]*Entrance to the Middle Way* VI.72-76. His commentary is 51b.6-54a.3. Cf. Huntington 166.

and there is the damage that if it is an other-experience, (1) it would follow that the experiencers would be endless and (2) it would follow that the later consciousness would not distinguish another object. The mode of establishment of the latter two reasons should be known from extensive statements in Dzongkaba's *Illumination of the Thought, Explanation of (Candrakīrti's) "Entrance."*[39]

Answer: The Prāsaṅgika School method of refuting those is that it is not feasible to prove [self-consciousness] by the

[39]See *Illumination of the Thought* 158 ff. According to Dzongkaba, both the Prāsaṅgika and Cittamātra Schools maintain that we ordinarily are able to remember not only objects such as a patch of blue that we have previously experienced, but also the awareness such as an eye consciousness which apprehended that patch of blue. For Cittamātrins following Dharmakīrti it is necessary that the original eye consciousness apprehending blue have been self-conscious; to them, unless that consciousness was in some way itself experienced at the time it occurred, there could be no memory of it. Prāsaṅgikas, on the other hand, have several ways of accounting for memory of a consciousness without resorting to the explanation of self-consciousness. These means are explained later in this chapter. Kensur Yeshey Tupden (12/14/83) defined "self-experience" as "experience of itself by itself." Self-experience is impossible, just as a lamp cannot illuminate itself by itself nor an eye see itself by itself. In other words, "self-experience" *(rang myong ba)* is not parallel to "self-illuminate" *(rang gsal ba)*, which, as was seen earlier, means only that fire has a *nature* of illumination, not that it illumines itself by itself. Instead, the term parallel to "self-illuminate" is "mere experience" *(myong ba tsam)*, meaning only that a consciousness does have an experience of an object. It is discussed later in this chapter. The Opponent mentions two consequences stemming from identifying the experiencer of an earlier consciousness as an other-experiencing consciousness: (1) there would be an infinite regress of consciousnesses and (2) that consciousness would be unable to distinguish another object. This person thinks that if one remembered an earlier consciousness apprehending blue, one would need yet another consciousness to apprehend that remembering consciousness while it apprehended the consciousness apprehending blue, and another to apprehend that consciousness, *ad infinitum*. Moreover, it is thought that this remembering consciousness would not be able to distinguish *blue* because it would be full of its apprehension of the *eye consciousness* apprehending blue. Kensur Yeshey Tupden took this to mean: if this consciousness were an other-experiencer, it and the eye consciousness apprehending blue would be different substantial entities, whereby they would not be simultaneous (and thus according to this opponent it would not be able to cognize the eye consciousness apprehending blue, since according to Cittamātra, a mind and its object must be simultaneous).

sign of memory because (1) if it were said, "Self-consciousness exists because inherently established memory exists," the sign would not be established, just as the probandum would not be established[40] and (2) if it were said that self-consciousness exists because memory exists, since the two, self-consciousness and memory consciousnesses, do not have the relation of [memory] not occurring if [self-consciousness] does not occur, the entailment is indefinite; it would be similar to the proof that since water and fire exist, a water-crystal and fire-crystal exist.[41] For Dzongkaba's *The Essence of the Good Explanations* says:[42]

> Candrakīrti's *Autocommentary on the "Entrance"* says:[43]
>
> > Here, if this is treated as proving a substantially established [memory consciousness], since such a memory consciousness does not exist, it is the same as what is being proved [i.e., self-consciousness, in terms of not existing and thus being incapable of serving as a proof]. If it is taken in terms of conventionalities, since self-consciousness is not established for the second party [i.e., a Prāsaṇgika], then it and memory are not established as cause and effect. Also, it is explained that the two, (1) the proof that since water and fire exist water-crystals and fire-crystals exist [respectively], and (2) the proof that since a memory exists, self-consciousness exists, are similar[ly fallacious].

---

[40]The sign "inherently established memory" is not established because there is no such thing.

[41]Fire and water crystals are believed to produce fire and water (the fire crystal is a magnifying glass). However, the existence of water or fire does not entail the existence of these crystals, since there are many other sources for those elements. Similarly, the mere existence of memory does not entail self-consciousness, since Prāsaṅgikas show that there are other explanations for the production of memory.

[42]*The Essence of the Good Explanations* 175.14-76.1.

[43]It would seem likely that this is from Candrakīrti's *Autocommentary on the "Entrance,"* but this passage does not appear there in exactly this way. Thurman (1984: 318) assumes this is Dzongkaba's statement based on Candrakīrti's *Entrance to the Middle Way* VI.72. Poussin's translation of VI.72-76 is in *Muséon* 11 (349-54).

> This is done in terms of treating [memory] as an effect sign and holding self-consciousness to be the predicate of what is proved.[44]

Objection: With respect to this [proof that self-consciousness exists by the sign of memory], if self-consciousness is held to be the predicate of the probandum [that is, what is to be proved], a concordant example would not exist.[45] Therefore, such is not to be stated. However, we will say, "With respect to the subject, an eye consciousness apprehending blue, an experiencer of it exists in the continuum of a common being who is seeing blue with his eyes because such a common being has a memory of it at a later time, for example, blue."[46]

---

[44]The Prāsaṅgikas refute all possible ways in which memory might serve as a sign for self-consciousness. In the first formulation, "self-consciousness exists because inherently (or substantially) established memory exists," the sign—inherently established memory—and the probandum (what is to be proved)—self-consciousness—are equally non-existent according to the Prāsaṅgika School. Inherently established memory is excluded because nothing inherently exists, and self-consciousness does not exist at all. With regard to the second formulation, "self-consciousness exists because memory exists," because memory does not depend on or is not contingent on self-consciousness, it is not entailed that if memory exists, self-consciousness necessarily exists. Just as the existence of fire does not entail the existence of a fire-crystal, the existence of memory does not entail the existence of self-consciousness. In both of these "proofs," memory has been put as the sign and the existence of self-consciousness, the probandum (what is to be proved). In particular, memory has been an *effect* sign, one which is held to be an effect of the probandum, self-consciousness. Similarly, in the example "On a smoky pass, fire exists because smoke exists," smoke, the effect of fire, is an effect sign indicating the existence of fire.

[45]The opponent now admits that there is no instance of self-consciousness to serve as an example in his proof, which would not be as much in dispute as the thesis and therefore could not serve as an example, which is supposed to be *easier* to understand than the thesis. In what follows, he argues for self-*experience* rather than self-consciousness.

[46]This is the third of four arguments made by a hypothetical Cittamātrin, the first two having been disposed of above. They were "Self-consciousness exists because inherently established memory exists" and "Self-consciousness exists because memory exists." This argument might be expressed, "A self-experiencer of an eye consciousness apprehending blue exists because a memory of that consciousness exists." Once again, the

Answer: Even though in this the sign and the predicate are present in the example, the entailment cannot be proven;[47] hence, it is similar to the former [statement]. This is because Dzongkaba's *The Essence of the Good Explanations* says:[48]

> Also, when it is taken that way, an example is not found. Therefore, even if one were to state, "An *experiencer* [rather than self-consciousness] of [a consciousness] apprehending blue exists because later memory exists, as is the case, for example, with blue" **[116b]**, although it is the case that the sign [later memory of it] and the predicate [an experiencer of it] are present in the example, the entailment [that if later memory exists, then an experiencer of it exists] cannot be proven. Hence, [specifying "an experiencer of a consciousness"] is the same as holding self-consciousness to be the predicate of what is to be proved. [If] therefore [you rephrased this such that] even if without explicitly stating [self-consciousness as the predicate of what is to be proved, you] prove mere experience....

Also, [that there is no entailment that because a memory of an eye consciousness apprehending blue exists, a self-experience of that consciousness exists] is because Śāntideva's *Engaging*

Prāsaṅgikas will not find the entailment—that the existence of memory entails the existence of a self-experiencer—to be acceptable. Jamyang Shayba says, in his *Great Exposition of the Middle Way* (711.2-3) that self-experience does not exist, even though there is a consciousness—a Buddha's omniscient consciousness—that directly realizes itself by itself. This is because it is not inherently established, whereas self-experience involves inherent establishment.

[47]The example is an instance of the recollection of blue. The sign—later memory—and predicate—an experiencer of an eye consciousness apprehending blue—exist in the example; that is, in the recollection of blue, there is a later memory and there is a recollection of the eye consciousness apprehending blue. However, as Dzongkaba will show, this person means by "experiencer" a self-experience (i.e., self-consciousness); hence, the entailment—that if later memory exists, a [self-]experiencer of it necessarily exists—cannot hold. It is exactly the same as the previous example.

[48]*The Essence of the Good Explanations* 176.1-5. Translated by Thurman, (1984: 318-19). Commentary by Geshé Rapten, *Annotations For the Difficult Points of (Dzongkaba's) "The Essence of the Good Explanations"* 350.3.1.

in the Bodhisattva Deeds (IX.23) says that memory is generated without experiencing the subject:[49]

> If self-consciousness did not exist,
> How would a consciousness be remembered?
> Memory [of consciousness] occurs due to the relation [of an object] with other-experiencers[50]
> Like [being mindful of] a rodent's poison.

Opponent: Mere experience exists because memory exists.

Response: That would be proving what is already established [for Prāsaṅgikas]; hence, there would be no purpose [in stating it]. That is because Dzongkaba's *The Essence of the Good Explanations* says:[51]

> Even if mere experience is being proved, since it is already established [for Prāsaṅgikas], such is not set forth [since it does not prove what the Cittamātrins seek to establish].

There are two modes of generating memory even without the existence of self-consciousness [as explained in Candrakīr-

---

[49]The quotation has been expanded to include the first two lines of the stanza. The Sanskrit (V. Bhattacarya, 191) is: *yadi nāsti svaṃsavittir vijñānaṃ smaryate kathaṃ / ānyānubhūte saṃbandhat smrtirākhuvishaṃ yathā*. Batchelor's translation is on 136-37. According to Geshay Belden Drakba, there is a very good commentary by Agya Yongdzin (Yangjen Gaway Lodrö) on this, but I have not yet located it. In Śāntideva's theory, when one originally cognized an object, the consciousness that saw, etc. the object was only subliminally experienced, not actually experienced. Later, remembering the original object, one remembers the consciousness that apprehended it. No mediating element such as self-consciousness is necessary. In the present example, a bear bitten by a rodent in winter becomes aware of the infection ("poison") in the spring, and that in turn causes it to remember having been bitten, something that it did not notice at the time.

[50]An "other-experiencer" is just any consciousness, i.e., any consciousness other than self-consciousness. In this case, the "other-experiencer" is a body consciousness aware of the pain of the bite of a rodent.

[51]*The Essence of the Good Explanations* 176.6. Material in brackets from Geshe Rapten 350.4. Translated by Hopkins (unpublished; chapter 4: 10) and Thurman (1984: 319), who says that the *zin bris* he used says that the opponents do not give formal proofs for self-consciousness in any case, because it is so unique that there is no concordant example to posit.

ti's *Entrance to the Middle Way* and Śāntideva's *Engaging in the Bodhisattva Deeds*. Candrakīrti's *Entrance to the Middle Way* (VI.75) says:[52]

> Because for me this memory is not [inherently] other
> Than that [consciousness] by which the object was experienced,
> One remembers, "I saw [this earlier]."
> This is also the way of worldly convention.

The meaning of this is as follows: The two, previous experience and later memory, are not others established by way of their own character. It has already been explained [earlier in the sixth chapter of the *Entrance*] that the conception of substantial cause and effect—for instance, seed and sprout—as others established by their own character does not exist in an ordinary worldly awareness.[53] Just so, the two, previous experience and later memory, not only are not conceived by an innate worldly awareness to be others established by their own character, but also when one later remembers the object seen in the previous apprehension of blue, one uses the verbal convention "*I* saw this previously also."

---

[52]*Entrance to the Middle Way* 7b.9. Dzongkaba's commentary is in *Illumination of the Thought* 159a.4-160a.4. Cf. Poussin *Muséon* 11: 353 and Huntington 166.

[53]Seed and sprout *are* conventionally different substantial entities, but in the world they are not ordinarily conceived to be so. They are ordinarily not even conceived to be *other*, as when we say, of a tree, "I planted this," when in fact we planted a seed. Similarly, we do not ordinarily conceive that the blue we experienced in the past and the blue of our current recollection are different. Here it should be noted that there is a difference between what is renowned to the world *('jig rten la grags pa)* and what is renowned to an ordinary worldly awareness *('jig rten rang 'ga' ba'i blo la grags pa)*. The first category is broader, including everything established for conventional valid cognition except emptiness, i.e., all conventional truths. The second category, however, precludes anything not obvious to an ordinary person; for example, that there is a difference between the seed that is the substantial cause of a tree and the tree itself is renowned to the world but is not renowned to an ordinary worldly awareness because an ordinary person does not conceive of the seed and tree as different.

Although such is indeed the case, one does not think "The self of the time of remembering is the self of the time of [previous] experience," and one does not use the verbal convention "Previously I saw the blue which was qualified by being the object which subsists [both] at the time of this utterance and the time of the [previous object]." Therefore, the verbal convention is not factually discordant. For example, it is like the fact that in the world, even though one uses the verbal convention "*I* hurt," when one's hand hurts, it is not a case of thinking "This hand is me," and so forth, and hence the verbal convention is not factually discordant.[54] An ordinary worldly [awareness] does not have the conception that such experience and memory or the two objects at those times are others established by their own character. Therefore, it is not the case that the [object] experienced and distinguished by the consciousness that earlier experienced it is not later experienced or distinguished by the consciousness which remembers that **[117a]**, whereby the remembering consciousness thinking, "I saw this earlier too," comes to be generated. This is the way of worldly convention; it is not to be taken as a case of positing something upon analysis by way of searching for an imputed object because it is a worldly convention that has a sense of

[54]When we utter statements such as these, we are not being strictly correct, but on the other hand we are not saying them within thinking that we are identical to ourselves at the time we previously saw the object, that the blue of the past and the blue of the present recollection are the same, or that I am my hand, etc. We are being correct, but within the context of no analysis. For instance, Kensur Yeshey Tupden noted that there is no innate conception of the present self and self of the past as a single substantial entity in the awareness of an ordinary being. Thus, "I saw that" does not indicate a wrong consciousness. Nor is there a conception that one's hand and oneself are different substantial entities (they are conventionally different entities because the hand is form and the person is an impermanent compositional factor which is neither form nor consciousness). Gelukbas tread a fine line by saying that we ordinarily have neither a conception that, for instance, seed and sprout are different substantial entities nor that they are the same substantial entity, even though we must be very close to the latter. Daktsang is said to contend that it is contradictory that seed and sprout be different substantial entities but that there be no production from other. Gelukbas reply that production from other means inherently other, whereas a seed and sprout are only conventionally other.

falseness in that when the imputed object is sought it is not found.

Those who assert self-consciousness say, "If self-consciousnesses did not exist, it would be contradictory that a memory of a subject would be generated because there is no generation of a memory without previous experience." The reason in that statement is *not* refuted by scriptural[55] passages such as:

> Because for me this memory is not [inherently] other
> Than that [consciousness] by which the object was experienced,
> One remembers, "I saw [this earlier]."
> This is also the way of worldly conventions.

[in Candrakīrti's *Entrance to the Middle Way*, cited earlier].[56] For otherwise [the syllogism being put forth] would have to be stated as:

> It is not contradictory that a later memory of the [consciousness] apprehending blue is generated even though one did not previously experience the [consciousness] apprehending blue, because for the perspective of an innate worldly awareness, the two, the previous apprehension of blue and the later memory, are not others established by way of their own character and the two, the previous apprehension of blue and later memory, have the same object.

---

[55]Candrakīrti's words are referred to as "scripture" *(lung, āgama),* for Candrakīrti is so revered that his words do indeed have the force of scripture.

[56]The quotation has been expanded; it is the same one cited at the beginning of this section. Cf. Huntington 166. Dzongkaba's commentary is in *Illumination of the Thought* 157.

in which case [the syllogism] would be senseless.[57] Therefore, this passage does not eliminate the "wrong" conception[58] that "There is no generation of memory without previous experience." Rather, the above passage in Candrakīrti's *Entrance to the Middle Way* eliminates the wrong conception that "If an eye consciousness apprehending blue did not experience itself by itself, when seeing blue is later remembered it would be contradictory to remember that oneself saw just that which was previously seen, [as in] 'I saw [it].'"[59] This is because Dzongkaba's *The Essence of the Good Explanations* says:[60]

---

[57]Candrakīrti's statement of a syllogism would be wrong if his stanza refuted that there is no memory without previous experience, for of course there can be no memory without any previous experience (though of course there can be memory without previous experience *of the subject*, as Śāntideva points out). In the syllogism, the reason (that the previous apprehension and later memory are not inherently different, etc.) is established—it is taken right from the verse—but there is no entailment (that because the previous apprehension and later memory are not inherently different it is not contradictory that there be later memory without previous experience), for it does not prove that there is no previous experience. If the assertion of the opponents at the beginning of the paragraph were refuted by Candrakīrti's statement, it would be established that there is generation of memory without previous experience. Thus, Candrakīrti would be advancing a syllogism that would demonstrate the possibility of memory without previous experience. However, such a syllogism would be senseless because the reason would not establish that there could be memory without experience, merely that the previous apprehension of blue and the later memory of blue are not inherently other (which would preclude any relationship) and that they engage in a single object, the previously existing blue, assertions with which Prāsaṅgikas are in agreement. Therefore, Candrakīrti's statement refutes only that memory is dependent on a consciousness experiencing itself by itself, i.e., being self-conscious.

[58]This is not a wrong conception. It *would* be wrong if he were trying to eliminate it.

[59]Geshay Belden Drakba strongly disagreed with saying that this passage does not eliminate that conception. He thought it was a scribal error and that later commentators struggled to get around it. Geshay Gönchok Tsayring argued that this *is* a wrong conception because according to the Prāsaṅgika School, it is possible to have memory without previous experience, e.g., memory of a subject (that is Śāntideva's argument). It is not possible to have memory without *mere* experience, however, that is, without any experience whatsoever; what would one remember?

[60]*The Essence of the Good Explanations* 176.11-20. Translated by Hopkins

> This [citation of Candrakīrti] does not eliminate the reason, previously explained, in the conception "It is contradictory that if self-consciousness does not exist, memory is generated [because there is no memory without previous experience]."[61] This is a conception that an earlier [eye consciousness apprehending blue] is self-conscious in dependence on there being a special mode of remembering which generates the memory: when the earlier seeing of blue is remembered later, just that earlier seeing—"I saw [that] earlier"—is remembered as one's own seeing. Therefore it is thought that it would be contradictory for that mode of memory to be produced if the previous experience of blue did not experience itself by itself, whereby the earlier [eye consciousness apprehending blue] would be self-conscious.[62]
>
> [According to Candrakīrti] this [mode of memory] does not occur through the power of self-consciousness, but nevertheless it is established that a memory consciousness thinking "I saw it previously," is generated through the force of the two, the earlier experience of the object, blue, and a later remembering consciousness, engaging in one object.

This can be known at length in just that [text].

The explanation in Śāntideva's *Engaging in the Bodhisattva Deeds* of the way in which it is not contradictory that there is

---

(1983a: 11) and Thurman (1984: 319).

[61]In other words, Candrakīrti does not intend to propound that memory is feasible without *any* previous experience. Rather, he means that it is possible to remember one's previous seeing of an object, as in "I saw *that* earlier," without it being the case that the earlier eye consciousness was a case of self-consciousness. Kensur Yeshey Tupden said that Candrakīrti *does* eliminate the conception that it is contradictory that memory be generated without self-consciousness because he shows there is memory without self-consciousness. On the other hand, he does not eliminate the reason here in the sense that he does not eliminate production of memory without previous experience. Thus, there is no fault in the printing. The memory consciousness realizes both blue and the eye consciousness realizing blue.

[62]Kensur Yeshey Tupden (12/14/83) reiterated that fire being self-luminous or consciousness being self-knowing (in the sense of having a nature of being clear and knowing) are acceptable; but fire does not illuminate itself by itself and consciousness does not know itself by itself. A butter-lamp must be self-luminous, having no other source of illumination.

generation of memory even though self-consciousness does not exist is indicated by (IX.23) **[117b]**:[63]

> If self-consciousness did not exist,
> How would a consciousness be remembered?
> Memory [of consciousness] occurs due to the relation [of an object] with other-experiencers
> Like [being mindful of] a rodent's poison.

This is to be known extensively from Dzongkaba's *Illumination of the Thought, Explanation of (Candrakīrti's) "Entrance"*[64] and Jamyang Shayba's *Great Exposition of the Middle Way*.[65] Because it is greatly renowned and easy to understand, I will not write [more about it] here.

---

[63]See the citation of the same verse earlier in this chapter.

[64]See *Illumination of the Thought* 160a.6 ff.

[65]*Great Exposition of the Middle Way* 709.2 ff.

8 *Pratyakṣa* and True Cessations

Jamyang Shayba:[1] The root text says:

When [an object and subject] are related, *pratyakṣa* (*mgon sum*) is for objects, not subjects.
True cessations are the element of a [Superior's] qualities (*chos dbyings, dharmadhātu*). [Therefore][2] Superiors perceive the absence of true establishment [directly].[3]

---

[1]*Great Exposition of Tenets cha* 39b.2.

[2]Jamyang Shayba does not explicitly connect the assertions that true cessations are the element of a [Superior's] qualities and that Superiors of all types realize emptiness. Probably, he means that since it is necessarily the case that Superiors realize true cessations (a Superior being a person who has completely destroyed every vestige of the obstructions to liberation), then if true cessations are indeed emptinesses it necessarily follows that those Superiors realize emptiness. Losang Gönchok, by his use of an instrumental grammatical particle after the first phrase, "True cessations are the element of a [Superior's] qualities," (*Word Commentary* 263.1-2), interprets Jamyang Shayba that way; on the other hand, Ngawang Belden's commentary links the two phrases only by "and" (*Three Commentaries* 511.2) and says nothing in his *Annotations* to indicate any causal relationship. It seems to me that it must be assumed that Jamyang Shayba sees a causal relationship, since he presents the two thoughts as a single topic, not as separate topics.

[3]"Directly" has been interpolated from Ngawang Belden, *Three Commentaries* 511.2. It is possible to realize the absence of true establishment in phenomena even before becoming a Superior, but only Superiors realize it

A. *Pratyakṣa* Refers to Objects, Not Subjects

It is not said that in general even a valid directly cognizing consciousness *(mngon sum tshad ma, pratyakṣa-pramāna)* is not a manifest object *(mngon sum, pratyakṣa)*.[4] However, the [Sanskrit] translation equivalent of *mngon sum, pratyakṣa,* was used for both *mngon sum* [which often refers to a directly perceiving consciousness] and *mngon gyur* ["manifest phenomenon," synonymous with manifest object]. Hence, when the two, a pot and the directly perceiving sense consciousness apprehending it, are considered together, it is asserted that the pot is the actual *pratyakṣa* and that the term *pratyakṣa* is used imputedly with respect to the directly perceiving sense consciousness. Candrakīrti's *Commentary on (Āryadeva's) "Four Hundred"* says:[5]

> In that way [when considering a subject and object together], a consciousness is not fit to be considered a *pratyakṣa.* It is fit for the object [to be considered a *pratyakṣa*].

His *Clear Words* says:[6]

> Furthermore, because the term *pratyakṣa* expresses the meaning, "not hidden," *pratyakṣa* means to manifest to a sense power. With respect to [*pratyakṣa*], since it is taken to mean "manifesting to a sense power," non-hidden phenomena such as a pot or blue are established as manifest objects *(mngon sum, pratyakṣa),* and the consciousnesses which thoroughly distinguish those are called manifest *(mngon*

---

directly.

[4]In general, minds themselves are manifest phenomena or manifest objects. A manifest object is one that need not be realized in dependence upon a logical mark or sign (Gönchok Jikmay Wangbo 58.9, translated in Sopa and Hopkins [232]). For instance, an eye consciousness seeing blue is a manifest object for a subsequent mental consciousness remembering it.

[5]P 5266, vol. 98, 259.3.4.

[6]*Clear Words* 48.1-3. The Sanskrit is in Poussin 71.10-11. The quotation has been restored to full length. Translations by Sprung (61) and Stcherbatsky (1927: 244).

sum, pratyakṣa) due to having as their cause a manifest object like hay-fire or grass-fire.[7]

Ngawang Belden:[8] It appears as if both this and Kaydrup's *Opening the Eyes of the Fortunate*[9] say that in general direct valid cognition *(mngon sum tshad ma)* is *pratyakṣa (mngon sum).* However, since they also explain that manifest object *(mngon sum),* sense object *(dbang po'i yul),* and manifest phenomenon *(mngon gyur)* are synonymous, this requires analysis.[10] Whatever is an established base is necessarily an actual manifest object *(mngon sum, pratyakṣa)* in relation to an awareness that clearly realizes it, and with regard to whatever consciousness is a valid directly perceiving consciousness with respect to an object, that consciousness is necessarily an imputed directly

[7]There are several etymologies for the term *pratyakṣa*. Poussin gives sources (1970: 71-72, n. 4); Stcherbatsky (1927: 250, n. 2) says Vasubandhu's definition in *Nyāyavārti* (42—edition unspecified) is quite different from Dignāga's in *Pramāna-samuccaya* I.15 (P 5700, vol. 130, Toh. 4203) but I have not had access to the former to compare. The etymology followed by the Prāsaṅgika School appears to be "before the eyes" (*prati*, before, + *akṣa*, eyes), in the sense of objects obvious to the senses. In general, the Prāsaṅgika School does not consider consciousnesses to be *pratyakṣa*. However, a consciousness that has its objects "before the eyes," that is, a directly perceiving consciousness, is also often called *pratyakṣa*. Candrakīrti explains that they come to have that name only by way of their association with their objects. Just as fire in the instances of a hay-fire or grass-fire has been given the name of its object, the substance being burned, so consciousnesses are given the name *pratyakṣa* ("manifest") because their objects are *pratyakṣa* ("manifest").

[8]*Annotations*, note *cha*, 117b.2.

[9]*Opening the Eyes of the Fortunate* 496.6 says that an eye consciousness is a *mngon sum*; however, Kaydrup later says that the fully-qualified *mngon sum* is the object, not the subject (502.2).

[10]In other words, there appears to be a contradiction. Ngawang Belden, pondering Jamyang Shayba's statement that in general, even consciousnesses are manifest objects, wonders how to reconcile this with other statements that sense objects are synonymous with manifest objects. The problem is that consciousnesses such as eye or ear consciousnesses are not themselves sense objects because they cannot be apprehended by any of the five sense consciousnesses. Rather, they are objects of the sixth consciousness, the mental consciousness.

perceiving consciousness *(mngon sum, pratyakṣa)* in relation to that object.[11]

B. True Cessations Are the Element of a [Superior's] Qualities; Therefore, All Superiors Realize Emptiness

Jamyang Shayba:[12] True cessations are understood to be the element of a [Superior's] qualities (*chos dbyings, dharmadhātu* [i.e., emptiness])[13] by way of how they are included in the four truths and two truths. Nāgārjuna's *Sixty Stanzas of Reasoning* (4cd) says,[14]

> Through [believing in inherent] existence one is not released.
> Through [believing in total] non-existence one does not transcend cyclic existence.

---

[11]Ngawang Belden himself thinks that not only is *pratyakṣa* not restricted only to sense objects (which would have excluded consciousnesses), but that all phenomena are *pratyakṣa* to awarenesses that clearly, i.e., directly realize them. This would imply that for Ngawang Belden, even a permanent phenomenon such as an emptiness can be considered a *pratyakṣa* in relation to the wisdom consciousness of meditative equipoise directly realizing it.

[12]*Great Exposition of Tenets cha* 39b.5.

[13]Maitreya, in his *Discrimination of the Middle and the Extremes* (I.15-16) explains that the term *chos dbyings (dharmadhātu)* is synonymous with emptiness and etymologizes it as "the cause *(= dbyings, dhātu)* of the qualities *(chos, dharma)* of Superiors" *('phags pa'i chos kyi rgyu, hetutvāccāryadharmā).* Tibetan is P 5522, vol. 108, 30.4.4-5. For Sanskrit, see Pandeya (1971: 38-39). Emptiness is the cause of the qualities of Superiors because meditation on it acts as a cause for becoming a Superior. Dzongkaba explains it this way in reliance on Vimuktisena's *Illumination of the 25,000 Stanza Perfection of Wisdom Sutra* (see Hopkins [1980: 178-79]; also see Ngawang Belden, *Annotations dbu* 8b.6 Hopkins [1983: 383]).

[14]P 5225, vol. 95, 11.2.6-7. The citation has been expanded by adding the first two lines. The Tibetan, and the Sanskrit reconstruction by Uriūtso Ryūshin, reproduced in Tola and Dragonetti (98), are: *yod pas rnam par mi grol te / med pas srid pa 'di las min. // idaṃ bhavaś ca nirvāṇam ubhayaṃ naiva vidyate / bhava eva parijñāto nirvāṇam iti kathyate.*

> By thoroughly understanding [the nature of] things and non-things *(dngos med, abhāva),*[15]
> The great beings are released.

Thereby, it is also explained that Superiors realize emptiness. Candrakīrti's *Commentary on (Nāgārjuna's) "Sixty Stanzas of Reasoning"* repeatedly explains this, as where it says:[16]

> It is thoroughly understood [by Superiors] that those two [things and non-things] do not inherently exist.... Those are called great beings who have many [qualities][17] of great essence; this refers to Superiors.[18]

---

[15]According to Candrakīrti (*Entrance to the Middle Way* VI.220 [14b.1]), *abhāva* means non-conditioned phenomena *('dus ma byas kyi chos, asaṃskra-dharma).* In other words, the "great beings" understand all phenomena, impermanent and permanent.

[16]It appears that this is not a direct quotation, but rather is a paraphrase of P 5265, vol. 98, 172.5.6-7 (= Toh. 3864, vol. 7, 3.3.2-3), which reads: "The thorough understanding [by Superiors] that those two [i.e., things and non-things] do not inherently exist, which has a nature of not conceiving a self-entitiness, and so forth, of things and non-things, is the non-erroneous thorough knowledge of things and non-things in that way. Through such thorough understanding the great beings posit [phenomena]. Therefore, they abide in the exalted wisdom of non-apprehension which totally transcends childish beings, whereby because just they are great, they are called 'great beings' and 'Superiors.'" *(de gnyis dngos po med par yongs su shes pa dgnos po dang dngos po med pa'i rang gi ngo bo la sogs yongs su mi rtog pa'i rang bzhin gang yin pa de ni de ltar dngos po dan dgnos po med pa phyin ci ma log par yongs su shes pa ste / de ltar yongs su shes pa des bdag nyid chen po rnams kyis rnam par gzhag go / de'i phyir de dag skye bo byis pa rnams las shin tu 'das pa dmigs pa med pa'i ye shes la gnas pas de dag nyid che ba'i phyir bdag nyid chen po zhes bya ste 'phags pa zhes brjod do.)*

[17]Kensur Yeshey Tupden. One of the great qualities is their thorough understanding of emptiness. He also thought that "great essence" might mean emptiness.

[18]According to Kensur Yeshey Tupden, Superiors realize that things and non-things are mutually related, hence dependently arisen; because of that they realize that those are not inherently established. All Superiors realize this directly. Jamyang Shayba does not attempt here to justify his identification of true cessations with emptiness; his point in using these two quotations seems to be to bolster the Consequentialist tenet that liberation depends upon realization of emptiness. Since true cessations are emptinesses, and Superiors necessarily realize true cessations, they must perforce realize emptiness.

Ngawang Belden:[19] Gyeltsap's *Commentary on (Nāgārjuna's) "Sixty Stanzas of Reasoning" (rigs pa drug bcu pa'i dar ṭīk)* explains:[20]

> A thing does not become a non-thing without depending on a thing because the disintegratedness which is its having become another thing is asserted to be the non-existence of a thing. A thing is not established without depending on a non-thing because a thing is not established without negating a non-thing. Therefore, the two, thing and non-thing, are thoroughly realized directly as having a nature of emptiness due to being mutually dependent. Therefore, because [the Superiors] are the basis of the exalted wisdom consciousness which does not observe [the basis of the emptiness it realizes][21] the great beings, the Superiors, are liberated.

---

[19]*Annotations*, note *ja*, 117b.4.

[20]*Collected Works*, vol. 5, 407.5-8.1. Gyeltsap also wrote a memorandum *(zin bris)* on this text, *Collected Works*, vol. 5, 461-82. There is a similar statement in Candrakīrti's *Commentary on (Nāgārjuna's) "Sixty Stanzas of Reasoning,"* P 5265, vol. 98, 172.5.5-6.

[21]According to Kensur Yeshey Tupden, sometimes it is also said that what is "not observed" is non-emptinesses, that is, positive phenomena and affirming negatives, which do not appear to the minds of non-Buddhas at the time they directly realize emptiness.

9 Nirvāṇas with Remainder and without Remainder

Jamyang Shayba:[1] The root text says:

Because it is explained that (1) it is unsuitable that [a remainderless nirvāṇa] be extinction of the aggregates [in the sense of cutting the continuum of mind and body], and (2) that feelings and discriminations are destroyed [only in the sense of being primordially extinguished into emptiness],
Without remainder *(lhag med myang bdas, nirupadhiśeṣa-nirvāṇa)* and with remainder *(lhag bcas myang bdas, sopadhiśeṣa-nirvāṇa)* [means] the extinction and non-extinction of mistaken [dualistic] appearances.[2]

---

[1]*Great Exposition of Tenets cha* 39b.6.

[2]A nirvāṇa is an emptiness in the mind of one who has completely and forever abandoned all the afflictions comprising the obstructions to liberation from cyclic existence. It occurs for Hearer Arhats and Solitary Realizer Arhats after the end of their paths of meditation and for Bodhisattvas at the beginning of the eighth of ten grounds of their path of meditation. An "uninterrupted path" realizing emptiness that is simultaneous with the cessation of the last of the afflictive obstructions is followed by a "path of release" in which they have nirvāṇa. The nirvāṇa experienced in meditative equipoise is a nirvāṇa without remainder because at that time there is a nirvāṇa but there is no remainder of appearance of mistaken dualistic appearances, that is, the appearance of true existence. It is followed by a

A. Contradictions in the Presentation of the Lower Schools

[According to] the Supramundane Victor, nirvāṇa has two aspects: that with a remainder of aggregates and that without a remainder. I have explained elsewhere the mode of assertion and mode of objection of certain[3] Cittamātrins and below—that the first [nirvāṇa with remainder] is the mere abandonment of the afflictions and the second [nirvāṇa without remainder] is the cutting of the continuum of the aggregates.[4]

If here we speak briefly [in accordance with the Prāsaṅgika School], this [explanation of the lower schools] is incorrect, because (1) in that case nirvāṇa [without remainder] would not be actualized, (2) it is explained that each Arhat also attains a nirvāṇa in which the contaminated aggregates are completely abandoned [in the sense that they are primordially extinguished into emptiness, not that they are irrevocably cut off] **[40a]**, and (3) there is a Hīnayāna sūtra in which Śariputra, having actualized such a nirvāṇa, set forth a repetition [of what he had accomplished].[5]

---

nirvāṇa with a remainder of the appearance of true existence because until one removes the obstructions to omniscience, phenomena appear to be truly existent.

[3]Jamyang Shayba says "certain" Cittamātrins because he does not include Dharmakīrti and his followers among those Cittamātrins who propound "three final vehicles," the doctrine that not all sentient beings eventually attain Buddhahood. Dharmakīrti and the Mādhyamikas assert that all beings eventually attain Buddhahood and that there is never a time when the continuum of mind is irrevocably cut off. Therefore, they cannot admit the position of the lower schools that the continuum of the aggregates is cut off in a nirvāṇa without remainder.

[4]For example, Vaibhāṣikas. See Gönchok Jikmay Wangbo, *Precious Garland of Tenets* 28.12, translated in Sopa and Hopkins (217).

[5]Jamyang Shayba adduces two faults to the definitions of nirvāṇa with and without remainder in the lower schools: first, if nirvāṇa without remainder involved the utter extinction of the mental and physical aggregates, there would be no one to experience the nirvāṇa. Second, the sūtras that say that Arhats extinguish their aggregates should be interpreted to mean that those aggregates are primordially extinguished into emptiness, not that they are utterly extinguished. Otherwise, there would be no way to explain how Śaripūtra repeated a sūtra after having actualized nirvāṇa. (I

[With respect to the first consequence, that nirvāṇa would not be realized,] Candrakīrti's *Commentary on (Nāgārjuna's) "Sixty Stanzas of Reasoning"* says:[6]

> Since there is nothing whatsoever in an entity which is a severance of the continuum of the aggregates, in whom is that cessation actualized? ...For the time being, as long as there is an impelling force for the continuation of those aggregates by the power of causes and conditions, so long can [the continuum of the aggregates] not be fully understood as extinct because it has production.[7]

---

have split the second objection into two parts for clarity.) See Candrakīrti, *Commentary on (Nāgārjuna's) "Sixty Stanzas"* 10b.3, for more.

[6]P 5265, vol. 98, 174.4.5. The second part of this quotation, the portion following the ellipses, seems to be a very loose paraphrase of the text following the first part. Perhaps it is based on a different translation into Tibetan.

[7]No person would be able to actualize a nirvāṇa without a remainder of aggregates because the mental and physical aggregates are the basis of imputation for persons. A person whose aggregates had been destroyed would be dead. In most Mahāyāna systems (the Mādhyamika School and the followers of Dharmakīrti in the Cittamātra School) there is no instance in which the aggregates of a person are completely extinguished in the sense of irrevocably cutting their continuum (although the form aggregate is temporarily absent in the case of persons born in the Formless Realm). All sentient beings eventually attain Buddhahood. Those who have attained nirvāṇa have purified their aggregates of afflictions and are no longer powerlessly reborn in cyclic existence, but the process of transformation from ordinary being to Arhat and from Arhat to Buddha does not disturb the basic continuum of the aggregates.

The lower schools would probably answer that there is after all an attainer of their version of nirvāṇa without remainder—one in which the continuum of the aggregates is cut off—because the person who is about to attain that nirvāṇa in the next moment may be designated as the attainer of a nirvāṇa without remainder. Such a designation would be a coarse worldly convention, analogous to the way in which the world refers to persons and death. For example, although it is not possible to posit a person who is dead (because persons are imputed in dependence on their aggregates, and a corpse has neither a living body nor a consciousness associated with it) people in the world often speak as though such a person could be posited. To Jamyang Shayba this is not a satisfactory answer. It is no more admissible to talk about persons who have attained a nirvāṇa in which the aggregates have been utterly destroyed than to talk about persons who are dead.

[With regard to the second reason, that Arhats attain a nirvāṇa in which the aggregates are extinguished into emptiness, but not irrevocably cut off,] a Hearer sūtra says:[8]

> This which is suffering is completely abandoned, definitely abandoned, purified, extinguished, freed from desire, stopped, thoroughly pacified, vanished, not connected to other sufferings, not arisen, not produced. This is peace, this is auspiciousness. It is like this: since all the aggregates are abandoned, attachment is extinguished, one is freed from desire, has cessation, nirvāṇa.

Moreover, it is explained in Candrakīrti's *Commentary on (Nāgārjuna's) "Sixty Stanzas of Reasoning"*[9] that the sūtra says, "completely abandoned...vanished" in terms of a present nirvāṇa and says, "not connected to other sufferings...nirvāṇa" in terms of a future mode of freedom from sufferings.

Ngawang Belden:[10] The meaning of this sūtra is as set forth in Dzongkaba's *Illumination of the Thought, Explanation of (Candrakīrti's) "Entrance"*:[11]

> Commenting on the meaning of this, [Candrakīrti] says that because the phrase "this which is suffering" uses the term of proximity "this," the passage "This which is suffering is completely abandoned...vanished" refers only to the sufferings of aggregates that exist presently in one's own continuum. The passage "not connected to other suffering...nirvāṇa" refers to future suffering.[12]

---

[8]This sūtra is cited in Candrakīrti's *Commentary on (Nāgārjuna's) "Sixty Stanzas of Reasoning"* but not identified by him or by Nāgārjuna, Dzongkaba, or Jamyang Shayba. According to Jamyang Shayba's *Great Exposition of the Middle Way* 188a.3 (Buxaduor edition), it is a sūtra set forth by Śariputra after his enlightenment, perhaps the *Repetition Sūtra*. Translated by Hopkins (1980: 170).

[9]P 5265, vol. 98, 174.4.6-5.2.

[10]*Annotations*, note *nya*, 117b.6.

[11]*Illumination of the Thought* 35b.5-6. Translated in Hopkins (1980: 170).

[12]This Hearer sūtra is apparently used by proponents of the lower schools of tenets to show that the continuum of the aggregates of an Arhat who has attained nirvāṇa is utterly cut off at the time of death (the meaning

of "nirvāṇa without remainder" for them). However, Candrakīrti and Dzongkaba argue that because the sūtra uses the term "this" it is referring to suffering, i.e., aggregates, in the continuum of someone who is alive. Thus it cannot be referring to a nirvāṇa without remainder in the sense that the lower schools use that term. Dzongkaba later explains that the first part of the sūtra refers to the primordial extinguishment of the aggregates into emptiness, that being the fact that all phenomena have a nature of emptiness and are primordially empty of inherent existence. According to Kaydrup, it specifically refers to the primordial extinguishment of the aggregates which is realized in meditative equipoise by someone who has attained nirvāṇa. Losang Dayang's *Grounds and Paths* (126.7-127.3) quotes Kaydrup's *Opening the Eyes of the Fortunate*:

> Since there is no remainder of the appearance of true existence for the perspective of a meditative equipoise which has actualized the cessation that is the primordial extinguishment of the aggregates, it is called a nirvāṇa without remainder; since there is a remainder of the appearance of true existence of the aggregates, and so forth, for the perspective of an [exalted wisdom of] subsequent attainment arisen from that [meditative equipoise], it is called a nirvāṇa with remainder.

It is possible that Dzongkaba means that the entire sūtra concerns primordial extinguishment into emptiness. However, it seems that Candrakīrti and Dzongkaba are distinguishing two parts to the sūtra, the first concerned with primordial extinguishment and the second actually concerned with the cessation of all the afflictions upon attainment of nirvāṇa. It is difficult to tell what is meant because neither of them comments on the second part of the sūtra and because the Tibetan of the sūtra gives no justification for their bifurcation. The first is a nirvāṇa that all phenomena have and that is experienced in the direct realization of emptiness. This nirvāṇa is not one brought about by the path. The second is the abandonment of an affliction due to the development of a path consciousness capable of permanently extinguishing an affliction.

Ngawang Belden considers Paṇchen Sönam Drakba to have a position similar to proponents of the lower tenet systems on nirvāṇa with remainder and without remainder. He probably bases this criticism on a passage from Paṇchen Sönam Drakba's *Commentary on the General Meaning of (Dzongkaba's) "Illumination of the Thought" (dbu ma'i spyi don;* see Losang Dayang 127.3-5, 127.7-28.1) that discusses a common mode of positing the two nirvāṇas for the upper and lower tenet systems. Paṇchen Sönam Drakba implies that a nirvāṇa in the continuum of an Arhat who has a remainder of aggregates and a remainder of the appearance of true existence is not only a nirvāṇa with remainder for the lower tenet systems but also a nirvāṇa with remainder for the Prāsaṅgika School. Similarly, he says that a nirvāṇa without a remainder of either aggregates or the appearance of true existence (presum-

[Dzongkaba continues:]

> *Objection:* "[This which is] suffering" and "[all] aggregates" are general terms used here for their instances, the afflictions.
>
> *Answer:* This also is not feasible. If general terms [such as "aggregates"] are not amenable to explanation with a general meaning, they must be explained as referring to [some of] their instances [i.e., the afflictions]; here, however, this can be explained in the context of a generality **[118a]**.[13]

Thus, if the meaning of this sūtra is explained according to the Proponents of True Existence, there would be no actualizing of nirvāṇa. With respect to how that is so, Dzongkaba, in that same text, says:[14]

---

ably at the time of meditative equipoise on emptiness) is a shared nirvāṇa without remainder. Paṇchen's analysis fails, it seems, because there could not actually be a shared nirvāṇa without remainder. That is because a nirvāṇa without remainder for the lower schools entails the total annihilation of the aggregates whereas in the upper schools there is never an irrevocable extinguishment of the aggregates. See Losang Dayang, *Grounds and Paths* 128.1-5. Paṇchen Sönam Drakba clearly does not fall into the camp of the proponents of the lower tenet systems because he recognizes that the system of the Prāsaṅgika School uniquely defines nirvāṇas with and without remainder and that is also unique with regard to the order in which those nirvāṇas are actualized.

[13]In their commentaries above, Candrakīrti and Dzongkaba replied to those who find the sūtra under consideration to be referring to a nirvāṇa without remainder in the sense of a nirvāṇa involving the irrevocable extinguishment of the aggregates. The present opponent takes an opposite tack, implying that the sūtra concerns a nirvāṇa with remainder in the sense of a nirvāṇa involving a remainder of aggregates. He thinks that perhaps "sufferings" and "aggregates" refer here only to the afflictions (of desire, hatred, and so forth); in that case this sūtra refers neither to the primordial extinguishment of the aggregates nor to the severance of the continuum of the mind and body of an Arhat at the time of that Arhat's death. Dzongkaba answers that it is not necessary to twist the literal meaning of "this which is suffering" and "all aggregates" because those phrases refer only to the fact that these phenomena have a natural extinguishment (that is, they are naturally or primordially without inherent existence). Dzongkaba's explanation follows.

[14]*Illumination of the Thought* 35a.2-5. Also translated by Hopkins (1980:

Otherwise, according to the Proponents of True Existence, it is not fit to explain [the Hearer sūtra] as primordial extinguishment in the sense that the aggregates have been primordially without inherently existent production, as in Maitreya's *Sublime Continuum of the Mahāyāna*, "The afflictions are primordially extinguished." It must be explained as an utter abandonment [of the aggregates] by means of the path.

[However, in that case] when the nirvāṇa that is to be actualized existed, the actualizer would not [and thus could not report on the extinguishment that was realized, as was done in the *Repetition Sūtra*]. Also, when the actualizer existed, the nirvāṇa to be actualized would not because the aggregates would not have been extinguished. Hence, they are unable to explain this sūtra.

According to us, it is permissible to explain extinguishment here in accordance with the statement:[15]

> Extinguishment [in this case] is not [caused] by means of an antidote;
> It is so called because of primordial extinguishment.

We are able to explain well the meaning of the sūtra [as referring to a natural or primordial absence of inherent existence in phenomena].[16]

170-71). The differences between this translation and that in *Compassion in Tibetan Buddhism* reflect Hopkins' subsequent reinterpretation of the passage.

[15]This passage appears in neither Maitreya's nor Asaṅga's texts. It may be in Gyeltsap's commentary.

[16]Since the Proponents of True Existence—the proponents of the lower tenet systems —interpret this sūtra as being concerned with a nirvāṇa without remainder in the sense of an irrevocable extinguishment of the aggregates, they would not interpret it as Dzongkaba has done or as Maitreya would, as being concerned with the primordial extinguishment of the aggregates into emptiness. In the section in which the quoted passage occurs, Maitreya speaks about the natural purity of the mind and the adventitious nature of the afflictions defiling it; he does not mean that the afflictions are removed by the path from beginningless time. They would then have the problem of explaining how there could be an actualizer of that nirvāṇa (since the aggregates would have been abandoned at the point of attaining the nirvāṇa), or, vice versa, how there could be an actualized nirvāṇa without remainder if there were a person who had actualized it.

Jamyang Shayba:[17] [With respect to the third reason for rejection of the explanations of the lower systems on types of nirvāṇa, that Śaripūtra set forth a Low Vehicle sūtra after actualizing a nirvāṇa without remainder,] the *Repetition Sūtra (rjes zlos kyi mdo)* says:[18]

> This sūtra called "Repetition"
> Was set forth by Śaripūtra
> After having actualized nirvāṇa.

Ngawang Belden:[19] Candrakīrti's *Commentary on (Nāgārjuna's) "Sixty Stanzas of Reasoning"* says:[20]

> If you think that because [for you] there being no remainder of aggregates is characterized by cutting the continuum of the aggregates, a nirvāṇa that has [a remainder of] aggregates is not asserted to be a [full-fledged] nirvāṇa even though the fetters such as desire have been abandoned, then how do you explain this which appears in a sūtra:
>
> > This sūtra called "Repetition"
> > Was set forth by Śāriputra
> > After having actualized nirvāṇa.

In accordance with that, if it were said, "As long as the continuum of aggregates is not severed, there is no full-fledged nirvāṇa," this would contradict the explanation that Śāriputra, having actualized nirvāṇa, subsequently repeated, "My births are extinguished," etc., to his other friends. That is what

---

[17] *Great Exposition of Tenets cha* 40a.5.

[18] A search of the *bka' 'gyur* revealed no sūtra of this name or containing the term "repetition" (which Ngawang Belden spells *rjes bzlas*). Its Sanskrit title might be *anuvīpsāsūtra*. Jamyang Shayba's *Great Exposition of the Middle Way* (343.5) says that according to "just that commentary" Śaripūtra spoke this sūtra after having attained enlightenment. Jamyang Shayba may be referring to Candrakīrti's *Commentary on (Nāgārjuna's) "Sixty Stanzas of Reasoning"* which he has quoted a little earlier.

[19] *Annotations*, note *ta*, 118a.4.

[20] P 5265, vol. 98, 175.1.3-6. The quotation has been expanded to include the previous phrase.

[Candrakīrti] is saying; he is not refuting the assertion by the Proponents of True Existence that initially one must actualize a nirvāṇa with remainder and subsequently one must actualize a nirvāṇa without remainder [though he would in fact disagree with them].

Moreover, the *Repetition Sūtra* is as explained above; Gyeltsap's *Commentary on (Nāgārjuna's) "Sixty Stanzas of Reasoning"* explains that the stanza uttered by the Superior Aśvajit[21] is not it.[22]

B. Definitions of Nirvāṇa with and without Remainder

Jamyang Shayba:[23] When the afflictions are abandoned along with their seeds, nirvāṇa is attained. Moreover, a nirvāṇa with remainder is:[24]

> a nirvāṇa which, although the afflictions are extinguished, involves a remainder of mistaken [dualistic appearance due to] the predispositions of those [afflictions].

---

[21]Tibetan: Datul *(rta thul)*. See *Mahāvyupatti,* vol. 1, n. 1037. He is identified as a Hearer.

[22]It is possible that Ngawang Belden is correcting Jamyang Shayba, or that he is making a reply to a hypothetical objection. What he says shows that nirvāṇa with remainder even in the Hearer sense of the term is an actual nirvāṇa. Hearers would otherwise have to deny that Śāriputra attained a full-fledged nirvāṇa, and they presumably would not want to do that. If it were thought that there is no actual nirvāṇa when there is a remainder of aggregates, one would have to deny that Śāriputra was able to explain a sūtra after having actualized nirvāṇa. Gyeltsap's commentary may confirm that the stanza that is cited as proof of Śāriputra's continued existence after actualizing nirvāṇa was indeed uttered by Śāriputra, not Aśvajit.

[23]*Great Exposition of Tenets cha* 40a.5.

[24]According to Jamyang Shayba's *Great Exposition of the Middle Way* (342.5), a nirvāṇa with remainder is: "a nirvāṇa of remainder that, although the afflictions have been abandoned, [involves] a mere remainder of the appearance of true existence of an object to any of the six manifest operating consciousnesses."

and a nirvāṇa without remainder is:[25]

> a nirvāṇa without a remainder of mistaken [dualistic appearance], because this extinguishment of the aggregates and so forth has the meaning of being extinguished into the element of qualities.

For with respect to the mode of abandonment in this [Hīnayāna] sūtra where it says, "these sufferings which are completely abandoned," and so forth, and the many profound [Mahāyāna] sūtras which say, "...unproduced, unceasing, primordially peaceful, and naturally beyond sorrow," the extinguishment mentioned in the former sūtra and non-production in this one are similar in necessarily being the element of qualities [and do not refer to a nirvāṇa that is attained on the path. For] (1) Nāgārjuna's *Precious Garland (rin chen phreng ba, ratnāvalī)* (III.86) says:[26]

> The teaching in the Mahāyāna of non-production
> And [the teaching] in the other, [the Hīnayāna, of] extinction are [of the same] emptiness.
> Extinction and non-production have the same meaning.
> Therefore let [the Mahāyāna] be accepted [as Buddha's word].[27]

---

[25]According to Jamyang Shayba's *Great Exposition of the Middle Way* (342.5-43.1), a nirvāṇa without remainder is: "a nirvāṇa in which not only have the afflictions been abandoned, but a remainder of the appearance of true existence to any of the operating consciousnesses and all the sufferings of the three times are extinguished in emptiness and which involves a meditative equipoise into which such appearances, manifest feelings, and so forth, are pacified." He mentions that all the sufferings of "the three times" are extinguished because of the reference to "future suffering."

[26]P 5658, vol. 129, 181.1.4. The quotation has been restored to full length. It has been translated in reliance on Hopkins (1975: 75).

[27]The Hīnayāna sūtras that teach that sufferings are extinguished and the Mahāyāna sūtras that teach that phenomena are unproduced are both referring to emptiness. The first is interpreted to refer to the natural or primordial extinguishment of all phenomena in emptiness, and the second is interpreted to refer to the utter non-production of anything inherently existent. Buddha explained in the *Descent to Laṅka Sūtra (laṅkāvatārasūtra)* that when he said, "no production," he meant, "no inherently existent production." See Suzuki (1932: 67).

(2) Also, Maitreya's *Sublime Continuum of the Mahāyāna (rgyud bla ma, uttaratantra* I.15) says:[28]

> Because [Superiors] realize phenomena as having a nature of quiescence,
> [They realize] the mode [of being, emptiness]; moreover, [this is]
> Because [the mind] is naturally pure
> And because the afflictions are primordially extinguished.[29]

(3) And Asaṅga's *Explanation of (Maitreya's) "Sublime Continuum of the Mahāyāna" (rgyud bla ma'i bstan bcos rnam bshad, uttaratantravyākhya)* says:[30]

[28]P 5525, vol. 108, 24.3.5. The Sanskrit, from E. H. Johnston (1950: 14): *prathāvattajjagacchāntadharmatāvagamāt sa ca prakrteḥ pariśuddhatvāt kleśasyādikṣayekṣaṇāt.* The quotation has been lengthened. See Obermiller (1931: 138) for this quotation and the Asaṅga quotation following it. *Sems,* which I have translated as "mind," is translated by Obermiller as "Spirit," which could easily mislead one into thinking that what Maitreya asserts is a permanent soul or self rather than a basically pure but adventitiously defiled impermanent continuum of mind.

[29]Takasaki's reading (174) is that Superiors realize phenomena as having a nature of quiescence—of being empty of their own nature—because the mind is pure and because they perceive the afflictions as being primordially extinguished. That is, he thinks that Superiors realize emptiness because they realize the primordial extinguishment of the afflictions. However, I think this puts the cart before the horse: because the afflictions are primordially extinguished, the mind is naturally pure; therefore, it is possible for Superiors to realize emptiness. If the mind were not naturally pure, it could not be transformed into a wisdom consciousness. The primordial extinguishment of the afflictions is not what they realize, but rather what enables them to realize emptiness (the quiescent nature of phenomena).

[30]P 5526, vol. 108, 35.4.1. Takasaki notes (7) that although the Tibetan tradition assumes that the commentary in which Maitreya's verses are embedded is Asaṅga's, there is no textual evidence that he is its author. The Sanskrit is (Johnson: 15) *atha ca punarbhagavan prakrtipariśuddhasya cittasyopakleśārtho duṣprativedhyaḥ.* Asaṅga says that Superiors realize the selflessness of persons and (other) phenomena for two reasons: (1) because the mind is seen to be naturally luminous and (2) because the afflictions are primordially extinguished. It is not clear whether one realizes selflessness in the dependence on these two reasons in the sense that realizing the luminous nature of the mind and the primordial extinguishment of the aggregates is itself realization of selflessness, or whether it is just meant that

> ...because the mind is seen to be naturally luminous and because the afflictions in proximity to that are seen to be primordially extinguished and ceased **[40b]**.[31]

Candrakīrti's *Clear Words* (XVIII.1) says:[32]

> Internal and external things are not observable [as truly existent]. Therefore, the consciousnesses conceiving the internal and external as [inherently existent] self and as [inherently existent] mine are extinguished totally. Here, this is suchness.

The meaning of this is set forth in Dzongkaba's *Great Exposition of the Stages of the Path (lam rim chen mo)*:[33]

> The total extinguishment of all conceptions of [inherently existent] I and mine through the thorough pacification of all these appearances of the varieties of internal and external phenomena as [their own] suchness, whereas they are not

---

these two factors make possible the realization of selflessness. Obermiller's translation (38) implies the first, it seems.

[31]Emptiness is the reality of phenomena and their total quiescence, meaning that all phenomena are "extinguished into emptiness" in the sense that they are primordially and forever devoid of inherent existence. Maitreya and Asaṅga explain that Superiors are in an important sense able to realize emptiness because the mind is naturally pure or luminous and because the afflictions are primordially empty of inherent existence. If the mind were not naturally pure with the afflictions being mere adventitious defilements staining it, it would not be possible to transform the mind. Also, if the afflictions were not empty of inherent existence, they could not be removed, for if something existed inherently it could not be eliminated. Asaṅga may also mean that the suchness of persons and phenomena is realized *because* Superiors see that the mind is naturally luminous and that the afflictions are primordially extinguished into emptiness. Those two facts make realization of suchness possible, and realizing them is realization of suchness. Jamyang Shayba's purpose in citing Maitreya and Asaṅga seems to be merely to provide more examples of writings in which extinguishment of the afflictions or aggregates refers to primordial extinguishment into emptiness rather than utter extinguishment.

[32]*Clear Words* 220.3. The Sanskrit is in Poussin 340.6-7: *ādhyātmikabāhyāśeṣavastvanupalambhenādhyātmaṃ bahiśca yaḥ sarvathāhaṃkāramamakāraparijñaya idamatra tattvaṃ*. Also translated by Sprung (165).

[33]Dzongkaba, *Great Exposition of the Stages of the Path*, 371b.2-3.

> [their own] suchness, along with their predispositions, is the suchness that is to be attained here, the Truth Body.

This explains that true cessations are ultimate truths.[34]

[34]The "suchness to be attained" is the adventitiously pure Nature Truth Body *(ngo bo nyid sku, svabhāvika-kāya)*, the emptiness of the Buddha's omniscient consciousness and the ultimate true cessation. "Suchness," i.e., emptiness, is explained to be the elimination of the object of the conception of an inherently existent I and mine. Thus, emptiness is being explicitly indicated by Candrakīrti and Dzongkaba to be a true cessation. This is an important source for establishing the Gomang College position that true cessations are emptinesses (in contradistinction to the Loseling College tenet that true cessations are ultimate truths but not emptinesses), and it is puzzling that Jamyang Shayba places it here instead of in the previous chapter. According to Jamyang Shayba, true cessations are ultimate truths and emptinesses and have both existent and non-existent objects of negation. On the other hand, Paṇchen Sönam Drakba of Loseling College held that true cessations, though ultimate truths, are necessarily *not* emptinesses because their objects of negation—the consciousness conceiving true existence—were not non-existent.

10 The Two Obstructions

Jamyang Shayba:[1] The root text says:

Predispositions [established by afflictions] are obstructions to omniscience. Non-afflictive ignorance is also asserted.
[Until] the afflictions are removed, abandonment of obstructions to omniscience is not begun.

A. Predispositions and Non-Afflictive Ignorance Are Obstructions to Omniscience

The [Prāsaṅgikas'] way of abandoning the two obstructions [to liberation and omniscience] is unique. Candrakīrti's *Autocommentary on the "Entrance"* says:[2]

With respect to [the existence of predispositions established by afflictions in the continua of Arhats] the predispositions [established by] ignorance are obstacles preventing thoroughly distinguishing objects of knowledge, and the exis-

---

[1]*Great Exposition of Tenets cha* 40b.2-3.

[2]P 5263, vol. 98, 164.2.1-2. This portion was not translated by Poussin. The quotation has been lengthened by filling in material indicated by "etc." *(sogs)*, beginning with "...and the existence of predispositions [established by] desire..." There is no available Sanskrit text.

> tence of predispositions [established by] desire, and so forth, is the cause of such engagement in body and speech [as spontaneously jumping like a monkey or saying "bitch!"].[3] Also, the predispositions of ignorance, desire, and so forth, are overcome only in exalted knowers of all aspects *(rnam pa thams cad mkhyen pa, sarvākārajñāna)* and Buddhas but not in others.

By that statement he [indicates that] the predispositions [established by] the three poisons [desire, hatred, and ignorance] are obstructions to omniscience.

Also, although the three poisons mentioned in Candrakīrti's *Autocommentary on the "Entrance"* when he says,[4] "The afflictions are ignorance, desire, and so forth..." are described as afflictions [and thus might lead one to think that all ignorance is afflictive], there is non-afflictive ignorance and ignorance that is an obstruction to omniscience because Candrakīrti says in his *Autocommentary on the "Entrance,"*[5] "...because of being thoroughly involved in ignorance that is not afflictive..." and his *Seventy Stanzas on the Three Refuges (skyabs gsum 'gro bdun cu pa, triśaraṇasaptati)* says:[6]

> For the sake of abandoning non-afflictive ignorance,
> [Arhats] are later urged on by the Buddhas.

---

[3]The line before this quotation (164.1.8) mentions Arhats "who formerly were monkeys, who go about jumping" and *mang mor bjod pa*—"one who formerly was a Brahmin, calling someone a low-caste woman." These are people who have predispositions from former lives as a monkey or Brahmin that cause them to act in strange ways, despite the fact that they have irrevocably destroyed the afflictions of desire, hatred, and ignorance. Just as predispositions established by ignorance—the obstructions to omniscience—continue to exist even though ignorance itself has been destroyed, so also the predispositions of desire and hatred exist despite the cessation of desire and hatred.

[4]P 5263, vol. 98, 164.1.3.

[5]Candrakīrti also mentions non-afflictive ignorance in his *Brilliant Lamp, Commentary on the Guhyasamāja Tantra (rgyud 'grel sgron gsal, pradīpoddyotana)*, which is cited in Losang Dayang 119.2.

[6]P 5366, vol. 103, 175.4.5. No Sanskrit text is extant.

And:[7]

> Since non-afflictive ignorance exists,
> [It must be] abandoned [in order to attain] omniscience.

The obstructions to omniscience are of two types, those that are consciousnesses and those that are not.

Ngawang Belden:[8] Janggya's *Presentation of Tenets* says:[9]

> In dependence on Candrakīrti's *Seventy Stanzas on the Three Refuges*, which says, "For the sake of abandoning non-afflictive ignorance..." and "...non-afflictive ignorance exists..." and his statement in his *Autocommentary on the "Entrance,"* "...ignorance that is not afflictive..." **[118b]**, Paṇchen Sönam Gyeltsen *(paṇ chen bsod nams rgyal mtshan)*[10] and the great scholar and adept Jamyang Shaybay Dorjay [Jamyang Shayba] say that the existence of obstructions to omniscience that are consciousnesses is correct.
>
> Nevertheless, with respect to the Foremost Omniscient [Dzongkaba's] interpretations of the ignorance that is an obstruction to omniscience, except for his interpretation [of it] as predispositions of mistaken dualistic appearance, he does not appear to have interpreted it as ignorance that is a consciousness.
>
> Most scholars and adepts, such as the omniscient Kaydrup, the lord of reasoning Jaydzün Chögyi Gyeltsen *(rje btsun chos kyi rgyal mtshan)* of Sera *(se ra)* and his [spiritual] sons, as well as the great treasure of wisdom Jamyang Gaway Lodrö *('jam dbyangs dga' ba'i blo gros)*, the foremost omniscient Gendün Gyatso *(dge 'dun rgya mtsho)*, and Paṇchen Sönam Drakba,[11] assert that there are no obstructions

---

[7]P 5366, vol. 103, 175.1.4.

[8]*Annotations*, note *tha*, 118a.8 ff. By citing Janggya, who disagrees with Jamyang Shayba about the existence of obstructions to omniscience that are consciousnesses, Ngawang Belden also obviously expresses his disagreement with Jamyang Shayba.

[9]Janggya, *Presentation of Tenets* 486.17-487.14.

[10]None of the half-dozen scholars I asked knew who this was.

[11]Kaydrup (1385-1438) is one of Dzongkaba's two chief disciples; Jaydzün Chögyi Gyeltsen (1469-1546) is the author of monastic textbooks for Jay college of Sera Monastery; I have not yet found biographical information

to omniscience that are consciousnesses. Also, the omniscient Paṇchen Losang Chögyi Gyeltsen *(paṇ chen blo bzang chos kyi rgyal mtshan)*,[12] a keeper of the teaching of both the transmission of explanation and the transmission of achievement of the Foremost Lama [Dzongkaba], says:

> The subtle obstructions [preventing] the perception
> Of the two truths directly and simultaneously by one consciousness
> Are designated "ignorance" [but] are not actual consciousnesses;
> Hence there is not even partial contradiction.

His statements along with his reasons are very concordant with the great mass of the speech of the Foremost [Dzongkaba]. Therefore, [this topic] still should be finely analyzed by the intelligent.

Jamyang Shayba:[13] Obstructions to omniscience and impedimentary obstructions *(thogs sgrib)* are equivalent.

Ngawang Belden:[14] Although there also is an explanation that the three—obstructions of attachment *(chags sgrib)*, impedimentary obstructions, and obstructions to omniscience—are equivalent, Gyel-tsap's *Commentary on (Maitreya's) "Sublime Continuum of the Mahāyāna" (rgyud bla ma'i dar ṭīk)*, at the point at which [the *Sublime Continuum of the Mahāyāna*] says, "Because there are no attachments in the stainless expanse and..." says:[15]

---

on Jamyang Gaway Lodrö, except for his dates (1429/30-1503); Gendün Gyatso (1476-1542) is the second Dalai Lama; and Paṇchen Sönam Drakba (1478-1554) is the author of monastic textbooks for Loseling College of Drebung Monastery.

[12]He is the first Paṇchen Lama (1569-1662). Losang Dayang (*Grounds and Paths* 119.4-5), calls him the All-Seeing Paṇchen Losang Chögyi Gyeltsen *(paṇ chen kun gzigs blo bzang chos kyi rgyal mtshan)*, and the name of his book is *Answer to the Objections of the Translator [Daktsang] Shayrap Rinchen (sgra pa shes rab rin chen gyi rtsod lan)*.

[13]*Great Exposition of Tenets*, 40b.6.

[14]*Annotations*, note *da*, 118b.5.

[15]*Collected Works*, vol. 3, 101.6.

> Because there are no attachments, i.e., consciousnesses conceiving *(zhen pa)* true existence, and no impediments to [knowing] all objects of knowledge in the naturally undefiled expanse, [the exalted wisdom of irreversible[16] Bodhisattvas] is pure of obstructions of attachments and of impediments.

And:[17]

> Moreover, in brief, for two reasons [those realizations of irreversible Bodhisattva Superiors are very pure relative to the perceptions] of partial exalted wisdoms that do not realize emptiness or do not engage all objects of knowledge. [With respect to the exalted wisdom of an irreversible Superior,] through the very seeing of the mode of existence [of things] it is [a consciousness] having as its object the naturally pure realm of sentient beings;[18] hence, it is without the attachments of consciousnesses conceiving true existence. Through the very seeing of the varieties [of phenomena] that exist, it is [a consciousness] having as its object the limitless things which are objects of knowledge; hence, it is without impediment **[119a]**.

Also, Dzongkaba's *Golden Rosary (gser phreng)* describes attachments as afflictive obstructions and impediments as obstructions to omniscience.

---

[16]Irreversibility *(phyir mi ldog pa)*, a definiteness as to attainment of liberation, is, according to Kensur Yeshey Tupden, attained even as soon as the path of preparation if the person's realization is strong, on the path of seeing if it is weaker.

[17]Gyeltsap, *Commentary on (Maitreya's) "Sublime Continuum of the Mahāyāna,"* 102.2-3. This quotation shows that "impediments" *(thogs pa)* are to be understood as obstructions to omniscience. The bracketed material comes from the context of the passage in Maitreya under discussion, which is cited in the next section of this chapter.

[18]The realm of sentient beings is seen by these Bodhisattvas to be pure because all beings have a "nature of omniscience," that is, a Buddha-nature, the capacity to develop into Buddhas. This is the subject of stanzas 13 and 15 of the first chapter of Maitreya's *Sublime Continuum of the Mahāyāna,* P 5525, vol. 108, 24.3.3-5.

B. Obstructions to Omniscience Are Not Abandoned until after the Afflictions Are Abandoned

Jamyang Shayba:[19] When one has abandoned all afflictions on the eighth [Bodhisattva] ground, one must [then begin to] abandon the obstructions to omniscience but not earlier than that because until the afflictions have been abandoned, there is no way to abandon their predispositions.[20] For example, until one removes the oil in something fouled with oil, one is unable to remove its befoulment. That is because: (1) Candrakīrti's *Autocommentary on the "Entrance"* says:[21]

> Those that are involved in stopping up and infusing the mental continuum are predispositions. "The aftermath of the afflictions," "conditioning of the afflictions," "the root of the afflictions," and "predispositions of the afflictions" are equivalent.
>
> Even though they have abandoned the afflictions by an uncontaminated path, all Hearer and Solitary Realizer [Arhats] are unable to abandon [the obstructions to omniscience]. This is like the fact that because a pot and [a piece of] woolen cloth have contacted [sesame oil and flowers, respectively], even though the sesame oil and flowers, and so forth, have been removed, a subtle quality [of those can be] observed.

(2) The *Questions of King Dhāraṇīśvara Sūtra (gzung rgyal gyis zhus pa, dhāraṇīśvararājaparipṛcchāsūtra)* says:[22]

---

[19]*Great Exposition of Tenets cha* 40b.6.

[20]In general, the antidote for obstructions to omniscience is the same as for obstructions to liberation, but one needs an enhancement of method, the power of compassion. Prāsaṅgikas assert that it is not possible to get rid of any of the obstructions to omniscience until all of the afflictive obstructions have been eliminated, because it is absurd to think that even before ignorance is entirely eradicated it would be possible to overcome the subtle predispositions causing things to appear as if truly existent.

[21]P 5263, vol. 98, 164.1.5-7. The quotation has been lengthened by filling in material indicated by "etc." *(sogs)*, beginning with, "This is like the fact..."

[22]This sūtra is part of the *de bzhin gshegs pa'i snying rje chen po nges par*

> The knowledge of a One Gone Thus *(de bzhin gshegs pa, tathāgatha)* that contamination has been eliminated is pure, stainless, thoroughly pure, luminous, and has thoroughly destroyed every connection to predispositions [of ignorance]. There is a limit to Hearers' elimination of contamination **[41a]**; they have not thoroughly destroyed the predispositions.

and so forth. (3) Also, Maitreya's *Sublime Continuum of the Mahāyāna* (I.17cd-18) says:[23]

> Because there are no attachments and no impediments in the stainless expanse,
> [The exalted wisdom of Bodhisattvas] is pure.
> Because their pure vision of exalted wisdom
> [Approximates the] Buddhas' unexcelled exalted wisdom,
> The irreversible Superiors [of the eighth ground and above]
> Are refuges for all beings.

(4) Concerning that, Asaṅga's *Commentary on (Maitreya's) "Sublime Continuum"* says:[24]

---

bstan pa (tathāgatamahākaruṇā-nirdeśa), P 814, vol. 32, 300.5.4 ff.

[23]P 5525, vol. 108, 24.3.6-7. The quotation has been lengthened by adding the last line, "Are refuges for all beings." Thus lengthened, it comprises the last two lines of the seventeenth stanza and all of the eighteenth stanza. The first two lines of the seventeenth stanza read: "Thus what is realized / Is seen with their distinct [exalted wisdom] consciousness."

I have taken the exalted wisdom consciousnesses of Superiors to be the antecedent of "pure" because the stanza suggests it and because Asaṅga's commentary says that the awareness that realizes the supramundane path is the Superiors' supramundane wisdom that is distinct in the sense of being unshared with others. The quotation seems to suggest that the exalted wisdom of Bodhisattvas is free both of attachments and of obstructions to omniscience. However, if that were the case, there would be no difference between Buddhas and Bodhisattvas. Rather, according to Ngawang Belden's comment following this series of quotations, it means only that these Bodhisattvas have overcome at least *some* of the obstructions to omniscience.

The Sanskrit has been edited by E. H. Johnston, *Ratnagotravibhāga-Mahāyānottaratantraśāstra*, 16.2, 16.9-10: *tacchuddhiramale dhātāvasaṇgāpratighā tataḥ* (17) / *jñānadarśanaśuddhyā buddhajñānādanuttarāt avaivartyādbhavantyāryāḥ śaraṇaṃ sarvadehinām* (18). English translation by Obermiller (141).

[24]P 5526, vol. 108, 35.5.4-5. Bracketed material has been taken from Gyeltsap's commentary.

> In brief, for two reasons the one [the exalted wisdom of an irreversible Superior in meditative equipoise on emptiness] is called very pure relative to the vision of a partial exalted wisdom consciousness [of a Superior not in meditative equipoise on emptiness or who has not attained the ground of irreversibility]. For which two [reasons]? Because it is without attachments and because it is without [some] impediments.

And:[25]

> In that way, the vision of exalted wisdom of such Bodhisattvas who abide on the grounds of irreversibility [i.e., the eighth ground and above] comes into proximity with the pure vision of the exalted wisdom of the Unexcelled Ones, the Ones Gone Thus.

The bottom limit of an exalted wisdom that releases one from any of the impedimentary obstructions [i.e., the obstructions to omniscience] is posited from the ground of irreversibility, the eighth [Bodhisattva] ground.[26] In consideration of many such meanings, Dzongkaba's *Illumination of the Thought, Explanation of (Candrakīrti's) "Entrance"* says:[27]

> ...because obstructions that are predispositions and that are different from those seeds [producing the afflictions] are posited as obstructions to omniscience, one does not [begin to] abandon them until one attains the eighth [Bodhisattva] ground.

Here there is much to be elaborated, but it should be known from other [texts].

---

[25]P 5526, vol. 108, 35.5-7-8. The quotation has been lengthened by completing the sentence, beginning with "...comes into proximity..."

[26]In an earlier note I cited Kensur Yeshey Tupden as saying that irreversibility—a definiteness with regard to liberation—could be obtained as early as the path of preparation. However, it appears that one does not attain the *ground* of irreversibility until the eighth Bodhisattva ground, when a Bodhisattva actually has become liberated.

[27]*Illumination of the Thought* 25b.1-2. Bracketed material comes from Dzongkaba's previous sentence. Also translated by Hopkins (1980: 147).

11 Avoiding the Two Extremes

Jamyang Shayba:[1] The root text says:

The extreme of [inherent] existence is avoided through appearance, and the extreme of [utter] non-existence is avoided through emptiness.[2]
For many unique [tenets] such as these, look in [the texts of the] Mādhyamika School.[3]

---

[1]*Great Exposition of Tenets cha* 41a.4.

[2]This is based on Dzongkaba's statement in his *Three Principal Aspects of the Path* (cited in Tenzin Gyatso, Dalai Lama IV [1984: 153], translated by Hopkins): "Further, the extreme of [inherent] existence is excluded [by knowledge of the nature] of appearances [existing only as nominal designations] / And the extreme of [total] non-existence is excluded [by knowledge of the nature] of emptiness [as the absence of inherent existence and not the absence of nominal existence]." The Dalai Lama adds (153): "Among all four Buddhist schools of tenets...it is held to be true that the extreme of non-existence—misidentification of what exists as not existing—is cleared away by appearance and the extreme of existence—misidentification of what does not exist as existing—is cleared away by emptiness. However, according to the uncommon view of the Prāsaṅgika-Mādhyamika School, the opposite also holds true: by way of appearance, the extreme of existence is avoided, and by way of emptiness, the extreme of non-existence is avoided. This doctrine derives from the pivotal point that the meaning of dependent-arising is the meaning of emptiness and that the meaning of emptiness is the meaning of dependent-arising."

[3]It is not clear whether by *dbu ma* Jamyang Shayba is referring to the great texts of the Mādhyamika School or his own extensive treatment of several of the unique Prāsaṅgika School tenets in his commentary on Candra-

Earlier, there was a short explanation at the point of [explaining] dependent-arising.[4] The reason for dissimilarity with the lower tenet systems must be known in detail.[5]

Ngawang Belden:[6] Dzongkaba's *Three Principal Aspects of the Path (lam gyi gtso bo rnam gsum*, stanza 13), says:[7]

> When [the two realizations of dependent-arising and emptiness exist] simultaneously without alternation
> And when from only seeing dependent-arising as infallible,
> Definite knowledge entirely destroys the mode of apprehension [of the conception of inherent existence],
> Then the analysis of the view [of reality] is complete.

For persons who have completed analysis of the view as in this passage, the extent to which they apply their minds to the meaning of dependent-arisings which are [understood to be] posited by names and terms decreases [to that extent] the force of the awareness conceiving inherent existence. This is the way the extreme of [inherent] existence is eliminated through appearance.

---

kīrti's *Entrance* entitled *Great Exposition of the Middle Way*, the title of which could be abbreviated as *dbu ma*. The first seems more likely, since Jamyang Shayba's commentary contains a list of the great texts of the Mādhyamika School. Also, Ngawang Belden takes the referent of *dbu ma* to be the Mādhyamika School texts of Nāgārjuna and Āryadeva and commentaries on them (*Three Commentaries* 512.4). Also, see Annotations 262.4. On the other hand, Losang Gönchok (*Word Commentary* 273.3) interprets *dbu ma* as the *Great Exposition of the Middle Way* and other works by Jamyang Shayba, as did Geshay Tupden Gyatso, a contemporary scholar from Jamyang Shayba's own Gomang College, when I asked him about this in March 1985.

[4]See translation in Hopkins (1983a: 675).

[5]Only the Prāsaṅgika School says that the extreme of conceiving of inherent existence is eliminated through the appearance of dependently-arisen phenomena and the extreme of annihilation through the realization of emptiness. This is also stated by Janggya in *Presentation of Tenets* 451.1-4, translated by Hopkins (1987:332-33, 418).

[6]*Annotations*, note *na*, 119a.1.

[7]P 6087, vol. 153. Thurman (1982) identifies this as Dzongkaba, *Collected Works*, vol. *kha*, 230b.4-31b.5. This translation follows that of Jeffrey Hopkins in Tenzin Gyatso, Dalai Lama XIV (1984: 148). Also translated by Hopkins and Sopa (43) and by Hopkins (1987: 22).

Also, for such persons, the extent to which they apply their minds to the emptiness of inherent existence decreases [to that extent] the force of the awareness that lacks conviction in the cause and effect of actions and conceives those to be non-existent. This is the way the extreme of non-existence [i.e., no conventional existence] is eliminated through emptiness.[8] The *[Questions of the Nāga King Anavatapta] Sūtra (klu rgyal ma dros pa'i zhus pa'i mdo, anavatapta-nāga-rāja-paripṛcchā-sūtra)* says:[9]

> That which is produced from conditions is not produced, [i.e.,]
> It has no inherently existent production.
> That which depends on conditions is explained to be empty.
> Those who understand emptiness are conscientious.

Āryadeva's *Four Hundred* (XII.5) says:[10]

---

[8]All Buddhist schools say that the extreme of existence is avoided through realizing selflessness and that the existence of non-existence is avoided through the appearance of conventional phenomena, but the Prāsaṅgikas are asserting that the opposite also is true. It seems that by switching these terms, the Prāsaṅgikas are emphasizing the compatibility of emptiness and dependent-arising. The observation of dependent-arisings is a sign of their lack of inherent existence, and the realization of emptiness makes possible one's understanding of conventionalities *as* conventionalities. Similarly, Dzongkaba says in the beginning of the sixth chapter of his *Illumination of the Thought* that understanding that phenomena are merely imputed by thought assists one in understanding emptiness, whereas usually it is said that until one has realized emptiness one is unable to understand conventionalities as mere conventionalities, imputed by thought.

[9]P 823, vol. 33. This sūtra is a development of the *Great Wisdom Perfection Sūtra (mahā-prajñāpāramitā-sūtra)*, according to Nakamura (1987: 165). This passage is cited in Dzongkaba's *Middling Exposition of Special Insight*, translated by Thurman (1982: 143). It is also cited in *Clear Words* 504.1 (Poussin ed.), and in Dzongkaba's *Great Exposition of Special Insight* (Dharamsala ed. 410a.5-6), along with an explanation. The point of the quotation seems to be that understanding emptiness assists one in understanding conventional appearances, thus avoiding the extreme of annihilation.

[10]P 5246, vol. 95, 139.1.4. This translation depends on Hopkins in Tenzin Gyatso, Dalai Lama XIV (1975: 83). Cf. Sonam 241 (stanza 241).

Whoever has generated doubt
Toward what is not obvious in Buddha's word
Will believe that only Buddha [is omniscient]
Based on [his profound teaching of] emptiness.

Also, the Foremost Great Being [Dzongkaba, in his *In Praise of Dependent-Arising (rten 'brel bstod pa)*] says:[11]

From [the concordance of appearances and emptiness] one
can well understand
[Nāgārjuna's] statement that there are no disputants
Who could factually oppose what you taught
Or find any possibility for censure in the Teaching.[12]
Why? This explanation
Puts far away the possibility
Of exaggerating or discrediting
Things seen and unseen.

It is greatly renowned nowadays that even though the mere assertion that the extreme of [inherent] existence is eliminated by appearance and the extreme of no [conventional] existence is eliminated by emptiness is not unique, the [Prāsaṅgika] *mode* of elimination is unique. However, I think that whether or not such an explanation exists in the texts of the Svātantrikas and below should be examined.[13]

Jamyang Shayba:[14] Moreover, the distinctive [presentation] of the absorption of cessation *('gog pa'i snyoms 'jug, nirodha-samāpatti)*,[15] the mode of generating the profound

---

[11]P 6016, vol. 153. It is translated in Geshe Wangyal (1973: 180-81); earlier, Jamyang Shayba cites a similar passage from Aśvaghoṣa (Hopkins 1983a: 586-87).

[12]Translation uncertain.

[13]Ngawang Belden doubts the prevailing Gelukba opinion that even proponents of the lower schools say that the extreme of existence is eliminated by the appearance of dependent-arisings and the extreme of annihilation through the realization of emptiness.

[14]*Great Exposition of Tenets cha* 41a.5.

[15]The absorption of cessation is a state of meditative equipoise that is the absence of the manifest activity of the six consciousnesses. It is a state achieved only by Superiors (see Hopkins [1983a: 207, 269]). Elsewhere,

view, and so forth,[16] should be known from the texts of the Father, the Superior (Nāgārjuna), and his spiritual son (Āryadeva), the two *Compendiums* [Nāgārjuna's *Compendium of Sūtra (mdo kun las btus pa, sūtrasamuccaya)* and Śāntideva's *Compendium of Learnings (bslab pa kun las btus pa'i tshig le'ur byas pa, śikṣāsamuccayakārikā)*], the two *Explanations* [Dzongkaba's *Illumination of the Thought, Explanation of (Candrakīrti's) "Supplement"* and his *Ocean of Reasoning, Explanation of (Nāgārjuna's) "Treatise on the Middle Way"*], Dzongkaba's [*Great, Middling,* and *Small*] *Exposition of the Stages of the Path,* and so forth.

Jamyang Shayba explains that it is the unique Prāsaṅgika assertion that one can realize emptiness even within the absorption of cessation (according to Losang Gönchok, *Word Commentary* 272.5). For a discussion on some problems involved with the concept, see Griffiths 1986.

[16]Regarding the "unique tenets" not listed, Ngawang Belden says they include unique Prāsaṅgika assertions on the absorption of cessation, the mode of generating the profound view (of emptiness), the basis of infusion of predispositions, the way to posit the illustration of the person, and so forth (*Three Commentaries* 512.2). Losang Gönchok explains that the other unique tenets are (1) one realizes even in the absorption of cessation that objects are not established from their own side; (2) an inferential consciousness realizing suchness is generated in dependence on a mere contradictory consequence (without the need for an autonomous syllogism to be stated); and (3) although inference meets back to direct perception, it is sufficient that the experience of that direct perception be incontrovertible—it need not be non-mistaken (i.e., it is not invalidated by the fact that objects appear to it to be inherently existent), etc. (*Word Commentary* 272.5-73.3).

Part Three

Janggya's "Unique Tenets of the Prāsaṅgika-Mādhyamika School"

from Janggya Rolbay Dorjay's *Clear Exposition of the Presentation of Tenets, Beautiful Ornament for the Meru of the Subduer's Teaching*

Translator's Introduction

During his twenties, while he oversaw the translation of the Indian treatise portion of the Tibetan canon into Mongolian, Janggya also composed his best-known work, the *Clear Exposition of the Presentation of Tenets*. He may have begun the project because of his interest in the doctrines of the Cittamātra School current in China, since he wrote that chapter first; but like Jamyang Shayba's *Great Exposition of Tenets*, his encyclopedic work discusses the prominent non-Buddhist systems of India as well as the major Buddhist tenet systems. Janggya's presentation is more straightforward than Jamyang Shayba's, without the latter's terseness, polemics, and copious citation of Indian sources. Janggya presents the tenet systems through a careful reading of the works of Dzongkaba, whom he clearly regards as having already done the fine analysis necessary to establish the supremacy of the Prāsaṅgika view.

A small group of American scholars has recently translated various portions of the *Clear Exposition of the Presentation of Tenets*. Anne C. Klein has published a translation of the "Sautrāntika School" chapter;[17] Donald S. Lopez has published a translation of the "Introduction to Mādhyamika" and "Svātantrika-Mādhyamika School" chapters;[18] Jeffrey Hopkins has published a translation of the first part of the "Prāsaṅgika

---

[17]In *Knowing, Naming, and Negation* (1991).

[18]In *A Study of Svātantrika* (1987).

School" chapter[19] (on the history of the school and the reasonings used in meditation on emptiness); and Guy Newland has translated the section on the two truths in the "Prāsaṅgika School" chapter.[20]

Two editions of the *Clear Exposition of the Presentation of Tenets* have been used for this translation.[21] The principal edition, chosen mainly for its legibility and availability, is the 1970 type-set edition published in Sarnath, India, by the Pleasure of Elegant Sayings Press *(legs bshad gter mdzod khang)*. Bracketed numbers found in the text of the translation are the page numbers of this edition. It has been compared to the xylograph edition edited by Lokesh Chandra and photoreproduced by Sharada Rani in 1977. Differences between the two editions (consisting mainly of minor printer's errors in the Pleasure of Elegant Sayings Printing Press edition) have been noted in the "emendations" section following the translation.

[19]In *Emptiness Yoga* (1987). The bulk of the book is his own commentary on Janggya's text, but it includes a running translation.

[20]Unpublished ms.

[21]I have not seen an edition that Mimaki (1982: xlvii) identifies as no. 82-85 in the Catalogue of the University of Tokyo, labeled "Ser byas," i.e., Jey College of Sera Monastery, n.d. Mimaki has compiled a concordance to these three editions (1982: 268-72). I have also heard about but have not seen an edition published by *gam bcar phan bde legs bshad gling grva tshang dang rgyud rnying slar gso tshogs pa* in the royal year 2109.

Janggya's Introduction

The explanation of the unique tenets of the Prāsaṅgika-Mādhyamika School has two parts: a brief explanation and an explanation of the eight chief distinguishing features **[472]**.

A. Brief Explanation of the Unique Tenets

The chief of the unique ways in which the Prāsaṅgika-Mādhyamika School comments on the thought of sūtra and of the Superior [Nāgārjuna] are these two:[1] (1) there is not even a mere speck of inherent establishment *(rang gyi mtshan nyid gyis grub pa, svalakṣaṇa-siddhi)*, and (2) it is permissible to posit all actions, agents, and objects as mere nominal imputations *(ming gis btags tsam)* without losing [even] a tiny piece [of a valid presentation of conventional phenomena].

In dependence on that, among the many pure tenets unshared with other commentators, the chief are renowned to our [Gelukba] scholars as explained by condensing them into eight difficult topics. [Inclusion into eight] appears to depend upon the statement by the Foremost Omniscient [Dzongkaba]

---

[1]According to Kensur Yeshey Tupden, these have been taken from Śāntideva's *Engaging in the Bodhisattva Deeds*, but such a statement is common in Gelukba literature on the Prāsaṅgika School.

in his *Illumination of the Thought, Explanation of Candrakīrti's "Entrance"*:[2]

> There are many pure tenets unshared with other commentators. What are they? Now, if the chief are expressed, they are:
>
> 1 The unique way of refuting a mind-basis-of-all that is a different entity from the six collections [of consciousness].
> 2 The unique way of refuting self-consciousness.
> 3 The unique way of not asserting that [it is feasible] to generate [realization of] suchness *(de bzhin nyid, tathatā)* just as it is in the continuum of another party by means of an autonomous syllogism.
> 4 The unique way of positing the need to assert external objects just as consciousnesses are asserted.
> 5 The unique way of positing that Hearers and Solitary Realizers realize that things do not have their own nature.
> 6 The unique way of positing the consciousness conceiving a self of phenomena *(chos kyi bdag, dharmātman)* as an affliction.
> 7 The unique way of positing disintegratedness as a [functioning] thing.
> 8 The unique way of positing that by reason of [disintegratedness being a functioning thing] the [Prāsaṅgika] way of positing the three times, and so forth.

From within "and so forth" there are also many features from the topics of the path and fruit that could be adduced.[3]

---

[2]*Illumination of the Thought* 124b.2-5.

[3]The basic division of the Prāsaṅgika chapter is into topics concerning bases, paths, and fruits. Janggya is indicating that this list of topics is being gleaned just from the "bases" section, and not from the path and fruit sections, which come immediately after the portion of the book translated herein. In fact, the fifth topic could be a "path" topic, and Dzongkaba, in another list (from his short text on the eight difficult points) adds a "fruit" topic concerning the qualities of a Buddha.

Objection: Refutation of a mind-basis-of-all[4] that is a different entity from the six collections [of consciousness] is not feasible as a unique Prāsaṅgika School tenet because the Sautrāntika-Svātantrika-Mādhyamika School also refutes that, and also affixes the same [negation or affirmation as the Prāsaṅgikas] to other tenets **[473]**. Also, the assertion that disintegratedness is a [functioning] thing cannot be unique because the Vaibhāṣika School also denies that [disintegratedness] is a [functioning] thing.

Response: [You] give a refutation of the literal reading of Dzongkaba's *Illumination of the Thought, Explanation of Candrakīrti's "Entrance."* Even some of our own followers, fearing damage by those reasonings, take up the well-intentioned burden of adding many word-patches to the literal reading of *Illumination of the Thought*. Both mutually indicate clearly the posture of not knowing even just how to read a great text, because the phrases in *Illumination of the Thought*—"unique system of refutation" and "unique way of positing"—are "indicators at the end" [of a list that apply to all members of that list][5] and it appears that [our followers] did not know anything about the purpose for what is excluded and included by those statements. That those with such a disposition take up the burden of explaining, disputing, and composing the major texts manifests a sign of great deterioration of the precious teaching and is only a source of extreme discouragement for the analytical.

Now, here I will briefly express some of the chief from among those unique features. This has three parts: (1) explana-

[4]"Mind-basis-of-all" translates *kun gzhi rnam par shes pa/ālayavijñāna*. I usually render *rnam par shes pa / vijñāna* as "consciousness," but in this phrase it will be translated as "mind" for the sake of brevity. According to Gelukbas the mind-basis-of-all is asserted by only the Cittamātra School.

[5]*Gsal bar byed pa*, an "illuminator" or "indicator" placed at the end of a list which is intended to apply equally to all members of that list. In Dzongkaba's list of eight chief difficult topics, "unique system of refutation" *('gog lugs thun mong ma yin pa)* appeared only after the statement of the second topic, but referred both to it and to the first topic; and "unique way of positing" *('jog tshul thun mong ma yin pa)* appeared only after the eighth topic but applied to all of the last six topics.

tion of the eight chief distinguishing features; (2) the way to refute inherent existence; and (3) in dependence on that, the way to differentiate definitive sūtras and those requiring interpretation.

Section A: Explanation of the Eight Chief Distinguishing Features of Prāsaṅgika-Mādhyamika

1 The Unique Way of Refuting a Mind-Basis-of-All

In a system that does not assert inherent existence, there is no assertion of a mind-basis-of-all, non-wastage *(chud mi za ba, avipraṇāśa)*, acquisition *(thob pa, prāpti)*, and so forth, but there is no need to assert those because [Prāsaṅgikas] are able to posit a presentation of actions and effects [without them].[1]

Question: How are you able to posit [actions and effects]?

Answer: Even without asserting a mind-basis-of-all, it is feasible to posit the arising of effects from an action *(las, karman)* that has been collected[2] and has ceased, because the cessation of actions is not inherently established **[474]**. There is a way in which that ["not inherently ceased"] serves as a reason for [the arising of effects from actions that have been collected and that have ceased] because the reason, "because it has not inherently ceased," establishes that later effects arise from an action's having disintegrated.[3]

The arising of effects from an action's non-inherently existent disintegratedness also has neither the fallacies of its fruition occurring endlessly nor of its fruition occurring in a

[1]These are theories set forth by various other schools. See note 2 of the Jamyang Shayba translation, chapter 6.

[2]That an action has been collected means that a seed for a future experience of pleasure or suffering has been established.

[3]This is the basic theory of *karman*, i.e., that effects of actions can arise even eons after their cessation. That is because the disintegratedness of an action—its cessation upon completion—is not inherently established.

confused fashion.[4] That is because just as it is definite that falling hairs appear to someone with cataracts whereas the horns of a donkey[5] do not appear, even though [the horns of a donkey and falling hairs] are the same in being non-existent, just so it is feasible to posit effects that do not arise from [actions] that have already fructified and to posit effects of virtuous and non-virtuous actions that are definite to be discrete, even though they are not inherently existent.

This does not contradict [Buddha's] statements in the *Descent to Laṅkā Sūtra*, the *Sūtra Unraveling the Thought*, and the *Mahāyāna Abhidharma Sūtra*, that the mind-basis-of-all exists, because he said such in terms of an intention to lead trainees who are temporarily not suitable vessels for the teaching of the profound reality [of emptiness] gradually to that profound doctrine. That was [Buddha's] purpose, and the basis of his thought was emptiness, [a phenomenon's] absence of establishment by its own nature.[6]

The damage to the literal teaching from *reasoning* is that if a mind-basis-of-all were asserted it would have to be asserted that [all phenomena] are exhausted as mere appearances as forms, sounds, and so forth, from the fruition of the predispositions in the mind-basis-of-all, and that there are no external objects.[7] However, that is not feasible because it is estab-

---

[4]If the disintegratedness inherently existed, it would be permanent and therefore would not cease upon issuing forth its effect; thus, its fruition could occur endlessly. Secondly, there is no reason why the effects of actions could not occur in an appropriate way, with virtuous actions leading to happy fruitions and non-virtuous actions leading to suffering, even though there is no inherently existent disintegratedness of an action to produce them.

[5]According to Kensur Yeshe Thupten (2/12/82), *bong bu'i rva* ("horns of a donkey") is equivalent to *ri bong rva* ("horns of a rabbit"). This is a famous example of something non-existent, since rabbits do not have horns (postcards from Wyoming of apocryphal "jackalopes" notwithstanding).

[6]The idea is that the Buddha taught the mind-basis-of-all provisionally, for the benefit of those who could be helped by believing in its existence but who would be harmed by hearing the teachings about emptiness. In his own mind, the basis of his teaching was emptiness.

[7]This is because the purpose of positing a mind-basis-of-all is supposed to be to provide a basis for experience without positing external objects.

lished by reasoning that the two, objects and consciousnesses, equally do not ultimately exist and equally conventionally exist, and so forth. [The damage to the literal teaching] from *scripture* is that the teacher himself indicates his thought explaining a mind-basis-of-all [in the *Descent to Laṅkā Sūtra* itself].

Question: In this system, what is asserted as the basis or support for establishing the predispositions of virtuous or non-virtuous actions?

Answer: The continual basis of predispositions is the mere I *(nga tsam)* or person, and it is also permissible to posit the mental continuum as the occasional basis of predispositions **[475]**.[8]

In dependence on those [points], what is the way to posit a basis, in the continuum of one on an uninterrupted path *(bar chad med lam, ānantarya-mārga)* of a path of seeing *(mthong lam, darśana-mārga)*,[9] for dormancies [i.e., predispositions], that are to be abandoned by the path of meditation?[10] Does or does not

---

[8]All schools must posit a place for karmic latencies to abide. The beginning of the chapter refers to some of the alternatives of other schools, e.g., "non-wastage." In the Prāsaṅgika School, the basis for the infusion of the latencies is the "mere I," the unanalyzed "I" of ordinary experience. When we refer to ourselves, saying "I," we do so without thinking that "I" is one with or different from the mind and body, etc., and this "mere I" is accepted as the basis of the latencies. Why the mental continuum is only an "occasional" basis is a mystery, since at least a subtle form of the mental consciousness always exists.

[9]The path of seeing is the designation for the initial direct realization of emptiness and the subsequent state of having abandoned the artificial conceptions of inherent existence (derived from parents, teachers, etc.). It has two parts, the exalted wisdom of meditative equipoise *(mnyam bzhag ye she, samahītajñāna)* and the exalted wisdom of subsequent attainment *(rje thob ye shes, pṛṣalabdhajñāna)*. The former has three parts: an uninterrupted path *(bar ched med lam, ānantarya-mārga)*, a path of release *(rnam grol lam, vimukti-mārga)*, and a path which is neither. On the uninterrupted path one is completely absorbed with realization of emptiness; it is said that emptiness and the mind realizing it are fused, like fresh water poured into fresh water.

[10]Kensur Yeshey Tupden (2/12/82) maintained that at that time, a consciousness that could be the basis of such latencies cannot be posited as existing, whereby the person *(gang zag, puruṣa)* must be posited as the basis of the infusion of latencies. Jambel Shenpen (6/9/82) added that although

the Mahāyāna altruistic mind generation exist in that person's continuum?[11] When uncontaminated minds are actualized in the continua of Superiors who have been born in [such a state as] the sphere of limitless space *(nam mkha' mtha yas skye mched, ākāśānantyāyatanam)*,[12] are they still transmigrators of that [level]? When the statements of the Foremost Precious [Buddha] and the texts of the great chariots[13] are arranged, there are limitless subtle points to be analyzed.

---

the Gomang College position is that predispositions *do not exist* at that time, according to Sera Monastery textbook author Jaydzünba, they exist with the mere I *(nga tsam)*. He also says that the Mahāyāna mind-of-enlightenment generation exists then but is *mngon du gyur med* (non-manifest). I have not yet found sources for these positions, but Paṇchen Sönam Drakba, the textbook writer for Drebung Loseling College, says that the mere I is the basis of latencies because the self-isolate *(rang ldog)* of the bodhisattva (i.e., the mere I) is imputedly existent whereas according to Cittamātra the mental consciousness which is the basis-isolate *(gzhi ldog)* is substantially existent and hence would not exist at that time. See his *General Meaning of Mādhyamika (dbu ma'i mtha' dbyod)*, 232.3-4 and 233.2-3.

[11]The question is: if one is absorbed in a non-conceptual realization of emptiness, is it possible to not lose one's mind of compassion?

[12]This is one of the formless absorptions *(gzugs med kyi snyoms 'jug, ārūpyasamāpatti)*, a meditative state and also a place of rebirth for those who have attained it. According to Jambel Shenpen (6/9/82), Paṇchen Sönam Drakba, textbook author for Loseling College, says that you are no longer of that level, whereas Sera's Jaydzünba says that you still are. I have not searched the texts.

[13]Nāgārjuna and Asaṅga are called chariots or "openers of the chariot-way" for having respectively opened up the Mādhyamika and Cittamātra "chariot-ways." Buddha found the path, but they prepared, through their teachings, a broad, smooth way to travel on it.

2 The Unique Way of Refuting Self-Consciousness

This section has two parts: the actual explanation and a presentation of valid cognition.

A. Explanation of Self-Consciousness

The way of asserting self-consciousness by our opponents is like [my previous] explanation in the chapter on the Cittamātra School.[14] In our system that refutes it, it is not feasible to establish self-consciousness by the sign, memory. If later memory is set as the sign within the context of being established by its own nature, that sign is not a proof, just as when one [posits] "object of apprehension by an eye [consciousness" as the sign] in the proof of sound as an impermanent phenomenon.[15] Even if [later memory is set as the sign]

---

[14]*Presentation of Tenets* 225.5-30.18.

[15]If the proof of sound as an impermanent phenomenon used as its sign (reason) "object of apprehension by an eye consciousness," it would be stated: "The subject, sound, is an impermanent phenomenon because of being an object of apprehension by an eye consciousness." Of course, such a "proof" would have no correlation of the subject and the reason, no "presence of the reason in the subject" *(phyogs chos, pakṣa-dharma)*, because sound is not an object of apprehension by an eye consciousness. The correlation of the subject and the reason is one of the three modes *(tshul gsum)* of a cor-

within the context of worldly conventions, it is not correct, because there is no memory that is a fruit of a self-consciousness. This is because when [it is established that] self-consciousness does not exist, a memory that is an effect of that is not established. Without a relation, no probandum is proved. It would be like inferring a water-crystal jewel from mere water and a fire-crystal jewel from mere fire.[16]

Objection: One infers the existence of the experience of the former consciousness in dependence on memory; self-consciousness is not proved by way of establishing self-consciousness and memory as cause and effect.[17] With respect to [the experience of a consciousness], it is limited to two [types], self-experience *(rang myong)* and other-experience *(gzhan myong)*, and since other-experience is refuted, self-experience is established.

Response: That is wrong, because a mind's knowledge of objects is not limited to the two, self-experience and other-experience, as they are posited by the Sautrāntikas and Cittamātrins **[476]**.[18]

---

rect sign *(rtags yang dag, samyakliṅga)*. Only a sign possessing all three modes, including this, serves as a proof. Similarly, there would be no correlation of subject and reason in a "proof" of the form "the subject, self-consciousness, exists because inherently other later memory [of an awareness] exists." That is, a later memory does not depend on self-consciousness. This example is used by Dzongkaba in *Illumination of the Thought* 158a.2-3.

[16]These are crystals that are believed to produce fire and water. The mere existence of water does not entail the existence of a water-crystal, nor the existence of fire a fire-crystal, since many other causes for water or fire exist. Just so, the mere existence of memory does not entail the existence of self-consciousness, since there are other ways of accounting for memory.

[17]For euphonic reasons, Janggya actually reads: "...memory and self-consciousness as cause and effect." I have reversed the order of "memory" and "self-consciousness" so that it would not be thought that memory is the cause and self-consciousness the effect, when what is under discussion is the reverse.

[18]According to Kensur Yeshey Tupden (2/19/82), by "other-experience" they mean that a consciousness that is a different substantial entity from the original awareness apprehends it, and by "self-experience" they mean self-consciousness, which is one substantial entity with that awareness. Both are untenable, the first because in their systems they assume the inherent existence of phenomena, which Prāsaṅgikas reject; the second because self-

These are reasonings that refute the proofs *(sgrub byed, sādhana)* [of self-consciousness by the signs of memory and self-experience], and the reasonings that refute the probandum *(bsgrub bya)*, that is, self-consciousness, are as follows.[19]

"An isolated phenomenon that has the aspect of an apprehender" *('dzin rnam yan gar ba)* is not feasible [as a definition of a self-consciousness] because (1) no matter how much one aims the mind, there is no appearance of [the mind] itself as the known and itself as the knower[20] and because (2) there is the fallacy that it would [absurdly] follow that if something's functioning naturally operated on itself, the three—action, agent, and object—would be one.[21] Also, it would [absurdly] follow that fire would burn itself, and so forth.

In our own system, even though self-consciousness does not exist, the generation of memory is feasible because (1) the two, the previous consciousness that saw blue and the later consciousness that remembers the eye consciousness apprehending blue, are not diverse [in terms of] inherent establishment,[22] and because (2) since my eye consciousness apprehending blue sees blue it can also be posited as *my* seeing blue, and because (3) just that blue that is previously seen by an eye consciousness apprehending blue is also distinguished by the later memory consciousness, whereby the experiencer and the

---

consciousness is rejected.

[19]The probandum is that which is to be proved, i.e., "self-consciousness exists." Previously, Janggya has just been concerned with showing (1) that there is no memory that is an effect of self-consciousness and that there is no inherently established memory; and (2) that "self-experience" means an awareness that is one substantial entity with an awareness, and therefore not possible. He has not yet actually dealt with the notion of self-consciousness itself.

[20]There is no directly perceiving valid cognition that can certify the existence of self-consciousness; therefore it will have to be logically inferred, if it exists at all.

[21]If consciousness operated on itself, there could be no distinction of agent, action, and object. This is supposed to imply absurdities such as that fire would burn itself as it burned something else.

[22]That is, they are not inherently different. If they were inherently different, there could be no way that one could perceive the other. This is a precondition for the other two reasons.

rememberer have the same object.[23] This reasoning can be found in the root text and autocommentary [of Candrakīrti's *Entrance to the Middle Way*].

Even though self-consciousnesses do not exist, the generation of memory [of a consciousness] is feasible because when a consciousness remembering blue is generated, what is seen previously is not remembered by way of dispensing with the previous eye consciousness, but rather blue and the eye consciousness apprehending blue are relatedly remembered [as in thinking], "Earlier I saw blue."

For instance, when [a bear's] body is bitten by a rodent in the wintertime, he experiences a bite but is not mindful of having been poisoned. However, later, when [the bear] hears the sound of thunder, it is not contradictory that a memory is generated, "Before, at the time of being bitten, poison entered in." These are reasons explained in [the ninth chapter of] Śāntideva's *Engaging in the Bodhisattva Deeds*.[24]

B. The Prāsaṅgika Presentation of Valid Cognition

This system gives the definition of valid cognition *(tshad ma, pramāṇa)* as only, "a consciousness that is incontrovertible

---

[23]Based on *Entrance to the Middle Way* VI.74-5 (7b.8-9). His own commentary is 53a.6-b.7 of *Autocommentary to the "Entrance"*; Dzongkaba's commentary is in *Illumination of the Thought* 158a.2-59a.4.

[24]*Engaging in the Bodhisattva Deeds* 190 (IX.23) explains: "If self-consciousness does not exist, / How would a consciousness be remembered? / Memory [of consciousness] comes about from its relation to experiencing another object / Like [the example of experiencing] a rodent's poison." Śāntideva apparently does not assert that a former consciousness is directly remembered; rather, through remembering the past object, one is able to put together something else that happened at the time. This concludes the section on self-consciousness, though Janggya has more to say about self-consciousness toward the end of the next section. Here, he has set forth arguments from Candrakīrti's *Entrance to the Middle Way* and Śāntideva's *Engaging in the Bodhisattva Deeds*; in the next section he will set forth arguments from Candrakīrti's *Clear Words* and Kaydrup's *Opening the Eyes of the Fortunate*.

with respect to its own object of the way of apprehension *('dzin stangs kyi yul)*. It is not necessary to affix the qualification of its being *newly* incontrovertible.

The etymology [of *pramāṇa*] is asserted to be: comprehended *(māna)* thoroughly or well *(pra)* **[477]**.

The divisions [of valid cognition] are explained in Candrakīrti's *Clear Words* as four: the two, direct perception and inferential cognition, as well as valid cognition of belief and valid cognition of comprehension through an example.[25] Nevertheless, it is not that [valid cognition] is not limited in number to two, direct perception and inferential cognition, because the latter two [types of] valid cognition [those of belief and those of comprehension through an example] are included within inferential cognition and also because [valid cognition] is explained as two in Āryadeva's *Four Hundred (bzhi brgya pa, catuḥśataka)*.

The enumeration of [types of] valid cognition is posited through the force of objects of comprehension *(gzhal bya, prameya)* because there are the three: manifest, hidden, and

---

[25]Jamyang Shayba (*Great Exposition of the Middle Way* 803.6-804.1) explains that "valid cognition through belief" is equivalent to "scriptural valid cognition" *(lung gi tshad ma)* and "valid scripture" *(lung tshad ma)* is equivalent to "scripture free from the three analyses" *(dpyad gsum gyis dag pa'i lung)*. Valid cognition through belief is an "inferential cognition that is incontrovertible with respect to the very hidden phenomenon that is its object of the way of apprehension." In other words, when the subject matter is a "very hidden phenomenon"—one that cannot be established through direct perception or by reasoning that does not depend on scripture, such as the subtle workings of karma and effect—one must rely on scripture that is not contradicted by direct perception, by reasoning, or by other scriptures. The scripture serves as one's reason. For instance, with regard to the scripture "From giving, resources; from ethics, a happy [migration]," one could reason, "it follows that good resources come from past giving, because such is stated in scripture." Valid cognition of comprehension through an example is nothing other than inference in which an example is used in the sign, e.g., "the [domesticated] ox *(ba lang)* has horns because of being like the wild ox *(ba men)*." (See *Great Exposition of the Middle Way* 804.5 ff.) As Janggya says, this division of valid cognition into four types is merely a terminological division, one that accounts for different expressions that people use; valid cognition can be condensed into two types, direct perception and inference, with valid cognition through belief and valid cognition of comprehension through an example being included in inference.

very hidden objects of comprehension.[26] Objects of comprehension [of valid cognition of] comprehension through an example are hidden phenomena with mutually similar attributes.[27] The entity [or definition] of direct valid cognition is:

> that which (1) is valid cognition and (2), without depending on a sign, is incontrovertible with respect to the directly perceived object of comprehension that is its object of the mode of apprehension.

Since [this system] does not assert self-knowing direct perception, there are [just] the two, valid cognition that depends on a physical sense power [as its] empowering condition *(bdag rkyen, adhipatipratyaya)* and valid cognition that depends upon a mental sense power [as its] empowering condition.[28]

With respect to mental direct perception, there are two [types]: that which does not depend on a union of calm abiding *(zhi gnas, śamatha)* and special insight *(lhag mthong, vipaśyanā)* and that which does depend on it. The former is mental direct perception and the latter is yogic direct perception *(rnal 'byor mngon sum, yogi-pratyakṣa)*. Although in general, yogic

---

[26]Manifest objects are those that can be comprehended through ordinary sense perception; the hidden are those that are accessible to reasoning without having to rely on scripture; and the very hidden are those that can be realized only by the power of belief in scripture. See Lati Rinbochay and Napper (78-79).

[27]Because it is inference, its object is a hidden or very hidden phenomenon; since it is not a case of inference through belief, its object is merely hidden, i.e., not obvious to the senses but accessible to reasoning (without requiring recourse to scriptural authority). It realizes something in dependence upon seeing the similar attributes of two things; e.g., even if one has never seen a *ba-men* (a wild ox), one can understand what it is like if someone says that it is basically like a domesticated ox, but different in minor ways—smaller or larger, shaggier or less shaggy, with longer or shorter horns, etc.

[28]Sense direct perception depends on physical sense powers—the eye, ear, nose, etc., sense powers—whereas mental direct perception depends on a mental sense power. A mental sense power is not the brain or anything like that, but merely a moment of any consciousness that causes the mental direct perception to be an entity of experience.

direct perception is indeed mental direct perception, at the time of distinguishing direct perception into three [types—sense, mental, and yogic—] those two are mutually exclusive.

The object of the way of apprehension for yogic direct perception is either the [sixteen] attributes of the four noble truths or a subtle or coarse selflessness. Svātantrika-Mādhyamikas and below assert that yogic direct perception is necessarily a Superior's exalted wisdom *(ye shes, jñāna)*.[29] However, in this system it is asserted that even before realizing subtle selflessness there is yogic direct perception that realizes the sixteen aspects—impermanence, and so forth—of the four noble truths as well as the coarse selflessness of the person, and so forth; therefore, there is yogic direct perception even in the continua of ordinary beings [on the paths of accumulation and preparation].[30]

[This system's presentation of] mental direct perception is also different from other [systems] **[478]**. [Mental direct perception] is not necessarily a non-conceptual consciousness that clearly realizes its object. Hence, even a memory consciousness or subsequent cognition induced by inferential cognition is [mental] direct valid cognition. Mental direct perception that experiences the feelings of bliss, misery, and so forth, accompanying a mental consciousness is not the same as self-consciousness. That is because it is asserted that a [consciousness that] looks inward does not necessarily have a vanishing of dualistic appearance, but rather it is asserted that to that awareness the experienced and experiencer appear to be just different.[31]

A manifest object of comprehension is a phenomenon that is necessarily an object of realization by the power of experience [of an ordinary being][32] without dependence on a sign. A

---

[29]In other words, they assert that it necessarily occurs only upon attaining a path of seeing.

[30]This topic is discussed by Jamyang Shayba and Ngawang Belden; see chapter 4 of translation.

[31]Whereas to a self-consciousness, they appear to be the same; or perhaps better, to a self-consciousness there is no appearance of difference.

[32]Buddhas are omniscient and therefore can realize objects without their own experience, since they know the experience of others.

hidden phenomenon is a phenomenon that is necessarily [initially][33] realized in dependence on a sign. The entity [or definition] of inferential valid cognition is:

> a consciousness that, explicitly in dependence on a sign, is incontrovertible with respect to the hidden object of comprehension that is its object of the way of apprehension.[34]

Also, with respect to [inferential valid cognition] there are three [types]:[35] inferential cognition by the power of the fact *(dngos stobs rjes dpag)*, inferential cognition of belief *(yid ches rjes dpag)*, and inferential cognition of comprehension through an example *(dpe nyer 'jal gyi rjes dpag)*.[36] [This system] also asserts the conventions of the two, inferential cognition that depends on only a consequence and inferential cognition that depends on a reason that has the three modes. With respect to [inferential cognition of] comprehension through an example, even though someone else does not state [to one] either a reason that has the three modes or a consequence, one comprehends [a thesis] in dependence on a logical mark; therefore, it is permissible to posit [this cognition] as depending on a sign.[37]

This system's way of certifying direct valid cognition apprehending blue is: an eye consciousness apprehending blue perceives the realized [blue] and realizer [itself] as different by the force of the dawning of the blue aspect from

---

[33]Something that is generally hidden, such as emptiness, can be directly realized; hence it is not always necessarily realized in dependence on a sign, even though it could only be realized *initially* in dependence on a sign.

[34]Kensur Yeshey Tupden (2/19/82) felt that this statement needed qualification because according to the Prāsaṅgikas, a consequence *(prāsaṅga)* is sufficient to cause another to make an inference—one does not need to state a syllogism.

[35]The Sanskrit equivalents are possible reconstructions.

[36]According to Kensur Yeshey Tupden (2/19/82), this is a variety of inferential cognition through the power of the fact; it is just an instance of the latter that involves an example in the sign.

[37]According to Kensur Yeshey Tupden (2/19/82), one does depend on a reason *(rgyu mtshan)* to realize the point of the example, but it is not stated (i.e., is just implicit).

outside to itself, and, due to its perceiving thus, the eye consciousness apprehending blue becomes [an instance of] valid cognition with respect to its own entity;[38] therefore, [valid cognition] does not have to be established by self-consciousness as in other systems. This is asserted to be the meaning of Candrakīrti's *Clear Words*: "Mere realization of the aspects of the objects of comprehension establishes the entity of the valid cognition." Since this appears to be very difficult, one must know how to analyze it with fine intelligence **[479]**.

A subsequent remembering consciousness also certifies [a consciousness] because (1) through the power of comprehending blue, without needing the mediation of any other valid cognition, an eye consciousness apprehending blue directly induces a consciousness remembering the apprehension of such and that remembering consciousness itself eliminates the superimpositions of both the non-existence of blue and the non-existence of the eye consciousness apprehending blue, and (2) the remembering consciousness itself validly cognizes the existence of the eye consciousness.[39]

This appears to be the thought also of Kaydrup's *Opening the Eyes of the Fortunate*, and it is a little easier to realize than the former [i.e., Candrakīrti's presentation in his *Clear Words*]. These topics can be known extensively elsewhere.

---

[38]Merely by having an appearance cast to it, an eye consciousness becomes a validly cognizing consciousness with respect to itself.

[39]This would appear to be just as difficult as Candrakīrti's explanation, but Janggya finds it "easier." He is saying that my present memory has been induced by my previous experience without any mediation. That is, my eye consciousness seeing my friend ten years ago is the direct cause of my memory of that friend today. There is no mention of the concept of "disintegratedness" *(zhig pa)* here, but the notion seems to be the same; just as it is not necessary that an intermediary entity be produced in order for an action to cause an effect years later because the mere disintegratedness of the action can cause the effect, so it is not necessary that there be an intermediary entity between the eye consciousness and the later memory, because the disintegratedness of the previous eye consciousness can cause the later memory.

3 The Non-Assertion of Autonomous Reasons

This section consists of the actual [explanation] and the way of asserting other-renowned reasons *(gzhan grags kyi gtan tshigs, parasiddhahetu).*

A. Why Autonomous Reasons Are Not Asserted

Svātantrikas assert that the mere establishment of the three modes of a sign[40] in the proof of non-true [existence] for either of the parties of a dispute is not sufficient; rather, [the three modes] must be established from within an objective way of subsistence *(don gyi sdod lugs).*[41] The meaning of auton

[40]A correct sign (reason) must possess three modes or qualities: the presence of the sign in the subject, the forward entailment, and the reverse entailment. For instance, in the syllogism "The subject, a pot, is impermanent because of being a product," all three modes are established. There is presence of the sign in the subject because the sign, product, is a quality of the subject, a pot. Roughly speaking, there is forward entailment because whatever is a product is necessarily impermanent; there is reverse entailment because whatever is not impermanent is necessarily not a product.

[41]That is, the subject, predicate, and reason (e.g., pot, impermanence, and being a product in the syllogism "The subject, a pot, is impermanent because of being a product") must be inherently existent and inherently related. In the Gelukba presentation of the Svātantrika School, Svātantrikas are held to propound that conventionally, objects inherently exist; i.e.,

omy *(rang rgyud, svatantra)* is asserted as: the generation of inferential cognition realizing the probandum *(bsgrub bya)* within the [context of the three modes] being established in that manner.[42] The reason for that is that in their system any non-conceptual or conceptual valid cognition must definitely be non-mistaken with respect to the inherent nature *(rang bzhin, svabhāva)* of the appearing object or referent object [respectively] with respect to which it is a valid cognition, because, if [a consciousness] is mistaken with respect to that, it cannot be posited that an object of comprehension is found by valid cognition. Furthermore, this meets back to the fact that they cannot posit a phenomenon as existent if conventionally it does not have its own nature that is not an imputedly existent nominality.[43]

Therefore, they think that if the bases [that is, the subjects] on which depend the predicates about which the two parties debate—permanence, impermanence, true existence, non-true existence, etc.—do not exist within being established as commonly appearing and as demonstrably established objectively, they are not able to prove the modes of the sign in terms of such [a subject] because it is not feasible that there be a predicate of a non-existent substratum. That is the meaning of a commonly appearing subject **[480]**.[44]

---

objects *do* exist the way they appear to non-defective sense consciousnesses. Prāsaṅgikas reject this, saying that even conventionally, nothing inherently exists. As will be seen later, Svātantrikas do not want to have to say that all sense consciousnesses, to which things appear to be inherently existent, are mistaken, for then how could objects be validly posited? Prāsaṅgikas take the plunge of asserting that even though sense consciousnesses are mistaken, they can validly posit objects (though not as existing the way they appear).

[42]The probandum is that which is to be proved, i.e., the thesis. To again use the "pot" syllogism, the probandum is "pot is impermanent."

[43]For them, a phenomenon cannot be a mere imputedly existent nominality, as for the Prāsaṅgikas; it *must* have its own inherent nature *(rang bzhin, svabhāva)*.

[44]For them, the stater and the hearer of a syllogism must agree on the way of existence of the subject of the syllogism. Therefore, the subject must be inherently existent, because objects appear to them and to their hearers alike as if they were inherently existent, and their hearers assent to that

According to this excellent [Prāsaṅgika] system, once such [a subject and sign] are demonstrable, both of those have become objects that exist by way of their own entity, and just that is the meaning of being ultimately established. Therefore, the assertion that there exists the establishment of a commonly appearing subject for both parties in a debate—that is, a way of proving a predicate within taking just that [subject] as the substratum—is very wrong. According to the Mādhyamika who is the first party, this is because existence by way of [an object's] own entity is not feasible even conventionally, whereby such [a commonly appearing subject] necessarily does not exist. As long as the other parties have not generated the [correct] view in their continua, they cannot distinguish the difference between existing by its own entity and mere [conventional] existence; therefore, until they realize the view, they cannot be shown the way of mere conventional existence.

Therefore, a way of objective establishment which exists in the manner of common appearance [in the systems of] both parties is asserted by those who do not just lead from an opponent's assertions [i.e., non-Prāsaṅgikas]; this way is not found, whereby it is asserted that a commonly appearing subject does not exist.

Also, this meets back to asserting or not asserting conventionally phenomena that exist by way of their own character. Even the essential points such as that Svātantrikas distinguish real and unreal conventionalities and that Prāsaṅgikas do not assert real conventionalities in their own system must be known in dependence on these [positions].[45]

---

appearance, conceiving of the objects as inherently existent. Prāsaṅgikas do not need to posit this, since their method is to reveal contradictions that arise from their opponent's convictions, without insisting, as the non-Prāsaṅgikas do, that the two systems agree that the inherent existence of objects is certified by the validly cognizing consciousnesses that certify the subject, etc. Therefore, for Prāsaṅgikas there need not be, nor could there be, a commonly appearing subject.

[45]According to Svātantrikas, in general, objects exist in terms of their inherent existence in the way they appear to non-defective sense consciousnesses, conventionally. However, some, such as a mirage, are unreal. Prāsaṅgikas assert that *all* appearances are unreal in the sense that they

B. The Prāsaṅgika Assertion of Other-Renowned Reasons

Although autonomous reasons are not asserted in the Prāsaṅgika School, signs with the three modes definitely must be asserted, and the three modes also must definitely be established by valid cognition. Also, that [establishment of the three modes] is accomplished by other-renowned reasons.

In accordance with the earlier explanation, there is no objective way of establishing, for the two parties of a debate, an object of comprehension that appears commonly [without contradicting their respective systems]. Therefore, leading from the assertions of an opponent, one states reasons that are renowned to the opponents themselves. [One may also state reasons that are] renowned to [the opponent who is] other in relation to the first party, i.e., a Mādhyamika. Therefore, the two, self-renowned reasons and other-renowned reasons, are equivalent **[481]**.[46]

Moreover, let us exemplify this in, for example, the explanation [in the second stanza] of the third chapter of Nāgārjuna's *Treatise on the Middle Way* that "The seer [just does not see] his own entity." The subject, "an eye"; the sign, "does not see itself"; and the example, "pot," are asserted by the opponent himself and do not need to be proved for him. The entailment is ascertained by way of the concomitance [of not seeing other with not seeing itself] and the obverse concomitance [of seeing self with seeing other]. With respect to the

---

appear to inherently exist whereas they do not, so there are no real conventionalities. However, from the point of view of the world they also say that most objects, with the exception of those of consciousnesses affected by superficial causes of error such as those that apprehend mirages as water, are real in relation to a worldly consciousness. See Lopez (1987: 207-12).

[46]The other party is self to himself, other to us, and vice versa. Prāsaṅgikas lead from an opponent's assertions, not from their own, so they would never use the expression "self-renowned" to indicate their own position; whether the expression is "self-renowned" or "other-renowned," it will refer to the opponent. See Jamyang Shayba, *Great Exposition of the Middle Way* 418.2-5.

way of entailment of not seeing itself by not seeing others inherently, the concomitance and obverse concomitance are ascertained in terms of an example that is renowned to the opponent himself.

The presentation of this reason is very important, and realization [of it] is difficult. No follower has appeared to have clearly explained this in accordance with the detailed statements in Dzongkaba's *Great Exposition of the Stages of the Path.*[47]

[47]This would seem to be an implicit criticism of Jamyang Shayba, who in both the *Great Exposition of Tenets* and in the *Great Exposition of the Middle Way* explains these topics extensively.

4 The Unique Way of Asserting External Objects

Asserting truly existent consciousnesses without external objects as the Cittamātrins do is incorrect because (1) neither objects nor consciousnesses can be posited in terms of being their own suchness *(de kho na nyid, tathatā)* as existing upon seeking them through reasoning and also because (2) objects exist just like consciousnesses in terms of worldly renown. For also the Supramundane Victor [Buddha] says in the Perfection of Wisdom Sūtras that all five aggregates are empty of inherent existence; therefore, they equally do not ultimately exist. Also, the *Mahāyāna Abhidharma Sūtra*[48] says that all five aggregates equally exist conventionally by way of their specific and general characteristics and so forth;[49] therefore, the distinguishing of a difference of existence or non-existence with respect to objects and consciousnesses would destroy these stages of the two truths.[50]

---

[48]It is interesting that Janggya cites this sūtra, since this is the very text from which Asaṅga draws Cittamātra arguments. It is even more interesting that he does not point out this apparent contradiction.

[49]The general characteristics of the aggregates are such shared qualities as their impermanence, etc. Their specific characteristics are their defining qualities; for instance, the aggregate of consciousness is clear and knowing, and so forth.

[50]The two truths are conventional and ultimate truths. The Cittamātra School is accused of destroying the conventional truths by denying the exis-

Question: Have not the Cittamātrins refuted directionally partless[51] external objects through the reasonings that, by [proving] the non-existence of partless particles, refute external objects that are composites of those?

Answer: There is no fault, because although it is not the case that [the Cittamātrins] do not refute such directionally partless external objects **[482]**, the mere negation of them does not necessarily negate external objects.

Similarly, it can be understood that even though a partless moment of consciousness and a continuum that is a connected series of those are refuted, consciousness is not necessarily negated. The Cittamātra School thinks that when partless external objects are refuted, sense consciousnesses that are non-mistaken with respect to their appearing [objects] are refuted;[52] in that case, since [for them,] mistaken sense consciousnesses are unable to posit objects, external objects would be negated.

In this excellent system the thought is that although it is true that a mistaken sense consciousness is unable to posit a true object of comprehension, such [mistaken sense consciousnesses] serve as assisters in positing false objects of comprehension; therefore, there is no proof of the non-existence of [external] objects.

In sūtra, the thought in setting forth Cittamātra is of two types. [First] the term "only" in the *Sūtra on the Ten Grounds* statement "The three realms are only mind" does not eliminate external objects; rather, [it means that] since all three realms[53]

---

tence of external objects conventionally as well as ultimately.

[51]The Vaibhāṣikas assert the existence of particles so subtle that further physical division is impossible; these are "ultimates" in their system. The refutation of such particles is a major plank in the Cittamātra denial of the existence of external objects.

[52]This is because for them only sense consciousnesses that apprehend partless particles or objects composed of them could be non-mistaken, since these consciousnesses apprehend external objects that would have to be composed of partless particles.

[53]The Desire Realm (*'dod khams, kāmadhātu*), Form Realm (*gzugs khams, rūpadhātu*), and Formless Realm (*gzugs med khams, ārūpyadhātu*), the realms of rebirth for sentient beings.

are constructed by actions and since actions are limited to the two, intention and thought [i.e., intentional and operational actions], the three realms are constructed by mind. Therefore, the term "only" is stated for the purpose of negating the existence of a creator of the world other than the mind, such as Īśvara, who is different than the mind, and so forth.[54]

[Second] also, in the *Descent into Laṅkā Sūtra* [Buddha] speaks of mind-only [in the sense of no external objects]:[55]

> [Objects] do not exist as external objects as perceived.
> The mind [appears] as various [objects through the power of predispositions].
> [Because the mind is generated] in the likeness of bodies [i.e., senses], enjoyments [i.e., the objects of the senses], and abodes [i.e., the physical sense organs and environments],
> I have explained [that all phenomena are] mind-only.

This is said in consideration of the thought of trainees who must gradually approach suchness; it is not fit to be taken literally [as refuting the existence of external objects] because it would be damaged by the reasonings explained earlier.

Another reason [for not taking literally sūtras setting forth mind-only] is that the Supramundane Victor says [in the *Descent into Laṅkā Sūtra*]:[56]

> Just as a doctor distributes
> Medicines to the ill **[483]**,
> So Buddha teaches
> Mind-only to sentient beings.

---

[54] "Īśvara" ("lord") is a general term for a high god and a particular term in thestic Yoga for the supreme *puruśa* ("soul" or "Self").

[55] P 775, vol. 29, 53.4.2. This is translated in reliance on the oral explanation of Kensur Yeshey Tupden (3/5/82) and differs little from Hopkins, *Meditation on Emptiness* 613. Cf. Suzuki 133 (33). For commentary, see Jñānaśrībhadra, P 5519, vol. 107, 138.1.8. Bracketed material is from Ngawang Belden's *Annotations dngos* 104a.8 ff.

[56] P 775, vol. 29, 34.3.5. This is in chapter 2. Cf. Suzuki 44 (123).

Moreover, the Cittamātra School offers [the instances of] a dream consciousness and a sense consciousness to which falling hairs appear[57] as examples of inherently established consciousnesses [that function] without there being external objects. When, in the root text and the autocommentary to his *Entrance to the Middle Way* (VI.50-55), [Candrakīrti] refutes this, he says that the examples are not correct. For at the time of those [consciousnesses], although there are no [dream-] elephants, falling hairs, and so forth, that are included within external objects, they appear as though they do exist. Therefore, the consciousnesses that have [such] as their objects are also false and [hence] do not inherently exist. Therefore, objects and consciousnesses are equally established by their own nature or not.[58] This is an extremely powerful reasoning that refutes the unfeasibility of external objects.

---

[57]Persons with an eye disorder (amblyopia) see wavy lines in the air.

[58]The very examples intended by Cittamātra to demonstrate the non-necessity of external objects serve as a very powerful example to refute the true existence of consciousness and make Candrakīrti's point—that both subject and object are equally not truly existent yet are conventionally existent.

5 The Proof That Hearers and Solitary Realizers Realize the Selflessness of Phenomena

The scriptural proof is in the *Sūtra on the Ten Grounds,* which says that Bodhisattvas on the seventh ground outshine Hearers and Solitary Realizers by way of their wisdom realizing the selflessness of phenomena but cannot outshine them on the sixth ground and below.[59] Additionally, there are three reasonings explained in Candrakīrti's *Autocommentary on the "Entrance."*

First, if Hearers and Solitary Realizers did not realize the subtle selflessness of phenomena, it would [absurdly] follow that just like sages *(drang srong, ṛṣi)* who, through worldly paths, are free from desire with respect to the state of [the absorption of] Nothingness *(ci yang med, ākiṃcanya)* and below, Solitary Realizers would be outshone even by Bodhisattvas who generate the first mind [i.e., ground] by way of [the Bodhisattvas'] wisdom realizing the absence of inherent existence.

Second, because Hearer and Solitary Realizer Arhats would not have generated in their continua a path whose

---

[59]This is discussed by Dzongkaba in *Illumination of the Thought* 26a.6 ff. (translated in Hopkins [1980: 150 ff.]). This establishes that at least some Hearers and Solitary Realizers have realized the emptiness of inherent existence, since even a first ground Bodhisattva has realized emptiness.

mode of apprehension is directly contradictory to the consciousness conceiving true existence—the root of all afflictions—it would [absurdly] follow that they, like the sages of the Outsiders [i.e., non-Buddhists] would not have abandoned all the afflictions—the subtle increasers *(phra rgyas, anuśaya)*—that are involved with the three realms **[484]**.[60]

Third, if Hearers and Solitary Realizers did not realize the subtle selflessness of phenomena, then, because they would have erroneous awarenesses due to observing the aggregates, such as the form aggregate, as truly existent, they [absurdly] would not realize a fully qualified form even of the selflessness of persons. This is because they would not have come to disbelieve the [referent] object of the consciousness observing the aggregates—the bases of imputation of the I or person—as truly existent. This indicates that without coming to disbelieve the referent object of the consciousness conceiving the aggregates—the bases of designation—as truly existent, one also would not come to disbelieve the referent object of the consciousness conceiving the person—the object designated—as truly existent.[61] This is asserted to be the thought of Nāgārjuna's *Precious Garland* (I.35), which says:[62]

> As long as the aggregates are [mis-]conceived,
> So long is there [mis]conception of an "I."

---

[60]Absurd because the afflictions are the very "foes" that an Arhat (literally, in Tibetan, a "foe destroyer") has vanquished.

[61]Kensur Yeshey Tupden (3/19/82) noted that it is easier to realize the emptiness of the person than of other phenomena, but it is not possible to realize the *fully qualified* selflessness of the person until one realizes that the aggregates, the bases of designation for a person, are not truly existent. The implication is that whoever realizes the selflessness of persons has already realized the selflessness of the aggregates. His Holiness the Dalai Lama told me (6/19/84) that one cannot realize the selflessness of the person while thinking that the aggregates are truly established—that superimposition cannot be present. Their understanding is that Nāgārjuna wanted to negate the possibility of understanding the selflessness of the person without understanding the selflessness of phenomena—to realize the selflessness of the person one must be *fully prepared* to realize the selflessness of phenomena.

[62]P 5658, vol. 129, 174.3.6-7. The quotation has been lengthened by adding the last three lines and translated in reliance on Hopkins and Lati Rinbochay (1975: 22).

When there is this conception of an "I,"
There is action that results in birth.

These [topics] can be known extensively in other places.

6 The Unique Way of Positing the Conception of a Self of Phenomena as an Affliction

A. The Self of Phenomena Should Be Posited as an Affliction

When Buddhapālita identifies the self that is non-existent in the statement in the Hearers' scriptural collection[63] "All phenomena are selfless," he explains that it [refers to] establishment by way of [the phenomenon's own] entity *(ngo bo nyid kyis grub pa)*. The glorious Candrakīrti also asserts it accordingly. Furthermore, [their assertions] are made in terms of a fully qualified selflessness or subtle selflessness.[64]

Therefore, since a fully qualified selflessness of persons must mean that persons are not established by way of their own entity, the two selflessnesses [of persons and other phenomena] are asserted not to differ in terms of coarseness or subtlety. The reason was already explained earlier. Therefore,

---

[63]That is, the non-Mahāyāna scriptures. Thus, even in the non-Mahāyāna scriptures, the selflessness of phenomena is taught, not only the selflessness of the person as non-Prāsaṅgikas maintain.

[64]They are saying that even in the Hearer scriptures there is mention of a fully qualified, or subtle, selflessness—the emptiness of inherent existence, as Janggya showed in the previous chapter—not merely a coarse selflessness such as the lack of the person being a self-sufficient substantial entity.

one who realizes a fully qualified selflessness of persons also definitely realizes the subtle selflessness of phenomena.[65] In accordance with these reasons, it must definitely be asserted that the consciousness conceiving phenomena to be truly established is an affliction [and not an obstruction to omniscience].

Both Candrakīrti's *Autocommentary on the "Entrance"* and his *Commentary on (Āryadeva's) "Four Hundred"* explain that both consciousnesses conceiving true existence—the consciousnesses conceiving persons and [other] phenomena to be truly existent—are afflictive ignorance and that those are [equally] abandoned by the three, the two [Hearer and Solitary Realizer] Arhats and Bodhisattvas who have attained forbearance with respect to the doctrine of non-production **[485]**.[66] The reason that proves this is: at the time of refuting establishment by something's own character *(rang gi mtshan nyid kyis grub pa, svalakṣaṇa-siddhi)* with respect to phenomena and persons by the reasoning that refutes the inherent existence *(rang bzhin gyis grub pa, svabhāva-siddhi)* of those two, the consciousness that conceives that those two are established as their own character is established as the consciousness that conceives of true existence and that is mistaken with respect to its referent object. When that is established, the consciousnesses that conceive that the two, persons and [other] phenomena, are truly existent are established as the two consciousnesses conceiving of self. When that is established, it is established that the consciousness conceiving true existence is the discordant class, the contradictory opposite of the

[65]The preceding chapter implies that one understands the subtle selflessness of phenomena (to the extent that one does not superimpose its opposite) even before one realizes the selflessness of persons.

[66]According to Jambel Shenpen (3/2/81), the doctrine of non-production is the doctrine that nothing is inherently produced or inherently not produced. One needs forbearance with respect to this doctrine because it is frightening. Those who have directly seen emptiness—Hearer Arhats, Solitary Realizer Arhats, and some Bodhisattvas—are able to bear it. Kensur Yeshey Tupden added (3/19/82) that non-production indeed refers to emptiness, but that it could also refer to the non-production of afflictions for those who have attained liberation.

exalted wisdom consciousness that is the knower knowing the meaning of suchness. Therefore, [the consciousness conceiving true existence] is established as ignorance. Also, since it can be proved that one does not remove even the view of the transitory [collection of aggregates as a real "I" and "mine"] until [the consciousness that conceives of true existence] is removed, those two [consciousnesses misconceiving self] are established as afflictive ignorance.

In dependence on the good explanations of the Foremost Precious [Dzongkaba], in the Prāsaṅgika School there are many who know merely that the consciousness that conceives a self of phenomena is just afflictive ignorance, but those who know how to explain the way to prove such in accordance with the Foremost One's thought seem to be rare.

Nevertheless, it is not that the afflictions explained in the two [treatises on] abhidharma [Vasubandhu's *Treasury of Higher Knowledge (chos mngon pa'i mdzod, abhidharmakośakārikā)* and Asaṅga's *Compendium of Higher Knowledge (chos mngon pa kun btus, abhidharmasamuccaya)*] are not asserted as coarse afflictions. The paths explained in those [texts] are able to suppress the manifest form of those coarse afflictions; however, at that time one is unable to suppress even the manifest form of the [subtle] desire, and so forth, induced by the subtle consciousness conceiving true existence, and so forth.[67] There are many such difficult points to be analyzed; [for instance, it should be noted that] the uncommon ignorance, view of the transitory [collection of aggregates as a real "I" and "mine"], and extreme views also have both artificial and innate forms.

B. Explanation of the Obstructions to Omniscience

In this system, the obstructions to omniscience are asserted to be predispositions established by afflictions. Also, with

---

[67]Since they do not teach the subtle emptiness of inherent existence, one cannot be liberated by following them.

respect to [predispositions], from among the two, the seeds of afflictions that are posited as predispositions and predispositions that are not seeds of afflictions, the latter are to be posited as the obstructions to omniscience **[486]**.[68]

Since the two [Hearer and Solitary Realizer] Arhats and Bodhisattvas who abide on the pure [eighth through tenth] grounds have removed all the seeds of the afflictions, the consciousness that conceives of true existence is not produced [in their continua]. However, since their [minds] are polluted by the predispositions [established by] those [afflictions], awarenesses are produced that are mistaken with respect to their appearing objects.

In that case, the predispositions [established by] the afflictions are the chief of the obstructions to omniscience, and the effects of those—the factors of mistaken dualistic appearance—are also included in those [obstructions to omniscience].

Most scholars following [Dzongkaba] agree with just this mere literal rendering of the Foremost One's speech. Gyeltsap, in his *Commentary on (Maitreya's) "Sublime Science,"* does indeed explain, for example, the existence of artificial obstructions to omniscience, but it is established by many scriptures and reasonings that obstructions to omniscience are necessarily innate. Therefore, Kaydrup's great *Opening the Eyes of the Fortunate* along with its followers assert that [Gyeltsap's] statement is not to be accepted literally.[69] It is good [to assert this point] in this way.[70]

---

[68]Although usually the terms "predispositions" and "seeds" are synonymous, the obstructions to omniscience are predispositions but are not seeds of the afflictions. They predispose one to have dualistic appearance (the appearance of the objects of one's experience as inherently existent) but do not ripen afflictions, etc.

[69]Kaydrup argues that if there were artificial obstructions to omniscience they would have to be abandoned on the path of seeing, in which case one would abandon some obstructions to omniscience even before the eighth ground, that is, even before one finished abandoning the obstructions to liberation. That would contradict a major Prāsaṅgika School tenet. See *Grounds and Paths* 120.7-21.2. According to Kensur Yeshey Tupden (3/19/82), the term "artificial" is reserved for consciousnesses, and obstructions to omniscience are *not* consciousnesses (but Jamyang Shayba disagrees).

[70]According to Losang Dayang (*Grounds and Paths* 120.5-6), Gyeltsap

The contemporary proponent of reasoning who has the name Prajñā[71] indeed propounds that: (1) there are artificial obstructions to omniscience; (2) since there is a mistaken consciousness explicitly indicated on the occasion of the word "mistaken" which is part of the phrase, "factors of mistaken dualistic appearance" in Dzongkaba's *Ocean of Reasoning, Explanation of (Nāgārjuna's) "Treatise on the Middle Way,"* it is the thought of the Foremost One that there is a common locus of something's being a consciousness and being an obstruction to omniscience; and (3) the thought of Kaydrup's *Opening the Eyes of the Fortunate* that explains that there are no artificial obstructions to omniscience is concerned only with the obstructions to omniscience that are predispositions.

However, these are not seen to be correct.[72] Although it is indeed stated in the *Sūtra Unraveling the Thought* that there are obscurations [i.e., the twenty-two thorough obscurations] that are objects of abandonment corresponding to each of the ten grounds, there is no source that on this occasion [of the Prāsaṅgika School] one needs to make assertions in a manner like the presentations of objects of abandonment and antidotes explained in that [sūtra].[73]

---

describes the "artificial obstructions to omniscience" as the awarenesses (and their seeds) that conceive that the appearance of true existence to a sense consciousness is logically correct.

[71]According to Geshay Tupden Gyatso, a contemporary Gomang scholar, "Prajñā" was the epithet of a scholar named Aku Shayrap Gyatso (Shayrap [*shes rab*] is the Tibetan translation of *prajñā*). Looking into this, I found that there is an Akhu Rinbochay whose name was Sherap Gyatso and who was known mainly by his Sanskrit name, Prajñāsāgara; however, he lived *after* Janggya, from 1803-75. According to Lokesh Chandra (1963: 60, n. 5), there is an earlier Shayrap Gyatso who was a Mongolian and collaborated in the translation of the Mongolian canon (a project supervised by Janggya). It is quite possible that this person was known also as Prajñā.

[72]Like Jamyang Shayba, "Prajña" thinks that there must be consciousnesses, not merely non-associated compositional factors (the predispositions established by the afflictions) that are obstructions to omniscience. As evidence, he adduces a statement of Dzongkaba in which there is a description of something included in the obstructions to omniscience as being "mistaken," a term he thinks could only apply to a consciousness.

[73]That is, there is no source stating that for the perspective of the Prāsaṅgika School there are artificial obstructions to omniscience to be aban-

In dependence on Candrakīrti's *Seventy Stanzas on the Three Refuges*, which says, "For the sake of abandoning non-afflictive ignorance..." and "...non-afflictive ignorance exists...," and his statement in his *Autocommentary on the "Entrance,"* "...ignorance that is not afflictive..." **[487]**, Paṇchen Sönam Gyeltsen[74] and the great scholar and adept Jamyang Shaybay Dorjay say that the existence of obstructions to omniscience that are consciousnesses is correct.

Nevertheless, with respect to the Foremost Omniscient [Dzongkaba's] interpretations of the ignorance that is an obstruction to omniscience, except for his interpretation [of it] as predispositions of mistaken dualistic appearance, he does not appear to have interpreted it as ignorance that is a consciousness.[75]

Most scholars and adepts such as the omniscient Kaydrup, the lord of reasoning Jaydzün Chögyi Gyeltsen *(rje bstun chos kyi rgyal mtshan)* of Sera and his [spiritual] sons, as well as the great treasure of wisdom Jamyang Gaway Lodrö *('jam dbyangs dga' ba'i blo gros)*, the foremost omniscient Gendün Gyatso *(dge 'dun rgya mtsho)*, and Paṇchen Sönam Drakba,[76] assert that there are no obstructions to omniscience that are consciousnesses. Also, the omniscient Paṇchen Losang Chögyi Gyeltsen *(paṇ chen blo bzang chos kyi rgyal mtshan)*,[77] a keeper of the teaching of both the transmission of explanation and the

---

doned on the first seven Bodhisattva grounds.

[74]None of the half-dozen scholars I asked knew who this was.

[75]Thus, according to Kensur Yeshey Tupden (3/19/82) they are named "ignorance" but are not.

[76]Kaydrup Gelek Belsangbo (1385-1438) is one of Dzongkaba's two chief disciples; Jaydzün Chögyi Gyeltsen (1469-1546) is the author of monastic textbooks for Jay college of Sera Monastery; other than his dates, I have not yet found any biographical information on Jamyang Gaway Lodrö (1429/30-1503); Gendün Gyatso (1476-1542) is the second Dalai Lama; and Paṇchen Sönam Drakba (1478-1554) is the author of monastic textbooks for Loseling College of Drebung Monastery.

[77]He is the first Paṇchen Lama (1569-1662). Losang Dayang (*Grounds and Paths* 119.4-5) calls him the "All-Seeing" Paṇchen Losang Chögyi Gyeltsen *(paṇ chen kun gzigs blo bzang chos kyi rgyal mtshan)* and the name of his book is *Answer to the Objections of the Translator [Daktsang] Shayrap Rinchen (sgra pa shes rab rin chen gyi rtsod lan)*.

transmission of achievement[78] of the Foremost Lama [Dzong-kaba], says:

> The subtle obstructions [preventing] the perception
> Of the two truths directly and simultaneously by one consciousness
> Are designated "ignorance" [but] are not actual consciousnesses;
> Hence there is not even partial contradiction.

His statements along with his reasons are very concordant with the great mass of the speech of the Foremost [Dzong-kaba]. Therefore, [this topic] still should be finely analyzed by the intelligent.

[78]I have not yet determined the difference between these transmission; perhaps this refers to teachings on sūtra and tantra, or, within tantra, to the lower and higher initiations of tantras of the Highest Yoga Tantra class.

7 The Unique Way of Asserting that Disintegratedness is a Functioning Thing

The modes of assertion, and so forth, of the Vaibhāṣika School have previously been explained. The Sautrāntikas, Cittamātrins, and Svātantrika-Mādhyamikas assert that (1) when a thing—a sprout, for instance—has disintegrated, everything that is a part of the sprout is obliterated, and (2) since no other thing, such as a pot, that is other than that [sprout] is obtained, that disintegratedness is utterly not a [functioning] thing. For they propound that any things that are individual sense-spheres *(skyed mched, āyatana)*, such as blue, and any things that are collections of parts are unsuitable to be illustrations of [that disintegratedness **[488]**. [These assertions] are [made] through the essential point that [according to them, phenomena] must be posited upon searching for the imputed object. Although this [Prāsaṅgika] system does not posit [phenomena] by way of such a search, since disintegratedness is suitable to be asserted as a [functioning] thing, disintegratedness is asserted to *be* a thing.[79]

---

[79]The point that is being made, rather obliquely, is that even though something's disintegratedness is not a thing like a patch of blue, it is possible to posit a disintegratedness as a thing because it is not necessary that a thing be something found upon analysis.

Moreover, with respect to scripture, the *Sūtra on the Ten Grounds*[80] says, "Aging and death are [produced] by the condition of birth." Thus, the death of a sentient being is said to be produced by a condition. Therefore, death must be posited as the disintegratedness of the sentient being who has died. Therefore [that disintegratedness is a functioning thing has been established by this scripture]. It also says:[81]

> Death subsists in two activities: it causes a composed phenomenon to disintegrate and (2) it issues forth the cause of the non-severance of the continuum of thorough non-knowingness [i.e., ignorance].

Thus, it is said that death is produced by a cause and also produces ignorance. Therefore, since that which is produced by its own causes and is able to produce effects must be asserted to be a [functioning] thing, [this passage also establishes that disintegratedness is a functioning thing]. Although [death] is the disintegratedness of a continuum, the disintegratedness of the first moment of something in its next moment is similar.[82]

The reasoning is: (1) the birth and death of a sentient being and (2) something not remaining for a second moment and not having remained for a second moment are proved to be thoroughly similar in terms of whether or not they are posited as [functioning] things and whether or not they depend on causes. This system asserts that even something's disintegratedness disintegrates, but other [systems] assert that disintegratedness and disintegration are contradictory.[83]

---

[80]761.3.1, vol. 25. A similar passage in the sūtra has been translated in Honda (190).

[81]761.3.1, vol. 25.

[82]In other words, just as death, the disintegratedness of the last moment of a sentient being's life, is both caused and acts as a cause, so also the disintegratedness of any other moment of a thing is both caused and acts as a cause. This disintegratedness has an effect, though it may be nothing more than to act as the cause of another moment of disintegratedness, etc.

[83]In other systems, since disintegratedness is regarded as a permanent phenomenon, it does not itself disintegrate. In the Prāsaṅgika School explanation, since disintegratedness is a functioning thing, it necessarily

The explanation, for instance, in Candrakīrti's *Commentary on (Nāgārjuna's) "Sixty Stanzas of Reasoning,"* which says that the exhaustion of the butter and wick is the cause of the butter-lamp's dying out, is the way to prove that the disintegratedness of a continuum is a [functioning] thing. The disintegratedness of the first moment [of something] in the next moment is a negative phenomenon due to the necessity of its being realized through eliminating an explicit object of negation, and, moreover, that which is destroyed is not a mere elimination, but rather implies a [functioning] thing that involves an elimination; therefore, it is an affirming negative.[84]

The two, the Vaibhāṣika School and this [Prāsaṅgika system], are similar in the mere assertion of the three times as [functioning] things but are very dissimilar in their modes of assertion **[489]**. This [Prāsaṅgika] system does not assert substantial existence in all [i.e., any] aspects and asserts that even the disintegratedness of a sprout is a [functioning] thing due to merely being produced in dependence on a thing that is destroyed. [Unlike the Vaibhāṣika School] they do not assert that [the disintegratedness of a sprout] is a thing due to positing, upon analysis by reasoning, the thing that is destroyed or

---

disintegrates; hence, disintegration and disintegratedness are not contradictory.

[84]A negative phenomenon *(dgag pa, pratiṣedha)* is one that must be realized through the explicit elimination of something, an object of negation. For instance, "treeless plain" must be realized through eliminating trees from the conceptualization of the object. See Gönchok Jikmay Wangbo's *Precious Garland of Tenets* 34.3-5 (translated in Sopa and Hopkins [230]).

Both mere eliminations and eliminations that are functioning things are negative phenomena, but a mere elimination is a non-affirming negative *(med dgag, prasajyapratiṣedha)*, a negative that implies nothing else in place of its object of negation. For instance, space, the mere absence of obstructive contact, or my lack of ability to speak Russian are negative phenomena, for they must be realized through the route of negating something, but they do not affirm anything else. "Treeless plain," however, which also must be realized by the route of a negation, implies a positive phenomenon, a plain, and is therefore an affirming negative. What is being argued here is that, for instance, "sprout's disintegratedness" implies something that has been caused. (In the next chapter, Janggya states that it implies that a sprout's disintegratedness occurs in dependence on a sprout.)

anything that is a type concordant with that [thing] as an illustration of the disintegratedness of a sprout.[85]

Since these are also said to be subtle points that are very difficult to realize, they must be known in detail from the great texts.

[85]The Vaibhāṣika School asserts that whatever is an ultimate truth—something that cannot be destroyed by physical breakage or mental analysis into parts, such as moments of consciousness too brief to be further subdivided (and thus called "partless"), or permanent phenomena, such as space—substantially exists *(rdzas yod, dravya)*, meaning that it is findable upon analysis. Hence, disintegratedness, which in their system is both a permanent phenomenon and a thing (a "permanent thing," which in other systems is an oxymoron), is substantially existent. Prāsaṅgikas, on the other hand, say that *nothing* substantially exists since all phenomena merely imputedly exist.

8 The Unique Presentation of the Three Times

If [the three times] are exemplified with a sprout, for instance, with respect to a sprout that has already been produced from causes and conditions, its disintegratedness in its second moment [i.e., the moment after] its own time[86] is the time of the sprout's pastness. The sprout's not having been produced at some place and time, like, for instance, a field in wintertime, due to the power of conditions that are, for the time being, incomplete, although the causes for the sprout's production exist, is the time of the sprout's futureness. The sprout's having been produced but not having ceased is the time of the sprout's presentness.

Therefore, since a pastness necessarily is a factor of disintegratedness of something that has already arisen, it not being sufficient for it to be merely not present, the great texts[87] also say, "Having arisen, ceased." "Arisen" refers to, for instance, a sprout that has passed.[88] Also, thinking of a special mode of

---

[86]A thing's "own time" is the moment in which it is present; the moment after its own time is the moment of its disintegratedness, when the thing itself does not exist and hence has no "own time."

[87]Such as Vasubandhu's *Treasury of Higher Knowledge*; see Jamyang Shayba's *Great Exposition of the Middle Way* 604.1.

[88]This is Dzongkaba's interpretation; his *Ocean of Reasoning* is cited in Jamyang Shayba's *Great Exposition of the Middle Way* 604.5 ff.

the future not having arrived, it is said, "although the causes exist, it is not [yet] arisen."

These points are the same in all [the systems] of the Sautrāntika School and above. However, Svātantrika-Mādhyamikas and below [excluding the Vaibhāṣika School] assert that the two, past and future, are not [functioning] things, and moreover, they assert that those are non-affirming negatives. In the Prāsaṅgika School, all three times are asserted to be [functioning] things, and the two, pastnesses and futurenesses, are asserted to be affirming negatives.[89]

The term "sprout's disintegratedness" serves both to eliminate a sprout's not having disintegrated and to imply that the disintegration of a sprout occurs in dependence on the sprout **[490]**. The term "sprout's futureness" serves both to eliminate sprout's having arrived and to imply that the futureness of a sprout is a [functioning] thing that is the non-completion of the conditions for a sprout's production.[90]

Each [functioning thing] such as a sprout cannot be treated as [three things due to] having three times, and since the two, pastnesses and futurenesses, must be posited by way of the disintegration and non-production of a [functioning] thing that is other than themselves, they are secondary. The present [functioning thing] itself is posited as present; since it does not have to be posited by way of the disintegration or non-disintegration and production or non-production of another [functioning] thing, it is chief.

Objection: It is not feasible to posit the disintegratedness of a sprout as a pastness, for, since in its own time it has been produced but has not ceased, it is present.

Response: There is no fault. At its own time, a sprout's disintegratedness is not a disintegratedness of itself, but rather is a disintegratedness of the sprout. Similarly, at its own time the disintegratedness of the disintegratedness of a sprout at its own time is not a disintegratedness of itself, but rather is the

---

[89]Concerning non-affirming and affirming negatives, see my note in chapter 7.

[90]With the further qualification that the causes for the sprout's production already exist.

disintegratedness of the first moment of the disintegratedness of a sprout. Therefore, since [the disintegratedness of a sprout] must be posited in general as a disintegratedness, it is not present, but only a pastness.

Because of that, no matter how many [moments] of similar type of a pastness have occurred, their entities must be posited by way of the disintegration of another thing, and however many [moments] of similar type of a futureness occur, their entities must be posited by way of the non-production of another [functioning] thing. For a present object—for instance, a sprout that has been produced but has not ceased—such is unnecessary. Therefore, the three times are mutually exclusive.

Nevertheless, it is not contradictory that the three times are also established in mutual dependence, because (1) the mode of dependence of the other two [on the present] is easy to understand, and (2) presentness must depend on the elimination, by the words "already produced," that it is a futureness, and the elimination, by the words "not ceased," that it is a pastness. The definition of a pastness is:

> a factor of disintegratedness of another [functioning] thing that has already been produced **[491]**.

The definition of a futureness is:

> a [factor of][91] non-production of another [functioning] thing due to the non-completion of its conditions, even though its causes exist.

The definition of a presentness is:

> that which is (1) neither a factor of disintegratedness nor a factor of futureness of another [functioning] thing and (2) has been produced but has not ceased.

---

[91]The material in brackets has been added to make these definitions identical to the definitions of the three times given in both Jamyang Shayba's *Great Exposition of Tenets* and his *Great Exposition of the Middle Way*, which may, in any case, have been Janggya's source.

Positing [the definitions] either as those or in accordance with what occurs in Kaydrup's *Opening the Eyes of the Fortunate* is permissible.[92]

The differences between that which is past at the time of a sprout and sprout's pastness, and so forth, should also be understood. They are greatly renowned and can be known from other [sources].[93]

[92]See *Opening the Eyes of the Fortunate*, 368.1-3. Kaydrup's definitions are very convoluted but seem to contain the same essential points. Cf. Cabezón 1992: 309-10.

[93]For example, a sprout's pastness is yet to come at the time of a sprout; that is, since a sprout has not yet disintegrated, its factor of disintegratedness is yet to come. On the other hand, if something has passed at the time of a sprout—for instance, the seed from which the sprout came—it is just a pastness that exists at the time of the sprout but is not that sprout's pastness.

Section B: The System of Refuting Inherent Existence

The ultimate root, the chief of all of these distinguishing features, is the [Prāsaṅgika School's] refutation of inherent existence. Four reasons are explained in the root text and auto-commentary of Candrakīrti's *Entrance to (Nāgārjuna's) "Treatise on the Middle Way"*:

(1) If things had their own inherent nature in the sense of being inherently existent, then, when Superiors realized that all phenomena lack inherent existence, their wisdom consciousnesses would have to observe those [inherently existent things]. However, because they are *not* observed, they are non-existent.[1] In that case, the later non-existence of a thing that existed earlier would be its disintegratedness, and since one would have to assert that those wisdom consciousnesses served as the cause of [the thing's] disintegration, it would [absurdly] follow that a Superior's meditative equipoise is the cause of the disintegration of things.

---

[1]A Superior's wisdom consciousness is capable of determining the final nature of phenomena; if phenomena existed inherently, it would have to perceive those phenomena. However, when a Superior's wisdom consciousness analytically searches for an inherently existent phenomenon, it does not find it; it "finds" only emptiness, and thus it is clear that phenomena lack inherent existence. The Svātantrikas might object that a Superior's wisdom consciousness is not looking for inherent existence as such, but rather is looking for ultimate inherent existence (in their system, nothing ultimately exists, but all existents must inherently exist). They might say that since the Superior was not searching for inherent existence, the failure to find it does not disprove its existence.

(2) If things were inherently existent, at the time of analysis with reasoning on the meaning of the designation of the verbal convention of "production," one would have to find, upon searching through reasoning, production in which the seed and sprout are either inherently one or inherently different, because otherwise they would be mere verbal conventions and would not be inherently existent. [This reason] flings the [absurd] consequence that conventional truths would be able to withstand analysis by reasoning.[2]

(3) If the conventional inherent existence of the production of things were not refuted by the reasoning that refutes production of the four extremes, ultimately established [production] also would not be refuted because if something inherently exists, it is necessarily ultimately established.[3] With respect to all three reasons, one must also know how the Svātantrika-Mādhyamikas answer them and also understand the reasons why the Svātantrikas' replies are nevertheless unable to eradicate fallacies.

(4) If [phenomena] were inherently existent, it would [absurdly] follow that statements in many sūtras such as the *Kāshyapa*

---

[2]Conventional truths, like production, cannot withstand analysis by a reasoning consciousness looking for a case of inherently existent production, that is, production in which a seed and sprout, for example, are either inherently one or inherently different. If they were inherently one, there would be no need for production. If they were inherently different, it would be impossible for them to be related as cause and effect.

[3]The Prāsaṅgika School, contrary to the Svātantrika School, asserts that there is no inherent existence not only ultimately but even conventionally. Inherent existence is not established either by ultimate valid cognition—a reasoning consciousness or directly perceiving consciousness realizing emptiness—or by conventional valid cognition, such as an eye consciousness apprehending a table. It is true that to the eye consciousness, the table appears to inherently exist, but only the table, and not the inherent existence of the table, is certified by that eye consciousness. Also, Prāsaṅgikas do not distinguish between inherent existence and ultimate inherent existence, for whatever would be inherently existent would have to be ultimately established.

Chapter Sūtra[4] that phenomena are empty of inherent existence would be incorrect. One must know in detail the reasons why [Prāsaṅgikas say that] the view of those sūtras as interpreted by the Cittamātrins and the Svātantrikas is not the final view.

[4]This is a chapter of the *Heap of Jewels Sūtra (dkon mchog brtsegs pa'i mdo, ratnakūṭa-sūtra).*

Section C: The Way of Distinguishing Definitive Sūtras and Those Requiring Interpretation in Dependence on [Unique Tenets and the Refutation of Inherent Existence]

In the first wheel [of doctrine as described in the *Sūtra Unraveling the Thought*, Buddha] explained the coarse, but not the subtle, mode of selflessness with respect to persons. Also, [he said that] the aggregates, and so forth, are inherently existent. These statements [require] interpretation.[1] That is because:

(1) the basis [of Buddha's] thought [when he turned the first wheel of doctrine] is the thought that [phenomena] merely conventionally exist;

(2) the purpose is that he spoke for the sake of trainees who are temporarily unsuitable vessels, since if they were taught the subtle selflessness, a view of annihilation would be produced; [he taught such] so that they might gradually train their continua and enter [into the profound teaching]; and

---

[1]Sūtras are interpreted in terms of the basis in (Buddha's) thought, his purpose, and damage to (i.e., refutation of) the literal teaching. For instance, when Buddha teaches the existence of a mind-basis-of-all, emptiness is the basis in his thought. However, because the person listening could not understand the presentation of the absence of inherent existence, he teaches the mind-basis-of-all instead. Thus, the purpose would be, for instance, to lead a person gradually to a more subtle level of understanding. Finally, one shows that the literal teaching is faulty—for instance, how a mind-basis-of-all could not exist. Phenomena also are divided into those requiring interpretation and those that are definitive. Conventional truths require interpretation whereas emptinesses are definitive. This means that conventional truths require interpretation in order to get at their final mode of subsistence, whereas such is not the case with emptinesses.

(3) the damage to the literal [teaching] is the reasonings that refute inherent existence.

[Buddha's] statement in the middle wheel [of doctrine] that persons and [other] phenomena merely conventionally exist, refuting that they inherently exist, is of final definitive meaning, and is set forth for sharp-facultied trainees having the Mahāyāna lineage who are able to realize emptiness as the meaning of dependent-arising.

Moreover, this excellent [Prāsaṅgika] system, unlike the two Svātantrika-Mādhyamika systems [the Yogācāra- and Sautrāntika-Svātantrika systems] asserts that all sūtras that teach the profound emptiness are similar in being sūtras of definitive meaning. [These include] not only, for instance, the *One Hundred Thousand Stanza Mother [Perfection of Wisdom] Sūtra (shes rab kyi pha rol tu phyin pa stong phrag brgya pa'i mdo, śatasāhasrikā-prajñāpāramitā-sūtra)*[2] in the middle wheel in which the qualification "ultimately" is explicitly affixed to the object of negation, but also, for instance, the *Heart of Wisdom Sūtra (shes rab snying po'i mdo, prajñāpāramitā-hṛdaya-sūtra)* in which the convention "ultimately" is not explicitly affixed [to the object of negation] but in which the qualification of emptiness of inherent existence, i.e., emptiness of existence by way of [the object's] own character, **[493]** is explicitly affixed, and in general those in which not even that [qualification] is affixed, as in, for instance, "no production, no cessation." This is because the qualification "ultimately," affixed in one sūtra, is affixed [implicitly] in other sūtras in which the objects of expression are concordant with those [of the first set] by way of meaning. For example, those [points] that occur in treatises of similar subject composed nowadays by one author must be carried over to places where they do not occur.

In the last wheel [of doctrine], statements that the three natures[3] have differences in terms of being or not being exis-

---

[2]P 730, Vols. 12-18.

[3]The three natures are the usual Cittamātra rubric for the discussion of phenomena. The Prāsaṅgika interpretation of them is found at the end of this section.

tent by their own character require interpretation. Moreover, the basis in [Buddha's] thought [when he made those statements] was the thought that the first two natures [other-powered and thoroughly established natures] and the latter nature [imputational natures] conventionally have a difference in terms of being posited and not being posited by terms and conceptions in the way they are asserted by the Cittamātra School.[4] [His] purpose was so that trainees who have the Mahāyāna lineage but who are temporarily unable to realize that the emptiness and the dependent-arising [that exists] with all phenomena have the same meaning might enter into [realizing] the subtle selflessness of phenomena after having trained their continua [in dependence on] having previously been taught the coarse selflessness of phenomena.

The damage to the literal [teaching] is (1) that there is not the slightest harm of reasoning with respect to the position that all phenomena are empty of existence by way of their own character and (2) that there are reasonings that prove that it is unsuitable to posit all objects and agents within the position of asserting that [they] exist by way of their own character.

Moreover, this is the mode of positing what is definitive and what requires interpretation within the three wheels as they are explained in the *Sūtra Unraveling the Thought*, but it is not asserted that *in general* [the sūtras of] the entire first wheel require interpretation, because statements in first wheel [sūtras] that persons and phenomena lack inherent existence

---

[4]The Cittamātra School says that other-powered phenomena and thoroughly established phenomena are not posited by terms and conceptions. This is because they are truly established (which is equated with being established by their own character but not with being inherently established or being established from their own side, which is true of all phenomena). Being posited by terms and conceptions is thus not equivalent to the Prāsaṅgika formulation "merely imputed by thought," since that includes *all* phenomena. In the Prāsaṅgika system, all three natures are posited by terms and conceptions, but even Prāsaṅgikas would agree that other-powered and thoroughly-established natures are not posited by terms and conceptions *as* the Cittamātra School uses that phrase.

are definitive.[5] In that case, the commentary by the Vijñāptikas (*rnam rig pa;* = Cittamātrins) on the three natures by way of distinguishing **[494]** a difference of existence or lack of existence by way of their own character is the meaning of the *Sūtra Unraveling the Thought* but is not the thought of the speaker, the Teacher [Buddha]. It is the meaning of the sūtra, since he taught, for instance, those subjects in accordance with the thoughts of trainees; however, there does not come to be a refutation of the meaning [of the thought] of the sūtra through refuting [what the sūtra says], and furthermore, it is not the case that the speaker has internal contradictions due to having set forth two discordant systems.[6]

With respect to this, most say that although such is the thought of the speaker, i.e., the Teacher, and the thought of the sūtra, it is not the *final* thought of those two. However, if one says, in accordance with a literal reading of Dzongkaba's *The Essence of the Good Explanations*, that it is not the thought of the speaker but is the meaning of the subjects of the scripture, it would accord with the meaning as well as with the words, because establishment by way of an object's own character cannot be posited with respect to other-powered phenomena in any place, time, or tenet system.[7]

Objection: However, Dzongkaba's *The Essence of the Good Explanations* says:

> In relation to the awarenesses of the trainees who are, temporarily, unfit to be vessels for the complete teachings on the

[5]Because Hīnayāna practitioners also must realize the subtle emptiness in order to be released from cyclic existence, there are statements in first wheel sūtras concerning emptiness. Nāgārjuna, for instance, quoted those sūtras to show that emptiness was taught even to Hearers. Janggya has discussed this in chapter 5.

[6]What is said in the sūtra is the meaning of the sūtra in the sense that it is the meaning for the intended trainees but it is neither Buddha's underlying thought nor the meaning of the *thought* of the sūtra.

[7]Janggya will not admit that the words Buddha says which require interpretation are his thought or the thought of the sūtra even if not the *final* thought. Janggya is opposed to inherent establishment being the thought of the sūtra even if it is said not to be the *final* thought of the sūtra.

meaning of the profound, [it is taught that] there is existence by way of [an object's] own character.

How can you interpret that statement?

Response: There is no fault, because this is merely an explanation that the teaching of existence by way of [an object's] own character *in relation to the awarenesses [of trainees]* is the meaning of the sūtra.

The presentation of the three characters *(mtshan nyid, svalakṣaṇa)* [i.e., natures] in our own Prāsaṅgika system is: those conventionalities that are the substrata [of emptiness] just like those appearing [to our minds now] are posited as other-powered phenomena *(gzhan dbang, paratantra)*; factors of superimposition that those are their own objective mode of subsistence or mode of disposition are posited as imputational natures *(kun btags, parikalpita)*; and the factors of the emptiness of such superimpositions are posited as thoroughly established phenomena *(yongs grub, pariniṣpanna)*.

Emendations of the Tibetan Texts

Jamyang Shayba Text (Musoori Edition)[8]

36a.5 "Also," reading *'ang* for *yang* in accordance with NG 1015.2.

36a.8 "Self-consciousness," reading *rang rig* for *rang rigs* in accordance with NG 1016.1.

36b.8 "Childish" *(byi, bāla)*, apparently short for *byis pa*, which is how both Losang Gönchok (*Word Commentary*) and Ngawang Belden cite the root text. NG edition (wrongly, I think) reads *phyi*.

37a.1 "Erroneous," reading *phyin ci log* for *phyin ci logs* in accordance with *Clear Words* 9b.4 and NG 1017.6 (*pha* 203a.6).

37a.2 "Unreal entities," reading *ngo bo log pa gang zhig* for *ngo bo log pa gang gis* in accordance with *Supplement to the Middle Way* 5b.9 and NG 1018.2 (203b.2).

37a.4 For "unsuitable," NG 1018.3 (203b.3) reads *mi rung ba* for *mi rung bar*.

37a.7 "Are seen," reading *mthong ba yin* for *mthong ba bzhin* in accordance with V. Bhattacharya (197) and NG 1019.1 (*pha* 204a.1).

37a.8 "I know," reading *bdag gis shes* for *bdag gis bshad shes*, omitting the superfluous *bshad*. Ngawang Belden notes this error.

37b.1 "Of"; NG 1019.5 (*pha* 204a.5) reads *pa'i* for *gyi*.

---

[8]The "Musoorie edition" was published by Dalama in 1962. It is compared to the "Drashikyil edition," recently reprinted by Gomang and also included in *The Collected Works of 'Jam-dbaṅs-bzad-pa'i-rdo-rje* published in New Delhi in 1973 by Ngawang Gelek Demo (NG).

37b.6 "Stated"; NG 1020.5 alternately reads *bkod* for *bkod pa.*

37b.8 "Realized," reading *rtogs* for *dmigs* in accordance with P.

38a.1 "Things," reading *gang dag dngos po* for *gang dag gi dngos po* in accordance with P.

38a.2 "Causeless," reading *rgyu med pa'i phyir ro* for *rgyu med pa nyid kyis phyir ro* in accordance with P.

38a.2 "Ceased," reading *de dag gi 'gag pa de dngos po* for *de dag gi ltar na 'gag pa de yang dngos po* in accordance with P.

38a.4 For "Previously," *Clear Words* 118.1 and NG 1022.1 read *sngar* for Jamyang Shayba's *snga na;* also, "and" *(dang)* is added from *Clear Words* 118.1.

38b.5 For "present," P alternately reads *da ltar byung ba ni* for *da ltar ba ni.* The *Great Exposition of the Middle Way* 624.6 also has *da ltar ba ni.*

38b.6 "Present time"; P alternately reads *da ltar byung ba'i dus* for *da ltar ba'i dus.*

38b.6 "Having disintegrated," reading *zhig nas* for *zhig* in accordance with NG 1024.2.

38b.6 "Actually," reading *dngos su* for *dngos* in accordance with NG 1024.2.

39a.1 For "not constitute a search," NG 1024.6 alternately reads *btsal bar mi 'gro* for *btsal mi 'gro.*

39a.3 "Valid cognition," reading *tshad ma rnams kyi* for *tshad ma rnams ni* in accordance with P 5228, vol. 98, 15.3.1.

39a.4 "Comprehension," reading *gzhal* for *gzhan* in accordance with P 5228, vol. 98, 15.3.2.

39b.4 "Manifest object," reading *mngon sum gyi* for *mngon sum gyis* in accordance with *Clear Words* 48.3 and NG 1027.3.

40a.1 For "nothing whatsoever," P reads *gang yang med na* for *'ga' yang mi srid pas* (same meaning).

40a.1 "Of," reading *phung po'i* for *phung po* in accordance with P.

40a.4 "Completely"; NG 1029.1 reads *ma lus par* for *ma lus pa.*

40b.2 "Attained," reading *thob par bya ba* for *thob dang bya ba* in accordance with *Great Exposition of the Stages of the Path* 371b.3 and NG 1030.3.

41a.1 "And," reading *chags med dang* for *chags med pa* in accordance with P.

41a.3 "Vision of exalted wisdom," reading *ye shes kyi gzigs* for *kyis gzigs* in accordance with P.

Ngawang Belden Text (Sarnath Edition)

108b.7 "In that case," reading *de ltar na* for *de lta na* in accordance with P.

109b.7 "And"; Ngawang Belden has added a *zhing* (Skt. *ca*) which is not present in the Peking edition and puts one syllable too many in the *pāda* but which is concordant with the meaning of Āryadeva's statement.

110b.1 "Path"; Ngawang Gelek edition of Gyeltsap's text (253.6) incorrectly reads *le'u* for *lam.*

111a.1 "Thing," reading *dngos po* for *dngos por.*

117b.4 "Disintegratedness," reading *gzhig* for *bzhig* in accordance with Gyeltsap, *Collected Works,* vol. 5, 407.6.

Janggya Text (Sarnath Edition)[9]

472.3 "Permissible," reading *chog pa* for *tshog pa* in accordance with SR 761.3.

472.6 "Explained," reading *'chad par* for *'tshad par* in accordance with SR 761.4.

472.9 "Chief," reading *gtso bo* for *gtso bor* in accordance with *Illumination of the Thought* 124b.2 and SR 761.5.

472.12 "Just as it is" (*ji lta ba bzhin*). SR (762.1) alternately reads *ji lta ba.* Kensur Yeshey Tupden (2/12/82) thought this should read "generate a view of suchness" *(de kho na nyid kyi lta ba skyed pa).*

472.20 "Affixes," reading *sbyor* for *spyor* in accordance with SR 762.4.

473.13 "Chief," reading *gtso bo* for *gtso bor* in accordance with SR 763.4.

476.9 "Sees blue," reading *sngon po mthong* for *sdon po ma mthong* in accordance with SR 767.3.

476.15 "Poisoned," reading *dmug pa* for *rmugs pa* in accordance with SR 768.1.

478.19 "Very difficult," reading *shin tu dka' bar* for *shan tu dka' bur* in accordance with SR 771.3.

478.20 "Subsequent," reading *rjes kyi* for *rjes kyis* in accordance with SR 771.3.

---

[9]The Sarnath (Pleasure of Elegant Sayings Printing Press) edition has been compared to the Sharada Rani (SR) edition.

479.9 "Parties," reading *phyi rgol* for *phyir rgol* in accordance with SR 772.1.

479.10 "Established," reading *'grub* for *grub* in accordance with SR 772.2.

479.10 "Being established," reading *grub nas* for *grub na* in accordance with SR 772.2.

479.16 "Permanence, impermanence," reading *rtag mi rtag* for *rtag* in accordance with SR 772.4.

480.1 "Both of those," reading *de gnyis ka* for *de nyid* in accordance with SR 773.1.

480.4 "First party," reading *sngar rgol* for *snga rgol* in accordance with SR 773.2.

480.19 "Relation," reading *ltos* for *bltos* in accordance with SR 774.3.

481.1 "Of"; SR 774.3 alternately reads *rtsa shes* for *rtsa she'i*.

481.13 "Victor," reading *bcom* for *bcon* in accordance with SR 775.3.

482.15 "Exist," reading *yod med* for *yongs med* in accordance with SR 777.1 and P 775, vol. 29, 53.4.2.

482.20 "The ill" (*nad pa nad pa*). SR reads *nad pa na ba*. I have not yet checked P.

484.11 "Identifies," reading *ngos bzung* for *ngos gzung* in accordance with SR 779.5.

485.7 "Contradictory opposite"; SR 781.1 reads *'gal ba* for *'gal zla*.

485.18 "Both," reading *gnyis gnyis* for *gnyis* in accordance with SR 781.5.

493.18 "Entire," reading *yin tshad* for *yin chad* in accordance with the *gam bcar phan bde legs bshad gling grva tshang dang rgyud rnying slar gso tshogs pa* edition 542.1.

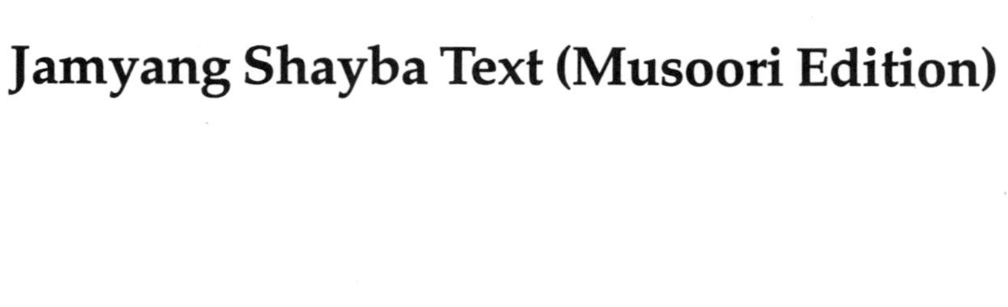

Jamyang Shayba Text (Musoori Edition)

༄༅། །ངེས་བདེན་གཉིས་ཟུང་འདྲེལ་གཅེས་ཏེ། དེ་ལ་མཐར་མ་ལྷུང་བ་དང་མི་ཕྱེད་བ་དང་ཚོགས་གཉིས་དང་དེའི་སྐུ་གཉིས་ཐོབ་པའི་པར་ཡིན་པའི་ཕྱིར་ཏེ། རིགས་པ་དྲུག་ཅུ་པ་ལས། བསོད་ནམས་ཡེ་ཤེས་ཚོགས་བསགས་ཤིང་། །བསོད་ནམས་ཡེ་ཤེས་ལས་བྱུང་བའི། །
དམ་པ་གཉིས་ནི་ཐོབ་ཅེས་དང་། འཇུག་པ་ལས། ཀུན་རྫོབ་དེ་ཉིད་སོགས་དང་། བདེན་གཉིས་ལས། བདེན་གཉིས་རྣམ་དབྱེ་ཤེས་པ་དག །ཐུབ་པའི་བཀའ་ལ་མི་རྨོངས་ཏེ། །དེ་དག་མ་ལུས་ཚོགས་བསགས་ནས། །ཕུན་ཚོགས་པ་རོལ་འགྲོ་བར་འགྱུར། །སོགས་སོ། ། །གཉིས་པ་ཞར་བྱུང་མཚན་
ཉིད་གསུམ་ནི། མཚན་ཉིད་གསུམ་མཚུངས་རང་བཞིན་གཞན་དབང་ལ། །བྲིས་པར་ཀུན་བརྟགས་རྒྱལ་ལ་ཡོངས་གྲུབ་བཞེད། །ཅེས་སྨོས་ཏེ། སྔར་བཤད་པས་རྟོགས་སླའོ།། ༈ །ཞི་བ་ཐུན་མོང་མ་ཡིན་པ་ལ། མདོར་བསྟན་རྒྱས་བཤད་གཉིས། དང་པོ་ནི། འཇུག་འགྲེལ་ལས། ལུགས་འདི་ནི་
ཐུན་མོང་མ་ཡིན་པའོ། །ཞེས་མཁས་པ་རྣམས་ཀྱིས་ངེས་པར་མཛད་དུ་གསོལ། ཞེས་པའི་རང་རྒྱུད་པ་མན་ཆད་དང་ཐུན་མོང་མ་ཡིན་པ་ཕྲ་མོ་མང་ཡང་ཁྱད་པར་ཆེ་བ་དག་བསྡུས་ན་ཡང་ཁྱད་པར་ཆེན་པོ་ཟུང་བརྒྱད་ཡོད་ཚུལ་རྣམ་བཤད་དང་འཇུག་འགྲེལ་སོགས་ལས་ཤེས་དགོས་ལ་སྔར་
བཤད་པ་དང་གཞན་དུ་ཡང་རྒྱས་པར་བཤད་པས་འདིར་མན་ཆད་པ་ཞུང་འགྲེལ་ཙམ་བྱས་ན། རང་མཚན་ཐ་སྙད་དུ་ཡང་མི་བཞེད་ཕྱིར། །ཁྱད་པར་ཐུན་མོང་མིན་པ་བརྒྱད་སོགས་མང་། །ཞེས་སྨོས་ཏེ། ཕྱིར་ཕྱི་དོན་ཡོད་པ་དང་ཀུན་གཞི་མེད་པ་སོགས་ཐུན་མོང་མ་ཡིན་པ་མིན་ཡང་རང་མཚན་
མི་བཞེད་པས་མིང་བཏགས་བཏགས་ཡོད་ལ་དེ་དང་དེ་ངེས་ལེན་པ་ནི་ཐུན་མོང་མ་ཡིན་པ་ཡིན་ཏེ། ཤེར་མདོ་དང་འཕགས་པ་ཡབ་སྲས་ཀྱི་དགོངས་པ་བླ་ན་མེད་པའོ། །ཇི་སྐད་དུ། འཇུག་པར། ལུགས་འདི་དགེ་སློང་ཟླ་གྲགས་ཀྱིས། །དབུ་མའི་བསྟན་བཅོས་ལས་བཏུས་ནས། །ལུང་ཇི་བཞིན་དང་
མན་ངག་ནི། །ཇི་ལྟ་བ་བཞིན་བརྗོད་པ་ཡིན། །འདི་ལ་གཞན་ན་ཆོས་འདི་ནི། །ཇི་ལྟར་མེད་པ་དེ་བཞིན་དུ། །འདིར་འབྱུང་ལུགས་ཀྱང་གཞན་ན་ནི། །མེད་ཅེས་མཁས་རྣམས་ངེས་པར་མཛོད། །ཅེས་སོ།། ༈ །གཉིས་པ་ལ། ཕྱི་དོན་དང་ཀུན་གཞི་ཡོད་མེད་དང་། བདག་མེད་གཉིས་ཀྱི་ཁྱད་པར་དང་
བཅད་ཤེས་ཚད་མ་དང་ཐ་སྙད་ཁྱད་པར་དང་། ཡིད་མངོན་དང་རྣལ་འབྱོར་མངོན་སུམ་ཁྱད་པར་དང་། བདེན་བཞིའི་རྣམ་པ་དང་དུས་གསུམ་འདོད་ཚུལ་ཁྱད་པར་དང་། ཞིག་པ་དངོས་པོ་དང་འབྲས་བུའི་འཕྲད་པ་རྟེན་སྦྱོར་དང་བཅས་པ་དང་། རང་རྒྱུད་རང་རིགས་མི་བཞེད་པ་དང་། མངོན

སུམ་དང་འགོག་བདེན་ཁྱད་པར་དང་། ལྷག་བཅས་ལྷག་མེད་ཀྱི་ཁྱད་པར་དང་། སྒྲིབ་གཉིས་དང་སྤང་ཚུལ་ཁྱད་པར་དང་། མཐའ་གཉིས་སེལ་ཚུལ་གྱིས་ཁྱད་པར་འཕྲོས་དང་བཅས་པ་བཅུ་གཅིག་ལས། དང་པོ་ནི་ཐ་སྙད་དཔྱོད་རྣམ་མི་རིགས་མི་འགྲུབ་ཕྱིར། །ཕྱི་དོན་ཡོད་དང་ཀུན་གཞིའི་མེད་པར་
བཞེད། །ཅེས་སྨོས་ཏེ། བྱང་ཆུབ་སེམས་འགྲེལ་དང་ཤེར་མདོ་ལས་གཟུང་བ་དང་འཛིན་པ་གཉིས་ཐ་སྙད་དུ་ཡོད་མཉམ་དང་དོན་དམ་དཔྱོད་པའི་སྐབས་སུ་མེད་མཉམ་དུ་གསུངས་ཤིང་། ཆོས་མངོན་པ་དག་ལས་རྒྱས་པར་བཤད་པ་དང་ཐ་སྙད་དཔྱོད་ནི་གང་གིས་ཀྱང་མི་ཁེགས་པས་ཕྱི་དོན་ཡོད་ལ། ཀུན་
གཞི་མདོ་དུ་མས་བཤད་ཀྱང་ཟབ་མདོ་དུ་མས་དྲང་དོན་དུ་བཤད་ཅིང་། དེ་འཇོག་པ་ལ་ལས་ཀྱི་རྣམ་སྨིན་གྱི་ས་བོན་དང་། བཏགས་དོན་མ་བཙལ་བར་འཇོག་མི་ཐུབ་པས་ཐ་སྙད་རིགས་པས་མི་གྲུབ་པའི་ཕྱིར་ཀུན་གཞི་མེད་དགོས་ཏེ། འདི་གཉིས་ཀྱང་བཏགས་དོན་དཔྱད་ནས་མེད་པ་ལ་ཐུག་པའི་ཕྱིར
ཐུན་མོང་མ་ཡིན་པའོ། །དེ་སྐད་དུ་འཇུག་པར། དེ་དག་ཤེས་རབ་ཚུལ་མཐོང་སངས་རྒྱས་ཀྱིས། །མཚུངས་པར་སྤངས་ཤིང་མངོན་པའི་ཆོས་ལས་གསུངས། །ཞེས་དང་། ཀུན་གཞི་ཡོད་ཅིང་གང་ཟག །སོགས་སོ།། ༈ །གཉིས་པ་ནི། དངོས་འཛིན་ཐར་མིན་དེ་ཕྱིར་བདག་མེད་མཚུངས། །ཞེས་སྨོས་ཏེ། སྤྱོད་
འཇུག་ལས། གང་ཕྱིར་ལུང་ལས་ལམ་འདི་ནི། །མེད་པར་བྱང་ཆུབ་མེད་པར་གསུངས། །ཞེས་གསུངས་པ་ལྟར་ཤེར་མདོ་ལས་དངོས་པོའི་འདུ་ཤེས་ཅན་ལ་ཐར་པ་མེད་པར་བཤད་པས་ན། བདེན་འཛིན་དེ་ཉོན་མོངས་པ་ལས་གྲོལ་ཏེ་ཐར་པ་འཐོབ་པ་ལ་བར་དུ་གཅོད་པའི་ཉོན་མོངས་
ཅན་དུ་ངེས་ལེན་དགོས་པས་ན་བདེན་འཛིན་ཉོན་སྒྲིབ་ཏུ་འདོད་པ་དང་། དེའི་རྒྱུ་མཚན་གྱིས་བདག་མེད་གཉིས་སྟོང་ཚུལ་ལ་ཁྱད་པར་མེད་ཀྱང་སྟོང་གཞིའི་སྒོ་ནས་འཇོག་དགོས་པས། བདག་མེད་གཉིས་ཕྲ་རགས་མཚུངས་ཏེ། འཇུག་པར། བདག་མེད་འདི་ནི་འགྲོ་བ་རྣམ་གྲོལ་ཕྱིར། །ཆོས་དང་གང་ཟག་
དབྱེ་བས་རྣམ་གཉིས་གསུངས། །ཞེས་དང་། བཞི་བརྒྱ་པ་ལས། ལུས་ལ་ལུས་དབང་ཇི་བཞིན་དུ། །གཏི་མུག་ཀུན་ལ་གནས་པར་གྱུར། །ཞེས་གསུངས་པས་རང་རྒྱུད་པ་མན་ཆད་ཀྱིས་བདེན་འཛིན་གྱི་ཆགས་སོགས་མི་འདོད་ཀྱང་། འདིར་བདག་འཛིན་རགས་པའི་རྣམ་པ་ཅན་དུ་མ་ཟད། བདེན་འཛིན་གྱི་རྣམ་པ་
ཅན་གྱི་དུག་གསུམ་བཞེད་དེ། མ་རིག་པ་ལ་དེ་གཉིས་ཡོད་པ་ལྟར་སྲེད་སོགས་ལ་ཡང་དེ་གཉིས་འདོད་པ་ཐུན་མོང་མ་ཡིན་པ་ཡིན་པའི་ཕྱིར་ཏེ། སྤྱོད་འཇུག་ལས། སྲེད་འདི་ཉོན་མོངས་ཅན་མིན་ཡང་། །ཀུན་རྨོངས་བཞིན་དུ་ཅི་སྟེ་མེད། །ཅེས་སོ།། ༈ །གསུམ་པ་ནི། མ་བརྟགས་མེད་དང་གསར་རྟོགས་མི

༄༅། །ཧྲུང་ཕྱིར། །ཁྱིམ་ཤེས་ཀུན་འཁྲུལ་བཅད་ཤེས་ཚད་མར་གྲུབ། །ཅེས་སྨྲས་ཏེ། ཚིགས་གསལ་ལས། ཕྱིན་ཅི་ལོག་དང་ཕྱིན་ཅི་མ་ལོག་པ་དག་ནི་ཐ་དད་པ་ཡིན་ནོ། །དེའི་ཕྱིར་གང་གི་ཚེ་རབ་རིབ་ཅན་གྱི་སྐྲ་ཤད་ལ་སོགས་པ་ལྟར་ཕྱིན་ཅི་ལོག་པས་གིས་ཡོད་པ་མ་ཡིན་པ་ཡོད་པ་ཉིད་དུ་འཛིན་པ་སོགས་དང་། འཇུག་པར། རབ་རིབ་མཐུ་ཡིས་སྐྲ་ཤད་ལ་སོགས་པ། །ངོ་བོ་ལོག་པ་གང་གིས་རྣམ་བརྟགས་པ། །སོགས་ལྟར་སངས་རྒྱས་མ་ཐོབ་པར་དུ་འཕགས་པའི་མཉམ་བཞག་ཡེ་ཤེས་མིན་པའི་མ་འཁྲུལ་བའི་ཤེས་པ་མེད་ལ། དེ་ལས་ཀྱང་བྱིས་པ་སྟེ་སོ་སོ་སྐྱེ་བོ་ལ་སྦྱོར་ལམ་ཆོས་མཆོག་པའི་མཉམ་བཞག་གི་ཡང་སྣང་བ་ལ་འཁྲུལ་བས་བསྣད་པའི་ཕྱིར། སོ་སྐྱེའི་ཤེས་པ་ཀུན་འཁྲུལ་པ་ཡང་ཐུན་མོང་མ་ཡིན་པ་ཡིན་ལ། རྩོད་ཟློག་ལས། དེ་ཡང་དང་པོ་གྲུབ་ཟིན་ལ། །བར་མ་མིན་ཞིང་ཐ་མ་མིན། །ཞེས་སོགས་ཀྱིས། གསར་རྟོགས་བཀག་ཅིང་རང་རིག་དང་གཞན་རིག་ཡང་བཀག་ནས་དེ་ལྟར་དཔྱད་མི་ཐུབ་པར་ཚིགས་གསལ་ལས་བཤད་ཅིང་མི་བསླུ་བའི་ཤེས་པ་ཚད་མའི་མཚན་ཉིད་དུ་བཤད་པའི་ཕྱིར། བཅད་ཤེས་ཡང་ཚད་མར་གྲུབ་སྟེ་ཐུན་མོང་མ་ཡིན་པ་དང་འདི་གཉིས་ཡང་རང་མཚན་ཁས་མི་ལེན་པར་ཐུག་གོ།། ། །བཞི་པ་ནི། ཚོར་བ་ཡིད་མངོན་བཅུ་དྲུག་མངོན་གྱུར་ཀྱང་། །འཕགས་པ་མིན་ཕྱིར་རྟོག་པའི་ཡིད་མངོན་དང་། །བདེན་ནམ་བཅུ་དྲུག་མངོན་གྱུར་སོ་སྐྱེ་བཞེད། །ཅེས་སྨྲས་ཏེ། དེ་ཡང་བརྒྱ་པའི་འགྲེལ་པར་ཚོར་བ་ལྟ་བུར་ཉམས་སུ་མྱོང་བའི་རྣམ་པ་ཅན་ཞིག་གམ་ཞེས་ཀུན་རྫོབ་རྣམ་ཅན་གྱི་ཚོར་བ་རང་དགའ་བ་རྣམས་ཡིད་མངོན་དུ་བཤད་ལ། ཚིགས་གསལ་ལས་ཀྱང་། ཕྱུང་ལས་ཀྱང་རྟོག་པ་དང་བྲལ་བའི་རྣམ་པར་ཤེས་པ་ཁོ་ན་མངོན་སུམ་ཉིད་དུ་མིན་པས་འདི་ནི་མི་རིགས་སོ། །ཞེས་གསུངས་པས་མངོན་སུམ་ལ་རྟོག་བྲལ་གྱིས་ཁྱབ་པ་བཀག་པའི་ཕྱིར་རྟོག་པར་གྱུར་པའི་ཡིད་མངོན་བཞེད་པ་དང་། སྤྱོད་འཇུག་ལས། ཉོན་མོངས་མེད་ཀྱང་དེ་དག་ལ། །ལས་ཀྱི་ནུས་པ་མཐོང་བ་བཞིན། །ཞེས་དག་བདག་སོགས་སུ་འཛིན་པའི་ཉོན་མོངས་མེད་པའི་མངོན་པ་ནས་བཤད་པ་ལྟ་བུའི་དགྲ་བཅོམ་པར་འདོད་པ་ལ་སངས་རྒྱས་ལ་ཐེ་ཚོམ་ཟོས་ནས་ལས་ངན་པའི་དམྱལ་བར་སྐྱེ་བ་མཐོང་བ་ཡིན་ཞེས་པ་སྟེ། བསམ་གཏན་དཔེ་འགྲུབ་ཀྱི་མདོ་ལས། དེ་གཅིག་ཏུ་དབེན་པར་སོང་ནས། ཞེས་པ་ནས། དེ་འདི་སྙམ་དུ་བདག་སྡུག་བསྔལ་ཐམས་ཅད་ལས་གྲོལ་བར་འགྱུར་རོ། ཡང་བྱིས་བྱ་བ་ཅི་ཡང་མེད་ཅིང་། བདག་ནི་དགྲ་བཅོམ་པར་གྱུར་ཏོ། །ཞེས་བྱ་བར་བདག་གིས་བཤད་ཤེས་སོ། །དེ་འཆི་བའི་ཚེ

བདག་ཉིད་སྐྱེ་བར་མཐོང་ནས། དེ་སངས་རྒྱས་ཀྱི་བྱང་ཆུབ་ལ་ཐེ་ཚོམ་དང་སོམ་ཉིར་འགྱུར་རོ། །དེ་སོམ་ཉིར་ལྟུང་སྟེ་འཆི་བའི་དུས་ལ་ནས་དམྱལ་བ་ཆེན་པོ་དག་ཏུ་ལྟུང་བར་འགྱུར་ཏེ། ཞེས་གསུངས་པ་འདིས་སྔར་སྨྲ་ལྟར་བདེན་བཞི་རགས་པ་མངོན་དུ་བྱས་ཀྱང་སངས་རྒྱས་བྱང་ཆུབ་ལ་ཐེ་ཚོམ་གྱི་དབང་གིས་དམྱལ་བ་ཆེན་པོར་སྐྱེ་བར་བཤད་པས་འཕགས་པ་ས་པར་མི་རང་བས་བདེན་བཞིའི་ཁྱད་ཆོས་རགས་པ་བཅུ་དྲུག་མངོན་གྱུར་རྟོགས་པའི་རྣལ་འབྱོར་མངོན་སུམ་རྒྱུད་ལྡན་གྱི་སོ་སྐྱེ་བཞེད་དེ་ཐུན་མོང་མ་ཡིན་པའོ།། ། །ལྔ་པ་ནི། སྟོང་ལ་ལྷག་མཐོང་སྦྱོར་ལམ་དུས་མཉམ་དང་། །ཞིག་པ་དངོས་ཕྱིར་བཅུ་དྲུག་མངོན་སུམ་གྱིས། །སྦྱོར་ལམ་འཆང་མི་སྲིད་དུས་གསུམ་དངོས་པོར་བཞེད། །ཅེས་སྨྲས་ཏེ། སྟོང་ཉིད་རྟོགས་པའི་ལྷག་མཐོང་ཐོབ་པ་དང་སྦྱོར་ལམ་ཐོབ་དུས་མཉམ་པས་དེ་ཐོབ་ན་ལོག་པའི་མངོན་ངའི་ང་རྒྱལ་དེ་ཙམ་མི་སྐྱེ་བས་ན་བདེན་བཞིའི་རྣམ་པར་རགས་པ་བཅུ་དྲུག་མངོན་སུམ་རྟོགས་ཙམ་གྱིས་སྦྱོར་ལམ་ཙམ་དུ་ཡང་མི་སྲིད་པ་དང་། ས་བཅུ་པ་དང་ཤེར་མདོ་སོགས་སུ་མས། སྐྱེ་བའི་རྐྱེན་གྱིས་ཀ་ཤི། ཞེས་གསུངས་པའི་ཕྱིར། སེམས་ཅན་ཤི་བ་དང་། ཞིག་པ་དང་འདས་པ་དངོས་པོར་གྲུབ་པས་ཤུགས་ལ་འདས་པ་མ་འོངས་པ་ད་ལྟར་བ་སྟེ་དུས་གསུམ་ཀ་དངོས་པོར་གྲུབ་སྟེ་འོག་ཏུ་འཆད་དོ།། ། །དྲུག་པ་ནི། བསྐྱེད་ཕྱིར་ཞིག་དངོས་ལས་འགགས་མང་སོང་ཡང་། །ཐོབ་རྒྱུན་ཆུད་མི་ཟ་ཆད་ངང་འབྲས་བུ་འབྱིན། །ཞིག་དངོས་སླ་ཙམ་དཔྱད་མིན་བུམ་དངོས་བཞིན། །དུས་སོང་ངག་རྒྱུན་ས་ཞིག་རྣམ་སྨིན་ལ། །སྣང་ན་སྔོན་བྱས་མཐའ་དག་མི་དྲན་ཅི། ཞེས་སྨྲས་ཏེ། འདི་ཞིབ་པར་མཐའ་པ་ཚད་དུ་ཤེས་པར་བྱ་ལ་འདོར་དུས་གསུམ་གྱི་རྒྱ་ཡོད་པས་དུས་གསུམ་དངོས་པོར་གྲུབ་པ་སོ་སོའི་མཚན་ཉིད་ཙམ་བཀོད་པ་ཡིན་འདས་མ་འོངས་ད་ལྟར་བ་གསུམ་ལས། འདས་པ་ནམ་ཞིག་པ་དངོས་པོ་ཡིན་ཏེ། དེའི་རྒྱུ་ཡོད་པས་རྒྱུ་འབྲས་གཉིས་ཀ་ཡོད་པར་ཁུངས་ལས་བཤད་དེ། སྒྲ་རྟོག་གཉིས་པའི་རྟེན་འབྲེལ་སྟོན་པའི་སྐབས་སུ། སྐྱེ་བའི་རྐྱེན་གྱིས་ཀ་ཤི། ཞེས་གསུངས་པའི་ཕྱིར་དང་། འབྲས་བུ་འབྱིན་པར་ཡང་ས་བཅུ་པ་ལས། འཆི་བ་ཡང་བྱ་བ་གཉིས་སུ་ཉེ་བར་གནས་པ་ཡིན་ཏེ། འདུ་བྱེད་འཇིག་པར་ཡང་བྱེད་པ་དང་། ཡོངས་སུ་མི་ཤེས་པ་རྒྱུན་མི་འཆད་པའི་རྒྱུ་ཡང་འབྱིན་པའོ། །ཞེས་དང་། དབུ་མ་ལས། དངོས་དང་དངོས་མེད་འདུས་བྱས་ཡིན། །ཞེས་དང་། ཡང་སྡོང་བུ་ཟད་པའམ་ཞིག་པ་མར་མེ་ཤི་བའི་རྒྱུར་གསུངས་པའི་ཕྱིར་ཏེ། རིགས་པ་དྲུག་ཅུ་པ་ལས། རྒྱུ་ཟད་ཉིད་ལས་ཞི་བ་ནི། །ཟད་ཅེས་བྱ་བར་དམིགས་པ་སྟེ། །ཞེས་དང་། དེའི་འགྲེལ་པར། གནས་པའི་རྐྱེན་མ་ཚང་ན

ཕྱིན་ཊཱི། ཀ སོ་བརྒྱད

༢༧༡ |འཇིག་པའི་ཕྱིར་རོ། །དེ་ལྟར་ན་འཇིག་རྟེན་ན་རྒྱུ་ཟད་པ་ཁོ་ནས་ཞི་ཞིང་ལོག་པ་གང་ཡིན་པ་དེ་ཟད་ཅེས་བྱ་བར་དགོངས་ཏེ། ཞེས་དང་། ཡང་དེ་ཉིད་ལས། ཁང་དག་གི་དངོས་པོ་རྣམས་ཀྱི་འགག་པ་རྒྱུ་མེད་པ་ཁོ་ནར་ངེས་པ་དེ་དག་གི་ལྟར་ན་འགག་པ་དེ་ཡང་དངོས་པོ་ལ་བརྟེན་པར་མི་འགྱུར་ཏེ། ནམ་མཁའི་མེ་ཏོག་ལ་སོགས་པ་བཞིན་དུ་རྒྱུ་མེད་པ་ཉིད་ཀྱིས་ཕྱིར་རོ། །ཞེས་སོ། །ཞིག་པ་དངོས་པོར་སྒྲུབ་བྱེད་ཡོད་དེ། འདུས་བྱས་ཀྱི་མཚན་ཉིད་དུ་དེ་བཤད་པ་མི་འཐད་པར་ཐལ་བ་དང་། གཞན་ཡང་རྒྱུ་ལས་མི་སྐྱེ་བར་ཐལ་བ་དང་སྟོང་མེད་གསར་སྐྱེའི་རིགས་པ་དང་། འཇིག་རྟེན་གྲགས་པ་རྣམས་ཀྱིས་སྒྲུབ་པའི་ཕྱིར། ཐལ་བ་དང་པོ་ནི། ཚིག་གསལ་ལས། གང་ཞིག་འཇིག་པ་རྒྱུ་མེད་པ་ཉིད་དུ་ཁས་བླངས་ནས་འདུས་བྱས་ཐམས་ཅད་སྐད་ཅིག་མར་སྒྲུབ་པ་དེའི་ལྟར་ན། ཞེས་པ་ནས། མི་འགྲིག་པ་ཉིད་དུ་འགྱུར་རོ། །ཞེས་སོ། །ཐལ་བ་གཉིས་ནི། ཚིག་གསལ་ལས། དངོས་པོ་ལ་ཡང་རྒྱུ་མེད་པར་འགྱུར་བ་མ་ཡིན་ནམ་ཞེས་པ་ནས། འདི་ཡི་མི་རིགས་སོ། །ཞེས་སོགས་གསུངས་པའི་ཕྱིར། རིགས་པ་གསུམ་པ་ཡོད་དེ། ཚིག་གསལ་ལས། གཞན་ཡང་ཇི་ལྟར་སྔ་ན་མེད་པའི་ཕྱིར་ཕྱིས་ཡོད་པའི་ཕྱིར། སྐྱེ་བ་རྒྱུ་དང་བཅས་པ་ཡིན་པ་དེ་བཞིན་དུ་འཇིག་པ་ཡང་ཡིན་པ་འདོད་པར་རིགས་སོ། །ཞེས་པ་གསུངས་པའི་ཕྱིར། རིགས་པ་བཞི་པ་འཇིག་རྟེན་གྲགས་པས་ཀྱང་གྲུབ་སྟེ། ཆུ་ཟད་ནས་མེད་པས་འབྲུ་རྣལ་བ་དང་། ཟས་ཟད་ནས་མེད་པས་བུ་བརླག་པོ་ཡང་མཐོང་བའི་ཕྱིར་དང་། འཇིག་རྟེན་པས་མཐོང་བ་ལ་རིགས་པས་དཔྱད་ནས་མེད་པར་བྱེད་མི་རུང་བའི་ཕྱིར་དང་། སངས་རྒྱས་ཀྱིས་ཀྱང་དེ་ལྟར་ཞལ་གྱིས་བཞེས་པའི་ཕྱིར་ཏེ། སྡོམ་པ་གསུམ་བསྟན་པའི་མདོ་ལས། གང་འཇིག་རྟེན་ན་ཡོད་པར་འདོད་པ་དེ་ང་ཡང་ཡོད་པར་འདོད། ཅེས་དང་། དེ་བཞིན་དུ་བུདྡྷ་པཱ་ལི་ཏ་དང་། ཟླ་བ་གཉིས་ཀས་བཤད་ཅིང་། འཕགས་པ་ལྷས་ཀྱང་། འཇིག་རྟེན་པ་ཡི་མ་གཏོགས་པར། །འཇིག་རྟེན་བརྫུང་བར་ནུས་མ་ཡིན། །ཞེས་པ་ཟླ་བ་མང་པོ་དང་། རིགས་པ་དྲུག་ཅུ་པའི་འགྲེལ་པ་ལས་ཀྱང་། འཇིག་རྟེན་པའི་དངོས་པོ་རྣམས་ནི་རྣམ་པར་དཔྱད་ཅིང་དཔྱད་ནས་ཁས་བླང་བར་བྱ་བ་མ་ཡིན་གྱི། འོ་ན་ཅི་ཞེ་ན། འཇིག་རྟེན་ན་གྲགས་པ་བཞིན་ནོ། ཞེས་དང་། ཡང་དེ་ཉིད་ལས། འཇིག་རྟེན་ན་མེད་པ་ཡང་རྒྱུ་ཉིད་དུ་ཡོད་དེ། འདི་ལྟར་ཆུ་མེད་ན་ངའི་འབྲུ་མ་རུང་བར་འགྱུར་རོ། །ཟས་མེད་པས་ངའི་བུ་ཤི་འོ། ཞེས་དེ་སྐད་དུ་འབྲུ་དང་བུ་དག་བརླག་པ་ཆུ་དང་ཟས་མེད་པས་བྱས་པར་སྨྲའོ། །གཞན་ཡང་། འཇིག་རྟེན་ན་གྲགས་པའི་དོན་ནི་འཇིག

རྟེན་ན་གྲགས་པ་པ་ཁོ་ནས་བཞག་པར་བྱ་ཡི། འཐད་པས་ནི་མ་ཡིན་ཏེ། འཇིག་རྟེན་པའི་ཐ་སྙད་ནི་འཐད་པ་དང་འགལ་བའི་ཕྱིར་རོ། །ཞེས་གསུངས་པའི་ཕྱིར། དེས་ན་འདི་ཟས་ཟད་པ་སོགས་ཀྱང་མ་ཡིན་དགག་ཡིན་གྱི་མེད་དགག་མིན་ཏེ། ཆགས་མེད་སྡང་མེད་གཏི་མུག་མེད་པ་དང་ཚེ་དཔག་མེད་འོད་དཔག་མེད་པ་ལྟ་བུ་ཡིན་ལ། དེས་ན་སྟག་ཚང་པས་ཟླ་བའི་རྗེས་སུ་འབྲངས་ཁུལ་བྱས་ཀྱང་། མདོ་སེམས་རིགས་པས་ཞིག་པ་དངོས་པོ་འགོག་ཅིང་། ཉ་ལས་པར་བྱེད་པ་ཡང་འཇིག་རྟེན་ཐ་སྙད་རགས་པ་དང་ཕྲ་བའི་ཁྱད་པར་གཉིས་དགོས་པ་མ་ཤེས་པས་ནོངས་ཤིང་ལུང་རིགས་འདི་དག་གང་ལའང་ལན་མི་ཐུབ་པས་དཔྱོད་ལྡན་རྣམས་ཀྱིས་དཔྱད་བཞིན་བོར་ཞིག །མ་འོངས་པ་ལའང་རྒྱུ་ཡོད་དེ། དེ་ལ་རྒྱུ་ཡོད་ཀྱང་། སྐབས་དེར་འོང་བའི་རྒྱུ་རྐྱེན་མ་ཚང་བ་དང་མ་ཚོགས་པའི་དབང་གིས་ཡིན་པའི་ཕྱིར་ཏེ། དེ་ཉིད་ལས། དེ་ལ་ནི་འོ་ན་ནི་རྐྱེན་མ་ཚང་བ་མ་འོངས་པ་མི་སྐྱེ་བ་ལ་རྒྱུར་གནས་ཏེ། ཀཱ་ལ་དེ་རྐྱེན་མ་ཚང་བར་མ་གྱུར་ན་ནོ། །དེ་ངེས་པར་སྐྱེ་བར་འགྱུར་རོ། །ཞེས་གསུངས་པའི་ཕྱིར། དངོས་པོ་གཞན་ཞིག་སྐྱེས་པ་ཞིག་ཆ་ནི་འདས་པའི་མཚན་ཉིད། མཚན་གཞི་སྨྱུ་གུ་ཞིག་པ་ལྟ་བུ། བརྒྱ་པའི་འགྲེལ་པ་ལས། འདས་པ་དེ་ཉིད་ལས་འདས་པའོ། །ཞེས་སོ། །དངོས་པོ་གཞན་ཞིག་ཆ་དང་མ་འོངས་པ་གང་ཡང་མིན་ཅིང་སྐྱེས་ལ་མ་འགགས་པ་ནི་ད་ལྟར་བའི་མཚན་ཉིད། སྨྱུ་གུ་ལྟ་བུ། བརྒྱ་པའི་འགྲེལ་པ་ལས། ད་ལྟར་བ་ནི་སྐྱེས་ལ་མ་འགགས་པའོ། །ཞེས་སོ། །དངོས་པོ་གཞན་ཞིག་རང་སྐྱེད་བྱེད་ཀྱི་རྒྱུ་ཡོད་ཀྱང་རྐྱེན་མ་ཚང་བས་མ་སྐྱེས་པའི་ཆ་དེ་མ་འོངས་པའི་མཚན་ཉིད། སྨྱུ་གུ་མ་འོངས་པ་ལ་རྒྱུ་ཡོད་ཀྱང་སྨྱུ་གུ་ད་ལྟར་བའི་དུས་སུ་མ་སྐྱེས་པ་ལྟ་བུ་ཡིན་ནོ། བརྒྱ་པའི་འགྲེལ་པ་ལས། དེ་ལ་མ་འོངས་པ་ནི་ད་ལྟར་བའི་དུས་སུ་མ་བྱུང་བའོ། །ཞེས་སོ། །ཞིག་པ་དངོས་པོ་ཡིན་པས་བྱས་བསགས་ཀྱི་ལས་ཞིག་བསྐལ་པ་དུ་མ་སོང་བས་ཀྱང་འབྲས་བུ་དངོས་འབྱིན་པས་ཐོབ་པ་དང་ཀུན་གཞི་དང་རྒྱུད་མི་ཟ་བ་དང་རྒྱུད་སོགས་ཁས་ལེན་མི་དགོས་པའི་ཕྱིར་ཏེ། བཞི་བརྒྱ་པའི་འགྲེལ་པ་ལས། བྱས་ཤིང་བསགས་པའི་ལས་འགགས་ནས་ཡུན་ཤིན་ཏུ་རིང་པོར་ལོན་པ་ལ་འགའ་ཡང་གནས་མེད་མོད་ཀྱི། འོན་ཀྱང་འགག་ནས་བསྐལ་པ་དུ་མས་ཆོད་པའི་ལས་ལས་ཀྱང་འབྲས་བུ་དངོས་སུ་འབྱུང་བ་དང་། ཞེས་སོ། །དེས་ཞིག་པ་དངོས་པོར་སྨྲས་ཙམ་ཞིག་པའི་བཏགས་དོན་ཚོལ་བ་མ་ཡིན་ཏེ། ཞིག་པ་དངོས་པོ་དང་དངོས་མེད་གང་ཡིན་དཔྱད་ཙམ་གྱི་དོན་དམ་དཔྱོད་པར་མི་འགྲོ་བའི་ཕྱིར་དང་། དཔེར་ན་བུམ་པ་དངོས་པོར་སྨྲས་པ་བཞིན། གཞན་དུ་ན་ཁྱེད་རང་གིས་ཞིག་པ་དངོས་མེད་དུ་སྨྲས་པའང་བཏགས་དོན་

༄༅། །བཙལ་བར་འགྱུར་བ་སོགས་གསོད་པ་དང་འཕལ་བ་མང་ལ་རྫོར་ལྟར་ཞིག་པ་ལ་རྒྱུ་ཡོད་མེད་དཔྱད་པ་ཙམ་གྱིས་ཀྱང་བཏགས་དོན་བཙལ་མི་འགྲོ་སྟེ། དེའི་ཕ་སྐད་དུ་རྒྱུ་རྐྱེན་བྱེད་ཚུལ་བཤད་པ་ཙམ་ཡིན་པའི་ཕྱིར། དཔེར་ན་ཆོས་མངོན་པར་འདུས་བྱས་ཀྱི་རྒྱུ་རྐྱེན་བཤད་པ་ལྟ་བུའོ། །ངག་རྒྱབ་སྐྱས་པ་སོགས་བྱས་པ་བསྐལ་བ་མང་པོ་སོང་ཡང་མ་ཞིག་པས་འབྲས་བུ་བསྐྱེད་ན་དེ་ལྟར་བའི་དུས་སྐབས་དེ་དག་འདས་བུ་མ་སྨིན་བ་དག་ཡོད་དགོས་པས་སྔོན་བྱས་པའི་ལུས་ངག་ཡིད་གསུམ་མ་ཞིག་ཀྱང་མི་མཐོང་བར་མ་ཟད་མི་དྲན་པ་ཅི་ཡིན་དེ། དེ་འདྲ་སུས་བཤད་བྱས་པ་སྔར་བཀག་ཟིན་ཏོ། །བདུན་པ་ནི། མ་དཔྱད་མིན་ཕྱིར་རང་རྒྱུད་རང་རིག་ཅིག །ཞེས་པ། བཏགས་དོན་དཔྱད་ནས་འཇོག་རྒྱུ་མ་རྙེད་པར་རང་རྒྱུད་ཡང་འཇོག་མི་ཐུབ་ལ། ཤེས་པའི་བཏགས་དོན་དཔྱད་འཐད་འདི་ལས་ལྷག་པ་དཔྱོད་ཚུལ་མེད་པས་རང་རིག་ཡང་ཆེད་པར་བཞེད་པ་ཐུན་མོང་མ་ཡིན་པ་ཡིན་ནོ། **ཚིག་གསལ་ལས།** དབུ་མ་པ་ཡིན་ན། སོགས་དང་། **རྩོད་ཟློག་ལས།** ཚད་མ་རྣམས་ནི་རང་ཉིད་ཀྱིས། །འགྲུབ་ཅིན་ཕན་ཚུན་གྲུབ་མིན་པ་འམ། །ཚད་མ་གཞན་གྱིས་མ་ཡིན་ལ། །གཞན་བྱས་མ་ཡིན་རྒྱུ་མེད་མིན། །ཞེས་དང་། གཙུག་ན་རིན་པོ་ཆེས་ཞུས་པ་ལས། དེ་སེམས་ཀུན་ཏུ་ཚོལ་བ་ན། །ཞེས་པ་ནས། འོན་ཏེ་དམིགས་པ་གང་ཡིན་པ་དེ་ཉིད་སེམས་ཡིན་ན་སེམས་ཀྱིས་སེམས་ཇི་ལྟར་མཐོང་བར་འགྱུར་ཏེ། འདི་ལྟ་སྟེ། དཔེར་ན་རལ་གྲིའི་སོ་དེ་ཉིད་ཀྱིས་རལ་གྲིའི་སོ་དེ་ཉིད་གཅོད་པར་མི་ནུས་ལ། སོར་མོའི་རྩེ་མོ་དེ་ཉིད་ཀྱིས་སོར་མོའི་རྩེ་མོ་དེ་ཉིད་ལ་རེག་པར་མི་ནུས་སོ། །ཞེས་དང་། **སྤྱོད་འཇུག་ལས།** འཇིག་རྟེན་གྱིས་ནི་མགོན་པོས་ཀྱང་། །སེམས་ཀྱིས་སེམས་མི་མཐོང་ཞེས་གསུངས། རལ་གྲིའི་སོ་ནི་རང་ལ་རང་། །ཇི་ལྟར་མི་གཅོད་དེ་བཞིན་ཡིན། །ཅེས་གསུངས་པ་སོགས་ཀྱིས་བཀག་ལ། །མར་མེས་རང་གཞན་གཉིས་གསལ་བ་ལྟར་སེམས་ཀྱིས་རང་གཞན་གཉིས་རིག་པ་ཡང་བཀག་སྟེ། **རྩོད་ཟློག་ལས།** མེ་ཡིས་རང་བདག་གསལ་བྱེད་ན། །འོ་ན་མེ་ཡིས་གཞན་བཞིན་དུ། །རང་ཉིད་སྲེག་པའང་བྱེད་པར་འགྱུར། །མར་མེ་བཞིན་དུ་སྨྲས་པ་ཡང་། །རང་གཞན་བདག་ཉིད་སྒྲིབ་པར་འགྱུར། །ཞེས་དང་། **དབུ་མ་ལས།** མར་མེས་རང་དང་གཞན་གྱི་དངོས། །གལ་ཏེ་སྣང་བར་བྱེད་འགྱུར་ན། །མུན་པས་རང་དང་གཞན་ཇིས་དངོས། །སྒྲིབ་པར་འགྱུར་བར་ཐེ་ཚོམ་མེད། །ཅེས་མུན་ངས་ཀྱང་རང་སྒྲིབ་ནས་མུན་པ་མི་སྣང་བར་ཐལ་བ་དང་། མར་མེ་ལས་བསལ་བྱེད་གཞན་མི་དགོས་ཏེ། དེ་ལ་མུན་པ་མེད་པའི་ཕྱིར་ཏེ། **ཞིབ་མོ་རྣམ་འཐག་ལས།** མ་ཡིན་ཏེ། དཔེ་དང་འགལ་བའི་ཕྱིར་རོ། །ཞེས་དང་། མར་མེ་ནི་རང་གི་བདག་ཉིད་གསལ་བར་བྱེད་པ་མ་ཡིན་ཏེ། མུན་པ་མེད་པའི་ཕྱིར་རོ། །ཞེས་དང་། **སྤྱོད་འཇུག་ལས།** མར་མེ་གསལ་བར་བྱ་མིན་ཏེ། །གང་ཕྱིར་མུན་གྱིས་སྒྲིབ་པ་མེད། །ཅེས་སོ།། །།

བརྒྱད་པ་ནི། ལྡོས་ཆོ་མངོན་སུམ་ཡུལ་ཡིད་ཡུལ་ཅན་མིན། །འགོག་བདེན་ཆོས་དབྱིངས་འཕགས་རྣམས་བདེན་མེད་གཟིགས། །ཞེས་སྨོས་ཏེ། སྤྱིར་མངོན་སུམ་ཚད་མ་ཡང་མངོན་སུམ་མིན་མི་ཟེར་ཀྱང་། མངོན་སུམ་གྱི་སྐད་དོད་པྲ་ཏྱཀྵ་མངོན་སུམ་དང་མངོན་གྱུར་པ་གཉིས་ཀར་འཇུག་པས། བུམ་པ་དང་དེ་འཛིན་དབང་མངོན་གཉིས་པར་ཚུན་ལྡོ་ཚེ་བུམ་པ་མངོན་སུམ་དངོས་དང་། དབང་མངོན་ལ་མངོན་སུམ་བཏགས་ནས་འཇུག་པར་འདོད་དེ། **བརྒྱ་པའི་འགྲེལ་པ་ལས།** དེ་ལྟར་རྣམ་པར་ཤེས་པ་ལ་མངོན་སུམ་དུ་རྟོག་པར་མི་རིགས་སོ། །ཡུལ་ལ་ནི་རིགས་ཏེ། ཞེས་དང་། **ཚིག་གསལ་ལས།** གཞན་ཡང་མངོན་སུམ་གྱི་སྒྲ་ནི་ལྐོག་ཏུ་མ་གྱུར་བའི་དོན་གྱི། ཞེས་པ་ནས། འདི་ལ་དབང་པོ་མངོན་དུ་ཕྱོགས་པས་ཞེས་བྱས་ནས། བུམ་པ་དང་སྔོན་པོ་ལ་སོགས་པ་ལྐོག་ཏུ་མ་གྱུར་བ་རྣམས་མངོན་སུམ་ཉིད་དུ་འགྲུབ་པར་འགྱུར་ལ། དེ་ཡོངས་སུ་གཅོད་པར་བྱེད་པའི་ཤེས་པ་ནི་རྩ་དང་སོག་མའི་མེ་བཞིན་དུ་མངོན་སུམ་གྱིས་རྒྱུ་ཅན་ཡིན་པའི་ཕྱིར་མངོན་སུམ་ཉིད་དུ་བརྗོད་དོ། །ཞེས་གསུངས་སོ། །འགོག་བདེན་ཆོས་དབྱིངས་ཡིན་པར་བདེན་བཞི་བདེན་གཉིས་ཀྱིས་བསྡུས་ཚུལ་གྱིས་ཤེས་ལ། **རིགས་པ་དྲུག་ཅུ་པ་ལས།** །དངོས་དང་དངོས་མེད་ཡོངས་ཤེས་པས། །བདག་ཉིད་ཆེན་པོ་རྣམ་པར་གྲོལ། །ཞེས་པས་འཕགས་པ་རྣམས་ཀྱིས་སྟོང་ཉིད་རྟོགས་པར་ཡང་བཤད་དེ། **དེའི་འགྲེལ་པ་ལས།** དེ་གཉིས་རང་བཞིན་མེད་པར་ཡོངས་སུ་ཤེས་པ། ཞེས་པ་ནས། འདི་དག་ལ་བདག་ཉིད་ཆེ་བ་མང་བའི་བདག་ཉིད་ཆེན་པོ་ཞེས་བྱ་སྟེ། འཕགས་པ་རྣམས་ལ་བརྗོད་དོ། །ཞེས་སོགས་ཡང་ཡང་བཤད་དོ།། །།

དགུ་པ་ནི། ཕུང་ཟང་མི་རུང་ཚོར་འདུ་འཇིག་བཤད་ཕྱིར། །ལྷག་བཅས་ལྷག་མེད་འཁྲུལ་སྣང་ཟད་མ་ཟད། ཅེས་སྨྲས་ཏེ། བཅོམ་ལྡན་འདས་ཀྱིས་མྱ་ངན་ལས་འདས་པ་རྣམ་པ་གཉིས་ཏེ། ཕུང་པོ་ལྷག་མ་དང་བཅས་པ་དང་ལྷག་མ་མེད་པའོ། །དང་པོ་ནི། ཉོན་མོངས་པ་སྤངས་ཙམ་མོ། །གཉིས་པ་ནི་ཕུང་པོ་རྒྱུན་ཆད་པ་ཞེས་སེམས་ཙམ་པ་ཁ་ཅིག་མཉམ་ཆད་འདོད་ཚུལ་དང་བརྟག་ཚུལ་གཞན་དུ་བཤད་ལ། འདིར་བསྡུས་ཙམ་སྨྲས་ན། མི་འཐད་དེ། དེ་ལྟར་ན་མྱང་འདས་མངོན་དུ་བྱེད་པ་མེད་པར་འགྱུར་བ་དང་། དགྲ་བཅོམ་པ་རེ་རེས་ཀྱང་མྱང་འདས་ཐོབ་པ་ཟག་བཅས་ཀྱི་ཕུང་པོ་མ་ལུས་པར་སྤངས་པར་བཤད་པ་དང་

ཕྱ་བ་ཨ་འགྲེལ། ཨ བཞི་བཅུ

༄༅། །ཕྲ་རིའི་བུས་དེ་འདྲའི་མྱང་འདས་མངོན་དུ་བྱས་ནས་རྗེས་ཟློས་བཤད་པའི་ཐེག་དམན་གྱི་མདོ་ཡང་ཡོད་པའི་ཕྱིར་ཏེ། དེ་སྐད་དུ་རིགས་པ་དྲུག་ཅུའི་འགྲེལ་པ་ལས། ཕུང་པོ་རྒྱུན་ཆད་པའི་ངོ་བོ་ལ་ནི་འགའ་ཡང་མི་སྨོད་པས་འགོག་པ་དེ་སུ་ལ་མངོན་སུམ་དུ་འགྱུར། ཞེས་པ་ནས། རི་ཞིག་ཇི་སྲིད་དུ་དེའི་ཕུང་པོའི་རྒྱུན་རྒྱུ་དང་རྐྱེན་གྱི་སྟོབས་ཀྱིས་འཕངས་པ་འབྱུང་བ་དེ་སྲིད་དུ་ཟད་པར་ཁོང་དུ་ཆུད་པར་མི་ནུས་ཏེ་སྐྱེ་བ་དང་ལྡན་པའི་ཕྱིར་རོ། །ཞེས་དང་། ཉན་ཐོས་ཀྱི་མདོ་ལས། གང་སྡུག་བསྔལ་འདི་མ་ལུས་པར་སྤངས་པ། ངེས་པར་སྤངས་པ། བྱང་བར་གྱུར་པ། ཟད་པ། འདོད་ཆགས་དང་བྲལ་བ། འགོག་པ། ཉེ་བར་ཞི་བ། ནུབ་པ། སྡུག་བསྔལ་གཞན་གྱི་མཚམས་མི་སྦྱོར་ཞིང་མི་འབྱུང་། མི་སྐྱེ་བ་འདི་ནི་ཞི་བ། འདི་ནི་གྱ་ནོམ་པ་སྟེ། འདི་ལྟ་སྟེ། ཕུང་པོ་ཐམས་ཅད་ངེས་པར་སྤངས་པས་སྲིད་པ་ཟད་པ། འདོད་ཆགས་དང་བྲལ་བ། འགོག་པ་མྱ་ངན་ལས་འདས་པའོ། །ཞེས་གསུངས་ལ། དེ་ཡང་མདོ་འདིའི་དགྲ་བཅོམ་གྱི་མྱང་འདས་དབང་དུ་བྱས་ནས་མ་ལུས་པར་སྤངས་པ་ནས། ནུབ་པ། ཞེས་པའི་བར་དང་། མ་འོངས་པའི་སྡུག་བསྔལ་བྲལ་ཚུལ་དབང་དུ་མཛད་ནས་སྡུག་བསྔལ་གཞན་གྱིས་མཚམས་མི་སྦྱོར་བ་ནས། མྱ་ངན་ལས་འདས་པའོ། །ཞེས་པའི་བར་དུ་བཤད་པར་འགྲེལ་པ་དེ་ལས་བཤད་པའི་ཕྱིར་དང་། རྗེས་ཟློས་ཀྱི་མདོ་ལས། རྗེས་བཟློས་ཞེས་བྱའི་མདོ་འདི་ནི། །ཕྲ་རིའི་བུ་ཡིས་མྱ་ངན་འདས། །མངོན་སུམ་བྱས་ནས་བཤད་པ་ཡིན། །ཞེས་གསུངས་པའི་ཕྱིར། ཉོན་མོངས་ས་བོན་དང་བཅས་པ་སྤངས་པ་ན་མྱང་འདས་ཐོབ་ལ་དེ་ཡང་ཉོན་མོངས་ཟད་ཀྱང་དེའི་བག་ཆགས་ཀྱི་འཁྲུལ་པའི་ལྷག་མ་དང་བཅས་པའི་མྱང་འདས་ནི་ལྷག་བཅས་མྱང་འདས་དང་། འཁྲུལ་ངའི་ལྷག་མ་མེད་པའི་མྱང་འདས་ནི་ལྷག་མེད་མྱང་འདས་ཡིན་ཏེ། འདིའི་ཕུང་པོ་སོགས་ཟད་པ་ནི་ཆོས་དབྱིངས་སུ་ཟད་པའི་དོན་ཡིན་པའི་ཕྱིར་ཏེ། མདོ་འདི་ལས། གང་སྡུག་བསྔལ་འདི་མ་ལུས་པར་སྤངས་པ་སོགས་ཀྱི་སྤངས་ཚུལ་དང་། ཟབ་མོའི་མདོ་དུ་མ་ལས། མ་སྐྱེས་པ། མ་འགགས་པ། གདོད་མ་ནས་ཞི་བ། རང་བཞིན་གྱིས་མྱ་ངན་ལས་འདས་པའོ། །ཞེས་པའི་མདོ་ཕྱི་མའི་ཟད་པ་དང་། འདིའི་མི་སྐྱེས་རྣམས་ཆོས་དབྱིངས་དགོས་པར་འདྲ་བའི་ཕྱིར་ཏེ། རིན་ཆེན་ཕྲེང་བ་ལས། ཟད་དང་མི་སྐྱེའི་དོན་དུ་ནི། །ཁ་ཅིག་པ་དེ་ཕྱིར་བཟོད་པར་བྱིས། ཞེས་དང་། རྒྱུད་བླ་མ་ལས། ཉོན་མོངས་གདོད་ནས་ཟད་ཕྱིར་རོ། །ཞེས་དང་། དེའི་ཐོགས་འགྲེལ་ལས། དེའི་ཕྱི་བའི་ཉོན་མོངས་པ་གདོད་མ་ནས་ཟད་ཅིང་འགག་པར་མཐོང་བའི་

ཕྱིར་རོ། །ཞེས་དང་། ཚིག་གསལ་ལས། ནང་དང་ཕྱིའི་དངོས་པོ་མ་དམིགས་པས། ནང་དང་ཕྱི་ལ་བདག་དུ་འཛིན་པ་དང་བདག་གིར་འཛིན་པ་རྣམ་པ་ཐམས་ཅད་དུ་ཟད་པ་འདི་ནི། འདིར་དེ་ཁོ་ན་ཉིད་དོ། །ཞེས་དང་། དེའི་དོན་ལམ་རིམ་ལས། ཕྱི་དང་ནང་གི་ཆོས་སྣ་ཚོགས་པ། དེ་ཁོ་ན་མིན་བཞིན་དུ་དེ་ཁོ་ན་ཉིད་དུ་སྣང་བ་འདི་ཐམས་ཅད་བག་ཆགས་དང་བཅས་པ་ཉེ་བར་ཞི་བས་བདག་དང་བདག་གིར་འཛིན་པ་རྣམས་ཐམས་ཅད་དུ་ཟད་པ་ནི། འཛིན་ཐོབ་དང་བྲལ་བའི་དེ་ཁོ་ན་ཉིད་ཆོས་ཀྱི་སྐུའོ། །ཞེས་སོ། །འདིས་འགོག་བདེན་དོན་དམ་བདེན་པར་བཤད་པ་ཡིན་ནོ།། ༎བཅུ་པའོ། །བག་ཆགས་ཤེས་སྒྲིབ་ཉོན་མིན་མ་རིག་འབའ་ཞིག །ཉོན་མོངས་མ་ཟད་ཤེས་སྒྲིབ་སྤོང་མི་ནུས། །ཞེས་སྨྲས་ཏེ། འདི་པའི་སྒྲིབ་གཉིས་སྤངས་ཚུལ་ཐུན་མོང་མིན་པ་ཡིན་ནོ། །འཇུག་འགྲེལ་ལས། དེ་ལ་མ་རིག་པའི་བག་ཆགས་ནི་ཤེས་བྱ་ཡོངས་སུ་གཅོད་པའི་གེགས་སུ་གྱུར་པ་ཡིན་ལ། ཞེས་སོགས་ཀྱིས། དུག་གསུམ་གྱི་བག་ཆགས་ཤེས་སྒྲིབ་དང་། འཇུག་འགྲེལ་ལས། ཉོན་མོངས་དག་ནི་མ་རིག་པ་དང་། འདོད་ལ་སོགས་པ་སྟེ། ཞེས་པའི་དུག་གསུམ་ཉོན་མོངས་སུ་བཤད་ཀྱང་ཉོན་མོངས་ཅན་མ་ཡིན་པའི་མ་རིག་པ་དང་ཤེས་སྒྲིབ་ཏུ་གྱུར་པའི་མ་རིག་པ་ཡོད་དེ། འཇུག་འགྲེལ་ལས། ཉོན་མོངས་པ་ཅན་མིན་པའི་མ་རིག་པ་ཀུན་ཏུ་སྤྱོད་པའི་ཕྱིར། ཞེས་དང་། སྐྱབས་འགྲོ་བདུན་ཅུ་པ་ལས། མི་ཤེས་ཉོན་མོངས་མིན་སྤངས་ཕྱིར། །ཕྱིས་ནས་སངས་རྒྱས་ཀྱིས་བསྒྲུབ་ངས། ཞེས་དང་། མ་རིག་ཉོན་མོངས་མེད་ཡོད་པས། །རྣམ་པ་ཀུན་མཁྱེན་སྤངས་པ་ཉིད། །ཅེས་གསུངས་པའི་ཕྱིར། ཤེས་སྒྲིབ་ལ་ཤེས་པ་ཡིན་མིན་གཉིས་ཡོད་ལ། ཤེས་སྒྲིབ་དང་ཐོགས་སྒྲིབ་དོན་གཅིག །ས་བརྒྱད་པར་ཉོན་མོངས་ཀུན་སྤངས་པ་ན་ཤེས་སྒྲིབ་སྤོང་བར་དགོས་ཀྱི་དེའི་སྔ་རོལ་དུ་མ་ཡིན་ཏེ། ཉོན་མོངས་མ་སྤངས་བར་དུ་དེའི་བག་ཆགས་སྤང་ཐབས་མེད་པའི་ཕྱིར་ཏེ། དཔེར་ན་སྣུམ་གྱིས་གོས་པའི་སྣུམ་མ་བསལ་བར་དེའི་གོས་པ་བསལ་མི་ཐུབ་པ་བཞིན་ཡིན་པའི་ཕྱིར་ཏེ། འཇུག་འགྲེལ་ལས། དེ་ནི་བག་ཆགས་ནི་ཉོན་མོངས་པའི་མཐར་ཐུག་པ་དང་སེམས་པ་དང་རྒྱ་བ་དང་བག་ཆགས་ཞེས་བྱ་བ་ནི་རྣམ་གྲངས་སོ། །དེ་ནི་ཟག་པ་མེད་པའི་ལམ་གྱིས་ཉོན་མོངས་པ་སྤངས་ཀྱང་ཉན་ཐོས་དང་རང་སངས་རྒྱས་ཐམས་ཅད་ཀྱིས་སྤངས་པར་མི་ནུས་ཏེ། དཔལ་མར་དང་ཞེས་སོགས་དང་། གཙང་རྒྱལ་གྱིས་ཞུས་པ་ལས། དེ་བཞིན་གཤེགས་པའི་ཟག་པ་ཟད་པ་ཤེས་པ་ནི་རྣམ་པར་དག་པ་དྲི་མ་མེད་པ་ཡོངས་སུ་དག་པ་འོད་གསལ་བ་བག་ཆགས་ཀྱི་མཚམས་སྦྱོར་བ་ཐམས་ཅད་ཡང་དག་པར་བཅོམ་པའོ། །ཉན་ཐོས་རྣམས་ཀྱི་ཟག་པ་ཟད་པ་ནི

༄༅། །ཚད་ཡོད་པ་བག་ཆགས་ཡང་དག་པར་མ་བཅོམ་པའོ། །སོགས་དང་། རྒྱུད་བླ་མ་ལས། དྲི་མེད་དབྱིངས་ལ་ཆགས་མེད་པ། །ཐོགས་མེད་ཕྱིར་དེ་དག་པ་ཡིན། །ཡེ་ཤེས་གཟིགས་པས་དག་པ་ནི། །སངས་རྒྱས་ཡེ་ཤེས་བླ་མེད་ཕྱིར། །འཕགས་པ་ཕྱིར་མི་ལྡོག་པ་ནི།
ཞེས་དང་། དེའི་ཐོགས་འགྲེལ་ལས། མདོར་བསྡུས་ན་རྒྱུ་གཉིས་ཀྱིས་ན་གཅིག་ཤེས་ཉི་ཚེ་བའི་ཡེ་ཤེས་ཀྱིས་མཐོང་བ་ལ་ལྟོས་ནས། ཤིན་ཏུ་རྣམ་པར་དག་པ་ཞེས་བརྗོད་དོ། །གཉིས་ང་གང་དག་ཡིས་ཞེ་ན། ཆགས་པ་མེད་པའི་ཕྱིར་དང་། ཐོགས་པ་མེད་པའི་ཕྱིར་རོ། །ཞེས་དང་། དེ་ལྟར་ཕྱིར་མི་
ལྡོག་པའི་ས་ལ་གནས་པའི་བྱང་ཆུབ་སེམས་དཔའ་རྣམས་ཀྱིས་གཟིགས་པ་དེ་ནི། ཞེས་གསུངས་ལ། ཐོགས་སྒྲིབ་ཅི་རིགས་ལས་གྲོལ་བའི་ཡེ་ཤེས་ཀྱི་མཐར་ཕྱིར་མི་ལྡོག་པའི་ས་སྟེ་ས་བརྒྱད་པ་ནས་བཞག་པའི་ཕྱིར་རོ། དོན་འདི་འདྲ་དུ་མ་ལ་དགོངས་ནས། རྣམ་བཤད་ལས་ས་བོན་དེ་ལས་
གཞན་པའི་བག་ཆགས་ཀྱི་སྒྲིབ་པ་ཤེས་སྒྲིབ་ཏུ་འཇོག་པ་ནི། ས་བརྒྱད་པ་མ་ཐོབ་པར་དུ་སྤོང་བ་མ་ཡིན་པའི་ཕྱིར་རོ། །ཞེས་སོ། འདིར་སྒྲོ་བ་མང་ཡང་གཞན་དུ་ཤེས་པར་བྱའོ།། །།བཅུ་གཅིག་པ་ནི། སྣང་བས་ཡོད་མཐའ་སྟོང་པས་མེད་མཐའ་སེལ། །དེ་སོགས་ཐུན་མོང་མིན་མང་དབུ་མ་
ལྟོས། །ཞེས་སྨྲས་ཏེ། སྔར་རྟེན་འབྱུང་གི་སྐབས་ཅུང་ཟད་བཤད་ལ། གྲུབ་མཐའ་འོག་མ་དང་མི་འདྲ་བའི་རྒྱུ་མཚན་ཞིབ་པར་ཤེས་དགོས་ལ། གཞན་ཡང་། འགོག་སྙོམས་ཀྱི་ཁྱད་པར་དང་ཟབ་མོའི་ལྟ་བ་སྐྱེད་ཚུལ་སོགས་འཕགས་པ་ཡབ་སྲས་ཀྱི་གཞུང་དང་མདོ་བཏུས་གཉིས་དང་རྣམ་བཤད་
གཉིས་ལམ་རིམ་སོགས་ལས་ཤེས་དགོས་སོ།། །།ལྔ་པ་དེ་དག་ངེས་འབྱེད་ཚད་མའི་ཁྱད་པར་འཁྲུལ་སྤོང་དང་བཅས་པ་ལ། ཚད་མའི་ཁྱད་པར་དང་། འཁྲུལ་སྤོང་གཉིས་དང་པོ་ལ་གྲུབས་ངེས་དང་མངོན་སུམ་གྱི་ཁྱད་པར་དང་། །རྗེས་དཔག་གི་ཁྱད་པར་བཤད་པ་གསུམ། དང་པོ་ནི། མངོན་
རྗེས་ཉེར་འཇལ་ལུང་གི་ཚད་མ་བཞིར། །བཤད་ཀྱང་གཞལ་བྱའི་དབང་གིས་མངོན་རྗེས་གཉིས། །ཞེས་སྨྲས་ཏེ། འདིར་ལུགས་འདིའི་ཚད་མའི་རྣམ་བཞག་མདོར་བསྡུས་ཞིག་སྨྲས་ན། ཚིག་གསལ་ལས། ཚད་མ་དག་ནི་དུ་ཞིག། མཚན་ཉིད་ནི་གང་། ཡུལ་དག་ནི་དུ་ཞིག། ཅི་བདག་ལས་སྐྱེ་བ
ཞིག་གམ་གཞན་ནམ་གཉིས་ཀའམ་རྒྱུ་མེད་པ་ལས་ཡིན་ཞེས་བྱ་བ་འདི་བརྗོད་པར་བྱའོ། །ཞེས་གསུངས་པ་ལྟར། སྤྱི་དོན་ཅུང་ཟད་བཤད་ན། མི་སླུ་བའི་ཤེས་པ་ཚད་མའི་མཚན་ཉིད། བརྒྱ་བའི་འགྲེལ་པ་ལས། མི་སླུ་བའི་ཤེས་པ་ནི་འཇིག་རྟེན་ན་ཚད་མ་ཉིད་དུ་མཐོང་ངོ། ཞེས་གསུངས་པའི་

Ngawang Belden Text (Sarnath Edition)

༄༅། །ཁ་རྣམས་དང་གཟུགས་དང་སྒྲ་ལ་སོགས་པ་རྣམས་ལ་ནི་ཚུལ་འདི་མི་རིགས་སོ། །འདི་ལྟར་འབྱུང་བ་ཆེན་པོ་དག་ནི་ལུས་ཀྱི་དབང་པོས་བཟུང་བར་བྱ་བ་ཡིན་ཞིང་མཉན་པར་བྱ་བ་མ་ཡིན་ལ། དེ་དག་ལས་གཟུགས་མིག་གི་གཟུང་བར་བྱ་བ་
དང་། མཉན་པར་བྱ་བ་སྒྲ་འབྱུང་བ་ཞེས་བྱ་བ་འདི་ནི་མཆོག་ཏུ་ངོ་མཚར་བ་ཞིག་གོ །ཞེས་གསུངས་པས་སོ། །དེའི་དར་ཊཱི་ཀ་ལས། ཅི་ནས་ཀྱང་དབང་པོ་རྣམས་ཡུལ་ལ་འཛིན་པ་མི་སྲིད་ལ། མིག་དང་གཟུགས་ལ་བརྟེན་ནས་མིག་གི་རྣམ་པར་ཤེས་པ་སྐྱེའོ་ཞེས་བྱ་བ་འདི་ནི་
ངོ་མཚར་བ་ཞིག་གོ་ཞེ་ན། དེ་ཁོ་ན་ངོ་མཚན་གྱི་རྒྱུ་མ་ཡིན་ཏེ། རིགས་པས་དཔྱད་པའི་ཚེ་ས་བོན་འགགས་པ་དང་མ་འགགས་པ་ལས་མྱུ་གུ་འབྱུང་བ་སོགས་གང་གི་ཚེ་ཁས་པ་ལ་ས་སྟེངས་ན། མིག་འབྲུབ་ལྟ་བུའི་ངོ་མཚར་ཅན་མིན་པ་ཅང་མེད་པ་དེའི་ཚེ་དབང་ཤེས
བདེན་མེད་ཀྱིས་དོན་རྟོགས་པ་དེ་འདྲ་ལ་དགོས་སུ་ཡ་མཚན་ཞེས་བྱ་བ་ཅི་ཞིག་ཡོད་ཀུན་གྱི་སྣ་མཐུན་ཡིན་པའི་ཕྱིར་རོ། །ཞེས་གསུངས་སོ། ། སྟོང་པ་ཉིད་ལ་ལྟ་ཉེས་ན་ལྟ་བ་པོ་ཕུང་བར་འགྱུར་བའི་ཚུལ་འདི་དག་སྟར་བཤད་ཟིན་ཏོ། །
འཇུག་པའི་རྣམ་བཤད་ལས། ཇི་ལྟར་དབུ་མའི་གཞུང་ལུགས་འདི་ལས་མ་གཏོགས་པར་བསྟན་བཅོས་གཞན་ན་སྟོང་པ་ཉིད་ཅེས་བྱ་བའི་ཆོས་འདི་ནི། ཕྱིན་ཅི་མ་ལོག་པར་བརྗོད་པ་མེད་པ་དེ་བཞིན་དུ། ཁ་ནོ་ཅག་གིས་འདིར་ལུགས་གང་ཞིག་བཀལ་ལན་དང་བཅས
པར་བསྟད་པ་འདིར་འབྱུང་བའི་ལུགས་ཀྱང་། སྟོང་པ་ཉིད་ཀྱི་ཆོས་ལྟར་བསྟན་བཅོས་གཞན་ན་ནི་མེད་དོ་ཞེས་མཁས་པ་རྣམས་ཀྱིས་ངེས་པར་མཛོད་དུ་གསོལ་ལོ། །དེའི་ཕྱིར་དབུ་མ་པ་ཁ་ཅིག་གིས་མདོ་སྡེ་པ་རྣམས་དང་། བྱེ་བྲག་ཏུ་སྨྲ་བ་རྣམས་ཀྱིས་གང་དོན་དམ
པར་སྨྲས་པ་དེ་ཉིད། དབུ་མ་པ་རྣམས་ཀྱིས་ཀུན་རྫོབ་ཏུ་འདོད་དོ་ཞེས་སྨྲས་པ་དེ་ནི། དབུ་མའི་བསྟན་བཅོས་ཀྱི་དེ་ཁོ་ན་ཉིད་མ་ཤེས་པས་སྨྲས་པ་ཡིན་ནོ། །འཇིག་རྟེན་ལས་འདས་པའི་ཆོས་ནི་འཇིག་རྟེན་པའི་ཆོས་དང་མཚུངས་པར་མི་རིགས་པའི་ཕྱིར་རོ། །ཞེས
རང་འགྲེལ་ལས་གསུངས་སོ། །འདིས་ནི་རང་གིས་ཐ་སྙད་དུ་རྣམ་པར་བཞག་པ་ཁས་བླངས་པ་ཐམས་ཅད་རང་མཚན་གྱིས་གྲུབ་པ་མེད་པ་ཉིད་ལ་འཇོག་པས། རང་གི་མཚན་ཉིད་ཀྱིས་གྲུབ་པ་ཁོ་ནའི་སྟེང་ནས་རྣམ་གཞག་བྱས་པའི་དོན་སྨྲ་གཉིས་ལ་སོགས་པའི་གྲུབ

མཐའ་རྣམས་རང་ལུགས་ཀྱི་དོན་དམ་དུ་མ་ཟད་ཐ་སྙད་དུ་ཡང་གྲུབ་པ་མེད་པར་འདོད་པའི་ལུགས་སོ། །དེས་ན་རང་གི་ལུགས་འདི་སེམས་ཙམ་པ་དང་ཡང་ཐུན་མོང་མ་ཡིན་པར་མ་ཟད། མགོན་པོ་ཀླུ་སྒྲུབ་དང་འཕགས་པ་ལྷའི་དགོངས་པ་འགྲེལ་བའི་དབུ་མ་པ་གཞན་གྱི་
ལུགས་དང་ཡང་ཐུན་མོང་མ་ཡིན་པར་ཤེས་པར་བྱེད་ཤིག་ཅེས་འདོམས་པའོ། །ཞེས་གསུངས་པ་ལྟར་ཡིན་ལ། སྔ་བ་གཉིས་ཀྱིས་དོན་དམ་དུ་འདོད་པ་རྣམས་དབུ་མ་པས་ཀུན་རྫོབ་ཏུ་ཁས་མི་ལེན་པ་ནི་ཆ་མེད་ལ་སོགས་པའི་དངོས་པོ་ལ་བྱ་ཡི་དེ་གཉིས་ཀྱིས་ངེས་བར
གང་འདོད་དབུ་མ་པས་ཀུན་རྫོབ་ཏུ་ཁས་མི་ལྷང་བར་སྟོན་པ་མིན་ཏེ་གཟུགས་སྒྲ་ལ་སོགས་པ་དེ་དག་གིས་བདེན་པར་འདོད་ཀྱང་དབུ་མ་པས་ཀུན་རྫོབ་ཏུ་འདོད་པ་བཞིན་ནོ། །ཞེས་ལྷག་མཐོང་ཆེན་མོར་གསུངས་ཀྱང་། ལེགས་བཤད་སྙིང་པོ་ལས། རང་གི་ལུགས་དབུ
མ་པ་གཞན་དང་ཐུན་མོང་མ་ཡིན་པའི་གནད་ཚིགས་ཀྱིས་དོན་སྨྲ་གཉིས་ཀྱི་དོན་དམ་པར་སྨྲས་པ་རྣམས་དབུ་མ་པའི་ཀུན་རྫོབ་ཏུ་འདོད་པས་དབུ་མའི་དེ་ཁོ་ན་ཉིད་མི་ཤེས་པར་འཇོག་པའི་རྒྱུ་མཚན་ནི། རང་གི་ལུགས་ལ་ཐ་སྙད་དུ་ཡང་རང་གི་མཚན་ཉིད་ཀྱིས་གྲུབ་པའི་ཆོས
མི་འདོད་ལ་དེ་དག་ནི་དེའི་སྟེང་ནས་འཇོག་པ་ཤ་སྟག་ཡིན་པའི་ཕྱིར་རོ། །བདེན་པ་གཉིས་གང་རུང་གཅིག་ལས་ཉམས་ན་ཅིག་ཤོས་ལས་ཀྱང་ཉམས་པར་འགྱུར་བས་བདེན་གཉིས་ཀྱིས་ཚུལ་ལས་མ་ཉམས་པའི་འཇིག་རྟེན་ལས་འདས་པའི་ཆོས་ནི་བདེན་གཉིས་ལས་ཉམས
པའི་འཇིག་རྟེན་པའི་ཆོས་དང་བདེན་གཉིས་གང་དུ་ཡང་མཚུངས་པར་མི་རིགས་པས་འཕགས་པའི་ལུགས་འདི་ནི་དོན་དམ་དུ་མ་ཟད་ཀུན་རྫོབ་ཏུ་ཡང་དངོས་པོར་སྨྲ་བའི་གྲུབ་མཐའ་དང་ཐུན་མོང་པ་མ་ཡིན་ནོ། །ཞེས་གསུངས་སོ། ། བྱང་ཆུབ
སེམས་འགྲེལ་ལས། ཤེས་པས་ཤེས་བྱ་རྟོགས་པ་སྟེ། །ཤེས་བྱ་མེད་པར་ཤེས་པ་མེད། །དེ་ལྟ་ན་ནི་རིག་བྱ་དང་། །རིག་བྱེད་མེད་ཅེས་ཅིས་མི་འདོད། །ཅེས་སོགས་ཀྱིས་དོན་ཤེས་ཡོད་མེད་མཚུངས་པར་གསུངས་ཤིང་། འཇུག་པ་ལས། གཟུགས་མེད་ན་ནི
སེམས་ཡོད་མ་འཛིན་ཅིག །སེམས་ཡོད་ཉིད་ནའང་གཟུགས་མེད་མ་འཛིན་ཅིག །དེ་དག་ཤེས་རབ་ཚུལ་མདོར་སངས་རྒྱས་ཀྱིས། །མཚུངས་པར་སྤངས་ཤིང་མངོན་པའི་ཆོས་ལ་གསུངས། །ཞེས་པས་ཕྱི་རོལ་གྱི་གཟུགས་མེད་པར་འདོད་ན་ནི་སེམས་ཡོད་པར་མ

དབུ་མ་པ། བརྒྱ་ དགུ

༄༅། །འཛིན་ཅིག །ང་གི་སེམས་ཡོད་པར་འདོད་ན་ཡང་ཕྱི་རོལ་གྱི་གཟུགས་མེད་པར་མ་འཛིན་ཅིག །ཕུང་པོ་ལྔ་པོ་དེ་དག་ནི་ཤེར་ཕྱིན་གྱི་མདོར་སངས་རྒྱས་ཀྱིས་ལྔ་ཆར་ཡང་མཚུངས་པར་རང་བཞིན་གྱིས་གྲུབ་པ་བཀག་ཅིང་། ཆོས་མངོན་པ་ལས་ནི་ལྔ་ཆར་ཡང་རང་དང་སྤྱིའི་མཚན་ཉིད་ལ་སོགས་པའི་སྒོ་ནས་མཚུངས་པར་གསུངས་སོ། །ཞེས་བཤད་དོ། །ཐལ་འགྱུར་བས་ཕྱི་དོན་ཐ་སྙད་དུ་ཡོད་པར་ཁས་ལེན་པའི་རྒྱུ་མཚན་མཐར་ཐུག་ནི་འདི་ལྟར་ཡིན་ཏེ། གཟུགས་སྒྲ་སོགས་ཕྱི་རོལ་གྱི་དོན་ཡིན་པ་ནི། དོན་དམ་དཔྱོད་བྱེད་ཀྱི་ཚད་མ་ལ་མ་ལྟོས་པར་ཐ་སྙད་དཔྱོད་བྱེད་ཀྱི་ཚད་མས་ཁེགས་པ་མ་ཡིན་ཏེ། ཕྱི་དོན་འགོག་བྱེད་ཀྱི་ཐ་སྙད་དཔྱོད་བྱེད་ཀྱི་ཚད་མ་མི་སྲིད་པའི་ཕྱིར་དང་། དོན་དམ་དཔྱོད་བྱེད་ཀྱི་ཚད་མས་དཔྱད་ན་ཤེས་པའང་མ་གྲུབ་པའི་ཕྱིར་རོ། །ཐ་སྙད་དཔྱོད་པའི་ཚད་མས་ཁེགས་པར་ནི་སེམས་ཙམ་པ་རང་ཡང་མི་སྨྲ་སྟེ། ཕྱི་དོན་འགོག་པ་ལྷན་ཅིག་དམིགས་ངེས་ཀྱི་རྟགས་ལ་སོགས་པའི་སེམས་ཙམ་པ་རང་ལུགས་ཀྱི་དོན་དམ་དཔྱོད་བྱེད་ཀྱི་ཚད་མ་ལ་ལྟོས་དགོས་པར་འདོད་པའི་ཕྱིར་དང་། ཕྱི་རོལ་དུ་སྣང་བ་ལྟར་གྲུབ་པས་སྟོང་པ་སེམས་ཙམ་པ་རང་ལུགས་ཀྱི་དོན་དམ་བདེན་པ་དང་དེ་བཞིན་ཉིད་ཡིན་པའི་ཕྱིར་རོ། །གཞན་ཡང་། ཐལ་འགྱུར་བའི་ལུགས་ལ། ཕྱི་དོན་ཐ་སྙད་དུ་མེད་ན་གཟུགས་སོགས་ཐ་སྙད་དུ་ཤེས་པའི་དངོས་པོར་ཁས་ལེན་དགོས་ལ། དེ་ལྟ་ན་དེ་ཉིད་རིགས་པས་མ་བརྟགས་མ་དཔྱད་པར་འཇོག་པའི་ཐ་སྙད་པའི་ཤེས་པ་རང་དགའ་བས་འགྲུབ་ས་མེད་པས་གཟུགས་སོགས་བེམ་པོ་འི་རང་བཞིན་དུ་གྲུབ་པ་ཡིན་ནམ་ཤེས་པའི་རང་བཞིན་དུ་གྲུབ་པ་ཡིན་དཔྱོད་པའི་རིགས་པས་དཔྱད་པ་ན་ཤེས་པའི་རང་བཞིན་དུ་རྟོགས་པར་འགྱུར་དགོས་ལ། དེ་ལྟ་ན་གཟུགས་སོགས་རང་གི་མཚན་ཉིད་ཀྱིས་གྲུབ་པར་འགྱུར་དགོས་པས། ཐལ་འགྱུར་བའི་ལུགས་ཡིན་པ་ལེགས་པར་ཉམས་པར་འགྱུར་རོ། །དེ་ལ་ཁ་ཅིག་ན་རེ། །དེ་ལྟ་ན་སེམས་ཙམ་པ་མདོ་སྡེ་པ་ལས་དམན་པར་ཐལ། ཤེས་པ་བདེན་གྲུབ་ཁས་ལེན་པར་མཚུངས། ཕྱི་དོན་མེད་པར་སྨྲ་བ་ལས་ཡོད་པར་སྨྲ་བ་བཟང་བའི་ཕྱིར། ཞེས་ལོག་པར་རྟོག་པ་ནི་གྲུབ་མཐའ་གོང་འོག་གང་ཡང་མི་ཤེས་པ་གསལ་བར་བྱེད་པ་སྟེ། མདོ་སྡེ་བས་རྡུལ་ཆ་མེད་དང་དེས་བརྩམས་པའི་རགས་པ་རིགས་པས་དཔྱད་ནས་ཁས་ལེན་པར་བྱེད་ལ། 218

སེམས་ཙམ་པས་དེ་འདྲའི་ཕྱི་དོན་རིགས་པས་ལེགས་པར་འགོག་ནུས་པའི་ཕྱིར་རོ། །འོན་ཀྱང་སེམས་ཙམ་པ་ཐ་སྙད་ཙམ་དུ་རིགས་པས་མ་བརྟགས་མ་དཔྱད་པར་གྲུབ་པའི་ཕྱི་དོན་འཇོག་མི་ནུས་པ་དང་། ཐལ་འགྱུར་བས་དེ་ལྟར་འཇོག་ནུས་པའི་ཁྱད་པར་ཡོད་པའི་ཕྱིར་ཕྱི་དོན་འདོད་མི་འདོད་ཀྱི་ཁྱད་པར་བྱུང་བ་ཡིན་ནོ། །དེའི་ཕྱིར་ཐལ་འགྱུར་བས་ཕྱི་དོན་དོན་ཁས་ལེན་པ་ནི་མང་རྒྱང་བདག་ཡོད་ཁས་བླངས་པ་ལ་ཐུག་པས་ན། ལེགས་བཤད་སྙིང་པོ་ལས། ཕྱི་དོན་འཇོག་ཅིང་ཀུན་གཞི་དང་རང་རིག་ཁས་མི་ལེན་པའི་ཐུན་མོང་མིན་པའི་ཁྱད་པར་དང་། ཞེས་དང་། ལུགས་འདིས་ཀྱང་ཕྱི་རོལ་རང་གི་མཚན་ཉིད་ཀྱིས་གྲུབ་པ་མི་སྲིད་པར་བཞེད་མོད་ཀྱང་དེ་ལ་ཕྱི་རོལ་མེད་དགོས་མི་དགོས་ཀྱི་སྒོ་ནས་མི་མཐུན་པ་ཡིན་ནོ། །དེའི་ཕྱིར་སྤྱིར་ཆོས་གང་རུང་ཞིག་རང་གི་མཚན་ཉིད་ཀྱིས་མེད་ཀྱང་ཡོད་པར་འཇོག་ཤེས་ན་དོན་ཤེས་ཡོད་མེད་འབྱེད་མི་ནུས་པའི་རིགས་པ་ལེགས་པོར་གོ་ནུས་ལ་དེ་མེད་ན་མི་ནུས་སོ། །ཞེས་གསུངས་སོ། །དེས་ན་སེམས་ཙམ་པས་ཕྱི་དོན་མེད་ཅིང་སེམས་བདེན་གྲུབ་ཏུ་འདོད་པ་ནི་བདེན་པ་གཉིས་ཀའི་རྣམ་བཞག་བཤིག་ཅིང་བདེན་པ་གཉིས་ཅར་ལས་ཉམས་པ་ཡིན་ཏེ། དེ་ལྟར་འདོད་པ་ལ་ཐ་སྙད་པའི་ཚད་མ་དང་དོན་དམ་དཔྱོད་བྱེད་ཀྱི་ཚད་མས་རིམ་བཞིན་གནོད་པའི་ཕྱིར་ཏེ། འཇུག་པ་ལས། བདེན་གཉིས་རིམ་པ་འདི་དག་བཤིག་ནས་ཀྱང་། །ཁྱོད་ཀྱི་རྫས་ནི་བཀག་བས་འགྲུབ་མི་འགྱུར། །ཞེས་དང་། ལེགས་བཤད་སྙིང་པོ་ལས། དེས་ན་དེ་འདྲ་བ་དེ་ལ་ཡོད་མེད་ཀྱི་ཁྱད་པར་འབྱེད་པ་ནི་འཇིག་རྟེན་པའི་ཐ་སྙད་ལས་ཀྱང་ཉམས་ལ་དོན་དམ་པའི་རྣམ་གཞག་ལས་ཀྱང་ཉམས་པས་བདེན་པ་གཉིས་ཅར་ལས་ཉམས་པ་ཡིན་ནོ། །བརྒྱ་པ་ལས། གཅིག་ཡོད་གཅིག་མེད་ཅེས་བྱ་བ། །དེ་ཉིད་མིན་ཞིང་འཇིག་རྟེན་ཉིད་བཟང་མིན། །དེས་ན་འདི་ཡོད་འདི་མེད་ཅེས། །བརྗོད་པ་ཉིད་དུ་ནུས་མ་ཡིན། །ཞེས་སོ། །ཞེས་གསུངས་པའི་ཕྱིར། །ཐལ་འགྱུར་བས་ཚོགས་དྲུག་ལས་ངོ་བོ་ཐ་དད་པའི་ཀུན་གཞི་རྣམ་ཤེས་མི་བཞེད་པའི་རྒྱུ་མཚན་ཡང་རང་བཞིན་གྱིས་འགྲུབ་པ་བདེན་པ་གཉིས་ཀར་ཞལ་གྱིས་མི་བཞེས་པ་དེ་ལ་ཐུག་པ་ཡིན་ནོ། །ཚོགས་དྲུག་ལས་ངོ་བོ་ཐ་དད་པའི་ཀུན་གཞི་རྣམ་ཤེས་འདོད་ན་ནི། མདོ་སྡེ་དགོངས་འགྲེལ་དང་ཐེག་བསྡུས་དང་གནད་ལ་དབབ་པའི་བསྡུ་བ་དང་དབུས་མཐའ་རྣམ་འགྲེལ་སོགས་ནས་བཤད་པ་ལྟར་འདོད་ 219

༄༅། །དགོས་ལ། དེ་ལྟར་འདོད་ན་མ་བརྟགས་མ་དཔྱད་པའི་ཐ་སྙད་པའི་ཤེས་པ་གནོད་མེད་ཀྱིས་འགྲུབ་ས་མེད་པས་ཀུན་གཞི་ཞེས་པའི་མིང་གིས་བརྟགས་པའི་དོན་ཇི་འདྲ་ཞིག་ཏུ་གྲུབ་བཙལ་ན་ནི་རིགས་པས་རྙེད་དགོས་ལ་དེ་ལྟར་ན་རང་བཞིན་གྱིས་གྲུབ་པའི་དོན་མི་འདོད་བཞིན་དུ་འང་ཁས་ལེན་དགོས་པར་འགྱུར་བའི་ཕྱིར་རོ། །གཞན་ཡང་། ཚིགས་དྲུག་ལས་ངོ་བོ་ཐ་དད་པའི་ཀུན་གཞི་རྣམ་ཤེས་འདོད་ན་ནི་དེ་ཉིད་ཉོན་ཡིད་དང་མཚུངས་ལྡན་གྱི་རང་འཛིན་པའི་འཇིག་ལྟ་ལྷན་སྐྱེས་ཀྱི་དམིགས་པ་ཡིན་པར་བཤད་པ་ལྟར་འདོད་དགོས་པས་ཀུན་གཞི་དེ་གང་ཟག་གི་མཚན་གཞི་དང་གང་ཟག་དེ་བཏགས་དོན་བཙལ་ན་རྙེད་རྒྱུ་ཡོད་པར་ཁས་ལེན་དགོས་པར་འགྱུར་རོ། །གཞན་ཡང་། ཐལ་འགྱུར་བས་ཕྱི་དོན་ཁས་ལེན་པའི་རྒྱུ་མཚན་གྱིས་ཀྱང་ཀུན་གཞི་མི་བཞེད་པར་གྲུབ་སྟེ། ལེགས་བཤད་སྙིང་པོ་ལས། ཕྱི་རོལ་ཁས་ལེན་པའི་གནད་ཀྱིས་ཀྱང་ཀུན་གཞི་མི་འཇོག་པ་ཡིན་ཏེ། དེ་ཁས་ལེན་ན་དབུ་མ་ཐལ་ལས། དོན་དང་སེམས་ཅན་བདག་རྣམ་རིག །སྣང་བའི་རྣམ་པར་ཤེས་པ་ནི། །རབ་ཏུ་སྐྱེའོ་དེ་དོན་མེད། །དེ་མེད་པས་ན་དེ་ཡང་མེད། །ཅེས་གསུངས་པ་ལྟར་འདོད་དགོས་པའི་ཕྱིར་རོ། །ཞེས་གསུངས་པས་སོ། །གཞན་ཡང་འཇུག་པ་ལས། ཀུན་གཞི་ཡོད་ཅིང་གང་ཟག་ཉིད་ཡོད་ལ། །ཕུང་པོ་འདི་དག་འབའ་ཞིག་ཉིད་ཡོད་ཅེས། །བསྟན་པ་འདི་ནི་དེ་ལྟར་ཆེས་ཟབ་དོན། །རིག་པར་མི་འགྱུར་གང་ཡིན་དེ་ལའོ། །ཞེས་པ་ལྟར། ཀུན་གཞི་རྣམ་ཤེས་ཡོད་ཅིང་གང་ཟག་རྫས་སུ་ཡོད་ལ་ཕུང་པོ་དེ་ཙམ་རྫས་སུ་ཡོད་ཅེས་མདོ་འགའ་ཞིག་ལས་བསྟན་པ་དེ་ནི་སྟོང་བཤད་པའི་ཟབ་དོན་རྟོགས་མི་ནུས་པའི་གདུལ་བྱ་ལ་དགོངས་ཏེ་གསུངས་སོ་ཞེས་ཀུན་གཞི་དང་གང་ཟག་དང་ཕུང་པོ་གསུམ་ཀ་རྫས་སུ་ཡོད་པར་གསུངས་པ་ཁྱད་པར་མེད་པར་དྲང་དོན་དུ་གསུངས་ཀྱང་། གང་ཟག་དང་ཕུང་པོ་རྫས་ཡོད་དུ་གསུངས་པའི་དགོངས་གཞི་ནི་གང་ཟག་དང་ཕུང་པོ་ཐ་སྙད་དུ་ཡོད་པ་ལ་དགོངས་ནས་གསུངས་པ་ཡིན་པས་དགོངས་གཞི་ལོགས་སུ་མ་གསུངས་ཀྱང་། ཀུན་གཞི་རྫས་ཡོད་དུ་གསུངས་པ་ནི་སྟོང་ཉིད་ལ་དགོངས་ནས་གསུངས་ཞེས་འཇུག་འགྲེལ་དུ་གསུངས་པ་ལྟར་དགོངས་གཞི་ལོགས་སུ་བཤད་པ་ངེས་ཀྱང་ཐལ་འགྱུར་བས་ཀུན་གཞི་ཐ་སྙད་དུ་ཡོད་པར་མི་བཞེད་པར་གོ་ནུས་སོ། །

སྒྲོན་འཇུག་དར་ཊཱི་ཀ་ལས། ཉན་རང་དགྲ་བཅོམ་པའི་འབྲས་བུ་ཐོབ་པ་ལ་ཡང་སྟོང་ཉིད་རྟོགས་པ་ངེས་པར་དགོས་པར་ཐལ། རྒྱ་མཚན་གང་གི་ཕྱིར་ན་ཤེས་རབ་ཀྱི་ཕ་རོལ་ཏུ་ཕྱིན་པའི་མདོ་སྡེའི་ལུང་ལས་སྟོང་ཉིད་རྟོགས་པའི་ལམ་འདི་ནི་གོམས་པ་མེད་པར་བྱང་ཆུབ་གསུམ་ག་ཐོབ་པ་མེད་པར་གསུངས་པའི་ཕྱིར་རོ། །སྒྲོན་འཇུག་འགྲེལ་ཆེན་ལས་ཡུམ་གྱི་མདོ་ལས། དངོས་པོ་འི་འདུ་ཤེས་ཅན་ལ་ཐར་བ་མེད་པ་དང་། དུས་གསུམ་གྱི་ཡང་དག་པར་རྫོགས་པའི་སངས་རྒྱས་དང་རྒྱུན་ཞུགས་ནས་རང་རྒྱལ་གྱི་བར་རྣམས་ཤེར་ཕྱིན་འདི་ཉིད་ལ་བརྟེན་ནས་ཐོབ་པར་གསུངས་པ་དྲངས་པ་ལྟར་ཡིན་གྱི་བླ་ན་མེད་པའི་བྱང་ཆུབ་ཀྱང་བ་ལ་བྱེད་པ་གཞུང་གི་དོན་མིན་ནོ། །ཞེས་པ་ལྟར་ཡིན་ལ། དངོས་པོ་འི་འདུ་ཤེས་ཅན་ཞེས་པ་ནི་བདེན་གྲུབ་ཀྱི་འདུ་ཤེས་ཅན་ཞེས་པ་དང་འདྲ་སྟེ། བདེན་གྲུབ་དང་དངོས་པོ་གཉིས་ལ་སྐད་དོད་ཐུན་མོང་པ་ཡོད་པར་གསུངས་པའི་ཕྱིར་རོ། ། འཇུག་པའི་རྣམ་བཤད་ལས། ཆོས་རྣམས་རང་བཞིན་གྱིས་གྲུབ་པ་མེད་པའི་བདག་མེད་འདི་ནི། བཅོམ་ལྡན་འདས་ཀྱིས་གང་ཟག་གི་བདག་མེད་པ་དང་། ཆོས་ཀྱི་བདག་མེད་པའི་དབྱེ་བ་རྣམ་པ་གཉིས་སུ་གསུངས་སོ། །དེ་གཉིས་སུ་འབྱེད་ཚུལ་ནི་ཡང་གཞི་གང་ཟག་དང་ཆོས་ཀྱི་སྟེང་དུ་མེད་རྒྱུའི་བདག་མི་འདྲ་བ་གཉིས་ཀྱི་སྒོ་ནས་ཕྱེ་བ་མིན་ཏེ། མེད་རྒྱུའི་བདག་ནི་རང་བཞིན་གྱིས་གྲུབ་པ་ཡིན་པས་སོ། །དེའི་ཕྱིར་གཞི་ཆོས་ཅན་ཕུང་རྣམས་ཀྱི་ཆོས་དང་གང་ཟག་གི་དབྱེ་བས་ཕྱེ་བའོ། །དགོས་པ་ཅིའི་ཕྱིར་དེ་གཉིས་བསྟན་ཞེ་ན། གང་ཟག་གི་བདག་མེད་ནི་ཉན་རང་གི་འགྲོ་བ་རྣམས་འཁོར་བ་ལས་རྣམ་པར་གྲོལ་བར་བྱ་བའི་ཕྱིར་བསྟན་ལ། བྱང་སེམས་ཀྱི་འགྲོ་བ་རྣམས་ཐམས་ཅད་མཁྱེན་པ་ཐོབ་པས་རྣམ་པར་གྲོལ་བར་བྱ་བའི་ཕྱིར་བདག་མེད་གཉིས་ཀ་བསྟན་ཏོ། །ཞེས་གསུངས་སོ། །ལུས་ལ་ལུས་དབང་ཞེས་སོགས་ཀྱི་དོན་ཡང་དེའི་དར་ཊཱི་ཀ་ལས། ལུས་ལ་ལུས་ཀྱི་དབང་པོ་མིག་ལ་སོགས་པའི་དབང་པོ་གཞན་རྣམས་ལ་ཁྱབ་ཅིང་། དེ་དག་གི་རྟེན་དུ་གནས་ལ་དེ་མེད་ན་དབང་པོ་གཞན་རྣམས་ཀྱང་མི་གནས་པ་ཇི་ལྟ་བ་བཞིན་དུ་དེ་ཉིད་འབྲེལ་བར་འབྱུང་བ་རང་བཞིན་གྱིས་གྲུབ་པས་སྟོང་པ་ལ་བདེན་པར་ཞེན་པའི་གཏི་མུག་ཉོན་མོངས་ཅན་གྱི་མ་རིག་པ་ནི། ཆགས་སྡང་ལ་སོགས་པའི་ཉོན་མོངས་ཀུན་ལ་ཁྱབ་ཅིང་གནས་པར་འགྱུར་ཏེ།

༄༅། །གང་ཟག་གིས་བཏགས་པའི་དངོས་པོར་རང་བཞིན་གྱིས་གྲུབ་པའི་ཡོད་དུ་འོང་བ་དང་མི་འོང་བར་ཞེན་ནས་འདོད་པ་དང་། རྒྱབ་ཀྱིས་ཕྱོགས་པ་སོགས་སུ་ཞེན་པའི་ཕྱིར་རོ། །དེས་ན་ཆགས་སྡང་གཉིས་ཀའི་འཛིན་སྟངས་ལ། བདེན་འཛིན་གྱི་འཛིན་སྟངས་དང་འདྲེས་པའི་ཚུལ་ཤེས་པར་བྱའོ། །ཞེས་པ་ལྟར་ཏེ། རྒྱས་པར་འཇུག་ཊཱི་ཀ་ཆེན་མོ་དང་ལེགས་བཤད་སྙིང་པོ་གཉིས་ལས་ཤེས་པར་བྱའོ། ། ཁྱད་དགྲ་བཅོམ་པར་འདོད་པའི་གང་ཟག་དེའི་རྒྱུད་ཀྱི་སྲིད་པ་འདི་མངོན་པ་ནས་བཤད་པ་ལྟར་གྱི་ཉོན་མོངས་ཅན་མིན་ཡང་། མངོན་པ་ནས་ཀུན་རྨོངས་མ་རིག་པ་ལ་ཉོན་མོངས་ཅན་ཡིན་མིན་གཉིས་སུ་འདོད་པ་བཞིན་དུ་སྲིད་པ་ལ་ཡང་མངོན་པ་ནས་བཤད་པ་ལྟར་གྱི་ཉོན་མོངས་ཅན་ཡིན་པ་གཅིག་དང་མིན་པ་གཅིག་ཀྱང་ཅི་སྟེ་མེད་དེ་འདོད་དགོས་སོ། །ཞེས་པའོ། ། ཤེས་བྱ་ཕྱིན་ཅི་ལོག་རྫུན་པ་དང་། ཤེས་བྱ་ཕྱིན་ཅི་མ་ལོག་པ་བདེན་པ་དག་ནི་ཐ་དད་པ་སྟེ་དངོས་འགལ་ཡིན་ནོ། །ཤེས་བྱ་ཕྱིན་ཅི་ལོག་དང་རྫུན་པ་དང་། ཤེས་པ་འཁྲུལ་བས་རྙེད་པའི་དོན་དང་ཀུན་རྫོབ་བདེན་པ་རྣམས་དོན་གཅིག་ཡིན་པས་སོ། ཀུན་རྫོབ་བདེན་པ་ནི། རབ་རིབ་ཅན་གྱིས་སྐྲ་ཤད་ལ་སོགས་པ་ཡོད་པ་མ་ཡིན་པ་ལ་ཡོད་པར་སྣང་བ་ལྟར་དོན་དམ་པར་ཡོད་པ་མ་ཡིན་པ་ལ་ཡོད་པར་སྣང་བའི་ཤེས་པ་འཁྲུལ་བས་རྙེད་པའི་དོན་ཡིན་ཞེས་པའོ། །རབ་རིབ་མཐུ་ཡིས་ཞེས་སོགས་ཀྱི་དོན་ནི། རབ་རིབ་ཅན་གྱིས་སྐྲ་ཤད་ལ་སོགས་པ་མཐོང་བ་ནི། སྐྲ་ཤད་ལ་སོགས་པ་གཞི་གང་དུ་མཐོང་བ་དེར་རབ་རིབ་མེད་པའི་གང་ཟག་གིས་མིག་གཏད་ཀྱང་སྐྲ་ཤད་ལ་སོགས་པ་མ་དམིགས་ཤིང་མེད་པར་མཐོང་ངོ་། །དེ་ལ་ཡིན་ཚུལ་ནི་རབ་རིབ་མེད་པས་མཐོང་བ་དེ་ཡིན་གྱི། རབ་རིབ་ཅན་གྱིས་མཐོང་བ་དེ་མིན་པ་བཞིན་དུ། མ་རིག་པས་བསླད་པའི་གང་ཟག་གིས་བདེན་པར་གྲུབ་པར་སྣང་བའི་གཞི་ཕུང་ཁམས་སྐྱེ་མཆེད་སོགས་ལ་མ་རིག་པའི་བག་ཆགས་སྤངས་པའི་སངས་རྒྱས་ཀྱིས་ཐུགས་གཏད་ཀྱང་གཞི་དེར་བདེན་པར་གྲུབ་པ་རྡུལ་ཙམ་ཡང་མ་དམིགས་ཤིང་མེད་པར་གཟིགས་པའི་ཡུལ་དེ་ནི་དོན་དམ་བདེན་པ་ཡིན་པར་ཤེས་པར་གྱིས་ཤིག །ཅེས་པའོ། ། དེ་ཡང་དང་པོ་གཞུང་ཆེན་ལ། ཞེས་སོགས་ཀྱི་དོན་ནི་རང་རྒྱུད་པའི་སྐབས་སུ་བཤད་ཟིན་ཏོ། །

སོ་སྐྱེའི་བློ་ཐམས་ཅད་འཁྲུལ་ཤེས་དང་བཅད་ཤེས་ཚད་མ་ཡིན་པར་འདོད་པ་གཉིས་ཀ་རང་མཚན་ཁས་མི་ལེན་པ་ལ་ཐུག་པ་ཡིན་ཏེ། སོ་སྐྱེའི་བློ་ཡིན་ན་རང་མཚན་གྱིས་གྲུབ་པར་སྣང་བས་ཁྱབ་པ་གང་ཞིག །གསར་དུ་མི་བསླུ་བའི་ཤེས་པ་ཡིན་ན་རིགས་ཤེས་ཀྱིས་དཔྱད་ནས་རྙེད་པའི་དོན་ཡིན་དགོས་པའི་ཕྱིར། དང་པོ་སླ། གཉིས་པ་གྲུབ་སྟེ། སྟོང་ཐུན་བསྐལ་བཟང་མིག་འབྱེད་ལས། རང་གི་འཛིན་སྟངས་ཀྱི་ཡུལ་དུ་གྱུར་པའི་གཞལ་བྱ་ལ་མི་བསླུ་བ་ཙམ་གྱིས་ཚད་མར་འཇོག་མི་ནུས་པའི་གསར་དུ་མི་བསླུ་བ་དགོས་པར་འདོད་པ་ནི་མི་འཐད་དེ། ཚད་མ་གསར་དུ་མི་བསླུ་བ་དགོས་པར་ཐ་སྙད་པའི་ཚད་མ་ཙམ་གྱིས་མ་འགྲུབ་ཅིང་དོན་དམ་དཔྱོད་བྱེད་ཀྱི་ཚད་མས་ཚད་མ་ཅུང་ཟད་ཀྱང་མི་རྙེད་པའི་ཕྱིར་རོ། །སྔ་མ་དེར་ཐལ། བློ་བུར་གྱི་འཁྲུལ་རྒྱུས་གནོད་པ་མེད་ཅིང་མ་བརྟགས་མ་དཔྱད་པར་འཇུག་པའི་འཇིག་རྟེན་པའི་བློ་ལྷན་སྐྱེས་རང་དགའ་བས་རང་གིས་གཞལ་བའི་དོན་ལ་མི་བསླུ་བ་ཙམ་ལ་ཚད་མར་ཐ་སྙད་བྱེད་ཀྱི་གསར་དུ་མི་བསླུ་བའི་བློ་ནས་ཐ་སྙད་བྱེད་པ་ཆུང་ཟད་ཀྱང་མེད་པའི་ཕྱིར་དང་། རྟོག་གེ་པ་དག་གིས་ཚད་མའི་མཚན་ཉིད་ཀྱི་ཟུར་དུ་གསར་དུ་ཅེས་པའི་ཚིག་སྨོས་དགོས་པའི་སྒྲུབ་བྱེད་གང་བཀོད་པ་ཐམས་ཅད་ཚད་མར་སོང་ཚུལ་རིགས་པས་དཔྱད་ནས་རྙེད་པའི་དོན་ལ་ཚད་མར་འཇོག་པའི་དབང་དུ་བྱས་པ་ཡིན་པའི་ཕྱིར་རོ། །ཞེས་གསུངས་པས་སོ། ། མངོན་སུམ་གྱི་ཚད་མ་ཡིན་ན་རྟོག་མེད་ཀྱི་ཤེས་པ་ཡིན་པས་མ་ཁྱབ་སྟེ། ཚད་མ་བ་ལ་གྲགས་པའི་འདོད་བསྟན་ཡིད་མངོན་དེ་སྐབས་འདིར་དྲན་ཤེས་སུ་འདོད་པའི་ཕྱིར་དང་། ཡིད་ཤེས་ཀྱི་ཆེ་རབ་ཡིད་མངོན་ཚད་མར་འདོད་པའི་ཕྱིར། དང་པོ་གྲུབ་སྟེ། རྣམ་བཤད་ལས། ཡིད་ཀྱི་མངོན་སུམ་ཡང་ཚད་མ་ནས་བཤད་པ་ལྟར་མི་བཞེད་དོ། བཞི་བརྒྱ་པའི་འགྲེལ་པ་ལས། ཆོས་མངོན་པ་ནས་གཟུགས་སོགས་ལྔ་རེ་རེ་ཞིང་དབང་པོ་དང་ཡིད་ཤེས་ཀྱིས་ཤེས་པར་བྱ་བར་གསུངས་པའི་དོན་འཆད་པ་ནི། རྣམ་པར་ཤེས་པ་གཉིས་ཀྱིས་དོན་གཅིག་རྣམ་པར་ཤེས་པ་མ་ཡིན་ཏེ། གཅིག་ནི་ཡུལ་གྱི་རྣམ་པ་དངོས་སུ་གཅོད་པར་བྱེད་པ་སྟེ་གང་དང་པོར་སྐྱེ་བའོ། །གཉིས་པ་ནི། དངོས་སུ་བྱེད་པ་ཉིད་དུ་རྣམ་པར་ཤེས་པ་མ་ཡིན་ཏེ། དབང་པོ་ནི་རྣམ་པར་ཤེས་པའི་སྟོབས་ཀྱིས་དེ་ལྟར་རྟོག་ཅིང་སྐྱེ་བས་ན། དེས་ཀྱང་དོན་དེ་རྣམ་པར་ཤེས་སོ་

༄༅། །ཞེས་ཏེ་བར་འདོགས་སོ། །ཞེས་དང་པོ་དབང་ཤེས་ཀྱིས་གཟུགས་སོགས་ཀྱི་དོན་དེ་དངོས་སུ་རིག་ལ། ཡིད་ཤེས་ཀྱིས་དབང་ཤེས་ཀྱི་སྟོབས་ཀྱིས་རིག་གི་དབང་ཤེས་བཞིན་དུ་དངོས་སུ་མི་རིག་པར་གསུངས་ཤིང་ནུབ་པར་ཡང་གསུངས་སོ།།
ཞེས་དང་། སྟོང་ཐུན་ལས་ཀྱང་། དབང་ཤེས་ཀྱི་གཟུགས་སོགས་ཀྱི་དོན་དེ་དངོས་སུ་གསལ་བར་རིག་ལ། ཡིད་ཤེས་ཀྱིས་དབང་ཤེས་ཀྱི་སྟོབས་ཀྱིས་རིག་གི །དབང་ཤེས་བཞིན་དུ་དངོས་སུ་གསལ་བར་མི་རིག་པར་གསུངས་ཤིང་། དབང་ཤེས་ཀྱི་སྟོབས་ཀྱིས
ཡུལ་རིག་པའི་ཡིད་ཤེས་རྣམས་ནུབ་པ་ཡིན་པར་གསུངས་པའི་ཕྱིར་རོ། །ཞེས་གསུངས་སོ། །གཉིས་པ་ཡང་གྲུབ་སྟེ། རྣམ་བཤད་ལས། ཡང་བཞི་བརྒྱ་པའི་འགྲེལ་པ་ལས། ཚོར་བ་ལ་སོགས་ལྟར་ཉམས་སུ་མྱོང་བའི་རྣམ་པ་ཡང་མ་ཡིན་ལ། གཟུགས་དང་སྒྲ་ལ
སོགས་པ་བཞིན་དབང་པོའི་སྒོ་ནས་ཡོངས་སུ་བཅད་པར་བྱ་བ་ཡང་མ་ཡིན་ནོ། །ཞེས་གསུངས་པས་མངོན་གྱུར་དུ་འཛལ་བ་ལ་དབང་ཤེས་ཀྱིས་གཟུགས་སོགས་གཅོད་ལྟ་བུ་དང་། ཚོར་བ་བདེ་སྡུག་ལ་སོགས་ལྟར་ནང་དུ་ཉམས་མྱོང་གིས་ཡོངས་སུ་གཅོད་པ་གཉིས
གསུངས་སོ། །དེ་གཉིས་ཀྱི་ཕྱི་མ་ནི་གཞི་དུས་ནས་ཀྱང་ཁས་བླང་དགོས་ལ། ཞེས་པ་ནས། དེ་ལྟར་ན་ཚོར་བ་ཞེས་པ་ནི་བྱེད་པ་པོ་དང་བྱེད་པ་དང་ལས་དང་འབྲེལ་བའི་ཚིག་ཡིན་པས་གང་ཟག་འདིས་ཚོར་བ་དང་། བྱེད་པ་འདིས་ཚོར་བ་དང་། འདི་འདྲ་བ་ཞིག
ཚོར་བ་ཞེས་པ་གསུམ་དུ་འགྱུར་རོ། །དེའི་གཉིས་པ་ནི་ཚད་མ་སྟེ་སེམས་བྱུང་ཚོར་བའོ། །གསུམ་པ་ནི་གཞལ་བྱ་སྟེ་བདེ་བ་དང་སྡུག་བསྔལ་དང་བཏང་སྙོམས་སོ། །འདི་ཡང་ཡིད་ཤེས་ཀྱི་དབང་དུ་བྱས་ཀྱི་དབང་ཤེས་ཀྱི་ཚོར་བ་གསུམ་གྱིས་གཟུགས་སྒྲ་སོགས་ཡོངས
སུ་གཅོད་དེ། ཞེས་དང་། འོན་ཡིད་ཤེས་ཀྱི་ཚོར་བས་བདེ་སྡུག་སོགས་མངོན་གྱུར་དུ་གཅོད་ན་རང་རིག་ཏུ་མི་འགྱུར་རམ་སྙམ་ན། སྐྱོན་མེད་དེ་བཀག་པའི་རང་རིག་ནི་ཤེས་པ་ཐམས་ཅད་ཁ་ནང་ལྟ་བ་རིག་བྱ་དང་རིག་བྱེད་ཐ་དད་པར་སྣང་བ་ནུབ་པའི་འཛིན་རྣམ
ཤར་བ་ཡིན་ཞིང་། འདིར་ནི་ཉམས་སུ་མྱོང་བ་ཁྱད་པར་ཅན་ཚོར་བའི་མཚན་ཉིད་དུ་བརྗོད་སྟེ་ན་གསུངས་ལ། འཇིག་རྟེན་གྱི་ཐ་སྙད་ལས་ཀྱང་བདེ་བ་དང་སྡུག་བསྔལ་ཉམས་སུ་མྱོང་ངོ་ཞེས་བརྗོད་པའི་ཕྱིར། མྱོང་བྱ་དང་མྱོང་བྱེད་ཐ་དད་པ་ཉིད་དུ་སྣང་བའི་ཕྱིར་ན

ཕྱོགས་སྔ་མའི་རང་རིག་དང་མི་གཅིག་གོ །ཞེས་གསུངས་པའི་ཕྱིར་རོ། ། (ཟ) ཁྱད་རང་གིས་དགྲ་བཅོམ་པར་འདོད་ངའི་གང་ཟག་གི་རྒྱུད་ལ་རེ་ཞིག་མངོན་པ་ནས་བཤད་པའི་ཉོན་མོངས་མངོན་གྱུར་དུ་རྒྱུ་བ་མེད་ཀྱང་ངས་ཀྱི་དབང་གིས་ཡ་སྲིད
ཕྱི་མ་འཕེན་པའི་ནུས་པ་མཐོང་བ་ཡིན་ཞེས་པའོ། ། (འ) ཡང་འཕགས་པ་བསམ་གཏན་པའི་དཔེ་མ་རྒྱུད་ཀྱི་མདོ་ཚིག་གསལ་དུ་དྲངས་པ་ལས། འཇམ་དཔལ་འཕགས་པའི་བདེན་པ་རྣམས་ཡང་དག་པ་ཇི་ལྟ་བ་བཞིན་དུ་མ་མཐོང་བས། སེམས
ཅན་ཕྱིན་ཅི་ལོག་གཞིས་སེམས་ཕྱིན་ཅི་ལོག་ཏུ་གྱུར་པ་རྣམས་འཁོར་བ་ཡང་དག་པ་མ་ཡིན་པ་འདི་ལས་འདའ་བར་མི་འགྱུར་རོ། །ཞེས་གསུངས་པ་ལ་འཇམ་དཔལ་གྱིས། བཅོམ་ལྡན་འདས་གང་ལ་ཉེ་བར་དམིགས་པས་སེམས་ཅན་རྣམས་འཁོར་བ་ལས་འདའ་བར་མི
འགྱུར་བ་བསྟན་དུ་གསོལ། ཞེས་སྟོན་པས་བདེན་བཞི་ཡང་དག་པ་ཇི་ལྟ་བ་བཞིན་དུ་མ་ཤེས་པས་འཁོར་བ་ལས་མི་གྲོལ་བར་གསུངས་པ་ལ། རྗེ་བཙུན་གྱིས་ཡུལ་གང་ལ་ཇི་འདྲ་བ་ཞིག་ཏུ་དམིགས་པས་འཁོར་བ་ལས་མི་ཐར་བ་བཤད་པ་ཞུས་པའི་ལན་དུ། བདག་ནི་འཁོར
བ་ལས་འདའ་བ་དང་། མྱང་འདས་འཐོབ་པར་འགྱུར་རོ་སྙམ་དུ་བདེན་པར་ཞེན་པའི་ཚུལ་གྱིས་རྟོག་པར་བྱེད་པས། མི་རྟག་པ་ལ་སོགས་པ་བསྒོམས་པ་ན། བདག་གིས་སྡུག་བསྔལ་ཤེས་སོ། །ཀུན་འབྱུང་སྤངས་སོ། །འགོག་པ་མངོན་དུ་བྱས་སོ། །ལམ་བསྒོམས་སོ་སྙམ
ནས་བདག་ནི་དགྲ་བཅོམ་པར་གྱུར་ཏོ་སྙམ་པ་འབྱུང་བར་གསུངས་ཏེ། ཐར་པ་བཤད་པ་ལྟར་གྱི་ཉོན་མོངས་མངོན་གྱུར་རེ་ཞིག་སྤངས་པ་ན། ཟག་པ་ཐམས་ཅད་ཟད་དོ་སྙམ་པ་སྐྱེས་པའོ། །དེ་འཆི་བའི་དུས་ཀྱི་ཚེ་དང་སྐྱེ་བ་ཡིན་པར་མཐོང་བ་ན། སངས་རྒྱས་ལ་ཐེ་ཚོམ
ཟོས་པའི་ཉེས་པས། དམྱལ་བ་ཆེན་པོར་ལྟུང་བར་གསུངས་སོ། །དེ་ནི་ལམ་དེ་ལྟ་བུ་ལ་གནས་པ་འགའ་ཞིག་ལ་ཡིན་གྱི། ཐམས་ཅད་ལ་ནི་མ་ཡིན་ནོ། །ཞེས་རྣམ་བཤད་ལས་གསུངས་སོ། །བདག་ནི་དགྲ་བཅོམ་པར་གྱུར་ཏོ། །ཞེས་བྱ་བར་བདག་གིས་ཤེས་སོ། །ཞེས
འདོན་པར་བྱའོ། ། (ཡ) གཞུང་མཐའ་སྒྲ་བ་གཞན་གྱི་ལུགས་ལ། ཞིག་འཇིག་འགལ་བ་ཡིན་པས། བྱས་པའི་འཇིག་པ་དང་བྱས་པའི་ཞིག་པ་གཉིས་འགལ་བ་ཡིན་ལ། བྱས་པ་རང་དུས་གཉིས་པར་མི་སྡོད་པ་ནི་བྱས་པ་འཇིག་པའི་དོན་དང་། བྱས་པ་

༄༅། །རང་དུས་གཉིས་པར་མ་བསྡད་པ་ནི་བུམ་པ་ཞིག་པའི་དོན་ཡིན་ཞིང་། དང་པོ་འདུ་བྱེད་ཀྱི་ཕུང་པོ་དང་གཉིས་པ་འདུས་མ་བྱས་སུ་འདོད་དོ། །ཐལ་འགྱུར་བའི་ལུགས་ལ། ཞིག་འཇིག་མི་འགལ་བས། བུམ་པ་ཞིག་པ་ཡང་བུམ་པའི་འཇིག་པ་ཡིན་ནོ། །གཞན་ཡང་། བུམ་པའི་འཇིག་པ་ཞེས་པ་ནི་བུམ་པ་འཇིག་པའི་བྱ་བ་ལ་འདོད་པ་ནི་མདོ་སྡེ་པ་ཡན་ཆད་འདོད་པ་མཐུན་པ་ཡིན་ཀྱང་ཐལ་འགྱུར་བས། བུམ་པ་རང་དུས་གཉིས་པར་མི་སྡོད་པ་དང་མ་བསྡད་པ་གཉིས་ཀ་བུམ་པའི་འཇིག་པའི་བྱ་བ་ཡིན་པར་འདོད་པའི་ཕྱིར་བུམ་པ་ཞིག་པ་ལ་མངོན་དུ་ཕྱོགས་པ་དང་བུམ་པ་ཞིག་པ་གཉིས་ཀ་བུམ་པའི་འཇིག་པའི་བྱ་བ་ཡིན་པར་འདོད་དེ། དཔེར་ན་མྱུ་གུ་སྐྱེ་བ་ལ་མངོན་དུ་ཕྱོགས་པ་དང་མྱུ་གུ་སྐྱེ་བ་གཉིས་ཀ་མྱུ་གུ་སྐྱེ་བའི་བྱ་བ་ཡིན་པ་བཞིན་ནོ་ཞེས་བཞེད་ལ། མདོ་སེམས་རང་རྒྱུད་པ་གསུམ་གྱིས་མྱུ་གུ་སྐྱེ་བ་ལ་མངོན་དུ་ཕྱོགས་པ་དང་མྱུ་གུ་སྐྱེ་བ་གཉིས་ཀ་མྱུ་གུ་སྐྱེ་བའི་བྱ་བ་ཡིན་ཀྱང་། མྱུ་གུ་ཞིག་པ་ལ་མངོན་དུ་ཕྱོགས་པ་དང་མྱུ་གུ་ཞིག་པ་གཉིས་ཀ་མྱུ་གུ་འཇིག་པའི་བྱ་བ་མིན་ཏེ། མྱུ་གུ་ཞིག་པ་ནི་མྱུ་གུའི་འཇིག་པའི་བྱ་བ་མ་ཡིན་པའི་ཕྱིར་ཏེ། དེ་དངོས་པོ་མ་ཡིན་པའི་ཕྱིར་ཞེས་འདོད་དོ། །ཐལ་འགྱུར་བའི་ལུགས་ལ། ཞིག་པ་དངོས་པོར་སྒྲུབ་པ་ལ་ལུང་རིགས་གཉིས་ཚིག་གསལ་ལས་གསུངས་པའི་དང་པོ་ནི། ས་བཅུ་པ་ལས། སྐྱེ་བའི་རྐྱེན་གྱིས་རྒ་ཤི་ཞེས་གསུངས་ཏེ། ཤི་བ་ནི་གང་ཤི་བའི་སེམས་ཅན་དེ་ཞིག་པ་ཡིན་ལ། དེ་སྐྱེ་བའི་རྐྱེན་གྱིས་བསྐྱེད་པར་གསུངས་པ་དང་། ཡང་དེ་ཉིད་ལས་འཆི་བ་ཡང་བྱ་བ་གཉིས་སུ་ཉེ་བར་གནས་པ་ཡིན་ཏེ་འདུ་བྱེད་འཇིག་པར་ཡང་བྱེད་པ་དང་། ཡོངས་སུ་མི་ཤེས་པ་རྒྱུན་མི་འཆད་པའི་རྒྱུ་ཡང་འབྱིན་པའོ། །ཞེས་འཆི་བས་བྱ་བ་གཉིས་བྱེད་པར་གསུངས་ཏེ། ཞི་བ་རྒྱུས་བྱེད་པ་དང་། ཞི་བས་ན་རིག་པ་བསྐྱེད་པར་ཡང་གསུངས་པས། ཞིག་པ་ལ་སྐྱེད་པའི་རྒྱུ་ཡོད་པ་དང་། ཞིག་པས་འབྲས་བུ་བསྐྱེད་ནུས་པ་ཡིན་ནོ། །འདི་ནི་རྒྱུན་གྱི་ཞིག་པ་ཡིན་ཡང་སྐད་ཅིག་མ་དང་པོ་དུས་གཉིས་པར་ཞིག་པ་ལ་ཡང་འདྲ་ལ། སྐད་ཅིག་མ་དང་པོ་དུས་གཉིས་པར་ཞིག་པའི་རྒྱུར་ཡང་བསྟན་ནོ། །དེས་ན་སེམས་ཅན་སྐྱེས་པ་དང་ཤི་བ་གཉིས་དང་སྐད་ཅིག་མ་གཉིས་པར་མི་སྡོད་པ་དང་། སྐད་ཅིག་མ་གཉིས་པར་མ་བསྡད་པ་རྣམས་ལ་དངོས་པོར་འཇོག་མི་འཇོག་དང་། རྒྱུས་བསྐྱེད

མི་བསྐྱེད་ཀུན་ནས་མཚུངས་སོ། །ཞེས་རྣམ་བཤད་ལས་གསུངས་སོ། །

དངོས་པོ་དང་དངོས་པོ་ཞིག་ནས་མེད་པ་གཉིས་ཀ་འདུས་བྱས་ཡིན་ཞེས་པ་སྟེ། དེ་ཡང་རང་མཚན་ཁས་མི་ལེན་པ་ལ་ཐུག་པའི་ཕྱིར་ཏེ། འཇུག་པའི་རྣམ་བཤད་ལས། དེ་ཡང་དངོས་པོ་རང་བཞིན་གྱིས་གྲུབ་པར་འདོད་པའི་ཕྱོགས་ཐམས་ཅད་ལ། ཞིག་པ་དངོས་པོར་མི་རུང་ལ་རང་བཞིན་གྱིས་མ་གྲུབ་པར་འདོད་པའི་དབུ་མའི་ཕྱོགས་ལ་ཞིག་པ་དངོས་པོར་འགྲུབ་པའི་གནད་དོ། །ལུགས་དང་པོ་ལ་ནི། མྱུ་གུ་སྣ་བུའི་དངོས་པོ་ཅིག་ཞིག་པ་ན། མྱུ་གུའི་ཆ་ཤས་ཀྱི་དངོས་པོ་ཐམས་ཅད་ནི་ལོག་པ། མྱུ་གུ་ལས་གཞན་པ་བུམ་པ་ལ་སོགས་པའི་དངོས་པོ་གཞན་གང་ཡང་མ་ཐོབ་པས། ཞིག་པ་དེ་དངོས་པོ་གཏན་མིན་པར་འདོད་དེ། སྔོན་པོ་ལ་སོགས་པ་སྐྱེ་མཆེད་རེ་རེ་བའི་དངོས་པོ་དང་། བུམ་པ་ལ་སོགས་པ་རང་གི་ཆ་ཤས་ཀྱི་དངོས་པོ་ཚོགས་པ་གང་ཡང་ཞིག་པ་དེའི་མཚན་གཞིར་མི་རུང་བའི་ཕྱིར་དངོས་པོ་མིན་ནོ་སྙམ་པའོ། །ལུགས་ཕྱི་མ་ལ་ནི། དཔེར་ན་ཉེར་སྤྲས་ཀྱི་ཕུང་པོ་ལྔ་རེ་རེ་བ་དང་ཚོགས་པ་གཉིས་ཀ་དང་། དེ་གཉིས་ལས་ངོ་བོ་གཞན་དུ་བ་གཅིག་ཉེར་སྤྲས་ཀྱི་མཚན་གཞིར་འཇོག་རྒྱུ་མེད་ཅིང་། ཉེར་སྤྲས་ཀྱང་དེ་གསུམ་གྱི་མཚན་གཞིར་མི་རུང་ལ། རང་གི་ཕུང་པོ་ལ་བརྟེན་ནས་ཉེར་སྤྲས་སུ་བཏགས་པ་དངོས་པོ་ཡིན་པར་མི་འགལ་བ་བཞིན་དུ། ཞིག་པ་ཡང་ཞིག་རྒྱུའི་དངོས་པོ་དང་། དེ་དང་རིགས་མཐུན་པའི་དངོས་པོ་གང་ཡང་མཚན་གཞིར་མེད་ཀྱང་། ཞིག་རྒྱུའི་དངོས་པོ་ལ་བརྟེན་ནས་སྐྱེས་པའི་ཕྱིར་དངོས་པའོ། །ཞེས་གསུངས་པས་སོ། །

དངོས་པོ་རྣམས་གནས་པ་ནི་གནས་བྱེད་ཀྱི་རྐྱེན་ལ་རག་ལས་ཏེ་གནས་པའི་རྐྱེན་མེད་ན་འཇིག་པར་འགྱུར་བའི་ཕྱིར། དེས་ན་གནས་བྱེད་ཀྱི་རྒྱུ་རས་སྡུམ་སོགས་ཟད་ཅིང་འགགས་པ་ཉིད་ལས་བྱུང་བའི་མར་མེའི་འོད་ཟད་ཅིང་འགགས་པའི་ཞི་བ་ནི་ཟད་པ་དང་འགགས་པ་ཞེས་བྱ་བར་དམིགས་པ་སྟེ། ཞེས་པའོ། །རྒྱ་བ་ལས་ཀྱང་། འབྲས་བུ་ཡིས་ནི་རྒྱུ་བཤིག་པ། །དེས་ན་མེད་པ་སྐྱེ་མི་འགྱུར། །ཞེས་རྒྱུ་འགགས་པ་འདས་པ་བྱ་སྐྱེ་བཞིན་པས་ཅུང་ཟད་པར་བཤད་པས་འཕགས་པ་ལྷ་ཡབ་སྲས་ཀྱི་བཞེད་པའོ། །མྱུ་གུ་ཞིག་པའི་འདས་པ་དངོས་པོར་བཞེད་པའི་གནད་ཀྱིས་མྱུ་གུའི་མ་འོངས་པ་ཡང་དེ་དང་འདྲ་སྟེ། དེས་ན་མེད་པ་སྐྱེ་མི་འགྱུར་གྱི

༄༅། །ཡང་དོན་ནི། །ཞེས་ཛ་ཤེའི་རྣམ་བཤད་ལས་གསུངས་སོ། ། ཐལ་བ་དང་པོའི་དོན་ནི། རང་སྡེ་ཞིག་འཇིག་འགལ་བར་འདོད་པ་རྣམས་ཀྱིས།དངོས་པོ་རྣམས་རང་གྲུབ་དུས་ལས་དུས་གཉིས་པར་མི་སྡོད་པའི་འཇིག
པ་ནི་དངོས་པོ་དེ་དང་དེའི་རྒྱུ་ཉིད་ལས་སྐྱེ་བས་རང་རྒྱུ་ལས་གཞན་པའི་ཕྱིས་འབྱུང་གི་རྒྱུ་ལ་མི་ལྟོས་པར་འདོད་ལ། སྐད་ཅིག་གཉིས་པར་ཞིག་པ་ནི་དངོས་མེད་ཡིན་པས་རྒྱུ་གཏན་མེད་དུ་འདོད་དོ། །དེ་ལ་འདིར་ཞིག་མ་ཞིག་གཉིས་རྒྱུས་སྐྱེད་མི་སྐྱེད་མགོ་མཚུངས་བྱས
ནས་གནོད་པ་སྟོན་པ་ཡིན་ཏེ་འདི་ལྟར་དུས་གཉིས་པར་མ་བསྡད་པ་ལ་རྒྱུ་མེད་ན་དུས་གཉིས་པར་མི་སྡོད་པ་ལ་ཡང་རྒྱུ་མེད་དགོས་པས་སྐད་ཅིག་མ་མེད་པར་འགྱུར་ལ། དེ་ལྟར་ན་འདུས་བྱས་སུ་ཡང་མི་འགྲུབ་ཅིང་འདུས་བྱས་སྐད་ཅིག་མར་སྨྲ་བ་ཡང་མི་འཐད་དོ་ཞེས
བྱ་བའི་དོན་ཏོ། །མདོར་ན་སྨྱུ་གུ་རྒྱུ་ལ་མ་ལྟོས་པར་ཞིག་པ་ཡོད་དམ་མེད། ཡོད་ན་སྨྱུ་གུ་རྒྱུ་ལ་མ་ལྟོས་པར་འཇིག་པ་མེད་པ་འགལ་ཞིང་། མེད་ན་སྨྱུ་གུའི་ཞིག་པ་རྒྱུ་ལ་མི་ལྟོས་པ་འགལ་ལོ། །འཇིག་པ་ཙམ་པ་ནི་ཞིག་པ་ལ་མངོན་དུ་ཕྱོགས་པ་ལ་བརྗོད་པ་ཡིན་པས་ཞིག
པ་ལ་མངོན་དུ་ཕྱོགས་པ་རྒྱུ་ལ་རག་ལས་ན་ཞིག་པ་རྒྱུ་ལ་རག་མ་ལས་པ་ཤིན་ཏུ་འགལ་ཏེ། གཞན་དུ་ན་སྐྱེ་བ་ལ་མངོན་དུ་ཕྱོགས་པ་རྒྱུས་བྱས་ཀྱང་སྐྱེས་པ་རྒྱུས་མ་བྱས་པར་ཐལ་བར་མཚུངས་སོ། །ཞེས་སྤྱོད་ཕྱུན་ལས་གསུངས་པ་ལྟར་རོ། །འདི་ཉིད་ལས། འདུས་བྱས་ཀྱི་མཚན
ཉིད་དུ་དེ་བཤད་པ་མི་འཐད་པར་ཐལ་བ་དང་། ཞེས་པ་དཔེ་དག་མ་དག་དཔྱད་པར་བྱ་སྟེ། དེའི་ཤེས་བྱེད་དུ་དྲངས་པའི་ཚིག་གསལ་གྱི་ལུང་དོན་སྟོང་ཕྱུན་དུ་བཤད་པ་ནི་དྲངས་མ་ཐག་པ་དེ་ཡིན་པའི་ཕྱིར་དང་། ཛ་ཤེའི་ཊཱི་ཀ་ཆེན་ལས་ཀྱང་སྔར་ལྟར་གསུངས་པའི་རྗེས་སུ།
དེ་ནི་རིགས་པས་འགོག་པ་ཡིན་ལ་ལུང་གིས་འགོག་པ་ནི། ཞེས་སོགས་ཀྱིས་སྔར་གྱི་སྒྲུབ་བྱེད་དེ་ནི་རིགས་པས་འགོག་པ་དང་། འདུས་བྱས་ཀྱི་མཚན་ཉིད་རྣམས་འདུ་བྱེད་ཀྱི་ཕུང་པོ་ནི་ནང་དུ་འདུ་བར་གསུངས་པ་དེ་ལུང་གིས་འགོག་པ་ཡིན་གསུངས་པའི་ཕྱིར་རོ། །
དེས་ན་འདུས་བྱས་སྐད་ཅིག་མར་སྨྲ་བ་མི་འཐད་པར་ཐལ་བ་དང་། ཞེས་འདོན་ན་འགྲིག་པར་འགྱུར་རོ། ། ཐལ་བ་གཉིས་པའི་དོན་ནི། གལ་ཏེ་སྨྱུ་གུ་ཞིག་པ་ནི་དངོས་མེད་ཡིན་ལ་དེ་ལ་རྒྱུས་ཅི་ཞིག་བྱེད་ངེས་ན་དེ་ལ་རྒྱུ་མེད་དོ་སྙམ་ན།

འོ་ན་སྨྱུ་གུ་ཡང་ཡོད་པ་ཡིན་པ་ན་དེ་ལ་ནི་རྒྱུས་དགོས་པ་ཅི་ཞིག་ཡོད་དེ་སྐྱེས་ཟིན་པ་སླར་ཡང་བསྐྱེད་དུ་མེད་དོ། །འདི་ནི་སྨྱུ་གུ་ཞིག་པ་ལ་རྒྱུས་ཅི་ཡང་བྱེད་མི་ནུས་ན་མ་ཞིག་པ་རྒྱུས་བྱེད་མི་དགོས་ཞེས་མགོ་མཚུངས་བྱས་པའོ། །འདི་ལ་མ་ཞིག་པ་གྲུབ་ཟིན་པས་ད
གཟོད་རྒྱུས་བྱ་མི་དགོས་ཀྱང་གྱུར་བ་ནི་ཉིད་རྒྱུས་བྱས་པ་ཡིན་པས་རྒྱུ་ཡོད་དོ། །ཞེ་ན། ཁོ་བོ་ཅག་ཀྱང་སྨྱུ་གུ་ཞིག་ཟིན་པ་ད་གཟོད་རྒྱུས་བྱེད་པར་མི་འདོད་ཀྱི་སྨྱུ་གུ་ཞིག་པ་དེ་ཉིད་རྒྱུས་བྱེད་པ་ཡིན་ཞེས་པའོ། ། ཐལ་བ་གསུམ་པའི་དོན་ནི།
སྔར་ས་བོན་གྱི་དུས་ན་མེད་ལ་ཕྱིས་ཡོད་པས་སྨྱུ་གུའི་སྐྱེ་བ་རྒྱུ་དང་བཅས་པ་ཡིན་པ་དེ་བཞིན་དུ་སྨྱུ་གུའི་ཞིག་པ་ཡང་སྔར་སྨྱུ་གུའི་དུས་ན་མེད་ལ་ཕྱིས་ཡོད་པའི་ཕྱིར་རྒྱུ་ཡོད་དེ་ཞེས་པའོ། ། རིགས་པ་བཞི་པའི་དོན་ནི་ཛ་ཤེའི་རྣམ་བཤད་ལས།
དེས་ན་ས་སྨུག་ལ་སོགས་པའི་རྒྱུ་འབྲས་འདི་དག་ནི་འཇིག་རྟེན་པས་མཐོང་བ་ལྟར་གཞག་དགོས་ལ་འཇིག་རྟེན་ན་ནི་ཆུ་མེད་པས་ང་ཡི་འབྲས་ཉེས་སོ། །ཟས་མེད་པས་ང་ཡི་བུ་ཤི་འོ་ཞེས་སྔ་མ་མེད་པས་ཕྱི་མ་བརྟགས་པ་བྱས་པར་སྨྲའོ། །དེ་ཡང་ཟས་དང་ཆུ་མ་ཟད་པ་བྱ
འཚོ་བ་དང་འབྲས་ལེགས་པའི་རྒྱུར་བྱེད་པ་བཞིན་དུ་དེ་དག་ཟད་པ་ཡང་དེ་རྣམས་ཟད་པའི་རྒྱུར་འཇོག་པའི་ཕྱིར། ཟད་པ་མིན་པའི་དེ་དག་མེད་པ་དང་མི་འདྲ་སྟེ་དེས་འབྲས་བུའི་ཕྱོགས་ཀྱང་ཤེས་པར་བྱའོ། །ཞེས་གསུངས་པ་ལྟར་རོ། །དེས་ནི་རྒྱུན་གྱི་ཞིག་པ་དངོས
པར་བཤད་ཅིང་། དེ་དག་ལ་གཏན་ཟད་དང་། གཏན་བརྟག་ཀྱང་ཡོད་པར་སྣང་བས་ན། དབུ་མའི་ཡིག་ཆར་ཤེས་སྒྲིབ་ཞིག་པ་སངས་རྒྱས་འཕགས་པའི་རྒྱུད་ལ་མེད་པར་གསུངས་པ་དང་། འདས་པ་མ་འོངས་སུ་འཇོག་པ་ལ་གཏན་ཟད་དང་གཏན་བརྟག་མ་ཡིན་པ
གཅིག་དགོས་པར་གསུངས་པ་དག་དཔྱད་གཞི་ཆེ་བར་སྣང་ཡང་མངས་སུ་དོགས་ནས་མ་བྲིས་སོ། ། ལུགས་འདིས་རང་རིག་འགོག་པ་ཡང་རང་མཚན་ཁས་མི་ལེན་པ་ལ་ཐུག་པ་ཡིན་པར་འདུག་པའི་རྣམ་བཤད་ལས་གསུངས་སོ། །དེའི་རྒྱུ
མཚན་ཡང་། གལ་ཏེ་རང་རིག་འདོད་ན་བཏགས་དོན་བཙལ་བའི་རིགས་པའི་དཔྱད་བཟོད་ཁས་ལེན་དགོས་པའི་རྒྱུ་མཚན་གྱིས་ཡིན་ཏེ། རང་གི་སྐྱོང་བཞམ་གཞན་གྱིས་སྐྱོང་བ་ཡིན་ཞེས་ཤེས་པའི་འཇོག་བྱེད་འཚོལ་བ་ནི་སྨྱུ་གུ་བདག་ལས་སྐྱེས་སམ་གཞན་ལས་སྐྱེས་

དབུ་མ་པ

༄༅། །ཞེས་བཙལ་བ་ལས་ཀྱང་ཚེས་ལྷག་པའི་བདགས་དོན་འཚོལ་ལུགས་ཡིན་པའི་ཕྱིར་རོ། ། མངོན་སུམ་དང་། རྗེས་དཔག་དང་། དཔེས་འཇལ་བ་དང་། ལུང་གི་ཚད་མ་སྟེ་བཞི་པོ་རྣམས་ཀྱི། མངོན་སུམ་ནི་མངོན་སུམ་རང་ཉིད་ཀྱིས་འགྲུབ་པ་མིན་པ་ནས་ལུང་གི་ཚད་མ་ནི་ལུང་གི་ཚད་མ་རང་ཉིད་ཀྱིས་འགྲུབ་པ་མིན་ནོ་ཞེས་འཆད་པར། ཚད་མ་རྣམས་ནི་རང་ཉིད་ཀྱིས། འགྲུབ་མིན་ཞེས་གསུངས་ཤིང་། མངོན་སུམ་ནི་རང་མ་གཏོགས་པའི་ཚད་མ་གསུམ་གྱིས་འགྲུབ་པ་མིན་པ་ནས་ལུང་གི་ཚད་མ་ནི་རང་མ་གཏོགས་པའི་ཚད་མ་གསུམ་གྱིས་འགྲུབ་པ་མིན་ནོ་ཞེས་འཆད་པར། ཕན་ཚུན་གྱིས་མིན་པའམ། ཞེས་གསུངས་ལ། མངོན་སུམ་ནི་མངོན་སུམ་གཞན་གྱིས་འགྲུབ་པ་མིན་པ་ནས་ལུང་གི་ཚད་མ་ནི་ལུང་གི་ཚད་མ་གཞན་གྱིས་འགྲུབ་པ་མིན་ནོ་ཞེས་འཆད་པར། ཚད་མ་གཞན་གྱིས་མ་ཡིན་ལ། ཞེས་གསུངས་པ་དང་། གཞལ་བྱ་རང་དང་གཞན་གྱི་ཡུལ་གྱིས་བསླུས་པ་མཐའ་དག་དང་རེ་རེས་ཀྱང་འགྲུབ་པ་མིན་ལ་རྒྱུ་མེད་པར་ཡང་འགྲུབ་པ་མིན་ནོ་ཞེས་འཆད་པར། གཞལ་བྱས་མ་ཡིན་རྒྱུ་མེད་མིན། ཞེས་གསུངས་སོ། ། འཇུག་པའི་རྣམ་བཤད་ལས། དེ་ལ་ཤེས་པ་དེ་ཉིད་ཀྱིས་ཤེས་པ་དེ་ཉིད་འཛིན་པར་ནི་མི་འཐད་དེ། རང་ལ་རང་གི་བྱེད་པ་འཇུག་པ་འགལ་བའི་ཕྱིར་རོ། །འདི་ལྟར་རལ་གྲིའི་སོ་དེ་ཉིད་ཀྱིས་དེ་ཉིད་མི་གཅོད་ལ། སོར་མོའི་རྩེ་མོ་དེ་ཉིད་ཀྱིས་དེ་ཉིད་ལ་མི་རེག་ཅིང་། ལེགས་པར་བསླབས་པའི་གཡེར་ཞིང་ཡང་བྲོར་ཅན་གྱིས་ཀྱང་རང་གི་ཕྲག་པ་ལ་ཞོན་པར་མི་ནུས་ཤིང་། མེས་རང་གི་བདག་ཉིད་མི་སྲེག་ལ། མིག་གིས་རང་གི་བདག་ཉིད་ལ་ལྟ་བ་མ་ཡིན་ནོ། །ཞེས་གསུངས་སོ། ། མི་ཤེས་རང་བདག་གསལ་བྱེད་ན། ཞེས་སོགས་ནི་རང་རྒྱུད་པའི་སྐབས་སུ་བཤད་ཟིན། སྐབས་འདིར་དྲངས་པ་འདི་ལ་ཡི་གེ་ཆད་པ་དང་ནོར་བ་ཡོད་པ་ཡང་དེ་ལས་ཤེས་པར་བྱའོ། ། འཇུག་པའི་རྣམ་བཤད་ལས། མར་མེས་རང་གིས་རང་གསལ་བར་མི་བྱེད་ཀྱང་། དེ་ལ་གསལ་བ་མི་ལྡོག་པ་བཞིན་དུ། ཤེས་པས་ཕྱོགས་སྔ་མས་འདོད་པ་ལྟར་དུ་རང་གིས་རང་སྟོང་བར་མི་བྱེད་ཀྱང་དེ་ལ་སྟོང་བ་ཙམ་མི་ལྡོག་པའི་ཕྱིར་རོ། །གལ་ཏེ་མར་མེས་རང་གིས་རང་གསལ

བར་བྱེད་དོ་ཞེ་ན། དེ་ལྟ་ན་མུན་པས་རང་གིས་རང་སྒྲིབ་པར་འགྱུར་ལ། དེ་འདོད་ན་མུན་ཁུང་དུ་བུམ་པ་མི་མཐོང་བ་བཞིན་དུ་མུན་པ་ཡང་མི་མཐོང་བར་འགྱུར་རོ། །ཞེས་གསུངས་པ་ལྟར་རོ། །ཞིབ་མོ་རྣམ་འཐག་ལས། མར་མེ་ནི་ཕྲད་པའམ་མ་ཕྲད་པའི་མུན་པ་བསལ་བར་བྱེད་པ་མ་ཡིན་ནོ། །གཟའི་གནོད་པ་བཞིན་དུ་འདིར་ཡང་འགྱུར་རོ་ཞེ་ན། མ་ཡིན་ཏེ། དགེ་དང་འགལ་བའི་ཕྱིར་རོ། །ཞེས་པའི་དོན་ཡོད་དེ། མར་མེས་རང་དང་ཕྲད་པའམ་མ་ཕྲད་པའི་མུན་པ་སེལ་བ་རང་གི་མཚན་ཉིད་ཀྱིས་ཡོད་པ་མ་ཡིན་ནོ་ཞེས་གསུངས་པ་ལ། ཕྱོགས་སྔ་སྨྲ་བས། ཀླུས་བྱིན་ལ་སོགས་པ་ལ་གཟས་བྱས་པའི་སྐྱོན་ཕྲད་ནས་གནོད་པ་བྱེད་པ་བཞིན་དུ་མར་མེས་ཀྱང་མུན་པ་དང་ཕྲད་ནས་གནོད་པ་བྱེད་དོ་ཞེ་ན། ཐལ་འགྱུར་བས། དེ་ནི་འཐད་པ་མ་ཡིན་ཏེ། དཔེ་དོན་མི་མཐུན་པའི་ཕྱིར་ཏེ། ཀླུས་བྱིན་དང་གཟས་བྱས་པའི་སྐྱོན་ཕྲད་པ་ཡོད་ཀྱང་མུན་པ་དང་མར་མེ་ཕྲད་པ་རི་སྲིད་པའི་ཕྱིར་ཏེ། སྣང་མུན་གཉིས་ལྷན་ཅིག་མི་གནས་འགལ་ཡིན་པའི་ཕྱིར་ཞེས་པའོ། །དེ་ནི་རྩ་ཤེས་ལས། གང་ཚེ་མར་མེ་སྐྱེ་བཞིན་པ། །མུན་པ་དང་ནི་ཕྲད་མེད་ན།། ཇི་ལྟར་མར་མེ་སྐྱེ་བཞིན་པས། །མུན་པ་སེལ་བར་བྱེད་པ་ཡིན། །མར་མེ་ཕྲད་པ་མེད་པར་ཡང་། །གལ་ཏེ་མུན་པ་སེལ་བྱེད་ན། །འཇིག་རྟེན་ཀུན་ལ་གནས་པའི་མུན། །འདི་ན་འདུག་པ་ངེས་བསལ་འགྱུར། །ཞེས་གསུངས་པའི་རིགས་པ་སྟེ། རྩ་ཤེའི་ཊཱི་ཀ་ཆེན་ལས། ཐ་སྙད་དུ་མར་མེས་མུན་པ་སེལ་བར་འདོད་པ་ལ་ཡང་མར་མེ་སྐྱེ་བཞིན་པ་དང་མུན་པ་གཉིས་ཕྲད་པ་དགོས་མོད་ཀྱང་། མར་མེ་སྐྱེ་བཞིན་པའི་དུས་ན་མར་མེ་མེད་པས་མུན་པ་དང་ཕྲད་མི་དགོས་སོ། །མར་མེས་མུན་པ་སེལ་བ་རང་གི་མཚན་ཉིད་ཀྱིས་གྲུབ་པར་འདོད་པ་ལྟར་ན་མར་མེ་སྐྱེ་བཞིན་པ་དང་མུན་པ་ཕྲད་ན་དེའི་དུས་སུ་མར་མེ་ཡོད་དགོས་པས་དེ་མེད་པའི་ཕྱིར། མར་མེ་སྐྱེ་བཞིན་པ་དང་ཡང་མི་ཕྲད་པས་མར་མེས་མུན་པ་སེལ་མི་འཐད་པར་སྟོན་པའི་རིགས་པའོ། །ཞེས་གསུངས་པའི་ཕྱིར། རྒྱས་པར་དེ་ཉིད་ལས་ཤེས་དགོས་སོ། །འདིར་རང་རིག་འདོད་ཚུལ་དང་དེ་འགོག་ཚུལ་འཇུག་པ་རྩ་འགྲེལ་ནས་གསུངས་པ་ལྟར་མདོར་བསྡུས་ཏེ་འགོད་ན། ཕྱོགས་སྔ་སྨྲ་བས། མིག་གིས་སྔོན་པོ་མཐོང་བཞིན་པའི་སོ་སོ་སྐྱེ་བོའི་རྒྱུད་ལ་ཡུལ་སྔོན་པོ་མྱོང་བ་དང་ཡུལ་ཅན་སྔོན་འཛིན

༄༅། །མྱོང་བ་གཉིས་ཀ་ཡོད་དེ། དུས་ཕྱིས་དྲན་པ་ན་སྔར་སྔོན་པོ་འདི་མཐོང་ངོ་ཞེས་ཡུལ་དྲན་པ་དང་ངས་མཐོང་ངོ་ཞེས་ཡུལ་ཅན་དྲན་པ་གཉིས་ཀ་ཡོད་པའི་ཕྱིར། འདོད་ན། སྔར་གྱི་ཡུལ་ཅན་མྱོང་བ་དེ་ཆོས་ཅན། རང་མྱོང་ཡིན་པར་ཐལ། རང་མྱོང་གཞན་མྱོང་གང་རུང་གང་ཞིག །གཞན་གྱི་མྱོང་ན་ནི་མྱོང་བ་ཐུག་མེད་དུ་ཐལ་བ་དང་། ཤེས་པ་ཕྱི་མས་ཡུལ་གཞན་མི་གཅོད་པར་ཐལ་བས་གནོད་པའི་ཕྱིར། ཞེས་ཟེར་རོ། །དགག་ཕྱི་མ་གཉིས་སྒྲུབ་ཚུལ་འཇུག་པའི་རྣམ་བཤད་དུ་གསུངས་པ་ལས་ཤེས་པར་གྱིས། ཐལ་འགྱུར་བས་དེ་འགོག་ཚུལ་ནི། དྲན་པའི་རྟགས་ཀྱིས་སྒྲུབ་པ་མི་འཐད་དེ། རང་རིག་ཡོད་དེ། རང་བཞིན་གྱིས་གྲུབ་པའི་དྲན་པ་ཡོད་པའི་ཕྱིར་ཞེས་བཀོད་ན་ནི། རྟགས་བསྒྲུབ་བྱ་དང་མཚུངས་པར་མ་གྲུབ་པའི་ཕྱིར་དང་། རང་རིག་ཡོད་དེ་དྲན་པ་ཡོད་པའི་ཕྱིར་ཞེས་འགོད་པ་ཡིན་ན། རང་རིག་དང་དྲན་པ་གཉིས་མེད་ན་མི་འབྱུང་བའི་འབྲེལ་བ་མེད་པས་ཁྱབ་པ་མ་ངེས་ཤིང་། ཆུ་དང་མེ་ཡོད་པས་ཆུ་ཤེལ་དང་མེ་ཤེལ་ཡོད་པར་སྒྲུབ་པ་དང་འདྲ་བར་འགྱུར་བའི་ཕྱིར། ཞེས་བཀག་པ་ཡིན་དེ། ལེགས་བཤད་སྙིང་པོ་ལས། འདིར་རྫས་གྲུབ་སྨྲ་བའི་དབང་དུ་བྱེད་ན་དེ་འདྲའི་དྲན་པ་མེད་པས་བསྒྲུབ་བྱ་དང་མཚུངས་ལ། ཐ་སྙད་ཀྱི་དབང་དུ་ཡིན་ན་རང་རིག་ཕྱིར་གྲོལ་ལ་མ་གྲུབ་པས་དེ་དང་དྲན་པ་རྒྱུ་འབྲས་སུ་མི་འགྲུབ་པ་དང་ཆུ་དང་མེ་ཡོད་པས་ཆུ་ཤེལ་དང་མེ་ཤེལ་ཡོད་པར་སྒྲུབ་པ་དང་དྲན་པ་ཡོད་པས་རང་རིག་ཡོད་པར་སྒྲུབ་པ་གཉིས་འདྲ་བར་བཤད་དོ། །འདི་འདྲས་རྟགས་ཡིན་ཞིང་བསྒྲུབ་བྱའི་ཆོས་སུ་རང་རིག་བཟུང་བའི་སྐབས་སུ་མཛད་དོ། །ཞེས་གསུངས་པས་སོ། །འདི་ལ་བསྒྲུབ་བྱའི་ཆོས་སུ་རང་རིག་བཟུང་ན་ནི་མཐུན་དཔེ་མེད་པས་དེ་ལྟར་མི་འགོད་ཀྱི། སྔོན་འཛིན་མིག་ཤེས་ཆོས་ཅན། མིག་གིས་སྔོན་པོ་མཐོང་བཞིན་པའི་སོ་སོ་སྐྱེ་བོའི་རྒྱུད་ལ་ཚོར་མྱོང་བྱེད་ཡོད་དེ། དེ་འདྲ་བའི་སོ་སོ་སྐྱེ་བོས་དུས་ཕྱིས་ཚོར་དྲན་པ་ཡོད་པའི་ཕྱིར། དཔེར་ན་སྔོན་པོ་བཞིན་ནོ། །ཞེས་འགོད་པ་ཡིན་ནོ་ཞེ་ན། འདི་ནི་དཔེ་ལ་རྟགས་ཆོས་ངེས་སུ་འགྲོ་བ་ཙམ་ཡོད་ཀྱང་ཁྱབ་པ་སྒྲུབ་མི་ནུས་པས་སྔ་མ་དང་འདྲ་བར་འགྱུར་ཏེ། དེ་ཉིད་ལས། དེ་ལྟར་བྱེད་ན་དཔེ་མི་རྙེད་པས་སྔོ་འཛིན་ནི་མྱོང་བྱེད་ཡོད་དེ་དུས་ཕྱིས་དྲན་པ་ཡོད་པའི་ཕྱིར་དཔེར་ན་སྔོན་པོ

བཞིན་ཞེས་འགོད་ན་ཡང་དཔེ་ལ་རྟགས་ཆོས་ངེས་སུ་འགྲོ་བ་ཙམ་ཞིག་ཡོད་མོད་ཀྱང་། ཁྱབ་པ་སྒྲུབ་མི་ནུས་པས་རང་རིག་བསྒྲུབ་བྱའི་ཆོས་སུ་བཟུང་བ་དང་འདྲ་བས་དངོས་སུ་མ་སྨོས་སོ། ཞེས་གསུངས་པའི་ཕྱིར་དང་། སྤྱོད་འཇུག་ལས་ཀྱང་། གཞན་མྱོང་བ་དང་འབྲེལ་བ་ལས། །དྲན་འགྱུར་བྱི་བའི་དུག་བཞིན་ནོ། །ཞེས་ཡུལ་ཅན་མ་མྱོང་བར་དྲན་པ་སྐྱེ་བ་ཡོད་པར་གསུངས་པའི་ཕྱིར་རོ། །གལ་ཏེ་མྱོང་བ་ཙམ་ཡོད་དེ་དྲན་པ་ཡོད་པའི་ཕྱིར་ཞེས་འགོད་ན་ནི་གྲུབ་ཟིན་སྒྲུབ་པར་འགྱུར་བས་དགོས་པ་མེད་པའི་ཕྱིར་རོ། ལེགས་བཤད་སྙིང་པོ་ལས། མྱོང་བ་ཙམ་སྒྲུབ་ནའང་གྲུབ་ཟིན་པས་དེ་དང་འདྲ་བར་མ་སྨོས་སོ། །ཞེས་གསུངས་པའི་ཕྱིར་རོ། །རང་རིག་མེད་ཀྱང་དྲན་པ་སྐྱེ་བའི་ཚུལ་ལ་གཉིས་ལས། འཇུག་པ་ནས་བཤད་པའི་ལུགས་ནི། གང་ཕྱིར་གང་གིས་ཡུལ་མྱོང་གྱུར་དེ་ལས། །དྲན་པ་འདི་གཞན་ང་ལ་ཡོད་མིན་པ། །དེ་ཕྱིར་ང་ཡིས་མཐོང་སྙམ་དྲན་འགྱུར་ཏེ། །འདི་ཡང་འཇིག་རྟེན་ཐ་སྙད་ཚུལ་ལུགས་ཡིན། །ཞེས་པས་སྟོན་ཏོ། །འདིའི་དོན་ནི། གང་གི་ཕྱིར་སྔར་གྱི་མྱོང་བ་དང་ཕྱིས་ཀྱི་དྲན་པ་གཉིས་རང་གི་མཚན་ཉིད་ཀྱིས་གྲུབ་པའི་གཞན་མིན་པ་དང་། ས་རྒྱུག་ལྟ་བུའི་ཉེར་ལེན་གྱི་རྒྱུ་འབྲས་ལ་རང་མཚན་གྱིས་གྲུབ་པའི་གཞན་དུ་འཛིན་པ་ནི་འཇིག་རྟེན་པའི་བློ་རང་དགའ་བ་ལ་མེད་པར་བཤད་ཟིན་པ་ལྟར། སྔར་གྱི་མྱོང་བ་དང་ཕྱིས་ཀྱི་དྲན་པ་གཉིས་ཀྱང་འཇིག་རྟེན་བློ་ལྡན་སྐྱེས་ལ་རང་གི་མཚན་ཉིད་ཀྱིས་གྲུབ་པའི་གཞན་དུ་འཛིན་པ་མེད་པར་མ་ཟད། སྔར་སྔོན་འཛིན་གྱིས་མཐོང་བའི་ཡུལ་ཕྱིས་དྲན་པ་ན་འདི་ངས་སྔར་ཡང་མཐོང་ངོ་ཞེས་ཐ་སྙད་བྱེད་དོ། །དེ་ལྟ་མོད་ཀྱང་དྲན་དུས་ཀྱི་བདག་དེ་མྱོང་དུས་ཀྱི་བདག་ཡིན་ནོ་སྙམ་དུ་མི་འཛིན་པ་དང་། དེ་སྐད་སྨྲ་དུས་ཀྱི་དུས་དང་དེའི་དུས་སུ་གང་ན་གནས་པའི་ཡུལ་གྱི་ཁྱད་པར་དུ་བྱས་པའི་སྔོན་པོ་སྔར་མཐོང་ངོ་ཞེས་ཐ་སྙད་བྱེད་པ་མིན་པས་ཐ་སྙད་དོན་མི་མཐུན་དུ་མི་འགྱུར་ཏེ། དཔེར་ན་འཇིག་རྟེན་ན་ལག་པ་ན་བ་ལ་བདག་ནའོ་ཞེས་ཐ་སྙད་བྱེད་ཀྱང་ལག་པ་འདི་ངའོ་སྙམ་པ་སོགས་མེད་པས་ཐ་སྙད་དོན་མི་མཐུན་དུ་མི་འགྱུར་བ་བཞིན་ནོ། །དེ་ལྟར་མྱོང་དྲན་དང་དེའི་དུས་ཀྱི་ཡུལ་གཉིས་རང་མཚན་གྱིས་གྲུབ་པའི་གཞན་དུ་འཛིན་པ་ནི་འཇིག་རྟེན་རང་དགའ་བ་ལ་མེད་པ་དེའི་ཕྱིར། སྔར་ཡུལ་ཉམས་མྱོང་གི་ཤེས་པས་མྱོང་བ་དང་བཅད་པ་དེ། ཕྱིས་དེ་དྲན་པའི་

༄༅། །ཤེས་པས་མ་མྱོང་བ་དང་མ་བཅད་པ་མིན་པས། འདི་སྔར་ཡང་ང་ཡིས་མཐོང་སྙམ་དུ་དྲན་པ་སྐྱེ་བར་འགྱུར་ཏེ། འདི་ཡང་འཇིག་རྟེན་གྱི་ཐ་སྙད་ཀྱི་ཚུལ་གྱི་ལུགས་ཡིན་གྱི། བཏགས་དོན་བཙལ་བའི་ཚུལ་གྱིས་དཔྱད་ནས་འཇོག་པར་མི
ནུ་སྟེ། བཏགས་དོན་བཙལ་ན་མི་རྙེད་པའི་རྫུན་པའི་དོན་ཅན་གྱི་འཇིག་རྟེན་གྱི་ཐ་སྙད་ཡིན་པའི་ཕྱིར་རོ། །ཞེས་པའོ། །རང་རིག་འདོད་མཁན་ཅིས། རང་རིག་མེད་ན་ཡུལ་ཅན་དྲན་པ་སྐྱེ་བ་འགལ་བ་ཡིན་ཏེ། སྔར་མ་མྱོང་བར་དྲན་པ་སྐྱེ་བ་མེད་པའི་ཕྱིར་ཞེས་པའི
རྒྱུ་མཚན་ནི། གང་ཕྱིར་གང་གིས་ཡུལ་མྱོང་བྱུང་དེ་ལས། ཞེས་སོགས་ཀྱི་ལུང་འདྲེན་སེལ་བ་མ་ཡིན་ནོ། གཞན་དུ་ན། སྔར་མྱོང་འཛིན་མ་མྱོང་ཡང་ཕྱིས་མྱོང་འཛིན་དྲན་པ་སྐྱེ་བ་མི་འགལ་ཏེ། འཇིག་རྟེན་པའི་བློ་ལྟན་སྐྱེས་ཀྱི་ངོར་སྔར་གྱི་མྱོང་འཛིན་དང་ཕྱིས
ཀྱི་དྲན་པ་གཉིས་རང་གི་མཚན་ཉིད་ཀྱིས་གྲུབ་པའི་གཞན་མིན་པ་དང་། སྔར་གྱི་མྱོང་འཛིན་དང་ཕྱིས་ཀྱི་དྲན་པ་གཉིས་ཡུལ་གཅིག་པའི་ཕྱིར། ཞེས་འགོད་དགོས་པས་འབྲེལ་མེད་དུ་འགྱུར་བའི་ཕྱིར་རོ། །དེས་ན་སྔར་མ་མྱོང་བར་དྲན་པ་སྐྱེ་བ་མེད་སྙམ་པའི་ལོག་རྟོག
ཁུང་འདྲིས་སེལ་བ་མིན་གྱི། སྔར་གྱི་མྱོང་འཛིན་མིག་ཤེས་དེ་རང་གིས་རང་མ་མྱོང་བ་ཡིན་ན་དེ་ཕྱིས་མྱོང་བ་པོ་མཐོང་བ་དྲན་པ་ན་ངས་མཐོང་ངོ་ཞེས་སྔར་མཐོང་བ་དེ་ཉིད་རང་གིས་མཐོང་བར་དྲན་པ་འགལ་ལོ་སྙམ་པའི་ལོག་རྟོག་སྔར་གྱི་འཇུག་པའི་ལུང་གིས་སེལ་བ་ཡིན
པའི་ཕྱིར་རོ། ལེགས་བཤད་སྙིང་པོ་ལས། རང་རིག་མེད་ན་དྲན་པ་སྐྱེ་བ་འགལ་ལོ་སྙམ་དུ་འཛིན་པའི་རྒྱུ་མཚན་སྔར་བཤད་པ་དེ་འདྲིས་སེལ་བ་མིན་ཏེ། འདི་ནི་དྲན་པ་སྐྱེ་བའི་དྲན་ཚུལ་ཁྱད་པར་བ་ལ་བརྟེན་ནས་སྔ་མ་རང་རིག་ཏུ་འཛིན་པ་ཞིག་གོ །དེ་ཡང་སྔར་མྱོང
བ་མཐོང་བ་ཕྱིས་དྲན་པ་ན་ངས་སྔར་མཐོང་ངོ་ཞེས་སྔར་མཐོང་བ་དེ་ཉིད་རང་གིས་མཐོང་བར་དྲན་པས། དྲན་ཚུལ་དེ་ནི་སྔར་གྱི་སྔོ་འཛིན་རང་གིས་རང་མ་མྱོང་ན་སྐྱེ་བར་འགལ་བས་སྔ་མ་རང་རིག་གོ་སྙམ་པའོ། །འདི་ནི་རང་རིག་གི་དབང་གིས་མ་བྱུང་ཡང་སྔར་གྱི
ཡུལ་སྔོན་པོ་མྱོང་བ་དང་ཕྱིས་ཀྱི་དྲན་ཤེས་གཉིས་ཡུལ་གཅིག་ལ་འཇུག་པའི་དབང་གིས་སྔར་ངས་མཐོང་སྙམ་དུ་དྲན་པ་སྐྱེའོ་ཞེས་སླབ་པོ། །ཞེས་སོགས་གསུངས་པའི་ཕྱིར། རྒྱས་པར་དེ་ཉིད་ལས་ཤེས་པར་བྱའོ། །རང་རིག་མེད་ཀྱང་དྲན་པ་སྐྱེ་བ་མི་འགལ་ཚུལ

ཀྱི་སྤྱོད་འཇུག་ལས་བཤད་པ་ནི། གལ་ཏེ་རང་རིག་ཡོད་མིན་ན། །རྣམ་ཤེས་དྲན་པར་ཇི་ལྟར་འགྱུར། །གཞན་མྱོང་བ་དང་འབྲེལ་བ་ལས། །དྲན་འགྱུར་བྱི་བའི་དུག་བཞིན་ནོ། །ཞེས་པས་སྟོན་ནོ། །རྒྱས་པར་འཇུག་པའི་རྣམ་བཤད་དང་དབུ་མའི་མཐའ་དཔྱོད་ལས་
ཞེས་པར་བྱ་སྟེ། གྲགས་ཆེ་ཞིང་གོ་སླ་བས་འདིར་མ་བྲིས་སོ། ། འདི་དང་སྦྱོང་ཐུན་གཉིས་ཀར་ཕྱིར་མངོན་སུམ་ཚད་མ་མངོན་སུམ་ཡིན་གསུངས་པ་ལྟ་བུར་སྣང་ཡང་། མངོན་སུམ་དང་དབང་པོའི་ཡུལ་དང་མངོན་གྱུར་རྣམས་དོན་གཅིག་ཏུ་བཤད
པའང་ཡོད་པས་དཔྱོད་དགོས་སོ། །གཞི་སྐབས་ན་རང་གསལ་བར་རྟོགས་པའི་བློ་ལ་ལྟོས་ནས་མངོན་སུམ་དངོས་ཡིན་པས་ཁྱབ་པ་དང་། ཤེས་པ་གང་ཡུལ་གང་ལ་མངོན་སུམ་ཚད་མ་ཡིན་ན་ཤེས་པ་ཡུལ་དེ་ལ་ལྟོས་ནས་མངོན་སུམ་བཏགས་པ་པ་ཡིན་པས་ཁྱབ་པ་ཡོད
དོ། ། དེའི་དར་ཊཱི་ཀ་ལས། དངོས་པོ་ལ་མ་བརྟེན་པར་དངོས་པོ་མེད་པར་མི་འགྱུར་ཏེ། དངོས་པོ་གཞན་དུ་གྱུར་པའི་བཞི་ག་པ་ལ་དངོས་མེད་དུ་འདོད་པའི་ཕྱིར། དངོས་མེད་ལ་མ་བརྟེན་པར་དངོས་པོ་མི་འགྲུབ་སྟེ། དངོས་མིན་མ
བཀག་པར་དངོས་པོ་མི་འགྲུབ་པའི་ཕྱིར། དེས་ན་དངོས་པོ་དང་དངོས་པོ་མེད་པ་གཉིས་ཕན་ཚུན་བལྟོས་པས་རང་བཞིན་སྟོང་པ་ཉིད་དུ་མངོན་སུམ་དུ་ཡོངས་སུ་ཤེས་པས་དམིགས་པ་མེད་པའི་ཡེ་ཤེས་ཀྱི་དེ་ཡིན་པས་ན་བདག་ཉིད་ཆེན་པོ་འཕགས་པ་རྣམས་རྣམ་པར་གྲོལ
བར་འགྱུར་རོ། །ཞེས་བཤད་དོ། ། མདོ་འདིའི་དོན་ནི་དགོངས་པ་རབ་གསལ་ལས། དེའི་འགྲེལ་པ་ན་སྡུག་བསྔལ་འདི་ཞེས་པའི་ཉི་བའི་ཚིག་གིས་གསུངས་པའི་ཕྱིར། ད་ལྟར་གྱི་རང་རྒྱུད་ཀྱི་སྡུག་བསྔལ་ལམ་ཕུང་པོ་ཁོ་ནའི་དབང་དུ་མཛད
ནས། མ་ལུས་པར་སྤངས་པ་ནས་ཞུབ་པའི་བར་དང་། མ་འོངས་པའི་སྡུག་བསྔལ་གྱི་དབང་དུ་མཛད་ནས། སྡུག་བསྔལ་གཞན་མཚམས་མི་སྦྱོར་བ་ནས། མྱ་ངན་ལས་འདས་པའོ་ཞེས་པའི་བར་དུ་གསུངས་སོ། །སྡུག་བསྔལ་ལམ་ཕུང་པོ་འདི་ཞེས་པ་དེ་གཉིས་ཀྱི
བྱེ་བྲག་ཉིད་མཐོང་ལ་འཇུག་པའི་སྤྱི་སྐད་བྱེ་བྲག་ལ་འཇུག་པའོ་སྙམ་ན། དེ་ཡང་མི་རུང་སྟེ་སྤྱི་སྐད་ནི་སྤྱིའི་དོན་ལ་བཤད་དུ་མི་རུང་ན་བྱེ་བྲག་ལ་བཤད་དགོས་མོད་ཀྱང་། འདིར་ནི་སྤྱིའི་སྐད་ནས་བཤད་དུ་ཡོད་པའི་ཕྱིར་རོ། །ཞེས་གསུངས་པ་ལྟར་རོ། །མདོ་འདིའི

༄༅། །དོན་དངོས་སྣང་བའི་ལུགས་ལྟར་བཤད་ན་སྣང་འདས་མངོན་དུ་བྱེད་པ་མེད་པར་འགྱུར་ཚུལ་ཡང་དེ་ཉིད་ལས། དེ་ལྟར་བྱས་ན་དངོས་པར་སྣང་བ་རྣམས་ལྟར་ན། རྒྱུད་བླ་མ་ལས་ཉོན་མོངས་གདོད་ནས་ཟད་ཕྱིར་རོ། །ཞེས་གསུངས་པ་ལྟར་
ཕུང་པོ་གདོད་མ་ནས་རང་བཞིན་གྱིས་སྐྱེ་བ་མེད་པས། གདོད་མ་ནས་ཟད་པ་ལ་བཤད་དུ་མི་རུང་བའི་ཕྱིར། ལམ་གྱིས་མ་ལུས་པར་སྤངས་པ་ན་བཤད་དགོས་ན། དེའི་ཚེ་མངོན་དུ་བྱ་རྒྱུའི་མྱ་འདས་ཡོད་པ་ན་མངོན་དུ་བྱེད་མཁན་མེད་པ་དང་། བྱེད་མཁན་ཡོད་པ་ན
ཕུང་པོ་མ་ཟད་པས་མངོན་དུ་བྱ་རྒྱུའི་མྱང་འདས་མེད་པར་འགྱུར་ བསམ་དོ་དེ་བཤད་མི་ནུས་པར་འགྱུར་རོ། །ཁོ་བོ་ཅག་ལྟར་ན། འདིའི་ཟད་པ་ནི། ཟད་པ་གཉེན་པོས་ཟད་པ་མ་ཡིན་ཏེ། །དེ་ནི་གདོད་ནས་ཟད་པས་ཟད་ཅེས་བྱ། །ཞེས་གསུངས་པ་ལྟར་བཤད་པས
ཆོག་པས་མདོ་འི་དོན་ལེགས་པར་བཤད་པར་ནུས་སོ། །ཞེས་གསུངས་པ་ལྟར་ཡིན་ནོ། ། རིགས་པ་དྲུག་ཅུ་པའི་འགྲེལ་བར། ཕུང་པོ་དང་བཅས་པའི་མྱ་ངན་ལས་འདས་པ་ལ་འདོད་ཆགས་ལ་སོགས་པའི་བཅིང་བ་སྤངས་ཀྱང་མྱ་ངན་ལས
འདས་པར་མི་འདོད་དོ་སྙམ་དུ་སེམས་ན་ནི། འོ་ན་མདོ་སྡེ་ལས། རྗེས་བཟླས་ཞེས་བྱའི་མདོ་འདི་ནི། །ཤཱ་རིའི་བུ་ཡིས་མྱ་ངན་འདས། །མངོན་སུམ་བྱས་ནས་བཤད་པ་ཡིན། །ཞེས་འབྱུང་བ་ཇི་ལྟར་བཤད། ཅེས་གསུངས་པ་ལྟར། ཕུང་པ་འདི་རྒྱུན་མ་ཆད
ཀྱི་བར་དུ་མྱང་འདས་མཚན་ཉིད་པ་མེད་ཟེར་ན། ཤཱ་རིའི་བུས་མྱང་འདས་མངོན་དུ་བྱས་ནས་གྲོགས་པོ་གཞན་ལ། བདག་གི་སྐྱེ་བ་ཟད་དོ་ཞེས་སོགས་རྗེས་སུ་བཟླས་པར་བཤད་པ་དང་འགལ་ཞེས་པ་ཡིན་གྱི། དངོས་སྨྲ་རྣམས། དང་པོར་ལྷག་བཅས་མྱང་འདས
མངོན་དུ་བྱེད་པ་དང་དེའི་རྗེས་སུ་ལྷག་མེད་མྱང་འདས་མངོན་དུ་བྱེད་དགོས་པར་འདོད་པ་འགོག་པ་མ་ཡིན་ནོ། །རྗེས་སུ་བཟླས་པའི་མདོ་ཡང་སྔར་བཤད་པ་ལྟར་ཡིན་གྱི། འཕགས་པ་ཉེ་དུལ་གྱིས་སྨྲས་པའི་ཚིགས་བཅད་དེ་མིན་པར་རིགས་པ་དྲུག་ཅུ་པའི་དར་ཊཱི་ཀ
ལས་བཤད་དོ། ། ཟུང་སྐྱ་གྲུབ་མཐའ། སྐབས་འགྲོ་བདུན་ཅུ་པ་ལས་མི་ཤེས་ཉོན་མོངས་མིན་སྤངས་ཕྱིར། །ཞེས་དང་། མ་རིག་ཉོན་མོངས་མིན་ཡོད་པས། །ཞེས་དང་། འཇུག་འགྲེལ་ལས། ཉོན་མོངས་པ་ཅན་མ་ཡིན་པའི་མ་རིག་པ

ཞེས་གསུངས་པ་ལ་བརྟེན་ནས་ཤེས་པར་བྱར་བའི་ཤེས་སྒྲིབ་ཡོད་པ་འཐད་ཕྱོགས་སུ་པཎ་ཆེན་བསོད་ནམས་རྒྱལ་མཚན་དང་མཁས་གྲུབ་ཆེན་པོ་འཇམ་དབྱངས་བཞད་པའི་རྡོ་རྗེས་གསུངས་སོ། །དེ་ལྟ་ན་ཡང་ཤེས་སྒྲིབ་ཀྱི་མ་རིག་པའི་འབྲུ་གནོན་རྗེ་ཐམས་ཅད་མཁྱེན་པས
མཛད་པ་རྣམས་སུ་གཉིས་སྣང་འཁྲུལ་བའི་བག་ཆགས་ལ་འབྲུ་གནོན་མཛད་པ་མ་གཏོགས་ཤེས་པར་བྱར་བའི་མ་རིག་པ་ལ་འབྲུ་གནོན་མཛད་པ་མི་སྣང་ངོ་། །མཁས་གྲུབ་ཐམས་ཅད་མཁྱེན་པ་དང་། རིགས་པའི་དབང་ཕྱུག་སེ་ར་རྗེ་བཙུན་ཆོས་ཀྱི་རྒྱལ་མཚན་པ་ཡབ
སྲས། མཁྱེན་རབ་གཏེར་ཆེན་འཇམ་དབྱངས་དགའ་བའི་བློ་གྲོས། རྗེ་ཐམས་ཅད་མཁྱེན་པ་དགེ་འདུན་རྒྱ་མཚོ། པཎ་ཆེན་བསོད་ནམས་གྲགས་པ་སོགས་མཁས་གྲུབ་ཕལ་མོ་ཆེས་ཤེས་པར་བྱར་བའི་ཤེས་སྒྲིབ་མེད་པར་བཞེད་ཅིང་། རྗེ་བླ་མའི་བཤད་རྒྱུད་དང་སྒྲུབ
རྒྱུད་གཉིས་ཀའི་བསྟན་པའི་བདག་པོར་གྱུར་པ་པཎ་ཆེན་ཐམས་ཅད་མཁྱེན་པ་བློ་བཟང་ཆོས་ཀྱི་རྒྱལ་མཚན་གྱིས་ཀྱང་། ཤེས་པ་གཅིག་གིས་བདེན་གཉིས་གཅིག་ཅར་དུ། །མངོན་སུམ་གཟིགས་པའི་སྒྲིབ་བྱེད་ཕྲ་བ་ལ། །མ་རིག་ཅེས་བཏགས་ཤེས་པ་དངོས་མིན་པས།།
དེ་ལ་འགལ་བ་སུ་ཙམ་ཡོད་མ་ཡིན། །ཞེས་རྒྱུ་མཚན་དང་བཅས་ཏེ་གསུངས་པ་རྣམས་རྗེའི་གསུང་ཕལ་མོ་ཆེ་དང་མཐུན་ཚབ་ཆེ་བར་འདུག་པས་ད་དུང་བློ་གྲོས་དང་ལྡན་པ་རྣམས་ཀྱིས་ཞིབ་ཏུ་དཔྱད་པར་བྱའོ། །ཞེས་ཀྱང་གསུངས་པ་ཡོད་དོ། །
ཆགས་སྒྲིབ་ཐོགས་སྒྲིབ་ཤེས་སྒྲིབ་གསུམ་རྣམ་གྲངས་སུ་བཤད་པའང་ཡོད་ཀྱང་། དྲི་མེད་དབྱིངས་ལ་ཆགས་མེད་དང་། །ཞེས་པའི་དར་ཊཱི་ཀ་ལས། རང་བཞིན་གྱིས་དྲི་མ་མེད་པའི་དབྱིངས་ལ་བདེན་པར་ཞེན་པའི་ཆགས་པ་མེད་པ་དང་། ཤེས་བྱ་ཐམས་ཅད་ལ་ཐོགས་པ་མེད
པའི་ཕྱིར་དེ། ཆགས་ཐོགས་ཀྱི་སྒྲིབ་པ་དག་པ་ཡིན་ནོ། །ཞེས་དང་། དེ་ཡང་མདོར་བསྡུ་ན་རྒྱུ་གཉིས་ཀྱིས་ནི་ཅིག་ཤེས་སྟོང་ཉིད་མ་རྟོགས་པ་དང་། ཤེས་བྱ་ཐམས་ཅད་ལ་མི་འཇུག་པའི་ཉི་ཚེ་བའི་ཡེ་ཤེས་ཀྱི་ཞེས་སོ། །དེ་ལ་ཇི་ལྟ་བ་བཞིན་ཡོད་པ་གཟིགས་པ
ཉིད་ཀྱིས་སེམས་ཅན་གྱི་ཁམས་རང་བཞིན་གྱིས་རྣམ་པར་དག་པའི་ཡུལ་ཅན་གྱི་ཕྱིར་ནི་བདེན་འཛིན་གྱི་ཆགས་པ་མེད་པ་ཡིན་ལ་ཇི་སྙེད་ཡོད་པ་གཟིགས་པ་ཉིད་ཀྱིས་ཤེས་བྱའི་དངོས་པོ་མཐའ་མེད་པའི་ཡུལ་ཅན་གྱི་ཕྱིར་ན་ཐོགས་པ་མེད་པ་ཡིན་ནོ། །ཞེས་གསུངས་ཤིང་།

དབུ་མ་པ
བཀྲ
བཅུ་དགུ

༄༅། གསེར་སྦྲང་ལས་ཀྱང་། ཆགས་པ་ཉོན་སྒྲིབ་དང་གྲོགས་པ་ཤེས་སྒྲིབ་ཏུ་བཤད་དོ། ། ནམ་ཞིག་རིས་འཛིན་མེད་པར་གཅིག་ཆར་དུ། །རྟེན་འབྲེལ་མི་བསླུར་མཐོང་བ་ཙམ་ཉིད་ནས། །ངེས་ཤེས་ཡུལ་གྱི་འཛིན་སྟངས་ཀུན་འཇིག་ན། །དེ་ཚེ་ལྟ་བའི་དཔྱད་པ་རྫོགས་པ་ལགས། །ཞེས་གསུངས་པ་ལྟར་གྱི་ལྟ་དཔྱད་པ་རྫོགས་པའི་གང་ཟག་གིས་མིང་དང་བརྡས་བཞག་ཙམ་གྱི་རྟེན་འབྱུང་གི་དོན་ཇི་ཙམ་ཡོད་ལ་བྱེད་པ་དེ་ཙམ་དུ་རང་བཞིན་གྱིས་ཡོད་པར་འཛིན་པའི་བློ་འི་ཞགས་ཐུང་དུར་འགྲོ་བ་ནི། སྣང་བས་ཡོད་མཐའ་སེལ་ཚུལ་དང་། དེ་འདྲ་བའི་གང་ཟག་གིས་རང་བཞིན་གྱིས་སྟོང་པ་ཇི་ཙམ་ཡོད་ལ་བྱེད་པ་དེ་ཙམ་དུ་ལས་རྒྱུ་འབྲས་ལ་ཡིད་མི་ཆེས་ཤིང་མེད་པར་འཛིན་པའི་བློ་འི་ཞགས་ཐུང་དུར་འགྲོ་བ་ནི། སྟོང་པས་མེད་མཐའ་སེལ་ཚུལ་ཡིན་ནོ། མདོ་ལས། གང་ཞིག་རྐྱེན་ལས་སྐྱེས་པ་དེ་མ་སྐྱེས། །དེ་ལ་སྐྱེ་བའི་རང་བཞིན་ཡོད་མ་ཡིན། །རྐྱེན་ལ་རག་ལས་གང་དེ་སྟོང་པར་བཤད། །གང་ཞིག་སྟོང་ཉིད་ཤེས་དེ་བག་ཡོད་ཡིན། །ཞེས་དང་། བཞི་བརྒྱ་པ་ལས། སངས་རྒྱས་ཀྱིས་གསུངས་ལྐོག་གྱུར་ལ། །གང་ཞིག་ཐེ་ཚོམ་སྐྱེ་འགྱུར་བ། །དེ་ཡིས་སྟོང་པ་ཉིད་བརྟེན་ཏེ། །འདི་ཉིད་ཁོ་ནར་ཡིད་ཆེས་བྱ། །ཞེས་དང་། རྗེ་བདག་ཉིད་ཆེན་པོས་ཀྱང་། ཁྱོད་ཀྱིས་ཇི་ལྟར་བསྟན་པ་ལ། །རྒོལ་བ་འགས་ཀྱང་ཆོས་མཐུན་དུ། །གླགས་མི་རྙེད་པར་གསུངས་པ་ཡང་། །འདི་ཉིད་ཀྱི་ནི་ལེགས་པར་ཁྲམས། །ཅི་སྐད་ཅེ་ན་འདི་བཤད་པས། །མཐོང་དང་མ་མཐོང་དངོས་པོ་ལ། །སྒྲོ་འདོགས་པ་དང་སྐུར་འདེབས་ཀྱི། །གོ་སྐབས་རིང་དུ་མཛད་ཕྱིར་རོ། །ཞེས་གསུངས་སོ། །སྣང་བས་ཡོད་མཐའ་དང་སྟོང་པས་མེད་མཐའ་སེལ་བར་ཁས་ལེན་པ་ཙམ་ཐུན་མོང་མ་ཡིན་པ་མིན་གྱི་སེལ་ཚུལ་ཐུན་མོང་མ་ཡིན་པ་ཡིན་ཞེས་དེང་སང་གྲགས་ཆེ་ཡང་། རང་རྒྱུད་པ་མན་ཆད་ཀྱི་གཞུང་དུ་དེ་ལྟར་བཤད་པའི་ཁུངས་ཡོད་མེད་འཚོལ་དགོས་སམ་སྙམ་མོ། ། ཚིག་གསལ་ལས། འདྲ་བ་ལས་ཉམས་སུ་མྱོང་བའི་དོན་རྟོགས་པ་ནི་ཉེར་འཇལ་བ་སྟེ། དཔེར་ན། བ་མེན་ནི་བ་གླང་དང་འདྲའོ། ལྟ་བུའོ། །ཞེས་གསུངས་པ་ལ། དབུ་མའི་མཐའ་དཔྱོད་ལས། མཚན་གཞི་ནི་བ་མེན་ནི་བ་གླང་འདྲའོ་སྙམ་པའི་རྗེས་དཔག་དང་། སྦྱ་ཀུ་ནི་ནི་བཞིན་

Janggya Text (Sarnath Edition)

བཤད་ཟིན་ཏོ། །གཉིས་པ་ནི། དབུ་མ་ཐལ་འགྱུར་བས་མདོ་དང་འཕགས་པའི་དགོངས་པ་འགྲེལ་ཚུལ་ཐུན་མོང་མ་ཡིན་པའི་གཙོ་བོ་ནི་རང་གི་མཚན་ཉིད་ཀྱིས་གྲུབ་པ་རྡུལ་ཙམ་ཡང་མེད་པ་དང་མིང་གིས་བཏགས་ཙམ་ལ་བྱ་བྱེད་ཐམས་ཅད་གྲུ་ཆ་ཉམས་པར་བཞག་པས་ཆོག་པ་འདི་གཉིས་ཡིན་པར་འདུག་ལ། དེ་ལ་བརྟེན་ནས་རྣམ་པར་དག་པའི་གྲུབ་མཐའ་འགྲེལ་བྱེད་གཞན་དང་ཐུན་མོང་མ་ཡིན་པ་མང་དུ་ཡོད་པ་ལས་གཙོ་བོ་ནི་དཀའ་བའི་གནས་བརྒྱད་དུ་བསྡུས་ནས་འཆད་པར་རང་རེའི་མཁས་པ་རྣམས་ལ་གྲགས་སོ། །དེ་ནི་རྗེ་ཐམས་ཅད་མཁྱེན་པས་འཇུག་པའི་རྣམ་བཤད་ཆེན་མོ་ལས། རྣམ་པར་དག་པའི་གྲུབ་མཐའ་འགྲེལ་བྱེད་གཞན་དང་ཐུན་མོང་མ་ཡིན་པ་མང་དུ་ཡོད་དེ། དེ་གང་ཞེ་ན། རེ་ཞིག་གཙོ་བོར་རྣམས་བརྗོད་ན། ཚོགས་དྲུག་ལས་ངོ་བོ་ཐ་དད་པའི་ཀུན་གཞི་རྣམ་ཤེས་དང་། རང་རིག་འགོག་ལུགས་ཐུན་མོང་མ་ཡིན་པ་དང་། རང་རྒྱུད་ཀྱི་སྦྱོར་བས་ཕྱིར་རྒོལ་གྱི་རྒྱུད་ལ་དེ་ཁོ་ན་ཉིད་རྗེ་ལྟ་བ་བཞིན་བསྐྱེད་པ་ཁས་མི་ལེན་པ་གསུམ་དང་། ཤེས་པ་ཁས་ལེན་པ་བཞིན་དུ་ཕྱི་དོན་ཡང་ཁས་བླང་དགོས་པ་དང་། ཉན་རང་ལ་དངོས་པོ་རང་བཞིན་མེད་པར་རྟོགས་པ་ཡོད་པ་དང་། ཆོས་ཀྱི་བདག་འཛིན་ཉོན་མོངས་སུ་འཇོག་པ་དང་། ཞིག་པ་དངོས་པོ་ཡིན་པ་དང་། དེའི་རྒྱུ་མཚན་གྱིས་དུས་གསུམ་གྱི་འཇོག་ཚུལ་ཐུན་མོང་མ་ཡིན་པ་སོགས་ཡིན་ནོ། །ཞེས་གསུངས་པ་ལ་བརྟེན་པར་སྣང་ཞིང་སོགས་ཁོང་ནས་འདོན་རྒྱུ་ལམ་དང་འབྲས་བུའི་གནས་སྐབས་ཀྱི་ཁྱད་པར་ཡང་མང་དུ་ཡོད་དོ། །ལ་ལ་དག་ཚོགས་དྲུག་ལས་ངོ་བོ་ཐ་དད་པའི་ཀུན་གཞིའི་རྣམ་ཤེས་འགོག་པ་ཐལ་འགྱུར་བའི་ཐུན་མོང་མ་ཡིན་པའི་གྲུབ་མཐར་མི་འཐད་དེ། མདོ་སྡེ་སྤྱོད་པའི་རང་རྒྱུད་པས་ཀྱང་དེ་འགོག་པའི་ཕྱིར་ཞེས་སོགས་གཞན་རྣམས་ལ་ཡང་དེ་འདྲ་དེ་སྦྱོར་ཞིང་།

༨

ཞིག་པ་དངོས་པོར་འདོད་པ་ཡང་ཐུན་མོང་མ་ཡིན་པར་མི་འཐད་དེ། བྱེ་བྲག་སྨྲ་བས་ཀྱང་དེ་དངོས་པོར་འདོད་པའི་ཕྱིར་ཞེས་རྣམ་བཤད་ཀྱི་ཚིག་ཟིན་ལ་དགག་པ་གནོང་···ཁྲེལ་བྱེད་པ་དང་། རང་རེའི་རྗེས་འཇུག་ཁ་ཅིག་གིས་ཀྱང་རིགས་པ་དེ་དག་གིས་གནོད་ཀྱིས་དོགས་ནས་རྣམ་བཤད་ཀྱི་སྐབས་ཟིན་ལ་ཚིག་གི་ལྷན་ཐབས་དུ་མ་ཞིག་སྦྱོར···པའི་ཞམས་པ་བཟང་པོ་འི་ཁྲར་ལེན་པར་འདུག་སྟེ། ཕན་ཚུན་གཉིས་ཀས་གཞུང་ཆེན་མོ་ཀློག་པ་ཙམ་ཡང་མི་ཤེས་པའི་རྣམ་འགྱུར་གསལ་བར་བསྟན་ཏེ། རྣམ་བཤད་ཀྱི་འགོག་ལུགས་ཐུན་མོང་མ་ཡིན་པ་ཞེས་དང་འཇོག་ཚུལ་ཐུན་མོང་མ་ཡིན་པ་ཞེས་པ་རྣམས་ཐ་མའི་གསལ་བྱེད་ཡིན་པ་དང་། གསུངས་རེ་དག་གི་རྣམ་བཅད་ཡོངས་གཅོད་ཀྱི་དགོས་པ་ཅི་ཡང་མ་ཤེས་པར་སྣང་བའི་ཕྱིར་རོ། །ངང་ཚུལ་འདི་ལྟ་བུར་གྱུར་པ་དག་གིས་ཀྱང་གཞུང་ལུགས་འཆད་རྩོད་རྩོམ་པའི་ཁྲར་ལེན་པ་ནི་བསྟན་པ་རིན་པོ་ཆེ···ཆེས་ཆེར་ཉམས་པའི་རྟགས་སུ་མངོན་ཞིང་དཔྱོད་ལྡན་མཆོག་ཏུ་ཡི་མུག་པའི་གནས་ཁོ···ནའོ། །ད་ནི་འདིར་ཐུན་མོང་མ་ཡིན་པའི་ཁྱད་པར་དེ་དག་ལས་ནི་གཙོ་བོ་འགའ་ཞིག་མདོ་ཙམ་བརྗོད་པར་བྱ་སྟེ། དེ་ལ་ཁྱད་ཆོས་གཙོ་བོར་བརྒྱད་བཤད་པ་དང་། རང་མཚན་འགོག་ལུགས་དང་། དེ་ལ་བརྟེན་ནས་མདོ་འི་དྲང་ངེས་འབྱེད་ཚུལ་གསུམ། དེའི་དང་པོ་ལ་བརྒྱད་ལས། དང་པོ་ཀུན་གཞི་རྣམ་ཤེས་འགོག་ཚུལ་ཐུན་མོང་མ་ཡིན་པ་ནི། རང་བཞིན་གྱིས་གྲུབ་པ་མི་འདོད་པའི་ལུགས་ལ་ཀུན་གཞི་དང་ཆུད་མི་ཟ་བ་དང་ཐོབ་པ་ལ་སོགས་པ་ཁས་མ་བླངས་ཀྱང་ལས་འབྲས་ཀྱི་རྣམ་གཞག་འཇོག་ནུས་པས་དེ་དག་ཁས་ལེན་དོན་མེད་དོ། །དེ་འཇོག་ནུས་ཚུལ་ཇི་ལྟར་ཡིན་ཞེ་ན་ཀུན་གཞི་ཁས་མ་བླངས་ཀྱང་ལས་བསགས་པ་འགགས་ཟིན་པ་ལས་འབྲས་བུ་འབྱུང་བའི་རྣམ···གཞག་བྱར་རུང་བ་ཡིན་ཏེ། ལས་འགགས་པ་རང་བཞིན་གྱིས་མ་གྲུབ་པའི་ཕྱིར།

དེ་དེའི་རྒྱུ་མཚན་དུ་འགྲོ་ཚུལ་ནི། གང་ཕྱིར་རང་བཞིན་གྱིས་ནི་མི་འགགས་པ། དེ་
ཕྱིར་ཞེས་པའི་རྒྱུ་མཚན་ཉིད་ཀྱིས་ལས་ཞིག་པའི་ཞིག་པ་ལས་ཕྱིས་ཀྱི་འབྲས་བུ་འབྱུང་
བ་འགྲུབ་པ་ཉིད་ཡིན་ནོ། །རང་བཞིན་གྱིས་མེད་པའི་ལས་ཞིག་པ་ལས་འབྲས་བུ་
འབྱུང་བ་ལ་རྣམ་སྨིན་ཐུག་མེད་དུ་འབྱུང་བ་དང་རྣམ་སྨིན་འཆོལ་བར་འགྱུར་བའི་སྐྱོན་
ཡང་མེད་དེ། ཡོད་པ་མ་ཡིན་པར་མཚུངས་ཀྱང་རབ་རིབ་ཅན་ལ་སྐྲ་ཤད་སྣང་གི་
བོང་བུའི་རྭ་མི་སྣང་བའི་ངེས་པ་ཡོད་པ་ལྟར། རང་བཞིན་མེད་ཀྱང་རྣམ་སྨིན་ཕྱུང་
ཟིན་པ་ལས་འབྲས་བུ་མི་འབྱུང་ཞིང་ལས་དགེ་མི་དགེའི་འབྲས་བུ་སོ་སོར་ངེས་པའི་
རྣམ་གཞག་འཐད་པའི་ཕྱིར། ལང་ཀར་གཤེགས་པ་དང་། དགོངས་འགྲེལ་དང་།
ཐེག་པ་ཆེན་པོའི་ཆོས་མངོན་པའི་མདོ་ལས་ཀུན་གཞི་ཡོད་པར་གསུངས་པ་དང་མི་
འགལ་ཏེ། དེ་ནི་ཆོས་ཉིད་ཟབ་མོ་རེ་ཞིག་སྟོན་པའི་སྣོད་དུ་མི་རུང་བའི་གདུལ་བྱ་
རྣམས་ཆོས་ཟབ་མོ་ལ་རིམ་གྱིས་དྲང་བའི་དགོངས་པའི་དབང་གིས་གསུངས་པ་ཡིན་
པའི་ཕྱིར། དགོས་པ་ནི་དེ་ཡིན་ལ། དགོངས་གཞི་ནི་རང་བཞིན་གྱིས་གྲུབ་པས་
སྟོང་པའི་སྟོང་ཉིད་དོ། །དངོས་ལ་གནོད་བྱེད་ནི། ཀུན་གཞི་ཁས་བླངས་ན་
ཀུན་གཞིའི་བག་ཆགས་སྨིན་པ་ལས་གཟུགས་སྒྲ་སོགས་སུ་སྣང་བ་ཙམ་དུ་ཟད་ཀྱི་ཕྱི་
རོལ་གྱི་དོན་མེད་པར་ཁས་བླངས་དགོས་ན། དེ་ནི་མི་འཐད་དེ། དོན་ཤེས་གཉིས་
དོན་དམ་དུ་མེད་མཉམ་དང་ཐ་སྙད་དུ་ཡོད་མཉམ་ཡིན་པ་རིགས་པས་གྲུབ་པའི་ཕྱིར།
ཞེས་སོགས་རིགས་པ་དང་། ལུང་ལས་ཀྱང་སྟོན་པ་རང་ཉིད་ཀྱིས་ཀུན་གཞི་བཤད་
པའི་དགོངས་པ་བསྟན་པ་རྣམས་ཡིན་ནོ། །འོ་ན་འདི་པའི་ལུགས་ཀྱི་དགེ་མི་དགེའི་
ལས་ཀྱི་བག་ཆགས་འཇོག་པའི་གཞི་འམ་རྟེན་དུ་ཅི་ཞིག་འདོད་པར་བྱ་ཞེ་ན། གདན་
དུ་བའི་བག་ཆགས་བསྒོ་གཞི་ནི་ངའམ་གང་ཟག་ཙམ་དང་རེས་འགའ་བའི་བག་ཆགས་

བསྒོ་གཞིར་སེམས་ཀྱི་རྒྱུད་ཀྱང་བཞག་ཆོག་པར་བཞེད་དོ། །འདི་དག་ལ་བརྟེན་ནས་མཐོང་ལམ་བར་ཆད་མེད་ལམ་པའི་རྒྱུད་ལ་སྒོམ་སྤང་གི་བག་ལ་ཉལ་གྱི་རྟེན་འཛིན་ཚུལ་དང་། དེའི་རྒྱུད་ལ་ཐེག་ཆེན་སེམས་བསྐྱེད་ཡོད་མེད་དང་། ནམ་མཁའ་མཐའ་ཡས་སྐྱེ་མཆེད་ལ་སོགས་པར་སྐྱེས་པའི་འཕགས་པའི་རྒྱུད་ལ་ཟག་མེད་ཀྱི་སེམས······མངོན་དུ་གྱུར་པ་ན་དེ་དག་གི་འགྲོ་བ་ལྡོག་མི་ལྡོག་སོགས་རྗེ་རིན་པོ་ཆེའི་གསུང་དང···ཤིང་རྟ་ཆེན་པོ་དག་གི་གཞུང་གུང་བསྒྲིགས་ན་དཔྱད་པར་བྱ་བའི་གནས་ཕྲ་མོ་མཐའ་··ཡས་པ་ཞིག་ཡོད་དོ། །གཉིས་པ་རང་རིག་འགོག་ཚུལ་ཐུན་མོང་མ་ཡིན་པ་ལ་གཉིས། དངོས་དང་། ཚད་མའི་རྣམ་གཞག་བཤད་པའོ། །དང་པོ་ནི། ཕྱོགས་སྔ་མའི་རང་རིག་འདོད་ཚུལ་ནི་སེམས་ཙམ་པའི་སྐབས་སུ་བཤད་པ་ལྟར་ཡིན་ལ། དེ་འགོག་ལུགས་ནི་དྲན་པའི་རྟགས་ཀྱིས་རང་རིག་སྒྲུབ་པ་མི་འཐད་དེ། རང་གི་མཚན་ཉིད་ཀྱིས་གྲུབ་པའི་དབང་དུ་བྱས་ནས་ཕྱི་དུས་ཀྱི་དྲན་པ་རྟགས་སུ་འགོད་ན་རྟགས་དེ་སྒྲུབ···བྱེད་མ་ཡིན་ཏེ། སྒྲ་མི་རྟག་པར་བསྒྲུབ་པ་ལ་མིག་གི་གཟུང་བྱ་བཞིན་ནོ། འཛིག་རྟེན་པའི་ཐ་སྙད་ཀྱི་དབང་དུ་བྱས་ན་ཡང་མི་འཐད་དེ། རང་རིག་པའི་འབྲས་བུ་དྲན་པ་མེད་པའི་ཕྱིར་ཏེ། རང་རིག་མེད་ན་དེའི་འབྲས་བུ་དྲན་པ་མི་འགྲུབ་པའི་ཕྱིར། འབྲེལ་པ་མེད་པར་ནི་བསྒྲུབ་བྱ་མི་འགྲུབ་སྟེ། ཆུ་ཙམ་ལས་ནོར་བུ་ཆུ་ཤེལ་དང་། མེ་ཙམ་ལས་མེ་ཤེལ་དཔོག་པ་བཞིན་ནོ། །གལ་ཏེ་དྲན་པ་དང་རང་རིག་རྒྱུ་འབྲས་སུ་གྲུབ་པའི་སྒོ་ནས་རང་རིག་བསྒྲུབ་པ་མིན་གྱི་དྲན་པ་ལ་བརྟེན་ནས་སྔར་གྱི་ཤེས་པ···ལ་མྱོང་བ་ཡོད་པར་དཔོགས་ལ། དེ་ལ་རང་མྱོང་དང་གཞན་མྱོང་གཉིས་སུ་ཁ་ཚོན་བཅད་ནས་གཞན་མྱོང་བཀག་པ་ལས་རང་མྱོང་འགྲུབ་བོ་ཞེ་ན། དེ་ཡང་མི་འཐད་དེ། ཤེས་པས་ཡུལ་རིག་པ་ལ་མདོ་སྡེ་པ་དང་སེམས་ཙམ་པས་གཞག་པ་ལྟར་གྱི···

རང་མྱོང་དང་གཞན་མྱོང་གཉིས་སུ་ཁ་ཆོན་མ་ཆོད་པའི་ཕྱིར། དེ་དག་ནི་སྒྲུབ་བྱེད་འགོག་པའི་རིགས་པ་ཡིན་ལ་བསྒྲུབ་བྱ་རང་རིག་འགོག་པའི་རིགས་པ་ནི། འཛིན་རྣམ་ཡན་གར་བ་མི་འཐད་དེ། ཡིད་ཛེ་ཙམ་གདད་ཀྱང་ཁོ་རང་ཁོ་རང་དང་རིག་བྱ་རིག་བྱེད་ཐ་དད་པའི་རྣམ་པ་མི་འཆར་བའི་ཕྱིར་དང་། རང་ལ་རང་གི་བྱེད་པ་རང་བཞིན་གྱིས་འཇུག་ན་བྱ་བྱེད་ལས་གསུམ་གཅིག་ཏུ་ཐལ་བའི་སྐྱོན་ཡོད་པའི་ཕྱིར། ཞེས་ཀྱང་རང་ཉིད་བསྲེག་པར་ཐལ་བ་ལ་སོགས་པའོ། །རང་ལུགས་ལ་རང་རིག་མེད་ཀྱང་དྲན་པ་སྐྱེ་བ་འཐད་དེ། སྔར་སྔོན་པོ་མཐོང་བའི་ཤེས་པ་དང་ཕྱིས་ཀྱི་སྔོ་འཛིན་མིག་ཤེས་དྲན་པའི་ཤེས་པ་… གཉིས་རང་བཞིན་གྱིས་གྲུབ་པའི་སོ་སོ་བ་མ་ཡིན་པའི་ཕྱིར་དང་། ངའི་སྔོ་འཛིན་མིག་ཤེས་ཀྱིས་སྔོན་པོ་མ་མཐོང་བས་ངས་སྔོན་པོ་མཐོང་བར་ཡང་འཇོག་ནུས་པའི་ཕྱིར་དང་། སྔར་སྔོ་འཛིན་མིག་ཤེས་ཀྱིས་མཐོང་བའི་སྔོན་པོ་དེ་ཉིད་ཕྱིས་ཀྱི་དྲན་ཤེས་ཀྱིས་ཀྱང་… གཅོད་པས་མྱོང་དྲན་ཡུལ་གཅིག་པའི་ཕྱིར། འཇུག་པ་རྩ་འགྲེལ་གྱི་རིགས་པའོ། །རང་རིག་མེད་ཀྱང་དྲན་པ་སྐྱེ་བ་འཐད་དེ། སྔོན་པོ་དྲན་པའི་ཤེས་པ་སྐྱེ་བ་ན་སྔར་གྱི་མིག་ཤེས་སྣངས་ནས་དྲན་པ་མ་ཡིན་པར་སྔར་སྔོན་པོ་འདི་མཐོང་ངོ་ཞེས་སྔོན་པོ་དང་སྔོ་… འཛིན་མིག་ཤེས་འབྲེལ་བར་དྲན་པའི་ཕྱིར། དཔེར་ན་དགུན་དུས་སུ་བྱི་བས་ལུས་ལ་རྨུགས་པ་ན་རྨུགས་པ་མྱོང་གི་དུག་མ་མྱོང་ཡང་ཕྱིས་འབྲུག་གི་སྒྲ་ཐོས་པ་ན་སྔར་མྱོང་པའི་དུས་སུ་དུག་ཞུགས་པར་འདུག་སྙམ་དུ་དྲན་པ་སྐྱེ་བ་མི་འགལ་བ་བཞིན་ནོ་ཞེས་པ་སྤྱོད་འཇུག་ནས་བཤད་པའི་རིགས་པའོ། གཉིས་པ་ཚད་མའི་རྣམ་གཞག་བཤད་པ་ལ། ལུགས་འདིས་ཚད་མའི་མཚན་ཉིད་ན་རང་གི་འཛིན་སྟངས་ཀྱི་ཡུལ་ལ་མི་བསླུ་བའི་…… ཤེས་པ་ཙམ་ལ་བྱེད་ཀྱི་གསར་དུ་མི་བསླུ་བའི་ཁྱད་པར་སྦྱར་མི་དགོས་སོ། །སྒྲ་བཤད་ཀྱང་རབ་ཏུ་འམ་ལེགས་པར་འཇལ་བ་ལ་བཞེད་དོ། །དབྱེ་བ་ནི། མངོན་རྗེས་

གཉིས་དང་། ཡིད་ཆེས་དང་། དཔེ་ཉེར་འཇལ་གྱི་ཚད་མ་སྟེ་བཞིར་ཚིག་གསལ་ལས་བཤད་དོ། །དེ་ལྟ་ན་ཡང་མངོན་རྗེས་གཉིས་སུ་གྲངས་མ་ངེས་པ་ཡང་མ་ཡིན་ཏེ། ཚད་མ་ཕྱི་མ་གཉིས་རྗེས་དཔག་ཏུ་འདུ་བའི་ཕྱིར་དང་། བཞི་བརྒྱ་པའི་འགྲེལ་པ་ལས་ཀྱང་གཉིས་སུ་བཤད་པའི་ཕྱིར་རོ། །ཚད་མའི་གྲངས་ནི་གཞལ་བྱའི་དབང་གིས་བཞག་པ་སྟེ། གཞལ་བྱ་མངོན་གྱུར་དང་ལྐོག་གྱུར་དང་ཤིན་ཏུ་ལྐོག་གྱུར་གསུམ་དུ་ཡོད་པའི་ཕྱིར་དང་། དཔེ་ཉེར་འཇལ་གྱི་གཞལ་བྱ་ནི་ཕན་ཚུན་འདྲ་བའི་ཆོས་ལྐོག་ཏུ་གྱུར་པའོ། །ཚད་མ་གང་། རྟགས་ལ་མ་ལྟོས་པར་རང་གི་འཛིན་སྟངས་ཀྱི་ཡུལ་གྱི་གཞལ་བྱ་མངོན་སུམ་པ་ལ་མི་བསླུ་བ་ནི་མངོན་སུམ་ཚད་མའི་ངོ་བོའོ། །རང་རིག་མངོན་སུམ་མི་བཞེད་པས་བདག་རྐྱེན་དབང་པོ་གཟུགས་ཅན་པ་ལ་བརྟེན་པའི་མངོན་སུམ་ཚད་མ་དང་། བདག་རྐྱེན་ཡིད་དབང་ལ་བརྟེན་པའི་མངོན་སུམ་ཚད་མ་གཉིས་སོ། །ཡིད་མངོན་ལ་ཞི་ལྷག་ཟུང་འབྲེལ་ལ་མ་བརྟེན་པ་དང་བརྟེན་པ་གཉིས་ཡོད་པའི་སྔ་མ་ཡིད་མངོན་དང་ཕྱི་མ་རྣལ་འབྱོར་མངོན་སུམ་མོ། །སྦྱོར་རྣལ་འབྱོར་མངོན་སུམ་ཡང་ཡིད་མངོན་ཡིན་མོད་ཀྱང་མངོན་སུམ་ལ་གསུམ་དུ་ཕྱེ་བའི་ཚེ་དེ་གཉིས་འགལ་བ་ཡིན་ནོ། །རྣལ་འབྱོར་མངོན་སུམ་གྱི་འཛིན་སྟངས་ཀྱི་ཡུལ་ནི་བདེན་བཞིའི་ཁྱད་ཆོས་སམ་བདག་མེད་ཕྲ་རགས་གང་ཡང་རུང་བའོ། །རང་རྒྱུད་པ་མན་ཆད་ཀྱིས་རྣལ་འབྱོར་མངོན་སུམ་ལ་འཕགས་པའི་ཡེ་ཤེས་ཀྱིས་ཁྱབ་པར་བཞེད་ཀྱང་། འདི་པའི་ལུགས་ལ་བདག་མེད་ཕྲ་མོ་མ་རྟོགས་པའི་སྔ་རོལ་དུ་ཡང་བདེན་བཞིའི་རྣམ་པ་མི་རྟག་སོགས་བཅུ་དྲུག་དང་གང་ཟག་གི་བདག་མེད་རགས་པ་སོགས་རྟོགས་པའི་རྣལ་འབྱོར་མངོན་སུམ་ཡོད་པར་བཞེད་པས་སོ་སོ་སྐྱེ་བོ་འི་རྒྱུད་ལ་ཡང་རྣལ་འབྱོར་མངོན་སུམ་ཡོད་དོ། ཡིད་མངོན་ཡང་གཞན་དག་དང་མི་མཐུན་ཏེ། རང་ཡུལ་གསལ་

བར་རྟོགས་པའི་རྟོག་བྲལ་མི་དགོས་པས་དྲན་ཤེས་དང་རྗེས་དཔག་གིས་དྲངས་པའི་བཅད་ཤེས་སོགས་ལ་ཡང་མངོན་སུམ་ཚད་མ་ཡོད་དོ། །ཡིད་ཤེས་འཁོར་གྱི་ཚོར་བ་བདེ་སྡུག་སོགས་ཉམས་སུ་མྱོང་བའི་ཡིད་མངོན་ནི་རང་རིག་དང་མི་འདྲ་སྟེ། ཁ་ནང་བལྟ་ལ་གཉིས་སྣང་ནུབ་པ་མི་དགོས་པར་མྱོང་བྱ་མྱོང་བྱེད་ཐ་དད་པ་ཉིད་དུ་བློ་ལ་སྣང་བར་བཞེད་པའི་ཕྱིར་རོ། །གཞལ་བྱ་མངོན་གྱུར་པ་ནི་རྟགས་ལ་མ་བརྟེན་པར་མྱོང་སྟོབས་ཀྱིས་རྟོགས་པར་བྱ་དགོས་པའི་ཆོས་སོ། །ལྐོག་གྱུར་བ་ནི་རྟགས་ལ་བརྟེན་ནས་རྟོགས་དགོས་པའི་ཆོས་སོ། །རྟགས་ལ་དངོས་སུ་བརྟེན་ནས་རང་གི་འཛིན་སྟངས་ཀྱི་ཡུལ་དུ་གྱུར་པའི་གཞལ་བྱ་ལྐོག་གྱུར་བ་ལ་མི་བསླུ་བའི་ཤེས་པ་ནི་རྗེས་དཔག་ཚད་མའི་ངོ་བོའོ། །འདི་ལ་ཡང་དངོས་སྟོབས་རྗེས་དཔག་དང་ཡིད་ཆེས་རྗེས་དཔག་དང་དཔེ་ཉེར་འཇལ་གྱི་རྗེས་དཔག་གསུམ་མོ། །ཐལ་འགྱུར་ཙམ་ལ་བརྟེན་པ་དང་ཚུལ་གསུམ་པའི་གཏན་ཚིགས་ལ་བརྟེན་པའི་རྗེས་དཔག་གཉིས་ཀྱི་ཐ་སྙད་ཀྱང་བཞེད་དོ། །དཔེ་ཉེར་འཇལ་ལ་ཚུལ་གསུམ་པའི་གཏན་ཚིགས་དང་ཐལ་འགྱུར་གཞན་གྱིས་བཀོད་པ་མེད་ཀྱང་རྒྱུ་མཚན་ལ་བརྟེན་ནས་འཇལ་བ་ཡིན་པས་རྟགས་ལ་བརྟེན་པར་བཞག་ཚོག་གོ། །ལུང་འདིས་སྔོ་འཛིན་མངོན་སུམ་ཚད་མ་འགྲུབ་ཚུལ་ནི་སྔོ་འཛིན་མིག་ཤེས་རང་ཉིད་ལ་ཕྱི་རོལ་ནས་སྔོན་པོའི་རྣམ་པ་ཤར་བའི་དབང་གིས་རྟོགས་བྱ་རྟོགས་བྱེད་ཐ་དད་དུ་སྣང་ཞིང་། དེ་ལྟར་སྣང་བས་སྔོ་འཛིན་མིག་ཤེས་རང་ཉིད་ཀྱི་ངོ་བོ་ཡོད་པ་ལ་ཡང་ཚད་མར་སོང་བ་ཡིན་པས་གཞན་གྱི་ལུགས་ལྟར་རང་རིག་སོགས་ཀྱིས་འགྲུབ་མི་དགོས་སོ། །འདི་ནི་ཚིག་གསལ་ལས། གཞལ་བྱའི་རྣམ་པའི་རྗེས་སུ་བྱེད་པ་ཙམ་གྱིས་ཚད་མ་དག་གི་རང་གི་ངོ་བོ་རྣམ་པར་འཇོག་པའི་ཕྱིར་ཞེས་པའི་དོན་དུ་བཞེད་དོ། །འདི་ཤིན་ཏུ་དཀའ་བར་སྣང་བས་བློ་གྲོས་ཞིབ་མོས་དཔྱོད་ཤེས་དགོས་སོ། །རྗེས་ཀྱིས་དྲན་

ཤེས་ཀྱིས་ཀྱང་འགྲུབ་ལ་དེ་ནི་སྔོ་འཛིན་མིག་ཤེས་ཀྱིས་སྔོན་པོ་གཞལ་བའི་སྟོབས······ ཀྱིས་ཚད་མ་གཞན་རྒྱུད་མི་དགོས་པར་དེ་ལྟར་བཟུང་བ་དྲན་པའི་ཤེས་པ་དངོས་སུ······ འདྲེན་ལ། དྲན་ཤེས་དེ་ཉིད་ཀྱིས་ཀྱང་སྔོན་པོ་མེད་པ་དང་སྔོ་འཛིན་མིག་ཤེས་མེད་པ་གཉིས་ཀའི་སྒྲོ་འདོགས་གཅོད་པའི་ཕྱིར་དང་། དྲན་ཤེས་དེ་ཉིད་མིག་ཤེས་ཡོད་པ་ལ་ཚད་མ་ཡིན་པའི་ཕྱིར་རོ། །འདི་ནི་སྟོང་ཐུན་གྱི་ཡང་དགོངས་པར་སྣང་ཞིང་སྤྱི་ལམ་ལས་རྩུང་ཟད་དོགས་སླའོ། །འདི་དག་རྒྱས་པར་གཞན་དུ་ཤེས་པར་བྱའོ། །

གསུམ་པ་རང་རྒྱུད་ཀྱི་གཏན་ཚིགས་ཁས་མི་ལེན་པའི་ཁྱད་པར་ལ། དངོས་དང་། གཞན་གྲགས་ཀྱི་འདོད་ཚུལ་ལོ། །དང་པོ་ནི། རང་རྒྱུད་པ་རྣམས་ནི་བདེན་མེད་སྒྲུབ་པའི་རྟགས་ཀྱི་ཚུལ་གསུམ་རྒོལ་ཕྱིར་རྒོལ་གང་ཡང་རུང་བའི་ངོར་གྲུབ་པ་ཙམ་གྱིས་མི་ཆོག་གི་དོན་གྱི་སྡོད་ལུགས་ཀྱི་སྟེང་ནས་གྲུབ་དགོས་ལ། དེ་ལྟར་གྲུབ་ན་བསྒྲུབ་བྱ་རྟོགས་པའི་རྗེས་དཔག་བསྐྱེད་པ་ཅིག་རང་རྒྱུད་ཀྱི་དོན་དུ་འདོད་དོ། །དེའི་རྒྱུ་མཚན་ཡང་དེ་དག་གི་ལུགས་ལ་རྟོག་པ་དང་རྟོག་མེད་ཀྱི་ཚད་མ་གང་ཡིན་ཀྱང་རང་ཉིད་ཚད་མར······ སོང་བ་སྣང་ཡུལ་དང་ཞེན་ཡུལ་རང་མཚན་ལ་མ་འཁྲུལ་བ་ཞིག་ངེས་པར་དགོས་ཏེ། དེ་ལ་འཁྲུལ་ན་ཚད་མ་དེས་གཞལ་བྱ་རྙེད་པར་འཇོག་མི་ནུས་པའི་ཕྱིར་རོ། །དེ་ཡང་ཐ་སྙད་དུ་མིང་རྐྱང་བཏགས་ཡོད་ཙམ་མ་ཡིན་པའི་རང་གི་རང་བཞིན་ཞིག་མེད་ན་ཆོས་དེ་ཡོད་པར་འཇོག་མི་ནུས་པ་ལ་ཐུག་པ་ཡིན་ནོ། །དེས་ན་རྟག་དང་བདེན་པར་
མི་རྟག
ཡོད་མེད་སོགས་རྒོལ་ཕྱིར་རྒོལ་གྱིས་རྩོད་པར་བྱ་བའི་ཁྱད་པར་གྱི་ཆོས་རྣམས་གང་ལ··· བརྟེན་པའི་གཞི་ཡུལ་སྟེང་ན་གྲུབ་གྲུབ་པ་ཞིག་སྟོན་རྒྱུ་མཐུན་སྣང་དུ་གྲུབ་པ་ཞིག་མེད་ན་དེའི་སྟེང་དུ་རྟགས་ཀྱི་ཚུལ་བསྒྲུབ་པར་མི་ནུས་ཏེ། ཁྱད་གཞི་མེད་པའི་ཁྱད་ཆོས་མི་འཐད་པའི་ཕྱིར་རོ་སྙམ་དུ་བསམ་པ་སྟེ། ཆོས་ཅན་མཐུན་སྣང་བའི་དོན་ཡང་དེ་ཡིན་

༄

སོ།། །།ཕྱང་དམ་པ་འདད་ལྟར་ན་འདད་འདྲ་ཞིག་སྟོན་རྒྱུ་ཡོད་ཕྱིན་དེ་ཉིད་རང་གི་ངོ་པས་ཡོད་པའི་དོན་དུ་སོང་ལ་དེ་ཉིད་དོན་དམ་པར་གྲུབ་པའི་དོན་ཡང་ཡིན་པས། དེ་ཉིད་ཁྱད་གཞིར་གཟུང་བའི་སྟེང་དུ་ཁྱད་པར་གྱི་ཆོས་གཞན་སྒྲུབ་ཚུལ་གྲོལ་ཕྱིར་གྲོལ་གཉིས་ཀ་ལ་མཐུན་སྣང་དུ་གྲུབ་པ་ཞིག་ཡོད་པར་འདོད་པ་ནི་ཤིན་ཏུ་མི་འཐད་དེ། སྔ་རྒོལ་དབུ་མ་པ་ལྟར་ན་རང་གི་ངོ་བོས་ཡོད་པ་ཐ་སྙད་དུའང་མི་འཐད་པས་དེ་ལྟ་བུ་ཞིག་མེད་དགོས་ཤིང་། ཕྱིར་རྒོལ་ལ་ནི་ཇི་སྲིད་ལྟ་བ་རྒྱུད་ལ་མ་སྐྱེས་ཀྱི་བར་དུ་རང་གི་ངོ་བོས་ཡོད་པ་དང་ཡོད་པ་ཙམ་གྱི་ཁྱད་པར་མི་ཕྱེད་པས་ཐ་སྙད་ཙམ་གྱི་ཡོད་ལུགས་ལྟ་བ་མ་རྟོགས་པར་དུ་སྟོན་མི་ནུས་པའི་ཕྱིར་རོ། དེས་ན་ཕྱིར་རྒོལ་གྱི་ཁས་བླངས་ལ་འཁྲིས་པ་ཙམ་མ་ཡིན་པར་ཡུལ་གྱི་སྟེང་ནས་གྲུབ་ལུགས་རྒོལ་ཕྱིར་རྒོལ་གཉིས་ཀ་ལ་མཐུན་སྣང་དུ་ཡོད་པ་ཞིག་མི་སྲིད་པས་ཆོས་ཅན་མཐུན་སྣང་བ་མེད་པར་བཞེད་པ་ཡིན་ནོ། །དེ་དག་ཀྱང་ཐ་སྙད་དུ་རང་མཚན་བཞེད་མི་བཞེད་ལ་ཐུག་ཅིང་རང་རྒྱུད་པ་ཀུན་རྫོབ་ལ་ཡང་ལོག་འབྱེད་པ་དང་ཐལ་འགྱུར་བས་རང་ལུགས་ལ་ཡང་དག་ཀུན་རྫོབ་མི་བཞེད་པ་སོགས་ཀྱི་གནད་ཀྱང་འདི་དག་ལ་བརྟེན་ནས་ཤེས་དགོས་སོ། །གཉིས་པ་ནི། ཐལ་འགྱུར་བའི་ལུགས་ལ་རང་རྒྱུད་ཀྱི་གཏན་ཚིགས་ཁས་མི་ལེན་ཡང་ཚུལ་གསུམ་པའི་རྟགས་ངེས་པར་ཁས་ལེན་དགོས་ལ་ཚུལ་གསུམ་ཡང་ཚད་མས་གྲུབ་པ་ཞིག་ངེས་པར་དགོས་སོ། །དེ་ཡང་གཞན་གྲགས་ཀྱི་གཏན་ཚིགས་ཀྱིས་བྱེད་པ་ཡིན་ཏེ། སྔར་བཤད་པ་ལྟར་རྒོལ་ཕྱིར་རྒོལ་གཉིས་ལ་ཡུལ་སྟེང་ནས་གཞལ་བྱ་འགྲུབ་ལུགས་མཐུན་སྣང་དུ་གྲུབ་པ་ཞིག་མེད་པས། ཕ་རོལ་པོའི་ཁས་བླངས་ལ་འཁྲིས་ནས་ཕ་རོལ་པོ་རང་ལ་གྲགས་པ་འམ་སྔ་རྒོལ་དབུ་མ་པ་ལ་བལྟོས་ཏེ་གཞན་ལ་གྲགས་པའི་གཏན་ཚིགས་འགོད་པ་ཡིན་པས་རང་གྲགས་དང་གཞན་གྲགས་ཀྱི་གཏན་ཚིགས་གཉིས་དོན་གཅིག

གོ། །དེ་ཡང་རྩ་ཤེའི་རབ་བྱེད་གསུམ་པ་ལས། ལྟ་དེ་རང་གི་བདག་ཉིད་ནི། ཞེས་སོགས་ཀྱིས་བཤད་པ་ལྟ་བུ་ལ་མཚོན་ན། ཆོས་ཅན་མིག་དང་། རྟགས་རང་ལ་མི་ལྟ་བ་དང་། དཔེ་བུམ་པ་རྣམས་ནི་ཕྱིར་རྒོལ་རང་ཉིད་ཀྱིས་ཁས་བླངས་པས་དེའི་ངོར་སྒྲུབ་མི་དགོས་སོ། །ཁྱབ་པ་ནི་རྗེས་སུ་འགྲོ་ལྡོག་གི་སྒོ་ནས་ངེས་པར་བྱེད་པ་སྟེ། རང་ལ་མི་ལྟ་བ་ལ་གཞན་ལ་ལྟ་བ་རང་གི་ངོ་བོས་མེད་པས་ཁྱབ་ལགས་ཁོ་རང་ལ་གྲགས་པའི་དཔེའི་སྟེང་ནས་རྗེས་སུ་འགྲོ་ལྡོག་ངེས་པར་བྱེད་པའོ། །གཏན་ཚིགས་འདིའི་རྣམ་གཞག་ཤིན་ཏུ་གནད་ཆེ་སྟེ་རྟོགས་ཀྱང་དཀའ་བར་ཡོད་ལ། ལམ་རིམ་ཆེན་མོ་ལས་ཞིབ་ཏུ་གསུངས་པ་ལྟ་བུ་རྗེས་འབྲངས་སུས་ཀྱང་གསལ་བར······བཤད་པ་མི་སྣང་ངོ་། །བཞི་པ་ཕྱི་དོན་ཁས་ལེན་པའི་ཁྱད་པར་བཤད་པ་ནི། སེམས་ཙམ་པ་ལྟར་ཕྱི་དོན་མེད་པར་ཤེས་པ་བདེན་པ་བ་འདོད་པ་ནི་མི་འཐད་དེ། དེ་ཁོ་ན་ཉིད་དུ་ན་དོན་ཤེས་གཉིས་ཀ་རིགས་པས་བཙལ་ནས་ཡོད་པར་འཇོག་མི་ནུས་ཤིང······འཇིག་རྟེན་གྲགས་པའི་དབང་ལས་ན་ཤེས་པ་ཡོད་པ་བཞིན་དུ་དོན་ཡང་ཡོད་པའི་ཕྱིར། བཅོམ་ལྡན་འདས་ཀྱིས་ཀྱང་ཤེས་རབ་ཀྱི་ཕ་རོལ་ཏུ་ཕྱིན་པའི་མདོ་ལས་ཕུང་པོ་ལྔ་ཆར···ཡང་རང་བཞིན་གྱིས་གྲུབ་པས་སྟོང་བར་གསུངས་པས་དོན་དམ་པར་མེད་མཉམ་དུ······གསུངས་ཤིང་། ཆོས་མངོན་པའི་མདོ་ལས་ནི་ཕུང་པོ་ལྔ་ཆར་ཡང་རང་དང་སྤྱིའི་མཚན་ཉིད་ལ་སོགས་པའི་སྒོ་ནས་ཀུན་རྫོབ་ཏུ་ཡོད་མཉམ་དུ་གསུངས་པས་ན་དོན་དང···ཤེས་པ་ལ་ཡོད་མེད་ཀྱི་ཁྱད་པར་འབྱེད་པ་ནི་བདེན་གཉིས་ཀྱི་རིམ་པ་འདི་དག་བཤིག··པར་འགྱུར་བའི་ཕྱིར་རོ། །འོ་ན་སེམས་ཙམ་པས་རྡུལ་ཆ་མེད་མེད་པས་དེ་བསགས་པའི་ཕྱི་དོན་འགོག་པའི་རིགས་པས་ཕྱོགས་ཀྱི་ཆ་མེད་ཀྱི་ཕྱི་དོན་མི་ཁེགས་པར་འགྱུར་རམ་སྙམ་ན། སྐྱོན་མེད་དེ། དེ་འདྲའི་ཕྱོགས་ཀྱི་ཆ་མེད་ཀྱི་ཕྱི་དོན་མི་ཁེགས་

པ་མ་ཡིན་ཀྱང་དེ་ཁེགས་པ་ཙམ་གྱིས་ཕྱི་དོན་ཁེགས་མི་དགོས་པའི་ཕྱིར་རོ། །དེ་བཞིན་དུ་ཤེས་པ་སྐད་ཅིག་ཆ་མེད་དང་དེ་འདུད་པའི་རྒྱུན་ཁེགས་ཀྱང་ཤེས་པ་ཁེགས་མི་དགོས་པ་ཡང་ཤེས་པར་བྱའོ། །སེམས་ཙམ་པའི་ལུགས་ཀྱིས་ནི་ཕྱི་རོལ་ཆ་མེད་ཁེགས་ན་སྣང་བ་ལ་མ་འཁྲུལ་པའི་དབང་ཤེས་ཁེགས་ལ། དེ་ལྟར་ན་དབང་ཤེས་འཁྲུལ་བས་དོན་འཛིན་མི་ནུས་པས་ཕྱི་དོན་ཁེགས་སོ་སྙམ་དུ་བསམ་པ་ཡིན་ནོ། །ལུང་དམ་པ་འདྲིས་ནི་དབང་ཤེས་འཁྲུལ་ས་པ་གཞལ་བྱ་བདེན་པ་འཛིན་མི་ནུས་པ་བདེན་མོད་ཀྱང་གཞལ་བྱ་རྫུན་པ་འཛིན་པ་ལ་དེ་གྲོགས་སུ་འགྲོ་བས་དེ་ཉིད་དོན་ཡོད་པའི་སྒྲུབ་བྱེད་ཡིན་གྱི་དོན་མེད་པའི་སྒྲུབ་བྱེད་མིན་ནོ་སྙམ་དུ་དགོངས་སོ། །མདོ་ལས་སེམས་ཙམ་དུ་གསུངས་པའི་དགོངས་པ་ནི་གཉིས་ཏེ་ས་བཅུ་པའི་མདོ་ལས། །ཁམས་གསུམ་པོ་འདི་ནི་སེམས་ཙམ་མོ། །ཞེས་པའི་མདོ་འི་ཙམ་སྒྲས་ཕྱི་དོན་གཅོད་པ་མ་ཡིན་གྱི་ཁམས་གསུམ་པོ་མཐའ་དག་ཀྱང་ལས་ཀྱིས་བྱས་ལ། ལས་ནི་སེམས་པ་དང་བསམ་པ་གཉིས་སུ་ངེས་པས་ཁམས་གསུམ་སེམས་ཀྱིས་བྱས་པར་གྲུབ་པས། དེའི་ཕྱིར་སེམས་ལས་གཞན་པའི་དབང་ཕྱུག་ལ་སོགས་པ་འཇིག་རྟེན་གྱི་བྱེད་པ་པོ་ཡོད་པ་དགག་པའི་ཆེད་དུ་ཙམ་སྒྲ་སྨོས་པ་ཡིན་ནོ། །ལང་ལང་གར་གཤེགས་པའི་མདོ་ལས། ཕྱི་རོལ་སྣང་བ་ཡོད་མེད་དེ། །སེམས་ནི་སྣ་ཚོགས་རྣམས་སུ་སྣང་། །ལུས་དང་ལོངས་སྤྱོད་གནས་འདྲ་བ། །སེམས་ཙམ་དུ་ནི་ངས་བཤད་དོ། །ཞེས་གསུངས་པས་ནི་སེམས་ཙམ་དུ་གསུངས་པ་ཡིན་མོད་ཀྱང་དེ་ཁོ་ན་ཉིད་ལ་རིམ་གྱིས་གཞུག་དགོས་པའི་གདུལ་བྱའི་བསམ་པའི་དབང་གིས་གསུངས་པ་ཡིན་གྱི་སྒྲ་ཇི་བཞིན་དུ་གཟུང་དུ་མི་རུང་སྟེ། གོང་དུ་བཤད་པའི་རིགས་པ་རྣམས་ཀྱིས་གནོད་པའི་ཕྱིར་དང་། བཅོམ་ལྡན་འདས་ཉིད་ཀྱིས་ཀྱང་། ཇི་ལྟར་ནད་པ་ནད་པ་ལ། །སྨན་

པས་སྐྱོན་རྣམས་གདོང་བ་ལྟར། །སངས་རྒྱས་དེ་བཞིན་སེམས་ཅན་ལ། །སེམས་ཙམ་དུ་ཡང་རབ་ཏུ་གསུངས། །ཞེས་གསུངས་པའི་ཕྱིར་རོ། །གཞན་ཡང་འཇུག་པ་རྩ་འགྲེལ་ལས། ཕྱི་དོན་མེད་ཀྱང་ཤེས་པ་རང་བཞིན་གྱིས་གྲུབ་པའི་དཔེར་རྨི་ལམ་གྱི་ཤེས་པ་དང་སྐྲ་ཤད་འཛག་སྣང་གི་དབང་ཤེས་དཔེར་བཀོད་པའི་སེམས་ཙམ་པའི····ལུགས་དགག་པ་ན། ད་དག་གི་ཚེ་ཕྱི་རོལ་གྱིས་བསྙུས་པའི་གླང་པོ་ཆེ་དང་སྐྲ་ཤད་སོགས་མེད་ཀྱང་ཡོད་པ་ལྟ་བུར་སྣང་བས་ཡུལ་ཅན་གྱི་ཤེས་པ་ཡང་རྫུན་པ་ཡིན་གྱི་རང་མཚན་གྱིས་མེད་པས། དོན་ཤེས་རང་བཞིན་གྱིས་གྲུབ་མ་གྲུབ་མཚུངས་པའི་རིགས་པས་དཔེ་མི་འཐད་པར་གསུངས་པ་ཡང་ཕྱི་དོན་མི་འཐད་པ་འགོག་པའི་རིགས་པ·····སྟོབས་ཆེ་བ་ཞིག་ཡིན་ནོ། །ལྷ་པ་ཉན་རང་ལ་ཆོས་ཀྱི་བདག་མེད་རྟོགས་པ་ཡོད་པར་བསྒྲུབ་པ་ལ་ལུང་ནི། ས་བཅུ་པའི་མདོ་ལས། ས་བདུན་པ་ལ་གནས་པའི་བྱང་སེམས་ཀྱིས་ཆོས་རང་བཞིན་མེད་རྟོགས་ཀྱི་ཤེས་རབ་ཀྱི་སྒོ་ནས་ཉན་རང་རྣམས····ཟིལ་གྱིས་གནོན་ལས་དྲུག་པ་མན་ཆད་དུ་ཟིལ་གྱིས་གནོན་མི་ནུས་པར་གསུངས་པའོ། །རིགས་པ་ལ་འཇུག་འགྲེལ་ལས་གསུམ་བཤད་པའི་དང་པོ་ནི། ཉན་རང་ལ་ཆོས་ཀྱི་བདག་མེད་ཕྲ་མོ་རྟོགས་པ་མེད་ན་འཇིག་རྟེན་པའི་ལམ་གྱིས་ཅི་ཡང་མེད་མན་ཆད་···ལ་ཆགས་པ་དང་བྲལ་བའི་དྲང་སྲོང་རྣམས་ལྟར་ཉན་རང་དེ་དག་སེམས་དང་པོ་བསྐྱེད་···པའི་བྱང་ཆུབ་སེམས་དཔས་ཀྱང་རང་བཞིན་མེད་རྟོགས་ཀྱི་ཤེས་རབ་ཀྱི་སྒོ་ནས་ཟིལ···གྱིས་གནོན་ནུས་པར་ཐལ་བ་དང་། རིགས་པ་གཉིས་པ་ནི། ཉན་རང་དགྲ་བཅོམ་པ་དག་གིས་ཉོན་མོངས་པ་ཐམས་ཅད་ཀྱི་རྩ་བ་བདེན་འཛིན་དང་འཛིན་སྟངས་དངོས་སུ···འགལ་བའི་ལམ་རྒྱུད་ལ་མ་སྐྱེད་པའི་ཕྱིར། དེ་དག་ཕྱི་རོལ་བའི་དྲང་སྲོང་བཞིན་དུ་ཁམས་གསུམ་ན་སྤྱོད་པའི་ཕྲ་རྒྱས་ཀྱི་ཉོན་མོངས་པ་ཐམས་ཅད་མ་སྤངས་པར་ཐལ་བའོ།

༨

རིགས་པ་གསུམ་པ་ནི། ཉན་རང་རྣམས་ཀྱིས་ཆོས་ཀྱི་བདག་མེད་ཕྲ་མོ་མ་རྟོགས་ན་གཟུགས་ལ་སོགས་པའི་ཕུང་པོ་ལ་བདེན་པར་དམིགས་པས་བློ་ཕྱིན་ཅི་ལོག་ཏུ་གྱུར་····པའི་ཕྱིར་གང་ཟག་གི་བདག་མེད་ཀྱང་མཚན་ཉིད་རྫོགས་པ་རྟོགས་པ་མེད་པར་འགྱུར་ཏེ། ངའམ་གང་ཟག་ཏུ་འདོགས་པའི་གཞི་ཕུང་པོ་ལ་བདེན་པར་དམིགས་པའི་ཡུལ་ཤུན་····ཕྱུང་པ་མེད་པའི་ཕྱིར་རོ། །ཞེས་པ་སྟེ། འདིས་གདགས་གཞི་ཕུང་པོ་ལ་བདེན་པར་འཛིན་པའི་ཞེན་ཡུལ་ཤུན་མ་ཕྱུང་བར་བཏགས་ཆོས་གང་ཟག་ལ་བདེན་པར་འཛིན་··པའི་ཞེན་ཡུལ་ཡང་ཤུན་མི་ཕྱིན་པར་བསྟན་ཏོ། རིན་ཆེན་འཕྲེང་བ་ལས། ཇི་སྲིད་ཕུང་པོར་འཛིན་ཡོད་པ། །ཞེས་སོགས་ཀྱི་དགོངས་པར་བཞེད་དོ། །འདི་དག་རྒྱས་པར་གཞན་དུ་ཤེས་པར་བྱའོ། །དྲུག་པ་ཆོས་ཀྱི་བདག་འཛིན་ཉོན་མོངས་སུ་འཛོག་པའི་ཁྱད་པར་བཤད་པ་ལ། སངས་རྒྱས་བསྐྱངས་ཀྱིས་ཉན་ཐོས་ཀྱི་སྡེ་སྣོད་ལས་ཆོས་ཐམས་ཅད་བདག་མེད་དོ་ཞེས་གསུངས་པའི་མེད་རྒྱུའི་བདག་ངོས་གཟུང་བའི་ཚེ་ངོ་བོ་ཉིད་ཀྱིས་གྲུབ་པ་ལ་བཤད་པ་ལྟར་དཔལ་ལྡན་ཟླ་བས་ཀྱང་བཞེད་དེ། དེ་ཡང་བདག་མེད་མཚན་ཉིད་རྫོགས་པའམ་བདག་མེད་ཕྲ་མོ་འདི་དབང་དུ་བྱས་པའོ། །དེའི་ཕྱིར་གང་ཟག་གི་བདག་མེད་མཚན་ཉིད་རྫོགས་པ་ཡང་གང་ཟག་ངོ་བོ་ཉིད་ཀྱིས་གྲུབ་པ་མེད་པ···ལ་བྱ་དགོས་པས་བདག་མེད་གཉིས་ལ་ཕྲ་རགས་ཀྱི་ཁྱད་པར་མེད་པར་བཞེད་དེ། རྒྱུ་མཚན་སྔར་བཤད་ཟིན་ཏོ། །དེའི་ཕྱིར་གང་ཟག་གི་བདག་མེད་མཚན་ཉིད་རྫོགས་པ་རྟོགས་པ་ལ་ཆོས་ཀྱི་བདག་མེད་ཕྲ་མོ་ཡང་ངེས་པར་རྟོགས་སོ། །རྒྱུ་མཚན་དེ་དག་ལྟར་ན་ཆོས་བདེན་པར་འཛིན་པ་ཉོན་མོངས་སུ་ངེས་པར་འདོད་དགོས་སོ། །ཆོས་དང་གང་ཟག་ལ་བདེན་པར་འཛིན་པའི་བདེན་འཛིན་གཉིས་ཀ་ཉོན་མོངས་པ་ཅན་གྱི་མ་རིག··པ་ཡིན་པ་དང་། དེ་དགྲ་བཅོམ་གཉིས་དང་མི་སྐྱེ་བའི་ཆོས་ལ་བཟོད་པ་ཐོབ་པའི་བྱང་

སེམས་གསུམ་གྱིས་སྦྱངས་པར་འདུག་འགྲེལ་དང་བཞི་བརྒྱ་པའི་འགྲེལ་པ་གཉིས་ཀ་ལས་བཤད་དོ། སྒྲུབ་བྱེད་ཀྱི་རིགས་པ་ནི། གང་ཟག་དང་ཆོས་རང་བཞིན་གྱིས་གྲུབ་པ་འགོག་པའི་རིགས་པས་དེ་གཉིས་ལ་རང་གི་མཚན་ཉིད་ཀྱིས་གྲུབ་པ་ཁེགས་པའི་ཚེ་དེ་གཉིས་རང་མཚན་དུ་གྲུབ་པར་འཛིན་པ་ཞེན་ཡུལ་ལ་འཁྲུལ་པའི་བདེན་འཛིན་དུ་བསྒྲུབ། དེ་གྲུབ་ན་གང་ཟག་དང་ཆོས་གཉིས་བདེན་གྲུབ་ཏུ་འཛིན་པ་བདག་འཛིན་གཉིས་སུ་འགྲུབ། དེ་གྲུབ་ན་བདེན་འཛིན་དེ་དེ་ཁོ་ན་ཉིད་ཀྱི་དོན་རིག་པའི་རིག་པ་ཡེ་ཤེས་ཀྱི་འགལ་ཟླ་མི་མཐུན་ཕྱོགས་སུ་འགྲུབ་པས་མ་རིག་པར་འགྲུབ་ཅིང་། དེ་མ་ཟད་པར་དུ་འཇིག་ལྟ་ཡང་མི་འདོད་པར་བསྒྲུབ་ནུས་པས་དེ་གཉིས་ཉོན་མོངས་ཅན་གྱི་མ་རིག་པར་འགྲུབ་པ་ཡིན་ནོ། །རྗེ་རིན་པོ་ཆེའི་ལེགས་བཤད་ལ་བརྟེན་ནས་ཐལ་འགྱུར་པའི་ལུགས་ལ་ཆོས་ཀྱི་བདག་འཛིན་ཉོན་མོངས་ཅན་གྱི་མ་རིག་པ་ཡིན་པ་ཙམ་ཤེས་མཁན་མང་བར་འདུག་ཀྱང་། དེ་ལྟར་ཡིན་པ་སྒྲུབ་ལུགས་རྗེའི་དགོངས་པ་ལྟར་འཆད་ཤེས་མཁན་དཀོན་པར་སྣང་ངོ་། །དེ་ལྟ་ན་ཡང་མངོན་པ་གཉིས་ནས་བཤད་པའི་ཉོན་མོངས་རྣམས་ཀྱང་ཉོན་མོངས་རགས་པར་མི་བཞེད་པ་མ་ཡིན་ཞིང་། དེ་ནས་བཤད་པའི་ལམ་གྱིས་ཉོན་མོངས་རགས་པ་དེ་དག་མངོན་གྱུར་མགོ་གནོན་ནུས་ལ། དེའི་ཚེ་ཡང་བདེན་འཛིན་ཕྲ་མོས་དྲངས་པའི་ཆགས་སོགས་མངོན་གྱུར་ཀྱང་མགོ་གནོན་མི་ནུས་པ་སོགས་དཔྱད་རྒྱུའི་དཀའ་གནས་མང་དུ་འདུག་གོ །ཉོན་མོངས་ཡིན་པའི་མ་རིག་པ་དང་འཇིག་ལྟ་མཐར་ལྟ་ལ་ཡང་ཀུན་བཏགས་དང་ལྷན་སྐྱེས་གཉིས་ཡོད་དོ། །ད་ནི་འདིར་བཤད་པར་བྱ་སྟེ། འདི་པའི་ལུགས་ཀྱི་ཤེས་སྒྲིབ་ནི་ཉོན་མོངས་པའི་བག་ཆགས་ལ་བཞེད་ཅིང་དེ་ལ་ཡང་ཉོན་མོངས་ཀྱི་ས་བོན་ལ་བག་ཆགས་སུ་བཞག་པ་ཞིག་དང་ཉོན་མོངས་ཀྱི་ས་བོན་མིན་པའི་བག་ཆགས་གཉིས་ལས་ཤེས་སྒྲིབ་ཏུ་

འཇོག་རྒྱུ་ནི་ཕྱི་མ་སྟེ། དགྲ་བཅོམ་གཉིས་དང་དག་ས་ལ་གནས་པའི་སེམས་དཔའ་ལ་ཉོན་མོངས་ཀྱི་ས་བོན་ཐམས་ཅད་ཟད་པས་བདེན་འཛིན་མི་སྐྱེ་ཡང་དེའི་བག་ཆགས་ཀྱིས་བསླད་པས་སྣང་ཡུལ་ལ་འཁྲུལ་བའི་བློ་སྐྱེ་བའོ། །དེ་ལྟར་ན་ཉོན་མོངས་པའི་བག་ཆར་ནི་ཤེས་སྒྲིབ་ཀྱི་ག་ཙོ་བོ་དང་དེའི་འབྲས་བུ་གཉིས་སྣང་འཁྲུལ་པའི་ཆ་རྣམས་ཀྱང་དེར་བསྡུ་བ་ཡིན་ནོ། །རྗེའི་གསུང་གི་སྒྲས་ཟིན་འདི་ཙམ་ལ་རྗེས་འབྲངས་མཁས་པ་ཕལ་མོ་ཆེ་མཐུན་ཅིང་། རྒྱུད་བླ་མའི་དར་ཊཱིཀ་ལས་ཤེས་སྒྲིབ་ཀུན་བརྟགས་ཡོད་པ་ལྟ་བུའི་བཤད་པ་ཞིག་མཛད་མོད་ཀྱང་ཤེས་སྒྲིབ་ལ་ལྷན་སྐྱེས་ཀྱིས་ཁྱབ་པ་ལུང་རིགས་དུ་མས་གྲུབ་པས་གསུང་དེ་སྒྲ་ཇི་བཞིན་དུ་ཁས་མི་ལེན་པར་སྟོང་ཐུན་ཆེན་མོ་རྗེས་འབྲངས་དང་བཅས་པས་བཞེད་པ་ལྟར་ལེགས་སོ། །ཕྱིས་ཀྱི་རིགས་པ་སྨྲ་བ་པཎྜི་ཏའི་མཚན་ཅན་ཀྱིས། ཤེས་སྒྲིབ་ཀུན་བརྟགས་ཡོད་པ་དང་ཊཱིཀ་ཆེན་གྱི་གཉིས་སྣང་འཁྲུལ་པའི་ཆ་ཞེས་པའི་ཚིག་ཟུར་གྱི་འཁྲུལ་པ་ཞེས་པའི་སྐབས་ནས་དངོས་སུ་བསྟན་པའི་འཁྲུལ་ཤེས་ཡོད་པས་ཤེས་སྒྲིབ་དང་ཤེས་པའི་གཞི་མཐུན་ཡོད་པ་རྗེའི་དགོངས་པ་ཡིན་ཞིང་། སྟོང་ཐུན་ལས་ཤེས་སྒྲིབ་ཀུན་བརྟགས་མེད་པར་བཤད་པ་བག་ཆགས་ཀྱི་ཤེས་སྒྲིབ་ཁོ་ན་ལ་དགོངས་སོ་ཞེས་སྨྲ་མོད་ཀྱང་འཐད་པར་མ་མཐོང་ངོ་། མདོ་དགོངས་འགྲེལ་ལས་ས་བཅུ་རེ་རེའི་ངོ་སྐལ་གྱི་སྤངས་བྱ་ཀུན་ཏུ་སྦྱོངས་པ་རེ་ཡོད་པར་གསུངས་མོད་ཀྱང་དེ་ནས་བཤད་པའི་སྤང་གཉེན་གྱི་རྣམ་གཞག་རྣམས་སྐབས་འདིར་ཇི་ལྟ་བ་བཞིན་ཁས་ལེན་དགོས་པའི་ཤེས་བྱེད་མེད་དོ། །སྐབས་འགྲོ་བདུན་ཅུ་པ་ལས། མི་ཤེས་ཉོན་མོངས་མིན་སྤངས་ཕྱིར། །ཞེས་དང་། མརིག་ཉོན་མོངས་མེད་ཡོད་པས། ། ཞེས་པ་དང་། འཇུག་འགྲེལ་ལས། ཉོན་མོངས་པ་ཅན་མ་ཡིན་པའི་མ་རིག་པ་ཞེས་གསུངས་པ་ལ་བརྟེན་ནས་ཤེས་པར་གྱུར་པའི་ཤེས་སྒྲིབ་ཡོད་པ་འཐད་ཕྱོགས་སུ

པཎ་ཆེན་བསོད་ནམས་རྒྱལ་མཚན་དང་མཁས་གྲུབ་ཆེན་པོ་འཇམ་དབྱངས་བཞད་པའི་རྡོ་རྗེས་གསུངས་སོ། །དེ་ལྟ་ན་ཡང་ཤེས་སྒྲིབ་ཀྱི་མ་རིག་པའི་འབྲུ་སྣོན་རྗེ་ཐམས་ཅད་མཁྱེན་པས་མཛད་པ་རྣམས་སུ་གཉིས་སྣང་འཁྲུལ་པའི་བག་ཆགས་ལ་འབྲུ་སྣོན་མཛད་པ་མ་གཏོགས་ཤེས་པར་གྱུར་པའི་མ་རིག་པ་ལ་འབྲུ་སྣོན་མཛད་པ་མི་སྣང་ངོ་། །མཁས་གྲུབ་ཐམས་ཅད་མཁྱེན་པ་དང་། རིགས་པའི་དབང་ཕྱུག་སེ་ར་རྗེ་བཙུན་ཆོས་ཀྱི་རྒྱལ་མཚན་ཡབ་སྲས། མཁྱེན་རབ་གཏེར་ཆེན་འཇམ་དབྱངས་དགའ་བའི་བློ་གྲོས། རྗེ་ཐམས་ཅད་མཁྱེན་པ་དགེ་འདུན་རྒྱ་མཚོ། །པཎ་ཆེན་བསོད་ནམས་གྲགས་པ་སོགས་མཁས་གྲུབ་ཕལ་མོ་ཆེས་ཤེས་པར་གྱུར་པའི་ཤེས་སྒྲིབ་མེད་པར་བཞེད་ཅིང་། རྗེ་བླ་མའི་བཤད་རྒྱུད་དང་སྒྲུབ་རྒྱུད་གཉིས་ཀའི་བསྟན་པའི་བདག་པོར་གྱུར་པ་པཎ་ཆེན་ཐམས་ཅད་མཁྱེན་པ་བློ་བཟང་ཆོས་ཀྱི་རྒྱལ་མཚན་གྱིས་ཀྱང་། ཤེས་པ་གཅིག་གིས་བདེན་གཉིས་ཅིག་ཅར་དུ། །མངོན་སུམ་གཟིགས་པའི་སྒྲིབ་བྱེད་ཕྲ་བ་ལ། །མ་རིག་ཅེས་བཏགས་ཤེས་པ་དགོས་མིན་པས། །དེ་ལ་འགལ་བ་ཆ་ཙམ་ཡོད་མ་ཡིན། ཞེས་རྒྱ་མཚན་དང་བཅས་ཏེ་གསུངས་པ་རྣམས་རྗེའི་གསུང་ཕལ་མོ་ཆེ་དང་མཐུན་ཚབས་ཆེ་བར་འདུག་པས་ད་དུང་བློ་གྲོས་དང་ལྡན་པ་རྣམས་ཀྱིས་ཞིབ་ཏུ་དཔྱད་པར་བྱའོ། །

བདུན་པ་ཞིག་པ་དངོས་པོ་ཡིན་པའི་བཞེད་ཚུལ་ཐུན་མོང་མ་ཡིན་པ་ནི། བྱེ་སྨྲ་རྣམས་ཀྱི་འདོད་ཚུལ་སོགས་ལྷུར་བཤད་ཟིན་ཅིང་མདོ་སེམས་རང་རྒྱུད་པ་རྣམས་ཀྱིས་ནི་སྨྱུ་གུ་ལྟ་བུའི་དངོས་པོ་གཅིག་ཞིག་པ་ན་སྨྱུ་གུའི་ཆ་ཤས་ཀྱི་དངོས་པོ་ཐམས་ཅད་ནི་ལོག་ལ་དེ་ལས་གཞན་བུམ་པ་ལ་སོགས་པའི་དངོས་པོ་གཞན་གང་ཡང་མ་ཐོབ་པས་ཞིག་པ་དེ་དངོས་པ་གཏན་མིན་པར་འདོད་དེ། སྔོན་པོ་ལ་སོགས་པ་སྐྱེ་མཆེད་རེ་རེ་བའི་དངོས་པོ་དང་ཆ་ཤས་ཚོགས་པའི་དངོས་པོ་གང་ཡང་དེའི་མཚན་གཞིར་མི་རུང་བའི་ཕྱིར་ཞེས

སྨྲ་སྟེ། བཏགས་དོན་བཅལ་ནས་འཇོག་དགོས་པའི་གནད་ཀྱིས་ཡིན་ནོ། །ཕྱུགས་
འདྲིས་ནི་དེ་ལྟར་ཅལ་ནས་མ་བཞག་ཀྱང་ཞིག་པ་དངོས་པོར་ཁས་བླང་དུ་རུང་བས་ཞིག་
པ་དེ་དངོས་པོ་ཡིན་པར་བཞེད་དོ། །དེ་ལ་ཡང་ལུང་ནི་ས་བཅུ་པ་ལས། སྐྱེ་བའི་
རྐྱེན་གྱིས་རྒ་ཤི་ཞེས་སེམས་ཅན་ཤི་བ་རྐྱེན་གྱིས་བསྐྱེད་པར་གསུངས་པའི་ཕྱིར་དང་།
ཤི་བ་ནི་གང་ཤི་བའི་སེམས་ཅན་དེ་ཞིག་པ་ལ་བཞག་དགོས་པའི་ཕྱིར་རོ། །ཡང་དེ་
ཉིད་ལས། འཆི་བ་ཡང་བྱ་བ་གཉིས་སུ་ཉེ་བར་གནས་ཏེ། འདུ་བྱེད་འཇིག་
པར་ཡང་བྱེད་པ་དང་ཡོངས་སུ་མི་ཤེས་པ་རྒྱུན་མི་འཆད་པའི་རྒྱུ་ཡང་འབྱིན་པའོ། །
ཞེས་ཤི་བ་རྒྱུས་བསྐྱེད་པ་དང་ཤི་བས་མ་རིག་པ་བསྐྱེད་པར་ཡང་གསུངས་པས་གང་···
རང་ཉིད་རྒྱུས་བསྐྱེད་པ་དང་རང་ཉིད་ཀྱིས་འབྲས་བུ་བསྐྱེད་ནུས་པ་དེ་ནི་དངོས་པོར་·······
འདོད་དགོས་པའི་ཕྱིར་རོ། །དེ་ནི་རྒྱུན་གྱི་ཞིག་པ་ཡིན་ཡང་སྐད་ཅིག་མ་དང་པོ་
དུས་གཉིས་པར་ཞིག་པ་ལ་ཡང་འདྲའོ། །རིགས་པ་ནི་སེམས་ཅན་སྐྱེས་པ་དང་ཤི་བ་
གཉིས་དང་སྐད་ཅིག་མ་གཉིས་པར་མི་སྡོད་པ་དང་སྐད་ཅིག་མ་གཉིས་པར་མ་བསྡད་པ···
རྣམས་ལ་དངོས་པོར་འཇོག་མི་འཇོག་དང་རྒྱུ་ལ་བལྟོས་མི་ལྟོས་ཀུན་ནས་མཚུངས·····
པར་བསྒྲུབ་པའོ། །ཕྱུགས་འདྲིས་ཞིག་པ་ཡང་འཇིག་པར་བཞེད་ལ་གཞན་དག་གིས་
ཞིག་འཇིག་འགལ་བར་འདོད་དོ། །རིགས་པ་དྲུག་ཅུ་པའི་འགྲེལ་པ་ལས་མར་དང་
སྙིང་པོ་ཟད་པ་མར་མེ་ཤི་བའི་རྒྱུར་བཤད་པ་ལྟ་བུ་རྣམས་ནི་རྒྱུན་གྱི་ཞིག་པ་དངོས་པོར་
བསྒྲུབས་པའི་ཚུལ་ཡིན་ནོ། །སྐད་ཅིག་དང་པོ་དུས་གཉིས་པར་ཞིག་པ་ནི་དངོས་སུ་
དགག་བྱ་བཅད་ནས་རྟོགས་དགོས་པས་དགག་པ་ཡིན་ལ། དེ་ཡང་ཞིག་རྒྱུ་དེ་བཅད་
པ་ཙམ་མ་ཡིན་གྱི་བཅད་པའི་དངོས་པོ་ཞིག་འཕངས་པས་ན་མ་ཡིན་དགག་ཡིན་ནོ། །
བྱེ་བྲག་སྨྲ་བ་དང་འདི་གཉིས་དུས་གསུམ་དངོས་པོར་འདོད་པ་ཙམ་དུ་མཚུངས་ཀྱང་···

འདོད་ཚུལ་ཤིན་ཏུ་མི་མཚུངས་ཏེ། ལུགས་འདིས་རྫས་ཡོད་རྣམ་པ་ཐམས་ཅད་དུ་མི་བཞེད་པ་དང་སྲུ་གུའི་ཞིག་པ་ཡང་ཞིག་རྒྱུའི་དངོས་པོ་ལ་བརྟེན་ནས་སྐྱེས་པ་ཙམ་གྱིས་དངོས་པོར་འདོད་ཀྱི་ཞིག་རྒྱུའི་དངོས་པོ་དང་། དེ་དང་རིགས་མཐུན་པའི་དངོས་པོ་གང་ཡང་སྲུ་གུ་ཞིག་པའི་མཚན་གཞིར་རིགས་པས་བཙལ་ནས་འཇོག་པའི་རྒྱུ་མཚན་གྱིས་དེ་དངོས་པོར་འདོད་པ་མ་ཡིན་པའི་ཕྱིར་རོ། །འདི་དག་ཀྱང་ཤིན་ཏུ་རྟོགས་དཀའ་བའི་གནས་ཕྲ་མོ་ཡིན་པར་གསུངས་པས་ཞིབ་ཏུ་གཞུང་ཆེན་མོ་རྣམས་ལས་ཤེས་དགོས་སོ། །བརྒྱད་པ་དུས་གསུམ་གྱི་རྣམ་གཞག་བྱེད་ཚུལ་ཐུན་མོང་མ་ཡིན་པ་ནི། སྲུ་གུ་ལྟ་བུ་ལ་མཚོན་ན་རྒྱུ་རྐྱེན་ལས་སྐྱེས་ཟིན་པའི་སྲུ་གུ་རང་གི་དུས་གཉིས་པར་ཞིག་པ་ནི་སྲུ་གུ་འདས་པའི་དུས་དང་། སྲུ་གུ་སྐྱེད་བྱེད་ཀྱི་རྒྱུ་ཡོད་ཀྱང་དགུན་དུས་ཀྱི་ཞིང་ལྟ་བུ་ཡུལ་དུས་འགའ་ཞིག་ཏུ་རྐྱེན་མ་ཚང་བའི་དབང་གིས་རེ་ཞིག་མ་སྐྱེས་པ་ནི་སྲུ་གུ་མ་འོངས་པའི་དུས་སོ། །སྲུ་གུ་རང་ཉིད་སྐྱེས་ལ་མ་འགགས་པ་ནི་སྲུ་གུ་ད་ལྟར་བའི་དུས་སོ། །དེས་ན་འདས་པ་ལ་ད་ལྟར་བ་ལས་ལོག་པ་ཙམ་གྱིས་མི་ཆོག་པར་བྱུང་ཟིན་ཞིག་པའི་ཆ་ཞིག་དགོས་པས་གཞུང་ཆེན་མོ་རྣམས་ལས་བྱུང་ལ་འགགས་པ་ཞེས་ཀྱང་གསུངས་སོ། །དེའི་བྱུང་ལ་ཞེས་པའི་གང་འདས་རྒྱུའི་སྲུ་གུ་ལྟ་བུ་ལ་བྱའོ། །མ་འོངས་པ་ཡང་མ་སླེབ་ལུང་ཕྲད་པར་བ་ཞིག་ལ་དགོངས་ནས་རྒྱུ་ཡོད་ཀྱང་མ་བྱུང་བ་ཞེས་གསུངས་སོ། །འདི་དག་ནི་མདོ་སྡེ་པ་ཡན་ཆད་ཐམས་ཅད་འདྲའོ། །འོན་ཀྱང་རང་རྒྱུད་པ་མན་ཆད་ཀྱིས་འདས་པ་དང་མ་འོངས་པ་གཉིས་དངོས་མེད་དུ་འདོད་ཅིང་དེ་ཡང་མེད་དགག་ཏུ་འདོད་དོ། །ཐལ་འགྱུར་བའི་ལུགས་ལ་དུས་གསུམ་ག་དངོས་པོར་བཞེད་ཅིང་འདས་དང་མ་འོངས་པ་གཉིས་མ་ཡིན་དགག་ཏུ་བཞེད་དེ། སྲུ་གུ་ཞིག་པའི་སྐབས་སྲུ་གུ་མ་ཞིག་པ་གཅོད་བ་དང་སྲུ་གུ་ཞིག་པ་སྲུ་གུ་ལ་བརྟེན་ནས་འབྱུང་བ་འཕེན་པ་གཉིས་ཀ་

བྱེད་པ་དང་། སྨྱུ་གུ་མ་འོངས་པའི་སྐབས་སྨྱུ་གུ་སླེབ་པ་གཅོད་པ་དང་སྨྱུ་གུ་མ་འོངས་པ་ཉིད་སྨྱུ་གུ་སྐྱེ་བའི་རྐྱེན་མ་ཚང་བའི་དངོས་པོར་འཕེན་པ་གཉིས་ཀ་བྱེད་པའོ། །སྨྱུ་གུ་ལ་སོགས་པ་རེ་རེ་ལ་དུས་གསུམ་གསུམ་དུ་བྱེད་པ་མ་ཡིན་ཞིང་འདས་པ་དང་མ་འོངས་པ་གཉིས་རང་ལས་གཞན་པའི་དངོས་པོ་ཞིག་ཞིག་པ་དང་མ་སྐྱེས་པའི་ཆ་ནས་འཇོག་དགོས་པས་ཕལ་པ་དང་། ད་ལྟར་བ་ནི་རང་ཉིད་ད་ལྟར་བར་འཇོག་པ་དངོས་པོ་གཞན་ཞིག་ཞིག་མ་ཞིག་དང་སྐྱེས་མ་སྐྱེས་ཀྱི་སྒོ་ནས་བཞག་མི་དགོས་པས་གཙོ་བོ་ཡིན་ནོ། །སྨྱུ་གུའི་ཞིག་པ་འདས་པར་འཇོག་བ་མི་འཐད་དེ། དེ་ཡང་རང་དུས་སུ་སྐྱེས་ལ་མ་འགགས་པའི་ཕྱིར་ད་ལྟར་བ་ཡིན་ནོ་ཟེར་ན། སྐྱོན་མེད་དེ། སྨྱུ་གུ་ཞིག་པ་དེ་ཉིད་རང་དུས་ན་རང་ཉིད་ཞིག་པ་མ་ཡིན་ཀྱང་སྨྱུ་གུ་ཞིག་པ་ཡིན་ལ། དེ་བཞིན་དུ་སྨྱུ་གུ་ཞིག་པའི་ཞིག་པ་ཡང་རང་དུས་ན་རང་ཉིད་ཞིག་པ་མ་ཡིན་ཀྱང་སྨྱུ་གུ་ཞིག་པ་སྐད་ཅིག་དང་པོ་ཞིག་པ་ཡིན་པས་ཕྱིར་ཞིག་པར་བཞག་དགོས་པས་ད་ལྟར་བ་མ་ཡིན་གྱི་འདས་པ་ཁོ་ན་ཡིན་ནོ། །དེའི་ཕྱིར་འདས་པའི་རིགས་འདྲ་རྗེ་སྐད་ཅིག་ཕྱུང་ཡང་དངོས་པོ་གཞན་ཞིག་ཞིག་པའི་སྒོ་ནས་རང་གི་ངོ་བོ་བཞག་དགོས་ལ་མ་འོངས་པའི་རིགས་འདྲ་རྗེ་སྐད་ཅིག་ཕྱུང་ཡང་དངོས་པོ་གཞན་ཞིག་མ་སྐྱེས་པའི་སྒོ་ནས་རང་གི་ངོ་བོ་བཞག་དགོས་སོ། །ད་ལྟར་བ་ནི་དེ་ལྟར་མི་དགོས་པར་རང་ཉིད་སྐྱེས་ལ་མ་འགགས་པའི་སྨྱུ་གུ་ལྟ་བུ་ཡིན་པས་དུས་གསུམ་པོ་འགལ་བ་ཡིན་ནོ། །དེ་ལྟ་ན་ཡང་དུས་གསུམ་ཕན་ཚུན་བལྟོས་ནས་གྲུབ་པ་ཡང་མི་འགལ་ཏེ། གཞན་གཉིས་ལྟོས་ཚུལ་གོ་སླ་ལ་ད་ལྟར་བ་ཡང་སྐྱེས་ལ་ཞེས་པའི་ཚིག་གིས་མ་འོངས་པ་གཅོད་པ་དང་མ་འགག་པ་ཞེས་པས་འདས་པ་གཅོད་པ་ལ་བལྟོས་དགོས་པའི་ཕྱིར། མཚན་ཉིད་ནི་དངོས་པོ་གཞན་ཞིག་སྐྱེས་ཟིན་ཞིག་པའི་ཆ་འདས་པའི་མཚན་ཉིད། དངོས་པོ་གཞན་ཞིག་

ང

རང་སྐྱེད་བྱེད་ཀྱི་རྒྱུ་ཡོད་ཀྱང་རྐྱེན་མ་ཚང་བས་མ་སྐྱེས་པ་དེ་མ་འོངས་པའི་མཚན་ཉིད། དངོས་པོ་གཞན་ཞིག་བ་དང་མ་འོངས་པའི་ཆ་གང་ཡང་མ་ཡིན་ཞིང་སྐྱེས་ལ་མ་འགགས་པ་དེ་ད་ལྟར་བའི་མཚན་ཉིད་ཅེས་འཇོག་པའམ་ཡང་ན་སྟོང་ཐུན་ལས་འབྱུང་བ་ལྟར་⋯⋯བཞག་པས་ཆོག་གོ །སྐུ་གསུའི་དུས་སུ་འདས་པ་དང་སྐུ་གསུའི་འདས་པ་སོགས་ཀྱི་ཁྱད་པར་ཡང་ཤེས་དགོས་ཏེ། གྲགས་ཆེ་པ་དང་གཞན་དུ་ཤེས་པར་བྱའོ། །གཉིས་པ་ཁྱད་ཆོས་དེ་དག་ཐམས་ཅད་ཀྱི་རྩ་བ་མཐར་གཏུགས་པ་རང་མཚན་འགོག་ལུགས་ལ། འཇུག་པ་རྩ་འགྲེལ་ལས་རིགས་པ་བཞི་བཤད་པའི་དང་པོ་ནི། དངོས་པོ་རྣམས་ལ་རང་གི་མཚན་ཀྱིས་ཉིད་གྲུབ་པའི་རང་བཞིན་ཡོད་ན་འཕགས་པ་རྣམས་ཀྱིས་ཆོས་ཐམས་ཅད་རང་བཞིན་མེད་པར་རྟོགས་པའི་ཆོ་ཡེ་ཤེས་དེས་དེ་དག་དམིགས་དགོས་པ་ལས་མ⋯དམིགས་པའི་ཕྱིར་དེ་མེད་པར་འགྱུར་རོ། །དེ་ལྟར་ན་དངོས་པོ་སྣང་ཡོད་པ་ཕྱིས་མེད་པ་ནི་དེ་ཞིག་པ་ཡིན་ལ། དེའི་འཇིག་རྒྱུ་ཡང་ཡེ་ཤེས་དེས་བྱས་པར་འདོད་དགོས་པས་འཕགས་པའི་མཉམ་གཞག་དངོས་པོ་འི་འཇིག་རྒྱུར་ཐལ་བའོ། །གཉིས་པ་ནི། དངོས་པོ་རྣམས་རང་གི་མཚན་ཉིད་ཀྱིས་གྲུབ་ན་སྐྱེ་བའི་ཐ་སྙད་བཏགས་པའི་བཏགས་དོན་ལ་རིགས་པས་དཔྱད་པའི་ཚེ་ས་ཕྱུག་རང་བཞིན་གྱིས་གཅིག་གམ་ཐ་དང⋯གང་རུང་གིས་སྐྱེ་བ་རིགས་པས་བཙལ་ནས་རྙེད་དགོས་ཏེ། གཞན་དུ་ན་ཐ་སྙད་ཙམ་དུ་འགྱུར་གྱི་རང་གི་མཚན་ཉིད་ཀྱིས་གྲུབ་པར་མི་འགྱུར་བའི་ཕྱིར་ཞེས་པ་སྟེ། ཐ་སྙད་བདེན་པ་རིགས་པས་དཔྱད་བཟོད་དུ་ཐལ་བ་འཕེན་པའོ། །གསུམ་པ་ནི། དངོས་པོ་རྣམས་ཀྱི་སྐྱེ་བ་ཐ་སྙད་དུ་རང་གི་མཚན་ཉིད་ཀྱིས་གྲུབ་པ་མཐའ་བཞིའི་སྐྱེ་འགོག་གི་རིགས་པས་མི་ཁེགས་ན་དོན་དམ་དུ་གྲུབ་པ་ཡང་མི་ཁེགས་པར་འགྱུར་ཏེ། རང་མཚན་གྱིས་གྲུབ་ན་དོན་དམ་པར་གྲུབ་དགོས་པའི་ཕྱིར་རོ། །རིགས་པ་འདི་གསུམ་

ག་ལ་རང་རྒྱུད་པས་ལན་འདེབས་ཚུལ་དང་དེ་ལྟ་ནའང་རང་རྒྱུད་པས་སྨྲས་པའི་ལན···
དེས་སྐྱོན་སྤོང་མི་ནུས་པའི་རྒྱུ་མཚན་རྣམས་ཀྱང་ཤེས་དགོས་སོ། །བཞི་པ་ནི། རང་
གི་མཚན་ཉིད་ཀྱིས་ཡོད་ན་འོད་སྲུང་གིས་ཞུས་པ་ལ་སོགས་པ་མདོ་དུ་མ་ལས་ཆོས་རྣམས་
རང་བཞིན་གྱིས་སྟོང་པར་གསུངས་པ་མི་འཐད་པར་ཐལ་བའོ། །འདི་ཡང་
མདོ་དེ་དག་གིས་སེམས་ཙམ་པ་དང་རང་རྒྱུད་པ་དག་གིས་བཀྲལ་བའི་ལྟ་བ་རྣམས···
ལྟ་བ་མཐར་ཐུག་མ་ཡིན་པར་གསུང་ལུགས་ཀྱི་རྒྱུ་མཚན་རྣམས་ཞིབ་ཏུ་ཤེས་དགོས་པ་
ཡོད་དོ། །གསུམ་པ་དེ་དག་ལ་བརྟེན་ནས་མདོ་འི་དྲང་ངེས་འབྱེད་ཚུལ་ནི།
འཁོར་ལོ་དང་པོར་གང་ཟག་ལ་བདག་མེད་ལུགས་རགས་པ་བཤད་ནས་ཕྲ་མོ་ལ་བཤད་
པ་དང་ཕུང་སོགས་རང་གི་མཚན་ཉིད་ཀྱིས་གྲུབ་པར་གསུངས་པ་རྣམས་དྲང་དོན···
ཡིན་ཏེ། དགོངས་གཞི་ཐ་སྙད་དུ་ཡོད་པ་ཙམ་ལ་དགོངས་ནས་དགོས་པ་བདག
མེད་ཕྲ་མོ་བསྟན་ན་ཆད་ལྟ་སྐྱེ་བས་རེ་ཞིག་སྣོད་དུ་མི་རུང་བའི་གདུལ་བྱ་རྣམས་རིམ་གྱིས་
རྒྱུད་སྦྱངས་ནས་གཞུག་པའི་ཕྱིར་དུ་གསུངས་པ་ཡིན་ལ། སྒྲ་ཇི་བཞིན་པ་ལ་གནོད་
བྱེད་ནི་རང་མཚན་གྱིས་ཡོད་པ་འགོག་པའི་རིགས་པ་རྣམས་ཡིན་པའི་ཕྱིར། འཁོར་
ལོ་བར་པར་གང་ཟག་དང་ཆོས་ལ་རང་གི་མཚན་ཉིད་ཀྱིས་གྲུབ་པ་བཀག་ནས་ཐ་སྙད···
ཙམ་དུ་ཡོད་པར་གསུངས་པ་ནི་ངེས་པའི་དོན་མཐར་ཐུག་པ་ཡིན་ཏེ། སྟོང་པ་རྟེན་
འབྱུང་གི་དོན་དུ་རྟོགས་ནུས་པའི་ཐེག་པ་ཆེན་པོ་འི་རིགས་ཅན་གྱི་གདུལ་བྱ་དབང་རྣོན་ལ་
གསུངས་པའོ། །དེ་ལ་ཡང་རང་རྒྱུད་པ་ལུགས་གཉིས་དང་མི་འདྲ་བར་ལུགས་དམ་
པ་འདི་བས་འཁོར་ལོ་བར་པའི་ནང་ཚན་གྱི་ཡུམ་འབུམ་པ་ལྟ་བུ་དགག་བྱ་ལ་དོན་དམ་
གྱི་ཁྱད་པར་དངོས་སུ་སྦྱར་བ་རྣམས་སུ་མ་ཟད་ཤེས་རབ་སྙིང་པོ་ལྟ་བུ་དོན་དམ་གྱི་ཐ···
སྙད་དངོས་སུ་མ་སྦྱར་ཡང་རང་བཞིན་གྱིས་སྟོང་པ་སྟེ་རང་མཚན་གྱིས་སྟོང་བའི་ཁྱད···

ང

པར་དངོས་སུ་སྨྲ་བ་དང་། དེ་ཙམ་ཡང་མ་སྨྲ་བར་སྤྱིར་སྐྱེ་བ་མེད་འགག་པ་མེད་ཅེས་པ་ལྟ་བུ་ཟབ་མོ་སྟོང་པ་ཉིད་སྟོན་པའི་མདོ་མཐའ་དག་ངེས་དོན་གྱི་མདོ་ཡིན་པར་འདུ་བར་བཞེད་དེ། བརྗོད་བྱ་རིགས་མཐུན་པའི་མདོ་སྡེ་གཅིག་ལ་དོན་དམ་གྱི་ཁྱད་པར་སྨྲ་ཕྱིན་དེ་དང་བརྗོད་བྱ་མཐུན་པའི་མདོ་སྡེ་གཞན་ལ་ཡང་དོན་གྱིས་སྨྲ་བ་ཡིན་པའི་ཕྱིར། དཔེར་ན་ད་ལྟར་གྱི་རྩོམ་པ་པོ་གཅིག་གིས་བརྩམས་པའི་བསྟན་བཅོས་བརྗོད་བྱ་མཐུན་པ་གཅིག་ཏུ་བྱུང་བ་རྣམས་དེ་མ་བྱུང་པའི་སར་ཡང་འཁྱེར་དགོས་པ་དང་འདྲའོ། །འཁོར་ལོ་ཐ་མར་མཚན་ཉིད་གསུམ་ལ་རང་གི་མཚན་ཉིད་ཀྱིས་ཡོད་པ་དང་མེད་པའི་ཁྱད་པར་གསུངས་པ་ནི་དྲང་བའི་དོན་ཏེ། དེ་ཡང་དགོངས་གཞི་ནི་ངོ་བོ་ཉིད་དང་པོ་གཉིས་དང་ཕྱི་མ་ལ་སེམས་ཙམ་པས་འདོད་པ་ལྟར་གྱི་མིང་བརྡས་བཞག་མ་བཞག་གི་ཁྱད་པར་ཐ་སྙད་ཙམ་དུ་ཡོད་པ་ལ་དགོངས་པའོ། །དགོས་པ་ནི་གདུལ་བྱ་ཐེག་ཆེན་གྱི་རིགས་ཅན་ཡིན་ཡང་རེ་ཞིག་ཆོས་ཐམས་ཅད་ཀྱི་སྟེང་གི་སྟོང་པ་དང་རྟེན་འབྲེལ་དོན་གཅིག་ཏུ་རྟོགས་མི་ནུས་པ་ལ་སྟོན་ཏུ་རུང་བའི་ཆོས་ཀྱི་བདག་མེད་བསྟན་ཏེ་རྒྱུད་སྦྱངས་ནས་ཕྱིས་ཕྲ་བའི་ཆོས་ཀྱི་བདག་མེད་ལ་གཞུག་པའི་ཕྱིར་ཡིན་ནོ། །སྒྲ་ཇི་བཞིན་པ་ལ་གནོད་བྱེད་ནི་ཆོས་ཐམས་ཅད་རང་མཚན་གྱིས་གྲུབ་པས་སྟོང་པའི་ཕྱོགས་ལ་རིགས་པའི་གནོད་པ་ཚུང་ཟད་ཀྱང་མེད་ཅིང་རང་མཚན་གྱིས་གྲུབ་པར་འདོད་པའི་ཕྱོགས་ལ་བྱ་བྱེད་ཐམས་ཅད་བཞག་ཏུ་མི་རུང་བར་སྒྲུབ་པའི་རིགས་པ་རྣམས་སོ། །དེ་ཡང་དགོངས་འགྲེལ་ནས་བཤད་པའི་འཁོར་ལོ་གསུམ་གྱི་དྲང་ངེས་འཇོག་ཚུལ་ཡིན་གྱི་སྤྱིར་འཁོར་ལོ་དང་པོ་ཡན་ཆད་དྲང་དོན་དུ་བཞེད་པ་མ་ཡིན་ཏེ། འཁོར་ལོ་དང་པོར་གང་ཟག་དང་ཆོས་ལ་རང་བཞིན་མེད་པར་གསུངས་པ་རྣམས་ངེས་དོན་ཡིན་པའི་ཕྱིར་རོ། །དེ་ལྟར་ན་རྣམ་རིག་པས་ངོ་བོ་ཉིད་གསུམ་ལ་རང་གི་མཚན་ཉིད་

English-Sanskrit-Tibetan Glossary

English	*Sanskrit*	*Tibetan*
abhidharma	abhidharma	chos mngon pa
able to set itself up	—	tshugs thub tu grub pa
absorption	samāpatti	snyoms 'jug
action	karma	las
affirming negation / negative	paryudāsapratiṣedha	ma yin dgag
afficted mind	kliṣamanas	nyon yid
affiction	kleśa	nyon mongs
afflictive obstruction	kleśāvaraṅa	nyon sgrib
aggregate	skandha	phung po
analysis	vicāra	dpyod pa
analytical cessation	pratisaṃkhyā-nirodha	so sor brtags 'gog
analytical meditation	—	dpyad sgom
Arhat	arhan /arhat	dgra bcom pa
artificial	parikalpita	kun btags
aspect	akārā	rnam pa
autonomous inference	svatantrānumāna	rang rgyud kyi rjes dpag
autonomous syllogism	svatantraprayoga	rang rgyud kyi sbyor ba
basis-of-all	ālaya	kun gzhi
basis of designation	—	gdags gzhi
belief	adhimokṣa	mos pa
bliss	sukha	bde ba
Blissful Pure Land	sukhāvatī	dbe ba can
Bodhisattva	bodhisattva	byang chub sems dpa'
body consciousness	kāyavijñāna	lus kyi rnam par shes pa
body sense	kāyendriya	lus kyi dbang po
Buddha	buddha	sangs rgyas
calm abiding	śamatha	zhi gnas
cause	hetu	rgyu
Cittamātra	cittamātra	sems tsam
clairvoyance	abhijñā	mngon par shes pa
coarse selflessness	—	bdag med rags pa
common being	pṛthagjana	so skye bo

English	*Sanskrit*	*Tibetan*
compassion	karuṇā	snying rje
Complete Enjoyment Body	saṃbhogakāya	longs spyod rdzogs pa'i sku
compositional factor	saṃskāra	'du byed
concentration	dhyāna	bsam gtan
conception of self	ātmagrāha	bdag tu 'dzin pa
condition	pratyaya	rkyen
conditionality	idaṃpratyayatā	rkyen 'di pa tsam nyid
Conqueror	jina	rgyal ba
conscientiousness	apramāda	bag yod pa
consciousness	jñā / vijñāna	shes pa / rnam shes
consequence	prasaṅga	thal 'gyur
constituent	dhātu	khams
contact	sparśa	reg pa
contaminated	sāsrava	zag bcas
contaminated action	sāsravakarma	zag bcas kyi las
contamination	āsrava	zag pa
continuum	saṃtāna	rgyun / gyud
contradictory consequence	—	'gal brjod thal 'gyur
conventional analysis	—	tha snyad pa'i dpyod pa
conventional existence	saṃvṛtisat	kun rdzob tu yod pa
conventional truth / truth-for-a-concealer / obscured truth	saṃvṛtisatya	kun rdzob bden pa
cooperative condition	sahakāripratyaya	lhan cig byed rkhyen
correct view	samyakdṛṣṭi	yang dag pa'i lta ba
counter-pervasion	vyatirekavyāpti	ldog khyab
creature / being / person	puruṣa	skyes bu
cyclic existence	saṃsāra	'khor ba
deed	karma	las
definitive	nītārtha	nges don
deity yoga	*devayoga	lha'i rnal 'byor
dependent-arising	pratītyasamutpāda	rten 'byung
dependent phenomenon	paratantra	gzhan dbang
desire	rāga	'dod chags
desire realm	kāmadhātu	'dod khams

English	*Sanskrit*	*Tibetan*
determining factor	viniyata	yul nges
dharma	dharma	chos
direct cognition	—	mngon sum du rtogs pa
direct perception / perceiver	pratyakśa	mngon sum
discipline	vinaya	'dul ba
discrimination	saṃjñā	'du shes
disintegration	naṣṭa	'jig pa
disintegratedness	naṣṭa	zhig pa
dissimulation	śāhya	gyo
doubt	vicikitsā	the tshom
ear consciousness	śrotravijñāna	rna ba'i rnam par shes pa
ear sense	śrotrendriya	rna ba'i dbang po
effort	vīrya	brtson 'grus
elaborations	prapañca	spros pa
element of [superior] qualities	dharmadhātu	chos dbyings
Emanation Body	nirmāṇkāya	sprul sku
embarrassment	apatrāpya	khrel yod pa
emptiness	śūnyatā	stong pa nyid
Enjoyment Body	saṃbhogakāya	longs sku
enlightenment	bodhi	byang chub
equanimity	upekṣkā	btang snyoms
established atomically	—	rdul tu grub pa
excitement	auddhatya	rgod pa
existence able to set itself up	—	tshugs thub tu grub pa
existence by way of its own character	svalakṣaṇasiddhi	rang gi mtshan nyid kyis grub pa
existence from the object's side	*svarūpasiddhi	rang ngos nas grub pa
existence through its own entityness / inherent existence	*svabhāvatāsiddhi	ngo bo nyid kyis grub pa
existence through its own power	*svairīsiddhi	rang dbang du grub pa
existent	sat	yod pa
existent base	*vastu	gzhi grub

English	*Sanskrit*	*Tibetan*
extreme	anta	mtha'
extreme of annihilation	ucchedānta	chad mtha'
extreme of permanence	śaśvatānta	rtag mtha'
eye consciousness	cakṣurvijñāna	mig gi rnam shes
feeling	vedanā	tshor ba
forbearance	kṣānti	bzod pa
form	rūpa	gzugs
Form Body	rūpakāya	gzugs sku
form-constituent	rūpadhātu	gzugs kyi khams
form for the mental consciousness	dharmāyatanarūpa	chos kyi skye mched pa'i gzugs
Form Realm	rūpadhātu	gzugs khams
form source	rūpāyatana	gzugs kyi skye mched
Formless Realm	ārūpyadhātu	gzugs med khams
fruit	phala	'bras bu
fruition consciousness	vipakavijñāna	rnam smin rnam shes
generally characterized phenomenon	sāmānyalakṣaṇa	spyi mtshan
generic object / generic image / meaning-generality	arthasāmānya	don spyi
giving	dāna	sbyin pa
great compassion	mahākaruṇā	snying rje chen po
ground	bhūmi	sa
Hearer	śrāvaka	nyan thos
hearing	śruta	thos pa
heat	uṣmagata	drod
higher knowledge	abhidharma	chos mngon pa
Highest Pure Land	akaniṣṭa	'og min
Highest Yoga Tantra	anuttarayogatantra	rnal 'byor bla med kyi rgyud
Hīnayāna	hīnayāna	theg dman
I	ahaṃ	nga
ignorance	avidyā	ma rig pa
imaginary	parikalpita	kun btags

English	Sanskrit	Tibetan
imaginary phenomenon	parikalpitadharma	kun btags pa'i chos
impermanent	anitya	mi rtag pa
imputedly existent	prajñaptisat	btags yod
inference	anumāna	rjes dpag
inferential valid cognition	anumānapramāṇa	rjes dpag tshad ma
inherent existence	svabhāvasiddhi	rang bzhin gyis grub pa
innate	sahaja	lhan skyes
innate affliction	sahajakleśa	nyon mongs lhan skyes
intention	cetanā	sems pa
introspection	samprajanya	shes bzhin
investigation	vitarka	rtog pa
Joyous Land	tuṣiṭa	dga' ldan
knowledge / higher knowledge	abhidharma	chos mngon pa
knowledge / wisdom	prajña	shes rab
liberation	vimokṣa / mokṣa	thar pa
lineage	gotra	rigs
love	maitrī	byams pa
Mādhyamika	mādhyamika	dbu ma pa
Mahāyāna	mahāyāna	theg chen
maṇḍala	maṇḍala	dkhyil 'khor
matter	kanthā	bem po
meditative absorption	samāpatti	snyoms 'jug
meditative stabilization	samāhita / samādhi	mnyam bzhag / ting nge 'dzin
mental and physical aggregates	skandha	phung po
mental consciousness	manovijñāna	yid kyi rnam shes
mental factor	caitta	sems byung
merit	puṇya	bsod nams
method	upāya	thabs
migrator	gati	'gro ba

English	*Sanskrit*	*Tibetan*
mind	citta	sems
mind-basis-of-all	ālayavijñāna	kun gzhi rnam shes
mind of enlightenment	bodhicitta	byang chub kyi sems
mindfulness	smṛti	dran pa
natural existence / existence by way of [the object's] own character	svalakṣaṇasiddhi	rang gi mtshan nyid kyis grub pa
natural nirvāṇa	*prakṛtiparinirvāṇa	rang bzhin myang 'das
nature	prakṛti	rang bzhin
Nature Body	svabhāvikakāya	ngo bo nyid sku
negation / negative phenomenon	pratiṣedha	dgag pa
neutral	avyākṛta	lung du ma bstan pa
Never Returner	anāgāmin	phyir mi 'ong
nirvāṇa	nirvāṇa	mya ngan las 'das pa
Noble / Superior	ārya	'phags pa
nominal existence	—	ming tsam du yod pa
non-affirming negation / negative	prasajyapratiṣedha	med dgag
non-analytical cessation	apratisaṃkhyānirodha	so sor brtags min gyi 'gog pa
non-application	anabhisaṃskāra	'du mi byed pa
non-associated compositional factor	viprayuktasaṃskāra	ldan min 'du byed
non-attachment	alobha	ma chags pa
non-conceptual wisdom	nirvikalpajñāna	rnam par mi rtog pa'i ye shes
non-conscientiousness	pramāda	bag med pa
non-existent	asat	med pa
non-person compositional factor	*apudgalaviprayukta-saṃskāra	gang zag ma yin pa'i ldan min 'du byed
non-produced phenomenon / uncompounded phenomenon	asaṃskṛtadharma	'dus ma byas kyi chos
non-revelatory form	avijñāptirūpa	rnam par rig byed ma yin pa'i gzugs

English	Sanskrit	Tibetan
non-thing	abhāva	dngos med
non-virtuous	akuśala	mi dge ba
non-wastage	avipranāśa	chud mi za ba
nose consciousness	ghrāṇavijñāna	sna'i rnam shes
nose sense	ghrāṇendriya	sna'i dbang po
not unable	anāgamya	mi lcogs med
object	viṣaya	yul
object of knowledge	jñeya	shes bya
object of negation	pratiṣedhya	dgag bya
object of observation	ālambana	dmigs yul / dmigs pa
objective existence	—	yul gyi steng nas grub pa
observed-object-condition	ālambanapratyaya	dmigs rkyen
obstructions to liberation / afflictive obstructions	kleśāvaraṇa	nyon mong pa'i sgrib pa
obstructions to omniscience / obstructions to objects of knowledge	jñeyāvaraṇa	shes bya'i sgrib pa
obtainer	prāpti	thob pa
odor	gandha	dri
omnipresent factor	sarvatraga	kun 'gro
omniscience / exalted knower of all aspects	sarvākārajñāna	rnam pa thams cad mkhyen pa
Once Returner	āgāmin	phyir 'ong
only imputed	prajñaptimātra	btags tsam
other-approved inference	parasiddhānumāna	gzhan grags kyi rjes dpag
other-approved reason	parasiddhaliṅga	gzhan grags kyi rtags
other-approved syllogism	parasiddhaprayoga	gzhan grags kyi sbyor ba
other-powered	paratantra	gzhan dbang
pain / suffering	duḥkha	sdug bsngal
path	mārga	lam
path of accumulation	saṃbhāramārga	tshogs lam
path of meditation	bhāvanāmārga	sgom lam

English	Sanskrit	Tibetan
path of no more learning	aśaikṣamārga	mi slob lam
path of preparation	prayogamārga	sbyor lam
path of release	vimuktimārga	rnam grol lam
path of seeing	darśanamārga	mthong lam
patience	kṣānti	bzod pa
peak	mūrdhan	rtse mo
perfection	pāramitā	phar phyin
Perfection Vehicle	pāramitāyāna	phar phyin kyi theg pa
permanent phenomenon	nitya	rtag pa
person	pudgala / puruṣa	gang zag
personal selflessness	pudgalanairātmya	gang zag gi bdag med
pervasions	vyāpti	khyab pa
phenomenon	dharma	chos
phenomenon-source	dharmāyatana	chos kyi skye mched
pleasure / bliss	sukhā	bde ba
position	pakṣa	phyogs
potency	vāsanā / bāla	bags chags / nus pa
Prāsaṅgika	prāsaṅgika	thal 'gyur pa
predisposition	vāsanā	bags chags
preparation	sāmantaka	nyer bsdogs
probandum	—	bsgrub bya
product	saṃkṛta	'dus byas
proof	sādhana	sgrub byed
Proponent of Annihilation	ucchedavādin	chad par smra ba
Proponent of Permanence	śaśvatavādin	rtag par smra ba
reality	dharmatā	chos nyid
reason	hetu	gtan tshigs
reasoning	yukti	rigs pa
referent object / determined object	—	zhen yul
requiring interpretation	neyārtha	drang don
resentment	upanāha	'khon 'dzin
root affiction	mūlakleśa	rtsa nyon
saṃsāra	saṃsāra	'khor ba
Sautrāntika	sautrāntika	mdo sde pa

English	Sanskrit	Tibetan
secondary affiction	upakleśa	nye nyon
seed	bīja	sa bon
self	ātman	bdag
self-approved inference	svasiddhānumāna	rang grags rjes dpag
self-approved reason	svasiddhaliṅga	rang grags kyi rtags
self-consciousness / self-knower	svasaṃvedanā	rang rig
self of persons	pudgalātman	gang zag gi bdag
self of phenomena	dharmātman	chos kyi bdag
self-sufficient	—	rang rkya ba
selflessness	nairātmya	bdag med
selflessness of persons	pudgalanairātmya	gang zag gi bdag med
selflessness of phenomena	dharmanairātmya	chos kyi bdag med
sentient being	sattva	sems can
Solitary Realizer	pratyekabuddha	rang sangs rgyas
sound	śabda	sgra
source	āyatana	skye mched
space	ākāśa	nam mkha'
special insight	vipaśyanā	lhag mthong
stabilization	samādhi	ting nge 'dzin
stabilizing meditation	—	'jog sgom
Stream Enterer	śrotāpanna	rgyun zhugs
subsequent cognition	*paricchinnajñāna	bcad shes / dpyad shes
substantial cause	upādāna	nyer len
substantial entity	dravya	rdzas
substantial existence	dravyasat	rdzas su yod pa
substantially established	dravyasiddha	rdzas su grub pa
substantially existent	dravyasat	rdzas su yod pa
suchness	tathatā	de bzhin nyid / de kho na nyid
Superior	āryan	'phags pa
suppleness / pliancy	praśrabdhi	shin tu sbyangs pa
supramundane	lokottara	'jig rten las 'das pa
sūtra	sūtra	mdo
Svātantrika	svātantrika	rang rgyud pa
syllogism	prayoga	sbyor ba

English	*Sanskrit*	*Tibetan*
synonym	ekārtha	don gcig
tangible object	spraṣṭavya	reg bya
tantra	tanra	rgyud
taste	rasa	ro
Tathāgata essence	tathāgatagarbha	de bzhin gshegs pa'i snying po
ten grounds	daśabhūmi	sa bcu
tenets / tenet system	siddhānta / siddhyanta	grub mtha'
thesis	pratijñā	dam bca'
thing / actuality	bhāva	dngos po
thinking	cintā	bsam pa
thoroughly established	pariniṣpanna	yongs grub
Three Refuges	triśaraṇa	skyabs gsum
tongue consciousness	jihvāvijñāna	lce'i rnam par shes pa
tongue sense	jihvendriya	lce'i dbang po
true establishment	satyasiddhi / bhāva	bden par grub pa / dngos po
true existence	satyasat	bden par yod pa
truly established	satyasiddha	bden par grub pa
truly existent	satyasat	bden par yod pa
truth	satya	bden pa
Truth Body	dharmakāya	chos sku
ultimate	paramārtha	don dam pa
ultimate analysis	—	don dam pa'i dpyod pa
ultimate existence	paramārthasiddhi	don dam par grub pa
ultimate truth	paramārthasatya	don dam bden pa
uninterrupted path	ānantaryamārga	bar chad med lam
Vaibhāṣika	vaibhāṣika	bye brag smra ba
vajra	vajra	rdo rje
valid cognition / valid cognizer	pramāṇa	tshad ma
validly established	*pramāṇasiddhi	tshad mas grub pa
vehicle	yāna	theg pa
view	dṛṣṭi	lta ba
view of the transitory collection	satkāyadṛṣṭi	'jig tshogs la lta ba

English	Sanskrit	Tibetan
virtuous/virtuous factor	kuśala	dge ba
visible form	rūpa	gzugs
wind/current of energy	prāṇa	rlung
wisdom	prajñā/jñāna	shes rab/ye shes
Wisdom Body	jñānakāya	ye shes chos sku
wrong view	mithyādṛṣṭi	log lta
Yogācāra	yogācāra	rnal 'byor spyod pa
yogic direct perception	yogi-pratyakṣa	rnal 'byor mngon sum

Tibetan-English-Sanskrit Glossary

To assist the non-specialist, Tibetan follows English alphabetical order.

Tibetan	*English*	*Sanskrit*
'bras bu	fruit	phala
'dod khams	desire realm	kāmadhātu
'dod chags	desire	rāga
'du mi byed pa	non-application	anabhisaṃskāra
'du byed	compositional factor	saṃskāra
'du shes	discrimination	saṃjñā
'dul ba	discipline	vinaya
'dus ma byas kyi chos	non-produced phenomenon/ uncompounded phenomenon	asaṃskṛtadharma
'dus byas	product	saṃkṛta
'gal brjod thal 'gyur	contradictory consequence	—
'gro ba	migrator	gati
'jig pa	disintegration	naṣṭa
'jig rten las 'das pa	supramundane	lokottara
'jig tshogs la lta ba	view of the transitory collection	satkāyadṛṣṭi
'jog sgom	stabilizing meditation	—
'khon 'dzin	resentment	upanāha
'khor ba	cyclic existence	saṃsāra
'og min	Highest Pure Land	akaniṣṭa
'phags pa	Noble/Superior	ārya
'phags pa	Superior	āryan
bag med pa	non-conscientiousness	pramāda
bag yod pa	conscientiousness	apramāda
bags chags/nus pa	potency	vāsanā/bāla
bags chags	predisposition	vāsanā
bar chad med lam	uninterrupted path	ānantaryamārga
bcad shes/dpyad shes	subsequent cognition	*paricchinnajñāna
bdag med rags pa	coarse selflessness	—
bdag	self	ātman

Tibetan	*English*	*Sanskrit*
bdag tu 'dzin pa	conception of self	ātmagrāha
bdag med	selflessness	nairātmya
bde ba	pleasure/bliss	sukhā
bde ba	bliss	sukha
bden par grub pa	truly established	satyasiddha
bden par yod pa	truly existent	satyasat
bden par grub pa/ dngos po	true establishment	satyasiddhi/bhāva
bden pa	truth	satya
bden par yod pa	true existence	satyasat
bem po	matter	kanthā
brtson 'grus	effort	vīrya
bsam gtan	concentration	dhyāna
bsam pa	thinking	cintā
bsgrub bya	probandum	—
bsod nams	merit	puṇya
btags tsam	only imputed	prajñaptimātra
btags yod	imputedly existent	prajñaptisat
btang snyoms	equanimity	upekṣkā
byams pa	love	maitrī
byang chub	enlightenment	bodhi
byang chub sems dpa'	Bodhisattva	bodhisattva
byang chub kyi sems	mind of enlightenment	bodhicitta
bye brag smra ba	Vaibhāṣika	vaibhāṣika
bzod pa	patience	kṣānti
bzod pa	forbearance	kṣānti
chad par smra ba	Proponent of Annihilation	ucchedavādin
chad mtha'	extreme of annihilation	ucchedānta
chos sku	Truth Body	dharmakāya
chos kyi bdag	self of phenomena	dharmātman
chos dbyings	element of [superior] qualities	dharmadhātu
chos kyi bdag med	selflessness of phenomena	dharmanairātmya
chos kyi skye mched pa'i gzugs	form for the mental consciousness	dharmāyatanarūpa
chos kyi skye mched	phenomenon-source	dharmāyatana

Tibetan	English	Sanskrit
chos mngon pa	abhidharma/higher knowledge	abhidharma
chos nyid	reality	dharmatā
chos	phenomenon	dharma
chud mi za ba	non-wastage	avipranāśa
dam bca'	thesis	pratijñā
dbe ba can	Blissful Pure Land	sukhāvatī
dbu ma pa	Mādhyamika	mādhyamika
de bzhin nyid/de kho na nyid	suchness	tathatā
de bzhin gshegs pa'i snying po	Tathāgata essence	tathāgatagarbha
dga' ldan	Joyous Land	tuṣiṭa
dgag bya	object of negation	pratiṣedhya
dgag pa	negation/negative phenomenon	pratiṣedha
dge ba	virtue/virtuous factor	kuśala
dgra bcom pa	Arhat	arhan
dmigs rkyen	observed-object-condition	ālambanapratyaya
dmigs yul/dmigs pa	object of observation	ālambana
dngos med	non-thing	abhāva
dngos po	thing/actuality	bhāva
don dam bden pa	ultimate truth	paramārthasatya
don dam pa'i dpyod pa	ultimate analysis	—
don gcig	synonym	ekārtha
don spyi	generic object/ generic image/ meaning-generality	arthasāmānya
don dam pa	ultimate	paramārtha
don dam par grub pa	ultimate existence	paramārthasiddhi
dpyad sgom	analytical meditation	—
dpyod pa	analysis	vicāra
dran pa	mindfulness	smṛti
drang don	requiring interpretation	neyārtha
dri	odor	gandha
drod	heat	uṣmagata
gang zag gi bdag med	selflessness of persons	pudgalanairātmya

Tibetan	*English*	*Sanskrit*
gang zag gi bdag med	personal selflessness	pudgalanairātmya
gang zag ma yin pa'i ldan min 'du byed	non-person compositional factor	*apudgalaviprayukta-saṃskāra
gang zag gi bdag	self of persons	pudgalātman
gang zag	person	pudgala/puruṣa
gdags gzhi	basis of designation	—
grub mtha'	tenets/system of tenets	siddhānta/siddhyanta
gtan tshigs	reason	hetu
gyo	dissimulation	śāhya
gzhan grags kyi rjes dpag	other-approved inference	parasiddhānumāna
gzhan grags kyi sbyor ba	other-approved syllogism	parasiddhaprayoga
gzhan dbang	other-powered	paratantra
gzhan dbang	dependent phenomenon	paratantra
gzhan grags kyi rtags	other-approved reason	parasiddhaliñga
gzhi grub	existent base	*vastu
gzugs	visible form	rūpa
gzugs sku	Form Body	rūpakāya
gzugs kyi skye mched	form source	rūpāyatana
gzugs med khams	Formless Realm	ārūpyadhātu
gzugs kyi khams	form-constituent	rūpadhātu
gzugs	form	rūpa
gzugs khams	Form Realm	rūpadhātu
khams	constituent	dhātu
khrel yod pa	embarrassment	apatrāpya
khyab pa	pervasions	vyāpti
kun rdzob bden pa	conventional truth/ truth-for-a-concealer/obscured truth	saṃvṛtisatya
kun gzhi	basis-of-all	ālaya
kun rdzob tu yod pa	conventional existence	saṃvṛtisat
kun gzhi rnam shes	mind-basis-of-all	ālayavijñāna
kun btags	imaginary	parikalpita

Tibetan	English	Sanskrit
kun btags pa'i chos	imaginary phenomenon	parikalpitadharma
kun btags	artificial	parikalpita
kun 'gro	omnipresent factor	sarvatraga
lam	path	mārga
las	action	karma
las	deed	karma
lce'i dbang po	tongue sense	jihvendriya
lce'i rnam par shes pa	tongue consciousness	jihvāvijñāna
ldan min 'du byed	non-associated compositional factor	viprayuktasaṃskāra
ldog khyab	counter-pervasion	vyatirekavyāpti
lha'i rnal 'byor	deity yoga	*devayoga
lhag mthong	special insight	vipaśyanā
lhan cig byed rkhyen	cooperative condition	sahakāripratyaya
lhan skyes	innate	sahaja
log lta	wrong view	mithyādṛṣṭi
longs spyod rdzogs pa'i sku	Complete Enjoyment Body	saṃbhogakāya
longs sku	Enjoyment Body	saṃbhogakāya
lta ba	view	dṛṣṭi
lung du ma bstan pa	neutral	avyākṛta
lus kyi rnam par shes pa	body consciousness	kāyavijñāna
lus kyi dbang po	body sense	kāyendriya
ma chags pa	non-attachment	alobha
ma yin dgag	affirming negation/ negative	paryudāsapratiṣedha
ma rig pa	ignorance	avidyā
mdo sde pa	Sautrāntika	sautrāntika
med pa	non-existent	asat
med dgag	non-affirming negation/ negative	prasajyapratiṣedha
mi dge ba	non-virtuous	akuśala
mi lcogs med	not unable	anāgamya
mi slob lam	path of no more learning	aśaikṣamārga
mi rtag pa	impermanent	anitya
mig gi rnam shes	eye consciousness	cakṣurvijñāna
ming tsam du yod pa	nominal existence	—
mngon par shes pa	clairvoyance	abhijñā

Tibetan	*English*	*Sanskrit*
mngon sum du rtogs pa	direct cognition	—
mngon sum	direct perception/ perceiver	pratyakśa
mnyam bzhag	meditative equipoise	samāhita
mos pa	belief	adhimokṣa
mtha'	extreme	anta
mthong lam	path of seeing	darśanamārga
nam mkha'	space	ākāśa
nga	I	ahaṃ
nges don	definitive	nītārtha
ngo bo nyid kyis grub pa	existence through its own entityness / inherent existence	*svabhāvatāsiddhi
ngo bo nyid sku	Nature Body	svabhāvikakāya
nyan thos	Hearer	śrāvaka
nye nyon	secondary affiction	upakleśa
nyer len	substantial cause	upādāna
nyer bsdogs	preparation	sāmantaka
nyon mongs lhan skyes	innate affliction	sahajakleśa
nyon yid	afficted mind	kliṣamanas
nyon mong pa'i sgrib pa	obstructions to liberation / afflictive obstructions	kleśāvaraṇa
nyon mongs	affiction	kleśa
nyon sgrib	afflictive obstruction	kleśāvaraṅa
phar phyin	perfection	pāramitā
phar phyin kyi theg pa	Perfection Vehicle	pāramitāyāna
phung po	mental and physical aggregates	skandha
phung po	aggregate	skandha
phyir mi 'ong	Never Returner	anāgāmin
phyir 'ong	Once Returner	āgāmin
phyogs	position	pakṣa
rang bzhin	nature	prakṛti
rang bzhin myang 'das	natural nirvāṇa	*prakṛtiparinirvāṇa

Tibetan	English	Sanskrit
rang gi mtshan nyid kyis grub pa	natural existence/ existence by way of [the object's] own character	svalakṣaṇasiddhi
rang dbang du grub pa	existence through its own power	*svairīsiddhi
rang gi mtshan nyid kyis grub pa	existence by way of its own character	svalakṣaṇasiddhi
rang grags kyi rtags	self-approved reason	svasiddhaliṅga
rang sangs rgyas	Solitary Realizer	pratyekabuddha
rang bzhin gyis grub pa	inherent existence	svabhāvasiddhi
rang rgyud pa	Svātantrika	svātantrika
rang rgyud kyi rjes dpag	autonomous inference	svatantrānumāna
rang rgyud kyi sbyor ba	autonomous syllogism	svatantraprayoga
rang grags rjes dpag	self-approved inference	svasiddhānumāna
rang rkya ba	self-sufficient	—
rang ngos nas grub pa	existence from the object's side	*svarūpasiddhi
rang rig	self-consciousness/ self-knower	svasaṃvedanā
rdul tu grub pa	established atomically	—
rdzas	substantial entity	dravya
rdzas su yod pa	substantially existent	dravyasat
rdzas su yod pa	substantial existence	dravyasat
rdzas su grub pa	substantially established	dravyasiddha
reg pa	contact	sparśa
reg bya	tangible object	spraṣṭavya
rgod pa	excitement	auddhatya
rgyal ba	Conqueror	jina
rgyu	cause	hetu
rgyun zhugs	Stream Enterer	śrotāpanna
rgyun / gyud	continuum	saṃtāna
rigs pa	reasoning	yukti
rigs	lineage	gotra
rjes dpag	inference	anumāna

Tibetan	*English*	*Sanskrit*
rjes dpag tshad ma	inferential valid cognition	anumānapramāṇa
rkyen 'di pa tsam nyid	conditionality	idaṃpratyayatā
rkyen	condition	pratyaya
rlung	wind / current of energy	prāṇa
rna ba'i rnam par shes pa	ear consciousness	śrotravijñāna
rna ba'i dbang po	ear sense	śrotrendriya
rnal 'byor spyod pa	Yogācāra	yogācāra
rnal 'byor bla med kyi rgyud	Highest Yoga Tantra	anuttarayogatantra
rnal 'byor mngon sum	yogic direct perception	yogi-pratyakṣa
rnam pa thams cad mkhyen pa	omniscience / exalted knower of all aspects	sarvākārajñāna
rnam pa	aspect	akārā
rnam par rig byed ma yin pa'i gzugs	non-revelatory form	avijñāptirūpa
rnam grol lam	path of release	vimuktimārga
rnam smin rnam shes	fruition consciousness	vipakavijñāna
rnam par mi rtog pa'i ye shes	non-conceptual wisdom	nirvikalpajñāna
ro	taste	rasa
rtag mtha'	extreme of permanence	śaśvatānta
rtag pa	permanent phenomenon	nitya
rtag par smra ba	Proponent of Permanence	śaśvatavādin
rten 'byung	dependent-arising	pratītyasamutpāda
rtog pa	investigation	vitarka
rtsa nyon	root affiction	mūlakleśa
rtse mo	peak	mūrdhan
sa	ground	bhūmi
sa bon	seed	bīja
sa bcu	ten grounds	daśabhūmi
sbyin pa	giving	dāna
sbyor ba	syllogism	prayoga

Tibetan	*English*	*Sanskrit*
sbyor lam	path of preparation	prayogamārga
sdug bsngal	pain / suffering	duḥkha
sems can	sentient being	sattva
sems tsam	Cittamātra	cittamātra
sems pa	intention	cetanā
sems byung	mental factor	caitta
sems	mind	citta
sgom lam	path of meditation	bhāvanāmārga
sgra	sound	śabda
sgrub byed	proof	sādhana
shes pa / rnam shes	consciousness	jñā / vijñāna
shes bya'i sgrib pa	obstructions to omniscience / obstructions to objects of knowledge	jñeyāvaraṇa
shes rab/ye shes	wisdom	prajñā/jñāna
shes bzhin	introspection	samprajanya
shes rab	knowledge/wisdom	prajña
shes bya	object of knowledge	jñeya
shin tu sbyangs pa	suppleness/pliancy	praśrabdhi
skyabs gsum	Three Refuges	triśaraṇa
skye mched	source	āyatana
skyes bu	creature/being/person	puruṣa
sna'i rnam shes	nose consciousness	ghrāṇavijñāna
sna'i dbang po	nose sense	ghrāṇendriya
snying rje	compassion	karuṇā
snying rje chen po	great compassion	mahākaruṇā
snyoms 'jug	absorption	samāpatti
snyoms 'jug	meditative absorption	samāpatti
so skye bo	common being	pṛthagjana
so sor brtags min gyi 'gog pa	non-analytical cessation	apratisaṃkhyānirodha
so sor brtags 'gog	analytical cessation	pratisaṃkhyā-nirodha
spros pa	elaborations	prapañca
sprul sku	Emanation Body	nirmāṇkāya
spyi mtshan	generally characterized phenomenon	sāmānyalakṣaṇa
stong pa nyid	emptiness	śūnyatā
tha snyad pa'i dpyod pa	conventional analysis	—

Tibetan	*English*	*Sanskrit*
thabs	method	upāya
thal 'gyur pa	Prāsaṅgika	prāsaṅgika
thal 'gyur	consequence	prasaṅga
thar pa	liberation	vimokṣa/mokṣa
the tshom	doubt	vicikitsā
theg pa	vehicle	yāna
thob pa	obtainer	prāpti
thos pa	hearing	śruta
ting nge 'dzin	meditative stabilization	samādhi
ting nge 'dzin	stabilization	samādhi
tshad mas grub pa	validly established	*pramāṇasiddha
tshad mas grub pa	valid establishment	*pramāṇasiddhi
tshad ma	valid cognition/ valid cognizer	pramāṇa
tshogs lam	path of accumulation	saṃbhāramārga
tshor ba	feeling	vedanā
tshugs thub tu grub pa	existence able to set itself up	—
tshugs thub tu grub pa	able to set itself up	
yang dag pa'i lta ba	correct view	samyakdṛṣṭi
ye shes chos sku	Wisdom Body	jñānakāya
yid kyi rnam shes	mental consciousness	manovijñāna
yod pa	existent	sat
yongs grub	thoroughly established	pariniṣpanna
yul	object	viṣaya
yul gyi steng nas grub pa	objective existence	—
yul nges	determining factor	viniyata
zag bcas	contaminated	sāsrava
zag bcas kyi las	contaminated action	sāsravakarma
zag pa	contamination	āsrava
zhen yul	referent object/ determined object	—
zhi gnas	calm abiding	śamatha
zhig pa	disintegratedness	naṣṭa

Sanskrit-Tibetan-English Glossary

To assist the non-specialist, Sanskrit entries follow English alphabetical order. However, long vowels (e.g., ā) follow short ones.

Sanskrit	*Tibetan*	*English*
abhidharma	chos mngon pa	higher knowledge
abhijñā	mngon par shes pa	clairvoyance
abhāva	dngos med	non-thing
adhimokṣa	mos pa	belief
ahaṃ	nga	I
akaniṣṭa	'og min	Highest Pure Land
akuśala	mi dge ba	non-virtuous
akārā	rnam pa	aspect
alobha	ma chags pa	non-attachment
anabhisaṃskāra	'du mi byed pa	non-application
anitya	mi rtag pa	impermanent
anta	mtha'	extreme
anumāna	rjes dpag	inference
anumānapramāṇa	rjes dpag tshad ma	inferential valid cognition
anuttarayoga-tantra	rnal 'byor bla med kyi rgyud	Highest Yoga Tantra
anāgamya	mi lcogs med	not unable
anạgāmin	phyir mi 'ong	Never Returner
apatrāpya	khrel yod pa	embarrassment
apramāda	bag yod pa	conscientiousness
apratisaṃkhyā-nirodha	so sor brtags min gyi 'gog pa	non-analytical cessation
*apudgalavipra-yukta-saṃskāra	gang zag ma yin pa'i ldan min 'du byed	non-person compositional factor
arhan/Arhat	dgra bcom pa	Arhat
arthasāmānya	don spyi	generic object/generic image/meaning-generality
asat	med pa	non-existent
asaṃskṛtadharma	'dus ma byas kyi chos	non-produced phenomenon/uncompounded phenomenon
auddhatya	rgod pa	excitement
avidyā	ma rig pa	ignorance
avijñāptirūpa	rnam par rig byed ma yin pa'i gzugs	non-revelatory form

Sanskrit	*Tibetan*	*English*
avipranāśa	chud mi za ba	non-wastage
avyākṛta	lung du ma bstan pa	neutral
aśaikṣamārga	mi slob lam	path of no more learning
āgāmin	phyir 'ong	Once Returner
ākāśa	nam mkha'	space
ālambana	dmigs yul/dmigs pa	object of observation
ālambanapratyaya	dmigs rkyen	observed-object-condition
ālaya	kun gzhi	basis-of-all
ālayavijñāna	kun gzhi rnam shes	mind-basis-of-all
ānantaryamārga	bar chad med lam	uninterrupted path
ārya	'phags pa	Noble/Superior
āryan	'phags pa	Superior
ārūpyadhātu	gzugs med khams	Formless Realm
āsrava	zag pa	contamination
ātmagrāha	bdag tu 'dzin pa	conception of self
ātman	bdag	self
āyatana	skye mched	source
bhāva	dngos po	thing/actuality
bhāvanāmārga	sgom lam	path of meditation
bhūmi	sa	ground
bodhi	byang chub	enlightenment
bodhicitta	byang chub kyi sems	mind of enlightenment
bodhisattva	byang chub sems dpa'	Bodhisattva
bīja	sa bon	seed
caitta	sems byung	mental factor
cakṣurvijñāna	mig gi rnam shes	eye consciousness
cetanā	sems pa	intention
cintā	bsam pa	thinking
citta	sems	mind
cittamātra	sems tsam	Cittamātra
darśanamārga	mthong lam	path of seeing
daśabhūmi	sa bcu	ten grounds
dāna	sbyin pa	giving
*devayoga	lha'i rnal 'byor	deity yoga
dharma	chos	phenomenon
dharmadhātu	chos dbyings	element of [superior] qualities
dharmakāya	chos sku	Truth Body
dharmanairātmya	chos kyi bdag med	selflessness of phenomena
dharmatā	chos nyid	reality

Sanskrit	*Tibetan*	*English*
dharmātman	chos kyi bdag	self of phenomena
dharmāyatana	chos kyi skye mched	phenomenon-source
dharmāyatana-rūpa	chos kyi skye mched pa'i gzugs	form for the mental consciousness
dhyāna	bsam gtan	concentration
dhātu	khams	constituent
dravya	rdzas	substantial entity
dravyasat	rdzas su yod pa	substantially existent
dravyasat	rdzas su yod pa	substantial existence
dravyasiddha	rdzas su grub pa	substantially established
duḥkha	sdug bsngal	pain/suffering
dṛṣṭi	lta ba	view
ekārtha	don gcig	synonym
gandha	dri	odor
gati	'gro ba	migrator
ghrāṇavijñāna	sna'i rnam shes	nose consciousness
ghrāṇendriya	sna'i dbang po	nose sense
gotra	rigs	lineage
hetu	rgyu	cause
hetu	gtan tshigs	reason
idaṃpratyayatā	rkyen 'di pa tsam nyid	conditionality
jihvendriya	lce'i dbang po	tongue sense
jihvāvijñāna	lce'i rnam par shes pa	tongue consciousness
jina	rgyal ba	Conqueror
jñeya	shes bya	object of knowledge
jñeyāvaraṇa	shes bya'i sgrib pa	obstructions to omniscience / obstructions to objects of knowledge
jñā/vijñāna	shes pa/rnam shes	consciousness
jñānakāya	ye shes chos sku	Wisdom Body
kanthā	bem po	matter
karma	las	action
karma	las	deed
karuṇā	snying rje	compassion
kāmadhātu	'dod khams	desire realm
kāyavijñāna	lus kyi rnam par shes pa	body consciousness
kāyendriya	lus kyi dbang po	body sense
kleśa	nyon mongs	affiction

Sanskrit	*Tibetan*	*English*
kleśāvaraṇa	nyon mong pa'i sgrib pa	obstructions to liberation / afflictive obstructions
kleśāvaraṅa	nyon sgrib	afflictive obstruction
kliṣamanas	nyon yid	afflicted mind
kṣānti	bzod pa	forbearance
kṣānti	bzod pa	patience
kuśala	dge ba	virtuous / virtuous factor
lokottara	'jig rten las 'das pa	supramundane
mahākaruṇā	snying rje chen po	great compassion
maitrī	byams pa	love
manovijñāna	yid kyi rnam shes	mental consciousness
mithyādṛṣṭi	log lta	wrong view
mādhyamika	dbu ma pa	Mādhyamika
mūlakleśa	rtsa nyon	root affiction
mūrdhan	rtse mo	peak
mārga	lam	path
nairātmya	bdag med	selflessness
naṣṭa	'jig pa	disintegration
naṣṭa	zhig pa	disintegratedness
neyārtha	drang don	requiring interpretation
nirmāṇkāya	sprul sku	Emanation Body
nirvikalpajñāna	rnam par mi rtog pa'i ye shes	non-conceptual wisdom
nitya	rtag pa	permanent phenomenon
nītārtha	nges don	definitive
pakṣa	phyogs	position
paramārtha	don dam pa	ultimate
paramārthasatya	don dam bden pa	ultimate truth
paramārthasiddhi	don dam par grub pa	ultimate existence
parasiddhaliṅga	gzhan grags kyi rtags	other-approved reason
parasiddhaprayoga	gzhan grags kyi sbyor ba	other-approved syllogism
parasiddhānumāna	gzhan grags kyi rjes dpag	other-approved inference
paratantra	gzhan dbang	other-powered
paratantra	gzhan dbang	dependent phenomenon
*paricchinnajñāna	bcad shes / dpyad shes	subsequent cognition
parikalpita	kun btags	artificial
parikalpita	kun btags	imaginary

Sanskrit	*Tibetan*	*English*
parikalpitadharma	kun btags pa'i chos	imaginary phenomenon
parinișpanna	yongs grub	thoroughly established
paryudāsapratiṣedha	ma yin dgag	affirming negation / negative
pāramitā	phar phyin	perfection
pāramitāyāna	phar phyin kyi theg pa	Perfection Vehicle
phala	'bras bu	fruit
prajña	shes rab	knowledge / wisdom
prajñaptimātra	btags tsam	only imputed
prajñaptisat	btags yod	imputedly existent
prajñā / jñāna	shes rab / ye shes	wisdom
prakṛti	rang bzhin	nature
*prakṛtiparinirvāṇa	rang bzhin myang 'das	natural nirvāṇa
pramāda	bag med pa	non-conscientiousness
pramāṇa	tshad ma	valid cognition / valid cognizer
*pramāṇasiddha	tshad mas grub pa	validly established
*pramāṇasiddhi	tshad mas grub pa	valid establishment
prapañca	spros pa	elaborations
prasajyapratiṣedha	med dgag	non-affirming negation / negative
prasaṅga	thal 'gyur	consequence
pratijñā	dam bca'	thesis
pratisaṃkhyānirodha	so sor brtags 'gog	analytical cessation
pratiṣedha	dgag pa	negation / negative phenomenon
pratiṣedhya	dgag bya	object of negation
pratyakśa	mngon sum	direct perception / perceiver
pratyaya	rkyen	condition
pratyekabuddha	rang sangs rgyas	Solitary Realizer
pratītyasamutpāda	rten 'byung	dependent-arising
prayoga	sbyor ba	syllogism
prayogamārga	sbyor lam	path of preparation
praśrabdhi	shin tu sbyangs pa	suppleness / pliancy
prāpti	thob pa	obtainer
prāsaṅgika	thal 'gyur pa	Prāsaṅgika
prāṇa	rlung	wind / current of energy
pudgala / puruṣa	gang zag	person

Sanskrit	Tibetan	English
pudgalanairātmya	gang zag gi bdag med	selflessness of persons
pudgalanairātmya	gang zag gi bdag med	personal selflessness
pudgalātman	gang zag gi bdag	self of persons
puruṣa	skyes bu	creature / being / person
puṇya	bsod nams	merit
pṛthagjana	so skye bo	common being
rasa	ro	taste
rāga	'dod chags	desire
rūpa	gzugs	form
rūpa	gzugs	visible form
rūpadhātu	gzugs khams	Form Realm
rūpadhātu	gzugs kyi khams	form-constituent
rūpakāya	gzugs sku	Form Body
rūpāyatana	gzugs kyi skye mched	form source
sahaja	lhan skyes	innate
sahajakleśa	nyon mongs lhan skyes	innate affliction
sahakāripratyaya	lhan cig byed rkhyen	cooperative condition
samprajanya	shes bzhin	introspection
samyakdṛṣṭi	yang dag pa'i lta ba	correct view
samādhi	ting nge 'dzin	meditative stabilization
samādhi	ting nge 'dzin	stabilization
samāhita	mnyam bzhag	meditative equipoise
samāpatti	snyoms 'jug	absorption
samāpatti	snyoms 'jug	meditative absorption
sarvatraga	kun 'gro	omnipresent factor
sarvākārajñāna	rnam pa thams cad mkhyen pa	omniscience / exalted knower of all aspects
sat	yod pa	existent
satkāyadṛṣṭi	'jig tshogs la lta ba	view of the transitory collection
sattva	sems can	sentient being
satya	bden pa	truth
satyasat	bden par yod pa	true existence
satyasat	bden par yod pa	truly existent
satyasiddha	bden par grub pa	truly established
satyasiddhi / bhāva	bden par grub pa / dngos po	true establishment

Sanskrit	*Tibetan*	*English*
sautrāntika	mdo sde pa	Sautrāntika
saṃbhogakāya	longs sku	Enjoyment Body
saṃbhogakāya	longs spyod rdzogs pa'i sku	Complete Enjoyment Body
saṃbhāramārga	tshogs lam	path of accumulation
saṃjñā	'du shes	discrimination
saṃkṛta	'dus byas	product
saṃskāra	'du byed	compositional factor
saṃsāra	'khor ba	cyclic existence
saṃtāna	rgyun / gyud	continuum
saṃvṛtisat	kun rdzob tu yod pa	conventional existence
saṃvṛtisatya	kun rdzob bden pa	conventional truth / truth-for-a-concealer / obscured truth
siddhānta / siddhyanta	grub mtha'	tenets / system of tenets
skandha	phung po	aggregate
skandha	phung po	mental and physical aggregates
smṛti	dran pa	mindfulness
sparśa	reg pa	contact
spraṣṭavya	reg bya	tangible object
sukha	bde ba	bliss
sukhā	bde ba	pleasure / bliss
sukhāvatī	dbe ba can	Blissful Pure Land
svabhāvasiddhi	rang bzhin gyis grub pa	inherent existence
*svabhāvatāsiddhi	ngo bo nyid kyis grub pa	existence through its own entityness / inherent existence
svabhāvikakāya	ngo bo nyid sku	Nature Body
*svairīsiddhi	rang dbang du grub pa	existence through its own power
svalakṣaṇasiddhi	rang gi mtshan nyid kyis grub pa	existence by way of its own character
svalakṣaṇasiddhi	rang gi mtshan nyid kyis grub pa	natural existence / existence by way of [the object's] own character
*svarūpasiddhi	rang ngos nas grub pa	existence from the object's side
svasaṃvedanā	rang rig	self-consciousness / self-knower

Sanskrit	Tibetan	English
svasiddhaliṅga	rang grags kyi rtags	self-approved reason
svasiddhānumāna	rang grags rjes dpag	self-approved inference
svatantraprayoga	rang rgyud kyi sbyor ba	autonomous syllogism
svatantrānumāna	rang rgyud kyi rjes dpag	autonomous inference
svātantrika	rang rgyud pa	Svātantrika
sādhana	sgrub byed	proof
sāmantaka	nyer bsdogs	preparation
sāmānyalakṣaṇa	spyi mtshan	generally characterized phenomenon
sāsrava	zag bcas	contaminated
sāsravakarma	zag bcas kyi las	contaminated action
śabda	sgra	sound
śamatha	zhi gnas	calm abiding
śaśvatavādin	rtag par smra ba	Proponent of Permanence
śaśvatānta	rtag mtha'	extreme of permanence
śāhya	gyo	dissimulation
śruta	thos pa	hearing
śrāvaka	nyan thos	Hearer
—	skye mched	source
śūnyatā	stong pa nyid	emptiness
tathatā	de bzhin nyid / de kho na nyid	suchness
tathāgatagarbha	de bzhin gshegs pa'i snying po	Tathāgata essence
triśaraṇa	skyabs gsum	Three Refuges
tuṣiṭa	dga' ldan	Joyous Land
ucchedavādin	chad par smra ba	Proponent of Annihilation
ucchedānta	chad mtha'	extreme of annihilation
upakleśa	nye nyon	secondary affiction
upanāha	'khon 'dzin	resentment
upekṣkā	btang snyoms	equanimity
upādāna	nyer len	substantial cause
upāya	thabs	method
uṣmagata	drod	heat
vaibhāṣika	bye brag smra ba	Vaibhāṣika
*vastu	gzhi grub	existent base
vāsanā	bags chags	predisposition
vāsanā / bāla	bags chags / nus pa	potency
vedanā	tshor ba	feeling
vicikitsā	the tshom	doubt

Sanskrit	Tibetan	English
vicāra	dpyod pa	analysis
vimokṣa / mokṣa	thar pa	liberation
vimuktimārga	rnam grol lam	path of release
vinaya	'dul ba	discipline
viniyata	yul nges	determining factor
vipakavijñāna	rnam smin rnam shes	fruition consciousness
vipaśyanā	lhag mthong	special insight
viprayuktasaṃskāra	ldan min 'du byed	non-associated compositional factor
vitarka	rtog pa	investigation
viṣaya	yul	object
vīrya	brtson 'grus	effort
vyatirekavyāpti	ldog khyab	counter-pervasion
vyāpti	khyab pa	pervasions
yāna	theg pa	vehicle
yogi-pratyakṣa	rnal 'byor mngon sum	yogic direct perception
yogācāra	rnal 'byor spyod pa	Yogācāra
yukti	rigs pa	reasoning

Bibliography

Sūtras and tantras are listed alphabetically by English translation (often with abbreviated titles), Indian and Tibetan treatises by author. "P" refers to the 1956 reprint of the Peking edition of the Tibetan canon (originally compiled in 1411), the *Tibetan Tripiṭaka* (Tokyo-Kyoto: Suzuki Research Foundation). Modern editions are listed where known.

1. Sūtras and Tantras

Buddha Garland Sūtra (*buddhāvataṃsakanāmamahāvaipulyasūtra, sangs rgyas phal po che zhes bya ba shin tu rgyas pa chen po'i mdo*)
P 761, vol. 25-26.

Chapter Showing the Three Vows Sūtra (*trisambaranirdeśaparivarta-sūtra, sdom pa gsum bstan pa'i le'u'i mdo*)
P 760.1, vol. 22.

Descent Into Laṅkā Sūtra (*laṅkāvatārasūtra, lang kar gshegs pa'i mdo*)
P 775, vol. 29.
Sanskrit: *Saddharmalaṅkāvatārasūtram*. P. L. Vaidya, ed. Buddhist Sanskrit Texts no. 3. Darbhanga: Mithila Institute, 1963; Also: Bunyiu Nanjio, ed. Bibl. Otaniensis, vol. I. Kyoto: Otani University Press, 1923.
English translation: D. T. Suzuki. *The Lankavatara Sutra*. London: Routledge and Kegan Paul, 1932.

Heap of Jewels Sūtra (*mahāratnakūṭadharmaparyāyaśatasāhasrikagranthasūtra, dkon mchog brtsegs pa chen po'i chos kyi rnam grangs le'u stong phrag bgrya pa'i mdo*)

P 760, vol. 22-24.

Mahāyāna Sūtra of Higher Knowledge (*mahāyānābhidharmasūtra, theg pa chen po'i mngon pa'i chos kyi mdo [?]*)

Questions of King Dhāraṇīśvara Sūtra (*dhāraṇīśvararājaparipṛccāsūtra gzung rgyal gyis zhus pa'i mdo*)
P 814, vol. 32.

Questions of the Nāga King Anavatapta Sūtra (*anavataptanāgarāja-paripṛccāsūtra, klu'i rgyal po ma dros pas zhus pa'i mdo*)
P 823, vol. 33.

Questions of Ratnacūḍa Sūtra (*atnacūḍaparipṛcchasūtra, gtsug na rin po ches zhus pa'i mdo*)
P 47, vol. 24, 229-51.

Repetition Sūtra *[?] (anuvīpsāsūtra [?], rjes zlos kyi mdo)*

Samyutta-nikāya
Pali: Feer, Leon M., ed. *Samyuttanikāya*. London: Pali Text Society, 1884-1904. Rpt. 1973.
English translation: C. A. F. Rhys-Davids and F. L. Woodward, *Book of the Kindred Sayings*. (5 Vols.). London: Pali Text Society, 1917-30.

Sūtra on the Heavily Adorned (*ghanavyūhasūtra, rgyan stug po bkod pa'i mdo*)
P 778, vol. 29.

Sūtra on the Ten Grounds (*daśabhūmikasūtra, mdo sde sa bcu pa*)
P 761.32, vol. 25.
Sanskrit: *Daśabhūmikasūtram*. P.L. Vaidya, ed., Buddhist Sanskrit Texts no. 7. Darbhanga: Mithila Institute, 1967.
English translation: M. Honda. "An Annotated Translation of the 'Daśabhūmika.'" in D. Sinor, ed., *Studies in Southeast and Central Asia*, Satapiṭaka Series 74. New Delhi: 1968, pp. 115-276.

Sūtra Unraveling the Thought (*saṃdhinirmocanasūtra, dgongs pa nges par 'grel pa'i mdo*)
P 774, vol. 29.
English translation: John Powers, *Wisdom of Buddha: the Saṃdhinirmocana Sūtra*. Berkeley, CA: Dharma Publishing, 1995.

French translation: Étienne Lamotte, *Saṃdhinirmocana-sūtra* (Paris: Louvain, 1935).

Teaching of Akṣhayamati Sūtra (*akṣayamatinirdeśasūtra, blo gros mi zad pas bstan pa'i mdo*)
P 842, vol. 34.

2. Sanskrit and Tibetan Works

Āryadeva (*'phags pa lha*, second to third century, C.E.)

Four Hundred / Treatise of Four Hundred Stanzas (*catuḥśataka-śāstrakārikā, bstan bcos bzhi brgya pa zhes bya ba'i tshig le'ur byas pa*)
P 5246, vol. 95.
Edited Tibetan and Sanskrit fragments along with English translation: Karen Lang, *Āryadeva's Catuḥśataka: On the Bodhisattva's Cultivation of Merit and Knowledge.* Indiske Studier VII, Copenhagen: Akademisk Forlag, 1986.
English translations: with translation of commentary by Gyeltsap: Ruth Sonam, trans. and ed., *The Yogic Deeds of Bodhisattvas: Gyeltsap on Āryadeva's "Four Hundred."* Ithaca: Snow Lion Publications, 1994. Chapters 3-5, 17, 23: William Ames, "Bhāvaviveka's Prajñāpradīpa," dissertation at University of Washington, 1986. Chapter 25: Malcolm David Eckel, *Miscellanea Buddhica*, Indiske Studier V, Copenhagen: Akademisk Forlag, 1985, pp. 25-75. Italian translation of the last half from the Chinese: Giuseppe Tucci, "La versione cinese del Catuhśataka di Āryadeva, confronta col testo sanscrito et la traduzione tibetana." *Rivista degli Studi Orientalia* 10 (1925): 521-567.

Asaṅga (*thogs med*, c. 310-390)

Actuality of the Levels (*bhūmivastu, sa'i dngos gzhi*)
P 5536-P 5538.

Explanation of (Maitreya's) "Sublime Continuum of the Mahāyāna" (*mahāyānottaratantraśāstravyakhā, theg pa chen po'i rgyud bla ma'i bstan bcos kyi rnam par bshad pa*)
P 5526, vol. 108.

Compendium of Ascertainments (*nirnayasaṃgraha* or *viniścaya-saṃgrahaṇī, gtan la dbab pa bsdu ba*)
P 5539, vol. 110-11.

Compendium of Knowledge (*abhidharmasamuccaya, mngon pa kun btus*)
P 5550, vol. 112. Sanskrit text: *Abhidharma Samuccaya*, ed. Pralhad Pradhan. Śantiniketan: Visva-Bharati, 1950.
French translation: W. Rahula, *Le Compendium de la Super-Doctrine Philosophie* (Paris: École Française d'Extréme Orient, 1971).

Compendium of the Mahāyāna (*mahāyānasaṃgraha, theg pa chen po bsdus pa*)
P 5549, vol. 112.
French translation: Étienne Lamotte, *La Somme du Grand Véhicule d'Asaṅga*, vol. II. (Louvain: 1939). German translation: (partial): Erick Frauwallner, *Die Philosophie des Buddhismus.* Berlin: Akademie-Verlag, 1958, pp. 335-350. Edward Conze, *Im Zeichen Buddhas: Buddhistische Texte.* Frankfurt: Fischer, 1957.

Explanation of the "Sūtra Unraveling the Thought" (*saṃdhinir-mocanabhāṣya, dgons pa nges par 'grel pa'i rnam par bshad pa*)
P 5481, vol. 104; Toh. 3981.

Asvabhāva (*ngo bo nyid med pa,* c. 450-530)

Connected Explanation of (Asaṅga's) "Compendium of the Mahāyāna" (*mahāyānasaṃgrahopanibandhana, theg pa chen po'i bsdud pa'i bsad sbyar*)
P 5552, vol. 113.

Atīśa (982-1054)

Explanation of (Śāntideva's) "Engaging in the Bodhisattva Deeds" (*bodhisattvacaryāvatārabhāṣya, byang chub sems dpa'i spyod pa la 'jug pa'i bshad pa*)
P 5872, vol. 146.

Lamp for the Path to Enlightenment (*bodhipathapradīpa, byang chub lam gyi sgron ma*)
P 5343, vol. 103.

English translation: R. Sherburne, *A Lamp for the Path and Commentary*, S. J. The Wisdom of Tibet Series—5. London: George Allen & Unwin.

Quintessential Instructions on the Middle Way (*madhyamakopadeśa, dbu ma'i man ngag*)
P 5324, vol. 102; P 5326, vol. 102; P 5381, vol. 103.

Avalokitavrata (*spyan ras gzigs brtul zhugs*, seventh century [?])

Commentary on (Bhāvaviveka's) "Lamp for (Nāgārjuna's) 'Wisdom'" (*prajñāpradīpaṭīkā, shes rab sgron ma'i rgya cher 'grel pa*)
P 5259, vol. 96-97.

Bhāvaviveka (*legs ldan 'byed*, c.500-570)

Blaze of Reasoning, Commentary on the "Heart of the Middle Way" (*madhyamakahṛdayavṛttitarkajvālā, dbu ma'i snying po'i 'grel pa rtog ge 'bar ba*)
P 5256, vol. 96.
Partial English translation by S. Iida in *Reason and Emptiness* Tokyo: Hokuseido, 1980, chap. III. 1-136, pp. 52-242.

Heart of the Middle Way (*madhyamakahṛdayakārikā, dbu ma'i snying po'i tshig le'ur byas pa*)
P 5255, vol. 96.
Partial English translation (chap. III. 1-136): S. Iida. *Reason and Emptiness*. Tokyo: Hokuseido, 1980.

Lamp for (Nāgārjuna's) "Wisdom," Commentary on the "Treatise on the Middle Way" (*prajñāpradīpamūlamadhyamakavṛtti, dbu ma rtsa ba'i 'grel pa shes rab sgron ma*)
P 5253, vol. 95.
English translation of chapters 18, 24, 25: Malcolm David Eckel, "A Question of Nihilism: Bhāvaviveka's Response to the Fundamental Problems of Mādhyamika Philosophy." Unpublished dissertation, Harvard, 1980.

Buddhapālita (*sangs rgyas bskyangs*, c. 470-540)

Buddhapālita's Commentary on (Nāgārjuna's) "Treatise on the Middle Way" (*buddhapālitamūlamadhyamakavṛtti, dbu ma rtsa *ba'i 'grel pa buddha pā li ta*)

P 5254, vol. 95; Toh. 3842, Tokyo *sde dge* vol. 1. Edited Tibetan edition: (Ch. 1-12): Max Walleser. Bibliotheca Buddhica XVI. Osnabrück: Biblio Verlag, 1970.

English translations: (Ch. 1): Judit Fehér. in Louis Ligeti, ed., *Tibetan and Buddhist Studies Commemorating the 200th Anniversary of the Birth of Alexander Csoma de Körös*, vol. 1. Budapest: Akadémiai Kiado, 1984, pp. 211-240. (Ch. 18): Christian Lindtner in *Indo-Iranian Journal* 23 (1981): 187-217.

Candrakīrti (*zla ba grags pa,* seventh century)

Autocommentary on the "Entrance to (Nāgārjuna's) 'Treatise on the Middle Way'" (*madhyamakāvatārabhāṣya, dbu ma la 'jug pa'i bshad pa / dbu ma la 'jug pa'i rang 'grel*)

P 5263, vol. 98. Also: New Delhi: Delhi Karmapae Chodhey Gyalwa Suagrab Partun Khang, n.d. Also: Dharamsala: Council of Religious and Cultural Affairs, 1968. Edited Tibetan: Louis de la Vallée Poussin. *Madhyamakāvatāra par Candrakīrti*. Bibliotheca Buddhica IX. Osnabrück: Biblio Verlag, 1970.

French translation: (up to VI.165): Louis de la Vallée Poussin. *Muséon 8* (1907): 249-317; ii (1910): 271-358; 12 (1911): 235-328. German translation: (VI. 166-226): Helmut Tauscher. *Candrakīrti-Madhyamakāvatāraḥ und Madhyamakāvatārabhāṣyam*. Wien: Wiener Studien zur Tibetologie und Buddhismuskunde, 1981.

Clear Words, Commentary on (Nāgārjuna's) "Treatise on the Middle Way" (*mūlmadhyamakavṛttiprasannapadā, dbu ma rtsa ba'i 'grel pa tshig gsal ba)*

P 5260, vol. 98. Also: New Delhi: Bel Gyelwa Karmapa, n.d. Also: Dharamsala: Tibetan Publishing House, 1968. Sanskrit: *Mūlamadhyamakakārikās de Nāgārjuna avec la Prasannapadā Commentaire de Candrakīrti*. Louis de la Vallée Poussin, ed. Bibliotheca Buddhica IV. Osnabrück: Biblio Verlag, 1970.

English translations: (Ch. I, XXV): T. Stcherbatsky. *Conception of Buddhist Nirvāṇa*. Leningrad: Office of the Academy of Sciences of the USSR, 1927; revised rpt. Delhi: Motilal Banarsidass, 1978, pp. 77-222. (Ch. II): Jeffrey Hopkins. "Analysis of Coming and Going." Dharamsala: Library of Tibetan Works and Archives, 1974. (partial): Mervyn Sprung. *Lucid Exposition of the Middle Way, the Essential Chapters from the P-*

rasannapadā of Candrakīrti translated from the Sanskrit. London: Routledge, 1979, and Boulder: Prajñā Press, 1979. French translations: (Ch. II-IV, VI-IX, XI, XXIII, XXIV, XXVI, XXVII): Jacques May. *Prasannapadā Madhyamaka-vṛtti, douze chapitres traduits du sanscrit et du tibétain*. Paris: Adrien-Maisonneuve, 1959. (Ch. XVIII-XXII): J.W. de Jong. *Cinq chapitres de la Prasannapadā*. Paris: Geuthner, 1949. (Ch. XVII): Étienne Lamotte. "Le Traité de l'acte de Vasubandhu, Karmasiddhiprakarana," MCB 4 (1936), 265-88. German translations: (Ch. V and XII-XVI): St. Schayer. *Ausgewählte Kapitel aus der Prasannapadā*. Krakow: Naktadem Polskiej Akademji Umiejetnosci, 1931. (Ch. X): St. Schayer. "Feuer und Brennstoff." *Rocznik Orjentalistyczny* 7 (1931): 26-52.

Commentary on (Āryadeva's) "Four Hundred Stanzas on the Yogic Deeds of Bodhisattvas" (*bodhisattvayogacaryācatuḥśatakaṭīkā, byang chub sems dpa'i rnal 'byor spyod pa gzhi brgya pa'i rgya cher 'grel pa*)
P 5266, vol. 98; Toh. 3865, Tokyo *sde dge*, vol. 8. Edited Sanskrit fragments: Haraprasād Shāstri, ed. "Catuḥśatika of Ārya Deva," Memoirs of the Asiatic Society of Bengal III, no. 8 (1914), pp. 449-514. Also (Ch. 8-16): Vidhusekhara Bhattacarya, ed. *The Catuḥśataka of Āryadeva: Sanskrit and Tibetan texts with copious extracts from the commentary of Candrakīrti*, part II. Calcutta: Visva-Bharati Bookshop, 1931.

Commentary on (Nāgārjuna's) "Seventy Stanzas on Emptiness" (*śūnyatāsaptativṛtti, stong pa nyid bdun cu pa'i 'grel pa*)
P 5268, vol. 99.

Commentary on (Nāgārjuna's) "Sixty Stanzas of Reasoning" (*yuktiṣaṣṭikāvṛtti, rigs pa drug cu pa'i grel pa*)
P 5265, vol. 98. Edited Tibetan: Louis de la Vallée Poussin. *Madhyamakāvatāra par Candrakīrti*. Bibliotheca Buddhica IX. Osnabrück: Biblio Verlag, 1970.
French translation: (up to VI.165): Louis de la Vallée Poussin. *Muséon* 8 (1907): 249-317; *Muséon* 11 (1910): 271-358; and *Muséon* 12 (1911): 235-328. German translation: (VI.166-226): Helmut Tauscher. *Candrakīrti-Madhyamakāvatāraḥ und Madhyamakāvatārabhāṣyam*. Wien: Wiener Studien zur Tibetologie und Buddhismuskunde, 1981.

Entrance to (Nāgārjuna's) "Treatise on the Middle Way" (*madhyamakāvatāra, dbu ma la 'jug pa*)
P 5261, P 5262, vol. 98. Also: New Delhi: Delhi Karmapae Chodhey Gyalwa Suagrab Partun Khang, n.d. Edited Tibetan: Louis de la Vallée Poussin. *Madhyamakāvatāra par Candrakīrti.* Bibliotheca Buddhica IX. Osnabrück: Biblio Verlag, 1970.
English translations: C. W. Huntington, *The Emptiness of Emptiness.* Honolulu: U. Hawaii, 1989. Peter Fenner, *The Ontology of the Middle Way.* Dordrecht: Kluwer, 1990. (Ch. I-V): Jeffrey Hopkins, *Compassion in Tibetan Buddhism.* Valois, NY: Gabriel / Snow Lion, 1980. (Ch. VI): Stephen Batchelor, trans., in Geshé Rabten's *Echoes of Voidness.* London: Wisdom, 1983, pp. 47-92. (Ch. VI, partial): Peter Fenner, "Candrakīrti's Refutation of Buddhist Idealism." In *Philosophy East and West* 33, #3 (July 1983).

Seventy Stanzas on the Three Refuges (*triśaraṇasaptati, gsum la skyabs su 'gro ba bdun cu pa*)
P 5366, vol. 103.

Chögyi Gyeltsen, Jaydzün (*rje btsun chos kyi rgyal mtshan*, 1469-1546, a.k.a. Sera Jaydzünba)

A Good Explanation Adorning the Throats of the Fortunate: A General Meaning Commentary Clarifying Difficult Points in (Dzongkaba's) "Illumination of the Thought: An Explanation of (Candrakīrti's) 'Entrance to (Nāgārjuna's) "Treatise on the Middle Way"'" (*bstan bcos dbu ma la 'jug pa'i rnam bshad dgongs pa rab gsal gyi dka' gnad gsal bar byed pa'i spyi don legs bshad skal bzang mgul rgyan*)
Collected Works, vol. ma. n.p.d. [Sera Jay College publication in India in early 1980s].

Presentation of Tenets (*grub mtha'i rnam gzhag*)
Bylakuppe: Se-ra Byes Grwa-tshaṅ, 1977.

Daktsang Shayrab Rinchen (*stag tshang lo tsā ba shes rab rin chen*, born 1405)
Freedom from Extremes through Understanding All Tenets (*grub mtha' kun shes nas mtha' bral grub pa*)
Thim-phu: Kun-bzang-stobs-rgyal, 1976.

Ocean of Good Explanations, Explanation of "Freedom from Extremes through Understanding All Tenets" (*grub mtha' kun shes nas mtha' bral grub pa zhes bya ba'i bstan bcos rnam par bshad pa legs bshad kyi rgya mtsho*)
Thimphu: Kun-bzang-stobs-rgyal, 1976.

Dharmakīrti (*chos kyi grags pa*, seventh century)

Commentary on (Dignāga's) "Compendium on Prime Cognition" (*pramāṇavārttikakārikā, tshad ma rnam 'grel gyi tshig le'ur byas pa*)
P 5709, vol. 13. Also: New Delhi: Delhi Karmapae Chodhey Gyalwa Suagrab Partun Khang, n.d. Also: Sarnath, India: Pleasure of Elegant Sayings Press, 1974. Sanskrit: Swami Dwarikadas Shastri, ed. *Pramāṇavārttika of Acharya Dharmakīrti*. Varanasi: Bauddha Bharati, 1968. Also: Miyasaka, Y., ed., *Pramāṇavārttika. Acta Indologica* #2-4.
Partial English translation: Vittorio A. van Bijlert, *Epistemology and Spiritual Authority: The Development of Epistemology and Logic in the Old Nyāya and the Buddhist School of Epistemology with an Annotated Translation of Dharmakīrti's Pramāṇavārttika II (Pramāṇasiddhi) VV. 1-7*. Wiener Studien zur Tibetologie und Buddhismuskunde, vol. 20. Wien: Arbeitskreis für Tibetische und Buddhistische Studien Universität Wien, 1989.

Dignāga (*phyogs-glang*, c. 480-540)

Compendium on Prime Cognition (*pramāṇasamuccaya, tshad ma kun las btus pa*)
P 5700, vol. 130.
Partial English translation by M. Hattori, *Dignāga, On Perception* (Cambridge: Harvard, 1968).

Drakba Saydrup (*grags pa bshad sgrub, co ne ba*, 1675-1748)

Condensed Essence of All Tenets (*grub mtha' thams cad kyi snying po bsdus pa*)
Delhi: May College of Sera, 1969.

Dzongkaba Losang Drakba (*tsong kha pa blo bzang grags pa*, 1357-1419)

The Essence of the Good Explanations, Treatise Differentiating the Interpretable and the Definitive (*drang ba dang nges pa'i don rnam par phye ba'i bstan bcos legs bshad snying po*)
P 6142, vol. 153. Also: Sarnath: Pleasure of Elegant Sayings Press, 1973 [on the cover in roman letters is *Dan-ne-leg-shed nying-po*].
English translation: Robert A. F. Thurman. *Tsong Khapa's Speech of Gold in the Essence of True Eloquence*. Princeton: Princeton University Press, 1984.

Explanation of the Eight Great Difficult Points of (Nāgārjuna's) "Fundamental Treatise on the Middle Way Called 'Wisdom'" (*rtsa pa shes rab kyi dka'gnas chen po brgyad kyi bshad pa*)
Sarnath: Pleasure of Elegant Sayings Press, 1970.

Extensive Commentary on the Difficult Points of the "Afflicted Mind and Basis-of-All," Ocean of Eloquence (*yid dang kun gzhi'i dka' ba'i gnas rgya cher 'grel pa legs par bshad pa'i rgya mtsho*)
Delhi: Lhalungpa, no date.

Golden Rosary of Eloquence / Extensive Explanation of (Maitreya's) "Treatise of Quintessential Instructions on the Perfection of Wisdom, Ornament for Clear Realization," As Well as Its Commentaries (*legs bshad gser gyi phreng ba / Shes rab kyi pha rol tu phyin pa'i man ngag gi bstan bcos mngon par rtogs pa'i rgyan 'grel pa dang bcas pa'i rgya cher bshad pa*)
P 6150, vol. 154.

Great Exposition of Special Insight (*lhag mthong chen mo*; part of *Great Exposition of the Stages of the Path*)
vol. 20 of *The Collected Works of Rje Tsoṅ-kha-pa Blo-bzaṅ-grags-pa*. New Delhi: Ngawang Gelek Demo, 1977. Also: Sarnath: Pleasure of Elegant Sayings Press, 1975.
Partial English translations: Elizabeth Napper, *Dependent-Arising and Emptiness*. London: Wisdom, 1988. (Parts on calm abiding and special insight:) Alex Wayman in *Calming the Mind and Discerning the Real*. New York: Columbia University Press, 1978; reprint New Delhi: Motilal Banarsidass, 1979. (Portion on Bodhisattva deeds:) Alex Wayman,

Ethics of Tibet. Albany: State University of New York Press, 1992.

Great Exposition of the Stages of the Path / Stages of the Path to Enlightenment Thoroughly Teaching All the Stages of Practice of the Three Types of Beings (*lam rim chen no / skyes bu gsum gyi rnyams su blang ba'i rim pa thams cad tshang bar ston pa'i byang chub lam gyi rim pa*)

P 6001, vol. 152. Also: Dharamsala: Shes rig par khang, 1964. Also: Delhi: Ngawang Gelek, 1975.

English translations: see *Great Exposition of Special Insight*.

Illumination of the Thought, Extensive Explanation of (Candrakīrti's) "Entrance to (Nāgārjuna's) 'Treatise on the Middle Way'" (*dbu ma la 'jug pa'i rgya cher bshad pa dgongs pa rab gsal*)

P 6143, vol. 154. Also: Dharamsala: Shes rig par khang. Also: Sarnath, India: Pleasure of Elegant Sayings Press, 1973. Also: The Collected Works (*gsuṅ 'bum*) of the Incomparable Lord Tsoṅ-kha-pa Blo-bzaṅ-grags-pa, vol. 16 *ma* (photographic reprint of the "1897 old żol [*dga'-ldan-phun-tshogs-gliṅ*] blocks"). New Delhi: Guru Deva, 1979 .

English translations: (first five chapters): Jeffrey Hopkins in *Compassion in Tibetan Buddhism*. Valois, New York: Snow Lion, 1980. (Portion of chapter six:) Anne Klein and Jeffrey Hopkins in *Path to the Middle*. Albany: State University of New York Press, 1994.

Middling Exposition of the Stages of the Path / Small Exposition of the Stages of the Path To Enlightenment (*lam rim 'bring / lam rim chung ngu*)

P 6002, vol. 152-53. Also: Dharamsala: Shes rig par khang, 1968. Also: Mundgod: Ganden Shardzay, n.d. (edition including outline of topics by Trijang Rinbochay).

English translations: (Section on special insight): by Robert Thurman, "The Middle Transcendent Insight" in *Life and Teachings of Tsong Khapa*. Dharamsala: Library of Tibetan Works and Archives, 1982, pp. 108-85; and by Jeffrey Hopkins, "Special Insight: From Dzongkaba's *Middling Exposition of the Stages of the Path to Enlightenment Practiced by Persons of Three Capacities* with supplementary headings by Trijang Rinbochay," unpublished manuscript.

Ocean of Reasoning, Explanation of (Nāgārjuna's) "Treatise on the Middle Way" / Great Commentary on (Nāgārjuna's) "Treatise on the Middle Way" (*dbu ma rtsa ba'i tshig le'ur byas pa shes rab ces bya ba'i rnam bshad rigs pa'i rgya mtsho*)

P 6153, vol. 156. Also, Sarnath, India: Pleasure of Elegant Sayings Printing Press, no date. Also: in rje *tsong kha pa'i gsung dbu ma'i lta ba'i skor*, vol. 1 and 2, Sarnath, India: Pleasure of Elegant Sayings Press, 1975.

In Praise of Dependent-Arising / Praise of the Supramundane Victor Buddha from the Approach of His Teaching the Profound Dependent-Arising, Essence of the Good Explanations (*rten 'brel bstod pa / sang rgyas bcom ldan 'das la zab mo rten cing 'brel bar 'byung ba gsung ba'i sgo nas bstod pa legs par bshad pa'i snying po*)

P 6016, vol. 153.

English translations: (with translation into Sanskrit and edited Tibetan): Gyaltsen Namdol and Ngawang Samten, *Pratītyasamutpādastutisubhāṣitahṛdayam of Ācarya Tsoṅkhāpā*. Dalai Lama's Tibeto-Indological Series, vol. 3. Sarnath: Central Institute of Higher Tibetan Studies, 1982. Geshe Wangyal, *The Door of Liberation*. Boston: Wisdom, 1995 (revised edition). Robert Thurman. in *Life and Teachings of Tsong Khapa*. Dharamsala: Library of Tibetan Works and Archives, 1982, pp. 99-107.

The Three Principal Aspects of the Path (*lam gtso rnam gsum / tsha kho dpon po ngag dbang grags pa la gdams pa*)

P 6087, vol. 153.

English translations: Geshe Wangyal, *The Door of Liberation*. Boston: Wisdom, 1995. Geshe Sopa and Jeffrey Hopkins, *Practice and Theory of Tibetan Buddhism*. New York: Grove Press, 1976, pp. 1-47. Jeffrey Hopkins, including commentary from the Dalai Lama, in Tenzin Gyatso's *Kindness, Clarity, and Insight*. Ithaca: Snow Lion, 1984, pp. 118-56. Robert Thurman in *Life and Teachings of Tsong Khapa*. Dharamsala, Library of Tibetan Works and Archives, 1982, pp. 57-58.

Gendün Gyatso, Dalai Lama II (*dge 'dun rgya mtsho*, 1476-1542)

Ship For Entering the Ocean of Tenets (*grub mtha' rgya mtshor 'jug pa'i gru rdzings*)

Vāranāsi: Ye shes stobs ldan, 1969.

Gendün Chöpel (*dge 'dun chos 'phel*, 1905?-1951?)

Ornament to Nāgārjuna's Thought, Eloquence Containing the Essence of the Profundities of the Middle Way (*dbu ma'i zab gnad snying pr dril ba'i legs bshad klu sgrub dgongs rgyan*)
Kalimpong: Mani Printing Works, no date.

Gomday Namka Gyeltsen (*sgom sde nam mkha' rgyal mtshan*, 1532-92)

Settling Difficult Points in the Opposite of the Consequences, Key to (Candrakīrti's) "Clear Words," Written by Jam-bay-yang Gom-day Nam-ka-gyel-tsen (*thal Bzlog gi dka' ba gnas gtan la 'bebs pa 'jam pa'i dbyang sgom sde nam mkha' rgyal mtshan gyis mdzad pa'i tshig gsal gyi lde mig*)
In *The Obligatory Texts (Yigcha) for the Study of Madhyamika of Byes Grwa-tshaṅ of Se-ra Monastery*. Madhyamika Text Series, vol. 4. New Delhi: Lha-mkhar yons-'dzin bstan-pa-rgyal-mtshan, 1973.

Gönchok Denbay Drönmay (*dkon mchog bstan pa'i sgron me*, 1762-1823)

Beginnings of Annotations on (Dzongkaba's) "The Essence of the Good Explanations" on the Topic of Mind-Only, Illumination of a Hundred Mind-Only Texts (*bstan bcos legs par bshad pa'i snying po las sems tsam skor gyi mchan 'grel rtsom 'phro rnam rig gzhung brgya'i snang ba*)
Tibetan blockprint in the possession of HH the Dalai Lama; no other data.

Explanation of the Difficult Points of (Dzongkaba's) "Afflicted Mentality and Mind-Basis-of-All," Entrance for the Wise (*yid dang kun gzhi'i dka' gnad rnam par bshad pa mkhas pa'i 'jug ngogs*)
Musoorie: Gomang College, no other data.

Gönchok Jikmay Wangbo (*dkon mchog 'jigs med dbang po*, 1728-91)

Precious Garland of Tenets / Presentation of Tenets, A Precious Garland (*grub pa'i mtha'i rnam par bzhag pa rin po che'i phreng ba*)
Dharamsala: Shes rig par khang, 1969.
English translations: Sopa and Hopkins in *Cutting through Appearances*. Ithaca: Snow Lion, 1989 (second edition of *Practice and Theory of Tibetan Buddhism*). H. V. Guenther, *Buddhist Philosophy in Theory and Practice*. Baltimore: Penguin, 1972.

Presentation of the Grounds and Paths, Beautiful Ornament of the Three Vehicles (*sa lam gyi rnam bzhag theg gsum mdzes rgyan*)
Buxaduor: Gomang College, 1965. Also: *The Collected Works of dkon-mchog-'jigs-med-dbang-po*, vol. 7. New Delhi: Ngawang Gelek Demo, 1972.

Gungtang—see Gönchok Denbay Drönmay

Gyeltsap Dharma Rinchen (*rgyal tshab dar ma rin chen*, 1364-1432)

Commentary on (Maitreya's) "Sublime Continuum of the Great Vehicle" (*theg pa chen po rgyud bla ma'i ṭīka*)
Collected Works (gsuṅ 'bum) of Rgyal-shab rje Dar-ma-rin-chen, vol. 3 (New Delhi: Ngawang Gelek Demo, 1981).

Eight Great Difficult Points of (Nāgārjuna's) "Treatise on the Middle Way" (*dbu ma'i rtsa ba'i dka' gnas chen po brgyad*)
Collected Works (gsuṅ 'bum) of Rgyal-tshab rje Dar-ma-rin-chen (New Delhi: Ngawang Gelek Demo, 1981), vol. 1. Also Pleasure of Elegant Sayings (Varanasi: 1973).

Explanation of (Śāntideva's) "Engaging in the Bodhisattva Deeds": Entrance of Conqueror Children (*byang chub sems dpa'i spyod pa la 'jug pa'i rnam bshad rgyal sras 'jug ngogs*)
Collected Works (gsuṅ 'bum) of Rgyal-tshab rje Dar-ma-rin-chen (New Delhi: Lama Guru Deva, 1982), vol. 4. Also: *Collected Works (gsuṅ 'bum) of Rgyal-tshab rje Dar-ma-rin-chen* (New Delhi: Ngawang Gelek Demo, 1981), vol. 3. Also: Pleasure of Elegant Sayings (Varanasi: 1973).

Notes on the Eight Great Difficult Points, Preventing Forgetfulness of the Foremost One's Speech (*dka' gnas brgyad gyi zin bris rje'i gsung bzhin brjed byang du bkod pa bcugs*)
Collected Works of Rje Tsoṅ-khapa Blo-bzaṅ-grags-pa (New Delhi: Ngawang Gelek Demo, 1975 -), vol. 23.

Jambel Sampel (*'jam dpal bsam 'phel*, ?-1975)

Presentation of Awareness and Knowledge, Composite of All the Important Points, Opener of the Eye of New Intelligence (*blo rig gi rnam bzhag nyer mkho kun 'dus blo gsar mig 'byed*)
Modern blockprint, no publication data, no date; reprinted in Lati Rinbochay and Napper.
English translation: Lati Rinbochay and Elizabeth Napper, *Mind in Tibetan Buddhism*. Valois, NY: Snow Lion, 1980.

Jambel Trinlay Yönden Gyatso (*'jam dpal 'phrin las yon tan rgya mtsho*)

Festival for the Wise, Good Explanation Collecting All Points of the Collected Topics (*bsdus grwa'i don kun bsdus pa legs bshad mkhas pa'i dga' ston*)
Mundgod, India: Drepung Loseling Printing Press, 1978.

Jamyang Shayba Ngawang Dzöndrü (*'jam dbyangs bzhad pa ngag dbang brtson 'grus*, 1648-1721)

Great Exposition of the Concentrations and Formless Absorptions / Treatise on the Presentations of the Concentrations and Formless Absorptions, Adornment Beautifying the Subduer's Teaching, Ocean of Scripture and Reasoning, Delighting the Fortunate (*bsam gzugs kyi snyons 'jug rnams kyi rnam par bzhag pa'i bstan bcos thub bstan mdzes rgyan lung dang rigs pa'i rgya mtsho skal bzang dga' byed*)
Folio printing in India; no publication data.

Great Exposition of the Middle Way / Analysis of (Candrakīrti's) "Entrance to (Nāgārjuna's) 'Treatise on the Middle Way,'" Treasury of Scripture and Reasoning, Thoroughly Illuminating the Profound Meaning [of Emptiness], Entrance for the Fortunate (*dbu ma chen no / dbu ma 'jug pa'i mtha' dpyod lung rigs gter mdzod zab don kun gsal skal bzang 'jug ngogs*)

Collected Works of 'Jam-dbyaṅs-bzad-pa'i-rdo-rje, vol. 9. New Delhi: Ngawang Gelek Demo, 1973. (Drashikyil edition). Also: Buxaduor: Gomang, 1967.

English translation (section on two truths): Guy Newland, "The Two Truths: A Study of Mādhyamika Philosophy as Presented in the Monastic Textbooks of the Ge-luk-ba Order of Tibetan Buddhism." Dissertation, University of Virginia, 1988.

Great Exposition of Tenets / Explanation of "Tenets," Sun of the Land of Samantabhadra Brilliantly Illuminating All of Our Own and Others' Tenets and the Meaning of the Profound [Emptiness], Ocean of Scripture and Reasoning Fulfilling All Hopes of All Beings (*grub mtha' chen mo / grub mtha'i rnam bshad rang gzhan grub mtha' kin dang zab don mchog tu gsal ba kun bzang zhing gi nyi ma lung rigs rgya mtsho skye dgu'i re ba kun skong*)

Mundgod: Gomang, n.d. (Drashikyil edition). Also: *Collected Works of 'Jam-dbyaṅs-bzad-pa'i-rdo-rje*. New Delhi: Ngawang Gelek Demo, 1973. Also: Musoorie: Dalama, 1962.

English translations: (beginning of the Prāsaṅgika chapter): Jeffrey Hopkins in *Meditation on Emptiness*. London: Wisdom, 1983. (Portion of Prāsaṅgika chapter): present volume.

Presentation of Tenets, Roar of the Five-Faced [Lion] Eradicating Error, Precious Lamp Illuminating the Good Path to Omniscience (*grub mtha'i rnam par bzhag pa 'khrul spong gdong lnga'i sgra dbyangs kun mkhyen lam bzang gsal ba'i rin chen sgron me*)

Folio printing in India; no publication data.

Janggya Rolbay Dorjay (*lcang skya rol pa'i rdo rje* II, 1717-86)

Presentation of Tenets / Clear Exposition of the Presentations of Tenets, Beautiful Ornament for the Meru of the Subduer's Teaching (*grub mtha'i rnam bzhag / grub pa'i mtha'i rnam par bzhag pa gsal bar bshad pa thub bstan lhun po'i mdzes rgyan*)

Varanasi: Pleasure of Elegant Sayings Printing Press, 1970. Also: an edition published by gam bcar phan bde legs bshad gling grva tshang dang rgyud rnying slar gso tshogs pa, in the royal year 2109 [n.d]. Also: *Buddhist Philosophical Systems of Lcaṅ-skya Rol-pahi Rdo-rje*. Edited by Lokesh Chandra.

Çata-piṭaka Series (Indo-Asian Literatures), vol. 233. New Delhi, 1977.

English translation: (Sautrāntika chapter): translated by Anne C. Klein, "Mind and Liberation: The Sautrāntika Tenet System in Tibet." Ann Arbor: University Microfilms, 1981. Anne C. Klein, *Knowing, Naming and Negation*. Ithaca: Snow Lion, 1988. (Svātantrika chapter): Donald S. Lopez, Jr., *A Study of Svātantrika*. Ithaca: Snow Lion, 1987. (Partial translation of Prāsaṅgika chapter): Jeffrey Hopkins in *Emptiness Yoga*. Ithaca: Snow Lion, 1987. (Portion of Prāsaṅgika chapter): present volume.

Jñānaśrībhadra (*ye-shes-dpal-bzang-po*)

Commentary on the "Descent into Laṅkā" (*laṅkāvatāravṛtti, lang-kar gshegs pa'i grel pa*)
P 5519, vol. 107.

Jñānavajra (*ye-shes-rdo-rje*)

Commentary on the "Descent into Laṅkā Sūtra," Ornament of the Heart of the Tathāgata (*laṅkāvatāranāmamahāyānasūtra-vṛttitathāgatahṛdayākaṅkāra, langkar gshegs pa zhes bya ba theg pa chen po'i mdo'i 'grel pa de bzhim gshegs pa'i snying po'i rgyan*)
P5520, vol. 107.

Kamalaśīla (eighth century)

Commentary on the Difficult Points of (Śāntarakṣita's) "Compendium on Suchness" (*tattvasaṃgrahapañjikā, de kho na nyid bsdus pa'i dka' 'grel*)
P 5765, vol. 138. Sanskrit edition: Dwarikadas Shastri (ed.), *Tattvasaṃgraha, with the Commentary 'Pañjikā' of Śrī Kamalaśīla*. 2 vols. Varanasi: Bauddha Bharati.

English translation: G. Jha, *The Tattvasaṅgraha of Çāntarakṣita with the Commentary of Kamalaśīla*, Gaekwad's Oriental Series, vols. 80 and 83 (Baroda: 1937-39).

Illumination of the Middle Way (*madhyamakāloka, dbu ma snang ba*)
P 5287, vol. 101.

Kaydrup Gelek Belsangbo (*mkhas sgrub dge legs dpal bzang po,* 1385-1438)

General Presentation of the Sets of Tantras, Detailed Explanation (*rgyud sde spyi'i rnam par gzag pa rgyas par bshad pa*)
English translatlon: Ferdinand Lessing and Alex Wayman. *Introduction to the Buddhist Tantric Systems.* The Hague, 1968. Rpt. Delhi: Motilal Banarsidass, 1978.

Thousand Dosages / Opening the Eyes of the Fortunate, Treatise Brilliantly Clarifying the Profound Emptiness (*stong thun chen no / zab no stong pa nyid rab tu gsal bar byed pa'i bstan bcos skal bzang mig 'byed*)
Stoṅ Thun Chen Mo of Mkhas-Grub Dge-Legs-Dpal-Bzaṅ and Other Texts on Madhyamika Philosophy: Madhyamika Text Series, vol. 1, ed. by Lha-mkhar Yoṅs-dzin Bstanpa Rgyal Mtshan. New Delhi, 1972 (no other data). Also: *The Collected Works of the Lord Mkhas-grub rje dge-legs-dpal-bzaṅ-po,* vol. 1, 179-702. New Delhi: Mongolian Lama Gurudeva, 1980. Also: Toh. 5459.
English translation: José Ignatio Cabezón. *A Dose of Emptiness.* Albany: State University of New York Press, 1992.

Longchen Rapjam (*klong chen rab 'byams / klong chen dri med 'od zer,* 1308-63)

Treasury of Tenets, Illuminating the Meaning of All Vehicles (*theg pa mtha' dag gi don gsal bar byed pa grub pa'i mtha' rin po che'i mdzod*)
Gangtok: Dodrup Chen Rinpoche, 1969[?].

Precious Treasury of the Supreme Vehicle (*theg pa'i mchog rin po che'i mdzod*)
Gangtok: Dodrup Chen Rinpoche, 1969[?].

Losang Dayang (*blo bzang rta dbyangs,* also known as *blo bzang rta mgrin,* 1867-1937)

Brief Expression of the Presentation of the Grounds and Paths of the Three Vehicles According to the System of the Perfection Vehicle, Essence of the Ocean of Profound Meaning (*phar phyin theg pa'i lugs kyi theg pa sum gyi sa dang lam gyi rnam bzhag pa mdo tsam du brjod pa zab don rgya mtsho'i snying po*)

Collected Works (Gsun 'Bum) of Rje-Btsun Blo-bzan-Rta-Mgrin, vol. IV, pp. 65-190. New Delhi: Lama Guru Deva, 1975.

Losang Gönchok *(blo bzang dkon mchog)*

Word Commentary on the Root Text of (Jamyang Shayba's) "Tenets," Clear Crystal Mirror *(grub mtha' rtsa ba'i tshig tik shel dkar me long)*

Part of *Three Commentaries on the "Grub Mtha' Rtsa Ba Gdon Lṅa'i Sgra Dbyaṅs" of 'Jam-Dbyaṅs-Bzad-Pa'i-Rdo-Rje Ṅag-Dbaṅ-Brston-'Grus.* Delhi: Chophel Legden, 1978.

Maitreya *(byams pa)*

-

Discrimination of Phenomena and the Nature of Phenomena *(dharmadharmatāvibhaṅga, chos dang chos nyid rnam par 'byed pa)*

P 5523, vol. 108.

Discrimination of the Middle Way and the Extremes (*madhyāntavibhaṅga dbus dang mtha' rnam par 'byed pa*)

P 5522, vol. 108. Sanskrit text: *Madhyānta-Vibhāga-Çāstra,* ed. Ramchandra Pandeya, Delhi: Motilal Banarsidass, 1971.

Partial English translation: T. Stcherbatsky, *Madhyānta-Vibhaṅga* (Calcutta: Indian Studies Past and Present, 1971). German translation: (chap. 1): Erich Frauwallner, *Die Philosophie Buddhismus.* Berlin: 1958, pp. 324-26.

Ornament for the Mahāyāna Sūtras (*mahāyānasūtralaṃkārakārikā, theg pa chen po'i mdo sde'i rgyan gyi tshig le' ur byas pa*)

P 5521, vol. 108.

English translation: (partial): W. T. DeBary, *The Buddhist Tradition.* New York: Random, 1972, pp. 94-95. Dutch translation: (partial): J. Ensink, *De grote weg naar het licht.* Amsterdam: 1973. German translation: (partial): Erich Frauwallner, *Die Philosophie Buddhismus.* Berlin: 1958, pp. 309-20.

Ornament for Clear Realization *(abhisamayālaṃkāra, mngon par rtogs pa'i rgyan)*

P 5184, vol. 88.

English translations: E. Conze, *Abhisamayālaṅkāra,* Series Orientale Roma VI (Rome: IS.M.E.O., July 1954); and by E. Obermiller, *Analysis of the Abhisamayālaṃkāra* (Calcutta

Oriental Series, no. 27, fasc. I, II, III, London: Luzac & Co. 1933, 1936, and 1943).

Sublime Continuum of the Mahāyāna (*mahāyānottaratantraśāstra theg pa chen po rgyud bla ma'i bstan bcos*)

P 5525, vol. 108. Sanskrit edition: E. H. Johnston, *Ratnagotra-vibhāga-Mahāyānottaratantraśāstra*. Patna Jayaswal Institute, 1950.

English translation: E. Obermiller, *Sublime Science of the Great Vehicle to Salvation* (Acta Orientalia, XI, ii,iii, and iv; reprint Talent, OR: Canon Publications, 1984). J. Takasaki, A *Study on the Ratnagotra-vibhāga* (Rome: I.S.M.E.O., 1966). Ken and Katia Holmes, *The Changeless Nature*. Eskdalemuir, Scotland: Kagyu Samye Ling Tibetan Centre, 1979; 2nd ed. 1985. (Verses #126, 169, 185): Edward Conze, *Buddhist Texts Through the Ages*. Oxford: Cassirer, 1954; New York: Harper & Row, 1964. German translations: (Verses 160, 176): Edward Conze, *Im Zeichen Buddhas: Buddhistische Texte*. Frankfurt: Fischer, 1957. Erich Frauwallner, *Die Philosophie Buddhismus*. Berlin: 1958, pp. 258-64.

Nāgārjuna (*klu sgrub*, first to second century, C.E.)

Commentary on "Seventy Stanzas on Emptiness" (*śūnyatāsaptati-vṛtti, stong pa nyid bdun cu pa'i 'grel pa*)

P 5231, vol. 95. Tibetan edition: Christian Lindtner, *Master of Wisdom*. Oakland: Dharma Publications, 1986, pp. 176-206.

Essay on the Mind of Enlightenment (*bodhicittavivarana byang chub sems kyi 'grel pa*)

P 2665, vol. 61; P 2666, vol. 61.

English translation: (with edited Tibetan and Sanskrit fragments): Christian Lindtner, *Master of Wisdom*. Oakland: Dharma Publications, 1986, pp. 32-71, 172-73.

Praise of the Supramundane [Buddha] (*lokātītastava, 'jig rten las 'das par bstod pa*)

P 2012, vol. 46. Edited Tibetan and Sanskrit along with English translation: Christian Lindtner in *Master of Wisdom*. Oakland: Dharma Publications, 1986, pp. 2-11, 158-62 and in *Nagarjuniana*. Indiske Studier 4, pp. 121-38. Copenhagen: Akademisk Forlag, 1982.

Precious Garland of Advice for the King (*rājaparikathāratnāvalī, rgyal po la gtam bya ba rin po che'i phreng ba*)
P 5658, vol. 129. Edited Sanskrit, Tibetan, and Chinese: *Nāgārjuna's Ratnāvalī, vol. 1, The Basic Texts (Sanskrit, Tibetan, and Chinese)*. Michael Hahn, ed. Bonn: Indica et Tibetica Verlag, 1982.
English translation: Jeffrey Hopkins in Nāgārjuna and the Seventh Dalai Lama, *The Precious Garland and the Song of the Four Mindfulnesses*. New York: Harper and Row, 1975.

Refutation of Objections (*vigrahavyāvartanīkārikā, rtsod pa bzlog pa'i tshig le'ur byas pa*)
P 5228, vol. 95. Tibetan and Sanskrit editions: Christian Lindtner, *Master of Wisdom*. Oakland: Dharma Publications, 1986, pp. 207-29.
English translation: K. Bhattacharya, *The Dialectical Method of Nāgārjuna*. Delhi: Motilal, 1978.

Seventy Stanzas on Emptiness (*śūnyatasaptatikārikā, stong pa nyid bdun cu pa'i tshig le'ur byas pa*)
P 5227, vol. 95. English translation with Tibetan edition: Christian Lindtner, *Master of Wisdom*. Oakland: Dharma Publications, 1986, pp. 94-119. Edited Tibetan and English translation: Christian Lindtner. In *Nagarjuniana*. Indiske Studier 4: 34-69. Copenhagen: Akademisk Forlag, 1982.
English translation: David Komito, *Nāgārjuna's "Seventy Stanzas."* Ithaca: Snow Lion, 1987.

Sixty Stanzas of Reasoning (*yuktiṣaṣṭikākārikā, rigs pa drug cu pa'i tshig le'ur byas pa*)
P 5225, vol. 95; Toh. 3825, Tokyo *sde dge*, vol. I. Also: New Delhi: Delhi Karmapae Chodhey Gyalwa Suagrab Partun Khang, n.d.
English translation: (with edited Tibetan with Sanskrit fragments): Christian Lindtner in *Master of Wisdom*. Oakland: Dharma Publications, 1986, pp. 72-93, 174-75, and in *Nagarjuniana*. Indiske Studier 4, pp. 100-19. Copenhagen: Akademisk Forlag, 1982.

Treatise Called "The Finely Woven" (*vaidalyasūtranāma, zhib mo rnam par 'thag pa zhes bya ba'i mdo*)
P 5226, vol. 95.

Treatise on the Middle Way / Fundamental Treatise on the Middle Way, Called "Wisdom" (*madhyamakaśāstra / prajñānāmamūlamadhyamakākarikā, dbu ma'i bstan bcos / dbu ma rtsa ba'i tshig le'ur byas pa shes rab ces bya ba*)

P 5224, vol. 95. Also: New Delhi: Delhi Karmapae Chodhey Gyalwa Suagrab Partun Khang, n.d. Edited Sanskrit: *Nāgārjuna. Mūlamadhyamakakārikāḥ.* J. W. de Jong, ed. Adyar: Adyar Library and Research Centre, 1977. Also: Christian Lindtner in *Nāgārjuna's Filosofiske Vaerker.* Indiske Studier 2: 177-215. Copenhagen: Akademisk Forlag, 1982.

English translations: Frederick Streng. *Emptiness: A Study in Religious Meaning.* Nashville, New York: Abingdon Press, 1967. Kenneth Inada. *Nāgārjuna: A Translation of his Mūlamadhyamakakārikā.* Tokyo, The Hokuseido Press, 1970. David J. Kalupahana. *Nāgārjuna: The Philosophy of the Middle Way.* Albany: State University Press of New York, 1986. Italian translation: R. Gnoli. *Nāgārjuna: Madhyamaka Kārikā, Le stanze del cammino di mezzo.* Enciclopedia di autori classici 61. Turin: P. Boringhieri, 1961. Danish translation: Christian Lindtner in *Nāgārjuna's Filosofiske Vaerker.* Indiske Studier 2: 67-135. Copenhagen: Akademisk Forlag, 1982.

Ngawang Belden (*ngag dbang dpal ldan,* b. 1797, a.k.a. Belden Chöjay)

Annotations for (Jamyang Shayba's) "Great Exposition of Tenets," Freeing the Knots of the Difficult Points, Precious Jewel of Clear Thought (*grub mtha' chen mo'i mchan 'grel dka' gnad mdud grol blo gsal gces nor*)

Sarnath: Pleasure of Elegant Sayings Press, 1964. Also: *Collected Works of Chos-rje ṅag-dbaṅ-dpal-ldan of Urga,* vol. II. Delhi: Mongolian Lama Guru Deva, 1983.

Partial English translation (portion of annotations on Prāsaṅgika chapter): in present volume.

Belden Chöjay's Partial Statement of a Word Commentary on the Root Verses (of Jamyang Shayba's "Tenets") Done on the Occasion of the Annotations on (Jamyang Shayba's) "Great Exposition of Tenets" (*dpal ldan chos rjes grub mtha' chen mo'i mchan 'grel gyi skabs su mdzad pa'i rtsa ba'i tshig 'grel zur du bkod pa*)

Collected Works of Chos-rje ṅag-dbaṅ-dpal-ldan of Urga, vol. III. Delhi: Mongolian Lama Guru Deva, 1984. Also: part of

Three Commentaries on the "Grub Mtha' Rtsa Ba Gdoṅ Lṅa'i Sgra Dbyaṅs" of 'Jam-Dbyaṅs-Bzad-Pa'i Rdo-Rje Ṅag-Dbaṅ-Brston-'Grus. Delhi: Chophel Legden, 1978.

Eliminating Doubts With Respect to the Meaning of (Vasubandhu's) "Treasury of Higher Knowledge," An Enjoyment for Those of New Intelligence *(mngon pa mdzod kyi don la 'dogs pa bcad pa blo gsar rol rtsed)*
Collected Works of Chos-rje ṅag-dbaṅ-dpal-ldan of Urga, vol. III. Delhi: Mongolian Lama Guru Deva, 1983.

Explanation of the Conventional and the Ultimate in the Four Systems of Tenets *(grub mtha' bzhi'i lugs kyi kun rdzog dang don dam pa'i don rnam par bshad pa legs bshad dpyid kyi dpal moi' glu dbyangs)*
Collected Works of Chos-rje ṅag-dbaṅ-dpal-ldan of Urga, vol. I. Delhi: Mongolian Lama Guru Deva, 1983.

Stating the Mode of Explanation in the Textbooks on the Middle Way and the Perfection of Wisdom In the Loseling and Gomang Colleges: Festival For Those of Clear Intelligence *(blo gsal gling dang bkra shis sgo mang grva tshang gi dbu phar gyi yig cha'i bshad tshul bkod pa blo gsal dga' ston)*
Collected Works of Chos-rje ṅag-dbaṅ-dpal-ldan of Urga, vol. III. Delhi: Mongolian Lama Guru Deva, 1983.

Ngawang Losang Gyatso *(ngag dbang blo bzang rgya mtsho,* Fifth Dalai Lama, 1617-82)

Sacred Word of Mañjusrī, Instructions on the Stages of the Path to Enlightenment *(byang chub lam gyi rim pa'i khrid yig 'jam pa'i dbyangs kyi zhal lung)*
Thimphu, Bhutan: kun bzang stobs rgyal, 1976.
English translation: ("Perfection of Wisdom" chapter): Jeffrey Hopkins, *Practice of Emptiness.* Dharamsala Library of Tibetan Works and Archives, 1974.

Paṇchen Sönam Drakba *(pan chen bsod nams grags pa,* 1478-1554)

General Meaning of (Maitreya's) "Ornament for Clear Realization" *(phar phyin spyi don / shes rab kyi pha rol tu phyin pa'i man ngag gi bstan bcos mngon par rtogs pa'i rgyan 'grel pa dang bcas*

pa'i rnam bshad snying po rgyan gyi don legs par bshad pa yum don gsal ba'i sgron me)
Buxaduor: Nang bstan shes rig 'dzin skyong slob gnyer khang, 1963.

Prajñamokṣha (*shes rab thar pa*)

Commentary on (Atīśa's) "Quintessential Instructions on the Middle Way" (*madhyamakopadeśavṛtti, dbu ma'i man ngag ces bya ba'i grel pa*)
P 5327, vol. 102.

Explanation of (Śāntideva's) "Engaging in the Bodhisattva Deeds" (*byang chub sems dpa'i spyod pa la 'jug pa'i bshad pa*)
P 5872, vol. 146.

Rabten, Geshé

Annotations for the Difficult Points of (Dzong-ka-ba's) "The Essence of the Good Explanations," Joyous Festival for the Unbiased with Clear Awareness (*drang nges rham 'byed legs bshad snying po dka' gnad rnams mchan bur bkod pa gzur gnas blo gsal dga' ston*)
n.p.d. [edition in India in the early 1970s].

Rongta Losang Tamchö Gyatso (*rong tha blo gzang dam chos rgya mtsho*, 1863-1917)

Mode of Asserting the Unique Tenets of the Glorious Prāsaṅgikas, A Few Letters of Beginning, Moonlight by Which the Intelligent Distinguish Errors (*dpal ldan bhal 'gyur ba'i thun mong ma yin pa'i bzhed tshul las brtsams pa'i yi ge nyung du blo gros kun da 'byed pa'i zla 'od*)
Collected Works of Blo-gzaṅ Dam-chos-rgya-mtsho, vol. 2. New Delhi: ??

Śāntarakṣita (*zhi ba 'tsho*, eighth century)

Compendium of Suchness (*tattvasamgrahakārikā, de kho na nyid bsdus pa'i tshig le'ur byas pa*)
P 5764. Sanskrit edition: Dwarikadas Shastri (ed.), *Tattvasaṃgraha, with the Commentary 'Pañjikā' of Śrī Kamalaśīla*. 2 vols. Varanasi: Bauddha Bharati.

English translation: G. Jha, *The Tattvasamgraha of Çāntarakṣita with the Commentary of Kamalaśīla*. Gaekwad's Oriental Series, vols. 80 & 83. Baroda 1937-39.

Śāntideva

Compendium of Learnings (*śikṣāsamuccayakārikā bslab pa kun las btus pai' tshig le'ur byas pa*)
P 5336, vol. 102.
English translation: C. Bendall and W. H. D. Rouse, *Cikṣā Samuccaya*. Delhi: Motilal Banarsidass, 1971.

Engaging in the Bodhisattva Deeds (*bodhisattvacaryāvatāra byang chub sems dpa'i spyod pa la 'jug pa*)
P 5272, vol. 99. Sanskrit and Tibetan edition: *Bodhicaryāvatāra*. Vidhushekhara Bhattacharya, ed. Calcutta: The Asiatic Society, 1960.
English translations: Stephen Batchelor. A *Guide to the Bodhisattva's Way of Life*. Dharamsala: LTWA, 1979. Marion Matics. *Entering the Path of Enlightenment*. New York: Macmillan, 1970. Contemporary commentary: Geshe Kelsang Gyatso. *Meaningful to Behold*. London: Wisdom, 1980.

Shamar Gendün Dendzin Gyatso (*zhwa dmar dge bdun bstan 'dzin rgya mtsho*, 1852-1910)

Lamp Illuminating the Profound Thought, Set Forth to Purify Forgetfulness of the Difficult Points of (Dzong-ka-ba's) "Great Exposition of Special Insight" (*lhag mthong chen mo'i dka' gnad rnams brjed byang du bkod pa dgongs zab snang ba'i sgron me*)
Delhi: Mongolian Lama Guru Deva, 1972.

Tomay Sangbo (*thogs med bzang po*)

Commentary on (Śāntideva's) "Engaging in the Bodhisattva Deeds," Ocean of Good Explanations (*byang chub sems dpa'i spyod pa la 'jug pa'i 'grel pa legs par bshad pai' rgya mtsho*)
Sarnath: Pleasure of Elegant Sayings Press, 1974.

Tügen Losang Chögyi Nyima (*thu'u bkvan blo bzang chos kyi nyi ma*, 1737-1802)

Mirror of the Good Explanations Showing the Sources and Assertions of All Systems of Tenets (*grub mtha' thams cad kyi khungs dang 'dod tshul ston pa legs bshad shel gyi me long*)
Sarnath: Chos Je Lama, 1963.
English translation of section on non-Buddhist and Indian Buddhist systems: K. K. Mittal, *A Tibetan Eye-View of Indian Philosophy*. Delhi: Munshiram Manoharlal, 1984.

Üba Losel (*dbus pa blo gsal*, fourteenth century)

Treasury of the Presentation of Tenets (*grub pa'i mtha' rnam par bzhad pa'i mdzod*)
Thimphu: Kunzang Tobgyel and Mani Dorji, 1979. Edition of Vaibhāṣika and Yogācāra chapters and edition and French translation of Mādhyamika chapter: Katsumi Mimaki, *Blo Gsal Grub Mtha'* (Kyoto: Kyoto University, 1982).

Vasubandhu (*dbyig gnyen, c.* 320-400)

Commentary on (Asaṅga's) "Compendium of the Mahāyāna" (*mahāyānasaṃgrahābhāṣya, theg pa chen po bsdus pa'i 'grel pa*)
P 5551, vol. 112.
English translation: (portion): Edward Conze, *Buddhist Texts through the Ages*. Oxford: Cassirer, 1954; New York: Harper & Row, 1964. French translation: (partial): Étienne Lamotte, *La Somme du Grand Véhicule d'Asaṅga (Mahāyānasaṃgraha)*. Louvain: Université de Louvain, 1973.

Commentary on (Maitreya's) "Discrimination of the Middle Way and the Extremes" (*madhyāntavibhāgaṭīkā, dbus dang mtha' rnam par 'byed pa'i 'grel pa*)
P 5528, vol. 108. Sanskrit edition: Ramchandra Pandeya, ed. *Madhyānta-Vibhāga-Çāstra, Containing the Kārikā-s of Maitreya, Bhāṣya of Vasubandhu and ṭīkā by Sthiramati*. Delhi: Motilal Banarsidass, 1971.

Demonstration of the Three Natures (*trisvabhāvanirdeśa, rang bzhin gsum nges par bstan pa*)
P 5559, vol. 113.

Explanation of the "Treasury of Knowledge" (*abhidharmakośabhāṣyam, chos mngon pa'i mdzod kyi bshad pa*)

P 5591, vol. 115. Sanskrit edition: P. Pradhan, *Abhidharmakośa-bhāṣyam*. Patna: K. P. Jayaswal Research Institute, 1975.
French translation: Louis de La Vallée Poussin, *L'Abhidharma-kośa de Vasubandhu*. Paris: Geuthner, 1923-31.

Thirty Stanzas (*triṃśikākarikā, sum cu pa'i tshig le'ur byas pa,* known as *sum cu pa*)
P 5556, vol. 113.
English translations: Isshi Yamada. "Vijñaptimātratā of Vasubandhu." *Journal of the Royal Asiatic Society*(1977), pp. 158-76. W. T. Chan in Radhakrishnan and Moore, eds. *Sourcebook of Indian Philosophy*. Princeton: Princeton University Press, 1957, pp. 333-37. Edward Conze, *Buddhist Texts through the Ages*. Oxford: Cassirer, 1954; New York: Harper & Row, 1964. German translations: Erich Frauwallner, *Die Philosophie Buddhismus*. Berlin: 1958, pp. 385-90. H. W. Schumann, *Buddhismus*. Darmstadt: 1973, pp. 152-55. Edward Conze, *In Zeichen Buddhas: Buddhistische Texte*. Frankfurt: Fischer, 1957.

Treasury of Knowledge (*abhidharmakośakārikā, chos mngon pa'i mdzod kyi tshig le'ur byas pa*)
P 5590, vol. 115.
French translation: Louis de La Vallée Poussin, *L'Abhidharma-kośa de Vasubandhu*. Paris: Geuthner, 1923-31.

Twenty Stanzas (*viṃśikākārikā, nyi shu pa'i tshig le'ur byas pa,* known as *nyi shu pa*)
P 5557, vol. 113. Sanskrit edition: N. Aiyaswami Sastrin, *Viṃśikākārikā*. Gangtok: Namgyal Institute of Tibetology, 1964.
German translation: Junyu Kitayama, "Metaphysik des Buddhismus, Versuch einer philosophischen Interpretation der Lehre asubandhu und Seiner Schule." *Veröffentlichungen des Orientalischen Seminars der Universität Tübingen*, #7, Heft, Stuttgart: 1934, pp. 234-68; reprint San Francisco: Chinese Materials Center, 1976.

Yeshay Gyeltsen (*ye shes rgyal mtshan,* 1713-93)

Clear Exposition of the Modes of Minds and Mental Factors, Necklace for Those of Clear Mind (*sems dang sems byung gi tshul gsal bar ston pa blo gsal mgul rgyan*)

The Collected Works of Tshe-mchog-gliṅ yoṅs-'dzin ye-śes-rgyal-mtshan, vol. 16. New Delhi: Tibet House, 1974.
English translation: H. V. Guenther and L. S. Kawamura, *Mind in Buddhist Psychology*. Emeryville: Dharma, 1975.

Special Instructions on the View of the Middle Way, the Sacred Word of Lo-sang *(zab no dbu ma'i lta khrid thun mong min pa blo bzang zhal lung)*
Appendix to Guenther's *Tibetan Buddhism without Mystification*, Leiden: Brill, 1966; English translation therein.

3. Other Works

Acton, H. B. "Idealism." In the *Encyclopedia of Philosophy*, vol. 4, pp. 110-18. Edited by Paul Edwards. New York: Macmillan, 1967.
Anacker, Stefan. *Seven Works of Vasubandhu*. Delhi: Motilal Banarsidass, 1984.
Asanga. *On Knowing Reality*. Translated by Janice Dean Willis. New York: Columbia University Press, 1979.
Bapat, Lata S. *Buddhist Logic: A Fresh Study of Dharmakīrti's Philosophy*. Delhi: Bharatiya Vidya Prakashan, 1989.
Bastow, David. "The Mahā-vibhāṣā Arguments for Sarvāstivāda." *Philosophy East & West* 44.3 (1994).
Batchelor, Stephen. *A Guide to the Bodhisattva's Way of Life*. Dharamsala: Library of Tibetan Works and Archives, 1979.
________, trans. *Echoes of Voidness*. London: Wisdom, 1983.
Bhattacharya, K. *The Dialectical Method of Nāgārjuna*. Delhi: Motilal, 1978.
Bhattacharya, Vidhushekhara, ed.*The Catuḥśataka of Āryadeva*. Calcutta, 1931.
________. *Bodhicaryāvatāra*. Bibliotheca Indica, vol. 280. Calcutta: The Asiatic Society, 1960.
Buescher, John. "The Buddhist Doctrine of Two Truths in the Vaibhāṣika and Theravāda Schools." Dissertation, University of Virginia, 1982.
Buswell, Robert. "The Wholesome Roots and Their Eradication: A Descent to the Bedrock of Buddhist Soteriology." In *Paths to Liberation: The Mārga and Its Transformations in Buddhist Thought*. Kuroda Institute. Studies in East Asian Buddhism 7. Honolulu: University of Hawaii Press, 1992.

Cabezón, José Ignatio. "The Concepts of Truth and Meaning in the Buddhist Scriptures." *Journal of International Association of Buddhist Studies* IV.1 (1981): 7-23.

———. "The Development of a Buddhist Philosophy of Language..." Ann Arbor: University Microfilms, 1986 [?].

———. "The Canonization of Philosophy and the Rhetoric of *Siddhānta* in Indo-Tibetan Buddhism." In Paul J. Griffiths and John P. Keenan, eds., *Buddha Nature: A Festschrift in Honor of Minoru Kiyota*. Las Vegas: Buddhist Books International, 1990, pp. 95-123.

———. *A Dose of Emptiness*. Albany: State University of New York Press, 1992.

———.*Buddhism and Language*. Albany: State University of New York Press, 1994.

Chandra, Lokesh, ed. *Eminent Tibetan Polymaths of Mongolia*. Śata-piṭaka series 16. New Delhi: International Academy of Indian Culture, 1961.

———. *Materials for a History of Tibetan Literature*. Śata-piṭaka series 28-30. New Delhi: International Academy of Indian Culture, 1963.

Chatterjee, A. K. *The Yogācāra Idealism*, 2nd ed. Delhi: Motilal Banarsidass, 1975.

Conze, Edward. *Abhisamayālankāra*. Series Orientale Roma VI. Rome: I.S.M.E.O., July 1954.

Cozort, Daniel. *Highest Yoga Tantra*. Ithaca: Snow Lion, 1986.

Dhargyay, Lobsang. "Tsong-Kha-pa's Understanding of Prāsaṅgika Thought." *Journal of the International Association of Buddhist Studies* 10.1 (1987).

Dhargyay, Geshe Ngawang. *Tibetan Tradition of Mental Development*. Dharamsala: Library of Tibetan Works and Archives, 1974.

Della Santina, Peter. *Madhyamaka Schools in India*. Delhi: Motilal Banarsidass, 1986.

de Jong, Jan W. "Le Madhyamakaśāstrastuti de Candrakīrti." *Bulletin de l'Ecole française d'Extrême Orient* (1924).

———. *Cinq chapitres de la Prasannapada*. Paris: Geuthner, 1949.

———. "La Madhyamakaśāstrastuti de Candrakīrti" in *Oriens Extremus*, Jahrg. 9 (1962): 47-56. Reprinted in *J. W. de Jong Buddhist Studies*. Taiwan: Asian Humanities Press, 1979, pp. 54-150.

———. "La Légende de Śāntideva." *Indo-Iranian Journal* 16.3 (1975).

Demieville, Paul. "L'origine des sectes bouddhiques d'apres Paramārtha. *Melanges Chinois et Bouddhiques* I (1931-32): 14-64.

Dragonetti, Carmen, and Fernando Tola. "The Yuktiṣaṣṭikākarikā of Nāgārjuna." *Journal of the International Association of Buddhist Studies* 6.2 (1983): 94-123.

Dreyfus, Georges. *Recognizing Reality; Dharmakirti's Philosophy and Its Tibetan Interpretations*. Albany: State University of New York Press, 1997.

Dreyfus, George, and Christian Lindtner. "The Yogācāra Philosophy of Dignāga and Dharmakīrti." *Studies in Central and East Asian Religions* 2 (1989).

Dutt, N. *Bodhisattvabhūmi*. Patna: K. P. Jayaswal Research Institute, 1966.

Eckel, Malcolm David. "A Question of Nihilism: Bhāvaviveka's Response to the Fundamental Problems of Mādhyamika Philosophy." Unpublished dissertation, Harvard, 1980.

________. "Bhāvaviveka's Critique of Yogācāra Philosophy in Chapter XXV of the Prajñāpradīpa." In C. Lindtner (ed.), *Miscellanea Buddhica*. Copenhagen: Akademisk Forlag, 1985.

________. *Jñānagarbha's Commentary on the Distinction between the Two Truths*. Albany: State University of New York Press, 1987.

Fenner, Peter G. "Candrakīrti's Refutation of Buddhist Idealism." In *Philosophy East and West* 33.3 (July, 1983).

Fifth Dalai Lama. "Practice of Emptiness" (the "Perfection of Wisdom Chapter" of the *Sacred Word of Mañjuśrī [dpal zhal lung])*. Jeffrey Hopkins, translator. Dharamsala: Library of Tibetan Works and Archives, 1976.

Franco, E."Once Again on Dharmakīrti's Deviation from Dignāga on Pratyakṣābhāsa." *Journal of Indian Philosophy*, trans V. M. Bedekar, (1984).

________."Did Dignāga Accept Four Types of Perception?" *Journal of Indian Philosophy* 21 (1993).

Griffiths, Paul J. "Indian Buddhist Meditation-Theory: History, Development, and Systematization." Dissertation, University of Wisconsin, 1983. Ann Arbor: University Microfilms International, 1986.

________. *On Being Mindless: Buddhist Meditation and the Mind-Body Problem*. LaSalle, IL: Open Court, 1986.

________. *On Being Buddha: The Classical Doctrine of Buddhahood*. Albany: State University of New York Press, 1994.

Griffiths, Paul J., Noriaki Hakamaya, John P. Keenan, and Paul L. Swanson, trans. *The Realm of Awakening: Chapter Ten of Asaṅga's Mahāyānasaṅgraha*. New York and Oxford: Oxford University Press, 1989.

Grupper, Samuel M. "Manchu Patronage and Tibetan Buddhism During the First Half of the Ch'ing Dynasty." *Journal of the Tibet Society* 4 (1984): 47-75.

Guenther, Herbert V. "*Saṃvṛtti* and *Pāramārtha* in Yogācāra According to Tibetan Sources." In M. Sprung (ed.) *The Problem of the Two Truths in Buddhism and Vedānta.* Dordrecht: Reidel, 1973.

Guenther, Herbert V., and Kawamura, Leslie S. *Mind in Buddhist Psychology.* Emeryville: Dharma, 1975.

Gyatso, Janet (ed.). *In the Mirror of Memory.* Albany: State University of New York Press, 1992.

Gyatso, Kelsang. *Meaningful to Behold.* London: Wisdom Publications, 1980.

Gyatso, Tenzin, The Fourteenth Dalai Lama. *The Buddhism of Tibet and The Key to the Middle Way.* London: George Allen and Unwin, 1975. Translated by Jeffrey Hopkins. Reprinted in a combined volume, *The Buddhism of Tibet.* London: George Allen and Unwin, 1983.

———. *Kindness, Clarity, and Insight.* Trans. and edited by Jeffrey Hopkins, coedited by Elizabeth Napper. Ithaca: Snow Lion, 1984.

———. *The Kālachakra Tantra: Rite of Initiation for the Stage of Generation.* Translated and introduced by Jeffrey Hopkins. London: Wisdom Publications, 1985.

Hall, B. C. "The Meaning of *Vijñāpti* in Vasubandhu's Concept of Mind." *Journal of the International Association of Buddhist Studies* 9.1 (1986).

Harris, Ian Charles. *The Continuity of Madhyamaka and Yogācāra in Indian Mahāyāna Buddhism.* Brill's Indological Library, vol. 6. New York: E. J. Brill, 1991.

Hattori, Masaaki. *Dignāga, On Perception.* Cambridge: Harvard, 1968.

———. "Realism and the Philosophy of Consciousness-Only." *Eastern Buddhist* 21.1 (1988).

Hayes, Richard P. "The Question of Doctrinalism in the Buddhist Epistemologists." *Journal of American Academy of Religion* 52.4 (1984).

———. *Dignāga on the Interpretation of Signs.* Boston: D. Reidel, 1988.

Herman, A. L. *Introduction to Buddhist Thought.* Lanham, MD: University Press of America, 1983.

Hirakawa, Akira. "The Rise of Mahāyāna Buddhism and Its Relationship to the Worship of Stūpas." In *Memoirs of the Research Department of the Toyo Bunko* 22 (1963): 57-106.

_______."The Meaning of "Dharma" and "Abhidharma." In *Indianisme et Bouddhisme*. Louvaine-la-Neuve: Institut Orientaliste, 1980.

Honda, M. "An Annotated Translation of the 'Daśabhūmika.'" *Studies in Southeast and Central Asia*, ed. by D. Sinor. Śatapiṭaka Series 74. New Delhi: 1968, pp. 115-276.

Hopkins, Jeffrey, trans. *Practice of Emptiness*. Dharamsala: Library of Tibetan Works and Archives, 1974.

_______, trans., with Lati Rimpoche. Nāgārjuna and the Seventh Dalai Lama. *The Precious Garland and the Song of the Four Mindfulnesses*. New York: Harper and Row, 1975.

_______, trans. *Analysis of Going and Coming*, by Chandrakīrti. Dharamsala: Library of Tibetan Works and Archives, 1976.

_______, trans. *Compassion in Tibetan Buddhism*. London: Rider and Co., 1980.

_______. *Meditation on Emptiness*. London: Wisdom, 1983.

_______, trans. *Meditative States in Tibetan Buddhism*. London: Wisdom, 1983.

_______. *Emptiness Yoga*. Ithaca: Snow Lion, 1987.

_______, trans. *Walking through Walls: A Presentation of Tibetan Meditation*, by Geshe Gedün Lodrö. Ithaca: Snow Lion, 1992.

Hopkins, Jeffrey, and Geshe Lhundup Sopa. *Cutting through Appearances* (revised edition of *Practice and Theory of Tibetan Buddhism*). Ithaca: Snow Lion, 1989.

Huntington, C. W., Jr. *The Emptiness of Emptiness: An Introduction to Early Indian Mādyamika*. Honolulu: University of Hawaii Press, 1989.

Iida, Shotaro. *Reason and Emptiness*. Tokyo: Hokuseido, 1980.

Jackson, D., ed. and trans. *The Entrance Gate for the Wise: Sa skya Pandita on Indian and Tibetan Traditions of Pramāṇa and Philosophical Discourse*. Vienna: Arbeitskreis für Tibetische und Buddhistische Studien Universität Wien, 1987.

Jackson, Roger Reid. "For Whom Emptiness Prevails: An Analysis of the Religious Implications of *Vigrahavyāvartanī* 70." *Religious Studies* 21.3 (1985).

_______. *Is Enlightenment Possible?* Ithaca: Snow Lion, 1993.

Jaini, Padmanabh S. "On the *Sarvajñatva* (Omniscience) of Mahāvīra and the Buddha." In L. Cousins, A. Kunst, and K. R. Norman, eds., *Buddhist Studies in Honour of I. B. Horner*. Dortrecht: D. Reidel, 1974.

———. "The Vaibhāṣika theory of Words and Meaning." *Bulletin of the School of Oriental and African Studies* 22 (1959).

Jha, G. *The Tattvasangraha of Çāntarakṣita with the Commentary of Kamalaśila*, Gaekwad's Oriental Series 1 and 13. Baroda: 1937-9.

Johnston, E. H. *Ratnagotravibhaiga-Mahāiyānottaratantraśāstra*. Patna Jayaswal Institute, 1950.

———. "Textcritical Notes on the Prasannapadā." *Indo-Iranian Journal* 20 (1978): 25-59, 217-52.

Kalupahana, David J. *Nāgārjuna: The Philosophy of the Middle Way*. Albany: State University Press of New York, 1986.

———. *A History of Buddhist Philosophy: Continuities and Discontinuities*. Honolulu: University of Hawaii Press, 1992.

Kapstein, Matthew. "Mereological Considerations in Vasubandhu's 'Proof of Idealism.'" *Idealistic Studies* 1.18 (1988).

Kawamura, L. S., ed. and trans. *Mādhyamika and Yogācāra: A Study of Mahāyāna Philosophies*. Albany: State University of New York, 1991.

Keenan, John P. "Original Purity and the Focus of Early Yogācāra." *Journal of the International Association of Buddhist Studies* 5 (1982): 7-18.

Kémpfe, Hans-Rainer. *ñi ma'i 'od zer / Naran-u gerel: Die Biographie des 2. Pekinger Lčaṅ skya-Qutuqtu Rol pa'i rdo rje* (1717-1786), Monumenta Tibetica Historica II.1. Wissenschaftsverlag, Sankt Augustin, 1976.

Keith, A. B. *Buddhist Philosophy in India and Ceylon* (2nd ed.). New Delhi: Oriental Books Reprint Corporation, 1979.

Klein, Anne C. *Knowledge and Liberation: Tibetan Buddhist Epistemology in Support of Transformative Religious Experience*. Ithaca: Snow Lion, 1986.

———. *Knowing, Naming and Negation*. Ithaca: Snow Lion, 1991.

———, trans. and ed. *Path to the Middle: The Spoken Scholarship of Kensur Yeshey Tupden*. Albany: State University of New York Press, 1994.

Kochumuttom, Thomas. *A Buddhist Doctrine of Experience*. Delhi: Motilal Banarsidass, 1982.

Lamotte, Étienne. *Saṃdhinirmocana-sūtra*. Paris: Louvain, 1935.

———. "Le traité de l'acte de Vasubandhu, Karmasiddhiprakaraṇa." *Melanges Chinoise et Bouddhique* 4 (1936): 265-88.

———, ed. and trans. *La Somme du Grand Véhicule d'Asaṅga*. 2 vols. Louvain: Muséon, 1938.

_______, trans. *Le Traité de la Grande Vertu de Nāgārjuna (Mahāprajñāpāramitāśāstra) avec une nouvelle introduction.* Louvain: Institute Orientaliste de l'Université de Louvain (originally Bibliothèque du Muséon, vol. 18), 1970-76.

_______. *La somme du grand véhicule d'Asaṅga (Mahāyānasaṃgraha).* Tome I: *Versions tibetaine et chinois.* Tome II: *Traduction et commentaire. Publications de l'institut Orientaliste de Louvain* 8. Louvain: Institut Orientaliste, 1973. First edition, Louvain: Bureaux du Muséon, 1935.

_______. "Passions and Impregnations of the Passions in Buddhism." In Cousins et al., *Buddhist Studies in Honour of I. B. Horner.* Dordrecht: Reidel, 1974.

_______. *History of Indian Buddhism.* Publications de l'Institut Orientaliste de Louvain no. 36. Louvain-la-Nueve: Institut Orientaliste, 1988. Original French edition: *Histoire du Bouddhisme indien,* 1958.

_______. "Assessment of Textual Interpretation in Buddhism." In D. O. Lopez, ed., *Buddhist Hermeneutics.* Honolulu: University of Hawaii Press, 1988.

la Vallée Poussin, Louis de, trans. *Madhyamakāvatāra. Muséon* 8 (1907): 249-317; 11 (1910): 271-358; and 12 (1911): 235-328.

_______, ed. *Prasannapadā.* Saint Petersburg: Bibliotheca Buddhica IV, 1913.

_______, ed. *Mūlamadyamakakārikās de Nāgārjuna avec la Prasannapadā Commentaire de Candrakīrti (Pras.).* St. Petersburg: Bibliotheca Buddhica IV, 1913.

_______. "Les quatre odes de Nāgārjuna." *Le Muséon,* 1913.

_______, trans. *L'Abhidharmakośa de Vasubandhu.* Paris: Geuthner, 1923.

_______, ed. *Madhyamakāvatāra par Candrakīrti.* Bibliotheca Buddhica IX. Osnabrück: Biblio Verlag (reprint of 1907 ed.), 1970.

_______, ed. *Mūlamadhyamakakārikās de Nāgāirjuna avec la Prasannapadā Commentaire de Candrakīrti.* Bibliotheca Buddhica IV. Osnabrück: Biblio Verlag, 1970

Lang, Karen. *Āryadeva's Catuḥśataka: On the Bodhisattva's Cultivation of Merit and Knowledge.* Indiske Studier VII, Copenhagen: Akademisk Forlag, 1986 and Delhi: Motilal Banarsidass.

_______. "sPa tshab Nyi ma grags and the Introduction of Prāsaṅgika Madhyamaka into Tibet," in *Reflections on Tibetan Culture: Essays in Memory of Turrell V. Wylie.* Ed. Lawrence Epstein and Richard Sherburne. Lewiston, NY: Edwin Mellon Press, 1990.

Lati Rinbochay. *Mind in Tibetan Buddhism.* Elizabeth Napper, trans. and ed. Valois, NY: Snow Lion, 1980.

_______, et. al. *Meditative States in Tibetan Buddhism,* trans. Jeffrey Hopkins, ed. and introduced Leah Zahler. London: Wisdom, 1983.

Lessing, Ferdinand, and Alex Wayman. *Introduction to the Buddhist Tantric Systems.* The Hague, 1968. Rpt. Delhi: Motilal Banarsidass, 1978.

Levi, S. *Asaṅga, Mahāyānsūtrālaṃkāra, exposé de la doctrine du Grand Véhicule selon le systême Yogācāra.* Paris: Champion, 1907.

Lindtner, Christian. *Nagarjuniana.* Indiske Studier 4. Copenhagen: Akademisk Forlag, 1982.

_______. "Bhavya's Critique of Yogācāra in the *Madhyamakaratnapradīpa,* Chapter IV." In R. D. Evans and B. K. Matilal, eds., *Buddhist Logic and Epistemology,* (1986): 239-63.

_______. *Master of Wisdom.* Oakland: Dharma Publishing, 1986.

Lodrö, Geshe Gedün. *Walking Through Walls: A Presentation of Tibetan Meditation.* Translated and edited by Jeffrey Hopkins. Ithaca: Snow Lion, 1992.

Lopez, Donald S. *A Study of Svātantrika.* Ithaca: Snow Lion, 1987.

_______. *Buddhist Hermeneutics.* Studies in East Asian Buddhism 6. Honolulu: University of Hawaii Press, 1988.

_______. *The Heart Sūtra Explained.* Albany: State University of New York Press, 1988.

Magee, William. "A Controversy in Tibet Regarding Sūtra Passages Indicated as Interpretable in Chandrakīrti's *Madhyamakāvatārabhāṣya.*" Unpublished ms.

Matilal, Bimal Krishna. *Epistemology, Logic, and Grammar in Indian Philosophical Analysis.* The Hague: Mouton, 1971.

_______. "A Critique of Buddhist Idealism." In L. Cousins, A. Kunst and K R. Norman, eds., *Buddhist Studies in Honour of 1. B. Horner.* Dordrecht: Reidel, 1974, pp. 139-69.

May, Jacques. *Prasannapadā Madhyamakavṛtti, douze chapitres traduits du sanscrit et du tibétain.* Paris: Adrien-Maisonneuve, 1959.

_______. "La philosophie Bouddhique idéaliste." In *Asiatische Studien / Etudes Asiatiques* 25 (1971).

McDermott, A. Charlene. "Asaṅga's Defense of *Alayavijñana.*" *Journal of Indian Philosophy* 2 (1973).

_______. "Direct Sensory Awareness: A Tibetan View and a Medieval Counterpart." In *Philosophy East and West* 23 (1973): 343-59.

_______. "Yogic Direct Awareness as Means of Valid Cognition in Dharmakīrti and Rgyal-tshab." In M. Kiyota (ed.), *Mahāyāna*

Buddhist Meditation, Honolulu: University of Hawaii Press, 1980.

Mimaki, Katsumi. *Blo Gsal Grub Mtha'*. Kyoto: Kyoto University, 1982.

Mittal, K. K. *A Tibetan Eye-View of Indian Philosophy*. Delhi: Munshiram Manoharlal, 1984.

Mizuno, Kogen. *Buddhist Sutras*. Tokyo: Kosei, 1980. English edition, 1982.

Murti, T. R. V. *The Central Philosophy of Buddhism*. London: George Allen and Unwin, 1955.

Nagao, Gadjin. "What Remains in *Śūnyatā*: A Yogācāra Interpretation of Emptiness." In M. Kiyoto and E. W. Jones, eds., *Mahāyāna Buddhist Meditation: Theory and Practice*. Honolulu: University of Hawaii Press, 1978.

_______. *The Foundational Standpoint of Mādhyamika Philosophy*. Trans. by John P. Keenan. Albany: State University of New York Press, 1989.

Nāgārjuna and Kelsang Gyatso. *Precious Garland and the Song of the Four Mindfulnesses*. London: George Allen and Unwin, 1975.

Nagatomi, Masatoshi. "*Mānasa-pratyakṣa*: A Conundrum in the Buddhist *Pramāṇa* System." In M. Nagatomi et al., eds. *Sanskrit and Indian Studies*. Boston: D. Reidel, 1980.

Nakamura, Hajime. *Indian Buddhism: A Survey with Bibliographical Notes*. Hirakata, Japan: Kurfs Publications, 1980. Rpt. Delhi: Motilal Banarsidass, 1987.

Napper, Elizabeth. *Dependent-Arising and Emptiness*. London and Boston: Wisdom, 1989.

Newland, Guy. "The Two Truths: A Study of Mādhyamika Philosophy as Presented in the Monastic Textbooks of the Ge-luk-ba Order of Tibetan Buddhism." Dissertation, University of Virginia, 1988.

_______. *The Two Truths*. Ithaca: Snow Lion, 1992.

Obermiller, E. *History of Buddhism by Bu-ston*. Rpt. Suzuki Reprint Series, 1931.

_______. "Sublime Science of the Great Vehicle to Salvation." *Acta Orientalia* 11.2-4. Rpt. Talent, OR: Canon Publications, 1984.

_______. "The Doctrine of the Prajña-pāramitā as exposed in the *Abhisamayalaṃkāra* of Maitreya." *Acta Orientalia*. Lugduni Batavorum: E. J. Brill, 1932. Rpt. Talent, OR: Canon Publications, 1984.

Pandeya, Ramchandra. *Madhyānta-Vibhāga-Çāstra*. Delhi: Motilal Banarsidass, 1971.

Paul, Diana. *Philosophy of Mind in Sixth Century China: Paramārtha's "Evolution of Consciousness."* Stanford: Stanford University Press, 1984.

Perdue, Daniel. *Debate in Tibetan Buddhism.* Ithaca: Snow Lion, 1992.

———. *Practice and Theory of Philosophical Debate in Tibetan Buddhist Education.* Ithaca: Snow Lion, 1992.

Powers, John. *The Yogācāra School of Buddhism: A Bibliography.* Atla Bibliography series 27. Metuchen, NJ and London: American Theological Library Association and The Scarecrow Press, 1991.

———, trans. *Two Commentaries on the Saṃdhinirmocana-Sūtra by Asaṅga and Jñānagarbha.* Lewistown, NY: Edwin Mellen Press, 1992.

———. *Hermeneutics and Tradition in the Saṃdhinirmocana-Sūtra.* New York: E. J. Brill, 1993.

———. *Introduction to Tibetan Buddhism.* Ithaca: Snow Lion, 1995.

Prebish, Charles, ed. *Buddhism: A Modern Perspective.* University Park: Penn State University Press, 1975.

Rabten, Geshé. *Echoes of Voidness.* London: Wisdom, 1983.

Rahula, Walpola. *Le Compendium de la Super-Doctrine Philosophie.* Paris: École Française d'Extréme-Orient, 1971.

Robinson, Richard H. *Early Mādhyamika in India and China.* Reprint Delhi: Motilal Banarsidass, 1976.

Rhys-Davids, C. A. F., and Woodward, F. L., trans. *The Book of the Kindred Sayings* (five volumes). London: Pali Text Society, 1917-30.

Ruegg, David Seyfort. *The Literature of the Madhyamaka School of Philosophy in India.* Wiesbaden: Otto Harrassowitz, 1981.

Sangharakshita. *The Eternal Legacy.* London: Tharpa, 1985.

———. *A Survey of Buddhism*, 6th edition. London: Tharpa, 1987.

Santina, Peter Della. *Madhyamaka Schools in India: A Study of the Madhyamaka Philosophy and of the Division of the System into the Prāsaṅgika and Svātantrika Schools.* Delhi: Motilal Banarsidass, 1986.

Sarachchandra, D. R. "From Vasubandhu to Śāntarakṣita." *Journal of Indian Philosophy* 4 (1976).

Schmithausen, Lambert. *Ālayavijñāna: On the Origin and Early Development of a Central Concept of Yogācāra Philosophy.* Studia Philogica Buddhica Monograph Series IVa. Tokyo: International Institute for Buddhist Studies, 1987.

———. "On the Problem of the Relation of Spiritual Practice and Philosophical Theory in Buddhism." In *German Scholars on India* II. New Delhi: Nachiketa Publications, Ltd., 1976.

Schubert, Johannes. *Tibetische Nationalgrammatik, Das Sum.cu.pa und Rtags.kyi.'jug.pa des Grosslamas von Peking Rol.pai.rdo.rje.* Leipzig: 1937.

Shastri, Swami D., ed. *Abhidharmakośa and Bhāṣya of Acārya Vasubandhu*, 2 vols. Varanasi: Bauddha Bharati, 1981.

———. *Pramāṇavārttika of Acārya Dharmakīrti.* Varanasi: Bauddha Bharati, 1968.

Sherbourne, R. F. *A Lamp for the Path and Commentary*, Wisdom of Tibet Series, vol. 5. London: George Allen and Unwin, 1983.

Siderits, M. "The Madhyamaka Critique of Epistemology, II." *Journal of Indian Philosophy* 8 (1981).

Sinha, Jadunath. *Indian Realism.* Delhi: Motilal Banarsidass, 1972. First edition, London: Routledge & Kegan Paul, 1938.

Smith, E. Gene. Introduction to N. Gelek Demo, *Collected Works of Thu'u-bkwan Blobzang-chos-kyi-nyi-ma*, vol. 1. Delhi, 1969.

———. *Tibetan Catalogue.* Seattle: University of Washington Press, 1969.

Snellgrove, David. *Indo-Tibetan Buddhism* (2 vols). Boston: Shambhala, 1987.

Sonam, Ruth, ed. and trans. *The Yogic Deeds of Bodhisattvas: Gyeltsap on Āryadeva's "Four Hundred."* Ithaca: Snow Lion, 1994.

Sopa, Geshe Lhundup, and Jeffrey Hopkins. *Cutting through Appearances* (second edition of *Practice and Theory of Tibetan Buddhism*). Ithaca: Snow Lion, 1989.

Sponberg, Alan. "Dynamic Liberation in Yogācāra Buddhism." *Journal of the International Association of Buddhist Studies* 2.1 (1979).

Sprung, Mervyn. *Lucid Exposition of the Middle Way.* London: Routledge, 1979.

Stcherbatsky, Theodore. *Buddhist Logic.* New York: Dover, 1962.

———. *Madhyānta-Vibhaṅga.* Calcutta: Indian Studies Past and Present, 1971.

———. *The Conception of Buddhist Nirvāṇa.* Leningrad: Office of the Academy of Sciences of the USSR, 1927; rev. rpt. Delhi: Motilal, 1977.

Steinkellner, Ernst. *Verse-Index of Dharmakīrti's Works.* Wien: Arbeitskreis für Tibetische und Buddhistische Studien Universität Wien, 1967.

———. "Is Dharmakīrti a Mādhyamika?" In David Seyfort Ruegg and Lambert Schmithausen, eds., *Early Buddhism and Madhyamaka.* Panels of the VIIth World Sanskrit Conference, vol. 2. Leiden: E. J. Brill, 1990.

Streng, Frederick J. *Emptiness.* Nashville and New York: Abingdon, 1967.

Sutton, Florin Giripescu. *Existence and Enlightenment in the Laṅkāvatāra-sūtra: A Study in the Ontology and Epistemology of the Yogācāra School of Mahāyāna Buddhism.* Albany: State University of New York Press, 1991.

Suzuki, Daisetz T. *The Laṅkāvatāra Sūtra.* London: Routledge and Kegan Paul, 1932.

Takasaki, J. *A Study on the Ratnagotravibhāga.* Rome: I.S.M.E.O., 1966.

Tāranātha. *History of Buddhism in India.* Trans. by Lama Chimpa and Alaka Chattopadhyaya. Calcutta Bagchi, 1970 (reprint 1980).

Thapkhay, Yeshe. "The Four Assertions: Interpretations of Difficult Points in Prasangika Madhyamika." Translated by Sangye Tandar and Richard Guard. *The Tibet Journal* 17.1 (Spring 1992): 3-35.

Tharchin, Geshe Lobsang, and Artemus B. Engle. *Nāgārjuna's Letter.* Dharamsala: Library of Tibetan Works and Archives, 1979.

Thurman, Robert, ed. *The Life & Teachings of Tsong Khapa.* Dharamsala: Library of Tibetan Works and Archives, 1982.

_______. *Tsong Khapa's Speech of Gold in the Essence of True Eloquence.* Princeton: Princeton University Press, 1984.

Tillemans, Tom J. F. "Indian and Tibetan Mādhyamikas on *Mānasapratyakṣa.*" *The Tibet Journal* 14.1 (Spring 1989): 70-85.

Tola, Fernando, and Carmen Dragonetti. "The *Yuktiṣaṣṭikākāirikā* of Nāgārjuna." *Journal of the International Association of Buddhist Studies* 6.2 (1983): 94-123.

Tulku, Doboom, ed. *Mind Only School and Buddhist Logic.* Dialogue Series 1. New Delhi: Tibet House and Aditya Prakashan, 1990.

Tucci, G. *On Some Aspects of the Doctrine of Maitreya and Asaṇga.* Calcutta: University of Calcutta, 1930.

Tuck, Andrew P. *Comparative Philosophy and the Philosophy of Scholarship: On the Western Interpretation of Nāgārjuna.* New York and Oxford: Oxford University Press, 1990.

Vaidya, P. L., ed. *Laṅkāvatārasūtra.* Darbanga: Mithila Institute, 1959.

_______, ed. *Bodhicaryāvatāra of Śāntideva with the Commentary of Pañjikā of Prajñākaramati.* Darbhanga: Mithila Institute, 1960.

_______, ed. *Prasannapadā.* Darbhanga: Mithila Institute, 1960.

_______, ed. *Daśabhūmikasūtra.* Darbhanga: Mithila Institute, 1967.

van der Kuijp, L. W. J. *Contributions to Tibetan Buddhist Epistemology.* Wiesbaden: Franz Steiner, 1983.

_______."Studies in the Life and Thought of mKhas grub rje I: mKhas grub rje's Epistemological Oeuvre and his Philological Remarks on Dignāga's *Pramāṇasamuccaya* I." *Berliner Indologische Studien*, Heft 1 (1985).

Waldron, William S. "A Comparison of the *Ālayavijñāna* with Freud's and Jung's Theories of the Unconscious." Shin Buddhist Comprehensive Research Institute Annual Memoirs 6.

Wangyal, Geshe. *Door of Liberation.* Boston: Wisdom, 1995.

Warder, A. K. *Indian Buddhism* (second ed.). Delhi: Motilal Banarsidass, 1980.

Warren, Henry. *Buddhism in Translations.* Cambridge: Harvard University Press, 1896.

Watson, Burton. *Chuang-tsu: Basic Writings.* New York: Columbia University Press, 1964.

Wayman, Alex. *Calming the Mind and Discerning the Real.* New York: Columbia, 1978.

_______. "Yogācāra and the Buddhist Logicians." *Journal of the International Association of Buddhist Studies* 2.1 (1979).

Williams, Paul. "On Rang Rig." In E. Steinkellner and H. Tauscher, eds., *Contributions on Tibetan and Buddhist Religion and Philosophy.* Wien: Arbeitskreis für Tibetische und Buddhistische Studien Universität Wien, 1983.

_______. *Mahāyāna Buddhism: The Doctrinal Foundations.* London and New York: Routledge, 1989.

_______."Introduction—Some Random Reflections on the Study of Tibetan Mādhyamaka." *The Tibet Journal* 14.1 (Spring 1989): 1-9.

Willis, Janice Dean. *On Knowing Reality.* New York: Columbia University Press, 1979.

Wilson, Joe B. *Chandrakīrti's Seven-fold Reasoning on the Selflessness of the Person.* Dharamsala: Library of Tibetan Works and Archives, 1980.

_______. "The Meaning of Mind in the Mahāyāna Buddhist Philosophy of Mind-Only *(Cittamātra)...*" Dissertation, University of Virginia, 1984. Ann Arbor: University Microfilms International, 1986.

Wood, Thomas E. *Nāgārjunian Disputations: A Philosophical Journey through an Indian Looking-Glass.* Honolulu: University of Hawaii Press, 1994.

Wylie, Turrell V. "A Standard System of Tibetan Transcription." *Harvard Journal of Asiatic Studies* 22: 261-67.

Yamada, Isshi. "*Vijñaptimātratā* of Vasubandhu." *Journal of the Royal Asiatic Society* (1977): 158-76.

Zahler, Leah, ed. *Meditative States in Tibetan Buddhism,* trans. Jeffrey Hopkins. London: Wisdom, 1983.

Index

Technical terms and book titles are listed by English translations.